THE PAPERS OF
THOMAS JEFFERSON

BARBARA B. OBERG
GENERAL EDITOR

THE PAPERS OF
Thomas Jefferson

Volume 32
1 June 1800 to 16 February 1801

BARBARA B. OBERG, EDITOR

JAMES P. McCLURE AND ELAINE WEBER PASCU,
SENIOR ASSOCIATE EDITORS

MARTHA J. KING, ASSOCIATE EDITOR

THOMAS M. DOWNEY, ASSISTANT EDITOR

LINDA MONACO, EDITORIAL ASSISTANT

JOHN E. LITTLE, RESEARCH ASSOCIATE

PRINCETON AND OXFORD
PRINCETON UNIVERSITY PRESS
2005

As INDICATED in the first volume, this edition was made possible by a grant of $200,000 from The New York Times Company to Princeton University. Since this initial subvention, its continuance has been assured by additional contributions from The New York Times Company Foundation; by grants of the Ford Foundation, the National Historical Publications and Records Commission, and the National Endowment for the Humanities; by grants of the Andrew W. Mellon Foundation, the Packard Humanities Institute, the Pew Charitable Trusts, the John Ben Snow Memorial Trust, and the L. J. Skaggs and Mary C. Skaggs Foundation to Founding Fathers Papers, Inc.; by benefactions from the Barkley Fund and the Lyn and Norman Lear Foundation through the National Trust for the Humanities, the Florence Gould Foundation, the Charlotte Palmer Phillips Foundation, Time Inc., the Dyson Foundation, and the Lucius N. Littauer Foundation; and by gifts and support from Sara and James Adler, Ruth and Sidney Lapidus, Sara Lee and Axel Schupf, Diane and John Cooke, Robert C. Baron, James Russell Wiggins, David K. E. Bruce, and B. Batmanghelidj. In common with other editions of historical documents, THE PAPERS OF THOMAS JEFFERSON is a beneficiary of the good offices of the National Historical Publications and Records Commission, tendered in many forms through its dedicated staff. For these and other indispensable aids generously given by librarians, archivists, scholars, and collectors of manuscripts, the Editors record their gratitude.

FOREWORD

"I HAVE never in my life enjoyed higher or more uninterrupted health," Jefferson reported in the summer of 1800. He may have been prompted to offer the declamation by rumors of his death that were causing alarm among his friends, but the statement of confidence and well-being also rings especially true for him in the eight and a half months covered by this volume. Jefferson spent the summer and most of the fall at Monticello. Although he tended to the necessary domestic matters, he was preoccupied with politics. On the 24th of November he set out for the new national capital and the opening of the Second Session of the Sixth Congress. He chose to postpone his arrival in Washington until after the start of the session, which was opened by the president's address to Congress and the Senate's formal answer. Expecting John Adams's message to contain some "silly things" on the grounds that it would be the president's "valedictory," and anticipating also that it would be "zealously" received and answered by the Federalist majority, Jefferson would not take part. Instead, he left the Senate on its own to deliver a response, as he had with every annual address since 24 May 1797. On that occasion, with reluctance, he delivered orally the Senate's response to President Adams's opening address.

Jefferson's stay on the mountain top was not an escape from the world of politics. As his correspondents tallied and passed on the results of the state legislative and gubernatorial races, they dispatched optimistic reports, and sometimes cautions about Republican prospects, either of victory or of an increased Republican vote. Encouraging predictions, from various quarters and with different degrees of accuracy, came regarding New Jersey, New York, Pennsylvania, Maryland, North Carolina, Georgia, Tennessee, and South Carolina. Jefferson worried about New England, a stronghold of federalism, but learned that Republicans were making inroads in Connecticut and Rhode Island. An optimistic Jefferson told James Madison that there was "good reason to believe" that even Massachusetts would see an increase in Republican representation in Congress. Delaware, however, was a disappointment, and Federalist Congressman James A. Bayard was re-elected. A young Joseph Alston from South Carolina, soon to become Aaron Burr's son-in-law, visited Monticello with information "full" and "recent" from the middle states in late October. Even in the face of disappointing returns Jefferson viewed the possible Republican majorities in the Congress as good, because "whatever may be the event of the Executive election," the legislature would be in good hands and the president could do "little mischief."

The Republicans, eager to garner votes for their candidates, did not agree beforehand on a mechanism to prevent a tie in electoral votes between Burr and Jefferson. In mid-December it became clear that the vote was tied, raising the prospect that hard-bitten Federalists might somehow prevent Jefferson's election. According to the Constitution, the election would then go to the House of Representatives. "Colo. Burr behaves with candour in this dilemma," Jefferson wrote to a son-in-law, John Wayles Eppes, on 23 December 1800, "but what is to be the issue of it no mortal can foresee." Although initial signals from Burr hinted that he would defer to Jefferson, in January came signs that the New Yorker, who had been displeased with the way in which his candidacy in 1796 had played out in Virginia and North Carolina, might accept the presidency if the voting in the House should favor him.

Even as the House embarked on its balloting to resolve the tie in mid-February 1801, Jefferson noted the rumor of an "intimacy of views" between Burr and the Federalist leader Robert Goodloe Harper. The prospect of a "last malevolent Effort of the Federalists" distressed a number of Republicans. The architects of the Constitution had not anticipated an election based on political parties and had provided neither guidance nor mechanisms. The uncertainty itself was enough to produce alarm. The outcome, as Jefferson saw it, would depend upon "a few moderate men." As this volume ends, however, that outcome was still in doubt. On Monday, 16 February 1801, at noon, the House cast ballots for the thirty-fourth time but remained equally divided between Aaron Burr and Thomas Jefferson.

ACKNOWLEDGMENTS

MANY individuals have given the Editors the benefit of their aid in the preparation of this volume, and we offer them our thanks. We particularly recognize the assistance of Amy Speckart, a 2004-2005 National Historical Publications and Records Commission (NHPRC) fellow in documentary editing, who has graciously and energetically helped with the late stages of preparation of the volume. Those who helped us use manuscript collections or answered research queries are Robert Darnton, Charles C. Gillispie, William C. Jordan, and Robert A. Kaster, Princeton University; in the libraries at Princeton, Karin A. Trainer, University Librarian, and Elizabeth Z. Bennett, Mary George, and Sooni K. Johnson; the late Rosemary A. Little and Lara Moore; Timothy Connelly, Dane Hartgrove, and Michael Meier of the NHPRC; James H. Hutson and his staff at the Manuscript Division of the Library of Congress, especially Fred Bauman, Jeffrey Flannery, Gerard W. Gawalt, Patrick Kerwin, Bruce Kirby, and Mary Wolfskill; Oona E. Beauchard, Anne E. Bentley, Peter Drummey, Nicholas Graham, Nancy Heywood, Brenda M. Lawson, and Virginia H. Smith at the Massachusetts Historical Society; Robert C. Ritchie, John Rhodehamel, and others at the Huntington Library; Lucia C. Stanton and Susan Stein of the Thomas Jefferson Foundation at Monticello; Michael Plunkett and the staff of the Special Collections Department, the University of Virginia Library; Susan A. Riggs, Swem Library, the College of William and Mary; the staff of the Missouri Historical Society; at the Library of Virginia, Marianne E. Julienne, Brent Tarter, and Minor T. Weisiger; Whitfield J. Bell, Jr., Robert S. Cox, Roy Goodman, and Martin Levitt at the American Philosophical Society; Rachel Onuf at the Historical Society of Pennsylvania; Leslie Fields at the Morgan Library; Charles T. Cullen and Lauren Matson at the Newberry Library; Douglas L. Wilson of the Lincoln Studies Center at Knox College; Victor Bers of Yale University; the staff of the New York Public Library; Jesse Teitelbaum and the Luzerne County Historical Society; Fr. Tom Buckley at the Jesuit School of Theology, Berkeley, California; Beth Bensman of the Presbyterian Historical Society; Jessica Kratz of the Center for Legislative Archives, National Archives and Records Administration; Richard A. Ryerson of the David Library of the American Revolution; Scott McClure; and our fellow editors at the Thomas Jefferson Retirement Series at Monticello, the Adams Papers at the Massachusetts Historical Society, the Papers of George Washington and the Papers of James Madison at the University of

ACKNOWLEDGMENTS

Virginia, and the Papers of Benjamin Franklin at Yale University. Alfred L. Bush of Princeton, Ellen G. Miles of the National Portrait Gallery, Stacey Kluck of the National Museum of American History, Smithsonian Institution assisted in obtaining illustrations, and Susan L. Siegfried of the University of Michigan provided advice. Alice Calaprice, Jan Lilly, Betsy A. McClure, and Gretchen Oberfranc improved the volume by their careful attention to its details. We thank the team at dataformat.com, especially Stephen Perkins. We are particularly grateful for those at Princeton University Press who always give these volumes the benefit of their expertise: Chuck Creesy, Dimitri Karetnikov, Neil Litt, Elizabeth Litz, Linny Schenck, and Brigitta van Rheinberg. And we take the occasion of Walter Lippincott's retirement to extend him our fondest appreciation and deepest gratitude. As director of the Press he has been a fine friend and an able partner in carrying the edition forward. We will miss his wise counsel and strong support.

EDITORIAL METHOD AND APPARATUS

1. RENDERING THE TEXT

Julian P. Boyd eloquently set forth a comprehensive editorial policy in Volume 1 of *The Papers of Thomas Jefferson*. Adopting what he described as a "middle course" for rendering eighteenth-century handwritten materials into print, Boyd set the standards for modern historical editing. His successors, Charles T. Cullen and John Catanzariti, reaffirmed Boyd's high standards. At the same time, they made changes in textual policy and editorial apparatus as they deemed appropriate. For Boyd's policy and subsequent modifications to it, readers are encouraged to consult Vol. 1: xxix-xxxviii; Vol. 22: vii-xi; and Vol. 24: vii-viii.

The revised, more literal textual method, which appeared for the first time in Volume 30, adheres to the following guidelines: <u>Abbreviations</u> will be retained as written. Where the meaning is sufficiently unclear to require editorial intervention, the expansion will be given in the explanatory annotation. <u>Capitalization</u> will follow the usage of the writer. Because the line between uppercase and lowercase letters can be a very fine and fluctuating one, when it is impossible to make an absolute determination of the author's intention, we will adopt modern usage. Jefferson rarely began his sentences with an uppercase letter, and we conform to his usage. <u>Punctuation</u> will be retained as written and double marks of punctuation, such as a period followed by a dash, will be allowed to stand. Misspellings or so-called slips of the pen will be allowed to stand or will be recorded in a subjoined textual note.

English translations or translation summaries will be supplied for foreign-language documents. In some instances, when documents are lengthy and not especially pertinent to Jefferson's concerns or if our edition's typography cannot adequately represent the script of a language, we will provide only a summary in English. In most cases we will print in full the text in its original language and also provide a full English translation. If a contemporary translation that Jefferson made or would have used is extant, we may print it in lieu of a modern translation. Our own translations are designed to provide a basic readable English text for the modern user rather than to preserve all aspects of the original diction and language.

[xi]

2. TEXTUAL DEVICES

The following devices are employed throughout the work to clarify the presentation of the text.

[. . .]   Text missing and not conjecturable.

[ ]   Number or part of a number missing or illegible.

[roman]   Conjectural reading for missing or illegible matter. A question mark follows when the reading is doubtful.

[*italic*]   Editorial comment inserted in the text.

<*italic*>   Matter deleted in the MS but restored in our text.

3. DESCRIPTIVE SYMBOLS

The following symbols are employed throughout the work to describe the various kinds of manuscript originals. When a series of versions is recorded, the first to be recorded is the version used for the printed text.

Dft   draft (usually a composition or rough draft; later drafts, when identifiable as such, are designated "2d Dft," &c.)

Dupl   duplicate

MS   manuscript (arbitrarily applied to most documents other than letters)

N   note, notes (memoranda, fragments, &c.)

PoC   polygraph copy

PrC   press copy

RC   recipient's copy

SC   stylograph copy

Tripl   triplicate

All manuscripts of the above types are assumed to be in the hand of the author of the document to which the descriptive symbol pertains. If not, that *fact is stated*. On the other hand, the following types of manuscripts are assumed *not* to be in the hand of the author, and exceptions will be noted:

FC   file copy (applied to all contemporary copies retained by the author or his agents)

Lb   letterbook (ordinarily used with FC and Tr to denote texts copied into bound volumes)

Tr   transcript (applied to all contemporary and later copies except file copies; period of transcription, unless clear by implication, will be given when known)

4. LOCATION SYMBOLS

The locations of documents printed in this edition from originals in private hands and from printed sources are recorded in self-explanatory form in the descriptive note following each document. The locations of documents printed from originals held by public and private institutions in the United States are recorded by means of the symbols used in the National Union Catalog in the Library of Congress; an explanation of how these symbols are formed is given in Vol. 1: xl. The symbols DLC and MHi by themselves stand for the collections of Jefferson Papers proper in these repositories; when texts are drawn from other collections held by these two institutions, the names of those collections will be added. Location symbols for documents held by institutions outside the United States are given in a subjoined list. The lists of symbols are limited to the institutions represented by documents printed or referred to in this volume.

CLU-C   University of California, Los Angeles, William Andrews Clark Memorial Library

CSmH   The Huntington Library, San Marino, California

CtHi   Connecticut Historical Society, Hartford

CtY   Yale University, New Haven

DeGH   Hagley Museum and Library, Greenville, Delaware

DLC   Library of Congress

DNA   The National Archives, with identifications of series (preceded by record group number) as follows:

        CD   Consular Dispatches

        LAR   Letters of Application and Recommendation

        LPG   Letters by Postmaster General

        MTA   Miscellaneous Treasury Accounts

InMuB   Ball State University, Muncie, Indiana

MHi   Massachusetts Historical Society, Boston

MWA   American Antiquarian Society, Worcester, Massachusetts

MoSHi   Missouri Historical Society, St. Louis

NHi   New-York Historical Society, New York City

NHC	Colgate University, Hamilton, New York
NIC	Cornell University, Ithaca, New York
NN	New York Public Library
NNMus	Museum of the City of New York
NNPM	Pierpont Morgan Library, New York City
NhHi	New Hampshire Historical Society, Concord
NjP	Princeton University
PHi	Historical Society of Pennsylvania, Philadelphia
PPAmP	American Philosophical Society, Philadelphia
PPL	Library Company of Philadelphia
PWacD	David Library of the American Revolution, Washington Crossing, Pennsylvania
PWbH	Wyoming Historical and Geological Society, Wilkes-Barre, Pennsylvania
ViHi	Virginia Historical Society, Richmond
ViU	University of Virginia, Charlottesville
ViW	College of William and Mary, Williamsburg, Virginia
WvLe	Greenbriar County Public Library, Lewisburg, West Virginia

The following symbol represents a repository located outside of the United States:

| AHN | Archivo Histórico National, Madrid |

5. OTHER SYMBOLS AND ABBREVIATIONS

The following symbols and abbreviations are commonly employed in the annotation throughout the work.

Second Series   The topical series to be published as part of this edition, comprising those materials which are best suited to a topical rather than a chronological arrangement (see Vol. 1: xv-xvi)

TJ   Thomas Jefferson

TJ Editorial Files   Photoduplicates and other editorial materials in the office of The Papers of Thomas Jefferson, Princeton University Library

TJ Papers   Jefferson Papers (applied to a collection of manuscripts when the precise location of an undated, misdated, or otherwise problematic document must be furnished, and always preceded by the symbol for the institutional repository; thus "DLC: TJ Papers, 4:628-9" represents a document in the Library of Congress, Jefferson Papers, volume 4, pages 628 and 629. Citations to volumes and folio numbers of the Jefferson Papers at the Library of Congress refer to the collection as it was arranged at the time the first microfilm edition was made in 1944-45. Access to the microfilm edition of the collection as it was rearranged under the Library's Presidential Papers Program is provided by the Index to the Thomas Jefferson Papers [Washington, D.C., 1976])

RG   Record Group (used in designating the location of documents in the National Archives)

SJL   Jefferson's "Summary Journal of Letters" written and received for the period 11 Nov. 1783 to 25 June 1826 (in DLC: TJ Papers). This register, kept in Jefferson's hand, has been checked against the TJ Editorial Files. It is to be assumed that all outgoing letters are recorded in SJL unless there is a note to the contrary. When the date of receipt of an incoming letter is recorded in SJL, it is incorporated in the notes. Information and discrepancies revealed in SJL but not found in the letter itself are also noted. Missing letters recorded in SJL are, where possible, accounted for in the notes to documents mentioning them or in related documents. A more detailed discussion of this register and its use in this edition appears in Vol. 6: vii-x

SJPL   "Summary Journal of Public Letters," an incomplete list of letters and documents written by TJ from 16 Apr. 1784 to 31 Dec. 1793, with brief summaries, in an amanuensis's hand. This is supplemented by six pages in TJ's hand, compiled at a later date, listing private and confidential memorandums and notes as well as official reports and communications by and to him as Secretary of State, 11 Oct. 1789 to 31 Dec. 1793 (in DLC: TJ Papers, Epistolary Record, 514-59 and 209-11, respectively; see Vol. 22: ix-x). Since nearly all documents in the amanuensis's list are registered in SJL, while few in TJ's list are so recorded, it is to be assumed that all references to SJPL are to the list in TJ's hand unless there is a statement to the contrary

V   Ecu

_f_   Florin

£   Pound sterling or livre, depending upon context (in doubtful cases, a clarifying note will be given)

s   Shilling or sou (also expressed as /)

d   Penny or denier

₶   Livre Tournois

℈   Per (occasionally used for pro, pre)

6. SHORT TITLES

The following list includes short titles of works cited frequently in this edition. Since it is impossible to anticipate all the works to be cited in abbreviated form, the list is revised from volume to volume.

Adams, *Diary*   L. H. Butterfield and others, eds., *Diary and Autobiography of John Adams*, Cambridge, Mass., 1961, 4 vols.

Adams, *Works*   Charles Francis Adams, ed., *The Works of John Adams*, Boston, 1850-56, 10 vols.

Ammon, *Monroe*   Harry Ammon, *James Monroe: The Quest for National Identity*, New York, 1971

ANB   John A. Garraty and Mark C. Carnes, eds., *American National Biography*, New York and Oxford, 1999, 24 vols.

Annals   *Annals of the Congress of the United States: The Debates and Proceedings in the Congress of the United States . . . Compiled from Authentic Materials*, Washington, D.C., Gales & Seaton, 1834-56, 42 vols. All editions are undependable and pagination varies from one printing to another. The first two volumes of the set cited here have "Compiled . . . by Joseph Gales, Senior" on the title page and bear the caption "Gales & Seatons History" on verso and "of Debates in Congress" on recto pages. The remaining volumes bear the caption "History of Congress" on both recto and verso pages. Those using the first two volumes with the latter caption will need to employ the date of the debate or the indexes of debates and speakers.

APS   American Philosophical Society

ASP   *American State Papers: Documents, Legislative and Executive, of the Congress of the United States*, Washington, D.C., 1832-61, 38 vols.

Bear, *Family Letters*   Edwin M. Betts and James A. Bear, Jr., eds., *Family Letters of Thomas Jefferson*, Columbia, Mo., 1966

Betts, *Farm Book*   Edwin M. Betts, ed., *Thomas Jefferson's Farm Book*, Princeton, 1953

Betts, *Garden Book*   Edwin M. Betts, ed., *Thomas Jefferson's Garden Book, 1766-1824*, Philadelphia, 1944

Biog. Dir. Cong.   *Biographical Directory of the United States Congress, 1774-1989*, Washington, D.C., 1989

Boand, *Lewis Littlepage*   Nell Holladay Boand, *Lewis Littlepage* Richmond, 1970

Brant, *Madison*   Irving Brant, *James Madison*, Indianapolis, 1941-61, 6 vols.

Brigham, *American Newspapers*   Clarence S. Brigham, *History* and Bibliography of American Newspapers, 1690-1820, Worcester, Mass., 1947, 2 vols.

Bryan, *National Capital*   Wilhelmus Bogart Bryan, *A History of the National Capital From Its Foundation Through the Period of the Adoption of the Organic Act*, New York, 1914-16, 2 vols.

Bush, *Life Portraits*   Alfred L. Bush, *The Life Portraits of Thomas Jefferson*, rev. ed., Charlottesville, 1987

Conway, *Omitted Chapters*   Moncure Daniel Conway, *Omitted Chapters of History Disclosed in the Life and Papers of Edmund Randolph, Governor of Virginia; First Attorney-General United States, Secretary of State*, New York, 1888

Cooke, *Coxe*   Jacob E. Cooke, *Tench Coxe and the Early Republic*, Chapel Hill, 1978

Cunningham, *Jeffersonian Republicans*   Noble E. Cunningham, Jr., *The Jeffersonian Republicans: The Formation of Party Organization, 1789-1801,* Chapel Hill, 1957

CVSP   William P. Palmer and others, eds., *Calendar of Virginia State Papers . . . Preserved in the Capitol at Richmond*, Richmond, 1875-93, 11 vols.

DAB   Allen Johnson and Dumas Malone, eds., *Dictionary of American Biography*, New York, 1928-36, 20 vols.

Dauer, *Adams Federalists*   Manning J. Dauer, *The Adams Federalists*, Baltimore, 1953

DeConde, *Quasi-War*   Alexander DeConde, *The Quasi-War: The Politics and Diplomacy of the Undeclared War with France, 1797-1801*, New York, 1966

Dexter, *Yale*   Franklin Bowditch Dexter, *Biographical Sketches of the Graduates of Yale College with Annals of the College History*, New York, 1885-1912, 6 vols.

DHSC   Maeva Marcus and others, eds., *The Documentary History of the Supreme Court of the United States, 1789-1800*, New York, 1985- , 7 vols.

Dictionnaire   *Dictionnaire de biographie française*, Paris, 1933- , 18 vols.

DNB   Leslie Stephen and Sidney Lee, eds., *Dictionary of National Biography*, 2d ed., New York, 1908-09, 22 vols.

DSB   Charles C. Gillispie, ed., *Dictionary of Scientific Biography*, New York, 1970-80, 16 vols.

Durey, *Callender*   Michael Durey, *"With the Hammer of Truth"*: *James Thomson Callender and America's Early National Heroes*, Charlottesville, 1990

EG   Dickinson W. Adams and Ruth W. Lester, eds., *Jefferson's*

Extracts from the Gospels, Princeton, 1983, *The Papers of Thomas Jefferson*, Second Series

Egerton, *Gabriel's Rebellion*   Douglas R. Egerton, *Gabriel's Rebellion: The Virginia Slave Conspiracies of 1800 and 1802*, Chapel Hill, 1993.

Ehrman, *Pitt*   John Ehrman, *The Younger Pitt: The Consuming Struggle*, London, 1996

Elkins and McKitrick, *Age of Federalism*   Stanley Elkins and Eric McKitrick, *The Age of Federalism*, New York, 1993

Evans   Charles Evans, Clifford K. Shipton, and Roger P. Bristol, comps., *American Bibliography: A Chronological Dictionary of all Books, Pamphlets and Periodical Publications Printed in the United States of America from . . . 1639 . . . to . . . 1820*, Chicago and Worcester, Mass., 1903-59, 14 vols.

Fitzpatrick, *Writings*   John C. Fitzpatrick, ed., *The Writings of George Washington*, Washington, D.C., 1931-44, 39 vols.

Ford   Paul Leicester Ford, ed., *The Writings of Thomas Jefferson*, Letterpress Edition, New York, 1892-99, 10 vols.

Gallatin, *Papers*   Carl E. Prince and Helene E. Fineman, eds., *The Papers of Albert Gallatin*, microfilm edition in 46 reels, Philadelphia, 1969, and Supplement, Barbara B. Oberg, ed., reels 47-51, Wilmington, Del., 1985

Gawalt, *Justifying Jefferson*   Gerard W. Gawalt, *Justifying Jefferson: The Political Writings of John James Beckley*, Washington, D.C., 1995

Gilpatrick, *Jeffersonian Democracy in North Carolina*   Delbert Harold Gilpatrick, *Jeffersonian Democracy in North Carolina, 1789-1816*, New York, 1931

Greene, *American Science*   John C. Greene, *American Science in the Age of Jefferson*, Ames, Iowa, 1984

Harrison, *Princetonians, 1769-1775*   Richard A. Harrison, *Princetonians—1769-1775—A Biographical Dictionary*, Princeton, 1980

HAW   Henry A. Washington, ed., *The Writings of Thomas Jefferson*, New York, 1853-54, 9 vols.

Heitman, *Dictionary*   Francis B. Heitman, comp., *Historical Register and Dictionary of the United States Army . . .* , Washington, D.C., 1903, 2 vols.

Heitman, *Register*   Francis B. Heitman, *Historical Register of Officers of the Continental Army during the War of the Revolution, April, 1775, to December, 1793*, new ed., Washington, D.C., 1914

Hening   William Waller Hening, ed., *The Statutes at Large; Being a Collection of All the Laws of Virginia*, Richmond, 1809-23, 13 vols.

JAH   *Journal of American History*, 1964-

Jefferson Correspondence, Bixby   Worthington C. Ford, ed., *Thomas Jefferson Correspondence Printed from the Originals in the Collections of William K. Bixby*, Boston, 1916

JEP   *Journal of the Executive Proceedings of the Senate of the United States . . . to the Termination of the Nineteenth Congress*, Washington, D.C., 1828, 3 vols.

JHD   *Journal of the House of Delegates of the Commonwealth of Virginia* (cited by session and date of publication)

JHR   *Journal of the House of Representatives of the United States*, Washington, D.C., 1826, 9 vols.

JS   *Journal of the Senate of the United States*, Washington, D.C., 1820-21, 5 vols.

Keane, *Paine*   John Keane, *Tom Paine: A Political Life*, London, 1995

King, *Life*   Charles R. King, ed. *The Life and Correspondence of Rufus King: Comprising His Letters, Private and Official, His Public Documents and His Speeches*, New York, 1894-1900, 6 vols.

Kline, *Burr*   Mary-Jo Kline, ed., *Political Correspondence and Public Papers of Aaron Burr*, Princeton, 1983, 2 vols.

L & B   Andrew A. Lipscomb and Albert E. Bergh, eds., *The Writings of Thomas Jefferson*, Washington, D.C., 1903-04, 20 vols.

Latrobe, *Virginia Journals*   Edward C. Carter II and others, eds., *The Virginia Journals of Benjamin Henry Latrobe, 1795-1798*, New Haven, 1977, 2 vols.

LCB   Douglas L. Wilson, ed., *Jefferson's Literary Commonplace Book*, Princeton, 1989, *The Papers of Thomas Jefferson*, Second Series

Leonard, *General Assembly*   Cynthia Miller Leonard, comp., *The General Assembly of Virginia, July 30, 1619-January 11, 1978: A Bicentennial Register of Members*, Richmond, 1978

List of Patents   *A List of Patents granted by the United States from April 10, 1792, to December 31, 1836*, Washington, D.C., 1872

Madison, *Letters*   William C. Rives and Philip R. Fendall, eds., *Letters and Other Writings of James Madison . . . Published by Order of Congress*, Philadelphia, 1865, 4 vols.

Madison, *Papers*   William T. Hutchinson, Robert A. Rutland, J. C. A. Stagg, and others, eds., *The Papers of James Madison*, Chicago and Charlottesville, 1962- , 28 vols.

Sec. of State Ser., 1986- , 6 vols.

Malone, *Jefferson*   Dumas Malone, *Jefferson and His Time*, Boston, 1948-81, 6 vols.

Marshall, *Papers*   Herbert A. Johnson, Charles T. Cullen, Charles F. Hobson, and others, eds., *The Papers of John Marshall*, Chapel Hill, 1974- , 11 vols.

MB   James A. Bear, Jr., and Lucia C. Stanton, eds., *Jefferson's Memorandum Books: Accounts, with Legal Records and Miscellany, 1767-1826*, Princeton, 1997, *The Papers of Thomas Jefferson*, Second Series

Miller, *Treaties*   Hunter Miller, ed., *Treaties and other International Acts of the United States of America*, Washington, D.C., 1931-48, 8 vols.

Monroe, *Writings*   Stanislaus Murray Hamilton, ed., *The Writings of James Monroe*, New York, 1898-1903, 7 vols.

NDQW   Dudley W. Knox, ed., *Naval Documents Related to the Quasi-War between the United States and France*, Washington, D.C., 1935-38, 7 vols.

Naval Operations from January 1800 to May 1800

Niemcewicz, *Under their Vine*   Julian Ursin Niemcewicz, *Under their Vine and Fig Tree: Travels through America in 1797-1799, 1805, with some Further Account of Life in New Jersey*, Elizabeth, N.J., 1965

Notes, ed. Peden   Thomas Jefferson, *Notes on the State of Virginia*, ed. William Peden, Chapel Hill, 1955

OED   Sir James Murray and others, eds., *A New English Dictionary on Historical Principles*, Oxford, 1888-1933

Parliamentary Manual, 1801   Thomas Jefferson, *A Manual of Parliamentary Practice. For the Use of the Senate of the United States*, Washington, D.C., 1801

Pasley, *Tyranny of Printers*   Jeffrey L. Pasley, *"The Tyranny of Printers": Newspaper Politics in the Early American Republic*, Charlottesville, 2001

Peale, *Papers*   Lillian B. Miller and others, eds., *The Selected Papers of Charles Willson Peale and His Family*, New Haven, 1983-2000, 5 vols. in 6

Peterson, *Jefferson*   Merrill D. Peterson, *Thomas Jefferson and the New Nation*, New York, 1970

PMHB   *Pennsylvania Magazine of History and Biography*, 1877-

Preston, *Catalogue*   Daniel Preston, *A Comprehensive Catalogue of the Correspondence and Papers of James Monroe*, Westport, Conn., 2001, 2 vols.

Prince, *Federalists*   Carl E. Prince, *The Federalists and the Origins of the U.S. Civil Service*, New York, 1977

PW   Wilbur S. Howell, ed., *Jefferson's Parliamentary Writings*, Princeton, 1988, *The Papers of Thomas Jefferson*, Second Series

Randall, *Life*   Henry S. Randall, *The Life of Thomas Jefferson*, New York, 1858, 3 vols.

Randolph, *Domestic Life*   Sarah N. Randolph, *The Domestic Life of Thomas Jefferson, Compiled from Family Letters and Reminiscences by His Great-Granddaughter*, 3d ed., Cambridge, Mass., 1939

Roider, *Thugut*   Karl A. Roider, Jr., *Baron Thugut and Austria's Response to the French Revolution*, Princeton, 1987

Saricks, *Du Pont*   Ambrose Saricks, *Pierre Samuel Du Pont de Nemours*, Lawrence, Kans., 1965

S.C. Biographical Directory, House of Representatives   J. S. R. Faunt, Walter B. Edgar, N. Louise Bailey, and others, eds., *Biographical Directory of the South Carolina House of Representatives,* Columbia, S.C., 1974-92, 5 vols.

Scott and Rothaus, *Historical Dictionary*   Samuel F. Scott and Barry Rothaus, eds., *Historical Dictionary of the French Revolution, 1789-1799*, Westport, Conn., 1985, 2 vols.

Shackelford, *Jefferson's Adoptive Son*   George Green Shackelford, *Jefferson's Adoptive Son: The Life of William Short, 1759-1848*, Lexington, Ky., 1993

Shaw-Shoemaker   Ralph R. Shaw and Richard H. Shoemaker, comps., *American Bibliography: A Preliminary Checklist for 1801-1819*, New York, 1958-63, 22 vols.

Shepherd, *Statutes*   Samuel Shepherd, ed., *The Statutes at Large of Virginia, from October Session 1792, to December Session 1806 . . .*, Richmond, 1835-36, 3 vols.

Smith, *Freedom's Fetters*   James Morton Smith, *Freedom's Fetters: The Alien and Sedition Laws and American Civil Liberties*, Ithaca, N.Y., 1956

Sowerby   E. Millicent Sowerby, comp., *Catalogue of the Library of Thomas Jefferson*, Washington, D.C., 1952-59, 5 vols.

Stafford, *Philadelphia Directory, for 1800*   Cornelius William Stafford, *The Philadelphia Directory, for 1800,* Philadelphia, 1800

Stets, *Postmasters*   Robert J. Stets, *Postmasters & Postoffices of the United States 1782-1811*, Lake Oswego, Oregon, 1994

Stewart, *French Revolution*   John H. Stewart, *A Documentary Survey of the French Revolution*, New York, 1951

Syrett, *Hamilton*   Harold C. Syrett and others, eds., *The Papers of Alexander Hamilton*, New York, 1961-87, 27 vols.

Terr. Papers   Clarence E. Carter and John Porter Bloom, eds., *The Territorial Papers of the United States*, Washington, D.C., 1934-75, 28 vols.

Tinkcom, *Republicans and Federalists*   Harry Marlin Tinkcom, *The Republicans and Federalists in Pennsylvania 1790-1801: A Study in National Stimulus and Local Response*, Harrisburg, 1950

TJR   Thomas Jefferson Randolph, ed., *Memoir, Correspondence, and Miscellanies, from the Papers of Thomas Jefferson*, Charlottesville, 1829, 4 vols.

Tucker, *Life*   George Tucker, *The Life of Thomas Jefferson*, Philadelphia, 1837, 2 vols.

Tulard, *Dictionaire Napoléon*   Jean Tulard, *Dictionnaire Napoléon*, Paris, 1987

U.S. Statutes at Large   Richard Peters, ed., *The Public Statutes at Large of the United States . . . 1789 to March 3, 1845*, Boston, 1855-56, 8 vols.

VMHB   *Virginia Magazine of History and Biography*, 1893-

Washington, *Diaries*   Donald Jackson and Dorothy Twohig, eds., *The Diaries of George Washington*, Charlottesville, 1976-79, 6 vols.

Washington, *Papers*   W. W. Abbot, Dorothy Twohig, Philander D. Chase, and others, eds., *The Papers of George Washington*, Charlottesville, 1983- , 44 vols.

   Pres. Ser., 1987- , 11 vols.

   Ret. Ser., 1998-99, 4 vols.

WMQ   *William and Mary Quarterly*, 1892-

Woods, *Albemarle*   Edgar Woods, *Albemarle County in Virginia*, Charlottesville, 1901

CONTENTS

1800

CONTENTS

CONTENTS

CONTENTS

CONTENTS

CONTENTS

CONTENTS

·«⟨ 1 8 0 1 ⟩»·

CONTENTS

CONTENTS

CONTENTS

CONTENTS

CONTENTS

ILLUSTRATIONS

Following page 328

PIANO BY JOHN ISAAC HAWKINS

Inventor John Isaac Hawkins obtained an American patent for his design of a compact, portable, upright piano in 1800. Calling it "the prettiest improvement in the Forte piano I have ever seen," Jefferson purchased a five-and-one-half octave model for $264 for his daughter Mary Jefferson Eppes to play at Monticello. Two years later, Jefferson returned the piano to Hawkins for repair or exchange because it would not stay in tune (TJ to Hawkins, 13 Apr. 1802). There is no record that Hawkins sent a substitute to Jefferson.

The major innovation in Hawkins's design was that the strings of the piano extended below the keyboard down to the ground. Other upright pianos at the time were inverted grand pianos, rising high above the players' hands. Hawkins changed the location of where the strings were struck, from one end of the string to the middle. When the piano case was shut, Jefferson observed, Hawkins's piano resembled "the under half of a book case, & may be moved, by it's handles, to the fire side." Jefferson's description suggests that the keyboard folded up into the cabinet, as can be done with the piano shown in the illustration, which was made in Philadelphia in 1801 according to a label on the instrument. The photographed piano measures approximately three-and-one-half feet high, three feet wide, and over a foot deep.

Described by Jefferson as a "very ingenious, modest & poor young man," Hawkins also invented the polygraph, a multiple-pen writing device that Jefferson used, before he returned to England, his native country, in 1803 at age 31. A close friend of Charles Willson Peale's family, Hawkins collaborated with Rembrandt Peale on a song titled "The People's Friend" that celebrated Jefferson's presidential inauguration in March 1801 (*The New Grove Dictionary of Music and Musicians*, 2d ed., 29 vols. [New York, 2001], 11:168; MB, 2:1014n; Vol. 31:365-6; TJ to Mary Jefferson Eppes, 4 July 1800; Mary Jefferson Eppes to TJ, 2 Feb. 1801; Charles Willson Peale to TJ, 8 Mch. 1801.)

Courtesy of the National Museum of American History, Smithsonian Institution.

QUERIES ON PARLIAMENTARY PROCEDURE

Illustrated here is one page of a set of questions by Jefferson on parliamentary procedure with answers written alongside in the smaller handwriting of Edmund Pendleton, one of Virginia's elder statesmen. As vice president of the United States and president of the Senate from March 1797 to February 1801, Jefferson was for the only time in his career the presiding officer of a legislative body. Finding no existing guide to procedure, he set out to compile one for his own use. The result, first printed in 1801 as *A Manual of Parliamentary Practice*, is still used (*Constitution, Jefferson's Manual and Rules of the House of Representatives of the United States, One Hundred Eighth Congress* [Washington, D.C., 2003]). To solve some of the riddles of legislative practice, Jefferson in February 1800 sent queries to his old Williamsburg law mentor George Wythe, whose legislative experience had included, along with service in the Virginia House of Burgesses and the Continental Congress, the clerkship of the Burgesses, 1768-76. Wythe, who was in his mid-seventies, was having difficulty writing and did not have most of his old notes and papers. After a reminder from Jefferson in April 1800, Wythe returned the queries unanswered, stating that he could be of little help on the subject of parliamentary procedure. Jefferson immediately sent the questions to Edmund Pendleton, whose experience from 1752 to 1778 encompassed membership in the House of Burgesses and the legislative bodies that succeeded it. Pendleton had also presided over the Committee of Safety, more than one of the state's legislative conventions during the Revolution, and a session of the House of Delegates. In 1788 he was president of the state's convention for ratification of the U.S. Constitution. Jefferson, by the time he sent the interrogatories to Pendleton on 19 Apr. 1800, said that he would be satisfied with the simplest "yea, or nay" response next to a question, but Pendleton was much fuller than that in most of his answers. The queries and responses are printed in this volume with Pendleton's letter of 17 June 1800. On 7 Dec. Wythe sent replies to a shorter set of queries from Jefferson (ANB; Leonard, *General Assembly*, 83, 85, 86, 88, 91, 94-105, 109, 112, 114, 117-22, 125, 172, 174; Vol. 31:400-1, 486-7, 494, 520-1).

Courtesy of the Library of Congress.

AARON BURR

Jefferson and Aaron Burr had some contact in Philadelphia in the early 1790s, when Burr was a senator and Jefferson secretary of state, but it was only in 1796 that they began any regular exchange of correspondence. Even then, with the exception of a long letter from Jefferson to Burr in June 1797 touching on several aspects of politics and matters of public interest, written communication between them tended to deal not with politics but with the business affairs of Dr. James Currie, for whom Jefferson had enlisted Burr's legal services. The lack of regular and trustworthy means of conveying letters accounts at least in part for the absence of political correspondence between them. "No freedom of communication, by letter, can be indulged consistently with any degree of discretion," Burr complained in the spring of 1798. Jefferson cited the "want of confidence in our posts," and writing to James Monroe he used code to disguise Burr's name in case the letter should fall into the wrong hands. Their political opponents were also anxious to monitor any face-to-face meetings between Burr and Jefferson. One of Alexander Hamilton's associates took care to note that Jefferson and Madison, in New York City in the spring of 1791, had met with Burr and Robert R. Livingston. And as the election of 1796 came on, Virginia Federalists made much of a brief stopover by Burr at Monticello in October 1795 (Vol. 20:434-5; Vol. 23:19-24; Vol. 25:66-7; Vol. 28:512; Vol. 29:72, 195-6, 198-9, 437-40, 447-8; Vol. 30:249, 356-7, 362-3, 366-7, 413-14, 576-7, 616-17; Vol. 31:300-1, 556n).

Burr was in his mid-forties in 1802 when John Vanderlyn painted this portrait of him, which measures approximately $28\frac{1}{2}$ by 22 inches. Vanderlyn, the son of a Kingston, New York, housepainter and sign maker, began to draw

and paint at a young age. After moving to New York City he attracted the attention of influential patrons, including Burr, whose attention was first drawn by Vanderlyn's copy of a Gilbert Stuart portrait of him. With Burr's financial support and contacts the young painter, who was then in his early twenties, worked in Stuart's Philadelphia studio for several months and studied in France from 1796 to 1801. Before Vanderlyn returned to Europe in 1803 for an extended stay, Jefferson paid him a subscription of $20 for two engravings of Niagara Falls. Jefferson received the engravings, which were produced by an English firm, in 1805 (ANB; Kline, *Burr*, 1:217n; MB, 2:1093).
Courtesy of the Yale University Art Gallery.

BENJAMIN RUSH

As Benjamin Rush recalled in a letter to Jefferson of 6 Oct. 1800, the two of them first met "on the banks of Skuilkill" in the year 1775. The occasion, a dinner to honor George Washington, made a lasting impression on Rush, who at the time was practicing medicine and teaching chemistry in Philadelphia. He and Jefferson corresponded sporadically during the 1780s and more regularly in the 1790s. In the period covered by this volume they wrote and conversed on a range of what the doctor characterized as "innocent & interesting subjects," including politics and muskmelon seeds. On 22 Aug. 1800 Rush reminded Jefferson of a promise to explain his "religious Creed." Jefferson framed his response of 23 Sep. within a specific context of current politics, denouncing criticism of him by New England clergymen and including a sentence that has become renowned: "for I have sworn upon the altar of god eternal hostility against every form of tyranny over the mind of man" (George W. Corner, ed., *The Autobiography of Benjamin Rush: His "Travels Through Life" together with his* Commonplace Book *for 1789-1813* [Princeton, 1948], 112-13; ANB).

This engraved portrait of Rush, made in Philadelphia in 1802, is one of about nine hundred profile portraits made in America by Charles Balthazar Julien Févret de Saint-Mémin (1770-1852). Saint-Mémin came to the United States in 1793. He taught himself engraving and printmaking in New York City, where he met another French émigré from whom he learned how to make profile portraits using a physiognotrace, a mechanical drawing device developed in France in the 1780s. The device's invention coincided with the publication of J. K. Lavater's theory of physiognomy, which held that facial features revealed moral character. Saint-Mémin's profile portraits also suited contemporary neoclassical taste. He worked in Baltimore, Washington (where he made a likeness of Jefferson in 1804), Richmond, and Charleston before returning to France in 1814 and becoming the director of the Musée des Beaux-Arts in Dijon. The image of Rush shown in this volume is from an album that Saint-Mémin gave to a friend in 1842. It has the standard measure of the artist's engraved profile portraits, $2\frac{1}{4}$ inches in diameter (Ellen G. Miles, *Saint-Mémin and the Neoclassical Profile Portrait in America* [Washington D.C., 1994], 27-45, 233, 383-4; Jane Turner, ed., *The Dictionary of Art*, 34 vols. [New York, 1996], 27:567; H. C. Rice, Jr., "An Album of Saint-Mémin Portraits," *Princeton Univ. Lib. Chronicle*, 13 [1951], 23-31; MB, 2:1140; Vol. 14:xli-xliv).
Courtesy of Princeton University Library.

ILLUSTRATIONS

JAMES A. BAYARD

As 1801 opened, James A. Bayard appeared to control the nation's "political destiny." The House of Representatives would ballot by states to resolve the electoral tie, and Bayard, as Delaware's lone representative, constituted one of the sixteen state votes. A resolute Federalist whose actions in Congress had not endeared him to the Republican interest, Bayard was nonetheless so rational and well-grounded, in Caesar A. Rodney's opinion, that Rodney considered him a friend despite their severe political differences. As rumors flew, some of Jefferson's supporters thought that Bayard was in their camp — "God grant it may be so!"—but unknown to them was Bayard's comment to Alexander Hamilton in January that "I am by no means decided" (Vol. 30:472-3, 615n; Vol. 31:357n, 408, 410n; Benjamin Hichborn to TJ, 5 Jan. 1801; TJ to Thomas Mann Randolph, 9 Jan.; Dr. John Vaughan to TJ, 10 Jan. 1801).

Saint-Mémin drew this portrait of Bayard in Philadelphia in 1801. As a drawing in black and white chalk on paper coated with a pink wash, this is a relic of the first part of Saint-Mémin's method of making profile portraits. Typically the artist's next step was to reduce the image to a copper plate for an engraving that was about one-tenth the size of the original drawing. This drawing of Bayard measures $20\frac{3}{4}$ inches by $15\frac{1}{2}$ inches (Miles, *Saint-Mémin*, 245; Turner, ed., *Dictionary of Art*, 27:567).

Courtesy of the Baltimore Museum of Art.

NAPOLEON BONAPARTE

When word of the coup of 18 Brumaire reached the United States in January 1800, some Americans believed that it foretold the restoration of monarchy to France. Jefferson was surprised that Bonaparte was not immediately assassinated by his fellow citizens—with justice—for usurping the government and putting an end to revolutionary progress. Yet Jefferson soon declared that "without much faith in Buonaparte's heart, I have so much in his head" as to allow the possibility that the general might use his new power for the benefit of republican government. In the months that followed, Bonaparte and France wrested peace from Austria, explored prospects of a settlement with Great Britain, and negotiated an agreement with American envoys Oliver Ellsworth, William R. Davie, and William Vans Murray to end the undeclared conflict between the two nations. Bonaparte took a personal interest in the shaping of the Convention of 1800 and had a prominent role in the celebration and banquet held at Môrtefontaine chateau in early October to mark the signing of the pact. This portrait in oils by the French artist Louis Léopold Boilly (1761-1845) depicts the sitter as first consul and dates from about 1800-02. Despite Jefferson's reservations about Bonaparte's "heart," the painting shows Boilly's predilection for emotional aspects of his subjects—in contrast to Jacques Louis David, who in about the same year portrayed Bonaparte as a heroic general on a spirited steed crossing the Alps (Turner, ed., *Dictionary of Art*, 4:241; Tulard, *Dictionnaire Napoléon*, 241, 572; Vol. 31:333, 336, 343-5, 351, 354, 357-8, 360, 395).

Private collection; courtesy of the Bridgeman Art Library.

ILLUSTRATIONS

PIERRE SAMUEL DU PONT DE NEMOURS

This sketch appropriately depicts Du Pont de Nemours at a writing table with quill and ink near at hand. In France the energetic physiocrat was a member of the National Institute, wrote on subjects as diverse as primary schools, international trade, and a *Philosophie de L'Universe*, and was himself a publisher. Arriving in the United States at the beginning of 1800, he was soon elected to membership in the American Philosophical Society and submitted a paper comparing plants, insects, and polyps. His response to Jefferson's request for his views on national education was so extensive that when Du Pont sent it on 24 Aug. 1800 he appropriately referred to it as a book: *voilà le livre*. This sketch dates no later than 1781, the year in which the artist, French painter and printmaker Noël Hallé, died. The signature on the work, "hallé pingebat," means "painted by Hallé." He exhibited in the Paris salons from 1746 to 1779 and was a court painter. A characteristic of his work, which is visible in this scene, was capturing figures in action. Initially scornful of Hallé's paintings, Du Pont held the artist's late work in higher regard. The pen and ink drawing on linen paper measures about $4\frac{1}{2}$ inches by 7 inches (Turner, ed., *Dictionary of Art*, 14:84-5, 29:599; Nicole Willk-Brocard, *Une Dynastie les Hallé: Daniel (1614-1675), Claude-Guy (1652-1736), Noël (1711-1781)* [Paris, 1995], 103, 161, 163; Vol. 30:501-3; Vol. 31:313-14, 495-6, 531n, 578).

Courtesy of the Winterthur Museum.

VIEW OF THE CITY OF WASHINGTON

This early view of the nation's capital city from a point above Georgetown, titled "George Town and Federal City, or City of Washington," shows the sparse urban development of the area when Jefferson arrived on 27 Nov. 1800 to take his place as presiding officer of the Senate. Buildings in the middle distance represent development at the mouth of the Anacostia River. Shown below and to the left is an arched bridge at K Street, an early public works project to link the city of Washington with Georgetown. According to the census, 3,210 persons lived in Washington in 1800. Georgetown had about 3,000 inhabitants, and Alexandria had nearly 5,000 residents. The scene was drawn by George Beck, an English landscape painter who arrived in the United States in 1795. Beck and his wife, who was also an artist, lived in Baltimore, Philadelphia, and after 1808 in Lexington, Kentucky. T. Cartwright engraved the image in London. The aquatint print measures about $16\frac{1}{2}$ inches by 23 inches and was published by Atkins and Nightingale in Philadelphia and London in 1801 (John W. Reps, *Washington on View: The Nation's Capital Since 1790* [Chapel Hill, 1991], 64; Bob Arnebeck, *Through a Fiery Trial: Building Washington 1790-1800* [Lanham, Md., 1991], 72, 124-5; Constance McLaughlin Green, *Washington, Village and Capital, 1800-1878* [Princeton, 1962], 21; George C. Groce and David H. Williams, *The New-York Historical Society's Dictionary of Artists in America, 1564-1860* [New Haven, 1957], 40).

Courtesy of the Library of Congress.

Volume 32

1 June 1800 to 16 February 1801

JEFFERSON CHRONOLOGY

1743 · 1826

1743	Born at Shadwell, 13 Apr. (New Style).
1760	Entered the College of William and Mary.
1762	"quitted college."
1762-1767	Self-education and preparation for law.
1769-1774	Albemarle delegate to House of Burgesses.
1772	Married Martha Wayles Skelton, 1 Jan.
1775-1776	In Continental Congress.
1776	Drafted Declaration of Independence.
1776-1779	In Virginia House of Delegates.
1779	Submitted Bill for Establishing Religious Freedom.
1779-1781	Governor of Virginia.
1782	His wife died, 6 Sep.
1783-1784	In Continental Congress.
1784-1789	In France as Minister Plenipotentiary to negotiate commercial treaties and as Minister Plenipotentiary resident at Versailles.
1790-1793	Secretary of State of the United States.
1797-1801	Vice President of the United States.
1801-1809	President of the United States.
1814-1826	Established the University of Virginia.
1826	Died at Monticello, 4 July.

VOLUME 32

1 June 1800 to 16 February 1801

3 June	James T. Callender convicted after sedition trial in Richmond.
30 June	Baltimore *American* publishes rumor of TJ's death.
4 July	Harvests good wheat crop at Monticello by this date.
13 Aug.	Outlines his principles of government to Gideon Granger.
16 Aug.	Insures buildings at Monticello through Mutual Assurance Society.
22 Aug.	Agrees to lease five fields to John H. Craven.
ca. 2 Sep.	Writes summary of his public service.
5 Sep.	Receives Du Pont's work on national education.
12 Sep.	Learns from James Monroe about Gabriel's revolt in Virginia.
23 Sep.	Responds to Benjamin Rush about his "religious Creed."
8 Oct.	Thomas Cooper released from jail.
ca. 1 Nov.	Visits Poplar Forest.
17 Nov.	Second Session of Sixth Congress opens.
27 Nov.	Arrives in Washington and boards at Conrad & McMunn's.
3 Dec.	Presidential electors meet in their respective states to cast ballots.
12 Dec.	Learns of electoral votes of South Carolina.
14 Dec.	Offers Robert R. Livingston secretaryship of the navy.
18 Dec.	Reports probability of electoral tie.
21 Dec.	Submits parliamentary manual to Samuel Harrison Smith.
3 Jan. 1801	Visits Martha Washington at Mount Vernon.
17 Jan.	Confirms plan to dine with John Adams on 22 Jan.
25 Jan.	Continues as president of the American Philosophical Society.
27 Jan.	Senate consents to Adams's nomination of Marshall as chief justice.
3 Feb.	Senate approves convention with France, with proviso.
11 Feb.	Presidential balloting begins in the House of Representatives.
13 Feb.	Judiciary Act of 1801 takes effect.

THE PAPERS OF

THOMAS JEFFERSON

·◅ ▬▬▬▬▬ ▻·

From Waller Holladay

Dear Sir   Louisa June 1st. 1800—

When Lewis Littlepage left America, he mentioned in the Presence of some of his friends, that he intended to hold a Correspondence with you, during his residence in Europe. He has now been absent nearly fifteen Years, in which time his relations have scarcely ever heard of him, but by doubtfull and unsatisfactory reports. He is my half-brother, and for the Communication of any Accounts you may have received of him, either by his Letters, or otherwise, you will have my own and the gratefull acknowledgments of his affectionate mother. From casual information I have reason to believe, he either now is, or has been at the Court of Russia, but where to address a Letter with any probability of it's reaching him, I know not. He requested his friends to write to him under cover to the Marquis de la Fayette, but the unhappy Situation of that unfortunate Nobleman, and their ignorance of his present place of residence,[1] have hitherto prevented them from pursueing that method. If there is an American Consul at Petersburg, it will be esteemed as a particular obligation, if you will inform me who he is—   I am with the greatest respect

Your most obdt. Servant   Waller Holladay

Dft (ViHi: Holladay Family Papers); addressed: "The Honble Thomas Jefferson Vice President of the United States Albemarle," with "Mr. Bullock" in lower left corner. Probably the retained copy of the letter recorded in SJL from Waller Holladay of 18 June and received on the 26th.

Waller Holladay (1776-1860) was the son of Elizabeth Lewis Littlepage, widow of James Littlepage, and Lewis Holladay, whom she married in 1774. Following six years of study with the rector of Berkeley Parish in Spotsylvania County, Holladay worked for a firm of Scottish import merchants in Fredericksburg, while studying law. He was admitted to legal practice in 1801 but, following the death of Lewis Littlepage in 1802, he abandoned the profession to administer his sizeable inheritance from his half-brother. He purchased land in western Spotsylvania County and built the estate, Prospect Hill, where he lived for the rest of his life. In 1819 he represented the county in the Virginia House of Delegates. He was also a member of the Constitutional Convention of 1829-30 (Horace E. Hayden, *Virginia Genealogies* [Washington, 1931], 361,

364-7; Leonard, *General Assembly*, 300, 353).

CORRESPONDENCE WITH YOU: the last letter TJ received from Lewis Littlepage was that of 26 Dec. 1791. At that time he was a diplomatic agent in the service of Stanislas II, king of Poland. According to SJL, TJ's last letter to Littlepage, a letter of introduction for Henry Middleton, was of 10 Sep. 1792 (TJ to Middleton, 11 Sep. 1792).

In November 1794 President Washington appointed John Miller Russell, a Boston merchant, to serve as AMERICAN CONSUL AT PETERSBURG but the Russian government refused to recognize him when he arrived in 1795 (JEP, 1:164; Nina N. Bashkina and others, eds., *The United States and Russia: The Beginning of Relations, 1765-1815* [Washington, D.C., 1980], 289-92, 357).

[1] Holladay first wrote "unhappy fate of that [fantastic] Nobleman, and their ignorance of his present Situation" before altering the passage to read as above.

From Count Rumford

SIR,
Royal Institution, Albemarle Street,
London, 1st June, 1800.

By direction of the Managers of the Royal Institution of Great Britain I have the honour to transmit to the President of the American Philosophical Society the enclosed Publication, in which an Account is given of an Establishment lately formed in this Metropolis for promoting useful Knowledge.

I have likewise the honour, in conformity to the Instructions I have received, to request that the Society may be assured of the sincere desire of the Managers of the Royal Institution of Great Britain to cultivate a friendly Correspondence with them, and to cooperate with them in all things that may contribute to the Advancement of Science, and to the general Diffusion of the Knowledge of such new and useful Discoveries, and mechanical Improvements, as may tend to increase the Enjoyments, and promote the Industry, Happiness, and Prosperity of Mankind.

I have the honour to be, with much Respect, Sir, Your most Obedient Humble Servant,
RUMFORD.

RC (PPAmP); at foot of text: "To the Honble. Thomas Jefferson, President of the American Philosophical Society Philadelphia"; endorsed by TJ as received 28 Nov. 1800 and so recorded in SJL; also endorsed by an officer of the American Philosophical Society. Enclosure: *The Prospectus, Charter, Ordinances and Bye-Laws of the Royal Institution of Great Britain: Together with Lists of Proprietors and Subscribers* (London, 1800).

Benjamin Thompson (1753-1814), a native of Massachusetts, was made a count (graf) of the Holy Roman Empire in 1790 and took as his title Rumford, the original name of Concord, New Hampshire, where he had lived as a young man. Although TJ was interested in Rumford's designs for fireplaces and chimneys (see Vol. 29:605), the letter above was the only correspondence between the two men. While teaching school in Concord in the early 1770s Thompson had improved his station in life by marrying a wealthy widow from whom he separated after three years. An unabashed Loyalist, he provided General Thomas Gage with information about American military capability, and early in the American War for Independence removed to Britain, where he became a protégé of Lord George Germain. During the latter part of the war, after the battle at Yorktown, he served in America as a lieutenant colonel of the King's American Dragoons. He was knighted by George III and became an adviser to the elector of Bavaria, in which role by energetic efforts toward military and social reform he attained his title. Interested in technological innovation, he made improvements to the designs of both fireplaces and oil lamps, and endowed medals to be given by the Royal Society and the American Academy of Arts and Sciences to promote scientific research. Mindful of Rumford's service

for the British during the American Revolution, John Adams turned down the count's proposal to establish a military academy for the United States. In 1799 Rumford was the prime mover in the creation of the Royal Institution of Great Britain. From 1805 to 1809, when they separated, he was married to the widow of Antoine Laurent Lavoisier. On Rumford's death his estate formed the endowment for a Harvard University professorship in science and mathematics (ANB).

On 16 Dec. 1800 TJ sent both Rumford's letter and the Royal Institution's *Prospectus* to Caspar Wistar. The American Philosophical Society received the letter and the publication on 16 Jan. 1801. The society sent a set of its published *Transactions* to the Royal Institution and early in 1803 elected Rumford to membership (APS, *Proceedings*, 22, pt. 3 [1884], 308-10, 332, 362).

From Gideon Granger

DEAR SIR.   Suffield June 4th. 1800—

Before I left Philadelphia you will recollect that I engaged to give some Information respecting the Issue of the late Election in Connecticut, and the State of the public mind in New England. The period has now arrived when I can speak with more confidence and with more accuracy, than I had even expected. Our Legislature closed it's Session last friday. when our Votes for Candidates for Congress were counted, it appeared that of five new Candidates, necessary to fill the list—Three of the Republican Ticket—Hart, Mather and Granger were elected—Upon the meeting of the Legislature which is composed of about One hundred & Ninety Representatives—The Republicans could count upon 63 in their Interest—while The Other party had not more than 40 who were known to be with them strongly, Altho' the rest went with the Current of N England politics—(their real opinions unknown) before this Time The Charge of Democracy as they Term it was Sufficient to displace any Judge, or Other Officer of Goverment—The party still confiding in their Strength made, at the Meeting of the Repl. for Hartford County, an Attack upon Judge Bull, and succeeded to displace him from his Offices. his defence in the Legislature devolved upon me solely. Their Attack was very violent, Illiberal and uncandid—But when the vote was called to their Utter Astonishment Two Thirds of the House were in favor of Mr: Bull. Their Disappointment exceeded discription. The Charm was broken. Many, very many of the Members, who were unknown—avowed themselves in favor of the Old principles of '76—We had sev'ral Other little Trials of Strength—in evry case we succeeded—In evry instance we gained Strength: and I think I may say with truth that for Ten days before our Session closed we had a clear and decided majority. I am not without Great hopes that Connecticut will afford strong aid towards effecting a change in the Administration and I feel the most perfect confidence, that if she should not and a change should take place, she will be one of the Strongest in Support of the New-Administration. This gives me great pleasure when I reflect, that I had to Support myself, allmost without even accidental—Aid, against a violent Tempest for Three years—Mr: Edwards has avowed himself openly—he will be a Candidate for Senator in the room of Tracey, and about the first of September will resign his offices & take a Seat in Our Legislature at the fall Session—evry possible exertion is making, (tho evry thing is perfectly Still) to effect a change in the Senate & House of Repes. of the UStates—and also in Our Own State Legislature, and also to carry Republican Electors—The whole arangement rests upon Three of Us. we all think the Chances equal at least and yet during all these Things I cannot learn that they apprehend any Such plan—from the habits of Our People & their mode of Electioneering evry Thing is lost, unless the most perfect Secrecy is observed—I am told Govenor Fenner has taken open ground with us. this leads me to believe that there are many chances for Success in Rhode Island—In Short as it respects New England generally, a mighty revolution in Opinion has taken place within One Year—The people are awakening to a True Sense of their Interest—they perceive that the late System of Measures will in a few years rob them of their Liberty and property, and they are fast rallying round the Standard of Republicanism—They cannot much longer be deceived by the Cry that we mean to destroy the Constitution & Govermt of Our Common Country—They must— They will know that all Such representations are false. Many of the proprietors here feel very uneasy at a report that Tracey is next fall to be Governor of the NorthWest Territory—There are many Republicans Who are removing into that Country that abhor his System of Terror—

you will recollect, Sir, that I had the pleasure of Introducing to Your Acquaintance at Philadelphia my Brother in Law Calvin Pease

Esq. who has removed onto the Connecticut Reserve—he is a Candidate for the Offices of Clerk of the County—Clerk of the quarter Sessions & Clerk of the Orphans Court in a new County to be formd of the Reserve, which offices are generally bestowed on the Same person—he has some Letters of Recommendation, is a man of very fair Character of good Abilities and decent Information, A Letter of Recommendation to Govr: St Clair, if consistent with your feelings & Sense of propriety will lay me under great Obligations—I have Sent this Letter inclosed in One to Mr. Beckley to whom I have communicated *only very generally*—An Answer would give me great pleasure—Sincerely devoted to the Liberty, the prosperity & happiness of my fellow Citizens I Am Sir With Great Esteem & Respect your friend   GIDN: GRANGER JUNR:

RC (DLC); addressed: "Thomas Jefferson Esq Vice-President of the United States Near Milton Virginia"; endorsed by TJ as received 26 June and so recorded in SJL.

Gideon Granger (1767-1822), a graduate of Yale, practiced law in his native Suffield, Connecticut, and entered politics by winning a seat in the state legislature in 1792. He unsuccessfully sought election to Congress in 1798, but retained his seat in the assembly and marked himself as an active Republican in a state seemingly dominated by Federalists. In 1801 TJ named him postmaster general of the U.S. His tenure in that office was controversial but he held the post until 1814. Long engaged in land speculation, he moved to Canandaigua, New York, where he involved himself in land development and politics (ANB).

Connecticut's congressional representation was chosen at large rather than by district, and elections in the state had been marked by poor voter turnout and little contest between parties. By quietly concentrating their votes, Republicans managed to surprise the political establishment in the spring of 1800 and place some of their number on the final slate of CANDIDATES FOR CONGRESS for the fall election. The 18 final candidates, culled from a field of 66 voted on by the state's freemen, included William HART and Granger. Charles Holt's New London *Bee* did not mention Hart, but instead identified Granger and Sylvester Gilbert as Republicans on the slate of candidates for the fall election. No one of the name Mather appeared even on the list of 66. Neither Granger, Hart, nor Gilbert succeeded in winning one of the state's seven House seats in the Seventh Congress (Hartford *American Mercury*, 22 May 1800; New London *Bee*, 21 May 1800; Richard J. Purcell, *Connecticut in Transition, 1775-1818* [Washington, 1918], 229-34; *Biog. Dir. Cong.*, 65).

Jonathan BULL, a Republican, was judge of probate and of the county court at Hartford (Kline, *Burr*, 1:545). Pierpont EDWARDS held the positions of state's attorney for New Haven County and U.S. attorney for the district of Connecticut (ANB).

In July, Arthur St. Clair, governor of the Northwest Territory, established Trumbull County from the Connecticut Reserve and appointed CALVIN PEASE, who like Granger was an attorney from Suffield, to the three clerkships (*Terr. Papers*, 3:525; DAB).

From Robert R. Livingston

DEAR SIR   ClerMont 4th. June 1800

I did not receive your favor of the 17th: Apl till on my Return to this place from New York, owing to its having gone on to my country residence while I was on my way down. I have also received the transactions of the Philosophical society with the model of your mould board. I have considered it with attention, & am satisfied that it is an important improvement, & the rather as it is constructed on principles that are so easily understood, that any mechanic of tolerable Ingenuity will find no difficulty in making it. If you have read my address to the Society for Arts agriculture &c. you will find that I have long considered this as an object of some moment in agriculture, & even ventured to place the invention in a more elevated rank than I was willing to afford to the whole tribe of politicians—Not however then thinking that the honour of this discovery would ever be claimed by the ablest of our statesmen. Permit me sir to acknowledge my obligations to you for this, & the other interesting communications that I received at the same time.

Your addition to the notes on Virginia leave no doubt on the subject of Cresops agency in the murder of the Logan family, & places the folly, & indiscretion of Luther Martin in a strong point of light. I however needed no other evidence on this subject than the impressions I had received of this transaction long before you favoured the world with your notes on Virginia.

I should have informed you before that the Society for the promotion of agriculture arts & manufactures in this State have done themselves honor to elect you a member. I need not tell you that they will be highly gratified by receiving from you occasionally such communications relative to the objects of their institution as your extensive observations enable you as you may find leisure to afford—

Enclosed is the sketch of a Steam engine which certainly avoids many of the inconveniences of Docr Watts as it works wh. less friction & wear & renders the escape of Steam from one to the other side of the cylinder almost impossible. Mr. Smith, one of the secretaries of the Philosophical society, supposed that the mercury might possibly be formed into globules by an admixture of water. But I think the following answer may be given to his objection. 1st. A very small portion of water or rather steam comes in contact with the mercury. It is only formed into globules when strongly agitated in water merely by being thrown out & separated from the mass, having then a strong attraction for itself it forms balls & when a number of these are collected on the surface their attraction for each other is less than they respectively have to their own centres—This can only happen when the quicksilver is thrown up in small particles, I found that mercury violently agitated for half an hour in cold water formed itself into globes. But agitation in hot water produced no such effect, nor wd any part of it be converted into a black powder, on the contrary the black powder formed in cold water by long continued triturations would be reduced by hot water to running mercury. Those objections being removed (and I have Docr. Priestlys opinion in confirmation of my own that they are not very important.) it is evident that this engine has many advantages over any yet known. These you will find stated in the enclosed description that I some time since sent to Docr Priestley

I am charmed with your idea of raising water into the upper part of the house as a security against fires, by means of the common Kitchen fire. I think it may be effected in the following manner at very little expence. In every large family a constant supply of hot water is required for culinary purposes. A boiler then should be fixed in the hearth furnished with a cock for family use. The top must be crewed on, from the upper part of the boiler a very narrow *copper* pipe must pass along the inside of the Chimney to the reservoir above, which must be close & large, the end of the pipe must be closed by a valve where[1] it enters the reservoir. When the water boils the steam will pass thro' the pipe into the reservoir where it will condense. In order to enable the boiler to supply itself from a well in the cellar if its depth is less than 30 feet a pipe may pass from the boiler into the well, this pipe to be furnished with a valve that opens upward. In this case whenever the fire goes down (which it will frequently do) the steam in the boiler will condense a vacuum being thus created the water will ascend from the well into the boiler. In this way many gallons of water may be carried into the garret & the Kitchen be supplied with water without labour. If at any time the fire should be continued so long as to exhaust all the water before the fire goes down, by opening the cock for a moment to let out the Steam & throwing cold water *on* the boiler a vacuum will be produced & the water will rise from the well.

If a larger quantity of water is required than the condensed steam will afford, it may be obtained by means of a Steam engine on the principle of Capt. Saveries which is extremely simply & is only exceptionable from the quantity of steam that it requires to raise a large body of water, which would be no object where the boiler requires to move fewer than that which is necessarily expended in the Kitchen for other purposes.

[9]

I sincerly congratulate you upon the returning good sense of our Countrymen. I am almost asshamed to own that I began to dispair of the republic, & to doubt whether there was not something in the nature of man that unfitted him for freedom in a state of society, where his real & imaginary wants seemes to doom him to a state of dependance, & to destroy his native dignity of character. Since I found even here, where these causes might be presumed to operate less than in the old world, such an unbounded desire for wealth, & honour, such a propensity to barter away the most substantial blessings peace, & liberty, for personal agrandizement, that I began almost to lament the many hours of my life, that I had (in conjunction with you, & others, who now think differently from us) employed in placing them, as I imagined, upon a firm & stable basis.

I thank god however the prospect brightens, the people are rouzing from their lethargy & I trust they will afford such a lesson to the future place men & office hunters of the United States, as will shew them the danger of violating their rights. What has alarmed & shocked me most in all our public measures, was the arbitrary dogmas of our courts of justice, & their avowed support of measures repugnant both to the letter & spirit of the constitution. I trust however, that under your auspices these dangers will be removed, that our great charter will undergo such a revision as to leave no hook whereon to hang a doubt, & that insurmountable barriers will be placed to the constructive powers of the Executive, Legislative, & judiciary. You will I dare say my dear Sir, consider it as a singular felicity, if, after having drawn the instrument that guarded us against foreign usurpation, you should give a fiat to that which secures us from domestic tyranny. I have purposely delayed replying to yr favours till you had returned home, I foresaw that I shd write a volume that might be read in Retirement, but which would have intruded too much on your time while acting on the busy theatre of Philadelphia. I will only add to its unreasonable length while I assure of the sincerity of the attachmt. with which I have the honor to be Dear Sir

Most respectfully Your Obt hum: Servt

ROBT R LIVINGSTON

RC (DLC); at foot of text: "The honbl Thomas Jefferson Esqr."; endorsed by TJ as received 31 July and so recorded in SJL. Dft (NHi: Robert R. Livingston Papers); incomplete, containing roughly the final third of the letter.

TJ had written Livingston no FAVOR OF THE 17TH: of April. Livingston meant TJ's letter of 30 Apr. 1800, in which TJ referred to having received, on the 17th, Livingston's of 28 Feb. In an ADDRESS to the New York Society for the Promotion of Agriculture, Arts, and Manufactures, Livingston had extolled the importance of agriculturalists against that of politicians and declared that anyone "who has invented a new implement of husbandry, or simply determined the angle the mould-board should make with plough-share, will be remembered with gratitude as the benefactor of society" (*Transactions of the Society, for the Promotion of Agriculture, Arts and Manufactures, Instituted in the State of New-York*, 2d ed., 1 [1801], 101).

Livingston was one of the people to whom TJ sent copies of the new addendum to the NOTES ON VIRGINIA; see Recipients of Appendix to the *Notes on the State of Virginia*, [ca. April 1800].

HONOR TO ELECT YOU A MEMBER: Livingston may have enclosed TJ's certificate of membership in the New York Society for the Promotion of Agriculture, Arts, and Manufactures, dated 19 Feb. 1800 (MHi, for "Thomas Jefferson, L.L.D.," signed by Benjamin DeWitt as secretary and Livingston as president; see illustration).

Livingston and Joseph PRIESTLEY had corresponded some months earlier about Livingston's ideas for a steam engine (Livingston to Priestley, 8 Aug., 22 Nov. 1799, Dfts in NHi: Robert R. Livingston Papers).

For TJ's IDEA OF RAISING WATER to a cistern for SECURITY AGAINST FIRES, see his letter to Livingston of 23 Feb. 1799. CAPT. SAVERIES: in 1698 Thomas Savery in England patented a machine that lifted water by means of the vacuum created by the condensation of steam (DNB).

DELAYED REPLYING TO YR FAVOURS: in New York on 2 Mch. 1800 Livingston drafted a letter to TJ that he did not send and may not have completed. In it, Livingston discussed the steam engine, announced TJ's election to the New York society, and said that he had "not yet sufficiently digested" his own thoughts about raising water to a cistern in the upper part of a house. He also mentioned that he had sent his letter of 28 Feb. by Thomas Peters Smith (Lb in NHi: Robert R. Livingston Papers; in Livingston's hand).

[1] MS: "were."

ENCLOSURE

Description of a Steam Engine

Description of mercurial engine

The figure represents an engine intended to work with very little friction. It must be observed that in order to simplify the drawg an ejection cock on the old principle is substituted for an air pump & condenser which however is to be preferred in practice—Nor can the enjection be made in the manner shewn in the drawing without a snifting valve for each side of the piston to carry off the air & water that would lodge above the mercury but as the object is only to shew the principle of the machine these are omitted

Mercury will rise by the ordinary pressure of the atmosphere if that pressure is taken from its upper surface, about 30 inches   If then a tube of sufficient length closed above was imersed in mercury to the depth of 30 inches, the quicksilver would stand at that hight on both sides of the tube: but if a vacuum was made within, It would then stand 30 inches higher within than without the tube as in the barometer. The mercury would then fall 15. inches without & rise as many within the tube or in other words would be 45 inches high within & 15 inches on the outside, in this case the tube might be raised 15 inches that is to the level of the external mercury before any air could pass into the tube. If this tube was covered by another, when a vacuum was made between them, the mercury would return to its original level [but if] the atmosphere is introduced into the inner tube, while the vacuum exists between the tubes, the position of the mercury would be reversed, & would stand 45 inches high between the tubes & only 15 in the inner one—The inner tube would then be pressed *up* with the whole weight of the atmosphere till it had risen so high as to let the air pass from one side to the other, so as to restore the equilibrium—

This principle being esstablished, a bare inspection of the drawing (which is a section of the engine) will explain the nature of the machine. a. Is a block of wood of not less than 48 inches high thro which the steam pipe & condensing pipe are passed, this is covered with a cylinder of sheet iron leaving a small space i & k of about $\frac{1}{6}$ of an inch between the block & the iron cylinder which is to operate as a piston. To this the working rod is to be fixed, this passes thro a stuffing box on the top of the external cylinder (omitted in the drawing)—C is the outward cylinder which may also be made of sheet iron. The intermediate space is to be filled with mercury to the hight of 30 inches if not more then a 16 inch stroke is required—If, as will generally be the case, a greater stroke, is sought, the depth of the mercury must be proportionably greater, 63 inches will admit of a four foot stroke, because 15 inches will be transferred from one side of the cylinder to the other by the pressure of the steam.

It is evident that if the steam is let into the inner cylinder or rather, middle cylinder or piston, thro the steam cock G & It is condensed by the condensing pipe H. while steam is admitted above, or between the piston & outward cylinder, that the piston must descend with the whole pressure of the steam, when on the other hand it is condensed without or above & admitted below the piston, it must rise with equal force. As it rises & falls in a fluid, it will feel little friction, but that of the working rod (& even that may be taken off if considered of moment by the use of mercury applied as above)—& that of the rollers placed at the bottom of the piston to prevent its vacilating. The only loss of power in the engine is that which arises from the action of the steam upon the mercury in the downward stroke but this would be extreamly small in an engine of 30 inches neither this, nor the frictions would amount to more than $\frac{1}{2}$ ℔ upon an inch. If air pumps are used they must be formed as the engine is, so as to work with little friction.

The advantages that this engine has over Docr. Watts are. 1st. the little friction, whereas the most approved engines of 30 inches, as I judge from actual experiment, including that of the air pump exceed $\frac{1}{3}$ of the whole power or 5 ℔ upon a square inch—2d The impossibility of any part of the steams escaping from one, to the other side of the piston, an evil that the greatest care can hardly prevent in Docr Watts engine, after it has run three days. This operates a very considerable loss of power   3d The saving of the time & trouble expended in repacking the piston which must be very frequently repeated, once in 14 days at least, & must therefore require the constant attendance of an artist. 4th. The freedom from wear, An engine on this construction must last for ages.

Water, or oil, may be used where the object is to raise water from mines instead of mercury since by this means the whole machinery may be of wood &

a stroke of 16 feet be obtained or any other required length. I have planed a variety of them, but thinking sufficient to shew the principle I will not trouble you with them—

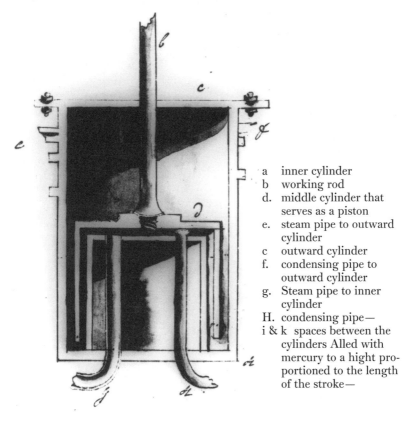

a inner cylinder
b working rod
d. middle cylinder that serves as a piston
e. steam pipe to outward cylinder
c outward cylinder
f. condensing pipe to outward cylinder
g. Steam pipe to inner cylinder
H. condensing pipe—
i & k spaces between the cylinders Alled with mercury to a hight proportioned to the length of the stroke—

MS (DLC); entirely in Livingston's hand; at head of text: "Cler Mont 5th. July 1800 by Robt. Livingston"; endorsed by TJ as received 31 July.

From Sir John Sinclair

DEAR SIR,   London 29 Parliament Street 6 June 1800.

Permit me to recommence our correspondence together, by requesting your Acceptance, of the Copy of a Work, in which, I am persuaded, you will feel yourself, in various respects, deeply interested. Being on the Eve of setting out for Scotland, I hope you will excuse me for using a borrowed hand, & for writing you a short letter. I cannot however avoid requesting your particular attention, to one point, respecting which I had the pleasure of corresponding with General Washington, namely the establishment of a Board of Agriculture in America, respecting which I have also taken the Liberty of writing Mr. Adams. Hoping by your united efforts, to see this important Object accomplished, I beg to subscribe myself,

With much respect & regard, Dear Sir, Your faithful and Obedient Servant   JOHN SINCLAIR

RC (DLC); in clerk's hand, signed by Sinclair; endorsed by TJ as received 29 Nov. but recorded in SJL at 28 Nov. 1800. Enclosure: probably *Letters from His Excellency George Washington, President of the United States of America, to Sir John Sinclair, Bart. M.P. on Agricultural, and Other Interesting Topics* (London, 1800).

For Sinclair's previous correspondence with Washington and TJ on the establishment of a BOARD OF AGRICULTURE IN AMERICA, see Sinclair to TJ, 15 July 1797. A facsimile of Washington's letter to Sinclair of 6 Mch. 1797 was included in Sinclair's *Letters from His Excellency George Washington*. In it Washington noted that Congress had made no decision on a board of agriculture but he hoped the next Congress would "bring this matter to maturity" (same, 41-2). LIBERTY OF WRITING MR. ADAMS: Sinclair to John Adams, 5 June 1800, in which Sinclair enclosed another copy of the publication he sent TJ and urged the president to use his influence to erect a board of agriculture as recommended by his predecessor (MHi: Adams Family Papers).

To George Jefferson

DEAR SIR   Monticello June 7. 1800.

I authorised mr Eppes in case he should purchase a horse which he was to get for me, to make me liable for 300. Dollars as the price; and as the seller was not acquainted with me, I gave him leave to draw on you for the sum at three months date, as he might consider your acceptance as more suitable to him. should such a draught be presented, be pleased to accept it, on full assurance that the money shall be placed in your hands before the day.—Colo. Gamble writes me there is an old balance of 5. Dollars due him from me. be so good as to pay it.

I thought I had desired you to send me a hogshead of molasses in the winter; but presume I am mistaken, as I do not find that any has been sent. as the weather is too warm now to move it in a large mass I will be obliged to you for thirty gallons double cased, or the watermen will spoil it.

I left with mr Gibson a draught on mr W. C. Nicholas on Picket Pollard & co. for 450. D. I drew lately in favor of John Watson for 148.29 D and the remaining 300. D[ols. is reserve]d for Henry

Duke, to whom be pleased to pay it on his application. I am not certain that he will apply

I am with great esteem Dr Sir Your friend & servt

TH: JEFFERSON

PrC (MHi); faint; at foot of text: "Mr George Jefferson"; endorsed by TJ in ink on verso.

The SELLER of the horse was William Haxall. COLO. GAMBLE WRITES ME: a letter from Robert Gamble to TJ of 20 May, recorded in SJL as received 6 June, has not been found.

For TJ's account with JOHN WATSON, merchant and factor for Alexander Brydie & Co. at Milton, see MB, 2:1021. TJ's payment included the sum of £93.15.0 for his brother-in-law Charles Lilburne Lewis, from whom he had purchased 125 barrels of corn at 15/ and £6 for Dabney Minor for 10 barrels of corn at 12/ (MB, 2:915, 1021). HENRY DUKE, brickmason at Monticello from 1797 to 1799, called for payment on 3 Sep. 1800 (MB, 2:958; TJ to George Jefferson, 13 Sep. 1800; Statement of Account with Gibson & Jefferson, 15 Jan. 1801).

A letter from TJ to George Jefferson of 26 May 1800, recorded in SJL as written from Eppington, has not been found.

From George Jefferson

DEAR SIR   Richmond 9th. June 1800

I am duly favor'd with yours of the 7th. and will attend to Mr. Eppes's draught should it appear.

I will also attend to your direction about the molasses; You did I recollect desire me to send up a Hogshead in the course of the winter provided it could be had at some certain price which you named, & I informed you immediately it could not be had at that price then, & I expected it would not be lower, and should therefore decline sending any.

I am Dear Sir Your Very humble servt.   GEO. JEFFERSON

RC (MHi); at foot of text: "Thos. Jefferson esqr."; endorsed by TJ as received 12 June and so recorded in SJL.

For TJ's request for MOLASSES the previous winter, see his letter to George Jefferson of 19 Dec. 1799. I INFORMED YOU: George Jefferson to TJ, 26 Dec. 1799.

To Amos Alexander

DEAR SIR   Monticello June 13. 1800.

Your favour of May 26. was recieved by our last post only, it having [unduly] loitered probably in some of the post offices. I am sorry that the subject of it's enquiry happens to be less known to me than almost to any other. [a] consciousness of my own inequality to the difficulties of the station which a portion of our fellow citizens seem desirous of assigning to me has rendered it a matter of duty as well as of [propriety] for me to avoid making enquiries as to the first & second destination of the [ensuing] election; & to leave to others to consider by whom they may most [use]fully be filled. while therefore I feel with sensibility & respect the favorable dispositions [entertain]ed towards myself in the disposal of those offices, I am quite unable to inform you who are the persons [associated] for them in the general [election.?] our representatives in the two houses of Congress have, equally with others, their anxieties on this subject, and by being brought together, have had other opportunities of learning the general wishes of the union. the information you desire could perhaps be obtained from them. I had understood too that committees of correspondence had been established in the different counties for the purposes of producing a concert of action in whatsoever is interesting to the republican cause. but neither on this subject can I speak with certainty. but while I regret my own inability to satisfy the enquiries of your letter, I am happy in the occasion it furnishes of expressing my attachment to those principles of general liberty which have excited the interest you take in this subject, and my sincere wish to see our constitution administered according to the constructions on which it was framed & [constituted?] by it's friends, & not according to those of which others thought it su[sceptible] and fearing this [. . .] for more explicit & pre[. . .]ous provisions.   I pray you to accept assurances of the great personal respect & esteem with which I have the honor to be Dr. Sir

Your most obedt. & most humble servt   TH: JEFFERSON

PrC (DLC); faint; at foot of text: "Amos Alexander esq."

Amos Alexander served as mayor of Alexandria in 1800. He and associates ran a stage line from Alexandria to Philadelphia via Baltimore. Alexander was a member of the charitable committee of Alexandria's Mechanical Relief Society, which held a dinner in May 1800 at which TJ was toasted with the wish that after 4 Mch. 1801 he would be "employed by the people, as their *first workman*" (CVSP, 9:137; *The Times; and District of Columbia Daily Advertiser*, 2 Oct. 1799, 2 May 1800, 6 Jan. 1801).

Alexander's FAVOUR OF MAY 26, recorded in SJL as received 9 June, has not been found.

For the COMMITTEES OF CORRESPONDENCE established by Virginia Republicans, see Philip Norborne Nicholas to TJ, 2 Feb. 1800.

To James Madison

In my last letter to you from Philadelphia I mentioned that I had sent for yourself[1] by mr Nicholas 160. Doll. recd from Lewis, and 110. Doll. for your father, part of 160.38 D delivered me by mr Hurt for him. the remaining 50. D. I brought & have here in half dimes ready to be delivered. I mentioned also that mr Nicholas would recieve from Barnes Generl Moylan's money (123. Dol. if my memory is right.) all this I hope has been right. I was charged by Barnes with 270. D. for mrs Key in this neighborhood. he had made up the parcels & labelled them. I gave that of 270 D. labelled by him for you, to mr Nicholas, as above mentd. yet when I came to open here the one he had labelled, *externally* for mrs Key, I found the *internal* divided into two parcels & labelled the one 160. D. for you & 110. D. for your father. not doubting that he had committed an error in cross-directing the external labels, & the sums happening to be precisely the same, I delivered this money to mrs Key. it would have been more satisfactory to me if a similar discovery of disagreement between the external & internal labels of the other parcel had been observed. but mr Nicholas tells me he returned that parcel to Barnes & took paper instead of it. however it suffices that yourself & your father have recieved your 270. D. I have here also for mrs Madison 2. small packets, about the size of letters and a third, containing a book, is on it's way in a trunk of mine which left Philadelphia about the 26th. Ult. by water. I have not yet heard of it's arrival in Richmond. I am not without hopes that you will soon recieve these things *here* yourselves. at present & for some days[2] you would find Dr. & mrs Bache with us. on Monday we expect mr & mrs Hollins on their return from Warren to Baltimore. tho' late occurrences have been wonderful, & furnish much matter for consideration; yet they are beyond the limits of a letter and not proper for one which is to go through the post office. there seems now to be one possibility which would furnish matter for very interesting consultation between us, & a consultation much desired: and unless you should find it convenient to come here soon, I propose to myself the pleasure of seeing you at your own house. but this cannot be till mr Eppes & my daughter, who are to leave us tomorrow, return again; which will not be till after his harvest. they take the wheels of my chair to equip the Phaeton for them. perhaps I may be able to borrow a chair in the neighborhood, tho' I do not know of one at present. should it be convenient for mrs Madison & yourself to solve the difficulty it will be sooner done & more to our gratification. mr Randolph & my daughter will participate of the pleasure of your company here. accept my sincere & affectionate attachments for mrs Madison & yourself. Adieu.

RC (DLC: Madison Papers, Rives Collection); addressed: "James Madison junr. esq. near Orange C. H."; franked and postmarked. PrC (MHi); endorsed by TJ in ink on verso.

LAST LETTER TO YOU: TJ to Madison, 12 May 1800.

GENERL MOYLAN'S MONEY: Moylan had arranged to be a tenant of Madison's at $200 per year; see Madison, *Papers,* 17:379. On 5 June TJ sent Ann KEY through John Barnes $296.97, the first two installments owed for her tobacco (Vol. 31:58, 236n, 242, 250, 388; MB, 2:1021).

John HOLLINS was a Baltimore merchant and acquaintance who also supplied TJ with plaster for Monticello (Betts, *Farm Book,* 197).

¹ TJ here canceled "& your father."
² Preceding three words and ampersand interlined.

To Samuel Latham Mitchill

DEAR SIR   Monticello June 13. 1800.

Your favor of May 15. happened to be written on the very day on which I left Philadelphia, and as I took a very circuitous route and was long on the way, it is but lately I have recieved it here. the interesting report it covered goes by this post to the Philosophical society at Philadelphia. the calamities which our great cities have experienced from the [new] infection render it important to discover what are those principles in nature which forbid the soil to be covered here with a solid block of buildings & men to be piled on one another, as they may with impunity in Europe. do our cloudless skies and the solar heat consequently accumulated generate effects here on the same materials which are innocent under the [bank] of clouds constantly hovering over Europe? however while those who, [with] yourself hold the clues to nature's secrets, are engaged in pursuing them, we of the multitude may rest in tranquility under the assurance that they will at length be laid open. nor is it in physics alone that we shall be found to differ from the other hemisphere. I strongly suspect that our geographical peculiarities may call for a different code of natural law to govern our relations with other nations from that which the conditions of Europe have given rise to there.   I sincerely join in your congratulations on the revival of those principles on which our republic has been founded. perhaps future ages may never know the real soporific which, in gentle slumbers, was carrying them to their grave. I am with great esteem & respect Dear Sir

Your most obedt. servt   TH: JEFFERSON

PrC (DLC); at foot of text: "Dr. Mitchell"; with faint passages interlined in pencil, possibly by TJ.

Some years earlier Dr. Samuel Latham Mitchill (1764-1831) had made a detailed study of the Hessian fly that was familiar to TJ, who also owned Mitchill's *Outline of the Doctrines in Natural History, Chemistry, and Economics* and *The Life, Exploits, and Precepts of Tammany; The Famous Indian Chief*. A native of Long Island, trained as a physician in Scotland, Mitchill was professor of natural history, chemistry, and agriculture at Columbia College, 1792-1807, and investigated a variety of scientific topics. He had also studied law and served in the legislature of New York. He served in the U.S. House of Representatives, 1801-4, 1810-13, and the Senate, 1804-9 (ANB; Vol. 20:446-8; Ezra L'Hommedieu to TJ, 10 Sep. 1791; TJ to Samuel Jones, Jr., 1 Dec. 1792; TJ to Henry Remsen, 17 Dec. 1795).

Mitchill's FAVOR OF MAY 15, recorded in SJL as received from New York on 4 June 1800, has not been found. The RE-PORT IT COVERED was a manuscript dated New York City, 14 May 1800, called "Observations on that vitiated condition of the atmosphere, which precedes and accompanies the endemic annual sickness of some of Atlantic cities of North America" (PPAmP; also endorsed as relating to "combinations of Azote and Oxygene, which constitute Pestilential Matter"; endorsed for the APS). Mitchill had been a member of the American PHILOSOPHICAL SOCIETY since 1791. His paper of 14 May, which TJ forwarded to Samuel Harrison Smith on 24 June, went before the APS on 15 Aug. Referred to Benjamin Smith Barton and Adam Seybert, it was not selected for publication. On 18 July the society had received another paper by Mitchill, on the composition of seawater and its potential for washing clothes without soap, which the APS did publish (APS, *Proceedings*, 22, pt. 3 [1884], 188, 301-2; APS, *Transactions*, 5 [1802], 139-47).

A letter from Mitchill to TJ, written 17 Feb. 1791 and received from New York on the 23d of that month, is recorded in SJL but has not been found.

From Pierre Samuel Du Pont de Nemours

MONSIEUR,   Good-Stay near New York. 15 Juin 1800

Je viens de finir l'ouvrage que vous avez bien voulu me demander sur l'Education nationale.

Comme la minute en est très barbouillée, je suis obligé de le faire mettre au net. On y travaille.

Hélas! C'est un livre.

J'ignore si vous le trouverez bon.

Mais tout n'y sera pas mauvais. Et il sera du moins un faible monument de mon attachement pour vous, et de mon Zêle pour les Etats-Unis.

Quelquefois je craignais que, ne recevant point de mes nouvelles, vous n'imaginassiez que je négligeasse la tâche que vous m'aviez donnée.

Je l'ai trouvée difficile, autant que belle.

Si l'on s'effrayait de sa faiblesse, on ne ferait rien. J'aime mieux me hazarder; et faire ce que désirent mes amis, ce que je crois avoir quelque utilité.

    Agréez mon respect.   Du Pont (de Nemours)

Peut-on vous adresser par la Poste un Cahier de deux ou trois cent pages?

Mme. Du Pont vous salue. Pusy en fait autant; Et mes Enfans y joignent leurs Sentimens respectueux.

EDITORS' TRANSLATION

Sir,   Good-Stay near New York. 15 June 1800

I have just finished the work on national education that you kindly requested of me.

As the draft of it is very messy, I am obliged to have a fair copy made. It is being worked on.

Alas, it is a book.

I don't know whether you will find it all right.

But not everything in it will be bad. And it will be at least a small monument of my affection for you and of my zeal for the United States.

Sometimes I feared that, not having any news of me, you might imagine that I was neglecting the task that you had given me.

I found it a difficult task, as well as a fine one.

If one took fright at one's weakness, one would do nothing. I prefer to put myself at risk; and do what my friends desire, which I think has some utility.

    Accept my respects.   Du Pont (de Nemours)

Is it possible to send you by mail a copybook of two or three hundred pages?

Mme Du Pont sends you greetings. Pusy does also; and my children join in sending their respectful sentiments.

RC (DLC); at head of text: "à Mr Jefferson"; endorsed as received 3 July and so recorded in SJL.

From George Jefferson

Dear Sir   Richmond 16th. June 1800

I some days ago receive a number of packages for you from Mr. Barnes, and likewise a cask & two boxes which were not mentioned in the bill of loading; the whole of which I forwarded by Thos. Priddy's boat a few days afterwards.

I also sent you a cask of molasses at the enormous price of 4/6 ℔. bill inclosed.

I am Dear Sir Your Very humble servt.   Geo. Jefferson

RC (MHi); at foot of text: "Thos. Jefferson esqr. Monticello"; endorsed by TJ as received 22 June and so recorded in SJL. Enclosure not found.

From Edmund Pendleton

DEAR SIR   Edmundsbury June 17th. 1800

When I view the date of yr. favor of April 19th., I am ashamed of having so long delayed to acknowledge it's reciept & comply with your small request. my Answers to your queries are now inclosed, which I fear will be a poor compensation for the delay, or for your trouble in forming the Questions. The truth is that when your letter came to hand, I was engaged in a very disagreable piece of business, not to be put by, wch. I found would employ me 'til you would have left Philadelphia, & since I gave way to an inclination to procrastinate, which I suppose the companion of old age, as I do not remember to have felt it in Youth. Another truth is that I am not only rusty in Parliamentary Rules, but never read much on the Subject; my small stock of knowledge in that way I caught from Mr. Robinson & Mr. Randolph, or was the result of my own reflections, dictated by the principle of having every question so put as to be well understood, & free as might be from embarrassment or complexity. My mite however is freely cast into your Treasury, and I wish it was of more value.

I had flattered my self with hopes of hearing that peace was concluded between France & Austria, as Negotiation was continued & hostilities not commenced so early, as Usual, notwithstanding the great preparations on both sides; but it seems treaty has failed, & Buonaparte Left to the event of his secondary means of procuring Peace, by beating them into it. If the French have been as successful on the Rhine (about which there are contradictory reports,) as in Italy, I fancy the Peace will not be long delayed. I hope that between France & America is 'ere now concluded.

Our early wheat crop, chiefly cultivated in this neigh[bour]hood, was very promising—free from the Fly, so destructive above, [. . .] Rust among that of the latter kind below—but we are much alarmed for the wet weather in the commencement of our Harvest. Accept my friendly Salutations, & assurance of Unchangeable & Affecte. esteem

EDMD PENDLETON

RC (DLC); torn at seal; endorsed by TJ as received 17 July and so recorded in SJL.

John ROBINSON was speaker of the Virginia House of Burgesses for 28 years. Upon his death in 1766 the office went to Peyton RANDOLPH, who held it until

Lord Dunmore dissolved the assembly in 1774. Randolph then became chairman of the first three Virginia Conventions, 1774-75, and first president of the Continental Congress (ANB).

Although the foreign ministers of FRANCE and AUSTRIA corresponded during the winter of 1799-1800, no terms of peace were reached and each nation read-ied its armies as the campaigning season approached. Initially Bonaparte intended to give emphasis to the RHINE, but move-ments by the Austrians made northern Italy the sudden focus of activity in the spring of 1800. In fact by the time Pendleton wrote TJ, Bonaparte had moved a newly formed reserve army through the Alps and managed to wring out a victory at Marengo on 14 June, re-sulting in an immediate armistice and the Austrians' withdrawal from the region. By mid-June, however, Americans were still seeing a mélange of reports and ru-mors from no later than April that ante-dated the decisive sequence of events (Roider, *Thugut*, 334-40; David G. Chandler, *The Campaigns of Napoleon* [New York, 1966], 264-98; *Universal Gazette*, 5, 12 June; *Philadelphia Gazette*, 6 June; *Aurora*, 7, 11 June).

ENCLOSURE

Queries on Parliamentary Procedure with Pendleton's Answers

In Committee.

The paper before a committee, whether select or of the whole, may be either such as originates with themselves, as a draught of an address a bill to be framed[1] Resolutions or a bill referred to them. in every case the bill or other paper is first read by the clerk, & then by the chairman by paragraphs. Scob. 49. pausing at the end of the paragraph, & putting questions for amending or striking out the paragraph, if proposed, & then on the paragraph as amended, or unamended: except that, in the case of a bill, no question is put on the paragraph; because all parts of the bill having been adopted by the house, stand of course, unless altered or struck out by a vote.

When through the whole a final question is put Whether the Address, or the Resolutions, or the Amendments to the bill shall be reported to the house? if decided negatively, what they have done falls; but in the case of a bill referred to them, the bill itself remains, & is to be reported without amendments.

Queries on the above passage.

It is believed to be certain that the chairman, in every case, reads the bill or other paper by para-graphs, and puts questions on amendments, or for striking out the paragraph, if proposed: but in what cases does he put a question Whether the paragraph is agreed to either as amended, or where no amendment has been made?

And in what cases does he put a final question on the whole?

If the propositn: be to strike out the whole Paragraph, the qn. is shall it stand as part of the Bill?

If to amend it is put upon that, & on that decision, or if no Amendment or striking out be proposed, no question is put on agreeing to the Paragraph, but, having in the latter case waited some time to permit a motion,

What is the form of that question? to wit is it whether they agree to the *address, resolutions, or bill* in the whole, even where they have already past a vote of agreement on all it's parts? or is it only Whether it shall be *reported* to the house?

you direct the Clk to proceed to read the next.

When through the whole, our usual mode was for a Member to move that the Commee may rise & the Chairman report the Amendmts., if on a Bill, to the house, & the qn. is put on agreeing to the Motion, but no qn. on the Bill.

If the Commee be to Originate an Address, or a Bill, altho' qns. on parts have been decided, one ought to be put on agreeing to the whole—a Resn. agd. to, or even Sevl., are difft. & do not reqe. that qn.—the final qn. in all is, upon the Commees rising & reporting.

In the House.

When the report of a paper originating with a committee is taken up by the house, they proceed exactly as in the committee, except that after the paragraphs have, on distinct questions, been agreed to seriatim, no question needs be put on the whole report.

On taking up a bill reported with amendments, the amendments only are read by the clerk. the Speaker then reads the first, & puts it to the question, & so on till the whole are adopted or rejected, before any other amendment be admitted, except it be an amendment to an amendment. then the Speaker reads the bill itself by paragraphs; as he does also if it has been reported without amendments, or if, on the 2d. reading, it has been taken up in the house without commitment; putting no questions but on amendments proposed, and when through the whole he puts the question Whether the bill shall be read a 3d time?

———

Much doubt is entertained on this whole passage.

1. After the amendments of a committee to a bill have been agreed to in the house, does the Speaker then *read* the whole bill over from beginning to end by paragraphs?
2. does he put a question on each paragraph as amended, or if unamended?
3. If the bill has been reported without amendments, the same questions arise
4. If the bill be not committed, on the 2d. reading,

1. Never with Us: on the 2d. reading the Speaker opened the Bill, in effect read it, & put the qn. as Commd., or ordd. it engrossed. On repg. Amendmts., when the Clk read one, the Speaker read the part of the Bill it related to, how it would be wth. the amendmt. & put the qn. on agreeing; when thro' all,

[23]

but is taken up & considered in the house, the same questions arise.

5. On a report of an Address or Resolutions framed in a committee when taken up in the house the same questions arise.

he did not repeat—either, but put the qn. if the Bill, wth. the Ammts. should be engross'd & read a 3d. time.

2. Only on Agreeing to the Amendmt, not on the Paragraph.

3. The qn. is put on the whole Bill, if it shall be ingross'd, a Negative produces a reject'n. of Course—without another question.

4. If on the 2d. reading, a Bill is not commd., the qn. upon engrossing, is the same, & wth. the same effect.

5. On report of an Original Address, it is sometimes refd. to a Commee of the whole, on whose report of Amendts. the proceedgs. are the same as on a Bill—& the same final qn. put on agreeing to it, as amended. & also, if amended in the House wth.out Commt.—

It is a general rule that the question first moved & seconded shall be first put. but this rule gives way to what may be called *Privileged questions*; & these privileged questions are of different grades among themselves.

I. a motion to adjourn *simply* takes place of all others, for otherwise the house might be kept sitting against it's will, & indefinitely.

II. Orders of the day take place of all other questions, except for adjournment.

III. After these there are other privileged questions which will require considerable explanation.

It is proper that every Parliamentary assembly should have certain forms of question, so adapted, as to enable them fitly to dispose of every proposition which can be made to them. such are 1. the Previous Question. 2. to Postpone indefinitely. 3. to adjourn a question to a definite day. 4. to lie on the table. 5. to commit. 6. to amend. the proper occasion for each of these questions should be understood.

1. When a proposition is moved, which it is useless or inexpedient now to express or discuss, the *Previous question* has been introduced for suppressing *for that time* the motion & it's discussion.

2. But as the Prev. Qu. gets rid of it only for that day, it may be *postponed indefinitely*, after which it cannot be moved again during that session.

qu. the exactness of these definitions of questions & their occasions?   the manner in which *postponement* is used in parliamt. has almost entirely escaped me.[2]

3. When a motion is made which it will be proper to act on, but information is wanted, or something more pressing claims the present time, it is *adjourned* to such day within the session as will answer the views of the house. sometimes however this has been irregularly used by adjourning it to a day beyond the session, to get rid of it altogether, as would be done by an indefinite postponement.

nor am I certain about the practice of adjourning a question. tho' I believe it is the mode of laying aside one question, to take up another.[3]

4. When the house has something else which claims it's present attention, but would be willing to reserve in their power to take up a proposition whenever it shall suit them, they order it to *lie on their table*. it may then be called for at any time.

5. If they are ready to take it up at present, but think it will want more amendment & digestion than the formalities of the house will conveniently admit, they refer it to a *Committee*.

6. But if the proposition be well digested, & may need but few & simple amendments, & especially if these be of leading consequence, they then proceed to consider & *amend* it themselves.

Though a question therefore has been first moved & seconded, yet the following if moved afterwards[5] are privileged to be first put, to wit, 1. the Previous Question 2. to postpone it. 3. to adjourn it to a definite day. 4. to lay it on the table. 5. to commit it. 6. to amend it.

But it may be asked Have these questions any privilege among themselves? or are they so equal that the common principle of 'the first moved first put,' takes place among them? this principle prevails among them in every instance, except that when a proposition has been moved, and a motion made to *amend* it, the whole subject may be postponed, adjourned, laid on the table, or committed, so that *amendment* gives way to the other privileged questions. qu.[6] if it does to the P. Quest. [qu. if Commitment. does not give way to postponement, definite adjournment or laying on the table? or are there any other inter-preferences?]

So far respects the case of two or more of the Privileged questions contending for privilege

If on difft. Bills, I suppose the motn. & Entry is to put off the furthr. consn. of that Bill. If the qn. be to postpone a questn. on one paragraph & take up another in the same Bill, it is done by Consent & no Entry.[4]

The definitions of questions & their Occasions, seem correct; but I confess I do not understand what is meant by an indefinite postponemt. wch. precludes the Subject from resumptn. in that Sessn., Suppose an Order entd. that the consn. of a Bill be postpd. (no time mentd.) will it's considn., even next day, be contrary to that Order*? Nor do I see the necessy. for it, since an Adjournmt. of it to the next Sessn., or to a day beyond the present, would answer the purpose, the latter is indeed a P–y trick, but not irregular, since there is not a Physical, nor natural impossibility that the Sessn. may continue to the day, however improbable.

*or is it like the continuance of a legal suit, sine die, making a discontinuance,

I suppose the prevs. qn. may be put on a proposed Amendmt., & therefore it has it's privilege in that instance, but posterior to the others between themselves, when both were moved on the original or Main Question. but suppose one of them to be moved, not on the original primary question, but on the secondary one. e.g. suppose a motion for the P. Qu. can a motion be made to postpone, adjourn, or lay that on the table? or suppose a motion to postpone, can we move to adjourn that question, or lay it on the table, or pre-question it? &c. &c. this is not allowed. because it would embarras questions too much to allow them to be piled one on another several stories high: & the same result may be had in a more simple way by deciding the secondary question itself negatively. but the useful character of *amendment* gives to that, & to that alone, a privilege of attaching itself to a secondary & privileged question, in the case of an amendment. that is there may be an amendment to an amendment. [qu. if there can be an amendment to a postponement, definite adjournment, or commitment?] but this is not admitted in another degree, to wit to *amend* an *amendment* to an *amendment* of a Main question. this would lead to too much embarrasment. the line must be drawn somewhere, & usage has drawn it after the *amendment* to the *amendment*. the same result may be sought by deciding against the amendment to the amendment, & then moving it again as it was wished to be amended. in this form it becomes only an amendment to an amendment.

IV. Another exception to the rule of priority is when a motion has been made to *strike out* a paragraph. it's friends may move any amendments for rendering it as perfect as they can, which shall be put to the question, before a vote is taken on striking out the whole paragraph.

other privileged questions, e.g. on order, privilege, reading papers &c present no difficulties.

Equivalent questions. Where questions are perfectly equivalent so that the negative of the one amounts to the affirmative of the other, & leaves no other alternative, the decision of the one concludes necessarily the other. thus the negative of striking out amounts to the affirmative of agreeing, & therefore to put a question on agreeing, after that on striking out, would be to put the same question in effect twice over; which is contrary to rule.

But in questions on amendments between the two houses, a motion to recede being negatived, does not amount to a positive vote to insist, be-

It seems to me that a qn. to adjourn is to be put, when moved, in preferance to all others. I think the rule is such, & that it is beneficial, in being interposed in heats, to give time to allay them
the other motions appear eql. for choice, & should be put as moved, where they can be properly put at all.

I suppose there may, to change it's effect, but not it's Nature,[7] e.g. to change the day proposed for a definite adjournment; but not where a Negative of the propn. will answer the purpose; as to change that for an indefinite Postpt. into a defe. Adjournment.

Very reasonable, since an Amendment may remove the Objection.

correct—but I suppose a motion to amend, may be made & a questn. put, after that for striking out is negatived. you must retain the substance, but may change the dress.

cause there is another alternative viz. to adhere. therefore another question is necessary.

———

Additional queries.

On a disagreement between the houses as to amendments to a bill, and a conference agreed on, can the conferees propose, or authorise either house to propose an amendment in a new part of the bill, having no coherence with the amendment on which they have disagreed?

———

When the Previous Question is moved, must the debate on the Main Question be immediately suspended?[8]

I suppose they may, as the Bill is still under the Power of both houses: tho' the Form is that "the Senate have agreed to the Bill wth. Amendments," implying their approbation of all other parts, yet since, if the Amts. are not agreed to, the Senate may reject the Bill, it would seem to follow, that if on a conference, to drop that & amend another part, will bring the houses to accord, it may be done, by the Senates receding from the former, & proposing the New Amendment.

When a Previous Question has been moved & seconded, may the Main Qu. be amended *before* putting the Prev. Qu.? we know it cannot afterwards; and that it is a vexata questio whether it may *before*:[9] I remember to have heard discussions on this subject between mr Pendleton, mr Wythe & the Speaker Randolph. what were their several opinions?

I do not recollect this discussion, nor of course any Opinions on it—nor remember any parly. rule for deciding the qn.—Upon principle, I see no reason for precluding the previous amendmt., since that might remove the objectione. part of the propn., & induce the withdrawing or negativing the Prev. questn.

———

When a member calls for the execution of an *order* of the house, as for clearing galleries &c. it must be carried into execution by the Speaker without putting any question on it: but when an *order of the day* is called for, I believe a question is put 'Whether the house will *now* proceed to whatever the order of the day is? is it so?[10]

Yes.

———

When a motion is made to strike out a paragraph, section, or even the whole bill, from the word 'whereas,' and to insert something else in lieu thereof, it is understood that the friends of the paragraph, section or bill, have first a right to amend, and make it as perfect as they can, before the question is put for striking out. suppose the question is then put on striking out, & that it passes in the negative. can any further amendment be made to the paragraph after it has been retained by a vote?

1. a motion is made to amend a bill or other paper by striking out certain words, and inserting others; & the question being divided, & put first

The right to amend is before stated—and if made & then the qun. for striking out Negatived, it may be doubted whether new Amendmts. can be proposed, since the dress, as well as substance, has been discussed—however I, who prefer Essentials to form where I can't have both, would decide for permitting it, on this ground, that an Enemy on striking out, it is negatived, and the insertion of course falls.

2. after this, a motion is made to strike out *the same words* and to insert others, of a different tenor altogether from those before proposed to be inserted. is not this admissible?

3. Suppose the 2d. motion to be negatived, would it not be admissible to move to strike out the *same words* & to insert nothing in their place?

So if the 1st. motion had been to strike out the words & to insert nothing, & negatived, might it not then have been moved to strike out the *same words* & insert other words?

———

When a paper is under the correction of the house, the natural order is to begin at the beginning, & proceed through it with amendments. but there is an exception as to a *bill*, the *preamble* which is last amended.

Does this exception extend to any other form of paper? e.g. a resolution &c. or would the *preamble* of the resolution be first amended according to the natural order?

Suppose a paper, e.g. a resolution, brought in without a preamble, & that a motion be made to prefix a preamble: can such a motion be recieved and acted on before the body of the paper is *acted* on?

to the clause, on finding it must stand, might propose an Amt. agreable to it's friends, tho' he would not strengthen the clause By doing it before—the Others should be cautious agt. a Clog. 1.2.3. When a qun. has been put for striking out certain words, and Negatived, altho' it was part of the motion, that certain others should be inserted, since the qns. are divided & put distinctly, no 2d. qun. for striking out the same words, either for the purpose of inserting others, or nothing, is admissible.

I see no reason for any distinction between this case & the other—nor indeed for the retrograde Progress in either. the preamble ought in both to shew the reason of Legislative Action; As the body does the Act.

I suppose not; since the paper can only enable the House to judge if a Preamble be necessary, & what it should be. it must be proposed as an Amendment & therefore, should be done before a question is put on the body of the paper, if that be meant by Acting on it.

MS (DLC: TJ Papers, 108:18470-2); queries in TJ's hand, including his brackets, printed on left side above; answers in Pendleton's hand, written in the wide margin TJ left for the purpose (see TJ to George Wythe, 28 Feb. 1800) and printed in right column above; TJ added final queries after making PrC (see note 10 below and TJ to Wythe, 7 Apr. 1800). PrC (same, 106:18240-4); entirely in TJ's hand, containing his unanswered queries in the form in which he sent them to Wythe on 28 Feb. (see note 9 below); variations recorded in notes below. MS enclosed in TJ to Wythe, 28 Feb. 1800, returned by Wythe, 10 Apr., and enclosed in TJ to Pendleton, 19 Apr.

SCOB. 49: a reference to a work by Henry Scobell (d. 1660), *Memorials of the Method and Manner of Proceedings in Parliament in Passing Bills, Together with Several Rules & Customs, which by Long and Constant Practice Have Obtained the Name of Orders of the House* (Sowerby, No. 2879; PW, xxv).

[1] Preceding five words interlined. Change lacking in PrC.

[2] TJ inserted this paragraph in the

margin alongside the two preceding numbered headings. Insertion lacking in PrC.

³ Pendleton inserted this paragraph after he had written the paragraph below it.

⁴ TJ wrote this paragraph in the margin alongside the preceding numbered heading. Insertion lacking in PrC.

⁵ Preceding three words interlined.

⁶ TJ interlined the clause from this abbreviation through "P. Quest."

⁷ Pendleton interlined this word in place of "purpose."

⁸ Below the line that follows this question TJ canceled: "May the Main question be amended *after* the Previous Question has been moved & seconded, *before* it be put?"

⁹ Remainder of paragraph interlined in place of "what is mr Wythe's opinion on it?" Changes lacking in PrC.

¹⁰ PrC ends here.

From George Jefferson

DEAR SIR   Richmond 23d. June 1800

I expected before this to have sent up the Hhd. of lime which you some time ago ordered, having spoken to a bricklayer to prepare one for you; I called on him to day to know why he had not sent it, and he informed me he had not been able to get it ready, but that I might depend upon receiving it tomorrow. You may therefore calculate upon getting it in a few days after you receive this.

The barrel of molasses I hope arrived safe. I omitted to inform you of the reason why I did not comply with your direction in having it cased.   The person from whom I bought it on my desiring him to have it done, assured me that it would burst if it had not vent, the weather having been extremely warm.   As I was partly of the same opinion I concluded it was better to risk a part than the whole— and particularly as I thought the boatman might be depended on, and he promised to be particularly careful of it

I am Dear Sir Your Very humble servt.   GEO. JEFFERSON

RC (MHi); at foot of text: "Thos. Jefferson esqr. Monticello"; endorsed by TJ as received 26 June and so recorded in SJL.

HHD. OF LIME: TJ added "1 gross porter 1 hhd. lime" to the endorsement on the letterpress copy of his letter to George Jefferson on 31 May 1800. These are the only substantive words, now legible, which indicate the content of the letter. TJ's uncharacteristic addition to the endorsement may indicate that he could not read the press copy (MHi).

From Joseph Priestley

Dear Sir   Northumberland June 23. 1800

Having a good opportunity of getting a letter conveyed to you, I make use of it to inform you, that a short time, as I thought, before the rising of Congress, I sent you some *thoughts on the subject of the College*, which you were so obliging as to request of me, but that I doubt whether my letter came to your hands. I shall be happy if my ideas in any measure meet with your approbation.

Having just heard from England, with an account of the prices of grain of several kinds, in the neighbourhood of Liverpool; and as it may be of use to you, or your friends, to know them, I shall transcribe the article.

"We have been in great want of wheat and grain of all kinds. The former is now selling for 24. S 6 d for 70 lbs Barley (the best) for 12.6; Oats 8.6 45 lb.; Rye 15; common peas 12 S per bushell; and Rice 45 S ℔ Cwt."

With the greatest respect, I am, dear Sir, yours sincerely

J Priestley

RC (DLC); endorsed by TJ as received 7 Aug. and so recorded in SJL.

Priestley sent TJ his THOUGHTS ON THE SUBJECT OF THE COLLEGE in his letter of 8 May.

To John Barnes

[Dear] Sir   Monticello June 24. 1800.

Your letters of May 24. & June 8. have been duly recieved, and but for an inadvertence as to the post day, should have been acknoleged by the last post. all the articles forwarded by you have come to hand except the half dozen square railed Windsor chairs bought in 4th. street. as these are not received, and mr Jefferson says nothing of them in his letters, I presume they never came to his hands, and consequently if put on board with the other things, must have been misdelivered by the captain. will you be so good as to enquire into this.—with respect to the loan the selling it above par is a new idea. however we must submit to this as to mr Short & Kosciusko rather than keep their money idle.

I shall be glad to recieve the young man recommended by mr Trump at the time you mention, as I had not employed another, in expectation of him, and in further dependance on him shall not employ another.[1] my want of him in the mean while presses as to time. if he has tools, he had better bring them, as when he shall have got through my work they will enable him to enter on work for others. he could not get tools here to set himself up. the only remaining commission I have for Philadelphia would be to obtain a gross of bottled porter from there. but I am so doubtful whether it could be removed in the hot season, that I shall leave it altogether to the result of your enquiries as to this: whether to send it or not. I am with great esteem Dr. Sir

Your friend & servt   TH: JEFFERSON

PrC (CSmH); faint; at foot of text: "Mr. John Barnes"; endorsed by TJ in ink on verso.

Barnes's letter of 8 JUNE, recorded in SJL as received on the 20th, has not been found. Also recorded in SJL, but missing, are a letter from TJ to Barnes of 30 May 1800 and one from Barnes of 15 June, received from Philadelphia on the 26th.

For the investment of William Short's and Tadeusz Kosciuszko's funds in the new government LOAN, see TJ to Short, 13 Apr. 1800, and Barnes to TJ, 24 May 1800.

The YOUNG MAN recommended by Daniel TRUMP to work as a carpenter at Monticello was named Forsyth. He did not go to Virginia, but Trump found a replacement in John Holmes (MB, 2:1028; Trump to TJ, 4 Aug. 1800).

[1] TJ interlined this word, and the sentence that follows it, in place of "him."

To Samuel Harrison Smith

DEAR SIR   Monticello June 24. 1800.

The inclosed communication from Dr. Mitchell to the Philosophical society was under cover of a letter to me dated at New York on the day I left Philadelphia. as I did not come directly home, it was but lately it came to my hands. I now inclose it to be laid before the society. I am with great esteem & respect Dr. Sir

Your most obedt. servt   TH: JEFFERSON

RC (DLC: J. Henley Smith Papers); addressed: "Samuel H. Smith one of the Secretaries of the Philosophical society Philadelphia. Chesnut street between 3d. & 4th"; franked; postmarked Milton, 28 June. Enclosure: Samuel Latham Mitchill, "Observations on that vitiated condition of the atmosphere . . ." (see TJ to Mitchill, 13 June 1800).

Samuel Harrison Smith (1772-1845), a native of Philadelphia, earned degrees at the University of Pennsylvania before becoming a printer and newspaper publisher. He published and edited the *New World*, 1796-97, and then the *Universal Gazette*. Elected a member of the American Philosophical Society in January 1797, that year he entered an essay in an APS competition on the subject of education and shared the first prize. He published his submission as *Remarks on Education: Illustrating the Close Connection between Virtue and Wisdom, To Which is Annexed, a System of Liberal Education* (Philadelphia, 1798). The society elected him to be one of its four secretaries in January 1798 and in each of the succeeding two years. In 1800 he married his cousin, Margaret Bayard, and, at TJ's urging and in expectation of a change in the presidency, moved the *Gazette* to Washington, where at the end of October it appeared as the *National Intelligencer*. During TJ's presidency Smith received lucrative government printing contracts and his newspaper's reports of debates in Congress, some taken down in shorthand by the editor himself, became the means by which much of the nation learned of congressional proceedings. Smith retired from the *Intelligencer* in 1810 and was a bank officer, serving briefly as secretary of the Treasury in 1814 (ANB; APS, *Proceedings*, 22, pt. 3 [1884], 246, 264-6, 277, 290).

From Samuel Morse

SIR   Danbury June 26. 1800

I have addressed a paper to you, the publication of which I have commenced in this town, and have dedicated to that cause, which in this state, and more in this town than any other part of the state, is universally spoken against. I mean the cause of Republicanism according to those ideas which were prevalent 6 years ago.

Persuaded, from the whole tenor of your public life, and from your acknowleged character, that this cause has one of the first places in your heart, I think you will not refuse this infant institution, your patronage, or slight the ardent efforts of a youth, in the cause of liberty.

If the times were perilous, during our revolutionary war, they are no less so at this day. We have against us multitudes of clamorous partizans who resigning their own right of thinking and acting, and guided wholly by those whose interest it is to decieve them, wish to crush the right of thinking and acting, and to introduce a class of men, who claiming under the title of gratitude, or confidence, should think for the whole society, and dictate the creed and the mode of conduct to all. The doctrine is now openly avowed, that while men were in office, we ought regard the dignity of the office too much to speak evil of the man. And why this?—Because all men are fallible, and because if we are not suited with their conduct, we can omit to re-elect them!!! Such is federal logic and such their aims, all this while they are scandalizing you as an atheist, a dishonest man, a friend to France and french depredations and the enemy of your own country, and its interests & constitution. This conduct and this language is not confined to the lower classes of this party, it is held by some whose information and intellects would teach them better. Lawyers of some repute do not scruple to say that the common law ought to govern the decisions of the federal courts, nor to defend Chase in declaring that a man had no right to the public documents, and that proof of a fact which came to the knowlege of the traverser after making his declarations could not be admitted in a court of justice. They are terrified to death at the idea of a peace with France, lest it should encrease infidelity in our land, while they can boast for themselves, scarce a christian virtue. But what is more surprizing, they are *afraid* of Great Britain, and say that altho they hate her as much as they did last war, (and some were warm whigs) yet as we are so much weaker than she is we must submit to what we cannot help without great danger to our property on the high seas, and even on our own coasts: that, is, *we must barter our independence for our safety*, and this to a nation which which 20 years ago, when weak and divided, when accounted her subjects, we beat in the field and forced to acknowlege our independence.

Situated among such a class of men you will imagine that my external circumstances are not very agreeable, and perhaps will wonder when I tell you I have no property, (scarce 100 dollars) that I should risque such an establishment in such a place. But the neighboring towns will furnish I believe a sufficient circulation to maintain the paper, and I hope (if it is patronized by influential characters) that it will afford a decent support to my family. Much however must I suffer by slander and insult, perhaps, by personal abuse as I am threatened with tar & feathers, and the destruction of my press, but nothing they can inflict will oblige me to give up the privilege of declaring the necessity of a change of Measures, when systems of encroachment has been carried to such a height as I think they have been. I would give you a history of my engaging in the business, but I am tired of saying so much about myself, and I believe you must by this time be tired of reading it.

The present appearances declare that you will be our next President, this event I sincerely pray for, hoping that when you are in office, we shall not have to pay 8 per Cent interest on loans nor be driven to the necessity of an encrease of taxes. I hope we shall not have a standing army raised without an object, a sedition law to guard your public character from public discussion and animadversion, or an alien law to subject the men we had invited to our shores, to the caprice of an individual. I hope we shall not uncensured behold another Jonathan Robbins delivered up to a British Court Martial, for escaping from his bondmen; the ipse dixit of one of the British officers held forth as a justification of his death, tho given long after his soul and body had separated, and received through a circular channel and that of 4 or 5 different persons. Nor do I hope to hear of a Secretary of State, condemning the conduct and denying the charge on oath of an injured fellow citizen, whose assertions were corroborated by the testimony of two others; merely on the honor of a British Captain.

Under your administration I hope to experience mild laws, a good government, light taxes, reduction of the public debt, economical expenditure, and peace with the world.

With a belief that as far as lies in your power you wi[ll pro]mote these objects, and persevere in pursuit of the true interests of the nation; I shall endeavor to promote your election to the next presidency, and if possible that you may get some of the votes from this State; this however is doubtful, though not altogether improbable.

But while I express my wishes, intentions and hopes, let me add that if you pursue those measures which have been pursued for some time past; I will be among the first to censure you before the public—

I might ask pardon for the freedom, with which I have written, but I think that Thomas Jefferson, the people's friend, will not be offended with the plainness and sincerity of an American youth

I am with respect, your well wisher   SAML MORSE

RC (DLC); torn at seal; addressed: "Thomas Jefferson, Esq. Vice President of the United States residing in Monti-Celli—Virginia"; franked; postmarked 30 June; endorsed by TJ as received 17 July and so recorded in SJL.

Samuel Morse (1778-1805), largely self-educated, began the study of medicine with a physician in 1795 and was granted a diploma by the Connecticut Medical Society in 1799. Unsuccessful in starting a medical practice in Danbury, Morse took a position as a schoolteacher. In April 1800 he began his career in journalism, establishing the Danbury *Farmers Journal* with Stiles Nichols. Apparently dissatisfied with his partner's business ethics and political conservatism, Morse withdrew from the publication in June 1800 and later that month printed the first issue of the Danbury *Sun of Liberty*. Because of his outspokenly Republican editorial policy, Morse was forced to move the newspaper first to Norwalk in October 1800 and then to New Haven, where the *Sun of Liberty* continued to appear from 26 Aug. until at least 4 Nov. 1801. In 1802 Morse moved

to Savannah, Georgia, where he and James Lyon brought out the first issue of the *Georgia Republican* on 21 Aug. Morse continued as co-editor of the newspaper until his death (Pasley, *Tyranny of Printers*, 162-6, 263, 269; Brigham, *American Newspapers*, 1:15, 18, 51, 63, 128; Savannah *Georgia Republican*, 2 Aug. 1805; Morse to TJ, 4 Feb., 9 Aug. 1802).

I HAVE ADDRESSED A PAPER TO YOU: *Sun of Liberty*, 24 June 1800 (see Sowerby, No. 549).

A MAN HAD NO RIGHT TO THE PUBLIC DOCUMENTS: during his trial Thomas Cooper unsuccessfully attempted to obtain authenticated copies of President Adams's answers to certain XYZ addresses. Judge Samuel Chase ruled that Cooper was mistaken to think he had "a right to obtain official copies" of documents he deemed necessary for his defense (Thomas Cooper, *An Account of the Trial of Thomas Cooper, of Northumberland; on a Charge of Libel Against the President of the United States* [Philadelphia, 1800], 12-13; Smith, *Freedom's Fetters*, 318-19).

For the JONATHAN ROBBINS case, see Vol. 31:181-2n, 410n, 421.

From Peyton Short

DEAR SIR,   Woodford (Kentucky) 28th. June 1800

I take the Liberty of enclosing you another Letter to my Brother— I very much fear that my Correspondence with him has given you more trouble than I ought to have imposed on your benevolent Disposition—but my Brother counts with Confidence on your friendship, and still urges me to continue my correspondence with him through the Channel. If therefore, my good Sir, I have stretched your permission to an unwarrantable Length, I pray you to lay the Burthen of your Disapprobation on the proper Shoulders—

I will endeavour to Wait on you some time in Octr. next in order to obtain the papers you mention in your Letter of the 16th. Octr. Last, respecting an unsettled Acct. between Colo., Skipwith and my Brother.

I am, Dear Sir, with the highest sentiments of Respect & Esteem Your Most Obt. Sert.   PEYTON SHORT

FC (Lb in DLC: Short-Harrison-Symmes Family Papers); at foot of text: "Mr Jefferson." Recorded in SJL as received on 23 Aug. 1800. Enclosure not found.

From William Dunbar

SIR,   Natchez, June 30, 1800.

MR. NOLAN'S man of signs has been here, but was so occupied that a long time elapsed ere I could have an opportunity of conversing with him, and afterwards falling sick was seized with such an invincible desire of returning to his own country, that I had little hopes of gaining much upon his impatience.

A commencement however we have made, and although little has been done, it is sufficient to convince me, that this language by signs has been artfully and systematically framed. In my last I took notice of some analogy which I conceived to subsist between the Chinese written language and our Western language by signs; I had not then read Sir George Staunton's account of the British Embassy to China. I will here beg your permission to transcribe a paragraph or two from that work, which appear to strengthen my ideas of the probability of their common origin. "Almost all the countries bordering on the Chinese sea or Eastern Asia, understand and use the written Chinese, though not the oral language. About 200 characters mark the principal objects of nature; these may be considered as roots of language, in which every other word or species in a systematic sense is referred to its proper genus or root. The heart is a genus represented by a curve line, somewhat of the form of the object, and the species referable to it, include all the sentiments, passions, and affections, that agitate the human breast, each species being accompanied by some mark denoting the genus or heart." Now Sir if the commencement of this extract was altered and we were to say "Almost all the Indian nations living between the Mississippi, and the Western American ocean, understand and use the same language by signs, although their respective oral tongues are frequently unknown to each other," the remainder of the paragraph would be perfectly descriptive of the organization of this language by signs, and would convey to an adept a full and complete idea of the systematic order which has been observed in its formation. Permit me to refer you to the short and very imperfect list of signs enclosed, where you will find water to be a genus, and rain, snow, ice, hail, hoar-frost, dew, &c. are species represented by signs more or less complex, retaining always the root or genus as the basis of the compound sign.

We are also informed that "if any uncertainty remains as to the meaning of a particular expression, recourse is had to the ultimate criterion of tracing with the finger in the air or otherwise, the form of the character and thus ascertaining at once which was meant to be expressed:" here also is a strong analogy between the language and practice of those countries so far separated from each other, for those Western Indians are so habituated to their signs that they never make use of their oral language, without instinctively at the same time tracing in the air all the corresponding signs, which they perform with the rapidity of ordinary conversation. I cannot avoid concluding that the custom of the Chinese of sometimes tracing the characters in the air, is a proof that this language by signs was at early periods of time universally used by them and by all the nations of the east coast of Asia; and perhaps if enquiry be made it may be found that the usage of this universal language is not yet totally neglected. In the above-mentioned account of the embassy, we are told only, I think, of three Chinese characters, the sun represented by a circle, the moon by a crescent, and man by two lines forming an angle representing the lower extremities; those three signs are precisely the same which are used by the Western people: in order to represent the two first mentioned, the thumb and fore-finger of the right hand are formed either into a Circle or Crescent, and the sign of man is expressed by extending the fore-finger of the right hand and bringing it down, until it rests a moment between the lower extremities.

It is probable that Chinese Sailors or others, may be found in your maritime towns, who might give some useful information, and it cannot I suppose be difficult to procure a collection of Chinese characters with English explanations, which would afford an opportunity of making farther comparisons upon a future investigation of this curious subject. I think Captain Cook says, some where, that in some of the Islands of the Western pacific he found persons who possessed a great facility of communicating their ideas by signs and made much use of gesticulations: this was probably no other than the language by signs; and if it is found that the Chinese actually use at this day upon some occasions a language by signs, actual experiment alone will convince me that it is not the same which is used by our Western Indians. Hence would spring forth an analogy and connection between the Continents of the New and Old World which would go directly to the decision of your question, without being involved in the ambiguity arising from the imperfect resemblance of words.

WILLIAM DUNBAR.

Text from APS, *Transactions*, 6 [1809], 1-3; extraneous quotation marks omitted; at head of text: "On the Language of Signs among certain North American Indians. By William Dunbar, Esq. of the Mississippi Territory, communicated by Thomas Jefferson, President of the Society"; below dateline: "Read 16th January, 1801"; at foot of text: "Thomas Jefferson, *President* A.P.S." Recorded in SJL as received on 23 Oct. 1800. Enclosure: "Signs made use of by the Indian Nations to the West of the Mississippi, refered to in the foregoing letter," printed in same, 4-8. Enclosed in TJ to Caspar Wistar, 16 Dec. 1800, first letter; transmitted to the American Philosophical Society, 16 Jan. 1801, and approved for publication on 6 Feb. (APS, *Proceedings*, 22, pt. 3 [1884], 308-9).

For Philip NOLAN'S MAN OF SIGNS, see Dunbar to TJ, 6 Oct. 1799; Daniel Clark to TJ, 12 Nov. 1799; TJ to Dunbar, 16 Jan. 1800; and Clark to TJ, 29 May 1800.

MY LAST: Dunbar to TJ, 6 Oct. 1799.

In 1792 Sir George Leonard Staunton became the secretary of a BRITISH EMBASSY TO CHINA led by Lord Macartney. Staunton wrote *An Authentic Account of an Embassy from the King of Great Britain to the Emperor of China; Including Cursory Observations Made, and Information Obtained, in Travelling through that Ancient Empire, and a Small Part of Chinese Tartary*, published in London in 1797 (DNB).

From George Jefferson

DEAR SIR   Richmond 30th. June 1800

After meeting with repeated disappointments I at length succeeded in getting the Hhd: of lime, which I sent up on Friday last by Henderson's boats.

The person of whom I got it promised to send in his bill but he has neglected to do so. he informed me it would be 5/. ℔ bushl.

The long delayed business of the nail-rod is at length in a train to be settled—Mr. Nicolson having a week or two ago received a remittance from his friend in Carolina in a bill on New York at 60 days.

From your last letter upon this subject I conclude that I must have omitted to informe you that I was induced to put this business into Mr. N's hands in consequence of my hearing that he was the agent of the underwriters on the vessel; together with my not having known any one else who had a correspondent in the place to which the vessel was carried.   but for these reasons I should have preferred getting almost any other person to have negociated the business, and the event has shewn that my unwillingness to avail myself of his offer, was not without foundation.

I am Dear Sir Your Very humble servt.   GEO. JEFFERSON

RC (MHi); at foot of text: "Thos. Jefferson esqr."; endorsed by TJ as received 3 July and so recorded in SJL.

LONG DELAYED BUSINESS OF THE NAILROD: in early January 1799 George Jefferson learned that the *Rising Sun*, a vessel carrying TJ's nailrod, had been abandoned at sea and subsequently brought into the customs district of Camden, North Carolina (George Jefferson to TJ, 8 Jan. 1799). For the LAST LETTER on the attempt to recover costs for the salvaged iron, see TJ to George Jefferson, 20 Mch. 1800. TJ may have also referred to the nailrod in the illegible letter to George Jefferson of 31 May (see note to George Jefferson to TJ, 23 June 1800). TJ did not receive payment from George Nicolson until September (George Jefferson to TJ, 22 Sep. 1800).

To John Breckinridge

DEAR SIR   Monticello July 4. 1800

This will be handed you by mr Monroe, a relation of our governour who proposes to pay a visit to Kentuckey to look out for a settlement. he is a lawyer of reputation, a very honest man and good republican. having no acquaintance in your state I take the liberty of recommending him to your attentions and counsel, which the worth of his character will entirely justify. we have no particular news but what you also have from the newspapers. mr Monroe will be able to give you the state of the public mind with us. I am with great esteem Dr. Sir

Your friend & servt   TH: JEFFERSON

RC (PWacD: Feinstone Collection, on deposit PPAmP); addressed: "John Breckenridge esq. Kentuckey by mr Monroe"; endorsed by Breckinridge. PrC (MHi); endorsed by TJ in ink on verso.

John MONROE, a resident of Staunton and member of the REPUBLICAN committee for Augusta County, Virginia, hoped for an appointment as U.S. attorney for Kentucky. Failing to attain that office, he put off his intended relocation and returned to Staunton (CVSP, 9:83; Marshall, *Papers*, 4:217; Preston, *Catalogue*, 1:73; John Monroe to TJ, 30 Apr. 1801).

A letter from James Monroe to TJ, written 3 July and received the same day, is recorded in SJL but has not been found. Also missing, but recorded in SJL, is a letter from TJ to Samuel Brown of 4 July "by mr John Monroe."

To Mary Jefferson Eppes

MY DEAR MARIA   Monticello July 4. 1800.

We have heard not a word of you since the moment you left us. I hope you had a safe & pleasant journey. the rains which began to fall here the next day gave me uneasiness lest they should have overtaken you also. Dr. and mrs Bache have been with us till the day before yesterday. mrs Monroe is now in our neighborhood to continue during the sickly months. our Forte-piano arrived a day or two after you left us. it had been exposed to a great deal of rain, but being well covered was only much untuned. I have given it a poor tuning. it is the delight of the family, and all pronounce what your choice will be. your sister does not hesitate to prefer it to any harpsichord she ever saw *except her own*. and it is easy to see it is only the celestini which retains that preference. it is as easily tuned as a spinette, & will not need it half as often. our harvest has been a very fine one. I finish to day. it is the heaviest crop of wheat I ever had.—a murder in our neighborhood is the theme of it's present conversation. George Carter shot Birch of Charlottesville, in his own door, and on very slight provocation. he died in a few minutes. the examining court meets tomorrow. as your harvest must be over as soon as ours we hope soon to see mr Eppes & himself. I say nothing of his affairs lest he should be less impatient to come & see them. all are well here except Ellen, who is rather drooping than sick; and all are impatient to see you. no one so much as he whose happiness is wrapped up in yours. my affections to mr Eppes & tenderest love to yourself. hasten to us. Adieu.

TH: JEFFERSON

RC (ViU); part of signature torn away, supplied from PrC; addressed: "Mrs. Maria Eppes at Montblanco in Chesterfield by the Petersburg mail." PrC (CSmH); endorsed by TJ in ink on verso.

The court decided GEORGE CARTER was insane when he murdered Samuel Burch and sentenced him to an asylum, where he remained until his death in 1816 (Woods, *Albemarle*, 155, 164).

To Waller Holladay

SIR   Monticello July 4. 1800.

Your favor of the 18th. ult. came to hand on the 26th. I have examined my papers on the subject of it, & find that I have recieved but one letter from mr Littlepage since I returned to America, & that was dated at Warsaw Dec. 26. 1791. the want of conveyances as well as the want of matter interesting to him in his then position, prevented my writing to him. I have since been informed (and I think it was by General Kosciuzko) that on the dismemberment of Poland he went to Petersburg & was employed by the emperor. I think the best means of obtaining intelligence of him would be to write to mr King, Minister Plenipotentiary of the US. at London, where a Russian minister resides, who in all probability can at once give information as to mr Littlepage. if he cannot, he can in a very short time obtain it from Petersburg, and will doubtless readily do it on mr King's request. I am satisfied mr King will with pleasure take the trouble of obtaining & communicating the information you desire, on your own application. I would willingly offer my service, but that I am not in correspondence with mr King, and am satisfied that your request alone will suffice to engage him in the enquiry.

I am Sir Your most obedt. servt   TH: JEFFERSON

RC (ViHi: Holladay Family Papers); addressed: "Mr. Waller Holladay Louisa to the care of Messrs. David & James Blair Fredericksburg"; franked; postmarked Milton, 5 July. Tr (same); in Lewis Holladay's hand with note at foot of text from Lewis Holladay to Waller Holladay, dated 18 July 1800, stating that the above is a true copy of the letter and that new writs are ready to be served on them.

The only extant copy of Holladay's FAVOR OF 18 June probably is the draft of his letter to TJ printed at 1 June.

In 1797, after the DISMEMBERMENT OF POLAND, King Stanislas II was removed to St. PETERSBURG, where he died in February 1798 before Lewis Lit-tlepage was able to join him. Littlepage remained in Warsaw until 1800. Waller Holladay sought news of his half-brother because suits seeking control over Littlepage's property had been brought by his sister Mary and her husband Robert S. Coleman. In May 1798 the Colemans contended that Littlepage had not been heard from and therefore was presumed to be dead. They were suing John Carter Littlepage and Lewis Holladay over ownership of slaves (Boand, *Lewis Littlepage*, 240-1, 255-76; Curtis Carroll Davis, *The King's Chevalier: A Biography of Lewis Littlepage* [Indianapolis, 1961], 362-3).

For TJ's efforts to gain INTELLIGENCE on Littlepage, see Julian Ursin Niemcewicz to TJ, 2 Aug. 1800.

To Harry Innes

DEAR SIR   Monticello July 4. 1800.

This will be handed you by mr Monroe, a relation of our governor, who proposes to pay a visit to Kentuckey to look out for a settlement. he is a lawyer of reputation, a very honest man, and good republican. having no acquaintance in your state, I take the liberty of recommending him to your attentions & counsel, which the worth of his character will fully justify. we have no particular news but what you also have from the newspapers. mr Monroe will be able to give you the state of the public mind with us. I am with great esteem Dear Sir

Your friend & servt   TH: JEFFERSON

RC (DLC: Harry Innes Papers); addressed: "The honble Judge Innes Kentuckey by mr Monroe."

From Pierre Samuel Du Pont de Nemours

Good-Stay near New York 6 Juillet 1800.

Rien ne peut égaler la douleur et la Consternation que m'a causé la triste et fausse nouvelle que les ennemis de l'Amérique et les vôtres avaient mise dans les journaux. Je croyais avoir perdu le plus grand homme de ce continent, celui dont la raison éclairée peut être le plus utile aux deux mondes, celui qui par la ressemblance de nos principes me donne l'esperance de la plus solide amitié, si nécessaire à qui *vit loin* de sa Patrie.

J'ai passé quelques jours dans un malheur inexprimable.

A présent je vous félicite, et les Etats-unis, et je me félicite moi même de ce que les tentatives et les bévues de la méchanceté retombent presque toujours sur sa tête.

Ils feront quelque faute, disait Mr. de Vergennes. Cette complaisance à laquelle l'ennemi ne manque jamais, nous sert toujours mieux que notre propre habileté.

L'ouvrage sur l'Education nationale en Amérique n'est encore qu'a demi copié.

C'est mon ami *Pusy* qui veut bien prendre la peine de la transcrire. La copie en sera bien plus correcte et souvent corrigée par ses sages avis. Mais il en résulte que je n'ai pas droit de le trop presser.

Agréez mon sincere et tendre et respectueux attachement.

Du Pont (de Nemours)

Ma Femme et mes Enfans ont bien partagé ma désolation et ma joie.

EDITORS' TRANSLATION

Good-Stay near New York 6 July 1800.

Nothing can equal the pain and dismay caused me by the sad and false news that the enemies of America and yourself had placed in the newspapers. I thought I had lost the greatest man of this continent, the one whose enlightened reason can be the most useful to both worlds, the one who by the similarity of our principles gives me the hope of the finest friendship, so necessary to one who *lives far* from his fatherland.

I spent several days in unutterable despair.

At present, I congratulate you, and the United States, and I congratulate myself that the attempts and the blunders of the wicked almost always fall back on their own head.

They will make some mistake, Mr. de Vergennes used to say. That neverfailing self-satisfaction of the enemy always serves us better than our own skill.

The work on national education in America is still only half copied.

It is my friend *Pusy* who has been willing to take the trouble to transcribe it. The copy will be much more correct, and often corrected by his wise counsels. But as a result I do not have the right to urge him on too much.

Accept my sincere and fond and respectful devotion.

Du Pont (de Nemours)

My wife and my children fully shared my grief and my joy.

RC (DLC); at head of text: "à Mr Jefferson"; endorsed by TJ as received 24 July and so recorded in SJL.

LA TRISTE ET FAUSSE NOUVELLE: on 30 June the Baltimore *American*, citing information that came by way of Winchester, Virginia, printed a report that TJ had died at Monticello on the 24th following "an indisposition of 48 hours." The *American* cast doubt on the rumor and no newspaper closer to Charlottesville seemed to have the news, but the report spread. It appeared in Philadelphia in the *True American* on 1 July, citing what seemed to be confirmation by way of Frederick, Maryland, and the next day the *Philadelphia Gazette* and the New York *Commercial Advertiser*, the latter drawing on the *True American*, carried versions of the story. Omitting details, the *Gazette of the United States* noted simply on 2 July: "The report of Mr. Jefferson's death appears to be entitled to some credit." The next day the *Aurora* printed the report from Baltimore without analysis, but Samuel H. Smith, in his *Universal Gazette*, took pains to review all available information and found it to provide "the strongest *presumptive* untruth of the report of Mr. Jefferson's death." Largely discredited by information published in New York and Philadelphia by 5 July, the story, which reached Boston by the 4th, only appeared in some New England papers for the first time on the 8th and 9th. As early as 3 July the *Gazette of the United States* tried to account for the origins of the tale by means of a second rumor from Virginia, to the effect that the death of a Monticello slave named Thomas Jefferson had sparked the confusion. Some Republicans, however, contended that the whole affair was no accident but a Federalist gambit to prevent TJ from receiving honorable notice on the 4th as the author of the Declaration of Independence (Charles Warren, *Odd Byways in American History* [Cambridge, Mass., 1942], 127-35; *Commercial Advertiser*, 2 July; Malone, *Jefferson*, 3:477-8).

From John Wayles Eppes

DEAR SIR,   Mont-Blanco July 6th. 1800

We reached Eppington safely on the third day from Monticello and this place two days afterwards. Our journey was extremely tiresome from the heat of the weather and slowness of our horses—The day after leaving Monticello we were twelve hours on the road and eleven of them actually travelling 36 miles—Maria bore the journey well and continues in good health.

I finished halling in my Wheat on the 4th. instant—It has been a terrible harvest in all the lower Country—The wheat is generally bad in quality and in many places lost totally by rust—I am so fortunate as to have a good crop having escaped the rust entirely.

I had occasion to go to Petersburg a few days since and met with Mr Haxhall. His horse cannot be purchased—He has refused four hundred dollars for him since I went up to Monticello—He is certainly in point of figure and appearance the first gelding[1] in the State—I called also on Mr. Bell who owns the horse Doctr. Walker rode up to Eppington—I find on enquiry I was mistaken in the age of Bells horse he is only 6 this Spring—Bell would sell, but asks far more than the value of his horse—300 dollars is his price—

We shall leave this place for Monticello on the 20th—We shall take Cumberland in our way up and I hope have the pleasure of meeting again by the last of the month—Accept from Maria & Myself the best wishes of affection

adieu yours sincerely   JNO: W: EPPES

PS. We had a severe hail storm on the 1st. instant. It continued about 20 minutes and the hail measured four Inches round—.

RC (MHi); endorsed by TJ as received 17 July and so recorded in SJL.   A letter from TJ to John Wayles Eppes of 30 May, recorded in SJL, has not been found.

[1] Word interlined in place of "horse."

From Daniel Smith

S<small>IR</small>,   Sumner County July 6th. 1800.

Judge Campbell was at my house a few weeks ago and shewed me a letter of yours to him in which you request him to procure you a vocabulary of the Cherokee language.—Just afterwards a Chickasaw family with whom I am acquainted passed by my house, and supposing that a vocabulary of the Chickasaw language might not be unacceptable to you I made use of this opportunity to take the enclosed. I had not your list of english words—but took down as many as I could think of in the time the indian family was with me one evening.

I am Sir with respect and esteem your obedt. Servt.

D<small>ANL</small> S<small>MITH</small>

Please to present my respects to Col. Lewis and Mrs. Lewis.

RC (PPAmP); endorsed by TJ as received 10 Aug. and so recorded in SJL. Enclosure: Vocabulary list, undated, giving 158 English words with Chickasaw equivalents for all but 6 of them; with a note on orthography and pronunciation and a note keyed to the English word "you" that reads: "in questioning them for their names of our pronouns they seemed not clearly to understand me" (MS in same; in Smith's hand; endorsed by TJ: "A Vocabulary of the Chickasaw language taken in 1800. by Genl. D. Smith of Tennissee from a chickasaw family who passed an evening at his house. see his lre July 6. 1800."); contains some of the same words that appear in the list provided by Benjamin Hawkins (see 12 July), but with different phonetic representation of the Chickasaw terms.

A LETTER OF YOURS: TJ to David Campbell, 14 Mch. 1800.

From Elijah Griffiths

D<small>EAR</small> S<small>IR</small>/   Alms-House July 8th: 1800

The republicans in general, & your particular friends in this quarter, have just recovered from sensations of the keenest regret & heartfelt sorrow; consequent to a Current report of your death. We have just congratulated each other on a satisfactory contradiction of what we considered a general calamity; and an individual affliction to ourselves.

We feel anxious to know what, or whether any extraordinary circumstance has occured to you, from which such a report could take its rise.

Among the number of those who felt every thing that a republican could feel on this occasion, was your friend Doctor Barton: I shall long remember the distress portrayed in his countenance, when we first met, after this inteligence appeared in the papers; he felt & expressed those sensations which alone flow from the heart of a sincere friend.—

The antirepublicans generally, but particularly that part of them, covered with disgrace, crimes & the speculated spoils of their country, swore the news was too good to be true: they however enjoy'd the short lived hope, that by your death their conduct would escape scrutanization & public detestation. They are now awok to those sensations, which fail not at times, to haunt the most callus consciences.—

I have not yet heard of any probable plan for effecting an election of electors for this state; but am sure the Governor will make use of every legal exertion to accomplish that end.—

The 4 of July 1800 exhibited a parade of republicans only; the other party gave no demonstrations of joy, the church bells were silent, & the were generally attending to their daily occupations.

This was shewing their true colors.—

I learn by a gentleman lately from Hagerstown, Mr FitzHugh is still of the same political faith he was when we seen him last. This gentle man was pretty certain if the election law in maryland stood as formerly, genl. D. Heister would be the elector for that district

I am now circulating letters among my friends in the neighbouring coun[ties] relative to the part you acted in procuring religious liberty in Virginia, this fact will be useful, tho' if the people have a chance, they are prepared to do themselves justice, without any new stimulus.—

There is a Mr B. Wood a clerk in the treasury department, and late a manager in this institution: I believe he is a real aristocrat at bottom, but prepared at all times to float with the strongest current; he is dependant, of course not very influential with his party, but recommends himself by invectives against you & the republicans generally. altho' I have never heard him speak on politics, my information, is by me, undoubted. Last winter this gentleman waited on you with some pecular kind of seeds from Mr Cummings, Steward to the alms-house. Whether Mr Woods motives were to pave the way to preferment, or to lay hold of & distort (if circumstances favored it) any unguarded expression or conversation: and thereby more fully recommend himself to his party I leave you to Judge; but I hardly think his motives honorable. my present situation forbids entering into any political disputes, more particularly so where the managers are concern'd, I have only given this information that you may know Mr Woods true cloth; I must beg therefore to be kept out of view. Mr Wood shortly moves to the Federal City.—

Since the late changes in the cabinet, & in politics at large, life has become not only tolerable, but somewhat comfortable, the Feds have exhibited a degree of order & civilization, not before witnessed for many years.

No diseases of a high inflamatory or bilious grade have yet appeared here this season; dysentery, diarrhea & remittent fevers of the common kind assume a pretty high tone at present, but this weather rouses all our fears for the future. I fear the water works will not be in a state to do much good this season.

Whether or not, the fever should appear this season, I shall remain at the alms-house, where I shall feel a particular pleasure in hearing from you by letter.—

With sentiments of great respect I am Dr sir your very humble Servant ELIJAH GRIFFITHS

RC (DLC); at foot of text: "Thomas Jefferson Esqr. Vice President of the United States"; endorsed by TJ as received 24 July and so recorded in SJL.

The Philadelphia *Aurora* noted that the Fourth of July, 1800, was celebrated by REPUBLICANS ONLY and that the Federalists acted as if "on some day of general mourning." The bells that were usually rung at Christ Church were silent. Many Republicans began their festivities with the reading of the Declaration of Independence (Philadelphia *Aurora*, 7, 8 July 1800; Simon P. Newman, *Parades and the*

Politics of the Street: Festive Culture in the Early American Republic [Philadelphia, 1997], 112-13).

Daniel HIESTER resigned as congressman from Pennsylvania in July 1796 and moved to Hagerstown, Maryland. From 1801 to 1804 he served as congressman from Maryland's fourth district in place of Federalist George Baer, Jr. (*Biog. Dir. Cong.*; Dauer, *Adams Federalists*, 267, 323, 328). For the retention of the district method for choosing electors in Maryland, see Stevens Thomson Mason to TJ, 11 July 1800.

To George Jefferson

DEAR SIR   Monticello July 9. 1800.

I wrote you last on the 7th. of June, since which your's of the 9th. 16th. 23d. & 30th. have been recieved—as have all the articles announced in them as forwarded. a half dozen stick chairs should have come with the other articles from Philadelphia, & as I left them in mr Barnes's wareroom with the other things, perhaps they did come, & have been mis-delivered by the Captain. tho' were this the case I suppose the bill of lading would shew it—I have written to mr Barnes on the subject. I have this day written to Joseph Roberts for $3\frac{1}{4}$ tons of nail & hoop iron, which be pleased to forward immediately on reciept. what you mention on the subject of the proceeds of that from Carolina is well. I yesterday drew on you for £24–11 in favor of W. J.

Aldridge or order which be pleased to honor on sight. should mr Eppes make a draught on you at all, it will probably be for something between 3. & 400. D. paiable after Oct. 1. before which day the money shall be placed with you by a draught on Mr. Barnes. I desired mr Archibd. Blair to pay into your hands 567.107 D for Philip Mazzei, which I will pray you to remit to mr Barnes, who will recieve direction[s on] transferring it to Hubbard.—send me, if you please, another dozen bottles of center. will you pass a part of the sickly season with us? it will always give [us] pleasure. I am Dear Sir

    Yours affectionately   Th: Jefferson

[can you] [. . .] [a big bundle] of [cord agreeable] to the sample enclosed [. . .] to our bi[. . .] [. . .] [you shew to me] [. . .] [the natural] [. . .] of the [. . .].

July 10. P.S. I have opened my letter again to [write] you to send me 15[0.] ℔ of bacon. it would be preferred to be all of medlings. it is to provision the family of a mr Powel, coming to take charge of my nailery, and who I expect will be calling on you about the 20th. instant to [. . .] him how to get up. I recommended to him to send his things by the boats, and even to bring his family in them. I shall thank you for any aid you [can give him].

PrC (MHi); faint; at foot of text: "Mr. George Jefferson"; endorsed by TJ in ink on verso.

I HAVE WRITTEN TO MR BARNES: see TJ to Barnes, 24 June 1800.

In SJL TJ noted that his letter to JOSEPH ROBERTS, Jr., of 9 July (now missing) was "for 3. tons rod, ¼ ton hoop."

The payment to William J. ALDRIDGE included £10.14.0 for groceries and the remaining £13.17.0 for the final payment to Chiles Terrell for Fitzpartner, the horse purchased by TJ in May 1799 (MB, 2:1022; Betts, Farm Book, 99). A letter from TJ to Aldridge of 14 Sep. 1800 and letters from Aldridge, the first recorded in SJL as received 12 Sep. 1800, but without date, and the second recorded as a letter of 6 Oct. 1800 received on the same day, have not been found.

A letter from TJ to Archibald BLAIR of 4 July 1800 and the response by Blair of 12 July, recorded in SJL as received five days later, have not been found. Letters from Blair to TJ of 11 and 28 June 1794 and 26 Dec. 1795, recorded in SJL as received on 18 June and 1 July 1794 and 4 Jan. 1796, respectively, the first two from Richmond, and a letter from TJ to Blair of 19 June 1794, are also missing.

SAMPLE ENCLOSED: probably cord (alongside the entry for this letter in SJL TJ recorded: "chairs. £24–11 Alldridge. A. Blair. Center. cord. bacon"). In his records TJ notes that he paid 15/ for six bunches of sash cord on 21 July (Statement of Account with Gibson & Jefferson, 15 Jan. 1801).

From Van Staphorst & Hubbard

SIR!   Amsterdam 10 July 1800

We are honored with your esteemed favor of 8 May, inclosing Letters for General Kosciuszko & the Baron de Geismar, which have been carefully forwarded, and to the former We likewise transmitted duly accepted, the Bill to his order sent us by Mr. John Barnes of Philadelphia.

Messs: Danl. Ludlow & Co. of Newyork advise us to have received from you Two Hundred Dollars, that We place to the Credit of your Account.

With singular Satisfaction, did We read your opinion of the State of your Country, and of the solidity of its Government, notwithstanding It had not escaped a Sensation of the Evils that have desolated a great part of Europe. We sincerely wish it may continue happy and prosperous, and afford one solitary proof at least, that a Government by free Representation, is capable of affording Security and the Enjoyment of real Liberty, to a nation that estimates and is determined to maintain its Independance, as the first and greatest of political Blessings.

We are with perfect Esteem and Respect Sir! Your mo: ob: hb: Servts.   N & J. VAN STAPHORST & HUBBARD

RC (DLC); in a clerk's hand, signed by the firm; at head of text: "Dupl."; at foot of first page: "The Honorable Thos. Jefferson Esqr. Vice president of the U.S."; endorsed by TJ as received 16 Oct. 1800 and so recorded in SJL.

From Stevens Thomson Mason

DEAR SIR   Rasberry Plain July 11th 1800

We have lately felt great anxiety at the report of your death, which was first circulated in a manner that gave us reason to fear its truth, and has for the two last posts deter'd me from writing to you. I hope that the report has originated with your political enemies and has not arisen from any indisposition that you have experienced.

I was a few weeks ago called into Maryland by the illness of my Uncle Mr John Barnes who died on the 23d Ulto.—I found whilst there that a considerable change in public opinion had taken place and I believe will manifest itself at the ensuing elections so as to confound the aristocracy of that State. this apprehension inclines many of them to attempt a change in the mode of chusing Electors. but the attention of the people is so alive on the subject that some of the hardiest of the

Tories hesitate at making the experiment and are fearful of the consequences. yet I believe it will be tried. the opinion of some well informed persons that I conversed with is, that should the present Legislature be called and take the choise of Electors from the people, the consequence would be such a change in the House of Delegates at the next election (in October) as to give the Republicans a majority on a joint ballot, and that the Senate would next year be all ousted. they are at present to a man aristocratic.

our friend Colo J F Mercer and several other men of Talents on the republican side are coming into their legislature. My brother JTM has at length been prevailed on to engage in politics, and is a candidate for the county of Montgomery. having entered into the business I am in hopes we shall be able to prevail on him to go further and that he may be elected for Craigs district next Spring.

I have obtained a subscription to the amount of $160 and expect to extend it to $200 for C.H. &c it would be well to know what is done in other parts of the State as the relief will soon be wanted.

I am like to have a good crop of Siccory seed. I think you have told me it might be sowed in the broad cast. I should be obliged to you to inform me the thickness and season of sowing in that way.

Have you ever seen the Peruvian Winter grass? I have a few sprigs in my garden which grew this year above six feet high. it is a very luxuriant and appears to be a very hardy grass. it is rather coarse but I think that might be corrected by thick sowing. if you have none of it, I can furnish you some of the seed to put you in Stock. it produces seed in great abundance. I had only forty which came up from which I got three quarts.

I should be glad to hear from you when convenient

And am Dear Sir With sincere regard Yours

STES. THON. MASON

RC (DLC); endorsed by TJ as received 24 July and so recorded in SJL.

MY UNCLE: Mason's mother was Mary King BARNES (DAB).

Federalists in Maryland were responsible for the state's MODE of choosing presidential ELECTORS by district, but, fearing the system would give the Republican candidate some electoral votes in 1800, hoped to give the selection of electors to the LEGISLATURE. The issue fostered much partisan debate, but in the end Governor Benjamin Ogle declined to call a special session of the legislature to make the change (L. Marx Renzulli, Jr., *Maryland: The Federalist Years* [Rutherford, N.J., 1972], 212-16).

John Francis MERCER represented Anne Arundel County when the Maryland House of Delegates convened in November (*Votes and Proceedings of the House of Delegates of the State of Maryland: November Session, One Thousand Eight Hundred* [Annapolis, 1801], 3). For the fate of Mason's BROTHER, John Thomson Mason, in the elections, see Stevens Thomson Mason's letters to TJ of 5 Sep. and 17 Oct. 1800.

C.H.: Charles Holt, whose fine under

the Sedition Act Mason was raising money to defray. TJ contributed $10 and also collected money from others (MB, 2:1024; enclosure to TJ to Madison, 29 Aug. 1800).

In SJL TJ recorded a letter to Mason of 26 July that has not been found (see descriptive note to TJ to Pierre Samuel Du Pont de Nemours, 26 July 1800). A letter from TJ to Mason of 14 May 1800 is also missing.

From Benjamin Hawkins

Creek agency 12 July 1800

I have had the pleasure to receive your favour of the 14 of march, to which I could have replied a few days sooner; but I have been in the expectation of seeing some chiefs of the neighbouring nations, from whom I could obtain the words, to compleat your vocabulary: that expectation will not soon be realized; and I now send you what I have obtained, with assurances that when I am able I will compleat it.

The Creek is obtained from the purest source, one of my assistants an interpreter, a chief of the nation, one of our greatest orators, aided by some chiefs selected for the purpose and by Mr. Barnard an assistant and interpreter. The Choctaw words were obtained by me some time past from a lad of that nation who spoke English. The Chickasaw from a Chickasaw who has resided several years among the Creeks, and had formerly acted as interpreter between the two nations.

I have been so much occupied with the affairs of this agency, that very little of my time is taken up with the political occurrencies alluded to by you. I shall never change my old friendships, nor the men of the times, of our first acquaintance, whom I esteem and venerate, for new ones. If the new are better, I am not dipleased, but for me to know this, requires proof that is not within my reach.

The communication you ask shall be sent you. The one to the war office, of necessity, was a hasty transcript from notes; but not less to be prized, as I have discribed only what I saw or believed to be true in the plainest language.

I am now in the woods like an arab chief in tents, with my stock and family around me, and at the moment I am writing I hear the language of Scotch French Spanish English Africans Creeks and Uches. and all in peace, considering themselves as forming one family, and executing my orders with pleasure. Colo. Gaither a worthy honest man, faithful in the execution of the duties enjoined on him by his command, is for the present with me.

You have heard of some of our embarrassments in this quarter upon the arrival of General Bowles among us. He had very unexpectedly aided by some Simenolies taken the fort of St. Marks, and a large supply of Indian goods, and military stores. The officers of his C.M having, after ten months of preparation roused by the unexpected surrender of this fortress, and the disgrace attending it, in a council of war of the 12 ultimo unanimously determined that the governor of Pensacola should form an expedition for the purpose of retaking that fortress and restoring order among the Simenolies "to this effect seven vessels of war and two merchant men armed were put in readiness and on board of them were embarked the troops and stores that were thought necessary for the undertaking" This force sailed from Pensacola on the 17 ultimo and have as I am informed retaken the fort without any loss. The general and his followers have fled to Mic,co,sooke a town of the Simenolies.

I shall write you soon, and enclose a letter for my most estimable friend your neighbour pray remember me to her, to Mr. Madison and Mr. Giles. It will be a source of happiness to me to hear from you some times, while I am labouring to carry into effect the plan intrusted to my agency, and I will endeavour to repay you by details from these wilds, which will satisfy you, that the plan has unquestionably succeeded.

I am very sincerely and truly My dear Sir Your affectionate friend and obt servt.

BENJAMIN HAWKINS

RC (PPAmP); at foot of text: "The Honble Thomas Jefferson Vice President of the U.S"; endorsed by TJ as received 8 Aug. and so recorded in SJL. Enclosure: Vocabulary of Creek and Chickasaw words, not found, but incorporated into "A Comparative Vocabulary of the Muskogee or Creek, Chickasaw, Choktaw and <in part of the> Cherokee languages, (with Some Words in the language of the old Indians of Keowa.) By the late Col. Benjamin Hawkins late Agent of the United States to the Creek Nation, & by him communicated to Mr Jefferson," the Historical and Literary Committee of the American Philosophical Society supplying the title and other notations on the document's cover page; containing Creek, Chickasaw, Choctaw, and Cherokee equivalents of 276 English terms in a sequence following TJ's standard list (see note to TJ to William Linn, 5 Feb. 1798, Vol. 30:81-2n); donated to the APS as a single list including all four languages (*Transactions of the Historical & Literary Committee of the American Philosophical Society*, 1 [1819], xlix), the APS committee subsequently adding some additional vocabulary from David Campbell's list (see TJ to Campbell, 14 Mch. 1800) and other sources; endorsed by TJ: "Vocabularies. Creek Chickasaw Choctaw Cherokee. from Benj. Hawkins" (MS in PPAmP).

Hawkins's SOURCE for Creek vocabulary was Alexander Cornells, also known as Oche Haujo, a CHIEF OF THE NATION whose father was a Scotsman (Florette Henri, *The Southern Indians and Benjamin Hawkins, 1796-1816* [Norman, Okla., 1986], 55-6). Hawkins did not send the CHOCTAW vocabulary until November (Hawkins to TJ, 6 Nov. 1800, 1 Mch. 1801). For the requested COMMUNICATION, see TJ to Hawkins, 14 Mch. 1800, and Hawkins to TJ, 1 Mch. 1801. UCHES: the Yuchis (Uchees) lived in the vicinity of the Creek Indians but were linguistically and culturally distinct. Lieutenant Colonel Henry GAITHER commanded the U.S. military garrison near the Creek agency (Joel W. Martin, *Sacred Revolt: The Muskogees' Struggle for a New World* [Boston, 1991], 137-8; C. L. Grant, ed., *Letters, Journals and Writings of Benjamin Hawkins*, 2 vols. [Savannah, 1980], 1:61n, 313). A letter from Gaither to TJ of 1 Aug. 1800, recorded in SJL as received from Fort Wilkinson on the 28th, has not been found.

In 1792 Spanish officials in the Floridas arrested William Augustus BOWLES, who used his influence among some bands of the Creeks and tacit support from British authorities to try to oust the firm of Panton, Leslie & Co. from its dominance over the region's trade. Taken to Spain and then the Philippines, Bowles escaped, restored his connection with the British, and in 1799 returned to the Creek coun-

try. Calling himself the "Director General of Muscogee," with a group of Lower Creeks and Seminoles he captured the Spanish outpost at ST. MARKS but could not hold it and withdrew to Miccosookee. Hawkins, who had urged the Spanish to take action against Bowles, reported to the secretary of war, but TJ in his letter of 14 Mch. said he did not usually see such papers, so Hawkins may have assumed that Andrew Ellicott had informed TJ of the recent events (same, 1:261, 265, 271-9, 334-8, 342, 361; DAB, 2:519-20; Vol. 26:415-16n).

C.M: Catholic Majesty (Carlos IV of Spain). ESTIMABLE FRIEND: Elizabeth House Trist (see TJ to Hawkins, 14 Mch. 1800).

From Jeremiah Moore

Farfax County

MR. THOMAS JEFFERSON SIR.   Moorsfields—July 12th. 1800

Having lived trough the American Revolution my political opinions were formed during that period of Tryal and danger and perhaps they are the more deeply rivited by the Circumstancies existing when they took their birth—However some how or other they have taken a disposition that all devouring time has not intirely Swallowed up—and while I See numbers that once were the advocates of republican principles bask in the Solar rays of arristocratical measures. I find my Self greatly at a loss how account for the Change that has taken place in the opinions of these men—the Virginia assembly above all others Surprise and astonish my understanding—Gentlemen who oppose with Such warmth the Measures of the general Goverment as Calkalated to Consolidate the united States in to one Grand Empire and Swallow up the State Goverments and with them the last remains of republickanism they say and Still there is no State in the union that more fully embraces the esential principles of arostocrasy than the State of Virginia—The rights of Humon Nature are atached to men and not to things and when any number of men all possest of the Same Natural rights do by Compact Cast all those rights into one Common Stock firm [Since] Certain aquired rights arise to each individual Stockholder in equal proportion and are as such a compensation for the Loss of those Natural rights which were lost by the

Compact—the first and most esential of those aquired rights I take to be that of Electing or being Elected as the Case may be but the Constitution of Virginia transfers this right from the man and places it in his property (and in the great wisdom of the State She has discovered the purcise quantity of Land be the same rich or poor that will confer this invalluable Blessing)—and of Course to be born poor in Virginia is to be born a Slave—I Should not Stranger as I am to you have given you the trouble these feble [observations] [. . .] I not heard it hinted a few days ago that you must be more aristocratical in your dispositions that Mr Adams the present president of the united States born as you were in Virginia it was insinuated that you must have approbated the Virginia aristocrasy at least you have been intirely Silent while the most glaring Violation of right that ever disgraced a free people prevailed and a great Number of respectable Citisins are thus deprived of all priviledges in the Goverment in which they live and which they rest both their lives and fortunes in the defence of—if Virginia may Say no man Shall be elligible to Elect or be Elected because he has not 50 acres of Land they may with equal propriety and Justice say he shall not unless he holds *5000* and so without end—it is a time when the political opinions of men high in office should be well understood—a time when Tyrants Spread the ravages of war. the instrument of their dignity and importance (with savage fury far and wide) a time when america Should with Caution trust her dearest intrest in the hands of those who give Evidence that they are not washed from the pullution of that Tyranny that has delluged the Earth with Humon Blood—it would gratify a number of your friends to hear you say you were in heart an enemy to the Doctrine of arristocrasy in Virginia and Every where Else—the part you took against the Religious Establishment when I had the honour with others of putting a petition into your hands Signed by 10000— Subscribers praying the disolution of those Tyrannical Chains Still lives in my memory—and has Sometimes afforded me pleasure in being able to Say without doubt that you were a friend to religious liberty and it would add to my happiness to able to Say with Equal Certainty that you were a friend to a general mode of Suffrage in opposition to that partial one which now prevails in this Commonwealth——I have no apolegy to plead for the intrution this Schrole will make on your time and patience but your own goodness which I trust will pardon the liberty [I have taken and] I have no doubt but you have been intruded on at Some time of your life by men whoes motives might not be more pure than those that occupy the heart of your obdt Hble Svt JEREMIAH MOORE

RC (DLC); torn; endorsed by TJ as received 21 July and probably the letter recorded in SJL as that of 9 July.

Born in Prince William County, Virginia, Jeremiah Moore (1746-1815) gave up his office as a lay reader in the Episcopal Church and became a Baptist itinerant preacher in the early 1770s. He was brought before the authorities in Alexandria several times before he obtained a license to preach in 1773. After the Revolution he returned to Fairfax County and from 1792 to 1813 attended meetings and played an active role in the Ketocton Baptist Association, composed of churches west of Philadelphia including Virginia. From about 1789 to 1815 Moore lived on his 600 acre estate at Moorefield in Fairfax County. He was one of the founders and pastor of the First Baptist Church in Alexandria to which TJ contributed $50 in 1805. He preached primarily in Maryland and Virginia but also traveled to churches in North and South Carolina, Tennessee, Kentucky, Pennsylvania, Delaware, New Jersey, and New York. William Wirt described Moore as "Not refined, but rough and strong, of copious and even impetuous volubility, keen, acute, witty, full of original observation, and as a reasoner I have seldom heard him surpassed. He was a most interesting preacher" (Thomas V. DiBacco, *Moorefield: Home of Early Baptist Preacher Jeremiah Moore* [Fairfax, Va., 1971], 3-27; James B. Taylor, *Lives of Virginia Baptist Ministers*, 2 vols. [Richmond, 1838-60], 1:209-13; Mary G. Powell, *The History of Old Alexandria, Virginia, From July 13, 1749 to May 24, 1861* [Richmond, 1928], 117; wmq, 2d ser., 13 [1933], 18-25; mb, 2:1146).

putting a petition into your hands: after TJ became governor in 1779 an unsuccessful effort was made to pass the Bill for Establishing Religious Freedom. TJ's bill was printed as a broadside in the summer of that year and petitions for and against it were presented (above in Vol. 2:547-8).

From William Dunbar

Sir   Natchez 14th. July 1800

Having been requested by a friend in London, to send him a Copy of such notes or remarks as I had made while upon the line of Demarcation, I have now complied with that request; while I was occupied in the preparation, I reflected, whether there could be any thing contained in those Notes worthy of being presented to you; and I had determined that there was not, being perfectly sensible how unimportant they are; knowing however that Men of learning and genius are indulgent to those of inferior talents, I have suffered my notes and observations to appear before you, with the expectation, that probably they may furnish you with the means or motives of asking some questions which it may be in my power to solve. Something more remains, which I have not been able to compleat by this opportunity, & will go to resolve your inquiries respecting the missisippi, and which at a future period I will have the honor of transmitting to you.

I have the honor to be with high respect Sir your most humble & Obedt. Servant   William Dunbar

N.B. After perusing the Notes, permit me to ask the favor of your directing the packet to be forwarded to its address at London.

RC (DLC); at foot of first page: "Honble Thomas Jefferson"; endorsed by TJ as received 23 Oct. and so recorded in SJL. Enclosures: (1) Dunbar's "notes or remarks . . . while upon the line of Demarcation," not found (see TJ to Caspar Wistar, 16 Dec. 1800, second letter, and TJ to Dunbar, 12 Jan. 1801). (2) "Description of a singular Phenomenon seen at Baton Rouge," describing a crimson, luminous object, "the size of a large house," that passed overhead and fell to earth in the night of 5 Apr. 1800; dated Natchez, 30 June 1800, printed in APS, *Transactions*, 6 [1809], 25; note at foot of page: "The above communication was accompanied by an account of the first invention of the Telegraphe extracted from the works of Dr. Hook," which was not selected for publication; enclosed in TJ to Wistar, 16 Dec. 1800, first letter; transmitted to the American Philosophical Society, 16 Jan. 1801, and approved for publication on 6 Feb. (APS, *Proceedings*, 22, pt. 3 [1884], 308-9).

According to TJ's second letter to Caspar Wistar on 16 Dec. 1800, Dunbar's FRIEND IN LONDON was named Smith. Dunbar corresponded with British scientists including Sir William Herschel, and perhaps Smith was James Edward Smith, the owner of Linnaeus's collections and library, founder of the Linnean Society, and botanist, who was interested in the efforts of American scientists and collected natural history information from throughout the world (DNB; DSB; Franklin L. Riley, "Sir William Dunbar—The Pioneer Scientist of Mississippi," *Publications of the Mississippi Historical Society*, 2 [1899], 86, 91; Greene, *American Science*, 9, 10, 23, 96).

INQUIRIES: apparently TJ's reference, in his letter to Dunbar of 24 June 1799, to the lack of knowledge about "the part of the continent you inhabit." Dunbar did not complete his "Description of the river Mississippi and its Delta," which concentrated especially on the river's floods and alluvial deposits, until early in 1804 (APS, *Transactions*, 6 [1809], 165-87, 191-201; Dunbar to TJ, 22 Aug. 1801, 5 Jan., 10 June 1803, 28 Jan. 1804).

From George Jefferson

DEAR SIR,   Richmond 14th. July 1800

Your favor of the 9th. is received. the chairs you mention were not inserted in the bill of lading with the other articles, unless they were for Colo. Saml. Cabell which I do not suppose; the same number came for him to the care of Mr. Brown, and were included in our bill of lading—but they were particularly stated in it to be for him, and were besides directed to him on the bottoms.

I received on saturday last the $:567–10:7 of Mr. Blair, which shall be remitted to Mr. Barnes by next post agreeably to your direction.

I am Dear Sir Your Very humble servt.   GEO. JEFFERSON

RC (MHi); at foot of text: "Thos. Jefferson esqr."; endorsed by TJ as received 17 July and so recorded in SJL.

Letters from TJ to Samuel J. CABELL of 10 Aug. and 22 Sep. 1800 and Cabell's responses of 26 Aug. and 6 Oct., recorded in SJL as received 28 Aug. and 11 Oct., respectively, the first from "Souldier's joy," have not been found.

From Pierre Samuel Du Pont
de Nemours

MONSIEUR,   Good-Stay, near New-York 17 Juillet 1800.

Votre Gouvernement propose à mon gendre Mr. de Pusy d'entrer au Service des Etats-Unis comme Colonel au Corps du Génie.

La Situation précaire de quelques uns de vos Ports lui persuade que, même dans les vues les plus pacifiques, il est nécessaire de les mettre à l'abri d'insulte. Il croit donc pouvoir par ce travail bien mériter de votre Patrie.

Mais si un homme d'Etat tel que vous, et dont l'amitié m'est si chere, en jugeait autrement, sa résolution serait très ébranlée; et je ne croirais pas qu'un travail que vous n'auriez point approuvé pût être réellement utile.

Dites nous donc votre pensée.

Salut et respectueux attachement.   DU PONT (DE NEMOURS)

Le Livre sur l'Education n'est pas encore achevé de transcrire.

Quoique mes Enfans se rendent à la campagne de peur de la Fievre, nous vous prions d'adresser toujours vos lettres à New York. On nous les envoie.

EDITORS' TRANSLATION

SIR,   Good-Stay, near New York 17 July 1800

Your government is proposing to my son-in-law, Mr. de Pusy, to enter as a colonel in the Corps of Engineers.

The precarious situation of some of your Ports has persuaded him that, even from the most peaceful perspective, it is necessary to shelter them from aggression. Thus he thinks by this work to render a good service to your country.

But if a statesman like yourself, whose friendship is so dear to me, should judge otherwise, his resolution would be severely shaken; and I should not think that a work that you would not have approved could be truly useful.

So please give us your opinion.

Greetings and respectful affection.   DU PONT (DE NEMOURS)

The book on education is not yet completely transcribed.

Even though my children are going to the countryside for fear of the fever, we request you to continue addressing your letters to New York. They are sent on to us.

RC (DLC); at head of text: "Mr. Jefferson"; endorsed by TJ as received 31 July and so recorded in SJL.

Jean Xavier Bureaux de PUSY did some work on fortifications for the approaches to New York harbor before returning to

France, where he became prefect of the department of Allier in November 1801 (*Dictionnaire*, 7:689; TJ to Du Pont de Nemours, 1 Aug. 1800; Du Pont de Nemours to TJ, 8 Nov. 1800).

To John Barnes

DEAR SIR   Monticello July 19. 1800

My last to you was of the 24th. of June, since which I have recieved yours of June 29. July 1. 3. & 7. I am sorry my omission to write a week sooner should have left you that much longer unable to contradict the useless fabrication on which you are so good as to express so much sensibility. I have never in my life enjoyed higher or more uninterrupted health than since I left you in Philadelphia & no circumstance had happened which could give the slightest pretext to the report.

I leave to yourself altogether the investment of Kosciuszko's and Short's money. in answer to my enquiry after the half dozen stickchairs purchased by me of Letchworth in 4th. street, you say that a half dozen Windsor chairs in your bill of lading for *Colo. Cabell* were addressed to mr Brown. there must be some mistake. you will see by your papers that I gave Letchworth an order of May 10. on you for 15.60 D for 6. stickchairs for myself. he carried the chairs to you & you paid him the money. are these the same which have been addressed to Brown for Cabell? mr Jefferson mentioned to me his recieving these & delivering them to Brown for Cabell & that no others came.—I am a good deal disappointed by the failure of the housejoiner to come. in consequence I write to mr Trump on the subject, & not knowing his address I inclose it to you to sup[erscribe?] his address, first reading & sealing it. according to your directions I address this to you at Georgetown. I am with sincere esteem Dear Sir

Your friend & servt   TH: JEFFERSON

P.S. I desired mr Jefferson to forward to you 567.107 D which I pray you to remit to Messrs. Van Staphorsts & Hubbard of Amsterdam for Philip Mazzei. they are his bankers.

PrC (MHi); at foot of text: "Mr. John Barnes"; endorsed by TJ in ink on verso. Enclosure: TJ to Daniel Trump, this date, not found (see below and Barnes to TJ, 26 July 1800).

Barnes's letter of JUNE 29, recorded in SJL as received on 10 July, has not been found. No letter from Barnes dated 1 July 1800 has been located or is recorded in SJL. His letters of 3 and 7 July, both of which TJ received on 17 July, are recorded in SJL but have not been found.

USELESS FABRICATION: the report of

TJ's death; see Pierre Samuel Du Pont de Nemours to TJ, 6 July.

MR JEFFERSON MENTIONED TO ME: George Jefferson to TJ, 14 July 1800.

A letter TJ wrote this day to Daniel TRUMP, recorded in SJL as pertaining to the house carpenter named Forsyth, has not been found (see also TJ to Barnes, 24 June 1800). A letter from TJ to Trump of 7 June 1800 is also recorded in SJL but is missing.

DESIRED MR JEFFERSON TO FORWARD: see TJ to George Jefferson, 9 July.

To George Jefferson

[DEAR SIR]   Monticello July 19. 1800.

Yours of the 14th. is recieved. I find that mr Barnes has made some mistake about the stick chairs. he recieved and paid for half a dozen for me. they were painted of a very dark colour, & were in this style. perhaps, if you saw those forwarded to Colo. Cabell you will recollect whether they were in this form, and may judge whether they were mine. if not, then mr Barnes has not forwarded mine at all.   I shall shortly draw on you for 168.62 D for my direct tax. I am Dear Sir

Your friend & servt   TH: JEFFERSON

PrC (MHi); endorsed by TJ in ink on verso.

From Uriah McGregory

DEAR & RESPECTED SIR   Derby (Connecticut) July 19th. 1800

On a tour to Albany, in the State of New York last week; I call'd on and dined with the Reverend Cotton Mather Smith of Sharon. he is an eminent Clergyman—has much influence and respectability—   I had not seen him in several years—I found him an *engaged federal* polititian—he soon found that my political feelings were not in unison with his—and ask'd whether my good wishes would really extend Mr. Jefferson to the Presidential Chair?—I answer'd in the affirmative—on which—accompanied with much other malicious invective, and in presence of five men and two women—he said that you, sir, "had obtain'd your property by fraud and robery—and that in one instance you had defrauded and robed a widow and fatherless Children of an estate, to which you was executor, of ten thousand pounds Sterling; by keeping the property and paying them in Money at the nominal amount, that was worth no more than forty for one"—I told him with some warmth that I did not believe it. he said that "it was true" and that "it could be proved"—I know, Sir, that you suffer'd much abuse in this State—And from faithful enquiry believe it to be unmerited and malicious—but never, untill the above instance, knew that the Vilest of your traducers—had ventur'd to impeach your honesty in pecuniary concerns—   I thought it my duty, Sir, to communicate the assertion—and no one knows that I have done it—you will therefore regard it as your own wisdom may dictate—it can be sufficiently proved—and tho' I have been long intimate in the family of Mr. Smith—and taught to revere him as a Father,—Still when the good of my Country calls I must not be silent, tho' my voice should condemn my friend—   I wish to have it in my power, Sir, to publish a clear and full refutation, together with the Vile assertion—

I have, Dear & Respected Sir, the honor to be with much Esteem, and faithfull attachment. Your friend and Very obedient Humble servant.   URIAH M,GREGORY

RC (ViW); at head of text: "Citizen Thomas Jefferson Vice President of the United States"; addressed: "The Honorable Thomas Jefferson Esquire Vice President of the United states at, or near Charlottesville Virginia"; franked; postmarked 22 July; endorsed by TJ as received 7 Aug. and so recorded in SJL.

Uriah McGregory married Lucretia Ely at the Second Congregational Church at Saybrook, Connecticut in 1792 (Frederic W. Bailey, ed., *Early Connecticut Marriages as Found on Ancient Church Records Prior to 1800*, 7 vols. [New Haven, 1896-1906; repr., Baltimore, 1982], 2:119).

COTTON MATHER SMITH, a graduate of Yale College in 1751, served as pastor of the Congregational church in Sharon, Connecticut, from 1755 until his death in 1806 (Dexter, *Yale*, 2:269-71).

To James Madison

TH:J. TO J. MADISON   Monticello July 20. 1800.

Since you were here I have had time to turn to my accounts, and among others undertook to state the one with you: but was soon brought to a non-plus, by observing that I had made an entry Aug. 23. 99. of nails delivered for you, but left the particulars & amount blank till mr Richardson should give them in to me. whether he omitted this, or I to enter them I cannot tell, nor have either of us the least recollection what they were. I am in hopes I may have sent you a bill of them, as I generally do if I see the messenger before departure. but sometimes I omit this. at any rate I am in hopes that either from the bill or the recollections of those who used them you may be able to fill up the blank in the inclosed account, conjecturally at least. I recieved from Mr. Barnes in Jan. a credit of 69.23 D on your account. not having the amount of nails, I could not tell what I ought to have recieved, but I remember that my idea at the time was that it must be a good deal more than you owed me, & that of course there would be a balance to return you: this shall be instantly done on recieving either your statement or conjecture of the amount, which I pray you to do.

I see in Gale's paper of July 8. an account of the 4th. of July as celebrated at Raleigh. the Governor presided at the dinner. among the toasts were the following. the U.S. may they continue free, sovern. & indepdt. not influenced by foreign intrigue, nor distracted by internal convulsions. the Pres. of the US. may his countrymen rightly appreciate his distinguished virtue patriotism, & firmness. the V.P. of the US. the militia of the US. may the valor of the souldier be combined with the virtue of the citizen. the Navy of the US. the benifits which have arisen from it's infant efforts is a just presage of it's future greatness & usefulness. the freedom of the press without licentiousness. the friends of religion & order. may they always triumph over the supporters of infidelity & confusion. &c my respects to mrs. Madison. Adieu affectionately

James Madison to Th: Jefferson for nails　　　　Dr.

			£ s d
1799. July 25. to 23 ℔ IVs. 1. ℔ inch brads	} @ $14\frac{1}{2}$ d		1– 9– 0
500. $1\frac{1}{2}$ I. brads @ $12\frac{1}{2}$ d pr. ℔			3– 8
26. ℔ Xs. @ $11\frac{1}{2}$ d			1– 4–11
35. ℔ XVId. brads @ $10\frac{1}{2}$ d			1–10– $7\frac{1}{2}$

Aug. 23. to

Cr.

1800. Jan. 28. By credit with J. Barnes 69.23 D = £20–15–5

RC (DLC: Madison Papers); addressed: "James Madison junr. Orange"; nail account written by TJ on verso of cover. PrC (DLC); lacks second page; endorsed by TJ in ink on verso.

For TJ's blank entry of NAILS DELIVERED to Madison, see Nailery Account Book, 1796-1800 at CLU-C.

Joseph Gales, a native Englishman who had settled in Philadelphia in 1795, established in North Carolina the Republican Raleigh Register, and North-Carolina Weekly Advertiser to counter Federalist sentiment in the state and to be a rival publication to William Boylan's Minerva. GALE'S PAPER first appeared with the 22 Oct. 1799 issue and after the General Assembly awarded him the public printing contract, its title changed to the Raleigh Register, and North-Carolina State Gazette on 25 Nov. 1800. TJ paid for a year's subscription to the Raleigh Register on 15 May (Robert Neal Elliott, Jr., The Raleigh Register, 1799-1863 [Chapel Hill, N.C., 1955], v, 20-1, 25; Brigham, American Newspapers, 2:774-5; Gilpatrick, Jeffersonian Democracy in North Carolina, 104-6; MB, 2:1019).

The 8 July 1800 issue of the Raleigh Register gave a local ACCOUNT OF THE 4TH. OF JULY. The festival, announced by a cannon charge, featured a gathering of about sixty citizens at Captain Rogers's spring. GOVERNOR Benjamin Williams and Colonel Polk presided for a reading of the Declaration of Independence, a dinner, and a series of sixteen toasts interspersed with patriotic songs and more cannon charges. Other toasts listed but not mentioned in TJ's letter above included: to the auspicious Fourth of July, to the memory of George Washington, to both houses of Congress, to agriculture and commerce, to envoys Davie, Ellsworth, and Murray, to the state of North Carolina, to the University of North Carolina,

and to the American fair "may their smiles excite deeds of valor in the youth of their country." The evening concluded as the group gathered at the state house "to meet the ladies of the city, where an elegant collation was provided, and 'the mazy dance' succeeded to the 'flowing bowl.'"

A CREDIT of 69.23 D: see Madison, *Papers,* 17:407.

A letter from Madison to TJ, dated 18 June and received on 24 June 1800, is recorded in SJL but has not been found.

From George Jefferson

DEAR SIR   Richmond 21st. July 1800

I sent you on Saturday last by A. Row's boat 155. ℔ bacon, 1 dozn. bottles of Center, and ½ dozn. bunches Cord, agreeably to your request; together with a box of fish which was left here by a Boston Captain, who did not know from whom he received it—not having signed any bill of lading for it.

I am Dear Sir Your Very humble servt.   GEO. JEFFERSON

I did not take particular notice of the chairs, but from my recollection of them do not think they can be yours.   G.J.

RC (MHi); at foot of text: "Thomas Jefferson esqr."; endorsed by TJ as received 27 July and so recorded in SJL.

From Giuseppe Ceracchi

Paris, 4 Thermidor Year 8 [i.e. 23 July 1800]. Mr. Bohlen, in repeated letters sent through Amsterdam, having advised him to write to TJ on the subject of the monuments to be built in America to the glory of liberty and to the memory of George Washington, he takes this occasion "to renew my correspondance and presente to you the sentiments of my estime." He is certain that TJ will not have forgotten his work on this subject and would only "apply" to "an Artist of superior merit" since "mediocrity in public works, would decrease the public expectation." Reviewing "the principles which gided my ideas in what i exibited in Philadelphia," he notes that his first model for a monument combined the equestrian statue of Washington desired by Congress with a monument to American liberty that illustrated the "deeds of the Nation." He subsequently decided that "it was improper; to let the Nation act a secondary part; an error that will be inavoidable when tow principals subject are put in competition." On his second visit to the United States he created a second model in which Liberty was "the protagonist of my poem" surrounded by statuary groups representing important national events. This work was to have a "grandeur of Stile and variations of wonders" that would produce a beautiful effect in spectators, and if TJ had been in Philadelphia at the time he would have been among those people who acclaimed it. A subscription was commenced in which even Washington himself agreed to take part, but a "malignant Spirit" that Ceracchi could not comprehend destroyed that plan and the artist was "sacrificed." He believes that the United States must have two monuments, one in marble showing the foundations of American independence and the other a bronze statue of Washington. He closes with friendly sentiments to TJ and asks to be remembered to Madison, Monroe, and others of his acquaintance.

2d Dft (Archives Nationales, Paris: Series F7, Records of Police Générale); 3 p.; at head of text: "Ceracchi to Mr Jefferson"; heavily emended; endorsed in French in an unidentified hand as No. 45 of a series. Dft (same); labeled as No. 44. Recorded in SJL as received 12 Oct. 1800. Probably enclosed in John Bohlen to TJ, 2 Oct. 1800, which has not been found but is recorded in SJL as received on 12 Oct.

Bohl and John Bohlen were merchants at No. 7 North Water Street in Philadelphia. They collected payment for Ceracchi's bust of TJ (Cornelius William Stafford, *The Philadelphia Directory, for 1797* [Philadelphia, 1797], 29; Stafford, *Philadelphia Directory, for 1800*, 22; MB, 2:961, 1013; Ceracchi to TJ, 11 May 1795; Joseph Marx to TJ, 29 May 1796; TJ to Marx, 4 June 1796). Letters to TJ from the firm of B. and J. Bohlen dated 27 Feb., 23 July, and 31 Aug. 1799, received on 28 Feb., 8 Aug., and 12 Sep., respectively, and one from TJ to the company on 19 Aug. 1799 are recorded in SJL but have not been found.

Congress in 1783 had authorized an equestrian sculpture to honor George Washington, and in 1791 Ceracchi made preliminary designs for an ambitious monument to American liberty that was to represent important events of the Revolutionary War and include several allegorical groups of sculpture around a statue of Washington. Again in the United States in 1794-95, Ceracchi once more

tried to solicit public funding for the monument, which in its new form portrayed Liberty as a chariot-borne goddess. Failing to obtain a congressional appropriation for the work, the sculptor commenced an ambitious subscription program, but Ceracchi, deciding that he had been misled, returned to Europe in 1795. Already exiled from Florence due to his Jacobin proclivities, he thought that Paris provided the best setting, in terms of costs and availability of materials, for creating the grand monumental works he envisioned. He had communicated with TJ once since his departure from the United States, a letter of 8 Mch. 1797, received from Paris on 29 June, that is recorded in SJL but has not been found (Ulysse Desportes, "Giuseppe Ceracchi in America and his Busts of George Washington," *Art Quarterly*, 26 [1963], 141-79; Ceracchi to TJ, 11 Mch., 13 Nov. 1794, 9 Mch., 11 May 1795).

In a case that may have involved entrapment by police agents, Ceracchi was implicated in the "Conspiration des Poignards" or "Dagger Conspiracy," a plot to assassinate Bonaparte at the Paris Opéra on 10 Oct. 1800. Arrested with three other men, Ceracchi lost any hope for clemency when another attempt was made on Bonaparte's life in December, and on 31 Jan. 1801 the artist was executed (Tulard, *Dictionnaire Napoléon*, 395, 488; Jean Tulard, *Napoleon: The Myth of the Saviour*, trans. Teresa Waugh [London, 1984], 98).

To Philip Ludwell Grymes

Dear Sir   Monticello July 24. 1800

Your father & the late Peyton Randolph, as securities for John Randolph were answerable to mrs Ariana Randolph for an annuity of an hundred & fifty pounds sterling a year from the death of her husband as long as she should survive him. John Randolph having died insolvent the debt falls on the representatives of your father & on mr E. Randolph as representative of Peyton Randolph, each being answerable for the other. £100. curry. is all which mrs Randolph has recieved of near 20. years arrearages now due. she desired me some years ago to act for her in this business; and mr E. Randolph engaging from time to time to make her remittances you were never troubled on the subject. but at length his failures, & her distresses obliged her to desire that coercive measures might be resorted to against the securities. the case being hard enough on them, even if responsible each for his own moiety only, I proposed to mrs Randolph, and she has authorised me, on either security's paying up his moiety of the arrearages, & securing her for the moiety still to accrue while she lives, to release him from responsability for his co-security. I act in this matter merely on principles of friendship & justice, and these dictate an equal regard to all the parties interested. you probably know that mr E. Randolph might be at a loss to pay his moiety; and can best judge for yourself whether it might not be for the interest of yourself & your family, by complying with mrs Randolph's conditions as to your moiety, to be released from the responsibility for the other. I submit this matter to your consideration, and assure you I shall have great pleasure in rendering this hard burthen as easy as the actual circumstances of all the parties will admit, and in exercising the powers committed to me towards relieving you as far as justice admits. mr J. B. Boardeley of Philadelphia is joined with me in the power of attorney, but it is several as well as joint and the desperate state of his health, will hardly permit his participation in the duties of the business. I am with great & constant esteem Dear Sir

Your most obedt. humble servt.   TH: JEFFERSON

RC (U.S. District Court for the Eastern District of Virginia, Richmond; photostat in Vi); addressed: "Philip L. Grymes esq. at Brandon near Urbanna"; franked; endorsed.

Philip Ludwell Grymes (1746-1805), a native of Middlesex County, Virginia, received his education in England at Eton School and Balliol College, Oxford. He returned to Virginia, serving in the House of Burgesses and as county sheriff while still in his twenties, and resided at Brandon, the Middlesex County estate he inherited from his FATHER, Philip Grymes, who died in 1762. Philip Ludwell Grymes's mother, Mary Randolph Grymes, was the sister of John and Peyton Randolph. The two families were linked again by the marriage of Philip L. Grymes's brother, John Randolph Grymes, to his cousin Susanna, one of John Randolph's daughters and a sister of Edmund Randolph. At the time of his death Philip Ludwell Grymes owned several properties and held a number of slaves (VMHB, 28 [1920], 91-6, 189-92b; H. J. Eckenrode, *The Randolphs: The Story of a Virginia Family* [Indianapolis, 1946], 42; Jonathan Daniels, *The Randolphs of Virginia* [Garden City, N.Y., 1972], xviii; Richard Arthur Austen-Leigh, *The Eton College Register, 1753-1790* [Eton, 1921], 236-7; Leonard, *General Assembly*, 98, 100).

ARIANA Jenings Randolph (1729-1801) was the widow of John Randolph, the last colonial attorney general for Virginia. They married about 1752 and lived at Tazewell Hall, his family's seat in Williamsburg, until 1775, when the breach between the colonies and Britain caused them to depart Virginia. Leaving behind their son Edmund, then in his early twenties, who refused to emigrate with them, they first took their two daughters to Lord Dunmore's estate in Scotland, then moved to the Brompton section of London. Ariana Randolph continued to reside there after the death of her husband in 1784 (ANB, 18:121-2, 128-9; Conway, *Omitted Chapters*, viii, 11). For her annuity, see also Mortgage of Slaves and Goods from Edmund Randolph, 19 May 1800.

SHE DESIRED ME SOME YEARS AGO: none of the correspondence between Ariana Randolph and TJ has been located. The first letter recorded in SJL is one from her to TJ of 6 Jan. 1797, received on 8 Apr. of that year, TJ replying on 29 May. She wrote from Brompton nine more times between 1 Nov. 1797 and 2 Nov. 1799, as well as letters of 2 and 6 Apr. 1800 that TJ received on 17 July and 12 June 1800, respectively. Her final letter to TJ, according to SJL, was of 8 July 1800 (received 11 Oct.). TJ wrote to her on 26 Jan. 1799, 1 Feb., 9 May, 30 Aug. 1800, and 9 Feb. 1801.

John Beale Bordley and Ariana Jenings Randolph had the same mother, who was born Ariana Vanderheyden, but were children of her second and third marriages, respectively (Elizabeth Bordley Gibson, *Biographical Sketches of the Bordley Family, of Maryland, for Their Descendants* [Philadelphia, 1865], 21-6; ANB, 3:211; Conway, *Omitted Chapters*, viii).

A letter to TJ from Edmund Randolph, dated 16 July and received on the 27th, is recorded in SJL but has not been found.

From John Barnes

DEAR SIR   George Town 26th. July 1800

I arrived here last Evening in 35 hours—and calling at the post Office this Morning I found—your Esteemed favr. 19th.—The One you addressed to Mr Trump I have forwarded & likewise wrote & given full directions Respecting the Young Mans going via Richmond ℔ water—Mr John Richard—whom I have left in Charge of my Bank a/c notes of hand &c: with directions to treat, & purchase a Bill of ex—(near as possible) to the Amot of $567.107—& to transmit Messrs. Van Staphorst & Hubbard & Co. Amsterdam on P.Ms: a/c when known shall Address said Gentn. particularly—Respecting the Chairs—they must (I think) be the same—I presume you bespok of and I paid for—how they came to be directed to Mr Brown for Colo

Cabell—I cannot now particularly—Recollect—Mr Letchworth—I presume must have recd two Orders—for ½ doz. each—but Were the Other ½ dozn. are—or were shipped & to whom—I cannot now Recollect. but I shall write—Mrs Ratcliffe to inquire particularly of Mr Letchworth abt them—I found your packages for Washington are all safely—stored here—

With great Esteem I am Dear Sir—Your Obedt: Hble servt:

JOHN BARNES

RC (ViU: Edgehill-Randolph Papers); at foot of text: "Thomas Jefferson Esqr: Monticello"; endorsed by TJ as received 7 Aug. and so recorded in SJL.

ARRIVED HERE LAST EVENING: anticipating the relocation of the national government, Barnes, who turned 70 during 1800, moved from Philadelphia to Georgetown in the Federal District (Cordelia Jackson, "John Barnes, A Forgotten Philanthropist of Georgetown,"

Records of the Columbia Historical Society, 7 [1904], 40, 42).

MR JOHN RICHARD: most likely John Richards, a grocer on Second Street in Philadelphia (Stafford, *Philadelphia Directory, for 1800*, 103).

P.M: Philip Mazzei.

Letters from Barnes of 20 and 23 July, both of which TJ received from Philadelphia on the 31st, are recorded in SJL but have not been located.

To Pierre Samuel Du Pont de Nemours

MY DEAR SIR   Monticello July 26. 1800.

I am much indebted to my enemies for proving, by their [little] tale of my death, that I have friends. the sensibility you are so good as to express on this occasion is very precious to me. I have never enjoyed better nor more uninterrupted health.

I ought sooner to have acknoleged your favor of June 15. which came to hand in due time as did that of the 6th. instant. [I] thank you for your assiduities on the subject of education. there is no occasion to incommode yourself or your friend by pressing it; as when recieved it will still be some time before we shall probably find a [good] occasion of bringing forward the subject. there are labors for which your reward will come when you will be no longer here to enjoy it.   we have had what is considered here as a very hot spell of weather. yesterday was the warmest day we have had this year. the thermometer was at 86.° at this place, & probably 2. or 3.° more in the vicinities.—when do you move on to Alexandria? for then I may expect to see you. I have much lamented you did not land here instead of New York. as you were determined to find the first spot you saw good enough to live on, this might in that case have become the object of your choice. we are anxious to hear of our treaty from Paris. when that arrives, I presume, I shall have to meet the Senate at Washington. and perhaps I may meet yourself there: for till then I can hardly flatter myself with your adventuring so far as this place. then, now, or whenever it best suits you I shall be most happy to recieve you. present my friendly salutations to Madame Dupont and to all the members of your family, & accept yourself assurances of my sincere & affectionate attachment.

TH: JEFFERSON

PrC (DLC); faint; at foot of text: "M. Dupont"; endorsed by TJ in ink on verso as a letter to Stevens Thomson Mason of this date (see note to Mason to TJ, 11 July 1800). Not recorded in SJL.

YOUR FRIEND: J. X. Bureaux de Pusy.

From Pierre Samuel Du Pont de Nemours

MONSIEUR,   Good-Stay, near New-York 26 juillet 1800.

Après avoir pleuré votre mort, comme un des plus grands malheurs qui pût arriver à l'Amérique et au monde, et mon cœur ajoutait qui pût m'atrister, je conçois aujourd'hui quelque inquiétude sur votre Santé.

Il y a environ six Semaines que je vous ai marqué que mon ouvrage sur l'Education nationale dans les Etats Unis était achevé, et que Pusy le mettait au net. Je vous demandais si l'on peut vous l'envoyer par la poste.

Depuis, je vous ai exprimé combien le triste bruit répandu par les Journaux m'avait pénêtré de douleur: avec quel plaisir j'apprennais sa fausseté; et mon opinion que ces bêtises méchantes tournent toujours à l'avantage du mérite et de la vertu.

Enfin je vous ai fait part de ce que l'on propose à Pusy; et je vous ai prié de nous en dire votre avis.

Je pense que vous êtes Cultivateur, et en tems de récolte.

Mais si vous êtiez malade, je vous prierais de me faire écrire. Et dites nous en même tems si le manuscrit sur l'Education peut être mis à la poste, ou par quelle voie je peux vous l'envoyer. Il est copié à présent, d'une écriture assez serrée, et ne tient qu'environ cent pages.

Vous connaissez mon bien respectueux attachement.

DU PONT (DE NEMOURS)

S'il fait beaucoup plus chaud en Virginie qu'ici, je trouverai que cela est fort.

J'ai envoyé mon Fils à Alexandrie chercher une Maison qui nous convienne. Ce sera dans celle là que J'habiterai le plus.

Il nous faut une maison à Alexandrie et une autre à New-York.

E D I T O R S '   T R A N S L A T I O N

SIR,   Good-Stay, near New York, 26 July 1800.

After having wept over your death, as one of the greatest misfortunes that could happen to America and the world—and, my heart added, that could sadden me—I now form some misgivings about your health.

About six weeks ago I indicated to you that my work on national education in the United States was finished, and that Pusy was making a fair copy of it. I asked you whether it could be sent by post.

Since then, I expressed to you how much the sad rumor spread by the newspapers had filled me with sorrow: with how much pleasure I learned that it was false; and my opinion that those wicked pranks always turn around to the advantage of worthiness and virtue.

Finally I advised you of what is being proposed to Pusy; and I begged you to tell us your opinion of it.

I am thinking that you are a farmer, and in harvest-time.

But if you should be ill, I beg you to have someone write to me. And tell us at the same time whether the manuscript on education can be sent by the post, or by what means I can send it to you. It is now copied, in a rather dense handwriting, and covers only about one hundred pages.

You know my very respectful affection.   DU PONT (DE NEMOURS)

If it is much hotter in Virginia than here, I shall find it very harsh.

I sent my son to Alexandria to look for a house that would suit us. That is the one in which I shall live the most.

We must have a house in Alexandria and another in New York.

RC (DLC); at head of text: "A Mr. Jefferson"; endorsed by TJ as received 7 Aug. and so recorded in SJL.

ENVIRON SIX SEMAINES: Du Pont recalled to mind his letters of 15 June, 6 July, and 17 July.

To Pierre Samuel Du Pont de Nemours

DEAR SIR   Monticello Aug. 1. 1800.

I wrote you on the 26th. of the last month, and on the [31st received] your favor of the 17th. my office relating altogether to the legislative [depart]ment, I am entirely unacquainted with the measures proposed in that of the Executive. I may know that the fortification of certain ports [to some] extent has been authorised by the legislature.

but whether the Executive will propose a greater extent I know not, or whether they [. . .] altogether fixed, or partly floating, as gun-boats, floating batteries &c. whatever they mean to do, I am happy that they propose to [. . .] it the [. . .] of a person of so much worth as your friend M. [. . .]. it is a tribute to his worth & sufferings which it is honorable to them to offer, and which I shall be happy to hear he accepts. it is extremely to be desired that such sums of money as the legislature agree to expend in works of defence should be employed with [. . .] & economy. it has been our misfortune sometimes, when a given sum has been [. . .] for a work, to undertake that work on double the scale desired & thus sacrifice the whole. of this our federal city furnishes some remarkable examples.—I am happy to hear you [are removed] into the [country] independantly of the danger of yellow fever, the country at this season is to be preferred for health & happiness. [wishing] yourself & family an [immense] share of both I proffer you assurances of my affectionate attachment & esteem.

Th: Jefferson

PrC (DLC); faint; at foot of text: "M. Dupont de Nemours"; endorsed by TJ in ink on verso.

From Julian Ursin Niemcewicz

Dear Sir   Eliz Town. N.J. 2 aug: 1800.

I had the pleasure to receive your favor of 23 July & hasten to give you immediately such Informations respecting Mr. Lewis Littlepage as are at present in my power. Owing to the events in Europe, & my particular Situation I receive but seldom & short letters from Poland, in one of them however dated 16 apr: 1799. a Lady giving me an account of the Society of Warsaw, says those words, *Mistriss S. . . Remains also in Warsaw Mr. Little page gallants her, he as formerly divides his time between Venus & Bachus*. I was very well acquinted with Mr. Littelpage, found him a very pleasant Compagnon & more so ful of genious & Information, but even at that time to muche European, the last time I saw him was at the Siege of Warsaw in the year 1794 in the month of Fbr. After my release from Russian Confinement, I heard in the beginning of 1797, that amongst other Creditors who presented their Notes to the Commissionair appointed to revise the King's of Poland Debts, Mr. Littlpage presented his to the amount of ten or twelve thousand pound: Sterling but he was not paid: I don't know how far all this is true, I have it only from general rapport. As you seem Sir to take a l[ively]

Concern to the family of that Gentelman I shall write to Poland, in order to get all possible Information respecting Mr Littlepage, I must however previously caution you, that one Year perhaps may elapse before I get an answer. The repport of my mariage Sir is true & I thank you for your kind Congratulations, if not by birth I am now an American by affection & choice; besides the happiness I find in Mrs. Niemcewicz's Society reasons points out, that rational Liberty all those blessings for which I fought bled, and sufferd have for ever forsaken Europe & fixed their Abode in America. You mention Sir you met a person who had for me Information from Poland rather agreable to me; I have not yet seen such person, & have not received the least pleasing Intelligence from that quarter. I should like very much to know the person & the Information. I Intend to write soon to Mrs. Bache, & beg you to remember me most affectionately to her & to the Dr. Remaining now in this Country I rejoice in the pleasing expectation that sooner or latter I shall have the opportunity of enjoing your Interesting Society. With the Sentiments of regard & attachement you inspired me with, from the first moment of our acquintence I remain Sir

    Your friend & obdt Serrvent   Ju: Niemcewicz

P.S. I had a letter from one of my friends in Sweden mentioning that he has seen persons returning from Paris, who were in Society with Gl: Kosc: & found him in very good health. If you hear any thing from him Sir, I shall be thankful to if you have the goodness to comunicate it to me. I hope Mrs. Bache has deliverd you gl: Mape of America by Arrow Smith.

RC (PWbH); addressed: "Thomas Jefferson Esqr Vice President of the United States. State of Virginia, Charlottesville Monticello"; franked and postmarked; endorsed by TJ as received 17 Aug. and so recorded in SJL.

TJ's FAVOR of 23 July is recorded in SJL but has not been found.

REPPORT OF MY MARIAGE: in June Niemcewicz had married Susan Livingston Kean, a widow. Following his release by the Russians in 1796, Niemcewicz had traveled with Tadeusz Kosciuszko by way of SWEDEN to reach Britain and the United States (Niemcewicz, *Under their Vine*, xxiv, 270). GL: KOSC: General Kosciuszko.

ARROW SMITH: by the mid-1790s English cartographer Aaron Arrowsmith produced maps of North America, culminating in his definitive 1802 version that showed the "Interior Parts" of the continent and was used by Lewis and Clark (DNB; Gary E. Moulton, ed., *Journals of the Lewis & Clark Expedition*, 13 vols. [Lincoln, Neb., 1983-2001], 1:5; Sowerby, No. 3846).

From John Wayles Eppes

DEAR SIR,   Eppington Aug. 4th. 1800.

We left Mont-Blanco on the 23d. of last month and expected by this time to have been safely landed at Monticello—We have been detained here however in consequence of the situation of my Father who has been so much injured in one of his legs by a kick from a horse as to be unable to move from home at a time when a heavy and serious business hangs over him—I went to Richmond for him a few days after coming up and am very apprehensive he will be obliged to raise in some way or other immediately the greater part of £2600 as security for Mr. Hylton—I do not know that my presence here will be useful to my Father after this week. While however my exertions can be atall useful or save him a single pang under his present difficulties nothing earthly would induce me to leave him—

Maria continues in good health and joins me in affectionate greetings to yourself and all at Monticello—We have remained below longer than we wished or intended and our feelings now plead powerfully for the immediate commencement of our journey—I hope we shall see you on the 15th—

adieu yours sincerely   JNO: W: EPPES

RC (ViU: Edgehill-Randolph Papers); endorsed by TJ as received 17 Aug. and so recorded in SJL.

Francis Eppes served as SECURITY for Richmond merchant Daniel L. HYLTON, who was married to Eppes's sister, Sarah. Before the Revolution Hylton owed the Bristol firm of Farell & Jones nearly £1,500 sterling, part of which Hylton paid under Virginia's sequestration law. In 1790 William Jones brought suit. When Jones died, the suit was continued by his administrator, John Tyndale Warre. In 1796 the U.S. Supreme Court reversed the decision of the U.S. Circuit Court for Virginia and declared Hylton responsible for the entire debt and ordered him to pay over $6,000. Hylton and Eppes defaulted on the bond rendered for the judgment in late 1797. Payment of this and other debts left Hylton without property, and he went to debtors' prison when other claims were filed against him (Marshall, *Papers*, 3:4-7; 5:295-9, 314-17, 327-9; MB, 1:340).

From Daniel Trump

SIR   Philadelphia August 4th 1800

I have now the Satisfaction to Inform you that I have at Last Succeeded in Engaging of a young man for you of the Name of John Holms a Native of the City of Philadelpia of a Good Carrecter a Sober Genteel young man a Good workman and understands Drawing he Studied under me three months and I found him Very active and

Ready to take any Design that was Given to him, his master was an Excellent workman and an Intimate acquaintance of mine he will Come on to Richmond by the first Vessel that Sails for that Place I had a good Deal of Difficulty to Get a Person that I Could Recommend I met with him on Saturday and Recd a final from this morning, but too Late for this Days mail. I was Very much Displeased with Forsyth for Disappointing us after Promising Mr Barns and me that he would go, I Shall forward your Sashes as Soon as Possibly I Can I have not been able to Get Mahogany Suitable for them as there was none of the Same kind of wood to be had at almost any Price but there is a quantity come in and I have Engag'd Some which I Expect to Get in the Course of a week. I Shall have to Give it a Little time to Dry as it is not Perfectly Season'd. I Shall a Letter as Soon as the young man Gets a Pasage and know the Day of Sailing I Remain Sir

yr obt Hle Servt   DANIEL TRUMP

RC (MHi); at foot of text: "Thos. Jefferson Esqr"; endorsed by TJ as received 17 Aug. and so recorded in SJL.

Daniel Trump was a Philadelphia house carpenter located on Fayette Street with several others in the trade in 1801.

For his previous effort to supply TJ with a qualified carpenter at Monticello, see TJ to John Barnes, 24 June and 19 July 1800 (Cornelius William Stafford, *The Philadelphia Directory, for 1801* [Philadelphia, 1801], 135).

From William Short

DEAR SIR   Paris Aug. 6. 1800

I have had the extreme pleasure of recieving your two letters of the 26th. of March & 13th. of April—the first was recieved & delivered to me by the American Envoys—the second was put into my hands by a Gentleman who I believe has the direction of the Flag ship which brought it—he promised to give me notice of his departure that I might write by him & I intended to have written to you at greater length than I shall perhaps be able to do as this letter is to go after him by post in order to overtake him at Bordeaux—I had written a volume to my brother on various subjects, which being ready, I sent to M. Testards lodgings together with three vols of *Les Connoissances des tems* for you—He has taken charge of these objects which he is to deliver to Mr. Barnes, & whom I desire to give you notice of their arrival, that you may direct as to the means of the books being sent to you, & the letter to my brother.—My servant on his return has brought me back word that this gentleman is to get off this morning.—You will observe that the *Connoissance des tems* is now divided according to the French Calendar—the volumes sent are for the years 8. 9. & 10. & commence therefore from last Septr.—I suppose from your letter that you have them up to the last year—If I am mistaken, be so good as to inform me, & they shall be sent to you as far back as you may desire.—You know that this work is now divided into two separate parts for each year—you have them both for the year 10—but for the years 8 & 9.—the second parts have not been sent, by an omission of the bookseller—If I shd. not find an opportunity for Bordeaux in time for this vessel, of which however I have hopes by an American who it is said will set off in two days, I will take care to send them by the return of the American Envoys, who have a vessel waiting for them at Havre—I suppose therefore it will not be postponed long, though I am not acquainted with the progress & state of their business, as I see them seldom, & continue the mode of life formerly mentioned to you, viz. at a distance from whatever concerns politics.—

I am glad you recieved the book on Pisé, that you may have some experiment made if it shd. be in your way—I know your well grounded aversion to wooden buildings—& at the same time the difficulty of substituting others in those parts of our country where there be no limestone—The pisé certainly succeeds in the neighborhood of Lyons & other parts of the south & I shd. suppose if there be a part of the world where it must succeed it would be in that region of our country, which is very extensive, where the only cement is derived from oyster-shells.—

I am much obliged to you for the care you were so good as to take of the watches I sent my sisters—My brother has informed me of their having been recieved in a perfect state—He informs me also that if you should appoint no other agent, he will endeavour to spare the time to come & settle the business with Colo. Skipwith—This would however be such a sacrifice as I should be sorry he should make, for I see with great satisfaction that he is actively & advantageously employed in his own affairs to the westward.—I have written to him therefore to desire him not to do this, & grounded it on the possibility of my being myself soon in America—But as in this I am obliged of course to consult the feelings of another, & cannot count on it with absolute certainty I have taken the precaution of sending him as full a state of the business as I was able, taking up the subject *above*, & referred him also to the extracts of Colo. Skipwith's letters which you were so good as to say you would furnish him with when he should have occasion for them—I have requested him to begin by writing to Colo. S. in order to obtain a statement of his acct, instead of leaving his business & coming in to Virga.—If I should have the pleasure which I desire most ardently of paying soon a visit to my country, this document will serve me to proceed on—If I shd. be disappointed, it will answer my brother's purpose, & will insure his being less detained if he should find it necessary to come at last to Virga. on this business.—I have at different times touched on Colo. Skipwith's conduct towards me— As it appears to me, it has been not just & is certainly not justifiable—But I ought not to be the judge, & do not desire to be so. I have never written to him since his letter of June 91.—Experience had shewn me it was useless, & this was confirmed by Browne's letter to me when I wrote to him in the early part of that year to settle the business with Colo. S.—Browne was an agent of his own chusing & of course ought to have been agreeable to him.

I have just mentioned my desire of paying you a visit—it has been long germing in my mind & I have frequently regretted having not executed this project when I set off, two years ago, & it has taken out a new lease as it were—The appearance of breaking entirely with one's country & remaining an absolute stranger to it, excites sensations in the mind of which it is impossible for any one to form an idea, but by real experience. This country is certainly of all others that which seems to hold out most temptations to a stranger, & to no one more than myself from the peculiar circumstances of my situation—I have seen here persons of different nations before & since the revolution who had planted here their tents & with the determination of ending their days without returning to their country—It is true that the most remarkable among them had their anchor still at home, though riding in this port—they were the representatives of their countries, Messrs. de Mercy—de Berkenrold—de Blome &c.—Had I continued in that situation I should perhaps have felt differently, & been able to hold out—but as it is, I have had a series of ideas I cannot describe, nor anyone concieve who has not experienced them—I have always felt a greater pride in being an American, than most foreigners whom I have known here have seemed to feel for their country—Whether it be because America from the nature of it's government, be more really one's country, or whether it arise from my particular character I cannot say—but the fact is that the length of time I have remained absent has in no one respect whatever diminished my attachment & from the time of my bonds having had the appearance of being dissolved, that is to say from the time of my quitting public service, I have felt in my new situation a certain kind of pain on which I had not counted. Although I knew that my situation would not admit of an immediate return & establishment in America, yet I have always had in view a visit of myself at least to my former home; and it has been constantly understood between us & still is so that that is to be regarded as our ultimate establishment. I for my own part had not the shadow of a doubt that it was the quarter of the world which furnished the best chance for rational happiness to reasonable people, & that without exception—It has been matter of some surprize therefore to me, & of pain also, to have seen the sentiments with which many of the French have returned here from their late residence in America, & I may say indeed all of them without exception who have come in my way since their return from America. You can form no idea of their acrimony & disgust with respect to America—Although I see myself clearly the source of their dissatisfaction & injustice towards us, arising out of the nature of their personal situation whilst there, yet that situation which was similar with their countrymen in other places, & produced often similar effects, does not seem to have done it with the same force & with the same universality. I have regretted this very sincerely as you will readily concieve on several accounts.—As to the precise time of my making this visit, I had hoped it would have been practicable during this summer, but the want of a good opportunity & the hesitation in the choice between such as were inconvenient run off the time until a circumstance took place which rendered it impossible for me to leave my friend during its existence—It has not ceased as yet, & before it does the equinox will have arrived—I must therefore aim at a passage during the fall so as to arrive on our coast before the winter—if this should not take place it will be postponed until the spring.—If in the mean time a peace shall have been made between the contending parties on the ocean, as is hoped & expected by some, my voyage will have become less hazardous.

I am extremely obliged by the information you give me, my dear Sir, in both your letters on the subject of the 9. M dollars, & for the steps you have been so good as to take respecting them.—You have certainly put the matter on the most advantageous footing which was possible for me. & I shall be extremely happy in its being finally settled in that way. It seems to me from your letter of March 26th. last— that the Sec. of State, wishes at present however to put it on a different ground from that acknowleged by him in 97.—it then appeared that the difficulty was as to the allowing interest—but as to the principal he acknowleged my right was good against the public.—At present he seems to make it dependent entirely on the issue of their suit against Randph.—Although it be impossible for me to suppose that any tribunal on earth should consider him as my agent, yet whatever depends on the judgment of man is more or less uncertain, & I therefore regret this circumstance. It seems to me that Government ought to have decided as to what passed between the Sec. of State & a foreign agent, & not to have made it dependent on the issue of a long law-suit & the judgment of a tribunal of law. If there were any thing human sufficiently clear not to be warped or darkened by a quibble I should suppose it would be the question whether E.R. were my agent in his private or his public capacity—but I have long known that words in the mouth of a man of address & directed to human ears,[1] produce such a variety of effects that they cannot be calculated with mathematical certainty. I shall not therefore be entirely exempt from uneasiness until I know the issue of the business.— When Mr. Marshall was here, although I saw him but two or three times, I think I mentioned to him the circumstances of this affair—I am sure I did to Mr. Gerry, & assure that to whomever I mentioned them, there appeared not the smallest doubt that I had a right to demand the sum of the public.—Having lately heard that Mr. Marshall was appointed Sec. of State I have some thoughts of writing to him on this business, in order to state it so as to keep up my claim & insist on the Government doing me justice, if contrary to all probability the court should admit of Mr. Rand's being my agent in his private capacity. I should hope that I might count on a remedy from Government for an evil which was brought on me by an act of Government, viz. the changing of the ordinary course (as to me) of the foreign agents recieving their salary, & tendering it to me in a depreciated paper; & this change made, (as mentioned in a letter of ER Sec. of State) in order to accomodate another foreign agent, then Minister at Lisbon.—. I should infer from the statement made of this business in your letters that if E.R. had acknowleged himself to have been not my agent, but to have acted in his capacity of Sec. of State, that this delay & difficulty in doing me justice would not have existed—If that be really the case his conduct towards me is as cruel as it was criminal against the public. If this were the only sum which he had embezzled, he ought to have felt that the loss would be less to the public than to me—but if he be also a defaulter for other sums he will shew himself to have made an abuse of both public & private confidence, & will thus occasion me an essential loss without saving or serving himself.—I cannot therefore concieve why he should insist on being considered as my agent—His letters to me & of which copies of course I suppose remain in the Dept. of State, if produced, will shew him in the most infamous light that it is possible to concieve—viz. setting down at his desk to write the most positive & most palpable lies.—In his letter of Nov. 9. 94. in the midst of public matter he says²—"As to the pecuniary part of the business (his remitting Jaudenes's bill for 9000 dol:) I can only say that my object was your accomodation & Mr. Jaudenes's object was to accomodate me. He has therefore readily returned me the 9. M dollars—*three thousand of which I have already invested in 6. pcts. for you*; & shall proceed to invest the remainder & give you a general acct. as soon as it is accomplished.—The reason why this sum was remitted was that Mr. Humphreys might draw for half a years salary. But I have informed him that this arrangement is changed."—In his letter of Feb. 25. 95. he says "*The 9. m. dol. have been applied*, as you have directed & have been already informed."—I suppose it at present highly probable that the letter in which he is supposed to have informed me of the investment of the whole sum was never written—it never came to my hands & was often mentioned in my letters—but if it were written it will of course be found in the Dept. of State—But you will see the base falsehood first as to the vestment of 3000. d.—& then months afterwards as to that of the 9000.—viz. a regular & continued system of infamous lying, since it is proved that he had not vested any part of the sum.—I am very anxious that this dirty business should be settled so that I may never more think of it: It is painful to see men of character so meanly disgracing themselves.

The affair with B. Harrison which you mention in your last is of a nature which may make it in fact appear to his Administrator to be finally settled without its being really so—This is the case—I first gave him £5000. certificates wch. he credited me on his books & he pd. that sum to Colo. S.—so that on his books the whole appeared balanced—But some days before my departure from Richmond I gave him an additional sum, which he omitted to enter on his books—On my reminding him of this circumstance after my arrival in France, he very candidly acknowleged his then recollection of it & his omission at the time to have entered it on his books—the sum was fixed between us at £150. certificates, as appears by his letter to me of Jan. 29th. 87—& of which I suppose a copy was of course entered on his letter-book—I have the original in my hands.—Colo. Skipth. says also in his letter to me of Dec. 1. 87. that Harrison had promised to pay him this £150, on his going down to Richmond, with the three years interest which had accrued on the 1st. of Jany. preceding.— From that time I have never been able to decide from the letters of Colo. S. whether he collected this article—no mention is ever made of it, nor any acct. rendered of it—but as I have never recd. an acct. from him, & only two little memoranda of partial operations it is possible this sum may have been recd. from Harrison at the time mentioned—that will easily appear from Harrison's accts. with Colo. S.—The bond of R. Randolph which you mention, was for an horse sold him before my departure—As he delayed paying the cash, B. Harrison at my request after my arrival here procured from him his bond—Colo. S. had undertaken after the affair got into his hands to have it collected I know not why he declined prosecuting it before Rand. became bankrupt—Mayo's bond has the same origin; I sold him a breeding mare for £100. certificates—the bond was obtained after my being here as he had failed in his promise to deliver the certificates, before the expiration of 84. that I might recieve the interest accruing the 1st. of Jany. 85.—In Mr. Browne's letter of May 91.—he notes having recd. of Mayo £37.15.8.—I suppose it was for the interest—I knew not why Colo. S. declined recovering this bond wch. had been so long due—nor do I know either why he let Mosby's bond run on, nor indeed why he took his bond at all, as it was procured with cash. It could not be expected by him that it was my wish or intention that he should dispose of my cash for bonds promising certificates—Cash would certainly at all times have commanded certificates—I have never heard from him how Griffin's bonds originated—It will certainly be a very extraordinary thing if he gave my cash for the bonds of a person in his situation & let them lye by until he became entirely bankrupt—the first & only mention ever made by him to me of Griffin or his bonds, is in the copy of Mr. Browne's rect. to him, which he inclosed me in his last letter of June 91. In the list of articles mentioned to have been recd. by Mr. Browne are two bonds of Griffin for £400 & for £192.—These bonds must of course have been procured after my letter recd. by him & acknowleged in which I request him to lay out without further delay every shilling of mine in his hands, in *Pierce's final settlements* a continental paper—I first limit him to 5/. in the pound, afterwards desire him to purchase them at the best price to be had.—At the time of his recieving this letter (in May. 88.—six months after the epoch he had fixed for ceasing to pay interest on the cash of mine he had taken into his hands & after requesting me to direct positively how to dispose of it,) their price was as he tells me 3/6. in the pound—To this day he has never paid one single shilling of that cash as far as I can judge—has kept it in his hands from year to year contrary to his request & to his most solemn promises made successively to lay it out in public paper—& for the cash which he recd. for me during the year 88 in interest warrants he desires to pass on me Griffin's bad bonds for Virga. certificates as far

as I can guess—for it is all guess work with me.—On later examination since I wrote you formerly & putting different circumstances together it wd. seem that he meant that these bonds of Griffin's should
represent at least in part the interest warrants accruing on my certificates the 1st. of Jany. 88.—For these warrants cash would have been
of course recd. from the treasury during the year 88—For the warrants issued for the interest of Jan 1. 87.—he recd. the cash from the
Treasury in Novbr. 87. & laid it out in certificates.—At that time he
acted under my desire to purchase the Virga. certificates—but by my
letters wch. he recd. May 23. 88, & wch. were written expressly for
that purpose, I requested him to purchase Pierces final settlements—
if to be had cheaper than the Virga. certificates & mention that these
are to be preferred only if they be at the same price—My letters of
wch. he acknowleged the rect. all at the same time, were dated Dec.
20th. 31st. *87*—& March 20. *88*.—You see by his answer that the
former were at that time much lower—& yet he would seem to desire
to pass on me instead of Pierce's settlements (thus directed) not even
certificates, but Griffin's bonds for certificates.—It is for him to shew
how it has happened after his having declined acting longer at discretion & insisting on positive instructions from me, how it has happened I say after recieving these instructions to purchase without
further delay *Pierce's final settlements*, if cheaper than certificates,
that he should have purchased *bonds for certificates* with such cash of
mine as he collected—& how under the same circumstances he still
kept in his hands cash of mine, which he had given me notice he had
no further occasion for & therefore shd. be unwilling to pay interest
on longer than the 25th. of Dec. 87. preceding—cash which he had
informed me early in the year 87.—he had credited me for in his
books, both principal & interest the moment he had wrested it from
Harvie's hands, & congratulated me on its being now in so good
hands, safe from a paper medium &c—& where I might always command it on a short notice—This debt of Harvies was for my negroes
sold to him—My brother had obtained a bond by which he was
obliged to pay the cash or certificates at 4. for 1. (at my choice)—on
the 1st. of Oct.br. 86—My brother went to Kentuckey & this passed
with my other business into Colo. Sks. hands during the summer of
86—Colo. Sk. gave the preference to the cash & by an arrangement
as he mentioned contrived himself to be my debtor, & [credited] me
for it as mentioned above & on the terms there stated—I regretted
much at the time that he had not preferred the certificates at 4. for
1.—& wrote him so—but mentioned at the same time that I was perfectly satisfied with his decision & better judgment, & as he had

expressed uneasiness at his responsability in such delicate matters I endeavored to remove it by assuring him I shd. be satisfied with whatever he shd. do &c.—his answer to this was declining absolutely to act at discretion & insisting absolutely on positive instructions—the same letter brought me notice of his unwillingness to pay interest on the cash in his hands (Harvie's debt) longer than Dec. 25. 87.—This letter was recd. only sixteen days, prior to the time fixed for the interest to cease, & he insisted on my saying positively wt. he should do with the money—I was extremely embarassed when I took up my pen to answer his letter, on the 20th. of Dec. 87. & really did not know what to say to him—He had avoided taking certificates at 4 for 1.—in Oct. 86.—& chose to take the matter into his hands as he informed me & to allow me an interest of 6. pct.—He now says he has no further occasion for the money & is unwilling to pay interest longer than the 25th. of that month—so that I found myself deprived of the certificates quadrupled, bearing a regular interest, & was to have only the original sum in cash, & not to bear interest longer—Whilst writing my letter of Dec. 20.—Mr. D. Parker called on me & accidentally gave me information of the nature of *Pierce's final settlements*, of which I knew nothing—I considered Parker an oracle in such a case, & immediately added a postscript to my letter, directing positively the purchase of this paper as high as 5/. in the pound—I repeated the same direction on the 31.st. of the same month—I wrote also to the same effect on the 20th. of March 88—In this last only I mention [the] Virga. certificates & that they are to be preferred if to be had at equal price with the settlements, because they bore an interest.—I wrote other letters also on the same subject—I mention these three because Colo. S. has acknowleged the rect. of them—In all I press the necessity of there being no delay—mention the inevitable loss from delay &c. &c.—The answer to these letters dated June 88—says his crop was appropriated & therefore it was impossible for him to execute my scheme in Final settlements on advantageous terms—but that the moment he is enabled to raise the cash I may depend it shall be laid out either in this paper or military certificates—From that time he ceased writing to me until Dec. 89.—& was then brought to it only on acct. of my letter which you delivered him—I had remained all this time under the impression of the last letter recd. of June 88. & could not doubt that all my cash in his hands & all recd. afterwards had been laid out in final settlements, wch. were then selling at 3/6. in the pound, as stated in his letter—On the contrary when he wrote in Dec. 89. having entirely forgotten his preceding letters, he says "*The money wch I am answerable to you for on acct. of Harvie has not yet been collected* owing to the uncommon scarcity of money tho' I can venture to assure you that prior to the ensuing fall it will be laid out in public securities agreeably to your wishes."—He here promised to carry with him to Monticello on the Feby. following a full statement of his accts. with me & put it into your hands to be forwarded to me—He went to Monticello as you wrote me, but not only did not send me the acct. promised but did not send me a single line—& never wrote me afterwards until he recd. from Mr. Browne's hands a letter from me in '91. & being obliged as it were to send some answer sent an extraordinary kind of one, in wch. he says, still forgetting what had preceded "The money recd. on Harvie's bond is not yet collected & consequently I am your debtor as security for the amount with an interest of 6. pct. deducting such payments as I have heretofore announced to you—Harvie's contract is in my possession—it shall be forwarded to Mr. Browne."—This is the last letter I have recd. from him.—I have formerly mentioned what passed between him & Browne.—How Colo. S. means to account, or explain his conduct towards me is what I am at a loss to concieve.—I regret extremely now having allowed the solution of this enigma to have been postponed so long, & not to have sent the necessary powers to my brother or some person after Mr. Browne's letter[—]I can compare it to nothing better than taking an emetic—one puts it off as long as possible, but if it be indispensable the best way is to swallow it as soon as possible. Nothing but the delusion of being soon in America could have made me delay it after my arrival here from Spain & meeting with a person with whom I had a good deal of conversation respecting Colo. Skip. & my affairs— he seemed to be better acquainted with him than I had been.—I have informed my brother in the case of Colo. S. making any difficulty as to paying into his hands as he has no direct power of me, that your power is general & adequate to all purposes & that the money may be recieved immediately by you under it.—I have authorized him also in the case of his collecting no money from Colo. S.—& in the case of his taking the Western lands from Colo. Harvie, instead of the dollar an acre, for them as agreed between him & Harvies agent last year (the alternative remained with my brother) to apply to you for such sums as may be wanted to execute a commission I have given him—This is the case: I have learned from one of the Envoys here who lives near Mush-Island that the negroes on that place had been sold by Harvie to a person whose creditors had lately siezed & sold them. I cannot describe to you the pain this circumstance has given me—Only a part of those negroes belonged to me, the rest belonged to my sisters; but as I am indirectly the cause of these poor unhappy people being now dispersed, separated from their nearest affections, husbands, wives, & children, and perhaps in the hands of cruel masters, I have desired him if perchance he shd. have any means of tracing any of them in this situation (though I fear he will have little opportunity) to purchase them for me & to put them into hands that will not treat them ill or work them too hard—Such as are able & careful enough to provide for themselves may be set free—the children to be bound out to the age of 21—Such as are not immediately set free I will leave so by will.—If I were on the spot I think I could render this scheme not too heavy, however numerous they might be, because I might allow all the able bodied to hire themselves out, & open an account with them so as to recover back the advances I should make for their purchase.—This circumstance brought into my mind the situation of these poor people who were on the Surrey estate, & who belonged partly to my brother & partly to my sisters—Some of them also may be in cruel hands, as they were sold there, on my family leaving that part of the country. I have extended my wishes to them also, & authorized my brother to re-purchase them in the same manner. If I should arrive as soon as I expect I shall be able to act in this business before him, but if this shd. not be the case I have authorized him to apply to you, & have mentioned that you would give directions to the person at Philadelphia, who recieves the interest on my funds, to pay him such sums as he may recieve for interest, & which may be in his hands—& shd. more be necessary, as it will not be wanted all at once I will thank you to be so good as to direct Mr. Bne. respecting it according to the sums & epochs at wch. my brother may want them—I mention this at present merely by way of precaution as it will necessarily be some time before any step can be taken in it either by my brother or myself.—I am much obliged to you for putting Mayo's & Mosby's bonds into Mr. Jefferson's hands & the directions you give respecting them—I should suppose Mayo would think he had had now sufficient indulgence—As to Mr. Mosby I know not who he is or any thing about him—if the amt. be collected so much the better—if not I shd. suppose that it wd. be for Colo. S. to shew how he comes to be my debtor, in the same manner as to Griffin—I do not see what has become of these bonds of Griffin—You mention in your letter of May 25. 95. that Colo. Skip. had informed you that Browne had secured the debt—& in your last of the 18th. of April,[3] that you presume from Browne's letter he recovered nothing from him—I observe also from the copy of Browne's letter to you wch. you sent me, of the 27th. Oct. 99.—he makes no mention of inclosing these bonds. I shall be much obliged to you to see by Mr. Jefferson what has been done with them, or if any thing remain to be done with Colo. Skip. respecting them.—. I observe what you say as to my canal shares & recollect perfectly the advantages wch. they presented at the time of their being purchased—it was my ardent wish that they should be purchased at the time & I still think that the speculation[4] was a most rational one—if posterior & unexpected circumstances have disappointed the whole of our expectations, yet a part may be still counted on & there is no reasonable ground of regret—The experiment has only served to shew now that it is best in similar cases to wait until the work be completed & in train, as the shares may be always had & in a good proportion of interest to capital—Shd. the assembly interfere in the way you mention it is probable that the chances will not be bettered of course, yet we may hope that these shares will be always worth something, although not the original purchase with the interest from the time of its being made.—At the time of this purchase & that of Indian camp though they both pleased me yet if I had been obliged to chuse between the two I should have given the preference to the canal myself—This only serves to shew what I knew before that events often decieve the most probable calculations.—I am more & more pleased with Indian camp—& if it were certain that tenants could be had I should be glad to have the whole Blenheim tract at a good clear interest on the purchase money: but I know this is impracticable. I am agreeably surprized however to see that those tenants pay their rents tolerably well, from the items of the account you were so good as to send me, & to see that the small part thus tenanted produces nearly three p.ct. on the money paid—so that if it were practicable to find three or four more such tenants it would be 6. p.ct. on the purchase money, & even then only a part of the land would be occupied—In such a case no placement could be more agreeable—the lands will certainly augment in time—& the interest would augment also in proportion as the whole of the lands were completely tenanted—There is only one consideration that darkens the prospect, as far as I can judge from here, & that is the number of slaves amongst us & the great difficulty if not impossibility of obtaining any reasonable precaution from the Legislature, composed necessarily of slave owners. I really cannot sufficiently express to you my gratitude for all the trouble you are so good as to take as to Indian camp, as to the leases &c—The plan you have adopted as to them seems to me the best possible.—If you think that on the lands being cleared, & huts or houses built, there would be a certainty of finding tenants, I should be glad you would apply the rents recieved

or to be recieved from Indian camp in that way.—By thus appropriating a given sum the subject is more easily reduced to a clear point
of view—one sees one's way, easily—& the value of the whole may
perhaps be ameliorated so as to yield a good interest as well on the
first purchase as the additional expences—And it seems to me that
the only sure way of calculating is the proportion of interest to capital. I know that our lands with difficulty admit of this & that is probably the reason why we see so many false calculations among our
countrymen or rather so much absence of all calculation—I have seen
with infinite pleasure by my brother's letter that he finds tenants in
Kentuckey—He tells me that he lives on a valuable estate of which he
is partly the cultivator himself, & partly under the cultivation of
about 30. tenants—they pay him in kind—he is also settling other estates in the same way, & I have seen with as much surprize as pleasure the revenue which he derives from them. I have long had reason
to rejoice at his having sold his patrimonial estate & adventured into
that country, although I was at first alarmed at it and disapproved
it—At the time of recieving your letter I was in *pourparler* with the
owner of Dover, or rather the person who considers himself the
owner of Dover, & would have certainly a right to consider himself so
if the *quantum* of price paid were to decide it—he purchased it of a
foreign minister residing here, who was the agent of Mr. R. Morris
for the sale, for the sum of £20000 stlg.—viz. the sum in livres which
produced that sum in bills on London—consequently £20000 stlg.
in effective money—this at least is what he tells me & of which I have
no doubt—He has recd. one years rent, & no more as well as I remember. & I believe never expects to recieve any more rent as he has
heard that all the moveables have been siezed by R.M's creditors—
Notwithstanding it has been a most ruinous purchase to him, &
notwithstanding he is extremely attached to his money, yet he does
not seem to be at all dissatisfied with the agent in this business.—My
expectation was that it might have been possible to have procured
Dover on exceedingly low terms, (& have been even of service to the
owner of Dover) by an exchange of lands in this country, on account
of their present extreme low price here—this would have been convenient to the friend who was united with me in this business. It was
a speculation which could not have failed I think at the price that I
contemplated, because I took into calculation the possibility of remaining some years without revenue from Dover, & as the property
that would have been given here was producing a revenue, that revenue was considered by me as so much additional capital—My ideas
were to give him in land here the same revenue as Dover could be

ascertained to be capable of being rented for, with the restrictions of such a course of agriculture as shd. not deteriorate the lands &c.—He was to have taken information on his side & I on mine, as the data to proceed on—I intended to have written to you on the subject & he I think to the person who sold it to him—I have since informed him that my ideas have changed, & that I should desist from the specula- tion—I thank you very sincerely for the information you were so good as to give me on this matter.—. As to the two other tracts of land you mention, there is no chance of any thing being done with them here—There is such a prejudice at present against American lands &c. & indeed many people here have been so cruelly taken in by land speculators from America, (though I thank God these speculators are not all of them Americans) that they would scarcely take them if offered for nothing—It would produce on the Parisians the same effect as is mentioned of an experiment made of a man crying on the Pont-neuf, a Guinea for 24. sols, & finding no purchaser—The pour- parler as to Dover was produced by the meer circumstance of my wishes alone, for without me my friend would not have it on any terms—& my wishes were produced by the expectation of changing lands here for lands there, with the prospect of greatly increasing the revenue with time—there are 2600. acres in this tract, & with proper management if good tenants could be found might be made a princi- pality.—The lands you mention are cheap according to our antient ideas of James River lands—but I should suppose it difficult to find tenants on 900. acres which would give you immediately the interest of £7000[5]—& if the revenue shd. not begin or tenants not be found immediately every year's delay must of course be calculated as so much added to the original purchase money.—And as to purchasing slaves, stock &c. to be put on these lands, under an overseer, it is so much the more capital you add, with little prospect of deriving an in- terest on your money—As to my own part, it is of all the kinds of rev- enue that wch. I shd. like the least—If any thing can render it tolerable to own slaves, it wd. be the having them under one's own eye, so as to see that they were well treated, & to form them as it were to industry by encouragement & by infusing into them an idea of property—that hoarding principle of wch. Ld. Kaims speaks, & wch. I consider the first & most important step in the moral education of these unfortunate people.—. I see by what you say of my Green sea land that I made a hard bargain in it—I was foolishly taken in by what was said,—by my own delusions,—& by not taking time to ex- amine the matter—If I had staid six months longer in Virga., viz. not have left it until the spring of 85. I might have almost doubled what

I have derived from M. Island—yet I do not regret the sale on the whole as it has turned out tolerably well from the part I took in certificates; although I then considered them the least valuable part, & should not have taken them but [on] the account of their producing me a more certain revenue by the means of the interest warrants than any thing else I could have; & at that time I had no expectation of being employed here & consequently had indispensable need of cash there.—. I am much obliged to you for the enquiries you were so good as to make as to the prices of lands in the middle states—but I see that I did not express my idea as I ought to have done—what I wished to know was the rent which lands there would yield on the purchase money—It is indifferent whether the price be 10. or 100. dollars an acre—they may be dear at 10. d. & cheap at an 100.— Should you have an opportunity without taking too much trouble, I should be much obliged to you to obtain as good information as you can of the rent of lands, & whether the *lesseés* be *farmers* or *metayers*, or in other words whether they be rich or poor—this is an important point for the *lessor*—I have seen & heard a good deal of the nature of leasing out lands in this country,—& I know that the perfection is to have *farmers* who are rich, who take long leases, & who have capitals to place in the exploitation of their farms—It will be a long time before we can aspire to this class of citizens even in our most peopled parts, & as to those where there are slaves it is beyond all kind of calculation—however it is some consolation to see that we are progressing in some places—I learn from the voyage of M. de Liancourt & from himself that lands near Philadelphia may be purchased in small parcels so as to produce an interest of 6. p.ct.—but he seems to have taken much more information as to the nominal price of the acres, than of the ordinary revenue of the lands, proportioned to the purchase money.— The statement wch. you were so good as to send me of my property in your care gave me a great deal of pleasure as well as the prospect wch. you mention of adding 3000 d. more of capital to it in the course of this year. I am extremely obliged to you also for having directed Mr. Barnes to correspond with me—To mercantile men who are obliged to be at their writing desk every day, letters cost nothing & they are therefore by habit regular, & also in the way of knowing how & when to forward their letters—Shd. my return be postponed I count on hearing from him regularly—In that case also I will send the joint power you desire, if you continue to desire it—I should have supposed that in the event you mention, he would have continued acting until I shd. send a new power, as he has only to draw my interest & replace it. You observe that you hold my certificates & Mr. Barnes recieves the interest, & that that is the safest way—You will see how ignorant I am in this kind of business when I tell you that I never in my life saw one of these kinds of certificates, & know not the nature of their tenor—but I had thought they were so arranged, that the funds being placed on my name in the Treasury books, these certificates were of a nature that being burned or lost or any thing else, that was of no importance, & had no effect on these funds & that no person could touch the capital but by an express authorization from the person in whose name they are placed.—. On the subject of the partial re-imbursement of five p.ct. on the 6. pcts., as far as I can judge from hence it would seem to me better to recieve the re-imbursements partially than to sell out at a depreciated rate—I know this kind of partial re-imbursement displeases the holder as it is eating out the capital, in *petits pâtés*—but this is the fault of the eater—if instead of eating this part of the capital he take care immediately to replace it, he certainly gains; for with this five p.ct. which the Government returns him at par in cash he can immediately purchase a larger sum in the funds as they are selling below par—I know not if I explain my idea—but it seems to me an arithmetical certainty that this re-imbursement (at the present price of the funds) is advantageous to the holder if he immediately revest it, & in every point of view disadvantageous to the public—I cannot concieve on what calculation it has been found to be an advisable measure of finance to re-imburse voluntarily & at par a capital bearing 6. p.ct.—& to borrow at 8. p.ct.—I am not acquainted with the circumstances & therefore do not pretend to decide, but as far as I can judge I cannot account for it on any of the acknowleged financial principles.—I should be sorry also that the 3. p.cts. shd. be sold to be re-invested in the 8 pcts.—On the whole I shd. think the 3. p.cts. the best funds to be kept on account of their having already undergone their reduction, & on account of their favor abroad from their being no danger of re-imbursement. &c—It is to be apprehended on the contrary if there shd. be any embarassments hereafter, or if any attack shd. be ever aimed at our funds, it will be by attempting a reduction of the interest of 8. p.ct. & in the first instance perhaps to 6. p.ct.—This is generally the way in wch. such things have begun in this part of the world—I shd. rather therefore unless there be good reasons to the contrary not diminish my 3. pcts. & in general not purchase the 8. pcts. above par—But as to this you will be the best judge & I refer it entirely to yourself after having made these observations.—. I have reserved for the last part of my letter an article wch. seems to give you uneasiness. I am very sorry my dear Sir, it should have given you that of a moment—So far as regards me it can be of no inconvenience whatever & I beg you to take no step which may be of any inconvenience to you. I cannot place this money in any hands where it can be so much to my satisfaction as in yours—that consideration alone I hope will satisfy you—I need not therefore add that under no consideration would I consent to your making any sale or any such thing to raise this money as you mention, even if I had any investment in view; but that in fact I have none & can have no interest whatever in your accelerating the term—I must insist for my own sake therefore that you will strike the word uneasiness out of the affair, as I shd. be really & extremely pained if my affairs in which you have been so good as to take so much trouble, were by any means whatever, to produce that sensation.—And in the present case you will see I hope clearly that there is not the smallest occasion for it.—I have on the contrary recieved great pleasure from seeing the successful branch of industry you have introduced into your quarter—I am persuaded it might be made a considerable source of prosperity, if various branches of industry were aimed at & applied to the various degrees of labour of wch. women & children are susceptible—how much better than to see a poor creature in a state of pregnancy, whose sex & situation renders her an object of sensibility & suffering, exposed to hard labour in a field of tobacco or corn!—On reading over my letter I find I have omitted mentioning at the article of Indian camp what I had intended, that is to say my disposition to augment it, in the following manner, if the prospect of finding tenants continues to grow better as mentioned in your last.—Should it get to such a point that there be good grounds for counting on tenants immediately so as to have a tolerable interest on the money laid out I shd. like to make small & gradual purchases, by appropriating thereto, the interest & re-imbursements recievable quarterly by Mr. Barnes. As the tract of Blenheim is separated into small portions, & as you mentioned some years ago that there wd. probably be for sale some of these portions, it is possible that a purchase might be made with the articles above-mentioned in the hands of Mr. Barnes—As matters stand at present he recieves about 400. dollars a quarter for interest, & about 300. dollars the 1st. of Jany. of re-imbursement—supposing in the course of this year the 3000. dollars of capital purchased as you mention & at such a rate as to produce 7. pct. interest, that will be about 50. dols. a quarter—thus the 1st. of Jany. next Barnes will recieve 450. d. of interest & 300. d. of capital re-imbursed—say 750. do. the 1st. of Jany. & afterwards 450. dollars quarterly—I shd. imagine that with 750. dol. cash, & the rest payable quarterly & with the certainty wch. may be thus counted on, lands might be purchased with that kind of credit, almost as for cash—If a good opportunity should present itself in the manner mentioned as to tenants & revenue, I should be obliged to you to make use of it provided it can be done without alienating capital & thus in the small & gradual way. Should I be in America as I hope, it will be a great object with me to look out for a good placement in land, merely as revenue & therefore with a view to solidity & regularity in the payments—or in other words with farmers as much at their ease as possible—I shd. suppose this must be somewhere far from slaves; & in the middle states.—The letters which you inclosed me in your two last have been all forwarded except one—that for the French family here was sent by my servant & delivered by him—that for the Cardinal was sent to the Spanish Ambassador near the Pope; this seemed the surest chanel & the most likely to find him out if he shd. not be at Rome, where you know perhaps or perhaps do not, that His Holiness now resides. The letter not sent remains with me as yet because it is certain it would not find him where directed & I know not where it would find him—As he has not probably been able to remain where he was, it is possible he may be now in America—I have now my dear Sir, to return you my thanks for the last parts of both your letters—You are perfectly right in supposing me, uninformed on these subjects—It would give me great pleasure to converse with you respecting them—It is so difficult to convey one's ideas fully by a desultory correspondence, & misconceptions often excite such painful ideas, that I have remained silent on them for a long time past.—I ought now to apologize for the length of this letter & I really fear you will not have patience to go through the whole, although I have endeavored that the hand-writing should be as legible as I could make it—I forget always that when you recieve my letters you have other things to attend to of more importance, & that you are not as I am who read yours over & over & over again, & never find them long enough, because I have a great deal of leisure on my hands, because your letters contain what regards me & my affairs, & interest me more than any of the newest & most interesting works that are published; & with all that I forget myself & write you letters three or four times as long as your longest, as one of my pages from the smallness of my hand contains a great deal more—Excuse me then my dear Sir & read me over only in lost moments—I cannot expect or desire to occupy any other. I am my dear Sir with the sentiments which you have ever known in me

Your affectionate friend   W Short

P.S. The opportunity I had hoped for of sending your two remaining vols. to Bordeaux, has failed—I must therefore send them by the Envoys when they shall return—I now inclose also another letter for my brother, wch. contains one that Mr. F Skipwith has just sent to me for him & wch. is on business—I will thank you to forward it by a different separate conveyance from that wch. Mr. Barnes will recieve for him & take your directions on, as this will multiply the chances of his hearing from me—I observe you direct my letters to the care of Mr. F Skipwith—I will thank you not to do this in future—but to the care of Messrs. DeLeport & Cie. Rue Coq-heron—when you send them directly to France—but if you shd. be so kind as to write me oftener, & send them to Hamburgh or Holland—the best way will be not to mention France, during the war, on account of cruisers—but simply put my name on the address, & send them to the care of Messrs Matthiessen & Sillem at Hamburgh—or N & J. V. Staphorst & Hubbard at Amsterdam—as the case may be—they will both know where to send me my letters—I hardly expect however that you will write me now as I have mentioned the chance of my going to America, & it was therefore with reluctance I mentioned this circumstance to you or my brother—but it will be a great gratification to me if you shd. not let this prevent your risking some lines.—Once more my dear Sir *Adieu.*

RC (PHi); not completed until 11 Aug.; endorsed by TJ as received 6 Nov. 1800 and so recorded in SJL. FC (DLC: Short Papers); a summary in Short's epistolary record of 26 Apr. 1799-30 Aug. 1800. Enclosure: William Short to Peyton Short, 11 Aug. 1800, enclosing a letter from Fulwar Skipwith (FC in same). Enclosed in William Short to John Barnes, 11 Aug. (FC in same), and probably enclosed by Barnes to TJ in a letter of 27 Oct. 1800 that is recorded in SJL as received on 6 Nov. but has not been found.

GENTLEMAN WHO I BELIEVE HAS THE DIRECTION OF THE FLAG SHIP: possibly François Testart, a Philadelphia merchant born in Bordeaux, or Jean Testart, also a merchant, who had Philadelphia connections but resided elsewhere (*Tableau des F.F. Composant la T. R. Loge Française l'Aménite, No. 73* [Philadelphia, 1802], 11, 13; Stafford, *Philadelphia Directory, for 1800*, 124). For the voyage of the *Benjamin Franklin* from Philadelphia to Bordeaux under a flag of truce, see Vol. 31:465-6n, 510n.

WRITTEN A VOLUME TO MY BROTHER: Short to Peyton Short, 28 July 1800, which according to its author's epistolary record was several pages longer than this letter to TJ—so lengthy that it was "divided into chapters" (FC in DLC: Short Papers). Short enclosed it in a letter he wrote on 5 Aug. to John BARNES (RC in same).

For François Cointeraux's BOOK ON PISÉ building, see Short's letter to TJ of 2 July 1799.

TO CONSULT THE FEELINGS OF ANOTHER: Short hoped to marry Alexandrine Charlotte Sophie de Rohan-Chabot, the Duchesse de La Rochefoucauld (Vol. 30:473-5, 488, 557, 577; Short to TJ, 2 July 1799). On 9 Oct. 1798 he had sent TJ EXTRACTS of his correspondence with Henry Skipwith.

Count Florimund Claude MERCY-Argenteau, Mattheus Lestevenon heer van Hazerswoude en Berkenrode (BERKENROLD), and Baron Otto von BLOME represented Austria, Holland, and Denmark, respectively, at the court of Louis XVI. In 1790 the Austrian government withdrew Mercy, who had become a confidant of Marie Antoinette, from Versailles for another diplomatic assignment. He continued to advise his government on policy toward France until his death in 1794. Berkenrode's government called him home in 1792, and Blome left France in 1793 (Roider, *Thugut*, 82, 89-90, 93, 164; Jean-Maurice Bizière, "La Révolution Française Vue de l'Ambassade de Danemark à Paris [1788-1794]," *Annales Historiques de la Révolution Française*, 286 [1991], 500, 508-9; Vol. 9:514; Vol. 14:613n, 647n; Vol. 24:333, 426, 561).

THEN MINISTER AT LISBON: David Humphreys; see Vol. 28:488.

Many recipients of PIERCE'S FINAL SETTLEMENTS—interest-bearing notes by which Paymaster General John Pierce settled back pay, bonuses, commutation of officers' pensions, and miscellaneous reimbursements owed to CONTINENTAL soldiers and officers after the War for Independence—sold their certificates. The notes represented approximately $11 million of the public debt and fueled an active speculative market (E. James Ferguson, *The Power of the Purse: A History of American Public Finance, 1776-1790* [Chapel Hill, 1961], 145, 164, 179-80, 183, 186-7, 252-3, 277).

Some years earlier John Harvie had bought from Short a tract of land at MUSH Island on the Roanoke River in Halifax County, North Carolina. William R. Davie owned land and slaves in the area. SURREY ESTATE: for several generations beginning in the middle of the seventeenth century the home plantation of Short's family had been at Spring Garden, in Surry County, Virginia, on the south side of the James River (Blackwell P. Robinson, *William R. Davie* [Chapel Hill, 1957], 374-5; Shackelford, *Jefferson's Adoptive Son*, 1-3, 15; William S. Powell, *The North Carolina Gazetteer* [Chapel Hill, 1968], 343; Harvie to TJ, 15 May 1798).

PERSON AT PHILADELPHIA: John Barnes.

At the time of Short's purchase of his INDIAN CAMP land in Albemarle County in 1795, TJ suggested the possibility of augmenting that tract with acreage from the Carter family's adjoining estate, BLENHEIM. The prospect faded somewhat when Edward (Ned) Carter elected to take up residence at Blenheim (Vol. 28:333, 354-5; Vol. 29:5; Vol. 30:148, 475).

MY BROTHER'S LETTER: probably one from Peyton Short, 29 Nov. 1799, mentioned in William Short's summary of the long letter that he wrote to his brother on 28 July 1800 (DLC: Short Papers).

ARTICLE WCH. SEEMS TO GIVE YOU UNEASINESS: TJ's utilization of Short's income; see TJ's letter of 13 Apr. The nailery at Monticello was the SUCCESSFUL BRANCH OF INDUSTRY.

TJ did not write the letter to the unidentified FRENCH FAMILY, but forwarded it on behalf of someone else. The letter to CARDINAL Dugnani, the papal nuncio, was TJ's, dated 7 May. The SPANISH AMBASSADOR through whom Short routed it may have been José Nicolás de Azara, who as Spain's ambassador to the Holy See and subsequently in a diplomatic position in Paris had influenced relations between the papacy and the French government. Of the letters that TJ had enclosed to Short, the one NOT SENT to its destination by Short was apparently from Antonio Giannini to an unidentified recipient (E. E. Y. Hales, *Revolution and Papacy, 1769-1846* [Garden City, N.Y., 1960], 93, 99, 139; Germán Bleiberg, ed., *Diccionario de Historia de España*, 2d ed., 3 vols. [1968-69], 1:429-30; TJ to Short, 26 Mch., 13 Apr. 1800).

[1] MS: "years."

[2] Preceding eight words interlined in place of "he says."

[3] Thus in MS, but Short meant TJ's letter of 13 Apr.

[4] Word interlined in place of "purchase."

[5] Figure interlined in place of "[your money]."

To Pierce Butler

DEAR SIR   Aug. 11. 1800.

Your favor of July 28. is safely recieved, and recieved with great pleasure, it having been long since we have been without communication. you will have percieved, on your return to Philadelphia, a great change in the spirit of this place. 'the arrogancy of the proud hath ceased, and the patient & meek look up.' I do not know how matters are in the quarter you have been in, but all North of the Roanoke has undergone a wonderful change. the state of the public mind in N. Carolina appears mysterious to us: doubtless you know more of it than we do. what will be the effect, in that & the two other states South of that, of the new maneuvre of a third competitor proposed to be run at the ensuing election, & taken from among them? will his personal interest, or local politics derange the votes in that quarter which would otherwise have been given on principle alone?—nothing ever passed between the gentleman you mention & myself on the subject you mention. it is our mutual duty to leave those arrangements to others, and to acquiesce in their assignment. he has certainly greatly merited of his country, and the Republicans in particular, to whose efforts his have given a chance of success. are we to see you at the Federal city, or will Philadelphia still monopol[ize] the time you spare from S. Carolina? I shall be happy to meet you there & at all times to hear from you. accept assurances of the high regard of Dr. Sir

Your friend & servt   TH: JEFFERSON

PrC (DLC); faint; at foot of text: "Pierce Butler esq."

Butler's FAVOR OF JULY 28, recorded in SJL as received from Philadelphia on 8 Aug., has not been found. The last COMMUNICATION between Butler and TJ is printed at 17 Aug. 1793. Butler, a wealthy planter who served as senator from South Carolina from 1789 to 1796 and from 1802 to 1804, began spending a majority of his time with his children in Philadelphia after the death of his wife in 1790 and continued to do so until his death in 1822. Although elected as a Federalist in 1795, his opposition to the Jay Treaty led

Republicans to consider him as a vice-presidential candidate in 1796 (Kline, *Burr,* 1:267; *S.C. Biographical Directory, House of Representatives,* 3:108-14).

THIRD COMPETITOR: Charles Cotesworth Pinckney. Some Federalists thought Pinckney had a chance to be elected president if the New England states chose electors for John Adams and Pinckney and South Carolina and part of North Carolina voted for Pinckney and TJ (see TJ to Thomas Mann Randolph, 7 May 1800). GENTLEMAN YOU MENTION: for the choice of Aaron Burr as the Republican vice-presidential candidate, see Tench Coxe to TJ, 4 May 1800.

To Pierre Samuel Du Pont
de Nemours

Dear Sir   Monticello Aug. 11. 1800.

In my letter by the last post I omitted to answer the question proposed in a former & repeated in your letter of July 26. whether your manuscript on education can be forwarded by post? it may; and will come safer through that than any other channel. accept in advance my grateful thanks for it; and my effort will not be wanting to avail my country of your ideas. success rests with the gods. — I had anticipated your question about the height of the thermometer. 86.° of Farenheit has been the maximum of the season at Monticello, & 88.° of course in it's vicinities. I rejoice to hear that you will stay chiefly at Alexandria. I shall then consider you within visiting distance. for tho' I suffered myself to consider as possible your meditated visit from N. York; in soberer moments I viewed the undertaking as too great for the object. be this as it may I shall be happy to see you & to hear from you at all times and places. present my respectful salutations to your family and accept assurances of my great & constant esteem.

Th: Jefferson

PrC (DLC); edge frayed; at foot of text: "M. Dupont de Nemours"; endorsed by TJ in ink on verso.

proposed in a former: Du Pont de Nemours to TJ, 15 June.

From George Jefferson

Dear Sir,   Richmond 11th. Augt. 1800

I some days ago forwarded to you by Martin Rowe's boat 120 bundles nail-rod, 7 bundles Hoop-iron, & a small paper parcel. These things arrived about ten days ago, but I could not sooner meet with an opportunity of sending them. There went with them a small Trunk for Miss Virginia Randolph.

It seems I think, as if Brown will scarcely ever pay the balance he owes Mr. Short—he still says he has not been able to get Mr. Ronalds acct. from Mr. Wiseham. Upon my representing to him however, to day, that the business has already been too long delayed considering it might be done in a few minutes as well as so many months—he promised more pointedly than he has heretofore done that he would endeavour to get it settled very shortly.   I have made enquiry respecting Moseby and am informed that he is a very honest punctual

Man. I therefore concluded it was best to wait until the fall, when he promises to make payment. Mayo is sued.

I am Dear Sir Your Very humble servt.   GEO. JEFFERSON

RC (MHi); at foot of text: "Thos. Jefferson esqr Monticello"; endorsed by TJ as received 17 Aug. and so recorded in SJL.

RONALDS ACCT: William Wiseham was the executor of Andrew Ronald's estate (Vol. 31:540). Letters recorded in SJL from TJ to Ronald of 19 Sep. 1794, 11 Jan. 1795, and 12 June 1796 have not been found. Ronald's letters to TJ, the first recorded in SJL without a date but as received 15 Oct. 1794 and the other of 8 Dec., recorded in SJL as received 30 Jan. 1795, are also missing.

From Samuel Miller

SIR,   New York August 11 1800.

I recieved, more than two months ago, the copy of the "Appendix to the Notes on Virginia," which you were so good as to send me. For this instance of attention, I beg you to accept my thanks. The perusal of this pamphlet has given me more than ordinary satisfaction. I was gratified to find the authenticity of so celebrated a morsel of savage eloquence, so fully established; & not less to see an opponent who had manifested so much insolence and brutality in his mode of warfare, completely vanquished. By this manner of treating the subject, you have given much pleasure & exultation to your friends in this part of the United States.—

I am not certain whether you have had an opportunity to see any copies of a periodical work, published in this city, under the title of the "Monthly Magazine & American Review." The principal conductor is a friend of mine, a young Gentleman of considerable talents & learning, some of whose productions, of the novel kind, I believe you have seen. How far you may consider this work as worthy of your attention & countenance, I am unable to decide. To me it seems the most respectable thing of the kind, which, within the compass of my memory, has been set on foot in this country. It is to be lamented that the small degree of taste for literature existing in this new world, and the scattered state of our population, render the support of American periodical works, so difficult, & for the most part so short-lived.—

I have the honor to be, Sir, with much respect, Your humble servant,   SAML: MILLER.

RC (DLC); endorsed by TJ as received 21 August and so recorded in SJL.

Charles Brockden Brown was the YOUNG GENTLEMAN OF CONSIDERABLE

TALENTS AND LEARNING whom Samuel Miller brought to TJ's attention. Brown boarded with Samuel Miller and his brother Edward, a physician in New York. The Millers and Brown also belonged to the Friendly Club, a literary society that prided itself on "unshackled intellectual intercourse" and that sponsored the founding of the *Monthly Magazine and American Review*, Brown's first magazine venture. The final issue of the magazine appeared in December 1800 although its popular review section continued under a different title. Samuel Miller praised the magazine to many of his contemporaries including Jedidiah Morse to whom he recommended the journal as "useful to the United States" and its editor as "a gentleman of undoubted learning and taste" (Walter H. Eitner, "Samuel Miller's Nation 'Lately Become Literary': The *Brief Retrospect* in Brockden Brown's *Monthly Magazine*," *Early American Literature* 13 [1978], 213-16; Bryan Elliott Waterman, "The Friendly Club of New York City: Industries of Knowledge in the Early Republic" [Ph.D. diss., Boston University, 2000]; 9, 11, 16; Vol. 31:276n).

To Philip Norborne Nicholas

DEAR SIR   Monticello Aug. 11. 1800

Having omitted for some days to turn my attention to your plan, when I reverted to it, some particulars of your desire had so escaped my memory that I could not recall them. be so good as to drop me a line stating what rooms are indispensable, & what more would be desireable. also what sizes would suit you best for a dining room & parlour, & particularly the former; for I believe you were satisfied for the latter with the 22. f. octagon in P. Carr's plan. will not your stay in the county, or your journies to or from it procure us the pleasure of seeing you? it will always be a sincere one. Affectionate salutations from
Your friend & servt   TH: JEFFERSON

Sep. 17. apprehending the original has miscarried, I send you a duplicate of the above. I wish you could see a particular construction for your middle room, now going on here, which would be a great beauty, and is very simple & easy; tho' without seeing it, you may apprehend difficulty & reject it.   TH:J.

Dupl (ViU); at head of text: "Duplicate"; addressed: "Philip Norborne Nicholas esq."; endorsed by Nicholas.

Nicholas's most recent extant letter to TJ is dated 2 Feb. 1800 and contains no mention of a PLAN. TJ recorded in SJL a letter from NICHOLAS of 15 Sep. 1800 received on 25 Sep., and also letters to Nicholas of 17 Sep. and 24 Oct. None of these letters has been found.

To Joseph Priestley

DEAR SIR   Monticello Aug. 11. 1800.

Your favor of June 23d. came to hand only four days ago. the former one, covering your thoughts on the plan of an university was recieved a little before I left Philadelphia. the journey, and pressure of other objects on my return home, had prevented my acknoledgments being made in their due time. accept now my sincere thanks for them. they come up perfectly to what I had wished from you; and if they are not turned to useful account for posterity, it will be from the insensibility of others to the importance of good education. as soon as we can ripen the public disposition, we shall bring forward our propositions. the prices you mention of the bread grains at Liverpool appear to be famine prices. I wish the government of that country could become as wise & well meaning as is the just character of the English as individuals.—the mind of this country is daily settling at the point from which it has been led astray during the latter years. I believe it will become what the friends of equal rights had ever hoped it would: and I trust the day is not distant when America will be proud of your presence, & be anxious only to find occasions of obliterating the pain which some of her degenerations stimulated by and countenanced by foreign malice, have been able to excite in your mind. can any future conduct of ours wipe out of the memories of men the follies & extravangancies we have for some time been committing and raise us again to the ground we before occupied? I fear that ages of wisdom[1] will not do it. accept my respectful & affectionate salutations.

TH: JEFFERSON

PrC (DLC); at foot of text: "Doctr. J.   [1] Preceding two words interlined.
Priestley."

To Gideon Granger

DEAR SIR   Aug. 13. 1800.

I recieved with great pleasure your favor of June 4. and am much comforted by the appearance of a change of opinion in your state: for tho' we may obtain, & I believe shall obtain a majority in the legislature of the US attached to the preservation of the Federal constitution according to it's obvious principles & those on which it was known to be recieved, attached equally to the preservation to the states of those rights unquestionably remaining with them, friends to the freedom of

[95]

religion, freedom of the press, trial by jury[1] & to economical government, opposed to standing armies, paper systems, war, & all[2] connection other than of commerce with any foreign nation, in short, a
majority firm in all those principles which we have espoused and the
federalists have opposed uniformly; still should the whole body of
New England[3] continue in opposition to these principles of government, either knowingly or through delusion, our government will be
a very uneasy one. it can never be harmonious & solid, while so respectable a portion of it's citizens support principles which go directly to a change of the federal constitution, to sink the state
governments, consolidate them into one, and to monarchize that. our
country is too large to have all it's affairs directed by a single government. public servants at such a distance, & from under the eye of
their constituents, will, from the circumstance of distance, be unable
to administer & overlook all the details necessary for the good government of the citizen; and the same circumstance by rendering detection impossible to their constituents, will invite the public agents
to corruption, plunder & waste: and I do verily believe that if the
principle were to prevail[4] of a common law being in force in the US.
(which principle possesses the general government at once of all the
powers of the state governments, and reduces us to a single consolidated government) it would become the most corrupt government on
the face of the earth. you have seen the practices by which the public
servants have been able to cover their conduct, or, where that could
not be done, the[5] delusions by which they have varnished it for the
eye of their constituents. what an augmentation of the field for
jobbing, speculating, plundering, office-building & office hunting,
would be produced by an assumption of all the state powers into the
hands of the general government. the true theory of our constitution
is surely the wisest & best, that the states are independant as to every
thing within themselves, & united as to every thing respecting foreign nations. let the general government be once reduced to foreign
concerns only, and let our affairs be disentangled from those of all
other nations, except as to commerce which the merchants will manage the better, the more they are left free to manage[6] for themselves,
and our general government may be reduced to a very simple organization, & a very unexpensive one: a few plain[7] duties to be performed
by a few servants. but I repeat that this simple & economical mode of
government can never be secured if the New England states continue
to support the contrary system. I rejoice therefore in every appearance of their returning to those principles which I had always imagined to be almost innate in them. in this state a few persons were

shaken by the XYZ duperies. you saw the effect of it in our last[8] Congressional representation chosen under their influence. this experiment on their credulity is now seen into, and our next representation will be as republican as it has heretofore been. on the whole we hope that by a part of the Union having held on to the principles of the constitution, time has been given to the states to recover from the temporary phrenzy into which they had been decoyed, to rally round the constitution & to rescue it from the destruction with which it had been threatened even at their own hands. I see copied from the American Mercury two Nos. of a paper signed Don Quixot, most excellently adapted to introduce the real truth to the minds even of the most prejudiced.   I would with great pleasure have written the letter you desire on behalf of your friend; but there are existing circumstances which render a letter from me to that magistrate as improper as it would be unavailing. I shall be happy on some more fortunate occasion to prove to you my desire of serving your wishes.

I sometime ago recieved a letter from a mr Mc.Gregory of Derby in your state.[9] it is written with such a[10] degree of good sense & appearance of candor as entitle it to an answer. yet the writer being entirely unknown [to me, and the] stratagems of the times very multifarious, I have thought [it best to avail] myself of your friendship & inclose the answer to you. you [will see it's] nature. if you find from the character of the person to whom it is addressed that no improper use would probably be made of it, be so good as to seal & send it. otherwise suppress it.

How will the vote of your state & R.I. be as to A. & P.

I am with great & sincere esteem Dear Sir Your friend & servt

TH: JEFFERSON

RC (MHi: Winthrop Collection); torn, with missing words supplied in brackets from PrC; addressed: "Gideon Granger esq. Suffield Connecticut." PrC (DLC). Enclosure: TJ to Uriah McGregory, 13 Aug. 1800.

LETTER YOU DESIRE: Granger requested that TJ write a letter to Arthur St. Clair on behalf of Calvin Pease, his brother-in-law (Granger to TJ, 4 June 1800).

TJ's letter from Uriah McGregory OF DERBY is printed at 19 July 1800.

A. & P.: John Adams and Charles C. Pinckney.

[1] Preceding three words interlined.
[2] TJ here canceled "political."
[3] TJ here canceled "remain."
[4] Preceding three words interlined.
[5] TJ here canceled "deceptions."
[6] Word interlined in place of "act."
[7] Word interlined in place of "simple."
[8] Word interlined.
[9] Preceding three words interlined.
[10] Preceding two words interlined in place of "that."

To Uriah McGregory

Your favor of July 19. has been recieved, and recieved with [senti-
ments] of respect due to a person who, unurged by motives of
personal friendship or acquaintance, and unaided by particular information, will so far exercise his justice as to advert to the proofs of
approbation given a public character by his own state, & by the
United states, & weigh them in the scale against the [fatherless?]
calumnies he hears uttered against him. these public acts are known
even to those who know nothing of my private life, & surely are
better evidence to a mind disposed to [the] truth, than slanders
which no man will affirm on his own knowledge, or even some men
who would. from the moment that a portion of my fellow citizens
[looked towards me] with a view to one of their highest offices, the
floodgates of calumny have been opened upon me; not where I am
personally known, where their slanders would be [instant]ly judged
& suppressed, from a general sense of their falshood; but in the
remote parts of the union, where the means of detection are not at
hand, & the trouble of an enquiry is greater than would suit the
hearers to undertake. I know that I might have filled the courts of
the United States with actions for these slanders, & have ruined perhaps many persons who are not innocent. but this would be no
equivalent in the [. . .] of character. I leave them therefore to the
reproof of their own consciences. if these do not condemn them,
there will yet come a day when the false witness will meet a judge
who has not slept over his slanders. if the reverend Cotton Mather
Smith of Sharon believed this as firmly as I do, he would surely
never have affirmed that 'I had obtained my property by fraud and
robbery: that in one instance I had defrauded & robbed a widow &
fatherless children of an estate to which I was executor of £10,000.
sterling, by keeping the property & paying them in money at the
nominal [amount] that was worth no more than 40. for one; & that
all this could be proved.' Every [tittle] of it is fable; there not having
existed a single circumstance of my life to which any part of it can
hang. I never was an executor but in two instances, [both of] which
having taken place about the beginning of the revolution, which
[withdrew] me immediately from all private pursuits. I never meddled in either executorship. in one of the cases only was there a
widow & children. she was my sister. she retained and managed the
estate in her own hands, & no part of it ever was in mine. in the

other, I was a copartner, & only recieved on [a divis]ion the equal portion allotted me. to neither of these executorships therefore could mr Smith refer. again, my property is all [patri]monial, except about 7. or 800. £'s worth of lands purchased by myself & paid for, not to widows & orphans, but to the very gentlemen from whom I purchased. if mr Smith therefore thinks the precepts of the gospel intended for those who preach them as well as for others, he will doubtless, some day, feel the duties of repentance & of acknowledgement in such forms as to correct the wrong he has done. perhaps he will have to wait till the passions of the moment are passed away. all this is left to his own conscience.

These, Sir, are facts, well known to every person in this quarter, which I have committed to paper for your own satisfaction, & that of those to whom you may chuse to mention them. I only pray that my letter may not go out of your own hands, lest it should get into the newspapers, a bear-garden scene into which I have made it a point to enter on no provocation.

I am Sir Your most obedt. humble servt   Th: Jefferson

PrC (DLC); faint; at foot of first page: "Mr. Uriah Mc.Gregory." Enclosed in TJ to Gideon Granger, 13 Aug. 1800.

TJ served as an EXECUTOR of Dabney Carr's estate upon his death in May 1773. Carr was married to TJ's SISTER Martha. In 1790 TJ wrote that he had "never actually meddled with the adminstration" of the estate. He did oversee the education of his nephews after the death of his brother-in-law and friend. TJ also administered the estate of his sister Elizabeth, who died unmarried in February 1774 at the age of 29. Her estate was valued at less than £150. TJ was an executor along with Francis Eppes and Henry Skipwith in the settlement of the estate of John Wayles, his father-in-law who died in 1773. The estate and its debts were divided equally between the three surviving daughters, Martha Jefferson, Elizabeth Eppes, and Anne Skipwith (MB, 1:329, 340, 349, 371, 380; Vol. 16:157-8, 191-2, 194-5; Vol. 17:677).

From James Madison

DEAR SIR   [before 14 Aug. 1800]

I have had an opportunity since my return of seeing Mr. McGee on the subject of the nails used by him last summer & of collecting through him the information of his brother who brought down the parcell delivered in July. They concur in saying that the Spriggs, the Xs. & XVId. alone formed that parcel & that the XVId. were not brads but nails owing to a mistake in executing the order. I recollect myself that no brads were recd. because the disappointment was felt at the time, and the floor of the Portico was laid with brads made in my father's shop, and a remainder of the Stock procured the preceding year. The IVd. cut nails, are accounted for by Mrs. M. and the driver of my carriage, who brought them down in Augst. The precise date is not recollected but from circumstances it must have been in an advanced Stage of the month. a part of them were used in lathing the Ceiling of the Portico. The balance is still on hand. It would seem therefore that you have enumerated all the nails sent: and that by filling the blank in Augst. with a transfer to that time, of the IVd. charged in July, the account will probably stand right. As this explanation however rests merely on memory, it must yield to any better evidence that may be found. None such is within my possession.   I have a letter from Mr. Dawson dated Hager's Town July 28: in which he says that the choice of Delegates in Maryland is to be made on the first Monday in Octr. that the contest in all the Counties is uncommonly warm, that he thinks it more thn. probable[1] the majority will be of the administrion party, and that in such event, it is understood the Legislature will be immediately called together for the purpose of appointg Electors. Adieu   J. M Jr

RC (DLC: Madison Papers); endorsed by TJ as received 14 Aug. and so recorded in SJL.

Madison set up Richard MCGEE of Louisa County as an overseer for one of Monroe's plantations (Madison, *Papers*, 17:408).

For Madison's letter from John DAWSON, see Madison, *Papers,* 17:399-400.

[1] Preceding four words interlined.

From James Thomson Callender

SIR   Richmond Jail, August, 14th. 1800

This letter will inclose a few pages of the second part of The Prospect. They contain nothing but what I fancy that You have seen already, as I sent You regularly the Petersburg paper, wherein they were printed. But next week, I Shall send some Sheets, that You have not seen before. A half volume will be ready, price half a dollar, in about a fortnight. I have by me as much manuscript as would fill two volumes, and materials, for twice as much more, so that, like the ass between the two bundles of hay, I am at a loss where to begin, or stop. I have been in very bad health, owing to the stink of this place, but I have got some better.

Mr. Rose, my worthy landlord, desires You to accept of his compliments.

I have the honour to be Sir your obliged servt.

J. T. CALLENDER.

RC (DLC); endorsed by TJ as received 21 Aug. and so recorded in SJL. Enclosure not found.

PETERSBURG PAPER: *The Republican*, published by James Lyon and Thomas Field (Brigham, *American Newspapers*, 2:1133; Callender to TJ, 21 Apr. 1800). According to tradition the 14th-century philosopher Jean Buridan used the example of the ass who starved to death, unable to choose between two equidistant, identical BUNDLES OF HAY (DSB, 2:603).

MY WORTHY LANDLORD: William Rose was the jailer at Richmond (CSVP, 9:121; Durey, *Callender*, 137).

From Tadeusz Kosciuszko

MY DEAR SIR   Paris 26 Thermidor [14 Aug.] rue de Lille No 545.
I have the honor to receive your letter of 7th: of May in which you gave me a notice of 1082. Dollars being the last dividents for me— and that you send over by Mr Barnes likwise a skitch of my land. I beg of you to send Thousands thanks from me to Colonel Armstrong for his goodnese, This Land require som settement. Can you procure one or more farmers of good reputation each for a Hundred acres, i should give them Land for nothing for five years on condition that after that terme will pay me the rente one procent Lesse than authers in that part of the Country, or upon any condition you thing proper. You have so many friends her that i most beforehand pay you the first my respects as to the President of the United States. I hope you will be the same in that new station always good, true Americane a Philosopher and my Friend, it may hapen under your helme i shall returne to America, but not otherwise, I do not see a great difficulty for your self to make accomodation with France what i know. I send you by this convey[anc]e a new book to remember me by. accept my thanks for the troubles i gave you and be assured of my friendship Esteem, Consideration, respect and Constante love for ever
Adieu   T: KOSCIUSZKO

The peace kwite made with Austria
I have received a letter of exchange from Mr Barnes for 1082 Dollars.

[101]

RC (MHi); damaged; English date supplied; endorsed by TJ as received 24 Apr. 1801 and so recorded in SJL.

The NEW BOOK may have been the work translated by Jonathan Williams and published in New York in 1808 as Kosciuszko's *Manœuvres of Horse Artillery: Written at Paris in the Year 1800 at the Request of General Wm. R. Davie, then Envoy from the United States to France*; see Sowerby, No. 1149.

After the battle at Marengo, Bonaparte offered Austria a PEACE settlement. The Austrians made a deliberately ambiguous response, but during July their messenger, Count St. Julien, concluded a negotiation in Paris without authorization. The Hapsburg foreign minister, Baron Thugut, tried to undo St. Julien's actions, but in September Emperor Francis accepted new armistice terms from the French and Thugut resigned (Roider, *Thugut*, 340-50).

To Jeremiah Moore

SIR   Monticello Aug. 14. 1800.

I have to acknolege the reciept of your favor of July 12. the times are certainly such as to justify anxiety on the subject of political principles, and particularly those of the public servants. I have been so long on the public theater that I supposed mine to be generally known. I make no secret of them; on the contrary I wish them known to avoid the imputation of those which are not mine. you may remember perhaps that in the year 1783. after the close of the war there was a general idea that a Convention would be called in this state to form a constitution. in that expectation, I then prepared a scheme of constitution which I meant to have proposed. this is bound up at the end of the Notes on Virginia which being in many hands, I may venture to refer to it as giving a general view of my principles of government. it particularly shews what I think on the question of the right of electing & being elected, which is principally the subject of your letter. I found it there on a year's residence in the county; or the possession of property in it, or a year's enrolment in it's militia. when the constitution of Virginia was formed I was in attendance at Congress. had I been here I should probably have proposed a general suffrage; because my opinion has always been in favor of it. still I find very honest men who, thinking the possession of some property necessary to give due[1] independance of mind, are for restraining the elective franchise to property. I believe we may lessen the danger of buying & selling votes, by making the number of voters too great for any means of purchase: I may further say that I have not observed men's honesty to increase with their riches.—I observe however, in the same scheme of a constitution, an abridgment of the right of being elected, which after 17. years more of experience & reflection, I do not approve. it is the incapacitation of a clergyman from being elected. the clergy, by getting themselves established by law, & ingrafted into the machine of government, have been a very formidable engine against the civil & religious rights of man. they are still so in many [countries] and even in some of these United States. even in 1783, we doubted the stability of our recent measures for reducing them to the footing of other useful callings. it now appears that our means were effectual. the clergy here seem to have relinquished[2] all pretensions to privilege, & to stand on a footing with lawyers, physicians &c. they ought therefore to possess the same rights.

I have with you wondered at the change of political principles which has taken place in many. in this state however much less than in others. I am still more alarmed to see, in other states, the general political dispositions of those to whom is confided the education of the rising generation. nor are all the academies of this state free from grounds of uneasiness. I have great confidence in the common sense of mankind in general: but it requires a great deal to get the better of notions which our tutors have instilled into our minds while incapable of questioning them; & to rise superior to antipathies strongly rooted. however, I suppose when the evil rises to a certain height, a remedy will be found, if the case admits any other than the prudence of parents & guardians. the candour & good sense of your letter made it a duty in me to answer it, and to confide that no uncandid use will be made of the answer: & particularly that it be kept from the newspapers, a bear-garden field into which I do not chuse to enter. I am with esteem Sir

Your most obedt. servt   TH: JEFFERSON

PrC (DLC); with faint passages interlined in pencil, possibly by TJ; at foot of first page: "Mr Jeremiah Moor."

SCHEME OF CONSTITUTION: see *Notes*, ed. Peden, 209-22.

[1] Word interlined.

[2] TJ first wrote "clergy appear to have relinquished [here?]" before altering the passage to read as above.

Memorandum on Postal Service
from Philadelphia

[15 Aug. 1800]

Memorandum for Dr. Bache to communicate to mr Duane

The post which branches off from Fredericksburg, & [carries the mail to] the counties of Louisa, Culpeper, Madison, Orange, Albemarle, [Bedford] & [Camp]bell leaves Fredericksburg Tuesday morning.

Since the change of the establishment which brings the mail [from] Philadelphia to Fredericksburg in three days, the Phila[delphia] papers of Friday reach Fredericksburg on Monday evening, [. . .] consequently to be sent through all the counties above [mentioned. yet] we never get the Aurora later than of the preceding [Monday]. If mr Duane therefore would put his [. . .] those counties into the mail which leaves Philadelphia [on] Friday at 9. aclock A.M. he would gain for his papers [four] days.—a proof of the delay they experience is that we recieve the Boston Chronicle of the same date with the Aurora by the same mail.

Greene's paper of Fredericksburg is taken by numbers because it gives them intelligence of several days later than the Aurora would. the [quickening] of this latter paper would [induce] many of these to take [. . .] instead [of] Greene's.

PrC (DLC); faint; undated, but endorsed by TJ in ink on verso: "Posts. mail day from Philada Aug. 15. 1800." The *Virginia Herald* was Timothy Green's PAPER OF FREDERICKSBURG (Brigham, *American Newspapers*, 2:1116).

Declaration for the
Mutual Assurance Society

Declaration for Assurance.

I THE underwritten *Thomas Jefferson* residing at *Monticello* in the county of *Albemarle* do hereby declare for Assurance in the Mutual Assurance Society against Fire on Buildings of the State of Virginia, established the 26th December, 1795, agreeable to the several acts of the General Assembly of this state, to wit:

My buildings on *my Plantation called Monticello* now occupied by *myself* situated between *the plantation of N. Lewis* and that of *Kemp Catlett* in the county of *Albemarle* their dimensions, situation, and contiguity to other buildings or wharves, what the walls are built of, and what the buildings are covered with, are specified in the hereunto annexed description of the said buildings on the plat, signed by me and the appraisers, and each valued by them as appears by their certificate hereunder to wit:

The	*Dwellinghouse*	marked	A. at	5000.	Dollars,	say	*five thousand*	Dollars.
The	*Office*	do.	B. at	400.	do.	"	*four hundred*	do.
The	*Joiners Shop*	do.	C. at	400.	do.	"	*four hundred*	do.
The	*Stone Outhouse*	do.	D. at	300.	do.	"	*three hundred*	do.
The	*Stable*	do.	E. at	200.	do.	"	*Two hundred*	do.
The		do.	F. at	—	do.			do.
The		do.	G. at	—	do.			do.

6300.

say *Six thousand and three hundred* Dollars in all.

    I do hereby declare and affirm that I hold the above mentioned buildings with the land on which they stand in fee simple, and that they are not, nor shall be insured elsewhere, without giving notice thereof, agreeable to the policy that may issue in my name, upon the filing of this declaration, and provided the whole sum does not exceed four-fifths of the verified value, and that I will abide by, observe, and adhere to the Constitution, Rules and Regulations as are already established, or may hereafter be established by a majority of the insured, present in person, or by representatives, or by the majority of the property insured represented, either by the persons themselves or their proxy duly authorized, or their deputy as established by law, at any general meeting, to be held by the said Assurance Society. Witness my hand and seal at *Monti*[*cello*] this *16*. day of *August 1800*.

TH: JEFFERSON

WE the underwritten, being each of us House Owners, declare and affirm that we have examined the [above menti]oned property of *Thomas Jefferson* and that we are of opinion that it would cost in cash *Six thousand and three hundred* Dollars to build the same, and is now (after the deduction of *(Nothing being in good repair)* Dollars for decay or bad repair) actually worth *Six thousand three hundred* Dollars in ready money, as above specified[1] to the best of our knowledge and belief, and he the said subscriber has acknowledged before us his above signature.

TH: M. RANDOLPH } RESIDING [*near*] *Albemarle*
WM. W. HENING. *residing in Albemarle*

A—	4000.	60.
		2:50.
B—	320.	5.80.
D—	240.	4.60.
C—	320.	10.60.
E—	160.	5.80.
		89.30.
U.S. Stamp[2]		2. –
		91.30.

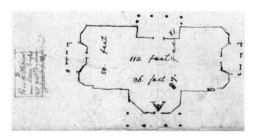

A built of Brick & Stone & covered with Wood—the Main Body is 96 feet long but the full length is 110 feet including porticoes. Wing is 50 feet broad and the Main body 87 feet wide.

The Buildings C D & E, are in a Rowe of small Wooden Buildings but none contiguous to them within 20 feet except D is within 20 feet of a small wooden Building without a Chimney. [stand?] it to be observed that these three Buildings lay on the South of the Main Building.

MS (Mutual Assurance Society, Richmond); printed form, signed by TJ, Randolph, and Hening, with blanks filled by an unidentified hand, possibly Hening's, reproduced in italics; portion of text above and below TJ's signature obscured by seal; text, calculations, and diagrams below signatures, with the exception of the plan of the main house, are in the same hand that filled the blanks in the form, the notes within the building plans reading: "B Brick Office one Story high 20 feet square Covered with Wood," "C Wooden Joiners Shop one Story high 57 by 18 feet," "D Stone Dwelling hse. one Story high 34 by 17 feet," and "E Wooden Stable one Story high 105 by 12 feet"; diagram of main house ("A") and notation of dimensions within it by TJ, probably predating the plans of the other buildings, which were added in an incorrect orientation to the main house; final paragraph written perpendicularly alongside diagrams of buildings "D" and "E"; near the calculation of premiums is a notation adding 320, 160, and 100, with a mark on the total perhaps converting it to 5.80 from 580; at head of text in an unidentified hand: "No. 389." Enclosed as a blank form in William Frederick Ast to TJ, 10 May 1800.

TJ recorded the premiums for the five buildings in his financial memoranda under 17 Aug., listing the estimated values of the dwelling house, "Outchamber" ("Office" above), stone house, joiner's shop, and stable as $5,000, $400, $300, $400, and $200, respectively, with insured costs of $4,000, $320, $240, $320, and $160. He recorded the buildings' premiums as $60, $4.80, $3.60, $9.60, and $5.80, respectively, for a total of $83.80, to which he added other charges of $7.50 to reach a total of $91.30 (MB, 2:1025). For his earlier description and plat of the buildings at Monticello, see the Declaration for the Mutual Assurance Society, [1796 or later], printed at Vol. 29:239-44, which he did not submit to the company.

[1] MS: "secified."
[2] MS: "Samp."

From James Lyle

DEAR SIR   Manchester Augt. 18. 1800

I was favord with a letter before you left Philadelphia; since that, I have not had the pleasure of hearing from you.

In order that you may see how matters stand between you and our Company I have made out a statement, which I now enclose, & hope on examining, you will find right. if any error, you will of course notice it. You will observe the first second & third bonds are paid, & part of the fourth, of this last there remained £99.3.8¾ principal with Interest from Novr. 12. 1798 due, also the fifth and sixth bond, besides that for your Mothers debt.   I have never been able to get payment from Coll. John Bolling (now decd) for the bond you put into my hands for R Harvie. Colo. Bollings sons assured me they are proposing to pay off all the Debts the Estate owed.

I was sorry to see by your last letter that you lost so much by not selling your Tobo. before the price fell. Yet on the whole I think you made the most of it; by selling at Phila.

I have Just now recd. an order from Christr. Clark for £29.12— which will be brot. to your Credit

I am with great Regard Dear Sir Your Mo hml st

                                                                JAMES LYLE

RC (MHi); at head of text: "The Honl. Thomas Jefferson Esqr."; endorsed by TJ as received 28 Aug. and so recorded in SJL. Enclosure not found.

A LETTER BEFORE YOU LEFT PHILADELPHIA: TJ to Lyle, 17 Mch. 1800.

For TJ's payments on his DEBT to Henderson, McCaul & Co., the firm Lyle represented, see Vol. 29:202-4. TJ questioned the accuracy of the 1775 bond of Richard HARVIE, which included an amount from TJ's mother to him that was later assigned to Henderson, McCaul & Co. Although the amount was reduced in 1803 to £132.12.0 principal and TJ made payments toward it, the debt was never paid in full during TJ's lifetime (MB, 1:393, 751).

Agreement with John H. Craven

The sd Thomas leases for 5. years to the sd John H. Craven five fields of land of his tract on the West side of the Rivanna of one hundred acres each cleared & to be cleared, the names of which fields are specified in a paper in the hand writing of the said Thomas delivered to the sd Craven; & also forty five negroes whose names are also specified in a paper in the hand writing of the sd Thos. delivered to the sd John H. Craven. The sd Thos. will sow for the sd John H. this fall one hundred acres of wheat, where he has corn & tobo. now growing; he will deliver to him all his stock of cattle & hogs, attached to the premisses, all the workhorses, such of the mules as are not wanting for himself; corn & fodder as to be hereafter more particularly fixed, prepare a house for him, & in the course of the winter remove the negro houses to a place to be agreed on.

The sd Craven will pay the sd Thomas annually a rent of three hundred & fifty pounds Virginia currency, deducting the first year fifty pounds in lieu of another hundred acres of wheat which ought to be sown, but cannot; he will observe respecting the lands & their culture the general covenants contained in the leases of the sd Thomas to mr Peyton & to John & Reuben Perry, and the conditions annexed to those leases: with respect to the negroes he will feed & clothe them well, take care of them in sickness, employing medical aid if necessary: he will in the last year of the lease sow two hundred acres of wheat where the sd Thomas shall direct, the sd Thos. finding seed for one hundred thereof, he will restore horses, mules, cattle, hogs, houses & fences equal in value to those he shall have recieved, both to be estimated by men mutually to be chosen. should the negroes be treated with unreasonable severity, or not be reasonably taken care of, the sd Thomas shall have a right to refer it to mutual arbiters whether the lease shall not be determined and the conditions on which. he reserves the right of passage to & from his house along the usual roads. this lease to commence on New Year's day ensuing. In witness whereof the parties have hereto set their hands this 22d. of August 1800.

TH: JEFFERSON
JNO H CRAVEN

Witness   TH: M. RANDOLPH
PHILIP DARRELL

MS (MHi); in TJ's hand, except for signatures; at head of text: "Heads of agreemt. between John H. Craven & Th: Jefferson committed to paper by way of memorandum to be reduced to form hereafter"; endorsed by TJ.

John H. Craven (d. 1845), a native of Bucks County, Pennsylvania, lived in Loudoun County, Virginia before he came to reside in Albemarle County. At the same time he leased the fields from TJ at Tufton and Monticello, he began purchasing land near Charlottesville and subsequently became a large landowner and slaveholder. In 1819 he bought Pen Park, the estate established by Dr. George Gilmer. Craven was noted as one of the best farmers in the county. He also owned a flour mill, which ground 15,000 bushels of wheat per year, and other enterprises, including a boat to transport his produce (Woods, *Albemarle*, 173-4; John Hammond Moore, *Albemarle: Jefferson's County, 1727-1976* [Charlottesville, 1976], 94-5, 124, 166; Betts, *Farm*

Book, 401, 516; MB, 2:1030; TJ to George Jefferson, 21 Sep. 1803).

For the FIELDS as SPECIFIED by TJ, see following document. TJ listed the slaves he leased to Craven in 1801 in his farm records. In an adjacent column he listed those slaves he retained at Monticello (facsimile in Betts, *Farm Book*, 60). For the GENERAL COVENANTS CONTAINED in previous leases, see TJ's Indenture with Craven Peyton for the Lease of Fields at Shadwell, 1 Oct. 1799. TJ's lease with JOHN & REUBEN PERRY, brothers who worked as carpenters at Monticello, has not been found (MB, 2:1000, 1023). A letter from REUBEN PERRY to TJ of 13 Dec. 1800, recorded in SJL as received six days later, has not been found.

List of Fields Leased to John H. Craven

[ca. 22 Aug. 1800]

The 5. fields leased to Mr. Craven

as

No. 1.   the River field. $33\frac{2}{3}$ ⎫
Indian field. $52\frac{2}{3}$ ⎬ to be cleared 1800-1
to be cleared adjact. $\underline{13\frac{2}{3}}$ ⎭
100.

No. 2.   Morgan's fields. $35\frac{1}{2}$ ⎫
to be cleared adjact. $\underline{64\frac{1}{2}}$ ⎬ to be cleared 1801-2
100

No. 3.   Outfield   40   ⎫
the Tuft $17\frac{3}{4}$ ⎬ to be cleared 1802-3
Highfield   40
adjact to be cleared $\underline{2\frac{1}{4}}$ ⎭
100.

No. 4.   Franklin's field   45   ⎫
Poggio   32   ⎬ to be cleared 1803-4
to be cleared adjact $\underline{23}$ ⎭
100

No. 5.   Long field   40
Park   20
Slatefield $\underline{40}$
100.

[109]

The order in which they are to be tended.

| | | 1806 | 1807 | 1808 | 1809 | |
		1801.	1802	1803	1804	1805.
No. 1.	Indian.		corn	wheat	clover	peas
2.	Milton	peas	wheat	corn	wheat	clover
3.	Tufton	clover	peas	wheat	corn	wheat
4.	Poggio	wheat	clover	peas	wheat	corn
5.	Meadow	corn	wheat	clover	peas	wheat

MS (MHi); entirely in TJ's hand, with the crop rotation plan perhaps added at a later sitting, and the years "1806" through "1809" interlined at a later date; undated, but see preceding document.

Tufton and Monticello were on the same side of the Rivanna River and had adjoining FIELDS. In his surveys TJ identified RIVER FIELD and the three fields included in No. 5 as part of Monticello, and the others with Tufton, although TJ evidently had a HIGHFIELD at both Monticello and Tufton and sometimes used various names for the same field (Betts, *Farm Book*, 336, and illustrations of TJ's surveys immediately following that page). TJ explained the crop rotation in his indenture with John H. Craven for the lease of fields and slaves at Tufton and Monticello, 23 Sep. 1800.

From Benjamin Rush

DEAR SIR/   Philadelphia August 22nd: 1800

The following thoughts have lately occurred to me. To whom can they be communicated with so much propriety as to that man, who has so uniformly distinguished himself by an Attachment to republican forms of government?

In the Constitution of the United States, titles are wisely forbidden, and pensions for public Services are considered as equally improper by many of our Citizens. There is a mode of honouring distinguished Worth which is Cheap, and which if directed properly, would stimulate to greater exploits of patriotism, than all the high sounding titles of a German, or the expensive pensions of a British Court. It consists in calling *States, Counties, towns, Forts,* and *Ships of War* by the names of men who have deserved well of their Country. To prevent an improper application of those names, the power of Confirming them Should be exercised only by our Governments. No man should have a town, County, Fort or Ship, called by his name 'till After his death; and to prevent any Ambiguity in the names thus given, the Act of Government which confers them, should mention the person's families, places of former Abode, and the Services, civil, military, philosophical or humane which they rendered to their Country. From the

Connection between *Words*, and *ideas*, much good might be done. A map of a State, and the history of travels through the United States, would fill the mind with respect for departed Worth, and inspire exertions to imitate it. Some Advantage likewise would arise to the public, by preventing the Confusion in business which arises from the multiplication of the same names in different States, and sometimes in the same State, and which is the unavoidable consequence of those names being given by Individuals. An end would likewise be put by the practice which is here recommended, to those indications of Vanity which appear in the numerous Names of towns given by their founders After themselves, and which too frequently suggest Other ideas than those of public or even private Virtue.

The Citizens of Boston in the republican years of 1776 & 1777 rejected the royal names of several Streets, and substituted in the room of them, names that comported with the new, and republican State of their town. Why has not Virginia imitated her example? If I mistake not, most of your old Counties bear the names or titles of several successive British Royal families. They are the disgraceful remains of your former degraded State as men, and Should by all means be changed for the names of those Worthies on whose characters death has placed his Seal, and thereby removed beyond the power of forfeiting their well earned fame.

A Spirit of moderation, & mutual forbearance begins to revive among our Citizens. What the issue of the present single & double elective Attractions in our parties will be, is difficult to determin. As yet appearances are turbid. much remains to be precipitated, before the public mind can become clear.—As a proof of the growing moderation of our citizens I shall mention two facts. Mr. Bingham lamented your supposed death in the most liberal & pathetic terms, and Judge Peters spoke of you yesterday at his table in my hearing, in the most respectful and even affectionate manner.[1] This is between ourselves.

You promised when we parted, to read Paley's last Work, and to send me your religious Creed.[2]—I have always considered Christianity as the *strong ground* of Republicanism. Its Spirit is opposed, not only to the Splendor, but even to the very *forms* of monarchy, and many of its precepts have for their Objects, republican liberty & equality, as well as simplicity, integrity & Oconomy in government.[3] It is only necessary for Republicanism to ally itself to the christian Religion, to overturn all the corrupted political and religious institutions in the World.

I have lately heard that Lord Kaims became so firm a Beleiver in

Christianity some years before he died, as to dispute with his former disciples in its favor. Such a mind as Kaims, could only yeild to the strongest evidence, especially as his prejudices were on the Other Side of the Question.

Sir John Pringle had lived near 60 years in a State of indifference to the truth of the Christian Religion.—He devoted himself to the Study of the Scriptures in the evening of his life, and became a Christian. It was remarkable that he became a decided Republican[4] at the same time. It is said this change in his political principles exposed him to the neglect of the Royal family, to Whom he was Physician, and drove him from London, to end his days in his native Country.

Our City continues to be healthy, and business is carried on with its usual Spirit. It is yet uncertain Whether we shall enjoy an exemption from the yellow fever. It is in favor of this hope, that vegetation has assumed its ancient and natural appearance, that all our fruits (the peach excepted) are perfect—that we have much fewer insects than in our sickly years, and that the few diseases we have had, in general put on a milder type than they have done since the year 1793.

An ingenious Work has lately arrived here by Dr Darwin,—full of original matter upon Botany and Agriculture. Dr Barton speaks of it in high terms. A translation of Sonnoni's travels into Egypt is likewise for Sale in our city. They will be memorable from the information they gave to Buonaparte in that Country. They contain a good deal of physical matter particularly upon the diet, diseases, and medicine of the inhabitants.—

A Dieu! From Dear Sir your sincere old friend of 1775

BENJN: RUSH.

RC (DLC); endorsed by TJ as received 5 Sep. and so recorded in SJL.

Rush used NAMES OF MEN he admired, including Anthony Benezet, John Coakley Lettsom, and John Fothergill, to name settlements on tracts of land that he developed (L. H. Butterfield, ed., *Letters of Benjamin Rush*, 2 vols. [Princeton, 1951], 2:821n).

TJ owned the 1795 Philadelphia edition of William PALEY's book, *A View of the Evidences of Christianity*, which was first published in London in 1794 (see Sowerby, No. 1519).

For the context of the letter above in Rush's efforts to elicit a statement of RELIGIOUS CREED from TJ, see EG, 17-19, 317-19.

The recent work by Erasmus DARWIN was *Phytologia; or, The Philosophy of Agriculture and Gardening* (London, 1800). SONNONI'S TRAVELS: Charles Nicolas Sigisbert Sonnini de Manoncourt's *Travels in Upper and Lower Egypt: Undertaken by Order of the Old Government of France*, trans. Henry Hunter, 3 vols. (London, 1799).

[1] Word interlined in place of "terms."
[2] Three lines heavily canceled here.
[3] Rush first wrote "and all its precepts have for their Objects, republican equality, and just government" before altering the clause to read as above.
[4] Rush here canceled a passage that may have read: "(from the [. . .] of Dr. Franklin)."

From Pierre Samuel Du Pont
de Nemours

MONSIEUR,   Good-Stay 24 Auguste 1800.

Je reçois avec reconnaissance votre lettre du 11. Voila le Livre. Je voudrais qu'il fut plus digne du Sujet et du Philosophe qui m'a demandé de le traiter.

Il est fait comme un Mémoire d'Administration, car c'en est un: non comme un Ouvrage qu'on destinerait au Public.

Il n'y a rien pour *le Lecteur*. Je n'ai travaillé que pour l'homme d'Etat. Puisse-t-il agréer mon inviolable et respectueux attachement!

DU PONT (DE NEMOURS)

Je vois dans les Gazettes que *Truxton* part et fera *l'impossible pour avoir un second combat avec la Vengeance*. D'où vient-cette fureur de tuer des Etrangers, et de faire tuer ses compatriotes, quand on sait que les deux Nations sont accommodées ou en accommodement?

Et l'on dit qu'il s'est hâté, de peur d'avoir les nouvelles officielles d'un armistice.

Combien la plus part des hommes sont de vaines et déraisonnables Créatures!

Ils seraient tout autres s'ils avaient été bien élevés, et de sorte que *la morale* leur fut devenue *une Religion*.

Ma Femme vous salue. Mes enfans vous présentent leur respect.

EDITORS' TRANSLATION

SIR,   Good-Stay 24 August 1800.

I am in grateful receipt of your letter of the 11th. Here is the book. I should wish that it were more worthy of the subject and of the philosopher who requested me to treat it.

It is presented as an administrative memorandum, for that is what it is; not as a work destined for the public.

There is nothing to *the Reader*. I have worked only for the statesman. May he accept my inviolable and respectful affection!

DU PONT (DE NEMOURS)

I see in the Gazettes that *Truxtun* is departing and will do *his utmost to have a second engagement with the Vengeance*. Whence comes this fury to kill foreigners and to have one's compatriots killed, when it is known that the two nations have made peace or are in the midst of making it?

And they say that he made haste, for fear of having official news of an armistice.

How much most men are vain and unreasonable creatures!

[113]

They would be completely different if they had been well brought up, and in such a way that *morality* had become a *Religion* for them.

My wife greets you. My children present their respects to you.

RC (DLC); at head of text: "Mr Jefferson"; endorsed by TJ as received 5 Sep. and so recorded in SJL. Enclosure: "Sur l'Éducation Nationale dans les Etats-Unis d'Amérique," 15 June 1800, a tract of 92 numbered pages in French (MS in DeGH; in hand of Jean Xavier Bureaux de Pusy, with scattered emendations probably by Du Pont); see below.

VOILA LE LIVRE: having made a similar request of Joseph Priestley, TJ on 12 Apr. 1800 asked Du Pont de Nemours for comments on curriculum and subject areas that might be appropriate for an institution of higher education. Although TJ posed the question in terms of a possible new university in Virginia, Du Pont, who had previously given some attention to the subject of education, covered all levels of schooling in the treatise he composed in response to the query. He finished it by mid-June, but then waited for Bureaux de Pusy, his stepdaughter's hus-

band, to correct it and make a fair copy. The definitive publication of the work was in Paris in 1812, labeled as the second edition (Du Pont de Nemours, *National Education in the United States of America*, trans. B. G. du Pont [Newark, Del., 1923], xi, xiii, 161; Mary Johnson, "Victorine du Pont: Heiress to the Educational Dream of Pierre Samuel du Pont de Nemours," *Delaware History*, 19 [1980], 89; Saricks, *Du Pont*, 290; Du Pont de Nemours to TJ, 21 Apr., 6 May, 15 June, 6 July 1800).

Captain Thomas Truxtun had been given command of the U.S.S. *President*, which had been launched in April, and the Navy Department had pressed forward the final outfitting of the frigate. In September Truxtun took the ship from New York to its station in the West Indies, where he was to intercept privateers who used Guadaloupe as a base (NDQW, Jan.-May 1800, 405-6; June-Nov. 1800, 76-8, 198-200, 321, 391).

From John Barnes

SIR   George Town, Potomac 28th. Augst: 1800

I had the pleasure addressing you 22d—Inst. since when, have been inabled to state—what I presume to be, the Nt Balce.—on your, & Mr Randolphs 4th: Instal[mt.] becoming payable 18th Next Mo, say $193.51 as ℔ a/c Annexed and should, your Occasional drafts, exceed that Amot:—do not, I pray you, hesitate in drawing them— Allowing me, time suitable, to the immediate Occasion—Your 1st: Octo. Compensation is drawing Near: Moreover I shall soon be inabled to get discounted. at Bank penna.[1] Mr Liepers last, $1000. Note payable 18th Novr:—P.Ms: $567.10 not noticed in this a/c I have Ordered—Mr Richards. to purchase—a sett of Bills ex. on best terms in the Name of, and transmit, to Messrs: VS. & Hubbards Amsterdam— whom I shall address ℔ same conveyance directing it. to be passed to the Credit of said P.M. accordingly—your draft, in favr of S.T. Mason have not yet made its Appearance? I am now got nearly settled—a Neat little two story house, 2 rooms on a floor—within 6 Minutes walk of my Store—garden & Cow house &ca &ca. better calculated, however, for the present season than Winter—under the Care—of Mrs Ratcliff, & Negro Girl, and for my Store—I would not—wish—a Better—Roomy—& compleatly shelved: Counting Room, with a fire place & small Bed room adjoining. for the Young Man who Assists me in tending it, and withal—a Compleat Cellar under the whole, sufficiently large to contain thirty or forty pipes & qr Casks Liqrs—Wine—Brandy &c—with which, I am induced to store it, against the Approaching meeting of Congress—GK $4,500 WS. $1500 & JB. $800—8 ⅌ Ct Stock—in 5 Certificates—have already issued. recd, & transferred to the Treasury Books City of Washington Mr Simpson—I find, notwithstandg: I gave him particular direction, to issue the two former in their respective Names have Nevertheless made the whole of them—in Mine Only—can be transferred again—at leisure—please favr me with your Usual letter—to Mr Steele—.

with great Esteem, I am sir—your mst Obedt: &c

JOHN BARNES

RC (ViU: Edgehill-Randolph Papers); addressed: "Thomas Jefferson Esquire Monticello—Virginia"; with subjoined statement of account in Barnes's hand, signed and dated by him on 28 Aug., charging TJ with $541.27 as a balance carried over from 24 May, plus $2 paid to William Russell Birch on 4 June for two "Views," apparently pictures from Birch's *City of Philadelphia* series (Barnes noting the entry as "with JB"), plus $28.77 paid on 19 July on an invoice concerning the sloop *Sally* and $5.50 paid on 11 Aug. for shipment and wharfage of seven packages sent from Philadelphia to Georgetown, the total of those debits placed against credits of $463.58½ for TJ and $307.46½ for Thomas Mann Randolph anticipated as Thomas Leiper's fourth installment of payment, due 18 Sep., for tobacco, giving a net balance of $193.51 in TJ's favor to be carried forward as of that date; endorsed by TJ as received 5 Sep. and so recorded in SJL.

Barnes's letter of the 22D, received by TJ from Georgetown on the 28th, is recorded in SJL but has not been found. Also recorded in SJL, but missing, is a letter from TJ to Barnes of 10 Aug.

4TH: INSTALMT.: the terms of Thomas Leiper's purchase of TJ's and Thomas Mann Randolph's tobacco called for five bimonthly payments, which began in March; see TJ to Randolph, 28 Jan., 17 Feb., 4 Mch. 1800, and Statement of Account from John Barnes, 12 May 1800.

P.M: Philip Mazzei.

At his new STORE Barnes offered for sale a variety of teas, coffee, sugar, spices, Madeira, sherry, brandy, English porter, gentlemen's hats from London, playing cards, pasteboard, wrapping paper, and Irish linen. NEGRO GIRL: Barnes was or became a slaveholder. After he died in Georgetown in February 1826 his will freed two slaves, Abigail and Nellie Gray, and granted them annuities for life (*Centinel of Liberty, or George-Town and Washington Advertiser*, 24 Oct. 1800; Cordelia Jackson, "John Barnes, A Forgotten Philanthropist of Georgetown," *Records of the Columbia Historical Society*, 7 [1904], 42-4).

GK: Tadeusz Kosciuszko. WS: William Short. Each quarter TJ, under power of attorney from Short, had written to Comptroller John STEELE authorizing Barnes to collect the proceeds of Short's federal securities; see, for example, notes to Barnes to TJ, 10 Mch. 1799, 24 May 1800.

[1] Interlined in place of "US."

To James Madison

DEAR SIR Monticello Aug. 29. 1800.

Before the reciept of your last favor, mr Mc.Gehee had called on me, and satisfied me that the entry of nails delivered in Aug. & left blank was really of nails charged in July & not then delivered. this[1] misconception on my part arose from imperfect entries made on the reports of mr Richardson who generally delivered out the nails. I am chagrined at it's having been the cause of my holding the whole of the 69.23 D of your order on Barnes, when so inconsiderable a portion of it was for me. I now send a statement of our account and the balance of £13–7–2 shall be sent by mr Barber from our court unless a more direct conveyance occurs.

I have recieved no letters of particular information since you were here: nor do I learn any thing lately respecting N. Carolina. the republican papers of Massachusets & Connecticut continue to be filled with the old stories of deism, atheism, antifederalism &c as heretofore & are very silent as to Pinckney.—P. Carr yesterday lost his son; & his daughter is understood to be hopeless. mr Trist has at length made a purchase of lands, those on which James Kerr lived, on the road to mr Divers's, @ 7. D. the acre. a purchaser has offered for Colo. Monroe's land above Charlottesville @ 6. D. he came from Loudon, with a mr Craven, recommended to me as a tenant by Genl. Mason. Craven has rented 5. fields of me of 100. acres each on this side the river,[2] with all the negroes belonging to the plantation (18 workers) stock, &c. at £350. a year for 5. years. I had before nearly compleated the leasing all my lands on the other side the river. my nailery & the erecting my mill are now to be my chief occupations. I hope to rent the latter advantageously. lands are rising sensibly here. several are wanting to buy, & there is little for sale. I imagine we shall hardly be summoned to Washington before the fixed time of meeting. present my respects to mrs Madison, & affectionate salutations to yourself.

TH: JEFFERSON

RC (DLC: Madison Papers, Rives Collection); statement of account written on verso (see below); addressed: "James Madison junr., near Orange court house"; franked. PrC (DLC); endorsed by TJ in ink on verso.

YOUR LAST FAVOR: James Madison to TJ, before 14 Aug. 1800.

TJ's STATEMENT of his ACCOUNT with Madison reflected charges dated 25 July and 23 Aug. 1799 for 23 pounds of fourpenny nails and one pound of one-inch brads at $14\frac{1}{2}$ pence per pound for a total of £1.9.0; 500 $1\frac{1}{2}$-inch brads at $12\frac{1}{2}$ pence per pound for 3 s. 8 d.; 26 pounds of tenpenny nails at $11\frac{1}{2}$ pence, totaling £1.4.11; and 35 pounds of sixteen-penny brads at $10\frac{1}{2}$ pence for a sum of £1.10.$7\frac{1}{2}$. On 12 May TJ paid, at Madison's request, £1.10.0 at the office of the *Aurora* for a subscription for Isaac Winston and on 10 Aug. transmitted to Stevens Thomson Mason, also at Madison's request, £1.10.0 for Charles Holt (MB, 2:1018, 1024). The total of these debits, £7.8.2½, was placed against Madison's credit—the January order on John Barnes for £20.15.4½—leaving TJ with a balance owed Madison of £13.7.2 (see note above; Tr in DLC, entirely in TJ's hand).

TJ's letter of 11 Sep. to James KERR of Charlottesville was recorded in SJL but has not been found. Kerr, a Scottish immigrant, came about 1762 to Albemarle County, where he purchased property at the head of Ivy Creek. He later leased and then, in 1773, bought from the trustees of John Dabney, the Birdwood plantation, which became his principal residence for 27 years. In 1800 Kerr sold the Birdwood property to Hore Browse Trist and bought a farm on Mechum's River. In 1808 he sold this property to James Kinsolving, Sr. and relocated to Kentucky (Woods, *Albemarle,* 244).

For details of TJ's 12 May and 10 Aug. payments, see MB, 2:1018, 1024.

[1] Word reworked from "the." PrC: "the."

[2] Preceding five words interlined.

To John Beale Bordley

DEAR SIR   Monticello Aug. 30. 1800.

Mrs. Randolph, your friend in England, & I believe your relation is entitled to large arrearages of an annuity settled on her by marriage contract, for the paiment of which Peter Randolph, Peyton Randolph & Philip Grymes were jointly & severally bound. Peter R's estate is no longer solvent, &. Peyton R's part devolves on Edmund Randolph, so that he and mr Grymes the son, are liable for the whole. a judgment is obtained against mr Grymes for 2250. ℔ sterl. arrearages, & he, by our law, can on motion & 10. days notice, come on E. Randolph for a moiety, which he is in no condition to pay. mrs Randolph having been apprised of this, and being desirous to indulge her son with further time, & yet not to make mr Grymes the victim of that indulgence, has inclosed me a power of attorney, giving to you & myself jointly & severally authority, of relinquishing to mr Grymes his responsibility for E.R's moiety on his (mr Grymes's) paying a moiety. knowing that the ill state of your health must render business irksome, I have taken the liberty to notify the parties of these circumstances to prevent inconvenience to them, until I could hear from you on the subject. the power of attorney is expressly to do this act; yet if there could be any reason against doing it, we might decline it. but I know of none. mr E.R. cannot pay his part, and mrs Randolph never meant to expose him to confinement. and as to mr Grymes, it is just he should not be sacrificed for that forbearance, & mrs Randolph expressly assents to it. still in proceeding in this business it would be a great satisfaction to me to recieve your approbation, bottomed on the hypothesis that the facts are accurately as I state them to you, as you can have no other knowlege of them. indeed I should gladly refer the whole to yourself as I know mrs Randolph's entire confidence in you, if your health & distance permitted you in your own opinion to undertake the sole agency. I pray you to drop me a line, & to accept assurances of my best wishes for your health & happiness being with sincerity Dear Sir

Your friend & servt　　　　　　　　　　　　　Th: Jefferson

RC (ViU); at foot of text: "John Beele Boardly esq."

TAKEN THE LIBERTY TO NOTIFY THE PARTIES: on this day TJ wrote letters to Ariana Jenings Randolph and Edmund Randolph that are recorded in SJL but have not been found. See also the following document.

To Philip Ludwell Grymes

DEAR SIR　　　　　　　　　　　　Monticello Aug. 30. 1800.

Your favor of the 21st. inst. is duly recieved. there were originally three securities for mrs Randolph's annuity, to wit Peter Randolph, Peyton Randolph & your father. Peter Randolph's estate I have long understood to be no further solvent. consequently the whole liability devolves on yourself and mr Edmund Randolph, each of you being liable for the whole in law, though in justice for only a moiety each. mrs Randolph desires to indulge her son with further time, & yet, as to yourself, not to make you the victim of that indulgence. at the time I wrote to you I did not know you had confessed judgment for the whole: however this ought not to prevent us from still doing what is right. mrs Randolph has authorised me by a power of attorney, on your *paying one moiety* of the arrearages, to relinquish your responsability for the other moiety; and so as to the growing annuity. but the actual paiment is a condition precedent to the relinquishment, & so expressed in the power of attorney. consequently, there can be no relinquishment till a full moiety is paid. if this takes place, as you have stipulated, by the 1st. day of Sep. 1801. or at any earlier period while this power of attorney is in force I shall be ready to relinquish your liability for the other moiety of the judgment. so far I go on the supposition that Peter Randolph's estate is not further solvent. if this is a mistake, then the law has given you the privilege of calling on them for their contribution at very short process. if you will accordingly direct your attorney or mr Copeland to proceed against them for one third, on the actual paiment of that third & of a third only for yourself, you can be released from the remaining third, all circumstances continuing as they now do. but you will be sensible that there are circumstances which, were they to happen before the actual relinquishment, might prevent that altogether. I sincerely wish you may anticipate them by the previous paiment of a moiety, or by the previous payment of one third, & recovery of another third from Peter R's. estate. I shall be happy in being instrumental to this relief. I write to mr Copeland in conformity herewith: & am with great esteem Dear Sir

Your most obedt. servt   TH: JEFFERSON

RC (U.S. District Court for the Eastern District of Virginia, Richmond); addressed: "Philip L. Grymes esq. at Brandon near Urbanna"; franked; endorsed by Grymes.

Grymes's FAVOR of 21 Aug., recorded in SJL as received on the 28th, has not been found. TIME I WROTE TO YOU: 24 July 1800.

I WRITE TO MR. COPELAND: TJ to Charles Copland of this date, recorded in SJL but not found. A letter from Copland, written on 21 Aug. and received on the 28th, is also missing.

From James Wilkinson

SIR   City of Washington Sept. 1st. 1800

I will rely on your goodness to excuse this intrusion produced by my desire to prevent interpretations, which I should be sorry to merit—

Your Letter of the 16th. Jany:, after some considerable lapse of time, reached my Hands at Natchez, & was answered by a Mr. Nolan, anterior to my departure from thence in May—

I had then cause for belief that Mr. N. would have presented Himself to you, long before this period, but a Letter which I have received from Kentucky, has induced a contrary apprehension, & hence the present trespass—

I left New Orleans on the 5th of June, at which time neither Mr. Clark or myself, had heard aught of the Boats, promised you by Mr M. Brown.—

The reperusal of your Letter Exposes to me my mistake of Nation & place—I am truly ashamed of the blunder, & have no apology to offer for it, except that the busy bloody Scenes of the Old World, had so fastened on my Mind, as to mislead my attentions to the ancient City, instead of the Infant Village of Palmyra—

I have in my possession a few productions of Nature & of Art, with several original modern Manuscripts of some Interest, which I am desirous to Submit to you, and as my continuance here & my future destination, appear equally precarious, I wish to be informed with whom I may deposit them, and should you think proper to direct me, I will thank you to put your Letter under cover to Col. Saml Hanson, Cashier of the Bank of Columbia Geo. Town.—

Colo. Orr who informs me he intends to visit you, in his route to Kentucky, has promised to call & take charge of this Letter—

With perfect respect & sincere attachment, I am Sir Your Obliged & Obedient Servant   JA. WILKINSON

RC (DLC); at foot of text: "Thos. Jefferson Esqr."; endorsed by TJ as received 3 Nov. and so recorded in SJL. Enclosure: Dupl of Wilkinson to TJ, 22 May 1800.

MISTAKE OF NATION & PLACE: see TJ to Wilkinson, 16 Jan. 1800, and Wilkinson's reply of 22 May, in which the soldier, unaware that Morgan Brown's PALMYRA was a town in Tennessee, called the American Indian sculptures that Brown was sending to TJ "Italian."

To Robert R. Livingston

DEAR SIR   Monticello Aug. [i.e. Sep.] 2. 1800.

I have to acknolege the reciept of your favor of June 4. and in the first place to return my thanks to the Agricultural society for the honour they have been pleased to confer on me in naming me one of their members. in affection indeed to the science I am a sincere brother; but it has been but a short portion of my life which has been free enough from other business to permit an indulgence of that affection. I fear therefore I shall be a very unprofitable member.

I recieve with great pleasure your description of the steam engine. whether mercury by attrition with steam would be reduced to globules can only be decided by experiment: but even should it be, I do not apprehend that it's specific gravity would be thereby so much changed as entirely to defeat your object.—your proposition to convey water to a reservoir on the top of a house in the form of steam, I think preferable, for the purpose I had suggested, to every possible steam engine. instead of a boiler to be used also for kitchen purposes, I should prefer a vessel, in form of a cannister, of cast iron inserted in the back of the hearth (instead of an iron back), containing as much water as you would wish to throw up in a day. then, in those places, where water can be got within 30. f. of the surface the supply by the weight of the atmosphere would make it the most beautifully simple contrivance that can be imagined. unfortunately for me, the water in my situation lies 64. feet below the level of the earth. if an engine, of any known construction, must be resorted to, Savary's would certainly be the simplest; because his receiver might be placed at 30. f. above the water of the well, and the force of the steam thrown down on the receiver[1] would raise the water the other 35. f. + the height of the house, say 70. feet in all. but this would soon overgo the demand, and require the attention of stopping it, or exhaust the well. I regret therefore again the impracticability of your contrivance in my situation.

I observe, in your address to the Agricultural society, a subject shortly touched on, which is of great importance, yet of great difficulty; the most profitable emploiment of land & labour. the subjects employed by the farmer are land & labour. his result is produce; his object the greatest gain from the whole, or the greatest profit on his capital: & the question interesting to him is what is the proportion of his capital which he should employ in labour & what in land, to produce a maximum of profit. this depends on the prices of land, labour & produce; and these vary so, that it would require a different calculation not only for every country, but for every part of the same country, and even for different periods of time in the same part. but would it not be practicable to reduce it to the form of a mathematical theorem, in which L. the price of land, l. the price of labour, and p. the price of produce should be so combined as to produce[2] M. a maximum of profit? so that in every place, & in every portion of time, we should only have to translate L. l. and p. into their actual equivalents of money at that place & time in order to see what proportion of each ingredient would then & there produce the Maximum? tho this is unquestionably one of the most difficult problems, if solvable at all, yet in reading the travels of Europeans through America, it would seem as if every man of them possessed the theorem & could apply it on the spot to every place he passed through. an Englishman ridicules the farmer of Genesee because he does not mix his land & labour in that place where land abounds & labour is scarce, exactly in the same proportions as in England where labour abounds & land is scarce. a Chinese travelling through England, would declaim in like manner against the ignorance laziness, & slovenliness of the English farmer, who would have but one stalk of wheat growing where, in China, they would have two by bestowing superior labour. but these travellers mistake the question, which is not how to make an acre yield the greatest quantity possible; but how to divide a given sum into land & labour so as to produce the greatest profit possible. the resolution of this question would save travellers a great deal of ink &

paper which they employ in censure; but to the farmer would be inestimable indeed. is it incapable of resolution?

I join you in taking shame for the depravity of our judges. who could have believed that a branch of government which was the last in England to yeild to the torrent of corruption, should have led the way here? seeing the extent to which party feuds may go here, it behoves us to try every means of forcing our judges to stand aloof from these, and to keep themselves pure & impartial administrators between the two parties. if *they* would continue firm in the principles of justice we shall be safe, in our persons & properties at least, amidst all the revolutions of party. impeachment is clearly nothing as at present provided.　　　with great & constant esteem I am Dear Sir

　　Your friend and servt.　　　　　　　　　　Th: Jefferson

RC (NNMus); addressed: "Chancellor Livingston"; endorsed by Livingston as a letter of 2 Aug. PrC (DLC); "Sep." interlined in ink by TJ in place of "Aug." in dateline; TJ also added Livingston's name to foot of first page in pencil. Recorded in SJL under 2 Sep. 1800.

[1] Preceding five words interlined.
[2] Word interlined in place of "[be equal to]."

Summary of Public Service

[after 2 Sep. 1800]

I have sometimes asked myself whether my country is the better for my having lived at all? I do not know that it is. I have been the instrument of doing the following things; but they would have been done by others; some of them perhaps a little later.

　　The Rivanna river had never been used for navigation. scarcely an empty canoe had ever passed down it. soon after I came of age, I examined it's obstructions, set on foot a subscription for removing them, got an act of assembly past & the thing effected, so as to be used completely & fully for carrying down all our pro[duce.]

1776.　　　The declaration of independance

1776.　　　I proposed the demolition of the church establishment, and the freedom of religion. it could only be done by degrees. towit 1776. c. 2. exempted dissenters from contributions to the church & left the church clergy to be supported by voluntary contributions of their own sect. continued from year to year & made perpetual 1779. c. 36. I prepared the act for religious freedom in 1777. as part of the revisal, which was not reported to the assembly till 1779. and that particular law not passed till 1785. and then[1] by the efforts of mr Madison.

1776.   c. 2. the act putting an end to entails.

1778.   c. 1. the act prohibiting the importation of slaves.

1779.   c. 55. the act concerning citizens & establishing the natural right of man to expatriate himself at will.

the act changing the course of descent and giving the inheritance to all the children &c equally I drew, as part of the revisal

the act for apportioning crimes & punishments, part of the same work, I drew. when proposed to the legislature by mr Madison in 1785[2] it failed by a single vote. G. K. Taylor afterwards in 1796[3] proposed the same subject, made & printed a long speech from which any person would suppose his propson was original[4] & that the thing had never been mentd. before: for he takes care not to glance at what had been done before:[5] and he drew his bill over again, carefully avoiding the adoption of any[6] part of the diction of mine. yet the text of mine had been studiously drawn in the technical terms of the law, so as to give no occasion for new questions by new expressions.[7] when I drew m[ine] public labor was thought the best punishment to be substituted for death. but while I was in France I heard of a society in England who had successfully introdu[ced] solitary confinement, and saw the drawing of a prison at Lyons in France formed on the idea of solitary confinement.[8] and being applied to by the Govr. of Virginia for a plan of a Capitol a[nd] prison, I sent them the Lyons plan, accompanying it with a drawing on a smaller scale better adapted to their use. this was in June 1786.[9] mr Taylor very judiciously adopted this idea (which had now been acted on in Philadelphia, probably from the English model) & substituted labor in confinement to the public labour proposed by the commee of revisal; which themselves would have done[10] had they been to act on the subject again. the public mind was ripe for this in 1796[11] when mr Taylor proposed it, and ripened chiefly by the experiment in Philada, whereas in 1785 when it had been before proposed to our assembly they were not quite ripe for it.

In 1789. & 1790. I had a great number of olive plants of the best kind sent from Marseilles to Charleston for S. Carola & Georgia. they were planted & are flourishing: & though not yet multiplied, they will be the germ of that culture in those states.

In 1790. I got a cask of the *heavy*[12] *upland* rice from the river Denbigh in Africa, about Lat. 9 H. 30' North, which I sent to Charleston, in hopes it might supercede the culture of the wet rice which renders S. Carola & Georgia so pestilential through the summer. it was divided, & a part sent to Georgia. I know not whether it has been attended to in S. Carola; but it has spread in the upper parts of Georgia so as to have become almost general, & is highly prized. perhaps it may answer in Tennessee & Kentucky. the greatest service which can be rendered any country is to add an useful plant to it's culture; especially a bread grain. next in value to bread is oil.

Whether the act for the more general diffusion of knowlege will ever be carried into complete effect, I know not. It was recd by the legislature with great enthusiasm at first. and a small effort was made in 1796. by the act to establish public schools, to carry a part of it into effect, viz. that for the establishmt of free English schools. but the option given to the courts has defeated the intention of the act.[13]

I have been drawn to this subject by a publication in Pleasant's paper of Sep. 2. 1800. wherein are some inaccuracies. viz. my father gave me an education in the languages, which was not quite compleat when he died. after compleating it, I went to the Coll. of W. & M— the Summary view was written[14] but not publd by me; but by some members of the convention. I was sick on the road.—I married Jan. 1. 1772. mrs Jefferson died in 1782.—I did not draw the Declaration of rights of Virginia. I believe George Mason drew it. I was absent at Congress. I drew a scheme of a constitution which arrived after the Convention had nearly finished theirs. they adopted the preamble of mine, & some new principles.—the writer speaks of one false return & the suppression of another preventing my being declared President. I know not on what this is founded. the return of 2. electors on the republican ticket of Pensva was delayed artfully so that two from the Federal ticket, who were *in truth* not elected at all, gave their votes. one of these however voted for me, so that I lost but one vote by the maneuvre. this made an apparent difference of 2. viz. 68. & 71. when the real vote was 69. & 70. so that mr Adams was duly elected by a majority of a single voice. these are the inaccuracies I note in that publicn.

MS (DLC: TJ Papers, 219:39161); undated; entirely in TJ's hand; frayed margin.

For TJ's efforts to make the RIVANNA RIVER navigable, including the organization of a subscription that raised £200, the appointment of trustees, and the passage of an act by the Virginia Assembly in 1765, see Vol. 1:87-8. DEMOLITION OF

THE CHURCH ESTABLISHMENT: the text of the bill for establishing religious freedom and its passage by the Virginia Assembly are considered in Vol. 2:545-53. For Madison's role in the passage of this act as part of the revisal of Virginia laws in 1785-86, see Madison, *Papers*, 8:401-2n. TJ's amendment to the "Bill to Enable Tenants in Fee Tail to Convey Their Lands in Fee Simple" resulted in the END TO ENTAILS in Virginia and has been characterized as the first of his "great reform bills," which TJ hoped would change an aristocracy of wealth into an "aristocracy of virtue and talent" (Vol. 1:560-2). For the debate over TJ's role in the authorship and passage of the ACT PROHIBITING THE IMPORTATION OF SLAVES, see Vol. 2:23-4n. The ACT CONCERNING CITIZENS is found in Vol. 2:476-9. Given his opposition to primogeniture TJ thought the legislation GIVING THE INHERITANCE TO ALL THE CHILDREN was among the most important features of the revision of the laws (same, 391-3). APPORTIONING CRIMES & PUNISHMENTS: see note to James Wood to TJ, 3 Mch. 1797.

TJ encouraged the introduction of OLIVE PLANTS in South Carolina and Georgia, being convinced that it is "one of the most precious productions of nature and contributes the most to the happiness of mankind." In 1787 the Agricultural Society of South Carolina appropriated funds and requested that TJ send olive trees for an experiment. TJ contacted Stephen Cathalan, Sr., at Marseilles to acquire "some plants of the best species of Olive-trees." They were sent in 1791 (Vol. 12:380-1, 614, 676; Vol. 13:180-1, 368-9; Vol. 15:101; Vol. 20:332-3). For TJ's acquisition of the heavy upland RICE from Africa, see Nathaniel Cutting to TJ, 6 July 1790 and TJ to Samuel Vaughan, Jr., 27 Nov. 1790, and to William Drayton, 1 May 1791.

For the legislative history of TJ's bill FOR THE MORE GENERAL DIFFUSION OF KNOWLEDGE presented to the Virginia House of Delegates in 1778, see Vol. 2:526-35. The act to establish primary schools passed by the Virginia Assembly in December 1796 left implementation to the discretion of county courts and relied on local funding (Vol. 29:178n, 288n).

John Beckley concluded his 4 July 1800 *Address to the People of the United States* with a biographical sketch of the Republican candidate for president. Signed "Americanus" the pamphlet has been described as the "first of all campaign lives." As TJ indicated, Samuel PLEASANT'S PAPER, the *Virginia Argus*, printed the biography, the concluding pages of the pamphlet, on 2 Sep. 1800. In a letter to Monroe, Beckley apologized for the "inaccuracies & insufficiencies" of the work, but concluded that although "destitute of materials" and in ill health, "having only designed a breif newspaper essay, and being urged by friends to give it its present form, and beleiving that it is materially founded in fact, I determined to set it forth" (*Address to the People of the United States; with an Epitome and Vindication of the Public Life and Character of Thomas Jefferson* [Philadelphia, 1800], Evans, No. 36917; Gawalt, *Justifying Jefferson*, 166-89, 191; Peterson, *Jefferson*, 640).

[1] Preceding two words interlined.

[2] Preceding four words and year interlined.

[3] Preceding word and year interlined.

[4] TJ first wrote "his was the first propson" before altering it to read as above.

[5] Preceding five words interlined in place of "it."

[6] TJ first wrote "so as to adopt no" before altering the preceding passage to read as above.

[7] Preceding sentence written in left margin.

[8] Preceding nine words interlined.

[9] Sentence interlined. TJ first wrote "this was about 1785 or 1786" before altering it to read as above.

[10] Word interlined in place of "proposed."

[11] Preceding word and year interlined here and again when date appears in this sentence.

[12] Preceding two words interlined.

[13] TJ left a large space here before his concluding paragraph.

[14] Preceding two words interlined.

To John Vanmetre

Your favor of Aug. 26. has been duly recieved and is entitled to my thankfulness for the personal considerations you are pleased to express in it. how far the measures proposed might have the expected effect, you can best judge. however in the great exercise of right in which the citizens of America are about to act, I have on mature consideration seen that it is my duty to be passive. the interests which they have at stake are entitled to their whole attention, unbiassed by personal esteem or local considerations: and I am far from the presumption of considering myself as equal to the awful duties of the first magistracy of this country. that there should be differences of opinion among our fellow citizens is to be expected always. men who think freely & have the right of expressing their thoughts will differ. it is true that these differences have of late been artificially increased. but they are now again subsiding to their natural level, and all will soon come right, if no acts of violence intervene. the great question which divides our citizens is whether it is safest that a preponderance of power should be lodged with the monarchical or the republican branch of our government? temporary panics may produce advocates for the former opinion even in this country; but the opinion will be as shortlived as the panic with the great mass of our fellow citizens. there is one circumstance which will always bring them to right: a preponderance of the executive over the legislative branch cannot be maintained but by immense patronage, by multiplying offices, making them very lucrative, by armies, navies, &c which may enlist on the side of the patron all those whom he can interest, & all their families & connections. but these expences must be paid by the labouring citizen. he cannot long continue therefore the advocate of opinions, which, to say only the least of them, doom the labouring citizen to toil & sweat for useless pageants.   I should be unfaithful to my own feelings were I not to say that it has been the greatest of all human consolations to me to be considered by the republican portion of my fellow citizens, as the safe depository of their rights. the first wish of my heart is to see them so guarded as to be safe in any hands, and not to depend on the personal disposition of the depository: and I hope this to be practicable as long as the people retain the spirit of freedom. when that is lost, all experience has shewn that no forms can keep them free against their own will. but that corrupt state of mind must be very distant in a country where, for ages to come, unoccupied soil will still offer itself to those who wish to reap for themselves what themselves have sown. our chief object at present should be to reconcile the divisions which have been artificially excited and to restore society to it's wonted harmony. whenever this shall be done it will be found that there are very few real opponents to a government elective at short intervals. accept assurances of the respect of Sir

Your very humble servt　　　　　　　　　　TH: JEFFERSON

PrC (DLC); at foot of first page: "John Vanmetre esq."

Probably John (Johannes) Vanmetre (d. 1818), the grandson of John Van Metre, an early settler in Berkeley County, Virginia, who bequeathed land he had purchased on Opequon Creek to his children and grandchildren. The grandson settled near Martinsburg (Samuel G. Smyth, *A Genealogy of the Duke-Shepherd-Van Metre Family. From Civil,*

Military, Church and Family Records and Documents [Lancaster, Pa., 1909], 31-40, 135; VMHB, 18 [1910], 461-4).

Vanmetre shared this letter with local Republicans who made copies of it, one of which reached Meriwether Jones at the Richmond *Examiner* (see Vanmetre to TJ, 28 Feb. 1801).

YOUR FAVOR: John Vanmetre's letter of 26 Aug., recorded in SJL as received from "Opeccon cr. Martinsbrg" on 1 Sep., has not been found.

To George Jefferson

DEAR SIR　　　　　　　　　　　　Monticello Sep. 5 1800.

On the 4th. of Aug. I drew on you in favor of Rhodes for 168.82 D. this by my statement would be somewhat over the funds I had in your hands, besides which you have paid articles of freight, drayage &c of which I have no account. I now inclose you a draught on John Barnes at George town[1] for 200. D. tho' it must be presented to him there, yet it is payable at the bank of the US. in Philadelphia. whether this kind of draught, or one payable at George town is most negociable with you I should wish to be informed, as in the 1st. week of the ensuing month mr Barnes will have funds of mine in his hands which I shall wish to draw.　　　Our sheriffs will be going to Richmond about the 22d. inst. (or a little before the 1st. of October) to pay up their collection. I shall give them draughts on you for my taxes, and also for some sums assumed by me for others. not possessing a statement of them, I do not know whether the inclosed draught will cover them, but you shall be furnished with another amply sufficient payable at Georgetown or Philadelphia as best suits you, the first week in Octob. if this can be disposed of for cash it will provide you for my draught. if not, they may perhaps leave me in arrears with you a few days. I pray you in that case to make the advance for me for a few days, as the sheriffs will be liable to a penalty if they do not pay into the treasury at a fixed day. by the next post I shall be able to inform you what my draught may be probably one or two hundred dollars beyond the bill inclosed—mr Barnes sent from Philadelphia directed to you,[2] in April I think, a [box] containing a pair of mahogany dining tables addressed to mr Eppes, marked probably I.W.E. I do not know by what vessel they came but they left Philadelphia while I was there. they came, I believe, alone. mr Eppes says that on application to you you cannot find them. still I think they must be in your warehouse. I pray you to search well. in the mean time I write to mr Barnes on the subject. I am Dear Sir

Your's affectionately   TH: JEFFERSON

PrC (MHi); faint; at foot of text: "Mr George Jefferson"; endorsed by TJ in ink on verso. Enclosure not found.

Matthew Rodes (RHODES) collected the federal direct tax enacted in 1798 on land, houses, and slaves. According to TJ's financial records, the tax on his Albemarle County lands amounted to $97.75; the tax on Monticello, valued at $6,000, was $30; the tax on 65 slaves amounted to $32.50; and the federal tax on his phaeton was $9. The correct total was $169.25, but TJ continued to refer to it as $168.62 (MB, 2:1023-4).

DRAUGHTS ON YOU FOR MY TAXES: TJ gave Alexander Garrett a payment of $104.63 for his taxes and fees in St. Anne's Parish, where Monticello was located. The amount included $10.24 for William Short's taxes. TJ's taxes in Fredericksville Parish amounted to only $11.15, but he gave Joel Yancey an order for $264.31. Of that $170 was for money TJ received from Yancey on 4 and 15 Sep., to be repaid in Richmond. The remainder was for SUMS ASSUMED by TJ FOR OTHERS, including $21.19 for William Davenport, $28.64 for Ann and Walter Key, $7 for James Key, and $26.33 for John H. Buck (MB, 1:40n; 2:1023-7).

[1] TJ interlined "for 200. D."
[2] Preceding three words interlined.

From Stevens Thomson Mason

DEAR SIR   Rasberry Plain Septr: 5th 1800

I recd yours of the 10th Ulto with the enclosure. I some time ago sent you some Peruvian winter-grass by post; it was certainly as justifiable that you should receive it under your privelege of franking as that Connecticut shirts and leather breeches should be sent home to wash under the same privilege. The contest in Maryland is very warm. I think they will get a republican House of Delegates. the people are every where much roused at the meditated attempt to take from them the right of voting for Electors   all the Aristocrats of Geo Town & the City of Washington are embodied agt my brother. I believe he will defeat them, tho' he is himself very doubtful of it. he writes me however that tho' he may probably lose his own election he shall get in two out of four agt changing the mode of election. their whole push is at him and he says that they lie with so much address and industry that he is fearful he shall not be able to counteract them. he spares no pains but he has a Host to contend with and but little assistance when ever he can bring them forth to public discussion (of which they are extremely shy) he gets the better of them. they seem now to depend upon circulating in private political misrepresentation and the most unfounded personal slander, there is scarce a County in the State in which he would have had such hardy Combatants.—J F Mercer is said to be very secure in his Election. can you believe that [. . .] will give a republican Vote? yet some good calculators count upon the whole of the Votes of that State in our favor. I confess I want faith.   I am Dear Sir with great respect & regard

    Your Friend & Servt   STES. THON. MASON

PS What are the accounts or expectations from N Carolina?

RC (DLC); endorsed by TJ as received 11 Sep. and so recorded in SJL.

I RECD YOURS: TJ's letter to Mason of 10 Aug., recorded in SJL, has not been found. According to TJ's financial records, the ENCLOSURE was a draft on John Barnes in favor of Mason for $100.

On 6 Aug. TJ received $75 from Peter Carr to be forwarded to Mason, to which TJ added $10 for Wilson Cary Nicholas, $5 for Madison, and $10 for himself to be part of the subscription for Charles Holt (MB, 2:1024; Mason to TJ, 11 July 1800).

From James Thomson Callender

SIR   Richmond Jail, Septr 8th. 1798 [i.e. 1800]

I had expected to have the honour this day of inclosing for your perusal 24 additional pages; but upon looking among my papers, I find only 8; and cannot get any more before the post goes off. The farther that I go, the more am I lost in amazement at the precipitation and absurdity which marked the acceptance of the federal constitution. I had more manuscript before I Came here, than would fill a large volume, but as my amusement I Continue to write, and wonder at what I have written; such a mass of deformity!

I have warned my readers that the present band did more mischief in 6 weeks than can be repaired in 4 Years; and that they must not blame the next administration for the continuance of the assessed tax. "Like the incendiary of the temple of Ephesus, Mr. — has taken full care that he shall be remembered by posterity."

One of my printers has fallen Sick, which greatly retards the publication. If I ever live to see better days, I Shall set up a printing office of my own here.[1] The expense will be small; the saving one half; and the certainty of getting a work done will be the greatest thing of all. I wish to dedicate the remainder of my life to the federal faction.

I hope that you will excuse this long letter

I am Sir Your most obed servt   J. T. CALLENDER.

RC (DLC); addressed: "The Honourable Thos. Jefferson Vice President of The United States Charllotesville"; franked and postmarked. Recorded in SJL as received 12 Sep. 1800. Enclosure not found.

INCENDIARY OF THE TEMPLE OF EPHESUS: to have his name go down in history Herostratus destroyed the temple to Artemis, the pride of the city, in 356 B.C.E. In response, the citizens of Ephesus passed a decree condemning his name to oblivion (Harry Thurston Peck, ed., *Harper's Dictionary of Classical Literature and Antiquities*, 2d ed., 2 vols. [New York, 1898], 1:808).

[1] Remainder of text written perpendicularly to first part of letter on same large sheet.

From George Jefferson

DEAR SIR   Richmond 8th. Septr. 1800.

I am by to-night's post favor'd with yours of the 5th. inclosing your dft: on Mr. Barnes for $:200—

I am apprehensive that the only way of getting money for such drafts will be by sending them on to Mr. Barnes with directions for him to remit the amount in Bank notes—as no person will like to be at the trouble of sending them to George Town for acceptance, and then of forwarding them on to Philada, when he can *at any time* get drafts direct on Philadelphia. As good a way therefore as any for you in future will be to direct Mr. B. to remit us in notes—in which we consider there is but very little risk, and which we are frequently ourselves compelled to do.

Mr. Eppes's Tables we find as you supposed are here. they came whilst I was absent, and with directions as I am told for their detention until further orders

I am Dear Sir Your Very humble servt.   GEO. JEFFERSON

My not being able to dispose of your dfts: need not make any difference in your drawing in favor of the Sheriffs, as the short advance which you will require will be perfectly immaterial.   G.J.

RC (MHi); at foot of text: "Thos. Jefferson esqr."; endorsed by TJ as received 12 Sep. and so recorded in SJL.

From James Monroe

DEAR SIR   Richmond Sepr. 9. 1800.

There has been great alarm here of late at the prospect of an insurrection of the negroes in this city and its neighbourhood wh. was discovered on the day when it was to have taken effect. Abt. 30 are in prison who are to be tried on Thursday, and others are daily discovered and apprehended in the vicinity of the city. I have no doubt the plan was formed and of tolerable extensive combination, but hope the danger is passed. The trial will commence on thursday, and it is the opinion of the magistrates who examined those committed, that the whole very few excepted will be condemned. The trial may lead to further discoveries of wh. I will inform you. We have nothing new from abroad. very sincerely I am yr. friend and servt.

JAS. MONROE

RC (DLC); endorsed by TJ as received 12 Sep. and so recorded in SJL.

Monroe had spent much of August traveling between Albemarle County, where his young son was seriously ill, and Richmond, where he and the Council of State took steps to quarantine Norfolk for yellow fever. In Richmond on the afternoon of Saturday, 30 Aug., he received information that an INSURRECTION by slaves in the surrounding area would strike the city that night. He communicated with the mayors of Richmond and Petersburg and called out militia to protect the capitol building and public stores of arms and ammunition. Heavy rainfall that made roads and bridges impassable forestalled the beginning of the revolt that night, but Monroe soon received information to convince him that the PLAN for rebellion was still in place. The legislature was not in session, but with the concurrence of the council on Tuesday, 2 Sep., the governor alerted all Virginia militia regiments and strengthened the guard on key locations in and around the capital city. He also communicated with local civil officials. The evening of 2 Sep. the first group of suspects was brought to Richmond from the vicinity of the Henrico County plantation of Thomas H. Prosser, whose slave Gabriel had been named as the primary leader of the intended revolt. Under Virginia law of more than a century's standing, the TRIAL of a slave accused of committing a capital offense was to take place without a jury before a court of oyer and terminer assembled for the purpose. According to a 1786 statute, which was a modified version of a bill in the great revision of the state's law code that TJ and others had drafted some years earlier, a slave could only be condemned to death by unanimous decision of the court of oyer and terminer, and the state would compensate the owner for the value of the executed slave. The first executions for participation in the conspiracy occurred on Friday, 12 Sep. (Monroe, *Writings*, 3:201-3, 216, 234-8, 242; CVSP, 9:134; Ammon, *Monroe*, 185-7; Philip J. Schwarz, *Twice Condemned: Slaves and the Criminal Laws of Virginia, 1705-1865* [Baton Rouge, 1988], 17-18, 25; Vol. 2:616-17).

The MAGISTRATES who first collected information from the slaves taken into custody were Gervas Storrs and Joseph Selden. Earlier in the year Storrs, a member of the Virginia Republicans' general committee, had been elected to the House of Delegates from Henrico County, to take his seat when the assembly convened in December. Selden, who in 1800 was on the Republican corresponding committee for Henrico County, would join Storrs in the assembly in 1803 (CVSP, 9:77-8, 138;

James Sidbury, *Ploughshares into Swords: Race, Rebellion, and Identity in Gabriel's Virginia, 1730-1810* [New York, 1997], 123; Leonard, *General Assembly*, 219-20, 232; Monroe to TJ, 23 Apr. 1800).

From Sylvanus Bourne

SIR   Amsterdam Sept 10 1800

I beg leave to acquaint you that Mr Lusac printer of the french Gazette at Leyden lately presented me an Account for his Papers, sent you in the years 93 & 94[1] while you filled the Office of Secretary of State requesting its transmission for payt. but presuming you received them in your official Capacity I veiwed it as a just debt from the U States & having explained myself accordingly to our Bankers they agreed to discharge it & I hope this procedure will prove to be right.

I proffit of this occasion to Solicit your aid & influence in favr. of an application to Govt. by a memorial in behalf of myself & Colleagues to be laid before Congress in the ensuing Session, praying for some due Compensation for our Services & indemnification for the loss of our Rights & privileges as Citizens of the U States involved in the acceptance of our places[2] as may be seen by the inclosed documents & to which other examples of the like sort might be added. I am at a loss to know exactly on what grounds the opinion of the Court at New york is founded. It certainly cannot be derived from the Laws of the U:S as these in cases where any doubt existed have been particular in confirming the rights of Citizens as appertaining to our Consuls in foreign Countries—nor can it be collected from the Laws of Nations as these are silent & even defective in duly explaining Consular Rights & Privileges—nor is to be explicitly deduced from the Custom or Usage of Nations as this is not sufficiently uniform to establish a principle so important in its consequences in many points of view— France has not acted upon it in this war as mr Johnsons property while Consul at London was I believe uniformly respected as neutral by that Govt. It is true Great Britain has acted on this principle because it is his interest to do it & in conformity to [a] favorite system of ruling the Seas—but I regret to say the solemn verdict of an American Court of Judicature adduced in Support of the Arbitrary procedings of any foreign nation in violation of the rights of other Nations. If we have not the prevent[3] the exercise this affirmed right we can at least forbear to avow or acknowlege it.[4]

If I recollect right you were formerly of opinion that some more valuable provisions ought to have been made for the due Support of our Consular Establishments & I humbly confide that this opinion will be confirmed on finding that our position has become so embarrassing from external Causes those unforeseen.

It was urged in Congress some years past (when a Bill was brought in for allowing due Compensation to our Consuls) that the advantages in trade which their public Situation would give them in Commerce ought to be deemed a due equivalent rendering any provision for them unnecessary & inexpedient—but as the Contrary of all this proves to be the fact—I presume every candid mind will be ready to acknowlege that the Contract between the Consuls was not duly understood by either & that Some remedy ought in future to be applied.

Should a Consular fee on vessels according to their tonnage or a pr Centum on the Cargoes not be deemed eligible—a fixed Stipend proportioned to the importance of the Several Stations may be allowed them over & above the fees they receive under the existing Laws—so as to make their combined Income to meet the Intent of Govt. in their regard—   Chearfully Submitting our Case to your patronage & to your Convictions of the propriety of complying with our request—I have the honor to be very respectfully Yr Ob. Sert

Sylvs Bourne

It appears by the principle of British Jurisprudence that residence makes an *Enemy* but *not a friend*. What [reciprocity] or justice in that?

RC (DLC); torn at seal; addressed: "The Honble Thomas Jefferson Esqr. Vice President of the U:States at the City of Washington Via Newyork"; endorsed by TJ as received 13 Jan. and so recorded in SJL. Dupl (same); dated 20 Sep. 1800; with variations in language from RC; at head of text: "Duplicate"; a postscript on verso of address sheet, which replaces final sentence and question above, reads: "PS. The *Main Source* of any emolument to Consuls under the existing Laws are from the Legalisation of Drawback Certificates so called & in prior times the revenue here from would not in the most frequented Station of any Consuls exceed 5 to 700 Dolls & even this depending on the uncertain Contingency whither American Navigation will have permission to bring West India produce to Europe after the War"; addressed: "The Honble Thomas Jefferson Eqr Vice President of the U:States of America City of Washington, Mr. Munroe"; endorsed by TJ as received 22 Apr. 1801 and so recorded in SJL. Enclosures not found.

On 20 Jan. 1801, Bourne's September 1800 MEMORIAL, requesting compensation for the services of consuls and indemnification for their losses in wartime, was presented to the House of Representatives on his behalf and that of many of his colleagues residing in Europe. The House rejected Bourne's request on 2 Feb. (*Annals*, 10:914; JHR, 3:768, 782; *National State Papers: Adams*, 23:52-3; Madison, *Papers, Sec. of State Ser.*, 1:10). For TJ's instructions to Bourne on an earlier consular bill, see Vol. 19:307-8.

¹ Dupl: "years 94 & 95."

² In Dupl remainder of sentence reads "as will be seen by the documents which accompany the memorial in hands of the Secy of State."

³ Dupl: "If we cannot prevent."

⁴ In Dupl Bourne here adds: "I have conveyed these Sentiments on the Subject to Brown & Relf at Phila desiring their insertion of them in their Gazette."

To Daniel Smith

DEAR SIR   Monticello Sep. 10. 1800.

Your favor of July 6. came safely to hand, & I thank you for the Chickasaw vocabulary it contained. it will aid me considerably in filling up a defective one I had recieved before. I have been long anxious to have as many of the Indian languages preserved as could be, because a comparison of them among themselves as well as with those of the red men in Asia, may lead to conjectures as to their history.

Your friends Colo. Lewis & mrs Lewis are well. you have probably heard of the death of mrs Gilmer. that family are in a very fair way to establish their title to the lands on Smith's river or Leatherwood. your old friend mr Davies too & his family were well at our last court. he continues able to come to court. the public papers giving you all the public news I know, I have thought these small details from a neighborhood where you have lived & are remembered with esteem would be more agreeable to you. I am with great esteem Dear Sir

Your friend & servt   TH: JEFFERSON

RC (Karl & Faber, Munich, Germany, 1951); addressed: "General Daniel Smith Knoxville Tenissee"; franked.

DEFECTIVE ONE I HAD RECIEVED BEFORE: possibly from Benjamin Hawkins in the 1780s; see Vol. 6:427; Vol. 9:640.

From George Smith Houston

SIR   Trenton New Jersey September 11th 1800

Known only to you as an american, I declare myself a Republican, a supporter of our Constitution & a true American—

I am one of your friends, and would support you for the Office of President, but I should wish to know, wether those publications which daily appear against you are Just or not, as they are acqusations of the Anglo-Federal Party, men void of all Justice, truth, or integrity, but we have little source to know from wether it be true & wishing to be acquainted from yourself I have taken the Liberty to write to you on the subject and to send you a Pamphlet which is circulated much to your injury through this State and several other principle cities in the ajacent States of New-York & Pennsylvania these industrous sycophants of the federal party are distributing them throughout this state gratis, I have just met with one & for the respect I have for you & our Republican party I have sent you one that, If you should think proper to answer & any of those charges refute—you may do it—any answer you may make to me or through the means of me Shall be ushered to the World if you wish it & through a very good sourse—

For my single self I believe you do not mean to infringe the constitution, I believe you to be a good & virtuous citizen, I believe you have not that mean contempt of Religion you are said to have by your *enemies*, and as for what is contained in your writings I find nothing to establish that opinion with me—It is my opinion that there would be no impropriety in contradicting those reports but on the contrary to contradict those lies that are published to the injury of your character—Hoping as every freeman ought, to see the people enlightened, enformed, free & united in the cause of Republicanism & the support of the Constitution—I remain respected Sir, your &c

GEORGE SMITH HOUSTON

of Wm C. Houston late member of Congress from this State—

RC (DLC); addressed: "Thomas Jefferson Vice President of the United States Monticello Virginia"; endorsed by TJ as received 18 Sep. and so recorded in SJL.

George Smith Houston, son of William Churchill and Jane Smith Houston, was orphaned with the death of his mother in 1796. His father died of tuberculosis in 1788. His maternal grandparents were Caleb Smith, a Presbyterian clergyman, and Martha Dickinson Smith, daughter of Jonathan Dickinson, the first president of the College of New Jersey. In 1789 Houston attended Trenton Academy. Ten years later he had not yet come of age and was still dependent on his guardian, the executor of his father's estate, for income. Thus he was quite young when he wrote this letter. He married Mary Forman, probably in the early 1820s. Their son William Churchill Houston became a prominent Philadelphia merchant (*Genealogy of Early Settlers in Trenton and Ewing, "Old Hunterdon County," New Jersey* [Trenton, 1883], 124-8; George Smith Houston to Maskell Ewing, 7 Oct.

1799 and 1 June 1805 in NjP:William Churchill Houston Papers; receipts from treasurer of Trenton Academy, 7 Jan. and 1 July 1789, in same).

The PAMPHLET was probably *Serious Considerations on the Election of a President: Addressed to the Citizens of the United States,* attributed to William Linn, the New York City clergyman who corresponded with TJ on Indian languages. On 2 Oct. William Duane noted that he had received an unsolicited copy of the pamphlet printed in Trenton, New Jersey, by Sherman, Mershon & Thomas. John Beckley, characterizing the piece as a virulent portrayal of TJ "as an Athiest and Deist," countered it with a series of four articles signed "Senex." These appeared in the *Aurora* on 27 Aug. and 2, 5, and 26 Sep., and were subsequently published as a pamphlet. DeWitt Clinton responded with essays under the signature of "Grotius," which were published in New York in 1800 as *A Vindication of Thomas Jefferson; Against the Charges Contained in a Pamphlet Entitled, "Serious Considerations,"*

&c. (Gawalt, *Justifying Jefferson*, 191-6; Philadelphia *Aurora*, 2 Oct. 1800; Cunningham, *Jeffersonian Republicans*, 223-7). According to SJL TJ did not answer this letter and there is no other correspondence with Houston.

William C. Houston, George's father, served as a New Jersey delegate to CONGRESS from 1779 to 1781 and 1784 to 1785. He attended the Annapolis Convention in 1786 and the Constitutional Convention in Philadelphia a year later, although he was ill at the time and did not sign the document (ANB; James McLachlan, *Princetonians, 1748-1768: A Biographical Dictionary* [Princeton, 1976], 643-7).

From James Thomson Callender

SIR   Richmond Jail, Septr. 13th. 1800.

Nothing is talked of here but the recent conspiracy of the negroes. One Thomas Prosser, a young man, who had fallen heir, some time ago, to a plantation within six miles of the city, had behaved with great barbarity to his slaves. One of them, named Gabriel, a fellow of courage and intellect above his rank in life, laid a plan of revenge. Immense numbers immediately entered into it, and it has been kept with incredible Secrecy for several months. A number of Swords were made in a clumsy enough manner out of rough iron; others by breaking the blade of a Scythe in the middle, which thus made two Swords of a most formidable kind. They were well fastened in proper handles, and would have cut of a man's limb at a single blow. The conspirators were to have met in a wood near Prosser's house, upon Saturday before last, after it was dark. Upon that day, or some very short time before it, notice was received from a fellow, who being invited, somewhat unguardedly, to go to the rendezvous, refused, and immediately Informed his master's overseer. No ostensible preparations were, however, made until the afternoon preceding the night of the rendezvous; and as the militia are in a State of the most contemptible disorganization, as the blacks are numerous, robust and desperate, there must have been bloody work. But upon that very evening, just about Sunset, there came on the most terrible thunder storm, accompanied with an enormous rain, that I ever witnessed in this State. Between Prosser's, and Richmond; there is a place called Brook Swamp, which runs across the high road, and over which there was a bridge. By this, the africans were of necessity to pass, and the rain had made the passage impracticable. Besides, they were deprived of the junction and assistance of their good friends in this city, who could not go out to join them.[1] They were to have Attacked the Capitol and the penitentiary. They could hardly have failed of success; for after all, we only could muster four or five hundred men, of

whom not more than thirty had Muskets. This was our stile of preparation, While several thousand stands of arms were piled up in the
Capitol and Penitentiary. I do not pretend to blame the executive
Council, for I really am not[2] sufficiently Master of the circumstances
to form an opinion. Five fellows were hung this day; and many more
will share the same fate. Their plan was to Massacre all the whites, of
all ages, and sexes; and all the blacks who would not Join them; and
then march off to the Mountains, with the plunder of the City. Those
wives who should refuse to accompany their husbands were to have
been butchered along with the rest; an idea truly wor[thy] of an
African heart! It consists with my knowledge that many of these
wretches, who were, or would have been partners in the plot, had
been treated with the utmost tenderness by their owners, and more
like children than slaves.

I hope, Sir, that You will excuse me [for] the freedom of sending
You the above details. I have been, for some days past, incommoded
with so great a dimness of my sight, that I was obliged to employ an
assistant in writing the last page. A great part of the above details I
had from your old acquaintance and Protegee, Mr. Rose. To a man of
liberal feelings, there are few Situations that can be more painful
than his; and I heartily wish that it were in my power to smoothe the
protuberancies of his descent along the down hill of life.

The news from Italy, from France, and from New Hampshire, is all
capital. I learn also by more ways than one (what you undoubtedly
know much better than I do) that there has been a very great revolution in the Sentiments of Connecticut. I Can hardly go on for the bel-
lowing of the banditti below Stairs, who were not carried directly, as
they Should have been, from the bar to the gallows.

I find much difficulty in getting the Prospect printed, from the
sickness of one hand, the laziness of another, and the difficulty of getting a third. If I live to see a republican president in the chair, I shall
have a press of my own in Richmond; and give the Aristocrats a cut
and thrust volume per annum for some years to come. This may be of
use; for it is not only proper to knock an adversary down, but to *keep*
him down; the best government will afford an ample verge for
damnatory criticism; and the federal viper will undoubtedly continue
to hiss; but I make no doubt of living to trample him in the mire of
universal detestation.

I hope, Sir, that you will pardon the tediousness of this letter. The
naval Remarks, of which I sent You a Copy last summer[3] will not get
into the first part of this volume.

I have the honour to be Sir Your most obed Servt

JAS. T. CALLENDER

P.S. By naval remarks, I mean the essays that were printed in the Republican, and which I sent you. The boy has not come this evening to take my letter to the Post office, So it stands till next week

RC (DLC); probably written over several sittings; torn; above postscript: "The Honourable Thos. Jefferson"; endorsed by TJ as received 26 Sep. and so recorded in SJL.

CONSPIRACY OF THE NEGROES: Callender sent a variant of this account (that part of the letter above the rule) to William Duane who published it in the Philadelphia *Aurora* on 23 Sep. 1800. It was identified as a letter to the editor dated 12 Sep. from Richmond. Responding to the *Aurora's* account, Meriwether Jones affirmed the accuracy of the statement except for the description of Prosser's treatment of his slaves, which Jones thought to be benevolent and humane (Richmond *Examiner*, 31 Oct. 1800).

GABRIEL, a tall, literate, 24-year-old blacksmith who was married to Nanny, also a slave, lived all of his life at Thomas Prosser's Brookfield estate, six miles north of Richmond. He was the same age as Thomas Henry Prosser, who inherited Brookfield upon the death of his father in 1798. In the spring of 1800 Gabriel began to plan and organize an uprising with slaves like himself who were skilled artisans often working away from the plantation in an urban setting. Slaves from Petersburg and Norfolk were brought into the conspiracy, as were black boatmen who served as couriers as the organization reportedly spread into ten counties. When the THUNDER STORM occurred on 30 Aug., the night set for commencing the attack, Gabriel and his wife tried to postpone the meeting, but two slaves belonging to the Sheppard family, Prosser's neighbors, had already informed Mosby Sheppard of the plan. Gabriel escaped and hid along the James River for almost two weeks before boarding a schooner for Norfolk. Captain Richardson Taylor aided Gabriel, but a slave crew member, who had heard of the $300 reward offered for the capture of the leader of the conspiracy, informed authorities at Norfolk. Gabriel was captured, returned to Richmond, and anticipating that he would make a confession, taken under heavy guard to the governor. He said little, however. On 6 Oct. Gabriel was tried and convicted of "conspiracy and insurrection." He was executed four days later (ANB, 8:598-9; Egerton, *Gabriel's Rebellion*, 19-22, 49-51, 68-71; Monroe, *Writings*, 3:211-13; CVSP, 9:152-6, 164-5; Richmond *Examiner*, 30 Sep. 1800).

FIVE FELLOWS WERE HUNG THIS DAY: according to the records on Friday, 12 Sep., the date of Callender's account to the *Aurora*, six slaves, convicted during the first day of trials held on 11 Sep., were executed. On 15 Sep. another four were hanged. On 16 Sep., however, the *Virginia Argus* reported that five slaves were hanged on the 12th and five on the 15th (CVSP, 9:140-1, 144-6; Egerton, *Gabriel's Rebellion*, 83-7; Philadelphia *Aurora*, 23 Sep. 1800).

In a chapter entitled "The American Navy" found in the second part of Volume 2, pages 42-58, of *The Prospect Before Us*, published in 1801, Callender examined the high cost of the British navy and criticized Adams's role in the establishment of the U.S. navy. He concluded: "It is pretended that this navy will preserve union; whereas all the world knows that the monstrous expence of it, and the leprosy of presidential jobs, which is to spring out of it, will break up union." Callender noted that the NAVAL REMARKS were written in April 1800.

[1] Text from this point to rule in Robert Richardson's hand.

[2] Word interlined.

[3] Word interlined in place of "Spring."

To George Jefferson

DEAR SIR   Monticello Sep. 13. 1800.

Yours of the 8th. came to hand yesterday, and I this day wrote to mr Barnes in consequence. I am sorry to find that Henry Duke has drawn 300. D. from you, as his letter informs me. as he did not draw the money when lodged for him in May, [he was] according to agreement to give me 3. months notice. this makes no other odds than the increasing your advance [and it] would have been convenient for me to have paid him the 1st. week in October. the amount of the two draughts which I mentioned in my last in favor of our sheriffs, as far as I can see at present will be 300.93 D perhaps a little more.—perhaps it would be better hereafter that instead of sending you my draughts on mr Barnes I should desire him to send you his on his agent at Philadelphia, which would avoid the risk & embarrasment of bank notes. I am Dear Sir

Your's affectionately   TH: JEFFERSON

PrC (MHi); faint; at foot of text: "Mr. George Jefferson"; endorsed by TJ in ink on verso.

TJ's letter of THIS DAY to John BARNES, recorded in SJL, is missing.

A letter from HENRY DUKE of 6 Sep., recorded in SJL as received 11 Sep. 1800, has not been found. Letters from TJ to Duke of 17 Mch., 20 and 29 Aug. 1800, and a letter from Duke of 24 Aug. 1800, recorded in SJL as received from Hanover four days later, are also missing. For the money previously LODGED FOR Duke, see TJ to George Jefferson, 7 June 1800. MY LAST: see 5 Sep.

From Samuel Hanson

DEAR SIR,   George-Town, 14th Septr., 1800.

The Interest you have had the Goodness to express for my well fare will excuse my troubling you with the Enclosed Letter from my friend, Judge Tilghman—and my informing you that in consequence of it, I was induced to relinquish my pursuit at Philadelphia. Indeed I should not have engaged in it had I known, what is now generally supposed to be the case, that the Salary will be less than my present one

The Resignation of Mr. Meredith was announced here a few days ago. The universal rumour of the district is that I am to succeed him. I do assure you, Sir, that no intimations, the most distant, of mine have given rise to it. Should, however, my pretensions be considered such as to warrant the appointment, it would lay me under infinite obligations

I felicitate you on the recent triumph of Republicanism in the Election of Democratic Electors of the Senate in the State of Maryland. In the district contiguous to the District of Columbia the progress of Democracy is remarkable, the Numbers having encreased, since the last Election, in the ratio of $2\frac{1}{2}$ to 1. During the contest I met with some of the electioneering Hand-Bills. In one of them the Federal Partizan dwelt a good deal upon the nefarious invitation to the Infidel Tom Paine. His opponent replied by descanting on the Eastern Sorcery which can convert Seven Black Horses into House-Hold Furniture. The Event of the Election has proved that even Infedelity is a crime more rancid, in the Eyes of the Sovereign People, than the Sin of Witchcraft.

Excuse my freedom—and do not, I pray you, Sir, imput it to any abatement of the perfect respect & Esteem with which I am

Dear Sir Your much-obliged & grateful Sert

S HANSON OF SAML

RC (DLC); endorsed by TJ as received 17 Sep. Enclosure not found.

Samuel Hanson (c. 1752-1830) of Port Tobacco Upper Hundred, Charles County, was a lieutenant colonel in the county militia from 1776 to 1778. He also served in the fifth Maryland convention in 1775, in the Maryland House of Delegates from 1782 to 1784, and as a Charles County justice from 1779 to 1786. By 1784 he had moved to Alexandria, Virginia, where he was a merchant and trustee of Alexandria Academy. He died in Washington, D.C., where he worked as cashier at the Bank of Columbia. He and his wife, Mary Key of Philadelphia, boarded several students, including George Washington's nephews, George Steptoe Washington and Lawrence Washington (T. Michael Miller, *Artisans and Merchants of Alexandria, Virginia 1784-1820*, 2 vols. [Bowie, Md., 1991-92], 1:183; Edward C. Papenfuse and others, eds., *A Biographical Dictionary of the Maryland Legislature, 1635-1789*, 2 vols. [Baltimore, 1979-85], 1:409; Madison, *Papers*, 17:533; Washington, *Papers, Pres. Ser.,* 1:29).

Samuel MEREDITH was first treasurer of the U.S. under the Constitution. Rumors may have circulated in 1800 about his intent to resign, but he did not retire from office until 31 Oct. 1801, when he cited his wife's ill health and unsettled business affairs (ANB; Meredith to TJ, 29 Aug. 1801).

To Samuel Miller

DEAR SIR   Monticello Sep. 14. 1800.

I have to acknowledge the reciept of your favor of Aug. 11. with a number of the Monthly magazine. I was before a subscriber to that work, and had read it's different numbers with much approbation.

On examining my papers I find only a single one which relates to the history of New York. this is a Chronological statement of English, French & Indian transactions in America from 1620. to 1691. it is far from being compleat, yet what it does state carries the mark of exactness. this paper was given to me by Wm. Burnet Brown of Salem, who removed to this country married & died here. he was the grandson (I think) of Govr. Burnet of Massachusets, & this paper was compiled by some one of his family, probably his father. he told me by whom, but I have forgotten. I have valued it because it possibly may contain notices of some facts, not otherwise now known. when you shall have taken from it therefore whatever suits you I will trouble you to return it. there is in Massachusets a historical society, within whose plan it would seem that such a paper might be printed entire. they too could supply the defects of my account of it. I have had a thought of sending it to them; but really our party feuds have bursted the bonds not only of society but of science. I know as to myself that I permit those passions to mingle themselves neither with my social or scientific intercourse: and perhaps I ought to judge as favorably of those who compose that society. yet being strangers, I have not yet determined to make advances.   The records referred to by Stith as mentd. in your letter of Mar. 4. are all lost. they were destroyed by the British partly[1] during their 24. hours possession of our seat of government, & partly in other places to which they had been removed. but Stith was a true & faithful narrator of facts. I knew him well, & that his word is equal to a record. he lived on the spot where ours were kept, & had the freest access to them. he studied them minutely, & they were then in a tolerably good state of preservation.

Health, respect & esteem.   TH: JEFFERSON

RC (NN: Lee Kohns Memorial Collection); at foot of text: "The revd. Samuel Miller." PrC (DLC). Enclosure not found.

Miller's letter of 4 Mch. asked TJ for information for a HISTORY OF NEW YORK.

[1] Preceding word interlined.

From Joel Barlow

DEAR SIR,   Paris 15 Sept. 1800—
I see by the testament of General Washington that he contemplated the establishment of a national University at the federal city, as he seems to have left something for the endowment of such an institution. Would it not be possible to take advantage of the veneration which the people have for the memory & opinions of that man to carry into effect a project of this sort? If so, could you not make of it an institution of much more extensive and various utility than any thing of the kind that has hitherto existed?

In all our colleges and universities with which I am acquainted there are so many useless things taught and so many useful ones omitted that it is difficult to say whether on the whole they are beneficial or detrimental to society. I mean to apply this observation only to those at the northward with which I have some acquaintance; but I pretend not to know how far it may be applicable to those in your state & neighbourhood. If those are all more or less defective in their plans, it is essential that we should embrace the present opportunity, when something new is to be attempted, to establish it on principles analogous to the object we have in view, the amelioration of society.

The present state of knowledge presents us with little more than a confused idea of the immense void of the unknown that lies before us; and we lose the principle advantages of the little that is known for want of proper methods of teaching it to our children. It appears to me that an institution that might properly be called national should embrace four principal objects: 1st. to extend the limits of general science: 2d. to explore the native resources of our own country and utilise its industry: 3d. to teach the method of teaching, or to point out what ought to be taught & the best manner of doing it: 4th. to aid the establishment or improvement of other schools similar to the great central one, to furnish them with professors where it can be done conveniently, to bear a part of the burthen of their salaries &c, to cultivate a strict adhereance to republican principles, and endeavour to encourage as great a uniformity as may be in manners, language & sentiments of the people. This last article would be of great utility in the United States; considering the extent of their limits, the variety of their pursuits, and how much their happiness depends on their political Union.

It seems proper that the twofold object of collecting & disseminating knowledge should be wrought into one system, the Institution to be called the Polysophic Society, or some such comprehensive name by which the variety of its labors should be designated. Its members to be chosen for their eminence in the Sciences, arts, trades and literature, after the manner of the learned Academies in Europe. These to be divided into about five or six classes according to their pursuits. Each Class to furnish one or more professors and demonstrators, who, being united in one body, will form the officiating branch of the Institution, and be employed in teaching. The president of the Polysophic society should be president of the Professorate, or officiating branch, whose members should recieve salaries and give their whole attention to the duties of their office.

A considerable fund would be necessary to begin this establishment on such a footing as to promise a permanent success,—to furnish the buildings, gardens, collections of natural history & mineraology, laboratories, books, mechanical & philosophical apparatus, implements of husbandry and of arts & trades. Some professors should likewise be employed in travelling for discovering & collecting the objects of improvement; and others if possible should be salaried by the society to profess in different[1] towns & colleges where their labours might be advantageously united with those of the few persons already employed there.

Should you be of opinion that any thing like this could be attempted with success at or near the seat of government in America I would make it a point to obtain & communicate to you the state of the New Institutions in France that may have come into being since you left this country. Some of them are highly worthy of imitation, and most of them are preferable to any of the old establishments that I am acquainted with. Indeed I regard the improvements in public instruction as one of the most solid advantages of the revolution, and one that no reverse of fortune in the republic will hardly be able to overturn. Ornamental literature is doubtless at a stand, & the fine arts are making no progress. This is scarcely to be regreted when we see that all the physical Sciences and all the useful arts are making more rapid strides than ever they have done before.

A countryman of ours, Robert Fulton of Philadelphia, has invented a new mode of submarine navigation which he is bringing to perfection. He hopes very soon to demonstrate the practicability of destroying military navies altogether, and with them the whole system of naval tyranny, & civilised piracy which seems worse than the barbarian, as it works its mischiefs on a larger scale and really threatens the existence of society. Should he thus succeed in setting commerce free, & in providing this cheap method of securing its freedom, he will merit well of his country and of mankind.

I have the honor to be Dear Sir, with great respect yr. obt. sert.

JOEL BARLOW

Dupl (DLC); at head of text: "To Mr. Jefferson" and "Copy"; endorsed by TJ as received 14 Jan. 1801 and so recorded in SJL. RC (same); with postscript: "I take the liberty to send you by Mr. Skipwith a little pamphlet I published last year on a subject which I thot useful" (see 3 Oct.); endorsed by TJ as received 13 Mch. 1801 and so recorded in SJL. Dupl enclosed in Barlow to TJ, 3 Oct. 1800.

George Washington's will bequeathed 50 shares in the Potomac Canal Company for the support of a NATIONAL UNIVERSITY in the District of Columbia. That project, which Washington had long pondered and mentioned in his last annual address to Congress, never came about, and the shares became worthless after the failure of the company in 1828 (Fitzpatrick, *Writings*, 37:280-1; James

Thomas Flexner, *George Washington: Anguish and Farewell (1793-1799)* [Boston, 1969], 199-200, 296-7, 326, 353).

Barlow later amplified his own concept of an educational INSTITUTION, publishing a *Prospectus of a National Institution* in Washington in 1806 (ANB).

NEW INSTITUTIONS IN FRANCE: for the French National Institute of Arts and Sciences, see Alexandre Lerebours to TJ, 17 May 1796. William Thornton and Volney had discussed prospects of incorporating a philosophical society into a national university in the U.S.; see Thornton to TJ, 22 May 1796.

In France Robert FULTON lived in an ambiguous relationship with Barlow and Barlow's wife, Ruth Baldwin Barlow. Beginning in 1797 the inventor, with some lobbying assistance from Barlow, had attempted to interest the French government in his design for a SUBMARINE warship. His working prototype operated successfully but failed to destroy any British ships during sea trials. Fulton ceased the development of his *Nautilus* in 1801 after failing to receive financial backing at the level he desired from Bonaparte's government (Cynthia Owen Philip, *Robert Fulton: A Biography* [New York, 1985], 72-84, 87, 94-117, 126-8).

[1] RC: "distant."

From James Monroe

DEAR SIR   Richmond Sepr. 15. 1800.

I find by yours of the 12. that Mr. Craven had not recd. my letter to him wh. was address'd to Leesburg abt. a fortnight since. I was apprized by Catlett & Miller of Charlottesville that Mr. Craven and Mr. Darrelle wished to purchase my land above that town, as they supposed in partnership, and communicated my terms to the former. I will take six dolrs. by the acre, of which I must have at least £1000. when possession is delivered, which may be immediately, and the balance as soon as possible. I wrote Miller and Catlett I must have the Whole in cash at that price, but will relax from that demand; tho' I think comparatively with the prices given for other land in the county, it wod. not be a hard bargain. The improvments cost me at least £600. they are new and good. The tract contains abt. 1000. acres. If those gentn. or either of them will give me a day I will meet them in Albemarle, to decide the affair.   We have had much trouble with the negroes here. The plan of an insurrection has been clearly proved, & appears to have been of considerable extent. 10. have been condemned & executed, and there are at least twenty perhaps 40. more to be tried, of whose guilt no doubt is entertained. It is unquestionably the most serious and formidable conspiracy we have ever known of the kind: tho' indeed to call it so is to give no idea of the thing itself. While it was possible to keep it secret, wh. it was till we saw the extent of it, we did so. But when it became indispensably necessary to resort to strong measures with a view to protect the town, the publick arms, the Treasury and the Jail, wh. were all threatened, the opposit course was in part tak[en.] We then made a display of our force and measures of defence with a view to intimidate those people. Where to arrest the hand of the Executioner, is a question of great importance. It is hardly to be presumed, a rebel who avows it was his intention to assassinate his master &ca if pardoned will ever become a useful servant. and we have no power to transport him abroad—Nor is it less difficult to say whether mercy or severity is the better policy in this case, tho' where there is cause for doubt it is best to incline to the former council. I shall be happy to have yr. opinion on these points.

yr. friend & servant — JAS. MONROE

RC (DLC); torn; endorsed by TJ as received 18 Sep. and so recorded in SJL.

TJ's letter to Monroe of 12 Sep. is recorded in SJL but has not been found.
DISPLAY OF OUR FORCE: on 6 Sep. the Council of State gave Monroe authority to order out the full militia of Henrico County, Chesterfield County, and the city of Richmond. On the 9th he called up two full regiments and part of another, and on the 13th, after he began to reduce the number of men in arms, he still had 650 militiamen at his disposal. It was unusual for a Virginia governor to call out militia to quell an insurrection that had not yet begun, but as Monroe later explained to the General Assembly, he and the council thought they needed troops already mustered and on the scene in case the many slaves who worked on contract in and around Richmond should become involved in any revolt. Believing also that the soldiers "inspired the citizens with confidence, and depressed the spirits of the slaves," he saw that the militia attended executions of slave conspirators and paraded in Richmond each day. Most of the citizen soldiers were sent home by 18 Oct. (Monroe, *Writings*, 3:205-7, 238-43; James Sidbury, *Ploughshares into Swords: Race, Rebellion, and Identity in Gabriel's Virginia, 1730-1810* [New York, 1997], 120-8; Ammon, *Monroe*, 187).
ARREST THE HAND OF THE EXECUTIONER: in the end, 26 slaves including Gabriel were hanged. The council agreed to some requests from Monroe for pardons or temporary reprieves of condemned men. In October, however, the council deadlocked, and so could not intervene, when a group of convicted slaves awaited execution and the governor asked "whether those less criminal in comparison with others" might be spared until the legislature could meet. In its first session after the discovery of the planned insurrection, the Virginia General Assembly did make it possible to TRANSPORT convicted slaves out of the state. By that means the lives of eight men convicted of participation in the aborted revolt were spared. They were sent to Louisiana under the provisions of an act of 15 Jan. 1801, which allowed the governor with the advice of the council to sell rather than execute condemned slaves—the purchaser to give bond to ensure that the convicts would be removed from the United States, and the transported slaves to be subject to execution if they ever returned to Virginia. On 15 June 1801 Monroe, at the legislature's request, wrote to TJ about the possibility of acquiring some location to which Virginia could transport condemned slaves. Monroe broadened the inquiry to include the subject of colonization in general, and TJ replied later that year, on 24 Nov. (Egerton, *Gabriel's Rebellion*, 151, 186-7; CVSP, 9:152, 156-9, 161, 164, 166; Ammon, *Monroe*, 188; Madison, *Papers*, 17:420; Philip J. Schwarz, "The Transportation of Slaves from Virginia, 1801-1865," *Slavery and Abolition*, 7 [1986], 216-17; Philip J. Schwarz, *Slave Laws in Virginia* [Athens, Ga., 1996], 103-7).

To James Madison

DEAR SIR   Monticello Sep. 17. 1800.

I now send by Bp. Madison the balance which should have gone from our last court by mr Barber: but not seeing him the first day of the court, & that breaking up on the first day contrary to usage & universal expectation, mr Barber was gone before I knew that fact.—is it not strange the public should have no information of the proceedings & prospects of our envoys in a case so vitally interesting to our commerce? that at a time when, as we suppose, all differences are in a course of amicable adjustment, Truxton should be fitted out with double diligence that he may get out of port before the arrival of a treaty, & shed more[1] human blood merely for the pleasure of shedding it?—I have a letter from mr Butler in which he supposes that the republican vote of N. Carolina will be but of a bare majority. Georgia he thinks will be unanimous with the republicans; S.C. unanimous either with them or against them: but not certainly which. Dr. Rush & Burr give favorable accounts of Jersey. Granger & Burr even count with confidence on Connecticut. but that is impossible. the revolution there indeed is working with very unexpected rapidity: before another Congressional election it will probably be complete. there is good reason to believe Massachusets will increase her republican vote in Congress, & that Levi Lincoln will be one. he will be a host in himself; being undoubtedly the ablest & most respectable man of the Eastern states. Health, respect & affection.

TH: JEFFERSON

44. D 53 c

RC (DLC: Madison Papers, Rives Collection); at foot of text: "James Madison." PrC (DLC); lacks sum at foot of text.

TJ sent by Bishop James Madison THE BALANCE of $44.53 to be transmitted to James Madison (MB, 2:1027).

A letter from Pierce BUTLER to TJ of 24 Aug. is recorded in SJL as received on 5 Sep. but has not been found.

Aaron Burr traveled to Rhode Island and CONNECTICUT in late August and early September, and while his first report on Republican prospects was optimistic, the Federalists won a majority in both branches of the Connecticut legislature. LEVI LINCOLN, a leader of the Republican Party in Massachusetts, was elected in 1800 to fill the remainder of Dwight Foster's term in the House of Representatives after Foster resigned. Although later elected to the Seventh Congress, Lincoln stepped down when TJ appointed him attorney general (Kline, *Burr,* 1:446-47; ANB).

[1] Preceding word interlined.

From William Short

DEAR SIR   Paris Septr. 18th. 1800.

I had the pleasure of writing to you on the 6th. ulto. & acknowleging your two kind letters of the 26th. of March & 18th.[1] of April—the first recieved from our Envoys here, the second from M: Testard of the flag ship arrived at Bordeaux—My letter was sent by the return of this same vessel, which probably sailed about the end of the last month, & will therefore if she arrive safe, have furnished you with that letter before you recieve this.—it is only therefore for greater caution that I shall repeat here several articles mentioned there—And first, my request not to address my letters to the care of Mr. S, as heretofore, but to that of Messrs. Deleport & Cie Rue Coqheron at Paris—Messrs. V. Staphorst at Amsterdam—& Messrs. Matthiessen & Sillem at Hamburgh—They will know how & where to forward my letters—& by their chanel the safest & speediest mode would be to make use of the English packets, both from America to England & from England to Hamburgh—or at any rate the last port.—   I sent you with my last letter such of the vols. of the Connoissances des tems, as had then appeared—the successive vols. shall be sent successively—I promised you in my last that I would send to you the *melanges astronomiques*, for the years 8 & 9.—You will recieve acordingly with this letter the part of the year 9.—that of the year 8.—cannot be procured any where—the stock is quite exhausted & Mr. Pougens as well as other booksellers to whom I have applied have hitherto searched for it in vain—As it is to be procured only by the accident of some sale, it is impossible to say when you can have it—But I have their promise to procure it if possible—& it is possible also that a second edition of that part of the work may be made, as the stock has been for some time exhausted—I am expecting also to recieve the vols of the year 11.—which will soon be ready—If in time, you shall recieve them with this—those of the year 10.—were sent with my last—I send you at present also a book which has been published lately in its present state, on the subject of Sheep—As it is by a man who unites practise to his precepts it is considered as valuable—there is a good deal of useful knowlege in it, but an affectation of the flourishing poetic style, gives a prejudice against it—There is no doubt however that the subject it treats of is one of the most interesting in the whole agronomical system.—I should suppose it peculiarly so in our country, & You will observe by this work the means of improving an indifferent breed of sheep & converting them finally into a race of the first blood—You are probably acquainted with the establishment made by the late King at Rambouillet, as it was in your time—The establishment has been preserved & has considerably extended the race of the Spanish sheep in this country—a certain number of the lambs are sold to the highest bidder every year, & as they sell high there is a certainty that those who purchase them mean to take care of them & preserve the race pure—There are besides, several private persons who have large flocks of this kind & find them extremely profitable as well from the high price of their wool as from the sale of the lambs—I know myself of three of these flocks of from four to five hundred within the distance of three leagues only of Paris.—The partisans of this business insist that the wool does not in the least degenerate in this climate—if it does, it is certainly in a small degree only & sells here regularly at so high a price that there can be no doubt the breed will become general—You may form some idea of the profits of this article here by this comparison which I take from a periodical work of great merit published at Geneva—In England the mean value of the fleece taken on fourteen of the best breeds there according to Arthur Young, is 6. livres 6 sols French money & that of the Spanish breed here nearly three times that amount—The authors of the work abovementioned, state in a late number that they procured last fall from Rambouillet twelve ewes of the Spanish breed,—they travelled from five to six leagues a day with bad weather & without accident, & each lambed soon after arriving at Geneva—They have been shorne this season, the fleeces of the ewes average six pounds French weight—& that of the Ram weighes eleven pounds—If he were to sell this fleece at the price he is offered for it, he would recieve 24.^{tt} 15. s—This breed is considered also as much more hardy, is much less subject to the rot, & preserves their teeth considerably longer than the common breed—Most of the breeds in France, as is here observed lose their teeth from five to eight years of age—this breed preserves them to fifteen years & sometimes more—The work abovementioned quotes an instance of an ewe at Nogent, brought from Spain in the year 86.—who had a lamb last winter & who still has all her teeth.—These qualities would be a great inducement I should imagine to introduce this breed amongst us, independent of the quality of the wool—As to the wool, it will be probably a long time before we shall find it advantageous to manufacture the superfine cloths which require the Spanish wool—but I think it highly possible that if this breed of sheep were introduced amongst us & properly attended to, that their fleece might in time be an object of exportation & rivalize with the Spanish exportations of this article—I ground my opinion on the following considerations—The method of producing this fine wool in Spain is extremely costly & prejudicial to agriculture from the vast quantities of land which it obliges to leave uncultivated on the route of the marching flocks—It will not be hereafter encouraged but rather the contrary from the complaints which are beginning to be made on the subject—The embarassment of the Spanish finances will for a long time oblige them to fiscalize on every article that commands money, & in that respect their wool in its production & exportation will be probably vexed & harassed—Besides the Government encourages as far as they can the manufacturing of this fine wool at home—Their politicians there see with pain this precious article go to aliment the manufactures of foreign nations & are pressing for premiums restrictions &c. &c. for the encouragement of this manufacture at home— Whilst I was in Spain the Government made considerable sacrifices to the establishment of this manufacture, & obtained very good cloth though at an high price—This will naturally bring them to throw obstacles in the way of the exportation of this article—Comparing this state with our situation & with the liberty of our productions & exportations, I should suppose that if this article were properly attended to with us we might in time enter into concurrence in foreign markets with this valuable article of Spanish exportation—It would seem to me that no situation would present greater advantages for this than Monticello & its environs—Colle & all that tract around & below it, which is considered as barren, would become a rich mine in this way—By means of our minister or some of our Consuls in Spain, I imagine you might procure this breed—If you should desire it, I would endeavor to procure the permission for the exportation by means of some of my old acquaintances there—I understand that this Government would be with difficulty prevailed on to admit of the exportation of these they have naturalized here—I have heard that a foreigner had been refused this permission—But I shd. imagine that a foreign minister might obtain it & I have advised one of ours to ask it & carry out some in the vessel they have waiting for them at Havre—I rather believe however he will not do it, though the opportunity is an extremely favorable one.—

You probably recieve the late publications in England on agricultural improvements—Their department of agriculture has given a rise & circulation to this kind of knowlege which must produce great effects. One is surprized to see what a variety of usages existed in the same little country, & how far some parts were behind hand with others—by the present measures the best methods will be known to all parts & become general—One sees also with astonishment notwithstanding the high improvement of British agriculture, what immense steps remain still to be made—the art may be almost considered as in its infancy—there are many things wch. would be incredible if not fully authenticated—You will certainly have seen the success of the farmer of the name of Bakewell, who has lately so far improved his breed of sheep for instance, as that he rented out a Ram to cover for one year for the enormous price of £1000. stlg.— Notwithstanding a part of this may be imputed to fashion or caprice, yet the improvement he had made in the raising of this animal was certainly immense, & shews what prodigies may be operated by the care & intelligence of man.

As I find that my brother attends to his estate I have recommended to him to procure some of the latest & best English publications on the improvements of agriculture. I have told him that you would certainly be acquainted with them, & taken the liberty to mention that I was persuaded you would if he decided it, point out the most useful to him.—As they will probably be to be had at Philadelphia I have authorized him to have them purchased by Mr Barnes on my acct. & forwarded to him—I have advised him at the same time not to adopt the systems prescribed in books, with too much enthusiasm, but to begin by degrees & to consider himself only as making experiments, until he should have fully ascertained that the prescription was applicable to his estate. It seems to me that is the true way to render book knowlege useful in agriculture.—I mentioned to you in my last that he found tenants for a part of his land in Kentuckey; a circumstance which I should not have expected in a country where land must be so cheap.—They are on the footing of a kind of *Metayers*— he recieves from them wheat, rye, & corn—he raises himself wheat & hemp—horses & cattle & has a flour-manufacture mill, & a distillery—& is employed in settling other tracts of land in the same way— If he shd. be able to find tenants, it would seem to me the best & most improving estate imaginable.

He writes me that he has come to a conditional arrangement with Harvie's agent as to my Western lands. The first agent or partner, Colo. Campbell, so contrived & neglected the matter, though he was to have an undivided third of the 15000. acres, that all his locations came to nothing—Of course my chance for the first choice lands, salt-springs &c. &c. which tempted me to make this purchase, has fallen to the ground—Harvie employed a new agent who could only make the locations two or three years ago, & consequently must have had the last choice—my brother refused to take these lands therefore, otherwise than on these conditions, which he consented to—that he shd. give his bond with security for the title & quality of the lands, & that in the case these lands did not answer the description, they should pay me a dollar an acre for the 10,000, acres—My brother informs me in his letter (of last November) that he was to meet them in a short time on the ground to examine the lands & decide whether he would take the money or the lands. He will be the best judge, being on the spot; but if I were to decide I own I should prefer the money to lands of the quality & situation which these must necessarily be— The option is of course made before this time; if in favor of the lands I shall probably request my brother to dispose of them or endeavour to exchange them for lands near him if he could be sure to find tenants for them, as for his.

I expressed to you in my last my thanks for the trouble you had been so good as to take in organizing the leases of Indian camp—It seems to me to promise so much advantage, that I think I shall be more & more satisfied with Indian camp—If such tenants could be found for the whole of the tract as those who are already there, & who should pay even as well as they do, there could be few placements which would please me better—for it would be a good interest on the money laid out & the most solid of all kinds of property according to my ideas—I asked you also in my last to apply the small rents recieved on Indian camp, to the clearing of other parts & building houses or huts thereon, if it would contribute to the procuring of more tenants.—I mentioned also that if this point could be secured I should be glad to have other small purchases made in the Blenheim tract or neighborhood, with the cash recievable quarterly at Philadelphia.—If a tolerable interest can be had & tolerably well paid on the cash laid out in such lands I should prefer it to almost any thing else—It is almost indispensable that there should be some rent in order to render the purchase not dearer than it would appear to be; because every year which produces no revenue is in fact so much to be added to the original price.—The rent present or probable on any given tract of land seems to me the best if not the only guide in ascertaining the value of it—And I therefore expressed my idea incorrectly when I requested you to inform me of the price of lands in the different States—I ought to have stated my idea to be the number of years purchase proportioned to the rent of the lands, or in other words the quantum of interest on the purchase money— Even this is not an infallible guide in all cases; of which the sale of Dover here by Mr. M. is a curious illustration. The purchaser paid for it £20000. stlg.—& Mr. R.M. obliged himself to take it on a lease I think of 9. years, at £1000. a year—Of course the purchaser considered the property obtained at twenty years purchase—It did not occur to him that in such a case the rent allowed by the seller on a lease for a term could be no indication of the real value of the land—Since one might afford in that way to allow an high rent on a lease for a term of lands, which he had begun by first selling for above its value—It is in fact saying, if you will begin by allowing me an high perpetual rent, I will allow you an equally high rent for the term of nine years.— I answered you in my last as to the two tracts of land on James River & informed you why nothing could be done with them here.—The best place for disposing of them will certainly be in the country where such lands have an high reputation. I am surprized to see that they have so fallen in that quarter—I should have supposed that lands there besides their annual production would have gone on gradually appreciating with the progress of the country—It was with that view that I had wished for Curles or Dover or some such estate. I should still think that persons on the spot, who would consent to employ slaves (as I suppose it impossible to find there proper tenants for agriculture *en grand*), might by introducing a new & intelligent system, improve the estates & augment the revenue beyond all conception—Take the Dover low grounds for instance & convert them into the best meadow—I am much mistaken if the hay cut thereon & sent to Richmond would not in a few years pay the purchase money of the low grounds so employed.—And every acre would produce still more if the hay were employed to raise a fine herd of horses—All the high ground might in time be converted into artificial meadow to alternate with other productions after some years—& then the meadow renewed &c. &c.—That estate well improved & covered with the best breeds of horses, sheep &c.—might be a principality in itself.—So it seems to me particularly when I consider what a variety of articles of the highest profit might be introduced there—One of the first should be *safran*—There is perhaps none which would yield so much Cash[2] on any given number of acres—& I am sure it would answer on the soil of Dover, from what I saw of it in Spain—It is cultivated also in some parts of France, & the produce of every acre is immense—It is cultivated also in England, & probably with more care as it sells higher at Amsterdam than that made in France—I shd. suppose it wd. answer also at Monticello; it would be worth your while to make the experiment—It must be of great importance for individuals as well as the public at large to vary the articles of culture.—The importance of improving one's estate as an augmentation of fortune is little known as well as I remember in Virga.—All those who aimed at an augmentation of fortune from agriculture were for adding to the number of their acres or their negroes.[3]—I have seen some agronomical calculations which induce me to believe it is not the most rapid way—Suppose two men with equal fortunes & capacities—The one pursues this route, viz. employs his disponible profits in the purchase of more lands & leaves them all in the same neglected state of improvement (this is the usage in France generally with those who aim at an augmentation of fortune)—With great care he may perhaps, they say, augment his property one third in the course of his life—The other on the contrary who should employ his disponible capital in improving his agriculture by all the means which cash & intelligence give, may double his fortune in the course of a few years—Although I concieve the advantage of purchasing more lands, greater in a new country than an old, yet I am persuaded that the owner of such an estate as Dover, for instance would for a long time to come find it more profitable to employ his capital & industry in carrying its improvement to the highest & most varied degree of culture, than in any other way.—As you are making experiments in this way, I hope I shall see my opinion confirmed by your success.—There is another article, & wch. I think you are aiming at, which I should suppose certain of success—the cultivation of the vine—If it should not be possible to make the best wines at first or if it shd. be difficult to find a market from the novelty of the thing, I should imagine it would answer to distill them as an affair of profit—It would be much more desirable however in a political point of view that the wine should be drunk—It would be a great point gained if wine could be made so cheap & common as with the aid of malted liquors to destroy the terrible abuse of the distilled, amongst us.—As to books on the vine, they must of course be French, & I don't doubt you have such as you have occasion for—Yet I am almost tempted to send you one which has lately appeared here—it is the tenth vol. of the Dictionary of Agriculture of the Abbe Rozier—& treats particularly of the vine—If I were sure you had the other vols, I should endeavor to prevail on the bearer to take charge of this notwithstanding its 4to. format—Should you wish for it or any other books be so good as to indicate them to me.

I expressed to you in my last my thanks for the statement you were so good as to send me of my affairs & the directions you had given on the subject to Mr Barnes—I wrote to him at the same time & sent him my address in order that he might forward me his letters, so that I hope to hear regularly from him, until I shall see him—My projected voyage of which I spoke to you in my last will be now necessarily deferred until the spring—particular circumstances render it impossible for me to leave my friend at this moment. I have been almost tempted to be silent as to this project of a voyage, lest it should prevent your writing. I should regret extremely the being deprived of your letters.—The mention of Mr. Barnes brings to mind the subject of funds—I know that the gradual re-imbursement of 2. p.ct of the capital depreciates the 6. pcts. in the eyes of most people—but it seems to me that it is an advantage to have a re-imbursement at par of a part of capital which is below par—provided the part re-imbursed be immediately placed in the purchase of more funds producing an interest—this seems to me a matter of demonstration—There is another observation also which I made, & that is that in general I do not think the funds bearing the highest nominal interest the most advantageous to possess, as for instance our 8. pcts.—because in the case of government's ever tampering with the funds, it is most probable they will begin with them—I do not mean to apply this observation to the original subscription to the 8 pct loan already made, but to the idea of disposing of my 6. & 3. pcts. to convert them into the 8. pcts.—   As to the canal shares; the accident which has happened to that undertaking is one of these chances which are inevitable in such things & ought to occasion no regret for the past—it is a lesson for the future & teaches that in such cases it will be best hereafter to wait until the work be completed before taking an interest in it—This was one of the speculations which pleased me the most, & I should still think that with intelligence the canal may be rendered highly productive—the great point is the employing the best & most-economical means for perfecting such a work—I apprehend that a skilful & experienced director or engineer will be difficult to be procured.   I say nothing here of the affair with Colo. Skipwith, because I have already said so much on it in my preceeding letters & particularly the last—My brother will endeavor to obtain from him some statement or acct. of his agency, which I have hitherto never been able to do.—On the subject of the 9. M dol. I had some thought of writing to Mr. Marshall on hearing he was Sec. of State—but I have postponed it hitherto—I should hope it would be settled by this time, though I saw with pain by your last, that the Government seemed now to make it dependent on the decision of a question between them & ER.—I should suppose it impossible that that question should be decided so as to prejudice me, yet I have long learned to consider the clearest points as questionable when dependent on the judgment of man—The conduct of E.R. towards me, in insisting on being my agent is as cruel as it was criminal; for it ought to be indifferent to him to owe the same sum to Peter or to Paul; & there is a great difference in the loss falling on the public or on me—This therefore is meer wanton infamy on his part—I hope by means of your friendly care in this instance that I shall not feel the effects of this disposition of Mr R.—   I have never heard from you whether you recd. a very long letter I wrote you some years ago of the date of Feb. 27. 98.—It was sent by an American who has returned here & who tells he put it in the post office I think at Boston—It went a good deal on a subject to which I think it of importance that our countrymen should pay attention—that of slaves—I know none more deserving of their most profound researches—It certainly presents serious difficulties in whatever way it is viewed—I wish that Genl. Washington had considered it maturely—his example would of course have had great weight—I own I do not think the manner, in which he has cut the Gordian knot,—the most advantageous either in policy or humanity—The turning a number of people, (grown up in chains) all at once loose on the wide world, seems to me at least impolitic—Would it not have been better for all if he had gone more gradually to work—To have provided for instance for their being in the hands of good masters—for the manumission of such as had shewn a capacity for self government—for the apprenticeship of the young &c. &c.—And in fine if he had established a permanent & productive fund vested in some corporate body (for wch. he might have obtained an act of the legislature) for the purchase & manumission & young women prior to their marriage—As this would have freed all their descendants, & as they would have been in a state of freedom, it would have gone in an increasing ratio—It is moreover highly probable if a fund of this sort had been established under the appellation of the Washington fund, & under legislative protection, that many people would have contributed to it, by imitation, who would of themselves never have thought of it—If Genl. Washington had left some such example, it is probable according to my way of seeing at least, that it would not have been the least important of the services for which his country has given him credit, & humanity at least would have erected him an altar.—   As it will probably be a long time before the legislatures of the Southern States will take up the subject of slavery on a wide political scale, it would seem to me that influential individuals, might in the mean time do good by proper examples—A great deal of useful information might be obtained on this head from the Northern parts of Europe, & particularly from the Holstein, if our public agents in those quarters were directed to turn their observation to that subject—Whilst we were multiplying foreign ministers I am sorry one of them was not sent to Copenhagen, not only as the best school of the doctrine of neutral rights, but also as the best position for learning the condition of persons in servitude, & the different circumstances respecting them— Besides the King of Denmark is now engaged in changing the condition of Serfs in the Holstein, a province whose privileges are respectable & respected, & of course this is a point of contact the more with us, as the general government is obliged to concert this measure with the provincial—It must be observed however that they are a degree before us, as they are converting the condition of their Serfs into a state of freedom, whilst we have to begin by aiming at a conversion of the condition of our slaves into that of serfs.—I am told that with respect to their serfs there were fixed rules which the owners were obliged to observe, as to their treatment, the hours of their labor &c. so that their condition was a paradise in comparison with our slaves, over & above the great & essential point of being fixed to the soil, so as never to be exposed to be put up at sale & separated from husbands, wives, & children, like cattle sold at a market.— Would it not be possible to obtain of the legislature an act somewhat of this nature—viz. which should authorize such persons as should chuse it to attach their slaves to the glebe, so as to avoid the horrible expectations, of being sold & dispersed by heirs or creditors—As the owners are authorized by law to set them free, I do not see why the legislature should not grant this lesser permission,—Many would profit of this who do not of the other, & humanity would certainly gain.—

I have long wished that the attention of our foreign agents were directed not only to meer news-monging, but to all such subjects & matters in the country where they reside, as might be transplanted & contribute to our improvement—There is a great variety of such from North to South, & I think I could draw up with time such permanent instructions as ought to be delivered to each & be a *vade mecum*. The subject should be divided so as to comprehend in a clear & separate point of view the animal & vegetable Kingdoms &c.—Whilst I were employed my situation was never one moment stable or satisfactory, & my mind never therefore in such a state as admitted of the doing all which ought to have been done. I saw then however & see still more clearly now the best road, although it were not then in my power to follow it. Others who will begin later[4] will I don't doubt see as well & follow it better.— It is time that I put an end to this long letter; but I cannot do it without repeating here my request that you would not be at all uneasy on the subject mentioned in your last. It is of no kind of inconvenience to me that the sum should remain in your hands—I have no placement at this time which would be so agreeable to me on every account, & this is peculiarly so from the idea that it is suitable to you.—I beg you therefore my dear Sir, not to let it give you one half moment's uneasiness, & to be persuaded that I should be dissatisfied with myself if I were to be, however indirectly, the means of your putting yourself to any kind of inconvenience.   I take the liberty of inclosing you two letters—one for my brother—the other from a person whom you probably recollect having seen often with Mde. D'Enville—As he is an extremely worthy man & I wish much to oblige him I hope you will excuse the trouble I give you on this subject which is of great importance to him—It is a power of attorney for his brother which he has sent me from the country & requested me to inclose to him with a letter which accompanies it—his brother resided a long time at Norfolk—he knows not whether he be there at present or returned to S. Domingue—I beg you therefore to be so good as to ascertain whether he be at Norfolk before sending the power of attorney there—this may be done I imagine by some person on the spot— Should he be gone from thence, then I beg you to be so good as to inclose the letter & power of attorney together & to send it by the best conveyance to be had, addressed thus "Au Citn. Patricot—sur l'habitation Patricot—Canton d'Ennery, Paroisse de la Marmelade St. Domingue."—It will crown all your kindness in this affair if you would be so good as to let me know as soon as possible what has been done with this letter & packet & whither directed.—   I have only one more favor to ask & that is that you would excuse this long letter & all the trouble I give you, & be assured of the sentiments of affectionate gratitude with wch. I am, my dear Sir,

Your friend & servant   W: SHORT

P.S. Sep. 29.—When I began this letter I did not know whether it would go by an American who then talked of setting out, or by the return of our Envoys who were drawing their business to a close— this latter circumstance having first taken place I shall make use of their offer to take charge of my letters—they set out in two or three days, as Mr Davie has just informed me.—I join to the books mentioned above for you, the Connoissances des Tems pour l'an 11.—& a pamphlet containing an instruction relative to wine-making— It has just appeared & is much approved here—I think you have Daubentons book on sheep, which had celebrity whilst you were here, otherwise I would send it to you—As I take it forgranted the treaty just concluded will be ratified, although I am unacquainted with its contents, I suppose the commercial intercourse between the two countries will be renewed immediately, & of course if there be any books which you may desire to have from hence, I shall be able to send them to you, immediately on your indicating them—I count also on this intercourse for facilitating my voyage in the spring, as I suppose there will be vessels here as early as I should wish to embark—In my absence M. Pougens will procure & furnish you with whatever you may want in this way, as you know.—I have reflected on the proposition which you made in your last of my sending a new power of attorney joint to you & Mr Barnes together, so that it might survive to the one in case of the death of the other—I suspend it until I shall have the pleasure of seeing you or hearing from you again—It seems to me that it would a greater power than I should wish to give to a person in Mr Barnes' situation, being in a line where great accidents happen, & where sometimes the most honest men may do injury, without intention when they have the capitals of others at their absolute disposal—I make this observation only by the way, & will adhere notwithstanding to your proposal if you still desire it—This makes me recollect a circumstance in the acct. of Mr Barnes wch. you sent me; namely that on the 1st of Jany. there was a trifling balance in his hands, wch. was increased on the 5th. of Feby. & on the 1st. of April was 1200. doll. & was not employed—It is not always easy perhaps to find funds for small sums, but I am told it is necessary from time to time to push these bankers who have your funds to dispose of—It might facilitate Mr Barnes if you were to authorize him to purchase bank stock also as that is at market always in small parcels—the share of the U.S. bank is I believe about 500. d. and that of other banks perhaps smaller— by this means even small sums need not lye idle in his hands, but he may purchase immediately on recieving each quarters interest—in this way it becomes compound interest as it were—Excuse, my dear Sir, these minutiæ; & believe me, that I would not trouble you with them, if I were not Yours affectionately   W.S.

RC (PHi); at foot of first page: "Thomas Jefferson, Vice President of the U.S."; endorsed by TJ as received 15 Dec. and so recorded in SJL. FC (DLC: Short Papers); a summary in Short's epistolary record. Enclosures: (1) Short to Peyton Short, 9 Sep. 1800 (FC in same). (2) Unlocated letter to Patricot in the United States from his brother in France, with power of attorney (see TJ to Patricot, 20 Dec. 1800, 24 Jan. 1801).

According to a notation in the FC, the recent book ON THE SUBJECT OF SHEEP was *Observations Pratiques sur les Bêtes à Laine* by Jean Marie Heurtault de Lamerville (Paris, 1800), a new edition of a work first published in 1786. The merino flock at the French royal estate of RAM-BOUILLET originated with Louis XVI's purchase of several hundred of the sheep from Spain in 1786 (G. Lenotre, *Le Château de Rambouillet: Six Siècles d'His-toire* [Paris, 1930], 93-4).

Robert BAKEWELL of Dishley, Leices-tershire, who died in 1795, earned fame for his selective breeding and innovations in the care of sheep, cattle, and other live-stock (DNB).

James M. Marshall was the MR. M. in-volved in the sale in Europe of the Vir-ginia land tract called Dover. MR. R.M. was his father-in-law, Robert Morris (Ellis Paxson Oberholtzer, *Robert Morris: Patriot and Financier* [New York, 1903], 266-7, 321-2; Marshall, *Papers*, 3:80; TJ to Short, 13 Apr. 1800).

DICTIONARY OF AGRICULTURE: François Rozier edited the early volumes of the *Cours Complet d'Agriculture Théorique, Pratique, Economique . . . ou Dictionnaire Universaire d'Agriculture*, parts of which first appeared in the 1780s. The tenth volume was published in Paris in 1800. See also Sowerby, No. 787.

ER: Edmund Randolph. AMERICAN WHO HAS RETURNED HERE: probably Stephen Higginson, Jr.; see Vol. 30:154n, 475, 482n.

The will of George WASHINGTON in-cluded the well-known provision that any slaves owned in his name would be freed upon his widow's death (Fitzpatrick, *Writings*, 37:276-7).

Through dynastic succession and diplomatic bargaining, HOLSTEIN be-longed to DENMARK, where reforms insti-tuted in 1788 and completed in 1800 abolished the compulsory labor system that had tied farm workers to particular estates (J. H. S. Birch, *Denmark in Histo-ry* [London, 1938], 277-8, 292, 296-7; Knud Ravnkilde, *From Fettered to Free: The Farmer in Denmark's History* [Hurst, Berkshire, England, 1989], 42-3, 65-6, 69).

According to a notation Short made on the FC of Enclosure No. 1 listed above, he expected William R. DAVIE to carry this letter. Davie departed from France in Oc-tober and arrived at Norfolk early in De-cember (Blackwell P. Robinson, *William R. Davie* [Chapel Hill, 1957], 356).

The PAMPHLET concerned with WINE-MAKING may have been the Baron Henri François Joseph Chapelle Jumilhac's *Sur la Fabrication et le Cuvage des Vins* [Ver-sailles?, 1800]. DAUBENTONS BOOK ON SHEEP: Louis Jean Marie Daubenton, *In-struction pour les Bergers: et Pour les Pro-priétaires de Troupeaux* (Paris, 1782). TJ later owned a translation published under the title *Advice to Shepherds* (Sowerby, No. 794).

TREATY JUST CONCLUDED: by mutual agreement, the result of the negotiations between the French government and Oliver Ellsworth, William Vans Murray, and William R. Davie from April through September was a "convention" rather than a "treaty." The two sides had not been able to agree on whether the 1778 treaties between the two nations would be affirmed or a new treaty created. Bona-parte insisted that indemnification of American commercial losses be tied to confirmation of the earlier treaties—oth-erwise, the French argued, the United States was responsible for denying the pacts of 1778 and for any spoliations that followed the abrogation. The first consul also would not agree to any new treaty that did not give France status with re-gard to commerce and access to American ports at least equal to the privileges that the Jay Treaty had accorded Great Britain. In the end, the 27 articles of the Convention of 1800 deferred the issue of compensation for American losses, gave France most favored nation status with regard to access to American ports, pro-vided for the recovery of debts and the restoration of ships and cargoes not yet formally condemned as prizes, estab-lished rules to regulate future maritime captures, affirmed the principle that free ships made free goods, and included many of the provisions of the earlier treaties. The document bore an official date of 30 Sep. but was signed first on 1 Oct., then again on 3 Oct. to recognize late changes. On the latter occasion Bona-parte presided over a great commemora-tive ceremony at Môrtefontaine, the es-tate of his brother Joseph, who had participated in the negotiations (Elkins and McKitrick, *Age of Federalism*, 682-7; DeConde, *Quasi-War*, 256-7; for the text of the convention, see ASP, *Foreign Relations*, 2:295-301, or DeConde, *Quasi-War*, 351-72).

ACCT. OF MR BARNES: Statement of John Barnes's Account with William Short, enclosed in TJ's letter of 13 Apr. 1800.

[1] Thus in MS, but Short meant TJ's letter of 13 Apr. He made the same error in the FC.

[2] Word interlined.

[3] Preceding three words interlined.

[4] Preceding two words interlined in place of "follow me."

To James Monroe

DEAR SIR   Monticello Sep. 20. 1800.

Mr. Craven, who was here at the receipt of your favor of the 15th. & will probably be here a week longer, desires me to inform you that he communicates by this day's post, your terms to mr Darrelle, and that he is thoroughly persuaded he will accede to them. he is very anxious you should retain the lands for Darrelle, who is his father in law, and whose removal into the neighborhood is therefore much wished for by him.

Where to stay the hand of the executioner is an important question. those who have escaped from the immediate danger, must have feelings which would dispose them to extend the executions. even here, where every thing has been perfectly tranquil, but[1] where a familiarity with slavery, and a possibility of danger from that quarter prepare the general mind for some severities, there is a strong sentiment that there has been hanging enough. the other states & the world at large will for ever condemn us if we indulge a principle of revenge, or go one step beyond absolute necessity. they cannot lose sight of the rights of the two parties, & the object of the unsuccessful one. our situation is indeed a difficult one: for I doubt whether these people can ever be permitted to go at large among us with safety. to reprieve them and keep them in prison till the meeting of the legislature will encourage efforts for their release. is there no fort & garrison of the state or of the Union, where they could be confined, & where the presence of the garrison would[2] preclude all ideas of attempting a rescue. surely the legislature would pass a law for their exportation, the proper measure on this & all similar occasions? I hazard these thoughts for your own consideration only, as I[3] should be unwilling to be quoted in the case; you will doubtless hear the sentiments of other persons & places, and will thence be enabled to form a better judgment on the whole than any of us singly & in a solitary situation. Health, respect & affection.   TH: JEFFERSON

RC (DLC: Monroe Papers); at foot of text: "Governor Monroe." PrC (DLC).

[1] Word interlined in place of "and," and TJ canceled "renders" after "quarter" later in the sentence.

[2] TJ here canceled "prevent."

[3] TJ apparently first wrote "and," then erased the word and substituted "as I." PrC: "as I" interlined in place of "and."

From George Jefferson

DEAR SIR,   Richmond 22d. Septr. 1800.

The long delayed (to say the least of it) business of the nail-rod is at last settled.

Mr. Nicolson a few days ago paid me on account of it £20.19.3, which is *something* to be sure, better, than to have lost the whole.

I have got 4 boxes of the ointment, and given them to the post-rider.

I am Dear Sir Your Very humble servt   GEO. JEFFERSON

RC (MHi); at foot of text: "Thos. Jefferson esqr. Monticello"; endorsed by TJ as received 26 Sep. and so recorded in SJL.

From James Monroe

DEAR SIR   Richmond Sepr. 22. 1800.

This will be delivered you by Mr. Peters with whom you are acquainted. He was presented me in a very favorable light by Mr. Beckly. Unfortunately my situation as he pass'd thro lately to Norfolk put it out of my power to profit of his acquaintance, and the dangerous indisposition of my child deprives now of that pleasure. Our Infant is in the utmost danger & I begin to fear that we shall want that consolation wh. I was abt. to offer to the afflicted Mr. & Mrs. Carr. This business of the insurrection increases my anxiety. The danger has doubtless passed but yet it wod. be unwise to make no provision agnst possibilities. The subject too presses in the points of view on wh. you have been so kind as favor me with some remarks. 15. have been executed. Several others stand reprieved for a fortnight so that shd. any thing occur in the interim will thank you to communicate it. I will attend darrelle when ever invited so to do. yr. affectionate friend & servt   JAS. MONROE

RC (DLC); endorsed by TJ as received 26 Sep. and so recorded in SJL.

A Swiss by birth, the MR. PETERS recommended to Monroe by John Beckley

[161]

was traveling in the United States to explore commercial prospects (Gawalt, *Justifying Jefferson*, 191).

The Monroes' INFANT son, James Spence Monroe, born in May 1799, was sick after suffering from whooping cough and complications of teething. He died on 28 Sep. (Ammon, *Monroe*, 185, 187-8; TJ to Monroe, 13 May 1799).

From David Humphreys

DEAR SIR   Madrid Sepr: 23d. 1800

After a long suspension of our correspondence, I take occasion of resuming it by enclosing to you a Prospectus for the publication of my works. To this measure I have been induced principally for the sake of inserting among the others a Poem on the death of Genl. Washington, of considerable length, in which I have paid the tribute of gratitude & have attempted to do whatever justice my talents would admit to the Memory of that most excellent Character.

Mr. Henry Preble, a respectable Citizen of the U.S., will have the honour of delivering this letter. I beg leave to recommend him to your favorable notice & good offices. He has for some time past performed the duties of Consul of the U.S. in this Capital (during the absence of Mr. Young) & of secretary to myself, very much to my satisfaction. He wishes to be named Consul of the U.S. for Cadiz whenever a vacancy may happen, and as I think him possessed of the qualities necessary for filling that place with credit to himself & utility to the Public, I should experience a real pleasure in his obtaining the appointment.

With Sentiments of great consideratn. & Esteem I am dear Sir Your Mo: Ot & Mo hble: Servt.   D. HUMPHREYS

RC (DLC); at foot of text: "Mr. Thos. Jefferson, V. President of the U.S of America &c. &c. &c."; endorsed by TJ as received 8 Jan. 1801 and so recorded in SJL.

LONG SUSPENSION: TJ's last letter to Humphreys that is extant is dated 3 Jan. 1794.

PUBLICATION OF MY WORKS: Humphreys's writings, *The Miscellaneous Works of Colonel Humphreys*, were first published in 1790. In 1800 he delivered his "Poem on the Death of General Washington" as a Fourth of July oration for Americans living in Madrid and included this poem in the 1804 edition of his works (Humphreys, *The Miscellaneous Works of*

David Humphreys. A Facsimile Reproduction with an Introduction by William K. Bottorff [New York, 1804; repr. Gainesville, Fla., 1968], 149-87; Sowerby, No. 4449).

HENRY PREBLE was appointed U.S. consul at Cadiz by John Adams but was not retained by TJ. A 22 Dec. 1801 entry from one of TJ's lists of appointments reads: "Joseph Yznardi consul at Cadiz. restored vice Henry Preble a midnight nomination." Relocating from Spain to France in 1801, Preble unsuccessfully sought appointments as U.S. commercial agent at Marseilles, Nantes, or Havre. In 1801 Preble also sailed to Italy with his wife and daughter hoping to open a mercantile house in Tuscany (George Henry

Preble, *Genealogical Sketch of the First Three Generations of Prebles in America* [Boston, 1868], 265-6; List of Appointments, 5 Mch. 1801-23 Feb. 1809 in DLC: TJ Papers, 186:33096; Preble to TJ, 23 Oct. 1801 and 26 Aug. 1802 in DNA: RG 59, LAR).

Indenture with John H. Craven for the Lease of Fields and Slaves at Tufton and Monticello

This indenture made on the 23d. day of Sep. 1800. between Thomas Jefferson[1] &c of the one part and John H. Craven[2] &c of the other part witnesseth that the said Thos. for the considerations hereinafter mentioned hath demised leased & hired unto the sd J.H. five fields of land part of his tract on the West side of the Rivanna river in Albemarle aforesd containing or to contain 500 as: & one other field adjacent called the Infield & containing 40. as. which said five fields are to be composed as follows to wit, one of them to be called No. 1 is to consist of the Low grounds adjacent to the Shadwell ford & the cleared lands between the Park branch & the Milton road to make up 40. as. & of the Indian field and as much land to be cleared adjacent thereto as will make up 60. as. more, in the whole 100. as.—One other to be called No. 2. is to consist of the cleared lands now occupied by Thos. Morgan & as much more to be cleared adjacent thereto as will make it up 100. as. which clearings to make up Nos. 1. & 2. are to be made in the ensuing winter & the winter following, to wit of 1800. 1. and 1801. 2.—One other to be called No. 3. is to consist of what are now called the Outfield & Highfield containing 40. as. each & as much more to be cleared adjacent thereto as will make up the same 100. as. which clearing is to be made in the 2d winter after the next, to wit of 1802. 3.—One other to be called No. 4. is to consist of what are now called Franklin & Poggio fields & as much more to be cleared adjacent thereto as will make them up 100 as. which clearing is to be made in the 3d. winter after the next to wit 1803. 4.—and One other to be called No. 5. is to consist of what are now called the Longfield of 40. as. the Slatefield of 40. as. & the Parkfield of 20. as.—Which 5. fields of 100. as. each together with the Infield of 40. as. compose the farm now meant to be demised of 540. as.

As also 48. negro slaves, to wit Bagwell & Minerva his wife & Mary Virginia, Esther, & Bec their children, Ned & Jenny his wife, and Ned, Fanny, Dick, Gill, Scilla, James & Aggy their children,

[163]

Isabel & Aggy, Lilly, Amy Thruston & Eldridge children of the sd Isabel, Jenny the wife of Lewis, & Jesse Sally, Jamy, Evelina & one unnamed, children of the said Jenny, Doll & Thenia & Dolly children of the said Doll, Rachael, & Nanny, Abram, [Laza]ria children of the sd Rachael, Patty & her child unnamed, Mary & her child Suckey, [James,] Caesar, Toby, Frank, Amy, Molly, Betty, Belinda, Squire & Juno with their increase.

To have and to hold the said lands so described & the sd negroes to him the said John H. his exrs & admrs from the 1st. day of Jan. 1801. for the term of 5. years to be counted therefrom.

Yielding & paying yearly for the same to the sd Thomas & his heirs 1166⅔ Dollars in the gold or silver coin of the US. the 1st. paimnt to be made on the last day of Decemb. 1801. and like paiments on the same day of every other year during the sd term, with a power to the said Thomas of distraining for the same or any part thereof whensoever it shall be due or unpaid: and if it shall happen that the sd yearly rent & hire or any part thereof shall be unpaid for the space of one whole year after it is due, then it shall be lawful for the sd Thomas or his heirs into the premisses to reenter, & the same to have again, repossess & enjoy as of his former estate. And the sd John H. doth covenant with the said Thomas that he will yearly & every year during the term hereby granted pay to the sd Thomas the sd yearly rent of 1166⅔ D. reserved on the days herein before limited for the paiment thereof, and that he will pay all taxes, levies & assesments laid or to be laid on the sd lands, negroes & other property demised, by public authority & which shall become due for the [same] during the sd term: and it is covenanted between the sd Thos. & John H. that if it shall happen that the value of the gold or silver coin of the US. or the quantity of the precious metals in them which shall constitute the dollar be increased or diminished during the said term, or any other thing be made a lawful tender except the sd coins & at the rates now by law established, neither party shall take advantage or suffer loss by such change, but that the said rent may & shall be paid & recieved still in the same coins & at the same rates as now by law established, each party expressly renouncing for himself the benefit of any law which may be made to authorize such paiment or demand in such substituted money or money of substituted value.

And the said Thomas doth covenant with the said John H. that he will deliver to the sd John H. all the horses, cattle & hogs, now appurtenant to the said farm, to be inventoried & appraised at the time of delivery by persons mutually chosen, & all the corn, fodder, & straw grown thereon this present year: that he will sow in wheat all the grounds which were in corn or tobacco this present year, and will deduct 166⅔ D. from the 1st. year's rent in consideration of what the grounds sowed shall fall short of 200. as. the quantity which ought to have been sown in wheat but cannot now be sown, that he will clear one half of the lands to be cleared in every winter as before specified: that he will put Morgan's cleared lands under a good fence in the course of the ensuing winter; that he will build a proper dwelling house for the sd John H. before the day on which he is to enter into possession of the premises: and will remove the negro houses to a more convenient position in the course of the ensuing winter: that he will allow to the sd John H. during the term aforesd sufficient timber to be cut & taken by him from any part of the Woodlands of the sd Thomas adjacent for firewood, fencing, building repairs, & utensils for the use of the sd farm, and that his stock shall have free range in all the uninclosed woods of the sd Thomas on the same side of the river.

And the sd John H. doth covenant with the sd Thomas that he will keep the fences & gates on the premisses in as good repair as he recieves them, & so deliver them at³ The determination of this lease; that he will keep the Houses built or to be built In repair except Against the decays of time; that no one of the aforesaid fields No. 1. 2. 3. 4. or 5. Shall be put into Indian Corn more than once in the Said term Of five years; that each of the Said fields Shall rest from culture (except of clover Or peas) two years during the Said term of five years, neither of which shall be Next after a year of Indian Corn; & that he will not during the Said term put Any thing but clover into the Said Infield: that he will during the term, permit To the Said Thomas & to all persons having Occasion of Communication with Him or his possessions at monticello free & reasonable use of the Said gates and Roads on the premises serving as communications between the Said Possessions or with the public roads; that he will feed and clothe the Said Negroes well, & take care of them in Sickness, employing medical aid When necessary; & useing towards them no unreasonable Treatment; and That Should they be treated Contrary to these Stipulations, the Said Thomas Shall have a right to refer to disinterested arbiters mutually Chosen whether the lease Shall not be determined, & the conditions, on Which According to the existing Circumstances it is reasonable that It Should be determined; that he will in the last year of the Lease Sow fifty acres of read clover, & will Sow in wheat the grounds He receives Sowed in wheat, and Also one hundred Acres more Wheresoever on the premises the Said Thomas Shall direct, the Said Thomas finding Seed for the Said Additional

hundred Acres; that He will at the determination of the lease, restore Horses, cattle, Hogs & Utensils equal each article, in Value to that of the same Article as appraised and delivered to him at Its Commencement, and corn Straw and fodder Equal in Quantity to what Shall be delivered to him; And it is Agreed that he Shall not have power to Assign this lease or Any part of it to any person without the Consent of the Said Thomas And the Said parties do mutually covenant that all the Obligations, burthens And Benefits here in Stipulated in their own names Shall be binding on A Result to their Respective Heirs, Executors and Administrators in like Manner as if they had been Specially named in every Several covenant. In Witness whereof the Said parties have hereto Set their hands & Seals On the day and year first Above written   THOMAS JEFFERSON
                                                    JOHN H. CRAVEN

Signed, Sealed & Deliverd
In presence of
John Holmes
Jas. Dinsmore
Rd. Richardson

PrC (MHi); incomplete, consisting of first two pages only, with remainder of text from Tr; faint, with words in brackets supplied from Tr. Tr (Albemarle County Deed Book No. 13, Albemarle County Circuit Court Clerk's Office, Charlottesville); with subjoined attestation by John Nicholas, Albemarle County Clerk, that on 6 Oct. 1800 the indenture was produced in court, acknowledged by TJ, and ordered to be recorded. An abstract of this text, entirely in TJ's hand and titled "Extract from the lease of Th: Jefferson to J. H. Craven, of certain articles relating to the lands" is in MHi and likely dates from a later time.

The INFIELD at Tufton was not included in TJ's list of fields leased to Craven that is printed at 22 Aug. 1800. In the list of slaves leased to Craven, which TJ included in his farm accounts, TJ altered NANNY to "Nancy" (see facsimile in Betts, *Farm Book*, 60).

Letters from Craven to TJ of 23 Jan. (from Loudoun), and 30 Aug., recorded in SJL as received 31 Jan. and 4 Sep., respectively, have not been found.

[1] Tr: "of Monticello in Albemarle" in place of "&c."
[2] Tr: "of the County of Loudon" in place of "&c."
[3] PrC ends here; remainder of text from Tr.

To Benjamin Rush

DEAR SIR   Monticello Sep. 23. 1800.

I have to acknolege the reciept of your favor of Aug. 22. and to congratulate you on the healthiness of your city. still Baltimore, Norfolk & Providence admonish us that we are not clear of our new scourge.[1] when great evils happen, I am in the habit of looking out for what good may arise from them as[2] consolations to us: and Providence has in fact so established the order of things as that most evils are the means of producing some good. the yellow fever will discourage the growth of great cities in our nation; & I view great cities as pestilential to the morals, the health and the liberties of man. true, they nourish some of the elegant arts; but the useful ones can thrive elsewhere, and less perfection in the others with more health virtue & freedom would be my choice.—I agree with you entirely in condemning the mania of giving names to objects of any kind after persons still living. death alone can seal the title of any man to this honour by putting it out of his power to forfeit it. there is one[3] other mode of rewarding merit which I have often thought might be introduced so as to gratify the living by praising the dead. in giving for instance a commission of chief justice to Bushrod Washington it should be in consideration of his integrity and science in the laws, and of the services rendered to our country by his illustrious relation &c. a commission to a descendant of Dr. Franklin, besides being in consideration of the proper qualifications of the person, should add that of the great services rendered by his illustrious ancestor B.F. by the advancement of science, & by inventions useful to man, &c. I am not sure that we ought to change all our names imposed during the regal government. sometimes indeed they were given through adulation, but often also as the reward of the merit of the times, sometimes for services rendered the colony. perhaps too a name when given should be deemed a sacred property.

I promised you a letter on Christianity, which I have not forgotten. on the contrary it is because I have reflected on it, that I find much more time necessary for it than I can at present dispose of. I have a view of the subject which ought to displease neither the rational Christian or Deist; & would reconcile many to a character they have too hastily rejected. I do not know however[4] that it would reconcile the genus irritabile vatum, who are all in arms against me. their hostility is on too interesting ground to be softened. the delusions into which the XYZ plot shewed it possible to push the people, the successful experiment made under the prevalence of that delusion, on the clause of the constitution which while it secured the freedom of the press, covered also the freedom of religion, had given to the clergy a very favorite hope of obtaining[5] an establishment of a particular form of Christianity thro' the US. and as every sect believes it's own form the true one, every one perhaps[6] hoped for it's[7] own: but especially the Episcopalians & Congregationalists. the returning good sense of our country threatens abortion to their hopes, & they believe that any position of power confided to me will be exerted in opposition to their schemes. and they believe truly.[8] for I have sworn upon the altar of god eternal hostility against every form of tyranny over the mind of man. but this is all they have to fear from me: & enough too in their opinion; & this is the cause of their printing lying pamphlets against me, forging conversations for me with Mazzei, Bishop Madison[9] &c which are absolute falshoods without a circumstance of truth to rest on; falshoods too of which I acquit Mazzei & Bishop Madison for they are men of truth.—but enough of this. it is more than I have before committed to paper on the subject of all the lies which have been preached or printed against me.—I have not seen the work of Sonnoni which you mention. but I have seen another work on Africa, Parke's, which I fear will throw cold water on the hopes of the friends of freedom. you will have seen[10] an account of an attempt at insurrection in this state. I am looking with anxiety to see what will be it's effect on our state. we are truly to be pitied.—I fear we have little chance to see you at the Federal city or in Virginia, & as little at Philadelphia. it would be a great treat to recieve you here. but nothing but sickness could affect that: so I do not wish it.[11] for I wish you health & happiness, and think of you with affection. Adieu.

TH: JEFFERSON

RC (DLC: Benjamin Rush Papers); addressed: "Doctr. Benjamin Rush Philadelphia"; franked; endorsed by Rush. PrC (DLC); faint, with portions overwritten by TJ in ink, presumably, because of variations from RC described in notes 7, 8, and 10 below, sometime after he had forgotten some wording of the letter. TJR, 3:440-2; HAW, 4:335-7; L & B, 10:173-6; Ford, 7:458-61; and versions derived from them, transcription follows the emended PrC with variations from RC; also printed in EG, 319-21, where PrC was misnamed a Dft.

Oliver Ellsworth was still CHIEF JUSTICE, although in France on 16 Oct. he penned a letter of resignation, citing poor health. Adams received that document on 15 Dec. (DHSC, 1:123; TJ to James Madison, 19 Dec. 1800).

Horace's remark on the "irritable tribe of poets (or prophets)," GENUS IRRITABILE VATUM, is from the second book of his *Epistulae*, letter 2, line 102.

LYING PAMPHLETS: according to the

Serious Considerations pamphlet attributed to William Linn, Philip MAZZEI had related an anecdote to clergyman John Blair Smith of Virginia, who had since died, in which Mazzei and TJ passed a dilapidated church and Mazzei expressed surprise that the local people would let the building fall into disrepair: "'*It is good enough*,' rejoined Mr. Jefferson, '*for him that was born in a manger!!*'" (*Serious Considerations on the Election of a President* [Trenton, N.J., 1800], 13-14).

WORK ON AFRICA: Mungo Park, *Travels in the Interior Districts of Africa: Performed under the Direction and Patronage of the African Association, in the Years 1795, 1796, and 1797*, first published in London in 1799 and in American editions the next year. TJ's attention may have been drawn to the work by an anticipatory comment in William Short's letter of 27 Feb. 1798.

[1] Preceding three words interlined in place of "it."

[2] Preceding two words interlined in

place of "[when a]," and TJ first wrote the word that follows as "consolation."

³ TJ here canceled "kind."

⁴ Word inserted in margin.

⁵ Word written over a partial erasure, "[establish]."

⁶ Word interlined.

⁷ Word illegible in PrC, overwritten by TJ as "his."

⁸ Word illegible in PrC, overwritten by TJ as "rightly."

⁹ TJ first wrote "conversations with Mazzei & Bishop Madison" before altering the phrase to read as above.

¹⁰ Preceding two words illegible in PrC, overwritten by TJ as "hear <*of*>."

¹¹ Word and period interlined in place of a colon.

To John McDowell

SIR   Monticello. Sep. 24. 1800.

I find the sale of my nails [at your place] to be so very dull as to be no longer [an object.?] of those sent [through] [. . .] proportion were still unsold at the date of your last letter. as ready money must be paid for every pound of nail rod nothing but short payments for the nails can support their manufacture. I must therefore request you to return me by the first waggon whatever nails remain unsold, as I can at any time dispose of them here in the course of a [month?] or two. if delivered to Colo. Bell he will recieve them & pay transportation. I inclose you a short statement of our account, [which] you will be pleased to certify as to the quantity of nails sold [and list?] [. . .] [unsold?]. whatever balance of cash may be [. . .] be so good as to remit by any safe conveyance to [. . .]

Your very humble servt   TH: JEFFERSON

PrC (DLC); faint; at foot of text: "Mr. M[cDow]ell"; TJ later added in ink below his signature: "May 8. 07. a copy sent to mr Coulter"; with enclosure pressed below text on left side of same sheet obscuring part of closing; endorsed by TJ in ink on verso. Enclosure: Statement of Account with John McDowell, 24 Sep. 1800, entirely in TJ's hand and signed by him (PrC in MHi, letterpressed on same sheet as letter above, large portions illegible, with date added by TJ in ink below signature).

LAST LETTER: McDowell to TJ, 14 Feb. 1800. In the enclosed SHORT STATEMENT of the nailery account TJ included the payments of £34.13.9, £27.16.0, and £40 received from the Staunton merchant on 12 July and 24 Oct. 1798 and 15 Apr. 1799, respectively, the first brought by Archibald Stuart and the last by Jacob Kinney. The totals in the credit and debit columns are illegible, but in a letter to John Coalter of 8 May 1807, TJ reported that McDowell still owed him almost £50, plus interest. McDowell paid TJ $70 later that year (MB, 2:988, 991, 1000, 1211).

From James Madison

DEAR SIR   [before 25 Sep. 1800]

I recd. by Bishop M. the 44. D 53. c committed to his care. The silence which prevails as to the negociations of our Envoys, is not less surprizing to my view than to yours. we may be assured however that nothing of a sort to be turned to the party objects on the anvil, has been recd. unless indeed the publication shd. be delayed for a moment deemed more critically advantageous. As we are left to mere conjectures, the following, have occurred to me. The long continuance of the Envoys at Paris, of itself indicates that difficulties of some sort or other have sprung up or been created. As the French Govt. seems to have provided for the future security of our commerce by repealing the decrees under which it had been violated, and as the ultimatum of the Ex. explained by former instructions permitted a waver at least of claims for past spoliations, it would seem that no insuperable obstacles would be likely to arise on these articles. In looking for other solutions, my attentions have fallen on the articles contained in the Treaty of 1778. relating 1. to free ships freeing their cargoes. 2. to the permissions granted to prizes. 3. to convoys. That a difficulty may have happened on the first, is rendered not improbable by the late transaction with Prussia. the 2d. is suggested by the circumstances under which the stipulation was sought & obtained by G.B. & the 3d. by the late occurrences & combinations in Europe. Should any one or more of these conjectures be just, the explanation will also coincide with the reports from different quarters, which speak of the Treaty of 78 as at the bottom of the impediments, and if so it seems more likely that they would be found in such parts of it as have been alluded to, than in the guaranty which cannot be needful to France, and which her pride would be more ready to reject than to claim. I cannot but flatter myself, that your letter from Mr. B. is to be otherwise explained than by admitting the accuracy of his information. Mr. Dawson now with me has a letter from Macon of Aug: 15. which with apparent confidence promises of Repub: votes in N.C. and in general seems to be pleased with the present temper of it. As to S.C. I learn in various ways that there is thought to be no danger there, and that the adverse party openly relinquish expectation. From the North your intelligence will be later as well as better than mine.

Yrs. always & affecly.   JS. MADISON JR.

RC (DLC); undated; endorsed by TJ as received 25 Sep. 1800 and so recorded in SJL.

For observations on the ARTICLES CONTAINED in the 1778 Treaty of Amity and Commerce with France, see Madison, *Papers*, 17:411-12.

YOUR LETTER FROM MR. B.: Pierce

Butler to TJ, 24 Aug. 1800; see TJ to James Madison, 17 Sep.

To John Barnes

DEAR SIR   Monticello Sep. 26. 1800.

Your two favors of the 10th. & 18th. came to hand yesterday. the post which leaves Alexandria Monday morning gets here Thursday morning. a recollection of this may shorten the passage of our letters. mine of Saturday morning ought to be at Alexandria Wednesday evening & with you Thursday morning. so that 11. or 12. days are requisite for a letter & it's answer.

I will thank you on the reciept of my compensation to remit to Henry Sheaff of Philadelphia 154.70 D to Roberts & Jones (formerly Joseph Roberts) 406.32 D and to Gibson & Jefferson of Richmond 680. D. this being the method seeming most convenient to us both. as to draughts on Stamped paper, they are out of the question. our distributor living 20. or 30. miles off through a mountainous country, to hire a person & horse to go for a 10. cent stamp would cost me a half eagle. I write to those several gentlemen by this post that you will contrive them paiment in the first week of Octob. the time to which my engagements stood. mrs Key will also thank you to remit to Gibson & Jefferson in Richmond her 3d. & 4th. instalments.—it will not be necessary to remove my boxes to mr Conrad's till I go myself, unless they are in your way.—I am in hopes you find your new position agreeable. it can hardly be as much so as the old one. at our time of life we do not accomodate ourselves to new society so quickly as we should have done 30. years ago. to me the new residence will be almost as my own state, the manners, customs & some of the inhabitants familiar. I am with great esteem Dear Sir

Your friend & servt   TH: JEFFERSON

PrC (CSmH); at foot of text: "Mr. Barnes"; endorsed by TJ in ink on verso.

Barnes's favors of the 10th. & 18th., both recorded in SJL as received on 25 Sep., have not been found. Also in SJL, but unlocated, are letters written by TJ to Barnes on 5 and 13 Sep.

In anticipation that his quarterly salary payment would be available for Barnes to draw on, TJ paid Henry SHEAFF for wine

(MB, 2:1028). He wrote Sheaff a letter of this date that is recorded in SJL but has not been found. Also recorded in SJL are a letter to Sheaff of 2 Aug. and ones from the merchant to TJ of 9 May and 2 June, received on 9 May and 22 June, respectively. None of that correspondence has been located.

The remittance to ROBERTS & JONES covered nailrod ordered in July (MB, 2:1028; TJ to George Jefferson, 9 July

1800). A letter from TJ to the firm of this date and correspondence from Roberts & Jones dated 18 July and 3 Oct. 1800, received on 31 July and 16 Oct., respectively, are recorded in SJL but have not been found.

To George Jefferson

DEAR SIR   Monticello Sep. 26. 1800.

By a letter by this day's post addressed to John Barnes of Georgetown I desire him to remit you in the first week of October six hundred & eighty dollars. this is the mode which appears most convenient to you both. I have also desired him to remit you a sum of not quite 300. D. for mrs Anne Key & Walter Key which place to their own account, subject to their orders. I expect some stoves from Roberts & Jones of Philadelphia will shortly come to your address, which be pleased to forward by the Milton boats. Higginbotham's boats should have a preference when they are down, because of their care & responsibility. I am Dear Sir

Your's affectionately   TH: JEFFERSON

P.S. the boxes of ointment are recieved.

PrC (MHi); at foot of text: "Mr. George Jefferson"; endorsed by TJ in ink on verso.

From Joseph Barnes

Naples Sepr. 27th 1800

When I had the pleasure of addressing you Mr Jefferson, from Hamburg the 4th of March Last, I Suggest'd, that "all circumstances Seem'd to presage a change in the political affairs of the Unit'd States highly favorable to the Man of the Peoples Choice" Exulting as I do on the presumption from a calculation & Statement of the votes made & publish'd in the English Papers that my Said predictions will be *verified*, I Should violate my feelings & do injustice were I not to *congratulate* you & *felicitate* myself & fellow Citizens on the propitious prospect which Lies before us—for, adverting to the great influence of the advice & recommendations of the President on the Legislature, what may we not hope from him who possesses not only Such eminently *Superior abilities* but *disposition* to promote the happiness of his fellow citizens particularly but of the great family of the human race generally? as far as circumstances will permit—

Should the funding System be abolish'd, (the curse of every Country in which it is introduc'd) Should peace with the whole world be maintain'd, the Navy & Army dissolv'd & a well regulat'd Militia be effect'd, & one general, Uniform Liberal System of Education be establish'd thr'o out the Unit'd States on the genuine principles of *Morality & Virtue*, presided, *not* by fanatics, but by the most eminent Sages as the only *Sure means* of promoting & perpituating *true republican* principles & *Virtue* in the Unit'd States; 'tis *Mr Jefferson* who will have been the *cause*!—

Notwithstanding 'tis report'd here that the negotiation between our Envoys & the French Commissioners, a Paris, is, from Some obstacles arising from the existing infamous treaty with England, Suspend'd!, hope however a mutual good understanding will Shortly be effect'd between the French Nation & the Unit'd States; on which, Should the English recommence their unprovok'd Spoilations on the American Commerce, under the Presidence of Mr Jefferson, Knowing his disposition I rest Satisfied they will be promptly punish'd by the only Means of bringing them to their Senses, Viz, *Shuting all* our ports & *Sequestering all* british property, which if we pleas'd under present circumstances would Soon bring the haughty British Minister to his knees, to make prompt Satisfaction for past & present offences;[1]—hope however peace will be preserved.—

Permit me to Suggest from mature consideration & good information, having been well introduc'd to the Secretary of State & by him to the Vice Roy here, that a mutually & very advantageous commerce might be establish'd between the Subjects of his Majesty King of the two Cicilies & the Unit'd States, provid'd an Agent possessing the requisite powers & abilities was Sent here, for the purpose, especially Should the port of Naples be made *free* to the commerce of the Unit'd States; which I have no doubt might be effect'd by Such means.—

Knowing your disposition to patronize, merit[2] when in your power, I need not remind you, you will Serve me as Soon as circumstances will admit in the object Suggest'd in my previous Letters or Such other as you may deem me qualified—believe me, no circumstance could possibly afford me more real Satisfaction than to have it in my power to be useful in any degree to my fellow Citizen or the Unit'd States as the *approbation* of my fellow beings especially those of Native Country is the *Summit* of my *wishes*.—

Being aware of the great evils which result from foreigners filling the offices of Consul of the Unit'd States in various parts of Europe, who, possessing neither Common feelings nor interest with the Citizens of the Unit'd States, instead of protecting often conspire to *rob* them—This has been the case at Marseilles in France, of which I have been Specially inform'd—hope under the presidency of Mr Jefferson the cause will be removed by the appointment of *Natives* to fill all foreign offices who alone can have a common interest & common feelings with the Citizens of the Unit'd States.—

With most grateful Sentiments of esteem I remain Mr Jefferson yours most respectfully   JOS: BARNES

P.S. the Consul here is neither a man of business nor a Native—the Consul at Genoa is English, & at Hamburg, the greatest commercial City of Germany Scotch, at other places Irish &c—

RC (DNA: RG 59, LAR); addressed: "Thomas Jefferson Esqr. V.P. of the U.S. Philadelphia," with the city struck through and "Washington City" substituted by another hand; franked; postmarked at Philadelphia, 19 Dec.; endorsed by TJ as received 22 Dec. and so recorded in SJL.

The incumbents of the U.S. OFFICES OF CONSUL were Stephen Cathalan, Jr. (vice consul, Marseilles), John S. M. Matthieu (consul, Naples), Frederick H. Wallaston (Genoa), and Joseph Pitcairn (Hamburg); see JEP, 1:48, 52, 209, 249-50, 253-4.

¹ Remainder of sentence interlined.
² Word interlined.

From James Thomson Callender

SIR   Richmond Jail Septr. 29th. 1800.

I have not been able to get any more of the Prospect; but next week I shall be able to Send either the whole, or nearly so. I beg leave to inclose the Copy of a letter to W. Duane on the negro business. It contains some trifles, which may amuse. Governor Monroe has, last night, lost his only Son. It has come out that the fire in Richmond, within these two years, was the work of negroes.

I have the honour to be Sir Your obed servant

JAS. T. CALLENDER

RC (DLC). Recorded in SJL as received 2 Oct. Probable enclosure printed below.

ENCLOSURE

Account of Richmond Trials

[ca. 18 Sep. 1800]

The tryal of the conspirators is going on. Fifteen have been hanged. Three others were in the Cart, and had got about half way to the gallows, when they were intercepted by an order from the executive council. This was in consequence of a Petition that had been presented a few minutes before, by some Ladies of Richmond, who lived not far distant from the place of execution. perhaps you will suppose that the prayer of their petition was to save the lives of these wretches. but it was only that they might be hung *in some other place*, because the exhibition was offensive. I do not design to make the slightest insinuation at the expense of female sensibility, for the application for mercy would have been very ill timed, and I trust that it would have been refused. These men have not yet been hung. Several others are since condemned, and it is expected that there will be a general clearance upon the third of next month. Much blame has been cast, but I cannot say with what justice, and it is probable with very little, upon the baptists, for having put impracticable notions of liberty into the heads of these fellows. But this I can say with certainty; that one of the baptist Ministers who chanced to be upon the bench, acted in a very unaccountable manner. The circumstances are worth relating. You must observe that, by a very humane Law, no negroe can be condemned in Virginia to Capital punishment unless the Judges are unanimous in their Opinion. This gives the prisoner the greatest possible chance for safety. A baptist Minister acted as one of the five Judges, in the case of the negroe *George*, who was himself a *baptist preacher*, and the property of one Billy Burton. It was proved, by such evidence as had been thought Sufficient for the execution of other blacks, that this Minister of the Gospel of *peace* had made the following declaration to Wit; That he would Wade up to his hands and his knees, in the blood of the White people, rather than desist from the completion of his purpose. There could not be a stronger proof of guilt than such an expression. The four other Judges voted for hanging him. But his neck was saved by the negative of the fifth one. This fact, every syllable of which is incontestibly true, was stated in civil, but in plain terms, in the Examiner.

A prodigious racket was raised against the Editor, as if he had designed to insult the whole sect of Baptists. Thus you see that illiberal superstition, and the most rancourous prejudice, are not excluded from this state. On the tryal, a very curious circumstance occured. It had been sworn that *George*, the prisoner, was at a Meeting of the conspirators upon a certain day. His master, Burton, swore that, upon that day, and at the Hour specified, the man was in his service. This proof of an *Alibi* was said to be the Cause of his acqutal. Burton soon after the tryal was over began to recollect himself, and acknowledged, that his *alibi* was founded upon a mistake. Reports have been circulated that in King William, in Glouster, and in some other counties, numbers of the negroes had refused to work, but I believe that the story has been without foundation.

MS (DLC: TJ Papers, 108:18568); undated, with date supplied from internal evidence (see below); in Robert Richardson's hand.

In response to the petition presented by SOME LADIES OF RICHMOND, the executive council had the five slaves scheduled for hanging on 18 Sep. taken outside of Richmond for execution. According to a report in the Richmond

Examiner, George Williamson, a BAPTIST MINISTER, voted for acquittal in the case of the slave George, owned by William Burton. The trial took place on 12 and 13 Sep. The OTHER JUDGES in the case were William Mayo, Daniel L. Hylton, Pleasant Younghusband, and Joseph Selden. Referring to Williamson as a "quondam Anabaptist preacher," the article concluded: "It is to be hoped that the natural instinctive sense of shame, which even a dog is capable of feeling, will prevent this *humane* magistrate from ever ascending the bench again." Although Callender did not sign the piece, it was dated 15 Sep. 1800 from the Richmond jail. PRODIGIOUS RACKET: in the next issue of the *Examiner*, Meriwether Jones denied responsibility for the article, assured his readers that he had due respect for all religious societies, and described Williamson as an "old and respectable Citizen." (Richmond *Examiner*, 16, 19 Sep. 1800; Egerton, *Gabriel's Rebellion*, 87-8, 92).

A Course of Reading for Joseph C. Cabell

A course of English History—recommended by Mr. Jefferson.

Rapin to the end of Stephen.
Ld. Lyttleton's Henry II.
Rapin's R. 1. John. H. 3. E. 1.
Edward 2. by E.F.
        by Sr. Thos. More.
E. 3. R. 2. H. 4. 5. 6. Rapin.
E. 4. Habington.
E. 5. R. 3. Sr. Thos. Moor.
R. 3. Rapin.
Henry VII. Ld. Bacon.
Henry 8. Ld. Herbert of Cherbury.
E. 6. his own journal.
E. 6. Mary Bp. of Hereford.
Eliz. Cambden.
    the Stewarts. Mc.Caulay.
                  Clarendon.
                  Ludlow.
                  Burnet.
Wm. & Mary   Burnet.
                  Dalrymple.
Wm. & M. to G. 3. Belsham.
Geo: 3. first 10 years. Burke.
Scotland. Robertson.
Ireland. Warner.
        Septr. 1800.
= = = = = = = = = = = = = = = = = =
A List of Books on various subjects recommended to a young man by
    Mr. Jefferson.
Antient Potter's antiquities of Greece 2. v. 8vo.

[176]

History. Histoire Ancienne de Milot. 4. vol. 12mo.

Voiages d'Anacharsis. 8. v. 8vo.

Livy.

Sallust.

Caesar.

Florus.

Plutarch.

Cornelius Nepos.

Middleton's life of Cicero.

Tacitus.

Suetonius.

Xiphilinus.

Herodian.

Gibbon's history. 12. v. 8vo.

Vie privee des Romains par D'arnay. 12mo.

Kennet's antiquities

Mallet's Northern Antiquities. 2. v. 8vo.

Priestley's historical Chart.

Priestley's biographical Chart.

Dictionnaire historique par Lavocat 4. v. 12mo.

Modern
History. Histoire moderne de Milot. 5. v. 12mo.

Tablettes Chronologiques de l'histoire universelle par
　　Langlet du Fresnoy. 2. v. 8vo.

Marianna's history of Spain.

Revolutions de Portugal de Vertot. 12mo.

Histoire de France de Millot. 3. v. 12mo.

Davila's history of France.

Memoires de Sully. 8. v. 12mo.

Robertson's Charles. V.

Watson's Philip II. 3. v. 8vo.

Watson & Thompson's Philip III. 2. v. 8vo.

Oeuvres de Frederic roi de Prusse, 17. v. 8vo.

British. Baxter's history of England. 1. vol: 4to.

Hume's hist: of England. 8. v. 8vo.

Macaulay's hist. of the Stewarts.

Ld. Clarendon's revolution. 6. v. 8vo.

Ludlow's memoirs. 3. v. 8vo.

Burnet's history of his own times 6. v. 8vo.

Belsham's history of Wm. Anne, & the Brandenburgs.
　　5. v. 8vo.

Burke's hist: of G III. 8vo.

Ld. Orrery's history of England. 2. v. 12mo.

Robertson's history of Scotland. 2. v. 8vo.

American. Robertson's history of America. 2. v. 8vo.

Douglass's summary of the British Settlements of America. 2. v. 8vo.

Gordon's history of the Am: war. 4. v. 8vo.

Ramsay's history of the Am: revn. 2. v. 8vo.

Belknap's hist: of N. Hampshire. 3. v. 8vo.

Trumbull's hist: of Connecticut

Williams's Natl. & Civil history of Vermt. 8vo.

Smith's history of N. York. 8vo.

Smith's history of Jersey. 8vo.

Proud's history of Pensylva. 2. v. 8vo.

Stith's history of Virginia. 8vo.

Keith's history of Virginia. 4to.

Beverley's history of Virga. 12mo.

Williamson's hist: N. Carolina (not yet pub:)

Hewett's history of S. Carolina. 2. v. 8vo.

Physics. Dr. Franklin's philosophical works. 4to.

Agricul-
ture   Dickson's husbandry of the Ancients 2. v. 8vo.

Tull's husbandry. 8vo.

Ld. Kaim's Gentleman farmer. 8vo.

Young's Rural economy. 8vo.

Kirwan on Manures & soils. 8vo.

Chemistry Lavosier. 2. v. 12mo.

Fourcroy. 4. v. 12 mo.

Surgery. Water's abridgment of Bell's Surgery. 8vo.

Medicine. Cullen's Materia Medica. 2. v.

the newest London Dispensatory. 8vo.

Tissot's advice. 8vo.

Buckan's domestic medicine. 8vo.

Cullen's Practice of Physic. 4. v. 8vo.

Cheselden's Anatomy. 8vo.

Natl.
history.   Linnaei systema naturae. 4. v. 8vo.

Histoire naturel de Buffon, & cepede. 75. v. 12mo.

Adams on the Microscope. 8vo.

Botany. Linnaei Philosophia botanica. 8vo.

Linnaei Genera plantarum 8vo.   ⎫ latest

Linnaei Species plantarum 2.v. 8vo. ⎭ editions

Clayton's Flora Virginica. 4to.

Minerals. Cronstedt's Mineralogy by Magellan. 2. v. {8vo.

Dachosta's elements of Conchology. 8vo.

Ethics.   Locke's essay on the human unders. 2. v. 8vo.

Stewart's Philosophy of the human mind.

Oeuvres de Helvetius. 5v. 8vo.

Progrés de l'esprit humain par Condorcet. 8vo.

Ld. Kaim's Natural religion. 8vo.

Puffendorf des devoirs de l'homme et du citoyen. 2. v. 12mo.

Ruines de Volnay. 8vo.

Locke's Conduct of the mind in search after truth {12mo.

Lettres d'Euler de Physique par Condorcet 3. v. 12mo.

Cicero de officiis.

Senecae philosophica.

Les moralistes anciennes par Leveque. 18 v. {petit format

Les maximes de Rochfoucault. 12mo.

Oeconomy of human life. 12mo.

Gregory's legacy. 12mo.

Gregory's comparative view. 12 mo.

Ld. Bacon's essays. 12 mo.

L. of   Vattel. Droit des gens. 4to.
nations.   Droit des gens moderne par martens. 2 v. {12mo.
Religion. Paley's evidences. 8vo.

Middleton's Miscelli works. 5. v. 8vo.

Priestley's Hist: of the corruptions of christianity. 2. v. 8vo.

Sterne's sermons.

Enfield's sermons.

&c. &c. this article is ad libitum

Politics. Locke on government. 8vo.

Sidney on government.

Beccaria on crimes & punishmts. 12mo.

Chipman's sketches on the principles of government. 12mo.

Priestley's principles of govt. 12mo.

Montesquieu.

De Lolme sur la constitution D'angl: {12mo.

Ld. Bolingbroke's works.

Burgh's political disquisitions. 3. v. 8vo.

Callendar's Political progress of B. 8vo.

Junius's letters. 2. v. 12mo.

Hatsell's Precedents in parlm: 3. v. 8vo.

Petty's Political Arithmetic. 8vo.

The Federalist. 2. v. 12mo.

Debates in the conventions of Massachesetts, Pensylva, N. York, Virga. 4. v. 8vo.

Franklin's political works. 8vo.

Anderson's history of Commerce. 6. v. 8vo.

Smith's wealth of Nations. 3. v. 8vo.

Distribution de richesses par Turgot. 8vo.

Hume's essays. 4. v. 12mo.

Vie de Turgot par Condorcet. 8vo.

Mathe matics. } Pike's Arithmetic. 8vo.

Cours de mathematiques pour la marine, de Bezout. 5. v. 8vo.

Histoire de math: par Montucla. 2. v. 4to.

Euclid.

Love's surveying 8vo.

Hutton's Mathematical tables. 8vo.

Physica Mathem. } Nicholson's Nat: philosophy. 2. v. 8vo.

Mussenbrock. Cours de Physique par Sigaud. 3. v. 4to.[1]

Lettres d'Euler de Physique par Condorcet. 3. v. 12 mo

Ferguson's mechanics. 8vo.

Astronomy. Ferguson's Astronomy. 8vo

Astronomie de De la Lande. 4. v. 4to

Geography. Busching's geography. 6. v. 4to

Atlas portatif de Grenet. 4to

Guthrie's geographical Gramr: 8vo

Morse's Am: Geography. 8vo

Travels ad libitum.

Poetry. ad libitum.

Oratory. Blair's lectures in rhetoric. 3. v. 8vo

Sheridan's on elocution. 8vo

Mason on Poetical & Prosaic numbers. 8vo

Criticism. Dictionaries. Grammars &c. ad lib:

Polygraphics L. Encyclopedie de Diderot et Dalambert, eds: de Lausanne 39 v. 8vo

Owen's dictionary of Arts & Sciences. 4. v. 8vo

Oeuvres de Rousseau. 31. v. 12mo

Ciceronis opera.

———

12mos are now about 3/6 Ster: in Europe

8vos about 7/.

4tos. about 18/.   Sept: 1800

folios about 30/.

in France they are about $\frac{1}{5}$ cheaper.

MS (ViU: Cabell deposit); in hand of Joseph C. Cabell; incomplete. Tr (H. Trevor Colbourn, "The Reading of Joseph Carrington Cabell: 'A List of Books on Various Subjects Recommended to a Young Man...,'" *Studies in Bibliography*, 13 [1960], 179-88). See note 1.

Joseph Carrington Cabell, who was at this time twenty-one years old, was an alumnus of William and Mary. Cabell was a legislator, visitor, and rector who labored for more than three decades on behalf of the University of Virginia (John Hammond Moore, *Albemarle: Jefferson's County, 1727-1976* [Charlottesville, 1976], 129).

[1] Text from here to end of document taken from Colbourn, "The Reading of Joseph Carrington Cabell," *Studies in Bibliography*, 13 (1960), 187.

From Delamotte

MONSIEUR   havre le 1r. 8bre. 1800.

Aprés que nous avons été si Longtems privés de moyens de correspondre avec l'Amérique, je Saisis avec joye une Occasion bien interessante de me rappeller á vous. C'est celle du retour de vos Commissaires, aprés avoir Signé un traité qui retablit les liens d'amitié qui éxistoient entre les deux nations & qui n'auroient point dû etre rompûs. Voilá donc ces liens d'amitié retablis dans un moment oú la france va reconquerir, j'espere, celle de toutes les nations, oú elle va pouvoir se livrer de nouveau au Commerce á l'exercice de son industrie & jouir enfin de la tranquilité qu'elle a perdûe pendans dix longues années. dix années qui tiennent lieu de trente á tous les individus qui ont survecû á cette terrible révolution. puisse cette harmonie entre nous & vous n'etre plus jamais interrompuë! J'ignore les articles du traité mais quelque qu'il soit, J'y prévois de grands Avantages pour l'Amerique qui est toute agricole, tandis que la france, dont le territoire sera probablement bien aggrandi, doublera ses rapports avec l'Amerique et par cette Augmentation de territoire & par l'Augmentation immense que recevra son industrie, puisqu'il faut aujourdhuy que tout le monde se livre á quelqu'occupation industrielle & proffitable. plus de biens de l'eglise, plus de faveurs de la Cour, plus de charges vénales, plus de noblesse. il faut que tout le monde fasse quelque chose d'utile. le commerce sera l'etat de tout le monde, tandis que nous n'attachions la Considération qu'á l'oisiveté. En verité, Monsieur, nous sommes bien changés de ce que vous nous avés Connûs; ce n'est plus la même nation, mais je me console, en esperant que ce Sera pour le mieux & je fonde cette esperance sur l'abolition de quelques préjugés qui etoient bien nuisibles á notre prosperité tant publique, que particuliere.

tous les Americains me disent qu'il est bien probable que vous Serés élû president des Etats unis, cette Année. Je ne vous en ferai point mon Compliment, je le regarde comme une chose toute naturelle, mais j'y prends un grand interet. Je tenois il n'y a pas trois jours la lettre que vous m'avés fait l'amitié de m'ecrire en 1795, la derniere que j'aye recû de vous, Monsieur; je la relisois avec émotion & me promets bien de la transmettre á mes enfans. C'est le gage d'estime le plus flatteur que j'aye jamais recû. & c'est de vous, que je l'ai recû! oui, Monsieur, je prends un grand interet á votre élection á la premiere place de votre pays. j'en prendrai toujours á quoi que ce soit, qui vous touche & mon attachement ira toujours de pair avec mon respect pour vous.

Je m'appuye si bien sur cette lettre pour compter sur votre amitié, que je crois pouvoir me permettre de vous dire ce qui me touche aussi. vous m'avés Connû lorsque je venois de perdre ma femme, qui ne m'avoit laissé que deux filles de son premier mariage, que j'ai eû le bonheur de bien marier. Je me suis remarié en 1793, avec une autre veuve qui a trois filles & qui m'a donné une fille et deux fils. tout ce monde lá se porte bien et fait á l'envi mon bonheur. du Coté de la fortune, je n'ai point á m'en louër, ni á m'en plaindre non plus. Il seroit trop heureux d'avoir pû passer ces dix dernieres Années, sans éprouver beaucoup de pertes. Il faudra les reparer maintenant & S'estimer heureux d'avoir encore quelque facultés á exerçer pendant la paix que tout nous fait esperer d'obtenir incessament. Il y a deux Ans & demi que j'ai donné ma demission au gouvernement des Etats unis. notre Constitution ne vouloit pas que les Citoyens françois fussent agens des puissances etrangeres & je voyois notre gouvernement d'alors prendre le chemin de Véxer les Citoyens françois qui persistoient á garder leur diplome. J'ai scû depuis, que tout ce train n'avoit été fait que pour exclure un ministre d'Espagne né francois & envoyé par l'Espagne en france, oú il n'a en effet point été recû. Il n'est pas douteux que notre gouvernement actuel agira differemment & quoique notre Constitution actuelle contienne encore Cette même exclusion, j'ai lieu de Croire qu'on ne refusera pas l'Exequatur aux Citoyens françois qui auront la Commission de Consul (ou d'agent Commerçial c'est le nouveau terme) d'une puissance etrangere. En effet, les Consuls ou Agens du Commerce maritime des nations, tiennent de Si loin á la diplomatie, que ce n'est guerre la peine pour la politique de faire ces distinctions & je n'ai jamais compris dans quel dessin la Constitution s'en etoit expliquée. Avec ce changement de tems & de Circonstances, je regrette d'avoir donné ma démission, parceque si je ne l'avois point donnée, il n'en Auroit, je crois, rien été. Je suis donc toujours bien au service des Etats unis & soit que je lui appartienne, ou non, je reste attaché de Coeur á votre gouvernement & á bien des hommes d'un grand mérite, que j'ai eû l'occasion de Connoitre, Comme Mr. Munroe, M. Gerry, M. Short, que j'ai le plaisir de Cultiver & de voir assés fréquemment á Paris. puisse-je avoir également quelques occasions de vous Cultiver, Monsieur, & de mériter votre amitié. je les saisirois avec bien de l'empressement.

Veuïllés Agréer l'hommage de mon attachemt. constant & de mon respect trés particulier.

J'ai l'honneur d'etre Monsieur Votre trés humble Serviteur

DELAMOTTE

EDITORS' TRANSLATION

Sir   Le Havre, 1st Oct. 1800
After we have for so long been deprived of ways to communicate with America, I am seizing with joy a very interesting occasion to recall myself to your attention. That occasion is the return of your commissioners, after having signed a treaty that re-establishes the bonds of friendship that used to exist between the two nations and which should never have been broken. Now that those bonds of friendship are re-established at a moment when France is going to reconquer, I hope, the friendship of all nations, when she is going to be able to devote herself once again to commerce, and to the practice of her industry, and finally to enjoy the tranquility that she lost during ten long years, ten years that were like thirty for all the individuals who have survived that frightful revolution. May that harmony between us and you never more be interrupted! I am unaware of the articles of the treaty, but whatever it may be, I foresee therein great advantages for America, which is completely agricultural, whereas France, whose territory will probably be greatly enlarged, will increase her relations with America twofold, both by this territorial increase and by the immense increase that her industry will receive, since now it is necessary that all devote themselves to some industrial and profitable occupation. No more church property, no more court favors, no more venal sinecures, no more nobility. Everyone must do something useful. Commerce will be everyone's condition, whereas we used to attach esteem only to idleness. Indeed, sir, we are very much changed from what we were when you knew us; it is no longer the same nation, but I console myself by hoping that it will be for the best, and I base that hope on the abolition of some prejudices that were quite harmful to our prosperity, both public and private.

All the Americans tell me that it is quite probable that you will be elected president of the United States this year. I shall not compliment you on it; I consider it quite a natural thing, but I do take a great interest in it. I was holding not three days ago the letter that in friendship you wrote me in 1795, the last one that I received from you, Sir; I was rereading it with emotion, and I promised myself to transmit it to my children. It is the most flattering token of esteem that I have ever received. And it is from you that I received it! Yes, Sir, I take a great interest in your election to the highest position in your country. I will always feel thus about whatever it may be that concerns you, and my devotion will always go hand in hand with my respect for you.

I lean so much on that letter to count on your friendship that I believe I may allow myself to tell you what concerns me as well. You knew me when I had just lost my wife, who had left me only two daughters from her first marriage, whom I have had the good fortune to see properly married. I myself remarried in 1793, to another widow who has three daughters and who gave me a daughter and two sons. All of them are well and they make me as happy as one can be. As far as wealth is concerned, I have reason neither to rejoice nor to complain. It would be too fortunate to have been able to spend these last ten years without suffering many losses. Now it will be necessary to make up for them and consider oneself lucky to have still some capacities to exercise during the peace that everything makes us hope to obtain without delay. It has been two and a half years since I gave my resignation to the government of the United States. Our Constitution required that French citizens not be agents of foreign powers, and I saw our government of the time taking the path of harassing French citizens who were persisting in keeping their commission. I have learned since that all that agitation had been made merely in order to exclude a Spanish minister, of French birth and sent by Spain into France, where in fact he was not received. There is no doubt that our present government will behave differently, and, even though our present Constitution still contains that same exclusion, I have reason to believe that the consular exequatur will not be withheld from French citizens who will have the commission of consul (or commercial agent, that is the new term) from a foreign power. Indeed, consuls, or agents of maritime commerce, are so far from diplomacy, that it is hardly worth the trouble for politics to make those distinctions, and I have never understood for what purpose the Constitution had spelled that out. With that change of times and circumstances, I regret having given my resignation, because if I had not submitted it, I believe that nothing would have come of it. Hence I am still very much in the service of the United States, and whether I belong to it or not, my heart remains attached to your government and to many men of great worth whom I have had the occasion to know, like Mr. Monroe, Mr. Gerry, Mr. Short, whom I have the pleasure to see and visit with quite often in Paris. I wish I had likewise some occasions to visit with you, Sir, and to earn your friendship, I would seize them with great haste.

Kindly accept the offering of my constant devotion and my most particular respect.

I have the honor to be, Sir, your very humble servant   DELAMOTTE

RC (DNA: RG 59, LAR); endorsed by clerk; endorsed by TJ as received 13 Dec. and so recorded in SJL.

LA LETTRE: probably TJ to Delamotte, 26 May 1795, which has not been found but was an enclosure to TJ's letter to Monroe of that date.

MINISTRE D'ESPAGNE: in refusing to receive the French-born Spanish banker François Cabarrus as ambassador, the Directory cited his nationality but was probably more concerned about royalist ties (Scott and Rothaus, *Historical Dictionary*, 1:137).

Delamotte had been made U.S. vice CONSUL at Havre de Grâce in June 1790, with Nathaniel Cutting in the position of consul after February 1793. Article 10 of the Convention of 1800 specified that each nation might appoint commercial agents (JEP, 1:52, 129-31; DeConde, *Quasi-War*, 358).

From James Madison

DEAR SIR   OCR. 1. 1800

Mr. Trist left with me yesterday on his way home, the inclosed pamphlet which I return to him thro' your hands, that you may have an oppy. of perusing it, in case a copy should not yet have reached you. I understand from Mr. T. who left Philada. on monday the 22d. that the prospect of a vote by Pennsa. was rather clouded by the uncertainty of the elections in one or two of the Senatorial districts. He seems to think that a favorable vote from N.J. may be expected. The idea collected by him as to Maryland in his passage thro' that State, is neither flattering, nor altogether hopeless. In general he speaks of the impression among all parties as strong in favor of republican issue to the main question. In the federal city he was told by Mr. R. Harrison, that late accounts had come to hand, which tho' not official were credited, that our Envoys in consequence of the form taken by the negociations, were on board the vessel which was to bring them home, and had refused the invitation of Buonaparte[1] to stay three days longer. No particulars whatever were explained by Mr. H. nor any indication given of the effect of the intelligence on the feelings of the Cabinet. You will do well in making your arrangements for the arrival of the Hessian fly among you next season. Many fields sown this fall in our neighbourhood, must be resown or given up for some other crop, and a little to the North of us the destruction is still greater.

Yrs. affecy.   JS. MADISON JR

RC (DLC: Madison Papers); endorsed by TJ as received 2 Oct. and so recorded in SJL. Enclosure not found.

MR. TRIST: Hore Browse Trist.

[1] Preceding four words interlined.

From Thomas Paine

Paris 9 thermidor[1] year 9

DEAR SIR   Octr. 1. 1800—

I wrote to you from Havre by the Ship Dublin Packet in the year 1797. It was then my intention to return to America, but there were so many british frigates cruising in sight of the port, and which after a few days, knew that I was at Havre waiting to go to America, that I did not think it to trust myself to their discretion, and the more so, as I had no confidence in the Capt. of the Dublin Packet, (Clay)

I mentioned to you in that letter, which I believe you received thro' the hands of Colo. Burr, that I was glad, since you were not President, that you had accepted the nomination of Vice President,[2]

The Commissioners Elsworth and Co. have been here about eight Months, and three more useless rascals never came upon public business. Their presence appear to me to have been rather an injury that a benefit. They set themselves up for a faction as soon as they arrived. I was then in Belgia. —

Upon my return to Paris I learned they had made a point of not returning the Visit of Mr. Skipwith and Barlow because, they said, they had not the confidence of the executive. Every known republican was treated in the same manner. I learned from Mr Miller of Philadelphia, who had occasion to see them upon business, that they did not intend to return my visit if I made one. This, I supposed was intended I should know that I might not make one. It had the contrary effect. I went to see Mr Elsworth. I told him, I did not come to see him as a Commissioner, nor to congratulate him upon his Mission; that I came to see him because I had formerly known him in Congress. —I mean not, said I, to press you with any questions, or engage you in any conversation upon the business you are come upon, but I will nevertheless candidly say, that I know not what expectations the government, or the people, of America may have of your Mission, or what expectations you may have yourselves, but I believe you will find you can do but little—the treaty with England lies at the threshold of all your business—the American [governmt.] never did two more foolish things than when it signed that Treaty, and recalled Mr. Monroe who was the only Man could do them any service. Mr Elsworth put on the dull gravity of a Judge and was silent.—I added, you may, perhaps, make a treaty, like that you have made with England, which is a surrender of the rights of the American flag; for the principle that Neutral ships make Neutral property must be general, or not at all.—I then changed the subject, for I had all the talk to myself upon this topic, and enquired after Sam Adams (I asked nothing about John) Mr Jefferson, Mr. Monroe and others of my friends, and the Melancholy case of the yellow fever; of which he gave me as circumstantial an account as if he had been summing up a Case to a Jury. There my Visit ended, and had Mr. Elsworth been as cunning as a Statesman, or as wise as a Judge, he would have returned my Visit that he might appear insensible of the intention of mine.

I now come to the affairs of this Country and of Europe. You will, I suppose, have heard before this arrives to you, of the battle of Maringo in Italy where the Austrians were defeated—of the Armistice in consequence thereof, and the surrender of Milan Genoa

&c to the french—Of the successes of the french Army in Germany—and the extention of the armistice in that quarter— Of the preliminaries of Peace signed at Paris—Of the refusal of the Emperor to ratify those preliminaries—Of the breaking of the Armistice by the french Governt. in consequence of that refusal—Of the *gallant* expedition of the Emperor to put himself at the head of his Army—Of his pompous arrival there—Of his having made his Will—Of prayers being put in all his churches for the preservation of the life of this Hero—Of General Moreau announcing to him, immediately on his Arrival at the Army that hostilities would commence the day after the next at sun rise unless he signed the treaty or gave security that he would sign within 45 days.—Of his surrendering up three of the principal Keys of Germany, Ulm, Philipsbourg, and Ingolstad, as security that he would sign them. This is the state things are now in at the time of writing this letter; but it is proper to add that the refusal of the Emperor to sign the preliminaries was motived upon a Note from the king of England to be admitted to the Congress for negociating Peace, which was consented to by the french upon the Condition of an Armistice at Sea, which England, before knowing of the surrender the Emperor had made, had refused. From all which it appears to me, judging from Circumstances, that the Emperor is now so compleatly in the hands of the french, that he has no way of getting out but by a peace. The Congress for the peace is to be held at Lunéville a Town in france. Since the Affair of Rastad the french Commissioners will not trust themselves within the Emperor's territory.

I now come to domestic Affairs.—I know not what the Commissioners have done but from a paper I enclose to you, which appears to have some authority, it is not much. The paper as you will perceive is considerably prior to this letter. I know that the Commissioners before this piece appeared intended setting off: It is therefore probable that what they have done is conformable to what this paper mentions—which certainly will not atone for the expence their mission has incurred, neither are they by all the accounts I hear of them Men fitted for the business.

But independantly of these matters there appears to be a state of circumstances rising, which, if it goes on, will render all partial treaties unnecessary. In the first place, I doubt if any peace will be made with England; and in the second place, I should not wonder to see a coalition formed against her, to compel her to compel her to abandon her insolence on the Seas. This brings me to speak of the manuscripts I send you.

[187]

The piece No. 1, without any title, was written in consequence of a question put to me by Bonaparte. As he supposed I knew England and English Politics he sent a person to me to ask, that in case of negociating a Peace with Austria, whether it would be proper to include England. This was when Count St Julian was at Paris, on the part of the Emperor negociating the preliminaries;—which as I have before said the Emperor refused to sign on the pretence of admitting England.

The piece No. 2, entitled, *On the Jacobinism of the English at Sea*, was written when the English made their insolent and impolitic expedition to Denmark, and is also an auxiliary to the politic of No. 1— I shewed it to a friend who had it translated into french and printed in the form of a Pamphlet, and distributed Gratis among the foreign Ministers, and persons in the Government. It was immediately copied into several of the french Journals, and into the official Paper, the Moniteur. It appeared in this paper one day before the last dispatches arrived from Egypt; which agreed perfectly with what I had said respecting Egypt. It hitt the two cases of Denmark and Egypt in the exact proper Moment.

The Piece No. 3 entitled *Compact Maritime* is the sequel of No. 2 digested in form. It is translating at the time I write this letter, and I am to have a meeting with the Senator Garat upon the subject. The pieces 2. & 3. go off in Manuscript to England by a confidential person where they will be published.

By all the news we get from the North there appears to be something meditating against England. It is now given for certain that Paul has embargoed all the English Vessels and English property in Russia, till some principle be established for protecting the Rights of Neutral Nations and securing the liberty of the Seas. The preparations in Denmark continue notwithstanding the Convention that she has been made with England, which leaves the question with respect to the right set up by England to stop and search Neutral Vessels, undecided. I send you the paragraphs upon this subject.

The tumults are great in all parts of England on account of the excessive price of Corn and bread, which has risen since the harvest.—I attribute it more to the abundant increase of paper, and the non-Circulation of Cash, than to any other Cause. People in Trade can push the paper off as fast as they receive it, as they did by continental Money in America; but as farmers have not this opportunity, they endeavour to secure themselves by going considerably in advance.

I have now given you all the great Articles of Intelligence for I trouble not my self with little ones, and consequently not with the

Commissioners, nor any thing they are about, nor with John Adams otherwise than to wish him safe home, and a better and wiser Man in his place.

In the present state of Circumstances and the prospects arising from them, it may be proper for America to consider, whether it is worth her while to enter into any treaty at this Moment, or to wait the event of those Circumstances, which, if they go on will render partial treaties useless by deranging them. But, if, in the Mean time, she enters into any treaty it ought to be with a Condition to the following purpose "Reserving to herself the right of joining in an Association of Nations for the protection of the Rights of Neutral Commerce and the security of the liberty of the Seas."

The pieces 2, 3, may go to the press. They will make a small pamphlet, and the printers are welcome to put my name to it. It is best it should be put. From thence they will get into the Newspapers. I know that the faction of John Adams abuses me pretty heartily. They are welcome. It does not disturb me, and they love their labour; and in return for it I am doing America more service, as a Neutral[3] Nation, than their expensive Commissioners can do, and she has that service from me for nothing. The piece No. 1 is only for your own Amusement and that of your friends.—I come now to speak confidentially to you on a private subject.

When Mr Elsworth and Davies return to America, Murray will return to Holland, and in that case, there will be nobody in Paris but Mr. Skipwith that have been in the habit of transacting business with the french Governt. since the revolution began. He is on a good standing with them, and if the chance of the day should place you in the presidency you cannot do better than appoint him for any purpose you may have occasion for in France. He is an honest Man and will do his Country Justice, and that with Civility and good Manners to the government he is commissioned to act with; A faculty which that Northern Bear Timothy Pickering wanted and which the Bear of that Bear, John Adams, never possessed.

I know not much of Mr Murray, otherwise than of his unfriendliness to every [. . .] American who is not of his faction. But I am sure that Joel Barlow is a much fitter Man to be in Holland than Mr. Murray. It is upon the fitness of the Man to the place that I speak for I have not communicated a thought upon the subject to Barlow, neither does he know, at the time of my writing this (for he is at havre) that I have intention to do it.

I will now, by way of relief, amuse you with some account of the progress of Iron Bridges.

[189]

The french revolution and Mr. Burke's attack upon it, drew me off from any pontifical Works. Since my coming from England in 92, an Iron Bridge of a single arch 236 feet span, versed sine 34 feet, has been cast at the Iron Works of the Walkers where my Model was, and erected over the river Waer at Sunderland in the County of Durham in England. The two Members in Parliament for the County Mr Bourden and Mr. Milbank were the principal subscribers; but the direction was committed to Mr. Bourden. A very sincere friend of mine Sir Robt. Smyth who lives in france, and whom Mr. Monroe well knows, supposing they had taken their plan from my Model, wrote to Mr. Millbank upon the subject. Mr. Milbank answered the letter, which answer I have by me, and I give you word for word the part concerning the Bridge. "With respect to the Bridge over the river Waer at Sunderland it certainly is a Work well deserving admiration both for its structure [. . .] and utility, and I have good grounds for saying that the first Idea was taken from Mr. Paine's bridge exhibited at Paddington. But with respect to any Compensation to Mr Paine, however desirous of rewarding the labours of an engenious Man, I see not how it is in my power, having had nothing to do with the bridge after the payment of my subscription, Mr Bourden being accountable for the whole; But if you can point out any Mode by which I can be instrumental in procuring for Mr. P. any compensation for the advantages which the public may have derived from his engenious Model, from which certainly the outlines of the Bridge at Sunderland was taken, be assured it will afford me very great satisfaction."

I have now made two other Models, One in pasteboard five feet span and five inches of height from the cord. It is in the opinion of every person who has seen it one of the most beautifull objects the eye can behold. I then cast a Model in Metal following the Construction of that in paste-board and of the same dimensions. The whole was executed in my own Chamber. It is far superior in Strength, elegance, and readiness in execution to the Model I made in America, and which you saw in Paris. I shall bring these Models with me when I come home, which will be as soon as I can pass the Seas in safety from the piratical John Bulls.

I suppose you have seen, or have heard of, the Bishop of Landaff's Answer to my second part of the Age of reason. As soon as I got a copy of it I began a third part which served also as an Answer to the Bishop; but as soon as the Clerical society for promoting *Christian knowlege* knew of my intention to Answer the Bishop, they prosecuted, as a society, the printer of the first and second part to prevent that answer appearing. No other reason than this can be assigned for their prosecuting at the time they did, because the first part had been in circulation above three years, and the second part more than one, and they prosecuted immediately on knowing that I was taking up their Champion. The bishop's Answer, like Mr Burke's attack on the french revolution, served me as a back ground to bring forward other subjects upon with more advantage than if the back ground was not there. This is the motive that induced me to answer him, otherwise I should have gone on without taking any Notice of him. I have made and am still making additions to the Manuscript and shall continue to do so, till an opportunity arrive for publishing it.

If any American frigate should come to france and the direction of it fall to you I will be glad you would give me the opportunity of returning. The abscess under which I suffered almost two years is entirely healed of itself, and I enjoy exceeding good health. This is the first of October and Mr Skipwith has just called to tell me the Commissioners sett off for Havre tomorrow. This will go by the frigate but not with the knowlege of the Commisrs.—Remember me with much affection to my friends and accept the same to yourself.

THOMAS PAINE

RC (DLC); torn; month in dateline corrected by TJ (see note 1 below); closing quotation marks of shorter quoted passage supplied by Editors, extraneous quotation marks in margin of longer quoted passage omitted; endorsed by TJ as received 6 Jan. 1801 and so recorded in SJL. Enclosures: (1) Untitled manuscript by Paine, referred to in the letter above as "piece No. 1," being a memorandum on whether France should, in making peace with Austria, take steps toward a negotiated peace with Great Britain; Paine mentioning the obvious answer in the negative, that Britain should be isolated from its last ally on the Continent and not allowed to use linked negotiations to its advantage and Austria's disadvantage; but going on to note the present weakened state of the British government from popular dissatisfaction with the monarchy, immense fiscal problems, and war weariness, arguing that instead of making peace France should go on the offensive, building a large flotilla of oar-powered gunboats to attack England's vulnerable North Sea coast from Belgium and Holland; Paine arguing that with such a strategy "the fate of the Government of England is decided" (MS in same; entirely in Paine's hand, undated and unsigned; endorsement by TJ associating the enclosure with the cover letter). (2) Manuscript, not found, of "On the Jacobinism of the English at Sea, and the means of preventing it," called "piece No. 2" in the letter above; presumably conveyed by TJ to Samuel Harrison Smith, who published it as the second of four short works by Paine collected as a pamphlet under the title, Compact Maritime (Washington, 1801), 10-15; Shaw-Shoemaker, No. 1087; Sowerby, No. 3242. (3) Manuscript, not found, of "Compact Maritime, Of an association of nations for the Protection of the rights and commerce of nations that shall be neutral in time of war," presumably conveyed by TJ to Smith; published as the third of the "heads" of Compact Maritime, 15-21, and called on the title page of that work "Compact Maritime for the protection of Neutral Commerce, and securing the Liberty of the Seas"; consisting of a proposed frame of ten articles for a pact of association of neutral countries; Paine's "piece No. 3" in the letter above. Enclosed in Stephen Thorn to TJ, 27 Dec. 1800.

Paine's letter by the DUBLIN PACKET was that of 1 Apr. 1797; see Vol. 29:340-5, 366.

Immediately before news of the battle of Marengo and the resulting ARMISTICE between the French and Austrian armies arrived in Vienna, Austrian officials had agreed to a treaty with Britain that prohibited either nation from making a separate peace settlement. The French demanded an ARMISTICE AT SEA as a condition for British participation in peace talks. Under the proposed terms, Britain would lift its blockade of French naval ports and also allow France to re-provision the besieged Mediterranean island of Malta, which actually surrendered to the British on 4 Sep., soon after the naval truce was proposed. The French also wanted to resupply their army in Egypt. Some negotiation over the proposed naval armistice took place, but ceased in October without a pact (Roider, *Thugut*, 339-40; Ehrman, *Pitt*, 384-6).

In August 1800 the French and Austrian governments agreed to hold negotiations at LUNÉVILLE, in Lorraine. The Austrians continued to insist on British involvement as those talks opened during the autumn (Roider, *Thugut*, 345-6, 351-5).

THE AFFAIR OF RASTAD: in April 1799, as a chaotic military situation broke up negotiations at Rastatt (Rastadt), a town on the Rhine where representatives of Austria, several German states, and France had met since late 1797, horsemen fell upon three homeward-bound French delegates, killing two of them and wounding the third. Although the attackers were never identified, some rumors blamed Austrian hussars and presumed that they had acted under orders (same, 258, 262-3, 282, 304-8).

Britain's IMPOLITIC EXPEDITION TO DENMARK took the form of a naval squadron sent in the summer of 1800 to the Øresund (known in English as the Sound), the narrow strait between Denmark and Sweden. The action was the culmination of a series of incidents in which Danish convoys in various waters had resisted searches by British warships. Although the British government also sent an envoy to Copenhagen to negotiate

a settlement, the appearance of the squadron prompted Denmark to mobilize its coastal defenses. Britain's show of force at the mouth of the Baltic Sea also moved Paul, the Russian emperor, to embargo British ships in his country's ports, confiscate British property, and invite Denmark, Sweden, and Prussia to join Russia in an alliance of armed neutrality (Ehrman, *Pitt*, 394-5; *Gazette nationale ou le Moniteur universel*, 23, 26, 27 Fructidor Year 8 [10, 13, 14 Sep. 1800]).

Nicolas de Bonneville of Paris was the FRIEND who put Paine's work into print, in pamphlet form and in the columns of Bonneville's newspaper, *Le bien informé* (Keane, *Paine*, 354, 435, 437-40). The MONITEUR published an abstract of the French pamphlet of Paine's "On the Jacobinism of the English at Sea" in September, just prior to the arrival of news from Cairo reporting the assassination of Jean Baptiste Kléber, the commander of the French army in EGYPT. Paine had argued in his tract that Britain shunned a treaty with France over Egypt in the expectation of displacing France in that region and monopolizing access to India (*Gazette nationale ou le Moniteur universel*, 18-22 Fructidor [5-9 Sep.]; Paine, *Compact Maritime*, 13-14; Tulard, *Dictionnaire Napoléon*, 1005).

Late in August the Danes agreed to a CONVENTION with Britain under which the latter nation would return some captured Danish vessels and Denmark would cease using warships to guard its convoys except as protection against Mediterranean pirates (Ehrman, *Pitt*, 394; *Gazette nationale ou le Moniteur universel*, 30 Fructidor [17 Sep.]). The PARAGRAPHS that Paine enclosed about Russia and Denmark were probably newspaper clippings; for a comparable instance, see his letter of 16 Oct.

WELCOME TO PUT MY NAME TO IT: Samuel H. Smith published the *Compact Maritime* pamphlet as Paine's work. The second and third items in the compilation, the manuscripts of which Paine presumably enclosed in the letter above, each included the subheading: "Addressed to the Neutral Nations, by a Neutral."

Beginning in the 1780s Paine experimented with the design of IRON

BRIDGES. The Walker Iron Works in Yorkshire had fabricated a bridge of his design that spanned 110 feet and was erected in a field in Paddington in 1790 as a demonstration. The bridge built on the Wear River at Sunderland on Rowland Burdon's initiative was completed in 1796 (Keane, *Paine*, 268-82; Philip S. Foner, ed., *The Complete Writings of Thomas Paine*, 2 vols. [New York, 1945], 2:1051-7; see also Paine's correspondence with TJ, 1787-89, printed in Vols. 12-15).

An Apology for the Bible, a response by the BISHOP of Llandaff, Richard Watson, to Paine on religious grounds, appeared in various English and American editions in 1796-97. In the latter year Thomas Williams received a prison sentence for printing Paine's *Age of Reason*. Paine's rejoinder to Watson was not published during Paine's life (Foner, *Writings*, 2:727-48, 764-88).

[1] TJ struck through the name of the month and interlined "Vendèmiaire."

[2] Paine here canceled a passage that appears to read: "that you might keep an eye on [John Adams] whose talent was to blunder and [offend?]. [His] fractious untractable disposition has justified this opinion of him. Like his Secretary Timothy he mistakes Arrogance for greatness, and sullenness for wisdom. Were you in Europe you would feel afflicted, as I do, for the degradation of the American Character. The [. . .] hypocrisy of Washington ([. . .]) gave the first [stab] to the [fame] of America, and the [. . .] of Adams has deepened the wound." The illegible portions contain an estimated one word, four words, and two words, respectively.

[3] Paine here canceled "power."

From Joel Barlow

DEAR SIR   3 Oct. 1800—

I took the liberty to write you a few days ago on a subject of some importance. Finding that Mr. Skipwith who was to be the bearer did not go I sent my packet by an occasion which is probably less safe. This induces me to address you a copy of that letter and likewise to send you by Col. Swift a little pamphlet I published last year, which has probably not yet found its way to America. The idea of a Maritime Convention as sketched in the latter part of this work may appear chimerical; but I am confident it is more owing to the want of reflection than it is to the want of power in the nations most interested in such a system, that something like it is not adopted with success. Is there no way of framing these ideas into a proposable project and submitting them to those governments whose interest so loudly calls for some check to the maritime Despotism which is making such alarming strides towards the destruction of civilization?—Perhaps nothing can be done while the present war continues; but there is a prospect now that this campagne may be the last, even with England. If so the approaching interval of peace will be the moment to be seized for this object; but it should be an early part of that interval, before the impression of present grievances shall be worn away.

I believe, whatever indications to the contrary may have gone abroad in the world, that the French government may be easily brought into a system founded on the most liberal principles relative to the rights of Nations and the protection of neutral commerce. I know that some of its most influencial members are full of these ideas, and only wait a moment of tranquility to bring them forward; but it would be convenient to such persons, & facilitate their perception of the practicability of the measure, to have it presented in such shape & from such a quarter as shall show them that men in other countries whom they respect have thought as they have.

You will not be surprised to find that nothing approaching towards a liberal system has been attempted during the negotiation now drawing to a close in Paris. There were many reasons for not expecting it. One was a constant scene of mystery, distrust & ill humour which prevailed from beginning to end.—

I have the honor to be, Dear Sir, with great respect your obt. & most hume. Sert. JOEL BARLOW

RC (DLC); at foot of first page: "Mr. Jefferson"; endorsed by TJ as received 14 Jan. 1801 and so recorded in SJL. Enclosure: Dupl of Barlow to TJ, 15 Sep. 1800.

Zephaniah SWIFT, Barlow's friend from the Yale College class of 1778, was secretary to the American envoys in France (ANB; James Woodress, *A Yan-*

kee's Odyssey: The Life of Joel Barlow [Philadelphia, 1958], 38, 49, 52).

PAMPHLET: *Joel Barlow to his Fellow Citizens of the United States of America. Letter II. On Certain Political Measures Proposed to their Consideration*, dated Paris, 20 Dec. 1799. It had as an appendix, dated 5 Dec., a "Memoir on Certain Principles of Public Maritime Law. Written for the French Government."

From Nathaniel Cutting

Paris, 3 Oct. 1800. He has not written since his letter of 27 Aug. 1798 by Dr. Logan, in part because he felt isolated by the trend of politics in the United States, which is now taking a more favorable turn. Although the American commissioners were not the best suited individuals to make progress in relations with France, they have negotiated an agreement and it seems probable that they will improve American impressions of France. An amicable relationship between the two countries is of primary importance. It will bring the disadvantage of worsened relations with Britain, which "with its usual arrogance" may interfere with trade, drawing the United States into a war that it has so far managed to avoid. It is too early to know if a breach with Great Britain "might not *eventually* prove advantageous to our rising Empire." The British government has acquired too much influence in the United States, so "*perhaps* it might be good policy even to *seek* a cause of rupture *if none presented of itself.*" Cutting's views have of course ostracized him with those who have held power in the U.S., and it came as no surprise when Timothy Pickering dismissed him from his position as consul. He would have considered it "a disgraceful burthen" to stay in the office under a secretary of state "of so contemptible a spirit and such prostituted abilities." President Adams deserves praise for removing from his cabinet a man of Pickering's "imperious, perverse temper, and political cunning." True republicanism is poorly understood in the Republic of France, the latest government being a despotism, although it may bring about political order by controlling "the inordinate rage of contending Factions." France has been fortunate both at home and abroad in the last year, with the peace now pending in Europe promising security for a long time to come. The "military Genius of *Bonaparte*" is more than a match for the English, who seek inclusion in the peace negotiations but will be hurt for having taken Malta, which is important to French trade in the Mediterranean. France has never been stronger, and if the war continues it is likely that the northern maritime powers will form a league of armed neutrality, which Cutting hopes the United States will join. Only that association and a revitalization of French naval power can guarantee the rights of neutral commerce, for British arrogance and defiance of law "put Algerine Marauders to the blush!"

RC (DLC); 3 p.; at foot of recto of each sheet: "M. Jefferson"; endorsed by TJ as received 22 Dec. and so recorded in SJL.

From Thomas Paine

DEAR SIR   Paris Octr. 4 1800

I understand there is an Article in the Treaty to the following purport, that the duties payable upon Articles brought from America into france shall not go to the revenue, but shall be appropriated as a fund to pay such of the condemned Cargoes as shall be proved to be American property. If you should be in the Chair, but not otherwise, I offer myself as one upon this business, if there should be occasion to appoint any. It will serve to defray my expences untill I can return. but I wish it may be with the condition of returning. I am not tired of working for Nothing but I cannot afford it. This appointment will aid me in promoting the Object I am now upon that of a law of Nations for the protection of Neutral Commerce

Salut et respect   THOMAS PAINE.

RC (DLC); endorsed by TJ as received 6 Jan. 1801 and so recorded in SJL. Enclosed in Stephen Thorn to TJ, 27 Dec. 1800.

The Convention of 1800 contained no ARTICLE such as that described by Paine, and in fact according to Articles 2 and 5 the issue of indemnification for captured property would have to be worked out in a separate negotiation (DeConde, *Quasi-War*, 352-3, 355).

Paine's work in progress on a LAW OF NATIONS was probably his "Dissertation" on that subject (see Paine to TJ, 6 Oct. 1800).

Notes on John Adams's Replies
to XYZ Addresses

[before 6 Oct. 1800]

1. Favor to England.

Smith. 1798.	Oct. 18. pa.	1.	Answer to Grand jury of Ulster county N.Y. 'if by a coalition—of aiding each other.' 26. lines.
Folsome.	pa. 51.		to Inhabitants of Concord in Massachus. 'as I have ever wished—useful to remember it.' 25. lines
Fenno. 1798.	July. 6. pa.	2.	to Officers & souldiers of Morris county N.J. 'had not the measures—& perhaps better founded. 30. lines.

2. Abuse of the French.

Smith. 1798.	Apr. 26. pa.	3.	to the inhabitants of the borough of York Pensva.¹ 'after years of depredations—of this country.' 9. lines.
Fenno.	May. 19.	3.	to the Jurors of the District of Maryland. 'the French revolution—candid mind.' 21. l.
Smith.	June 7.	4.	to the young men of Brunswick. 'I understand—audience.' 6. l.
Fenno.	June. 8.	2.	to the inhabitants of Mount Bethel in Northampt. Pensva. 'the depredations—on decent terms.' 7. li.
	9.	3	to the light infantry of the boro' of Easton Pensva. 'the nation—will be lost.' 16. l.
	23.	2.	to the citizens of Hudson in Columbia. N.Y. 'the reign of terror—ignominy' 8. l.
	July 2.	2.	to the Judges &c of Somerset county, N. Jersey. 'it is impossible—exaggerated.' 9. l.
	3.	2	to the inhabitants of Franklin county N. Carolina. 'our conciliatory—contumelious language'. 16. li.
	14.	1.	to the 62d. battalion of militia in Prince George Virginia. 'it is to be regretted—beginning.' 43. li.
Smith.	Aug. 2.	4.	to the Inhabitants of Rockingham county N.C. 'the revilers—avowal of it.' 24. l.
	14.	2.	to the officers & men of the militia of Mont-

gomery N.Y. 'when a foreign power—of sovereignty.' 12. l.

Nov. 15.   2. to the Cincinnati of S. Carolina. 'the French & too many Americans—acted accordingly.' 10. l.

Dec. 27.   1. to the H. of Representatives of Pensva. 'the French nation from their numbers—servile imitation.' 35. l.

Folsom.   pa. 11.   to the inhabitants of the towns of Arlington &c Vermont. 'I have seen in the conduct—yet escaped.' 14. l.

19.   to the legislature of N. Hampshire. 'the indignities which have—more justice than yourselves.' 13. l.

31.   to the legislature of Massachusets. 'if the object of France—liberties will be in danger.'² 8. l.

47.   to the Grand jury of Plymouth in Massachusets. 'while occupied in the—to similar abuses.' 10. l.

164.   to the inhabitants of Burlington. 'there is nothing in the conduct of *our enemies*—be decieved.' 12. l.

178.   to the inhabitants of the townships of Windsor &c. 'the depredation committed &c—smallest agitation. 8. l.

190.   to the Students of N. Jersey college. 'the passions of avarice, ambition & pleasure have dictated the aim—friendship.' 5. l.

194.   to the citizens of Philadelphia. 'many of the nations of the earth—dogmas by the sword.' 8. l.

239.   to the students of Dickinson college. 'two of your envoys—question to a decision.' 24. l.

244.   to the officers of the militia of Newcastle county. 'there is too much reason to believe—measure of right & wrong. 17. l.

262.   to the inhabitants of Washington county Maryld. 'when you say that—as the antient monarchy.' 7. l.

265.   to a committee of the citizens of Worcester county. 'the dispatches exhibit a scene—to human nature.' 3. l.

3. Libels against his fellow citizens.

Fenno. 1798. May 24. pa. 2. to the inhabitants of Perth Amboy. N. Jersey. 'it is too much to expect—foreign power.' [18. l.]

July. 6.   2 to the militia of Morris county N. Jersey. 'who were the people who depreciated—preserved from depreciation.' 10. l.[3]

Aug. 25.   2 to the officers & souldiers of Burlington in Vermont. 'your opinion of the opposition—studies & contempla[tion 14.] l.

to the inhabitants of Amesbury. Massachusets. 'your indignation, abhorrence—support of the people.' 12. l.

Smith.   Aug. 30.   1. to the field officers of Bath in Virginia. 'more depends upon Virginia—offended country.' 6. l.

Oct. 25.   4. to the freeholders of the town of Kittery. Massachusets. 'in the last extremity—their supposed friends.' 5. lines.[4]

Dec. 27.   1. to the H. of Representatives of Pensva. 'Candour must own—ought to be sought.' 18. l.

Fenno.   Dec. 7.   2 to the Grand lodge of Freemasons in Vermont. 'it seems to be agreed—have been suspected.' 17. lines.[5]

Smith. 1799.   Jan. 3.   2. to the Senate of Pensva. 'whether any change of men—have placed it.' 19. l.

Folsom.   pa. 11.   to the inhabitants of the town of Arlington &c Vermont. 'sentiments like yours—feet of France, so have [I.'] 13. l.

37.   to the young men of Boston. 'the state of the world—truth, reason, or justice.' 11. l.

133.   to the inhabitants of the town of Hartford in Connecticut. 'if the designs of foreign—are purely American.' 23. l.

145.   to the citizens of Albany in N.Y. 'that a perfidious attachment to France lurks among us is certain.' 2. l.

152.   to the Grand jury of the county of Columbia. N.J. 'if there are citizens—of foreign domination, all is lost.' 5. l.

168.   to the citizens of Newark in N. Jersey. 'the delusions & misrepresentns—calamities in this country.' 6. l.

184. to the Souldier citizens of N. Jersey. 'the degraded characters—the lines of an invading enemy.' 5. li.

192. to the Mayor, Aldermen & citizens of Philada. 'at a time when all the old republics—defaming our government.' 13. l.

239. to the students of Dickenson college.[6] 'if there are any who—greatest enemies.' 4. l.

244. to the officers of the militia of Newcastle county. 'the unjust & imperious—deluded Americans.' 5. l.

297. to a committee of the 48th. regiment of militia in Botetourt, Virginia. 'the confidence of the—of the federal goverment.' 9. l.

4. Anti-republican heresies.

Fenno. 1798. May 15. pa. 2. to the inhabitants of the boro' of Easton Pensva. 'I trust &c—again increase.' 2. lines.

June 1. 2. to the citizens of Queen Anne's county Maryld. 'I cannot profess—with you.' 7. l.

30. 2. to the Court of the county of Onondago. N.Y. 'the delusive theories—afraid to write.' 12. li.

July. 3. 2. to the companies of artillery &c of Rutland in Vermt. 'the words republican government—despotism itself.' 11. [l.]

Aug. 14. 2. to the regiment of militia of Montgomery cnty. N.Y. 'your government has indeed—in many years. 17. l.

Folsom. pa. 27. to the students of Dartmouth university. N.H. 'let me intreat you—at least in Italy.' 10. l.

37. to the young men of Boston. 'the state of the world is such—truth, reason or justice.' 7. li.

54. to the inhabitants of the town of Haverhill in Massachus. 'the interference of the people—the present is one.' 12. l.

69. to the inhabitants of Dedham in Massachus. 'I know very well that—by their conquerors.' 13. l.

96. to the Boston marine society. 'whatever pretexts the French people—spirit, or patriotism.' 39. l.

117. to the inhabitants of Providence. 'when we were the first—foresight of it's consequences.' 5. l.

125.	to the students of Rho. isld. college. 'the 15. years of peace—a sacrifice of honour.' 9. li.
152.	to the Grand jurors of Columbia in N.Y. 'in contemplating our government—disgraceful to human nature.' 20. l.[7]
159.	to the inhabitants of the county of Oneida N.Y. 'the cause of a certain species—progress of humanity.' 12. [l.]
177.	to the inhabitants of the township of Windsor &c. 'the very modern history—good government.' 6. l.
197.	to the young men of Philadelphia. 'for a long course of years—was at length secured.' 15. l.
223.	to the inhabitants of the boro' of Harrisburg. 'the rage for innovation—suffering humanity.' 12. l.
252.	to the citizens of Baltimore. 'the fate of every republic—friends and ourselves.' 5. l.
288.	to the young men of Richmond. 'it might have been as well—from bad to worse.' 11. l.
316.	to the inhabitants of Harrison county. 'I believe that the distinction of aristocrat—animosities between them.' 21. l.

5. Egotisms.

31.	to the legislature of Maryland. 'the first 40. years of my life—ardent wishes gratified.' 11. l.
62.	to the inhabitants of the town of Cambridge in Mass. 'difficulties were the inheritance—them to censure.' 9. l.
70.	to the inhabitants of Dedham in Massachus. 'that we have thought too well—witness for 20. years.' 3. l.
91.	to the Grand lodge of the Freemasons of Massachus. 'as I never had the honour—the felicity to be initiated.' 11. l.
96.	to the Marine society of Boston. 'floating batteries and wooden—establishing the practice.' 12. li.[8]
171.	to the inhabitants of Bridgeton in N.J. 'in preparing the project of a treaty—pursued until this time.' 18. l.

190.   to the students of the N. Jersey college. 'if the choice of the people will not defend their rights who will'? 2. l.

197.   to the young men of Philadelphia &c⁹ 'I have long flattered—independce of our country.' 10. l.

202.   to the inhabitants of the county of Lancaster. 'I submit with entire resignation—invited to become.' 2[7. l.]

206.   to the citizens of the boro' of Carlisle. 'when you acknowledge that—assemble and declare it.' 10. li.

227.   to the people of Pott's town. 'your confidence that I will not surrender—ignominious deed.' 5. l.

231.   to the inhabitants of the towns of Sunbury & Northumbld. 'when you assure me that— my warmest gratitude.' 6. l.

302.   to the inhabitants of the county of Middlesex. 'for reasons that are obvious—peculiarly agreeable.' 4. li.

Smith. 1799. Jan. 17. pa. 1. to the legislature of Maryland. 'as the course of my life—from the trial. 9. li.

Dft (photostat at Papers of Thomas Jefferson, Princeton, New Jersey); undated, but see note below; entirely in TJ's hand; torn at margin, with letters and numerals in brackets supplied by consulting source texts, described below.

In compiling these notes TJ meticulously organized the sentiments, he believed, John Adams expressed as he penned replies to the addresses that came to him from all over the country in support of his administration following the publication of the XYZ dispatches in April 1798. Many newspapers printed the addresses and Adams's replies. On 18 May Abigail Adams observed, "he answers all of them and by this means has an opportunity of diffusing his own sentiments, more extensively & probably where they will be more read and attended to than they would have been through any other channel." In his correspondence TJ criticized the president for increasing the XYZ hysteria and further damaging relations with France. TJ observed that the president's answers were "full of extraordinary things" and were "more Thrasonic than the addresses" themselves (Stewart Mitchell, ed., *New Letters of Abigail Adams, 1788-1801* [Boston, 1947], 174-5; Vol. 30:322-3, 326, 331, 353).

In his compilation above TJ referred to three sources for the texts of the president's responses. The Republican editor Samuel H. SMITH had printed a number of the XYZ addresses and the president's replies in his weekly Philadelphia *Universal Gazette*. Late in 1798, William Austin edited and John W. FOLSOM (Folsome) printed *A Selection of the Patriotic Addresses, to the President of the United States. Together with the President's Answers* (Boston, 1798; Sowerby, No. 3525). The publication included 107 addresses arranged by state of origin, along with Adams's replies to about 90 of them.

The edition did not include the dates of the addresses. TJ's third source was John and John Ward FENNO, who had printed 87 addresses in the *Gazette of the United States*, more than any other newspaper (Thomas M. Ray, "'Not One Cent for Tribute': The Public Addresses and American Popular Reaction to the XYZ Affair, 1798-1799," *Journal of the Early Republic*, 3 [1983], 408).

TJ communicated the notes above to William Duane. Perhaps William Bache carried the manuscript to Philadelphia along with TJ's memorandum on the postal service (printed above at 15 Aug.). The document above perhaps served as TJ's retained copy, with the manuscript taken to Philadelphia being in Bache's or some other hand so that TJ would not be associated with the document. Selections from Adams's addresses as compiled by TJ appeared in the Philadelphia *Aurora* on 6, 8, 9, 10, and 13 Oct. 1800. Duane captioned the series "The Beauties of John Adams's Political Opinions." He introduced it by stating, "We now, take up Mr. *Adams's* answers to the memorable addresses of the reign of terror in 1798 when Mr. *Adams* exposed himself to the condemnation of history, by his *Fast day* and the *furious denunciation* of his fellow

citizens; when he insulted religion while he breathed *War*." He consistently began the column with selections from TJ's third category, LIBELS AGAINST HIS FELLOW CITIZENS, changed slightly by Duane to "Libels on His Fellow Citizens." ANTI-REPUBLICAN HERESIES: Duane's caption, "Hostility to Republican Government," usually appeared second in the column. Duane always ended, as TJ did, with EGOTISMS. All but thirteen of the passages selected by TJ were printed in the *Aurora*.

[1] The entry to this point at first appeared as the last entry under "Favor to England" before TJ canceled it and entered it here.
[2] Preceding five words written over partially erased, illegible passage.
[3] Entry interlined by TJ.
[4] Entry interlined by TJ.
[5] Entry interlined by TJ.
[6] TJ here canceled "Who of your envoys."
[7] Entry interlined by TJ.
[8] Entry interlined in place of "'whatever pretexts the French—spirit or patriotism.' 38 l."
[9] TJ here canceled "for a long course of years."

From Nathan Haley

SIR   Havre de Grace. 14 Vendemiaire L'an 9 [i.e. 6 Oct. 1800]

I recived a few days since a letter from citizen Thomas Paine, requesting me to forward you, by the Portsmouth, some copies of a work lately published by him, called the maritime compact. which accordingly I have the honour of inclosing you, it was his Intention to send a letter for you by the same conveyance, but as the Persons composing the american Embassy, are arrived, the wind fair, & the vessell ready to go to Sea next Tide, I apprehend she will Sail before it arrives.—with respect to the news of this country, the victories obtained by the french armies in the last campaign, their Imposing aspect in the present, and the Disorganized state of those of austria, have obliged the Emperor to solicit a continuance of the armistice, that had existed for some time, and to Deliver into the possession of the French Republick, the three Important fortresses of Ulm, Ingoldstad, & Philipsbourg, as a proof of his sincerity, those places are now actually Garrisoned by french troops, & as the communication between the armies of Itally, & those of the Rhine, & Reserve, are by that means secured, it will be in their power in the event of hostilities being renewed, to Destroy the Emperor's Italian army, tak his Capital, & penetrate into the hereditary Dominions. it is Gennerally Imagined that those serious Dangers, which threaten him will oblige the Emperor to make a speedy peace, the congress for the purpose of conclding it is to be held at Luneville a Town of the French Republick.—the British have Demanded that this congress should be a Genneral one of all the parties concerned in the War, and that they should be permitted to send a person to Negociate for her, this has been consented to by france on condition of their agreeing to a Naval armistice, the utmost anxiety now exists in this country to Know what their Determination will be, it is however pretty Gennerally supposed that Britain will not agree to a condition, that would oblige them to raise the Blockade of several ports & enable the french to transport Timber for constructing vessells of war, & naval stores to their principal Ports when they would not enjoy any advantage to counterballance those & the many others the French Republique would Derive from a naval armistice. It is an Important moment in Europe, the Publick mind is every where anxious and agitated, & amidst the number of events that Interest them the Election of a President of the united states is a principal one. it is Gennerally believed & I will say hoped that you sir will be the person Elected, give me leave [to] anticipate this event and rejoice with all [the] true friends of my country in a circumstance so Happy for it, and for the Genneral cause of Liberty. and to assure you that I am with the Highest Respect

your Most obedent Humble Sevent

NATHAN HALEY

Lieutenant de Vasseau in the service of the French Republique

RC (DLC); English date supplied; words torn away at seal; addressed: "Thos Jefferson Vice President des Etats Unis de L'Amerique a Philadelphia," with the name of the city canceled and "Washington City" supplied in another hand; franked and postmarked; endorsed by TJ as received 30 Dec. and so recorded in SJL.

Nathan Haley (1766-1841), who signed himself here as a French naval lieutenant, came from Stonington, Connecticut. In France, Thomas Paine borrowed over 7,000 livres from Haley to meet various expenses, including the printing of the *Pacte maritime* (see Paine's letter to TJ at 16 Oct., below). From August to December 1803 Paine visited Haley, then the owner of at least one ship, in Stonington and temporarily became a local celebrity. Haley continued to travel between France and the United States and in 1839 received an appointment as U.S. consul at Nantes (Keane, *Paine*, 489-92; Richard Anson Wheeler, *History of the Town of Stonington, County of New London, Connecticut, from its First Settlement in 1649 to 1900, with a Genealogical Register of Stonington Families* [New London, Conn., 1900; repr. Mystic, Conn., 1966], 408-9; JEP, 5:186, 197; Paine to TJ, 23 Sep. 1803; TJ to Haley, 14 July 1808; Haley to TJ, 8 Sep. 1808).

MARITIME COMPACT: Paine's "*Compact Maritime*" essay was printed separately in English, its main title reversing Paine's usual ordering of the words— *Maritime Compact; or, an Association of Nations for the Protection of the Rights and Commerce of Nations that May be Neutral in Time of War*. The essay was dated 1 Oct. 1800, and the pamphlet did not specify the place of publication (Sowerby, No. 3241; Paine to TJ, 1 Oct.).

From Thomas Paine

DEAR SIR   Octr. 6

I enclose you a piece to serve as an introduction to the two other pieces which you will receive by the same Conveyance. I observe the Consul Le Brun at the entertainment given to the American Envoys gave for his toast.

A l Union de l'Amerique avec les puissances du Nord pour faire respecter la liberté des mers.   T. P—

RC (DLC); endorsed by TJ as received 6 Jan. 1801 and so recorded in SJL. Enclosure: probably a manuscript, not found, of Paine's "Dissertation on the Law of Nations. Respecting the Rights of Neutral Commerce and the Liberty of the Seas," conveyed by TJ to Samuel Harrison Smith and printed as the first paper in *Compact Maritime*, 3-9 (see Paine to TJ, 1 Oct. 1800). Enclosed in Stephen Thorn to TJ, 27 Dec. 1800.

Charles François Lebrun, third consul of France, delivered his TOAST at the festivities held at Môrtefontaine on 3 Oct. to mark the signing of the convention be-tween his country and the United States. Translated, it salutes "the union of America with the northern powers to give respect to the freedom of the seas." It followed a toast by Napoleon Bonaparte commemorating Frenchmen and Americans who died fighting for American independence and one by the second consul, Jean Jacques Régis Cambacérès, recognizing John Adams as the "successeur de Washington" (*Gazette nationale ou le Moniteur universel*, 14 Vendémiaire Year 9 [6 Oct. 1800]; Stewart, *French Revolution*, 773; Short to TJ, 18 Sep. 1800).

From Benjamin Rush

DEAR SIR/   Philadelphia October 6th 1800

I agree with you in your Opinion of Cities. Cowper the poet very happily expresses our ideas of them compared with the Country.

"God made the Country—man made Cities." I consider them in the same light that I do Abscesses on the human body viz: as reservoirs of all the impurities of a Community.

I agree with you likewise in your wishes to keep religion and government independant of each Other. Were it possible for St. Paul to rise from his grave at the present juncture, he would say to the Clergy who are now so active in settling the political Affairs of the World. "Cease from your political labors your kingdom is not of *this* World. Read my Epistles. In no part of them will you perceive me aiming to depose a pagan Emperor, or to place a Christian upon a throne. Christianity disdains to receive Support from human Governments. From this, it derives its preeminence over all the religions that ever have, or ever Shall exist in the World. Human Governments may receive Support from Christianity but it must be only from the love of justice, and peace which it is calculated to produce in the minds of men. By promoting these, and all the Other Christian Virtues by your precepts, and example, you will much sooner overthrow errors of all kind, and establish our pure and holy religion in the World, than by aiming to produce by your preaching, or pamphflets any change in the political state of mankind."

A certain Dr Owen an eminent minister of the Gospel among the dissenters in England, & a sincere friend to liberty, was once complained of by one of Cromwell's time serving priests,—that he did not preach to the *times*. "My business and duty said the disciple of St Paul is to preach—to *Eternity*—not to the *times*." He has left many Volumes of Sermons behind him, that are so wholly religious, that no One from reading them, could tell, in what country,—or age they were preached.—

I have sometimes amused myself in forming a Scale of the different kinds of *hatreds*. They appear to me to rise in the following Order. *Odium Juris-consultum, Odium medicum, Odium philalogicum, Odium politicum*, and *Odium theologicum*. You are now the Subject of the two last. I have felt the full force of the 2nd: and 4th degrees of hostily from my fellow Creatures. But I do not think we shall ultimately suffer from either of them. my persecutions have averted, or delayed the usual languor of 55 in my mind. I read, write, and think with the same vigor and pleasure that I did fifteen years Ago. As natural stimuli are sometimes supplied by such as are artificial in the production of human life, so Slander seems to act upon the human mind. It not only supplies the place of fame, but it is much more powerful in exciting Our faculties into vigorous and successful exercises.—

[205]

To persevere in benevolent exertions After ungrateful returns for former Services, it is only necessary to consider mankind as Solomon considered them several thousand years ago,—viz: as labouring Under madness. A few Cures, or even a few lucid intervals produced in a state, or nation, will repay the unsuccessful labors of many years. "No good effort is lost" was a favorite Saying of the late Dr: Jebb.— A truth cannot perish; Altho' it may sleep for Centuries. The Republics of America are the fruits of the precious truths that were disseminated in the Speeches and publications of the republican patriots in the British parliament one hundred and sixty years Ago. My first american Ancestor Jno: Rush commanded a troop of horse in Cromwell's Army. He Afterwards became a Quaker and followed Wm Penn in 1683 to Pennsylvania. My brother possesses his horseman's sword. General Darke of your state, who is descended from his youngest daughter, owns his Watch. To the sight of his Sword, I owe much of the Spirit which animated me in 1774, and to the respect & admiration which I was early taught to cherish for his Virtues, and exploits, I owe a large portion of my republican temper and principles.—Similar circumstances I believe produced a great deal of the Spirit and exertions of all those Americans who are descended from Ancestors that emigrated from England between the years 1645 and 1700.

I send you herewith some musk melon seeds of a quality as much Above the common melons of our Country, as a pine Apple is superior to a potatoe. They were brought originally from Minorca. The Ground must be prepared for them at the usual time, by having some brush burn't upon it.—The fire destroys the eggs of insects in the ground, & the ashes left by it, manures the ground so as to prepare it for the Seeds. No vine of any kind should grow near them. They are, when ripe, a little larger than a Child's head—round—and have a green rind. They are never mealy, but juicy, and cannot be improved by Sugar, pepper, salt or any Other Addition that can be made to them.

We have had a few Cases of yellow fever in our City, eno' to satisfy unprejudiced persons that we have not been defended from it by our Quarantine law. They were all evidently of domestic Origin.—

I reciprocate your kind expressions, upon the probability of our not meeting again, and feel sincere distress upon the Account of it. I shall always recollect with pleasure the many delightful hours we have spent together from the day we first met on the banks of Skuilkill in the year 1775 to the day in which we parted. If the innocent & interesting subjects of our occasional Conversations should be a delusive

One,—the delusion is enchanting. But I will not admit that we have been deceived in our early, and long Affection for republican forms of Government. They are, I believe, not only rational, but practicable. As well might we reject the pure and simple doctrines & precepts of Christianity, because they have been dishonoured by being mixed with human follies & crimes by the corrupted Churches of Europe, as renounce our republics because their name has been dishonoured by the follies and crimes of the French Nation. The preference which men, depraved by false government have given to monarchy, is no more a proof of its excellency, than the preference which men whose Appetites have been depraved by drinking Whiskey, is a proof that it is more wholesome than Water. Thousands have derived health and long life from that wholsome beveridge of nature, while tens of thousands have perished from the use of the former liquor.

Representative & elective Government appears to be a discovery of modern times. It has met with the fate of many Other discoveries which have had for their Objects the melioration of the Condition of man. It has been opposed, traduced, and nearly scouted from the face of the earth. The Science of medicine abounds with instances of new truths being treated in the same manner. The cool Regimen which Dr Sydenham applied with general success to the small pox, was exploded before he died by his Cotemporary physicians. In the year 1767 it was revived in London by Dr Sutton, and now prevails all over the World.

Excuse the length of this letter. my pen has run away with me.—Pray throw it in the fire as soon as you have read it. Not a line of it must be communicated to a human Creature with my name.

When you see Mr Madison please to tell him he is still very dear to *his*, and *your* sincere & Affectionate friend   Benjn: Rush

PS: From the difficulty of packing up the Melon seed so as to send them by the post, I have concluded to send them to you in the Winter at the federal city by a private hand.—

RC (DLC); endorsed by TJ as received 16 Oct. and so recorded in SJL.

As written by William cowper in *The Task*, first published in 1785, the line of poetry ran: "God made the country, and man made the town" (book 1, "The Sofa," line 749). It reflected phrasing from an earlier poem, "The Fire-Side: A Pastoral Soliloquy," by Isaac Hawkins Browne: "That the town is Man's world, but that this is of God" (William Cowper, *The Task and Selected Other Poems*, ed. James Sambrook [London, 1994], 24, 81; James King and Charles Ryskamp, eds., *The Letters and Prose Writings of William Cowper*, 5 vols. [Oxford, 1979-86], 3:284).

From Samuel Smith

Dr. Sir/   Montebello. Near Baltimore 8t. Octr. 1800

Mr. Iznardi Consul of the U:S—has arrived in Baltimore from Cadix, the Old Gentle[man] on his arrival wrote you, to which having no Answer [he] Concludes his Letter has miscarried either in the *us[ual] Way*, or for want of proper direction—He informs me from Philadelphia, that he brought with him from Cadix some particular Wine for his friends among Others two Casks for your Use which he [asks] me to forward—Do me the favor to say to w[hose] Care in Richmond they shall be sent—

The Elections for the City & County of Baltimore are Closed, both in favor of the Repub. The City—1100 to 294—The County 995 Fed.—2035 Repub—It has exceeded our most sanguine expectations—I [have] Reason to believe that 49 Republicans will be sent to our He. of Delegates—40 will be sufficient to prevent a Change in our present Mode of Elec[tion.] If no Alteration should take place I think we [can] with safety Count on 5 perhaps 6 Votes for the Republican Candidate for President & Vice President—I am sir

With sentiments of real Regard Your friend & servt

S. Smith

RC (DLC); frayed at margin; endorsed by TJ as received 16 Oct. and so recorded in SJL.

IZNARDI: for TJ's correspondence with Joseph Yznardi, Sr., see Yznardi to TJ of 4 Jan. 1801.

From Aaron Burr

Dear Sir   N, York 9th: Octr. 1800

The family of Alston of South Carolina is probably well known to you—The Young gentleman who will hand you this, bids fair to do honor to his Name and his Country—His Warmest wishes, and his influence which is already important, are engaged in promoting your election—He has passed through the eastern States and is now on his return to attend the Legislature of S.C. of Which he is a Member—I refer you to him for any thing regarding domestic politics—

With respectful attachment I am Dear Sir Your friend & st

A; Burr

RC (DLC); at foot of text: "The Hon. Thos Jefferson"; endorsed by TJ as received 23 Oct. but recorded in SJL under 16 Oct. "by Mr. Alston."

In 1800 Joseph ALSTON, scion of a family of wealthy rice planters, turned 21 years old and made an extended tour of the United States. He had read law with

Edward Rutledge but was actually not yet a member of the South Carolina legislature, where he began a political career in 1802. In his travels in 1800 Alston became acquainted with Burr's daughter Theodosia, whom he married in February 1801 (Kline, *Burr*, 1:442-3, 448-9; *S.C. Biographical Directory, House of Representatives*, 4:32-5; ANB).

From Thomas Leiper

DEAR SIR   Philada. Octr. 9th 1800

I received you very kind favor of the 26th Ult but too late to answer by last post—I am very much obliged for the offer of your Crop of Tobacco and more especially as you offer me a Credit till April—My letters from Richmond of the 18th Ult: Quote Tobacco of the first Quality at 26/ pr Ct. your Currency—and the common Run at 24/ pr Ct. Six months interest will make it 33/5 our Currency and the freight and Charges to Philadelphia 40/11. I will notwithstand give for your Crop of Tobacco delivered in good order in Philadelphia Six Dollars per Ct.—I will also take the Crops of Tobacco you mention for Four or Five years at One Guinea pr Ct. delivered in Richmond and if delivered in Philadelphia the freight, insurance & charges to Philadelphia. my reason for making my price at Richmond I expect the freight and insurance will be two thirds less—in a year or two than it is at present—I will engage to take your Tobacco at any time but as I cannot use them before the month of September I will not engage to pay for them before that period and should I not be able to pay then I will oblige myself to pay at the Rate of Six pr Ct. pr Annum untill the money is paid you obliging yourself to deliver me Albemarle Tobaccos equal in Quality to those I have heretofore received of you—Should Mrs. Keys or any of your neighbours whom you know of your own knowledge make good Tobacco and approve of the Terms I will take from One to Two Hundred Hhds pr Annum—I could wish also to have a promise that the Tobacco should be Cured without Smoke and when Packed into Hhds. the Plants should be selected the first Quality into One Hhd and those of an inferiour Quality into Another—Your opinion is perfectly correct as it respects Pennsylvania the people of 1776 think all alike and see as much necessity for being unanimous now as they were then—Our Ward Elections for inspectors of the election is Over and we have a majority of One some say [Two this] gives us an opportunity of appointing the Judges [which] is a point we have not gained since the Revolution. I informed Mr Dallas you had offered me you Crop of Tobo. and that I was going to write you respecting the price and that if he could give me any thing clever to inform you in the political line perhaps I might procure it One Dollar less pr Ct. Tell him from me we shall have a legal election in Pennsylvania for President & Vice President. Thomas Cooper was enlarged yesterday I had a Visit from him this morning and intend to Dine with him at 9 oclock he is in good health & spirits I am Dr Sir Your most Obedient St.

THOMAS LEIPER

RC (MHi); torn at seal, with words in brackets supplied from FC; franked and postmarked; addressed: "The Honble. Thomas Jefferson Vice Presedent of the U: States Monticello Virginia"; endorsed by TJ as received 16 Oct. and so recorded in SJL. FC (Lb in Leiper Papers, Friends of Thomas Leiper House, on deposit at PPL).

Thomas Leiper (1745-1825) was born in Scotland, educated in Glasgow and Edinburgh, and emigrated to America in 1763 after the death of his father. He served in the First Troop of Light-Horse in Philadelphia and the Jersey campaigns during the American Revolution and afterwards in the Whiskey Rebellion. Leiper became a wealthy tobacco merchant and landowner, first entering the tobacco business in Philadelphia through the employ of his cousin, Gavin Hamilton, but later venturing into business on his own. He advertised as a tobacconist in the 17 Oct. Philadelphia *Aurora*, in which he announced that his wares were newly available from No. 274 Market Street. An owner of two snuff mills on Crum Creek for more than twenty years, and a new tobacco manufactory, Leiper offered for sale a variety of tobaccos, cigars, and snuff (DAB; S. Gordon Smyth, *Thomas Leiper: Lieutenant of Light Horse, Patriot and Financier in the Revolution; and Pioneer in the Development of Industries and Inland Commerce in Pennsylvania* [Conshohocken, Pa., 1900], 7-8).

TJ's FAVOR OF THE 26TH ULT., recorded in SJL, has not been found.

In an act of 1 Mch., the Pennsylvania legislature increased the number of wards to fourteen and stipulated that two IN-SPECTORS OF THE ELECTION be chosen for each ward. Republicans adroitly established ward committees to their political advantage as the way of nominating all candidates for city office (Tinkcom, *Republicans and Federalists*, 260).

THOMAS COOPER had been imprisoned for six months for libel against John Adams (Vol. 31:492-3n).

From Tadeusz Kosciuszko

Paris 18. Vendemiaire An 9. [i.e. 10 Oct. 1800]

CHER AMI   rue de Lille No 545.

Enfin la Vertu triomphe si ce n'est pas encore dans le vieux du moins dans le nouveau Monde. Le peuple de moeurs et d'un jugement solide apperçoit qu'il faut vous nommer pour être heureux et independant et il ne se trompe pas. je joins mes voeux à la voix Generale. Souvenez vous cependant que le premier Poste de l'Etat qui est toujours entouré des flateurs, des intrigants, des hipocrites et des Gens mal pensants, soit environé par Les Gens à Carecter à talents honetes et d'une probite stricte, il faut que les places dans l'interieur comme l'exterieur soyent occupées par les Gens à principe et d'une conduite irreprochable jointe avec les connoissances et d'activité, et je vous recomande pour Paris au lieu de Mr Muray, Mr Barlaw, qui à tant des qualités que s'il étoit votre Ennemi personel (qu'il en faut beaucoup) je l'aurai tout de même recommandé a cette Place il à tout ce que vous souhaiteriez dans une personne pour cette poste importante pour vous. Les Gens de telle trempe vous aideront dans votre grand travaille pour le bonheur de votre Pays; ne Vous vous oubliez pas à votre poste Soyez toujours vertueux, Republicain avec justice et probité san faste et embition en un mot soyez Jefferson et mon ami

T Kosciuszko

E D I T O R S '   T R A N S L A T I O N

Paris 18 Vendémiaire Year 9.

DEAR FRIEND No. 545 rue de Lille.

Finally virtue triumphs, if not yet in the Old at least in the New World. The people, with solid morals and judgment, recognize that they must name you to be happy and independent, and they are not mistaken. I join my wishes with the public voice. Keep in mind, however, that the first position in the State, which is always encircled with flatterers, plotters, hypocrites, and evil-thinking people, must be surrounded by people of character with honest talents and strict probity; offices domestically as well as abroad must be held by people of principle and irreproachable conduct together with knowledge and activity; and I recommend to you for Paris, in place of Mr. Murray, Mr. Barlow, who has so many qualities that, if he were your personal enemy (which is far from the case) I should have recommended him just the same for the post. He is all that you could wish for in a person for that important post for you. People of such mettle will help you in your great work for the good fortune of your country; do not forget yourself in your post, always be virtuous, republican with justice and probity, without display and ambition. In a word, be Jefferson and my friend.

T. Kosciuszko

RC (MHi); English date supplied; endorsed by TJ. Recorded in SJL as received 18 Mch. 1801.

From James Thomson Callender

SIR Richmond October 11. 1800.

For some time past, I have regularly sent you, as far as they were printed, the Sheets of the 2d volume of *The Prospect*, because I flattered myself that, although neither the Stile nor matter could be exactly conformable to your ideas, or taste, yet that upon the whole, they would not be disagreeable. Whether I was right or wrong, or whether indeed You received my letters, I do not know.

Along with this letter come two others, containing 1 Set for you, and a second for Mr. Madison, of whom to balance the absolute necessity of condemning his Share in the Convention business, I have Spoke in the terms that his talents and his virtues, as well as my personal obligations to him do so eminently demand, in the Sheet which follows this. You have still 40 pages to receive. Most of it is set up, but various things prevent its being worked off. 3 of my Compositors have successively fallen sick, which has greatly retarded the progress of the work. If I Can manage the price of the paper, I mean to go right on with a second part, for the amusement of reading, writing, and printing is the only thing that has kept me from going out of my senses, in this den of wretchedness and horror. On friday last, 10 blacks were taken out and hung; and they were hardly gone, when 14 pirates, accused of murder, &ca. were brought in their places. I have kept my health and Spirits better than any white person I have seen here; partly because my mind is clear, and partly because, during the warm weather, I went often into Mr. Rose's, for fresh air; but on this Subject the marshal has interfered. I do not believe that the world ever saw such a Contemptible Set of Scoundrels.

I have been plucked by my Subscribers, numbers of whom went off without paying me. I advertised for payment but excepting 20 dolls. from one in Wythe county, have not got one farthing. I had advanced 14 dollars to one of the Journeymen, who was starving, and he has been struck with a dead palsy. Mr Lyon went off with about 70, or 80 dollars, I think in my debt, and that also is a desperate debt. I sent by Duane's desire 100 Copies to Philadelphia, and now, from motives of envy I presume, he refuses to advertise them, while the whole edition here is got sold, but a dozen or two, at most, so I have sent for them back again, and shall have to pay two freights for nothing.

I should be much obliged to you for sending me a few lines, at first or second hand, merely to let me know that the packets have, or have not, reached you. This I fancy could be here by the return of post. I, by no means, wish to take up time devoted to purposes so much more important, but just a few lines, if not improper, would be very welcome; and if you were to return Mr. Rose's notice, it would please the old Gentleman, who but that he is *timid*, has no fault upon earth; and his daughter is perhaps the most generous hearted creature under heaven.

The principal thing that vexed me in this business was the being prevented from going up to Pennsylvania to bring down my 3 boys, and to see a fourth person there, of whom I Can, by no letters gain an account. This disappointment put me, for some weeks, into an extasy of rage that no words can express, but time softens every thing. My boys, I hear, are well; and still, I hope, to be, what I once was, one of the happiest of human beings; and which I always would have been, if fortune had been half as kind as nature to

Sir Your most obliged & most obedt servt

JAS. T. CALLENDER

RC (DLC); endorsed by TJ as received 16 Oct. and so recorded in SJL.

PIRATES: Elihu Marchant and 12 other seamen were brought from Alexandria to Richmond in October for trial in the fall term of the U.S. circuit court. According to the indictment they "did unlawfully unjustly and Corruptly Confederate to run away" with the *Ranger*, an armed British brigatine. They were not, however, ACCUSED OF MURDER. All were found guilty and Captain Marchant was sentenced to two years in prison and a $100 fine (DNA: RG 59, Petitions for Pardons, 1801-9, No. 50; William Rose to TJ, 16 June 1801).

The SCOUNDRELS who complained that William Rose sometimes permitted Callender "a little health-inspiring air" were sardonically described in the Richmond *Examiner* of 10 Oct. as "federal christians, that is, *Church and State*

Christians" who were expected to show at least "external signs of humanity." I ADVERTISED FOR PAYMENT: in July a piece appeared in the *Examiner* reminding readers that Callender was confined to jail for sedition—"a martyr to the cause in which he has embarked"—and requesting payment of approximately $400 due him by various individuals. He needed the money to care for his children (Richmond *Examiner*, 18 July 1800). In August 1800 James LYON began publishing a newspaper, *The Cabinet*, in Georgetown (Brigham, *American Newspapers*, 1:87).

Advertisements for the forthcoming volume of *The Prospect Before Us* appeared in the *Aurora* with the notice that it could be purchased in Philadelphia from William DUANE (Philadelphia *Aurora*, 30 Sep. 1800). On 20 Oct. an extract from that volume, a description of Thomas Pinckney, also appeared in the *Aurora*.

From James Monroe

DEAR SIR   Richmond Octr. 12. 1800

Since yr. favor respecting my land above charlottesville I have heard nothing of Darrelle or Craven tho' I wrote the former by yr. advice, communicating my price. I wish much to know whether that gentln. takes it, as in the interim it suspends my negotiation with any other person. I have thoughts of visiting Albemarle the last of this week, with Mrs. M to whom a change of place may be useful, at wh. time it is possible Craven may be able to give me satisfactory information on the subject. In case I do sit out it will be on thursday, so that we shall be up before the post leaves you. But shd. we not be there by that time will thank you for what information you have respecting the view of Darrelle.

your friend & servant   JAS. MONROE

RC (DLC); endorsed by TJ as received   YOUR FAVOR: TJ to Monroe, 20 Sep.
16 Oct. and so recorded in SJL.   1800.

From Charles Pinckney

DEAR SIR,   October 12: 1800

I have written you very often lately but have never yet had the pleasure of a line from you or known whether you have received my Letters—indeed from the manner in which a Letter from Mr. Nicholas came to me after being opened, I have every reason to beleive very few if any of my friends Letters reach me, or those I write, the Gentlemen to whom they are Addressed—I wish to know how things will go in Maryland & Pennsylvania & Delaware & Jersey—the influence of the officers of the Government & of the Banks & of the British & Mercantile Interest will be very powerful in Charleston. I think we shall in the City as Usual, loose ⅔ds. of the representation, but the City has generally *not* much influence at Columbia—our Country Republican Interest has always been very strong, & I have no doubt will be so now—I have done every thing to Strengthen it & mean to go to Columbia to be at the Election of Electors—the *24* numbers of *the Republican* which I have written have been sent on to you, & I trust you have received & approve them—they are written in much moderation & have been circulated as much as possible—so has the *little Republican Farmer*, I shewed you in Philadelphia & which has been reprinted in all our *Southern States*—with these & my Speeches on Juries, Judges, Ross's Bill the Intercourse Bill & the Liberty of the Press, we have Literally sprinkled Georgia & No. Carolina *from the Mountains to the Ocean*—Georgia will *be Unanimous*. North Carolina 8 or 9—Tenessee—Unanimous & I am hopefull we shall also,—I suppose you must have got the Volume of my Speeches—one was sent you by Post & another by Water Via Philadelphia—I have done every thing that was possible here & have been obliged *alone to* take the whole abuse of the Parties United against us—they single me out, as the object; my situation is difficult & delicate, but I push Straight on in those principles which I have always pursued, & in which I would persevere if there were but *ten Men* left who continued to think with me

October 16th.—1800

Since the within written we have had the Election for Charleston, which by dint of the Bank & federal Interest, is reported by the Managers to be against us 11 to 4—that is the federalists are reported to have 11 out of 15 the number for the City representation, many of our Members run within 28 & 30 & 40 & we think we *get four* in,—I believe 5—to shew you what has been the Contest & the abuse I have been obliged to Bear, I inclose you some of the last days Publications—I suppose this unexpected opposition *to my Kinsman*, who has never been opposed here before as *member for the City*, will sever & divide[1] me from him & his Brother for ever—for the federalists all charge me with being the *sole cause* of any opposition, in this State, where all our intelligence from the Country convinces me, we shall have a *decided Majority* in our Legislature—besides we mean to dispute the Election of Charleston on the ground that many have Voted who had no right & are not Citizens—I am told 200—& that a Scrutiny is to be demanded—you may be assured that I have since June laboured as much as I was able—so will I continue if my health is spared, which I trust it will, to exert myself, to the Utmost, & have little doubt of succeeding; I long to hear from the Northern States— no doubt Pennsylvania will Vote & do right, & Jersey, so Genl. Mason writes me—being lame from a recent Accident to my arm Obliges me to write at intervals, I left off Yesterday & now resume my pen. since this our Accounts from the Country are still more favorable. I expect tomorrow to hear further & more favorably,—I never before this knew the full extent of the federal Interest connected with the British & the aid of the Banks & the federal Treasury, & all their officers—they have endeavoured to Shake *Republicanism in South Carolina* to its foundations—but we have resisted it firmly & I trust successfully—our Country Interest out of the reach of Banks & Custom Houses & federal officers is I think as pure as ever—I rejoice our Legislature meets 130 or 40 Miles from the Sea,—As much as I have been accustomed to Politics & to Study mankind this Election in Charleston has opened to me a new View of things—never certainly was such an Election in America—we mean to contest it for 8 or 9 of the 15—it is said several Hundred more Voted than paid taxes—*the Lame, Crippled, diseased and blind were either led lifted or brought in Carriages to the Poll.*—the sacred right of Ballot was struck at (for at a late hour when too late to Counteract it) in order to know how men, who were supposed to be under the influence of Banks & federal Officers & English Merchants, Voted, & that they might be *Watched to*

[215]

know whether they Voted as they were directed—the Novel & Un-warrantable measure was used of Voting with tickets printed *on Green & blue & red & yellow paper* & Men Stationed to Watch the Votes—the Contest lasted several days & Nights & will be brought before the House—in the Mean time I am charged with being the whole & *sole cause*, & so much abuse & public & private Slander, I beleive no man has ever yet sustained—on *some false private Charges* I have been obliged to come forward & deny them, & whenever it may be in their power, the British & federal Interest will consider it not only *as Meritorious*, but even as *a duty* to persecute me——

I request to have a line from you[2] saying if you recieve this safe.— I have kept up a correspondence in North Carolina & Georgia & sent there every thing I could—We hope from North Carolina 8 & per-haps 9 & I inclose You an Extract from Louisville that says Geor-gia—will be unanimous—. I congratulate you most sincerely on the Change in Maryland & the probable one in North Carolina & Rhode Island—In this State I have no doubt nor ever had—

October 26: 1800.—Our accounts respecting our State Legislature are every day more favourable. from those we have heard of We are sure now to have a decided majority & We still have to hear from other counties which have been always republican & which in fact we consider as our strong ground—. I send this under cover to Mr Madison & am hopeful you will get it safe & unbroken, my Letters have many of them come to me open which obliges me to use this [. . .] *Cover*—

From my going to Columbia to be at the Election of Electors & other circumstances it will be late before I can go to Washington this Year—besides my arm is not yet so strong as to risque too much with it in travelling & as I go by Land I must go slow—one great object I have in going by Land is to *see you at Monticello* & my esteemed Friends Mr Madison & Mr Monroe—I have just got a Letter from Mr: Dawson confirming from the authority of Mr: Burr the Business of Rhode Island—is it *possible*? can good come out of Galilee?

Tripl (DLC); first pages in unknown hand, with remainder and corrections in Pinkney's hand; torn at fold; at head of text: "Triplicate"; endorsed by TJ as a letter of 26 Oct. received 24 Nov. and so recorded in SJL. Enclosures not found. Enclosed in Pinckney to James Madison, 26 Oct. (see below).

I HAVE WRITTEN YOU VERY OFTEN

LATELY: according to SJL, TJ received letters from Pinckney of 22 and 26 Oct. on 3 and 24 Nov. 1800, respectively. They have not been found, but the contents pre-sumably are incorporated in the triplicate copy above. The only earlier letter in the fall of 1800 from Pinckney recorded in SJL is one of introduction delivered by Joseph Alston (see TJ to Pinckney, 4 Nov. 1800). Letters from Pinckney to TJ of 30 Oct. 1799 and 18 Mch. 1800, recorded in SJL as received on 14 Nov. 1799 and 18 Mch. 1800, respectively, are missing.

On 28 Aug. NUMBERS of a series "On the Election of a President of the United States" signed "A Republican" began appearing in the Charleston *City Gazette and Daily Advertiser*, the daily newspaper published by Peter Freneau and Seth Paine. By 6 Oct. the first 17 were in print, but numbers 18-22 did not appear. In 13 Oct. "No. XXIV" was published and the next day "No. XXIII." Pinckney's article signed a REPUBLICAN FARMER was first published in the New York *American Citizen and General Advertiser*, 22 Apr. (Brigham, *American Newspapers*, 2:1024-6; Madison, *Papers*, 17:428). MY SPEECHES: for the *Speeches of Charles Pinckney, Esq. in Congress*, published in 1800, probably in Philadelphia, see Evans, No. 38270. The first two of the five addresses in the pamphlet, delivered by the senator during the first session of the Sixth Congress, were in support of the bills he had introduced for selecting juries by lot in the federal courts and forbidding dual appointments for federal judges. In the last three addresses Pinckney registered opposition to the James Ross bill for deciding disputed presidential elections, the bill to further suspend commercial intercourse with France, and the action against the *Aurora* for breach of Senate privilege. MY KINSMAN: Charles Cotesworth Pinckney, who was not only the Federalist vice-presidential candidate but

also ran for a seat in the state senate to help the local Federalist ticket. He was the BROTHER of Thomas Pinckney, a South Carolina congressman in 1800. For campaign issues and practices that threatened to DIVIDE Charles Pinckney from his Federalist cousins, see Marvin R. Zahniser, *Charles Cotesworth Pinckney: Founding Father* (Chapel Hill, 1967), 219-27; John Harold Wolfe, *Jeffersonian Democracy in South Carolina* (Chapel Hill, 1940), 151-6; Frances Leigh Williams, *A Founding Family: The Pinckneys of South Carolina* (New York, 1978), 344-7.

LOUISVILLE, 40 miles southwest of Augusta, was the capital of Georgia in 1800.

I SEND THIS UNDER COVER TO MR MADISON: see Pinckney to Madison, 26 Oct. TJ undoubtedly received the letter when he visited Montpelier on his way to Washington (Madison, *Papers*, 17:xxviii, 427-8). A letter from John DAWSON to TJ of 30 Sep., recorded in SJL as received 3 Oct., and TJ's response on the same day he received the letter, have not been found. BUSINESS OF RHODE ISLAND: for Aaron Burr's optimistic forecast of an electoral victory for Republicans in the state, see Madison to TJ, 21 Oct. 1800.

GALILEE: the question posed in John 1:46 is "Can anything good come out of Nazareth?"

[1] Preceding word and ampersand interlined by Pinckney.
[2] Remainder of letter in Pinckney's hand.

From Caesar A. Rodney

HONORED & DEAR SIR,   Wilmington Octob 13. 1800

It is with much regret I inform you of the unfavourable result of the election in our State. Mr. Bayard is reelected by a majority of 300. votes. The Federal ticket having succeeded by about 90 votes in Kent County, the Governor is about convening the legislature, who will choose the Electors of a President & V. President. From what I have understood in conversation from some of our leading men on the Federal side I should doubt whether they will vote for Adams here, as Pinckney is undoubtedly their man. however on reflection I am rather inclined to believe they must run Adams with Pinckney least we might succeed, in consequence of their not having done so. Altho' our horizon be clouded the prospect brightens on turning our eyes to Pennsylvania &[1] Maryland. I trust in the old maxim "*Magna est veritas & prevalebit.*"[2] That you may judge better of our present situation I inclose you the Rolls for New Castle & Kent Counties. In Sussex they beat us 560. Our majority in this county ought to have been at least 600. as there were 2168 votes out but their Sheriff dragged them along, whilst ours pulled us back. The Fedl sheriff run much above his ticket & ours much below. The Governor is to commission theirs, tho' ours had a small majority of votes. Our State consists you know Sir of but three counties, the returns from Sussex except as to Rep: to Congress have not come to hand, but as their ticket succeeded there they have two thirds of the legislature

I remain Sir with great respect your Most Obedt.

C A RODNEY

RC (DLC); endorsed by TJ as received 24 Oct. and so recorded in SJL. Enclosure not found.

Born in Dover, Delaware, Caesar A. Rodney (1772-1824) was the son of Thomas and Elizabeth Fisher Rodney and the nephew of Caesar Rodney. He graduated from the University of Pennsylvania in 1789 and four years later began practicing law in Delaware and Philadelphia. In 1795 he protested against the Jay Treaty. The next year Rodney was elected to the state legislature, where he became a leader in the organization of the Republican Party. He served in the state legislature until 1802, when, at TJ's urging, he successfully challenged James A. Bayard for Delaware's seat in the House of Representatives. In Congress he became a prominent supporter of administration policy and served as a manager in the impeachment trials of John Pickering and Samuel Chase. He did not stand for reelection in 1804. In 1807 TJ appointed Rodney to serve as U.S. attorney general, a position he held until his resignation in 1811. During James Monroe's presidency he served as one of three commissioners to study and report on South American affairs.

Rodney was again elected to the House of Representatives in 1820, serving until January 1822 when he resigned to accept a seat in the U.S. Senate, being the first Republican elected to that position from Delaware. He served until January 1823 when he accepted appointment as the first U.S. minister to Buenos Aires. He died less than eight months after his arrival there (ANB; *Biog. Dir. Cong.*).

The official returns on 15 Oct. indicated that incumbent congressman Bayard was REELECTED, having defeated John Patten, the former Republican congressman, by 464 votes. In Kent County, Bayard received 811 to Patten's 720 votes, and in Sussex Bayard led with 963 votes to Patten's 373. Federalist GOVERNOR Richard Bassett, Bayard's son-in-law, convened the legislature. MAGNA EST VERITAS & PREVALEBIT: "truth is great and will prevail."

THIS COUNTY: in New Castle County, Patten received 1,247 votes to Bayard's 1,030. Each county sent seven representatives to the state legislature. The Republican candidates were victorious only in New Castle, where Rodney led the ticket with 1,244 votes; William Robinson led the Federalist ticket with 916. Joseph Israel was elected sheriff with

[1] Rodney here canceled "Delaware."
[2] Closing punctuation supplied by Editors.

From Matthew L. Davis and William A. Davis

SIR,   New York Oct 14th: 1800

We contemplate putting to press an Edition of your Notes on Virginia, and printing at the end of the Volume the *Appendix* recently published by you on the subject of Logans speech—If there are any alterations, corrections or additions that you are desirous of making, we shall be highly gratified in communicating with you on the subject. . . . If, however, the Copies at present extant, meet your approbation, then Sir, you will pardon our soliciting a line from you, stating whether the *Notes on Virginia*, or the *Appendix* have been presented by you to any Printer or Bookseller *exclusively*.

Should you consider it of consequence to suggest any amendments or additions, you may rely on a punctual and respectful attention to your suggestions.

We were the publishers of Mr Gallatins Sketch of the Finances of the United States, and also his late pamphlet entitled, Views of the Debt &c, both of which publications were entrusted to us by him, without his examining the proof sheets, and printed, amidst a pressure of business, in *very great haste*. We mention this circumstance, that you may not be deceived in us, as it respects our *Mechanical* talents. With Mr Gallatin we have the honor of a personal acquaintance. We are, with Respect, Sir, Your Most Obt. Serts—

M: L: & W: A: DAVIS

RC (DLC); in Matthew L. Davis's hand and signed by him; at head of text: "Thomas Jefferson Esqr"; endorsed by TJ as received 3 Nov. and so recorded in SJL.

Matthew Livingston Davis (1773-1850) was a Republican journalist and politician from New York City. He edited the *New-York Evening Post* with Levi Wayland from 17 Nov. 1794 until 25 May 1795. In 1797 and 1798 he collaborated

with Philip Freneau in editing the New York *Time Piece*. A member of the Society of Tammany in 1800, Davis was one of Aaron Burr's political lieutenants in the state election campaigns. He was also Burr's first biographer as the author of the two-volume *Memoirs of Aaron Burr,* published in 1836 (Syrett, *Hamilton,* 25:173; Kline, *Burr,* 1:xxx, 421; Sowerby, No. 4167).

TJ did not EXCLUSIVELY grant to any printer rights to the publication of *Notes on the State of Virginia,* as it went through multiple editions and publishers; see Coolie Verner, *A Further Checklist of the Separate Editions of Jefferson's Notes on the State of Virginia* (Charlottesville, 1950).

WE WERE THE PUBLISHERS: William A. Davis published Albert Gallatin's *Sketch of the Finances of the United States* (New York, 1796; Sowerby, No. 3523). The Davis brothers also printed Gallatin's *Views of the Public Debt, Receipts & Expenditures of the United States* (New York, 1800; Sowerby, No. 3230).

From George Douglas

SIR,   Petersburg 15th. Octr. 1800

I am the person to whom you were so obliging as to give some time ago, in Philaa., a description of the *Virginian Arms*—Since I came to this place, I took the liberty of sending to you a copy of a pamphlet, which I called a *Register*—also, a copy of a Collection entitled *Washingtoniana*—I did not send these pamphlets to you as being of any value, but as a mark, the only one I had in my power, of my respect for your person & character—

Crude & indigested as the Register was, I have been encouraged to publish another for the present year 1800—Altho' it will be very far from what it ought to be to answer its title, yet, what will be of it, I will endeavour to make more regular & systematical—And to render it more acceptable to the people of Virginia, I propose to have a frontispiece to it representing a view of the Capitol in Richmond, the plate for which is now actually engraving in Philadelphia

When in Richmond for the purpose of having the drawing taken, I endeavour'd, but in vain, to find some person who could give me an account of this building—The intention of this letter, therefore, is, to request (having been informed, that you, Sir, were the original & principal mover in having the building undertaken & executed) that you will have the goodness to give me a short account of it—such as, from what original the design is taken, from Greece or Italy, of what order, the drawers & builder's names, when the work was commenced & when finished, & the expence, with some account of the inside apartments, &c

Having thus candidly informed you of my intentions, it remains with your pleasure to give me the wished for account, or not, or to point out to me any other Gentleman who can—I know that your time must be employed in much more important matters, but I flatter myself with hoping, that you will have the goodness to excuse me when you consider the nature of the application—

Perhaps it may not be improper to say, that if the Public approves of my present attempt, I propose to continue, annually, a series of *American* views—but, in so pestiferous an atmosphere as that which covers & surrounds Petersburg, a man ought to speak with very great diffidence indeed of his future intentions, be they ever so laudable.   I have the honor to be, Sir   G: Douglas.

Please to direct to G. Douglas, bookseller, Petersburg.
P.S—I got the Virginian Arms cut agreeably to your description—I have never yet had occasion to use them—if I had, I should have been ashamed of them, they are so wretchedly executed—

RC (DLC); addressed: "Thomas Jefferson, Esqr. Monticello, *Charlottesville, Virginia*"; franked; endorsed by TJ as received 3 Nov. and so recorded in SJL.

George Douglas (1744?-1828), a bookseller in Philadelphia and Virginia, announced the opening of his Petersburg printing office in a 1 Sep. 1799 broadside in which he made known his readiness "to undertake any Kind of Printing Work with which Merchants, or Others, either in Town or Country, may be pleased to employ Him" (Evans, No. 35419). In May 1812 Douglas established a weekly Irish-interest newspaper in New York, *The Western Star and Harp of Erin*, which was discontinued the following year (Brigham, *American Newspapers*, 1:706).

For TJ's connection to a Virginia coat of ARMS, see Vol. 1:510-11 and illustrations facing 551.

Using the pen name "Americanus Urban," Douglas published an annual REGISTER for the purpose of inculcating the importance of religious and moral conduct and the Republican form of government. His *Annual Register, and Virginian Repository, for the Year 1800* (Petersburg, Va., n.d.) was advertised in the *Virginia & North Carolina Almanack of 1801* (Petersburg, Va., n.d.).

COPY OF A COLLECTION: *Washingtoniana: A Collection of Papers Relative to the Death and Character of General George Washington* (Petersburg, Va., 1800).

For TJ's SHORT ACCOUNT of the Virginia capitol, see TJ to George Douglas, 21 Dec. 1800.

A letter from Douglas in April 1800 is recorded in SJL as received 3 June at Monticello but has not been found.

From Thomas Leiper

DEAR SIR   Philada. Octr. 16th. 1800

I wrote you by last Post an answer to yours of the 26th. Ult: to which I refer—The Aurora of this day will inform you That we have carried our Member of Congress—Captain Jones—our State Senator John Pearson and Sheriff Israel Israel and one Member Samuel Wetheral for the Assembly—The old member Barton of Lancaster is returned against us but Bucks has given us Mr Rodman in our favor which is taking Two from them and giving Two to us in the Senate. Mr Dallas informs me he has information from every county in the State and says all is right—Pittsburg the Philadelphia of the West have carried their inspectors—

Inclosed you have the Governors Proclamation for a Call of the Assembly—This Proclamation has been sent to their proper places some time and there is no doubt but the Assembly will meet at the time appointed—It was observed that a number of Old Quakers did not come forward and give their votes if they had we should have lost our Member of Congress—I am with much esteem

Dear Sir Your most Obedient St. THOMAS LEIPER

RC (DLC); endorsed by TJ as received 3 Nov. and so recorded in SJL. Enclosure not found, but see below.

The 16 Oct. issue of the AURORA announced the Republican victories in the 14 Oct. Pennsylvania election, including Captain William Jones as a congressman for Philadelphia, John Pearson of Darby as senator representing Philadelphia and Delaware County, Israel Israel as sheriff, and Samuel Wetherill of Philadelphia as assemblyman. Matthias Barton, a Federalist from Lancaster, was reelected to the state senate in 1800 while Republican William Rodman took the Senate seat representing Chester, Bucks, and Montgomery counties (Tinkcom, *Republicans and Federalists*, 246-7, 321).

GOVERNORS PROCLAMATION FOR A CALL OF THE ASSEMBLY: on 18 Oct. Governor Thomas McKean convoked a special session of the General Assembly on 5 Nov. in Lancaster for the purpose of choosing presidential electors (Samuel Hazard and others, eds., *Pennsylvania Archives. Selected and Arranged from Original Documents in the Office of the Secretary of the Commonwealth*, 119 vols. [Harrisburg, 1852-1935], 4th ser., 4:452-3; Vol. 31:419).

From Thomas Paine

DEAR SIR   Paris 24 Vendre. year 9 [i.e. 16 Oct. 1800]

As the wind at one time and the tides at another prevented the Commissioners sailing at the time they intended it gives me the opportunity of sending you an addition to the other pieces.—We have nothing new since the date of my last. I send you a paragraph from a paper of yesterday. 15 Ocr—23 Vendre.[1]

The arrangement between Denmark is but tempory—the first Article is

The question respecting the right of visiting Neutral Ships going without convoy is sent (renvoya) to an ulterior discussion

3 Art—Pour empêcher que de pareilles rencontres. ne renouvellent des contestations de la meme nature. S. M. danoise suspendra ses convois jusqu'à ce que les *explications ulterieures* sur le meme objet aient pu effectuer une convention definitive"

fait Copenhagen le 29 Augst. 1800[2]

La politique des puissances du Nord se developpe de plus en plus. L'article publie par la gazette de Petersbourg, du 15 septembre, six jours après l'arrivée du courier danois, porteur de la nouvelle que les differens avaient été applanis entre l'Angleterre et le Dannemarck, confirme aujourd'hui positivement ce qu'on ne pouvait conjecturer, il y a quinze jours, savoir, que l'execution du plan dirigé contre l'ambition de l'Angleterre n'etait que differee de la part des trois puissances du Nord. Si le courroux de Paul 1er avait été calmé par la convention du 29 août, il n'aurait surement point publié le 15 septembre, que *diverses circonstances politiques font prévoir à S.M. qu'une rupture avec l'Angleterre pourrait avoir lieu.* Une chose remarquable, et qui semble prouver que notre cour ne prendra pas une part active dans cette querelle, c'est l'espèce de ménagement avec lequel la gazette de la cour a omis ce passage menaçant, en transcrivant la gazette de Petersbourg.[3]

This is by the way of Berlin, and is the latest News we have from Russia[4]

The translation of all the pieces I have sent you are in the press and I expect will be printed by tomorrow

  Salut et respect   THOMAS PAINE

RC (DLC); English date supplied; with two newspaper clippings, one now missing, attached within the body of the letter (see notes below); endorsed by TJ as received 6 Jan. 1801 and so recorded in SJL. Enclosure: probably a manuscript of "Observations on some passages in the Discourse of Sir William Scott, Judge of the Admiralty in England, in the affair of the Swedish vessel the Maria, captured by the English," not found, but printed as the fourth and final "head" of *Compact Maritime*, 21-4 (see Paine to TJ, 1 Oct. 1800). Enclosed in Stephen Thorn to TJ, 27 Dec. 1800.

MY LAST: Paine to TJ, 6 Oct. Paine reported, in English, the substance of the FIRST ARTICLE of the August 1800 convention between Denmark and Great Britain, which postponed the question of rights of NEUTRAL SHIPS. The agreement's third article was as he wrote it in French, with minor variations. The brief convention contained three other articles (Sir Francis Piggott and G. W. T. Omond, *Documentary History of the Armed Neutralities: 1780 and 1800* [London, 1919], 412-13; Paine to TJ, 1 Oct. 1800).

TRANSLATION OF ALL THE PIECES: the four brief essays that Paine sent to TJ—two on 1 Oct., one on 6 Oct., and one with the letter above, which were published together in the U.S. as *Compact Maritime*—also appeared as a French-language pamphlet, *Pacte maritime: addressé aux nations neutres, par un neutre* (Paris, 1800).

[1] Here Paine apparently attached a clipping, which has not been found, and then continued his letter below it.

[2] Translation: "Art. 3. To prevent similar encounters from renewing disputes of the same kind, His Danish Majesty will suspend his convoys until *further clarifications* on the same subject have been able to bring about a definitive convention. done at Copenhagen 29 Augst. 1800."

[3] This paragraph is from a newspaper clipping affixed to the letter. Translation: "The policy of the northern powers is becoming clearer and clearer. The article published in the Petersburg newspaper on 15 Sep., six days after the arrival of the Danish courier, bearer of the news that the disputes had been smoothed over between England and Denmark, confirms

positively today what one could not sur-mise two weeks ago, namely, that the execution of the plan directed against England's ambition had been merely postponed by the three northern powers. If the wrath of Paul I had been assuaged by the 29 Aug. convention, it would cer-tainly not have been published on 15 Sep. that *diverse political circumstances make His Majesty foresee that a rupture with England might take place*. A remarkable thing, and which seems to prove that our court will not take an active part in this quarrel, is the kind of tact with which the court gazette omitted that threatening passage when transcribing the Peters-burg gazette."

⁴ Paine wrote this sentence on the clipping.

From Andrew Ellicott

DEAR SIR   Philadelphia. October 17th. 1800

I wrote to you soon after my arrival in this City last May, but hav-ing received no answer, I suspect the letter has not reached you.—

My Astronomical Journal which contains the principal part of the report to the Executive of the U.S. and his Catholic Majesty has been ready for the press some weeks, but delayed for want of the plans, and charts; the originals being annexed to the report to our Execu-tive, and I had not time to take copies, expecting that I might again have them in my possession for that purpose, but in this I have been mistaken.—

From the conduct of administration towards me since my return, it is evident that I am marked out as a victim, but for what I know not, I am conscious of having served my country to the full extent of my abilities, without devoting one day to any kind of amusements, (my business excepted), during the three years, and eight months I was absent.—It is true that I did not aid Mr. Blunt's plans in the District of Natchez, and that I opposed the British party in that country which was headed by Mr. A. Hutchins, who was then, and is yet, a Major on the British Military establishment.—The original docu-ments to prove this fact as sworn to by himself, were intercepted, and forwarded to our Executive last February was a year.—Correct copies are now in my possession.—That our government and Mr. Blunt, in part of that disagreeable business, had an understanding I have no doubt, but on this subject, important as it is at this crisis, I am com-pelled to be silent.—The sedition law on the one hand, and the ne-cessity I am under on the other of obtaining my money which is yet witheld have tied up my hands.—

Our elections in this quarter have generally gone favourably for republicanism,—even in this City, we have carried a republican for

Congress!—This year, the beginning of a new century, I am in hopes will be distinguished as an epoch in which republicanism not only became triumphant, but be too firmly established ever again to be shaken by the advocates for Monarchy.—

I am this moment informed that the monarchists have carried the election in the county of Lancaster;—but to ballance this it is reported that the republicans have been successful in the State of N. Jersey.—

I am Sir with due respect and esteem your Hbl. Servt.

ANDW. ELLICOTT

RC (DLC); at foot of text: "T. Jefferson. President of the Senate and V.P—U.S"; endorsed by TJ as received 3 Nov. and so recorded in SJL.

Ellicott last WROTE to TJ on 28 May 1800. For the surveyor's conflict with Anthony HUTCHINS, see Ellicott to TJ, 25 Sep. 1797.

From Stevens Thomson Mason

DEAR SIR   Rasberry Plain Octr 17th 1800

You will probably have heard the issue of the Maryland Elections before this reaches you the aristocrats have sustained a great defeat. the numbers are 46 Reps, 34 Arists, at least. this Statement results from authentic returns that have been received. 5 Counties we have not heard from. we have some, but no great hopes, from them. should they however only give two Republicans, there will be a majority upon a joint ballot of both Houses in the choise of a Successor to Lloyd and in the appointment of their Governor & Council. The Tories of George Town and the Anglo federalist of Washington quite overpowered my brother JTM. they beat him more than two to one. The plan of taking the choice of Electors from the people is however, compleated upset. there will be certainly 5 and most probably 6 Republican Electors. I subjoin the returns of the different elections

I am Dear Sir with great regard and respect Your Obt Servt

STES. THON MASON

	Repn	Aristo
Washington	4	
Frederick	4	
Harford	4	
Baltimore	4	
Balt. town	2	
A. Arundel	4	

Annapolis	2		
Cecil	4		
Kent	4	Montgomery	4
QAnn	4	Charles	4
Caroline	4	P George	4.
Talbot	3		1
Calvert	3		1
	46		14

Allegany ⎫
St Marys ⎪
Somerset ⎬ Not heard from
Dorset ⎪
Worscester ⎭

RC (DLC); with election returns written perpendicularly at foot of page; endorsed by TJ as received 3 Nov. and so recorded in SJL.

NO GREAT HOPES: the Republicans failed to gain any of the twenty seats in the five counties not yet heard from and thus could not control appointments. William Hindman, a Federalist who had served in Congress from 1793 until his defeat in the election of 1798, succeeded James LLOYD, who had resigned his Senate seat (DAB, 9:62; Philadelphia Aurora, 24 Oct. 1800). MY BROTHER: according to returns published in the Virginia Argus on 14 Oct., John Thomson Mason received 560 votes while the four Federalist candidates each polled over 1,100.

A letter from TJ to Mason of 13 Sep. 1800, recorded in SJL, has not been found.

To James Monroe

DEAR SIR   Monticello Oct. 17. 1800.

Yours of the 12th. came to hand yesterday. we shall be happy to recieve mrs Monroe & yourself again among us, but as you speak of your coming with some uncertainty, I prepare the present for the post. Craven has been gone back some time. he was anxious to get his father in [law's] purchase of you concluded. he said indeed he would have taken on him[self to] conclude it, but that mr Darrelle had refused to sell his own lands till [he] could be sure of yours. that the purchaser was waiting with the money and therefore he viewed the thing as certain; but not so absolutely so as [to] justify his undertaking the conclusion. he is much interested in [effect]ing it; because the situation of his wife renders it necessary to move here immediately or not till the spring. the latter would ruin him; and he cannot get a house to bring her to till next month unless yours is purchased. in hopes of delivering these details to you in person I add no more to them. health respect & affection TH: JEFFERSON

PrC (DLC); faint; at foot of text: "Governr. Monroe"; endorsed by TJ in ink on verso.

On this day TJ wrote to John H. CRAVEN. That letter, recorded in SJL, has not been found.

To Samuel Smith

DEAR SIR   Monticello Oct. 17. 1800.

Your favor of the 8th. came to hand yesterday. I had in due time answered mr Yznardi, but not knowing where it would find him, I inclosed it to mr Barnes at Georgetown praying him to enquire for him & forward it. he has since written me he has done so. Mr. Yznardi had asked me to accept two casks of wine. my answer mentioned that I had made it a rule to accept no presents while in a public office: that as this rule was general it could not give offence to any body, and was necessary for my own satisfaction. I proposed at the same time to recieve the wines paying him their usual price; and expressed my thanks for his attention to me, of which I was as sensible as if I could have availed myself of it as he desired. supposing it will be a thing of course for mr Yznardi to assent to this, I will thank you to forward the casks to messrs. Gibson & Jefferson at Richmond. perhaps you may have learnt by some means the price of the wines. if so you will oblige me by the information, as it will enable me to remit the money to mr Yznardi should his motions prevent his reciept of my letter. —I congratulate you on the triumphs of republicanism in the city & county of Baltimore. the spirit of 76. had never left the people of our country. but artificial panics of rawhead & bloody bones had put it to sleep for a while. we owe to our political opponents the exciting it again by their bold strokes. whatever may be the event of the Executive election, the Legislative one will give us a majority in the H. of R. and all but that in the Senate. the former alone will keep the government from running wild, while a reformation in our state legislatures will be working and preparing a compleat one in the Senate. a President can then do little mischief. mr & mrs Carr are as well as their late catastrophe will permit. she is at Warren till she increases her family. I shall see you on the 17th. ensuing. health respect and esteem. TH: JEFFERSON

RC (Joseph E. Fields, Joliet, Illinois, 1946); addressed "Genl. Samuel Smith at Montebello near Baltimore"; franked. PrC (DLC).

TJ's correspondence with John BARNES regarding the wine from Joseph Yznardi, Sr., has not been found. TJ began purchasing wine from Yznardi and his son in 1793, but he recorded no payments to them during the later months of 1800. On 8 Apr. 1801 TJ noted receiving wine from Yznardi and recorded payments to him on 20 May 1801, but for deliveries at Washington not Monticello (MB, 2:921, 1029-32, 1037, 1115).

From Gideon Granger

DEAR SIR   Newhaven Oct: 18. 1800

I embrace the opportunity presented by Mr. Erwing with great Satisfaction. The receipt of your Letter inclosing one to Uriah McGregory gave me much pleasure—The Letter to Gregory I yet hold. I have not been able to satisfy myself respecting his Character. In the present state of things it appeared to me most prudent to retain the Letter untill I could be satisfied beyond a reasonable doubt of his moral Character & fidelity and I perfectly well know the withholding the Letter could produce not the least Injury. The Sentiments contained in your Letter were those which I have long felt to be just. The prospect of their being tested by experiment brightens, and it must certainly be matter of high Congratulatn and Joy, that we can rest with such Confidence upon the final success of our long and laborious exertions. In this State we have just come to a decision of Strength—We have been defeated—but *not conquered.* so far from that we have encreased & are encreasing—we may with great modesty claim one Third of the people on our Side—our votes between May & Octr. increased for the Republican Candidates from 1049. to 3012. our difficulties are great merely from a Consideration, that the persons in Authority both in State & federal Goverments, the Clergy & the Barr are formed, together with all Ambitious men, into a well formed body in favor of Aristocracy—There are at least four hundred Men of public Education & possessed of public Confidence for four or five of us to contend with—yet the contest is kept up on all Occassions, and to some advantage—I have long labored to rally the Physicians & Dissenting Clergy who are generally friends of equal liberty—This wished for event I have not yet been able to accomplish—we suffer much from an unceasing persecution and constant operation of the System of Terror—They are now bold enough to tell us that we must be destroyed *root and branch*—And—In the Legislature yesterday on the floor of the

House one of them was insolent enough to declare to me that tho' he esteemed me as a Man—yet we must all be crushed, and that my life was of little Importance, when compared to the peace of the State— At the last Election they practised evry possible fraud. In One place they denied its being the place & day for election to Congress—The Republicans tendered their votes—They were rejected—afterwards at 10 OC at Night—They opened the poll & took in 30 or 40. federal votes—In very many places They hissed when my name was calld.— pronouncd me Jacobin & the friend of the Atheist—Threatened to publish the name of evry person who dare vote for the Jacobin— Nay—They even forged a Letter, and circulated it in all distant parts of the State by newspapers & hand bills, with a view to destroy me. I trust in God that our relief draweth near. If the Republicans are defeated in their General Election there is certainly reason to fear that Edwards, Kirby Wolcott & myself shall be ruined or forced to leave the State. we feel as tho; even our Courts of Justice were not pure & uninfluenced, and being all of Us men Largely concerned in business—the Sources of Justice being corrupted—our ruin will be easy—yet We will persevere—Our cause is founded in Truth and our Sufferings cannot exceed the Sufferings of those who Achieved the revolution—we are constantly threatned with bloodshedding and civil war (if we succeed) and to what pitch their passions might carry them, if all New-England were united in one view is uncer- tain—But thanks to the Author of Our Existence we have formed a party sufficiently powerful to remove all possibility of their proceed- ing to overt Acts—by this means time for reflection and experiment will be given and these must and will produce public approbation & political Quietude. Our struggles here have allready produced good effects in the States of Massachusetts & Vermont, particularly in the eastern part of Vermont, who are generally Connecticut People—We took our ground, planted our Standard and shouted boldly—It resounded through half New England, and roused many from their Torpor—Our force was not equal to the Contest, but those who have advanced, cannot retire—These are our political Calculations— Rhode-Island, republicanized will afford democratic Electors— Vermt. is doubtfull Our chances are at least equal. I look for republn: Electors & Members of Congress—but it is uncertain. In New hampshire about $\frac{3}{10}$ths. right—all Officers the Other side—In Mass. $\frac{2}{5}$ths. right. & we believe 5 republican members in Congress— The Conduct of their Electors doubtfull—I cant believe they will vote for Pinkney—If they do Mr. Adams has lost all Influence—Our Condition I have stated, with all this leaven warm'd & fostered by the hand of a beneficent Govermt. we have nothing to fear.—A Letter by Mr Erwing will be pleasing.

Sincerly wishing you prosperity & happiness—I Am Sir—

GIDN GRANGER JR

RC (DLC); endorsed by TJ as received 7 Nov. and so recorded in SJL.

YOUR LETTER: see TJ to Granger, 13 Aug. 1800.

FORGED A LETTER: on 12 Sep. the *Middlesex Gazette* published a letter from *Springer's Weekly Oracle*, which did not name the author or recipient but was dated from Granger's hometown of Suffield, 17 Aug. 1800. The letter urged Republican organizers in Connecticut to stir up "the *ignorant multitude*," noting that "our dependance is principally on them, and when they are once hot, we must not suffer them to become cool, till our purposes are answered." The writer recommended that the New London *Bee* be put into the hands of as many "country people as possible." Republican organizers were especially encouraged to distribute pamphlets that countered the charge that TJ was a deist. The writer continued: "Probably he is so; but whether he be or not, to use his own expression, 'This neither breaks my leg nor picks my pocket.'" On 13 Sep. Granger responded from Hartford that the whole publication was a forgery "evidently designed to calumniate and injure my character" (New Haven *Connecticut Journal*, 17 Sep. 1800; Brigham, *American Newspapers*, 1:60; Granger to TJ, 4 June 1800).

From Caspar Wistar

DR SIR   Philada. Octobr 19th: 1800—

The unceasing calls of my profession have accasioned me to postpone my answer to your esteemed favour longer than I wished—You committed Chancellor Livingstons first paper on the Steam Engine to my care—it was read at the next meeting of the Society & referred to Messrs. Patterson & Latrobe. Those Gentlemen finding no references to the figure, in the descriptions which accompanied it, were much puzzled, & therefore wished to have the consideration of the Paper deferred—I handed the Second paper to Mr. P. & he has informed me since, that it renders the first much more intelligible, & that the Committee will report fully upon the subject in a short time—In consequence of a resolution of the Society to publish yearly, & to arrange their papers for that purpose in September; a Committee was appointed last month & they found a sufficient number of Papers for a volume of moderate size—Among them are two papers on the premature decay of Peach Trees wh[ich] appear very interesting—The paper you transmitted with a plan of an opening for common sewers was read at the Society, & referred to a Committee who appeared pleased with the box for collecting sand; but our fellow Citizens who are engaged in mechanical pursuits display great talents not only in the invention but the simplification of Machinery, & we now use a box at the opening of some of the common sewers which has completely the effect of a valve with out the inconveniences which arise from intricate structure. thus suppose a box with an aperture at each end A.B., at an equal heighth from the bottom, and a partition CD extending from the top, so as to divide the box cross-wise, but to leave an aperture at the bottom—if this box is placed horizontally & receives a stream of water at A, it will allways be filled up to the line A.B. while the partition CD will prevent any exhalations from passing out thro the aperture A.

Have you received any accounts respecting the large bones which have lately been found up the North River in the State of New York—The News papers informed us about two months Since that a large proportion of a Sceleton was found, I think near New-Burgh in that state—I have applied to two different Gentlemen at New York, & as yet have received no information respecting it—You remember that bones which seem to have resembled those of the Mammoth were found at the Wallkill (described in the 2d Vol: of the Academy at Boston)—I have long thought that we have neglected too much Dr Mather's story in the Abridgement of the Philosophical Transactions for I met with an Old Man at Claverack, who specified the spot in that neighbourhood where the large bone was found, & mentioned also a man whose father or Grandfather had seen it.

I am tempted by the importance of the subject, & the difficulty of procuring information elsewhere, to inquire if you have met with any accounts of diseases that resemble our yellow fever among the first Adventurers to America. I see in Robinson that the first Settlers at Darien were much reduced in their numbers, & the natives of Mexico were also attacked by Sickness after their Conquest—If you can refer me to any of the historians of those transactions who describe, or state the circumstances of those diseases, I will be greatly obliged to you—

To this long letter I will only add, that the returns of our Election have not yet been received from many of the Counties, but those which have appeared show that the Republican Party has acquired a great accession of strength in the Course of the last year—Our Governor is about to issue his writs for calling the Assembly immediately, & a short time will decide whether this populous State is to be deprived of her sufferage at the important election—I am not at all conversant with the maneuvres of parties, but I cannot believe any party will be hardy Enough to take such a meas[ure.] Our friends here are perfectly confident as to the result in general, & their confidence appears to increase daily—With sincere wishes that their calculations may prove just

I am, with respect & affection Yours &c   C. WISTAR JUNR

RC (DLC); damaged; endorsed by TJ as received 3 Nov. and so recorded in SJL.

YOUR ESTEEMED FAVOUR: TJ wrote Wistar on 9 Sep., according to SJL, but the letter has not been found.

After hearing from its secretaries and treasurer on the matter, the American Philosophical Society on 15 Aug. 1800 formed a committee, including Wistar, to collect material for a new VOLUME of the society's published *Transactions*. At the next meeting, on 19 Sep., the committee received instructions for proceeding, although the volume of the *Transactions* did not appear until 1802. The DECAY OF PEACH TREES had been an object of the society's attention for at least five years. On 3 Oct. 1800 the society concluded an essay competition on the subject by naming two essays to share the prize. Those papers appeared in an appendix to the next *Transactions* volume (APS, *Proceedings*, 22, pt. 3 [1884], 229-30, 301-3; APS, *Transactions*, 5 [1802], 325-8; Vol. 30:37).

With his letter of the 9th TJ evidently enclosed for the APS a two-paragraph description of an apparatus for the street drains of city SEWERS. By retaining some runoff water in a catch basin, the device would block the escape of air and fumes from the sewer. TJ wrote the paper in his own hand and called it a "Description of a stopper for the openings by which the sewers of cities receive the water of their drains," but his title line continued: "by mr John Fraser, of Chelsea, London." Fraser, born in Scotland, had begun his career as a draper and hosier but became a botanist and horticultural collector and established the "American Nursery," a commercial enterprise, in Chelsea. He traveled widely, searching for plants in South Carolina and Georgia in 1786-88 and meeting TJ in France not long after. Fraser maintained gardens in South Carolina to supply his nursery in England,

and visited them more than once in the 1790s. He was in the United States in 1800, traveling in the Carolinas, Virginia, and elsewhere to collect plants for Emperor Paul of Russia. It seems likely that the botanist described the concept of the sewer stopper to TJ on a visit to Monticello during those travels, since there is no indication of any correspondence between them in this period. TJ's brief paper discussed, and illustrated by diagrams, both the basic device and a modified form that included attachments for catching the SAND that commonly ran into drains in Charleston and Savannah, cities familiar to Fraser. The paper was read at the APS meeting of 19 Sep. 1800, and at the next meeting Charles Willson Peale and Robert Leslie, to whom it had been referred, recommended its publication. It appeared in the next volume of the *Transactions* (PrC in DLC: TJ Papers, 107:18354-5, entirely in TJ's hand; Dft in DLC: TJ Papers, Ser. 9, entirely in TJ's hand including emendations; APS, *Transactions*, 5 [1802], 148-9; APS, *Proceedings*, 22, pt. 3 [1884], 302-3; ANB; MB, 1:736; Vol. 12:655n; Vol. 14:278, 390; Vol. 15:47-8, 296).

The LARGE BONES that farm workers found while digging marl for fertilizer near Newburgh, New York, were the most recent of a series of similar discoveries in the area. This newest find gave hope that a complete skeleton of the animal, which had not yet been identified, might be recovered. Georges Cuvier later classified the fossils from the Hudson Valley and named the animal the mastodon (*Medical Repository*, 4 [1801], 211-14; Paul Semonin, *American Monster: How the Nation's First Prehistoric Creature Became a Symbol of National Identity* [New York, 2000], 316-17; Charles Coleman Sellers, *Mr. Peale's Museum: Charles Willson Peale and the First Popular Museum of Natural Science and Art* [New York, 1980], 113; Peale, *Papers*, v. 2, pt. 2:1189-90).

In 1785 clergyman Robert Annan reported to the American ACADEMY of Arts and Sciences in BOSTON that immense teeth and bones had been found five years earlier on his farm on the Walkill River, in New York State about fifteen miles west of the Hudson River and seventy miles north of New York City (Robert Annan, "Account of a Skeleton of a Large Animal, found near Hudson's River," *Memoirs of the American Academy of Arts and Sciences*, 2, pt. 1 [1785], 160-4). Cotton MATHER'S discussion of fossils from CLAVERACK, also in the Hudson Valley, appeared in a letter of November 1712 that was reported in the Royal Society's *Philosophical Transactions*, 29 (1714), 62-3. Mather decided that the remains must be those of gigantic humans mentioned in the Bible. A few years earlier the governor of New York had sent the Royal Society a huge tooth from the same vicinity. As the earliest reported evidence of an American "mammoth," the finds at Claverack generated speculation and discussion in scientific and theological circles, including correspondence between TJ and Ezra Stiles in 1784. TJ traveled through Claverack in May 1791, taking note of the azaleas in bloom but saying nothing in his journal of the trip about the early fossil discoveries there (Semonin, *American Monster*, 9-11, 15-40; Vol. 7:312-17, 364-5; Vol. 20:453).

ROBINSON: William Robertson's *History of America*, first published in 1777, which chronicled Spanish colonization in the Americas. TJ did not hold the work in the highest regard, considering it to be an uncritical reflection of the views of Buffon and Raynal; see Vol. 8:185; Vol. 13:397; Vol. 14:698; Sowerby, Nos. 468-9.

From James Thomson Callender

SIR   Richmond Jail [ca. 20] Octr. 1800.

I am afraid of being troublesome. I wrote you last week with some pages of The Prospect, and now inclose a few more. I expect to have two pieces in tomorrow's Argus, and a defence of Mr. Coxe in the Examiner. Mr Larkin Stannard of Spotsylvania was here this minute, and says that some of my Subscribers that he got me, were shy of taking the books after they heard of my being imprisoned. It almost requires an effort of my credulity to believe that such wretches Can exist. How Congress contrived to raise the fabric of a revolution upon such scaffolding is wonderful indeed!

Certainly a people thus buried in the kennel of servility require very much the Aid of a political apostle; and I have contemplated, for some time, the setting up, next Summer, or Autumn, a printing office in Richmond, providing we succeed in turning out the aristocracy. By a press of my own, I would not only get the work much more easily, and thankfully, but much more cheaply done; and among such drones, I Could not fail of plenty of business. The Editorship of a news paper, and the probable profit of a volume per annum, would Come to a thousand dollars per annum, 500, for the former, the Argus or Examiner, and 500 for the latter; and upon a smaller sum it is not possible to exist. 2 or 300 dollars would be quite enough to buy a press, &ca.

[233]

RC (DLC); partially dated, with day determined by internal evidence; signature torn away. Recorded in SJL as received 24 Oct. 1800. Enclosure not found.

TWO PIECES: only one piece in the 21 Oct. issue of the *Virginia Argus* is clearly by Callender. As a "Scots Correspondent" in the Richmond jail, Callender predicted TJ's victory in the presidential election and analyzed probable electoral outcomes in various states, including North Carolina, Maryland, New Jersey, Delaware, and Pennsylvania. A piece by Callender in defense of Tench COXE, dated 20 Oct. 1800 from the Richmond jail, appeared in the Richmond *Examiner* the next day.

Larkin Stanard (STANNARD) served in the Virginia House of Delegates from 1798 to 1804 (Leonard, *General Assembly*, 213, 217, 221, 225, 229, 233).

From James Madison

DEAR SIR   OCT. 21. 1800

This will be handed to you by Mr. Altson of S. Carolina, who proposes to call at Monticello on his return from a Northern tour. He will probably be made known to you by other introductions; but those which he has brought to me, as well as a short acquaintance with him make me feel an obligation to add mine. He appears to be intelligent, sound in his principles, and polished in his manner. Coming fresh from N.Y. through Pena. & Maryld. he will be able to furnish many details in late occurrences. The fact of most importance mentioned by him and which is confirmed by letters I have from Burr & Gilston, is that the vote of Rho: Island will be assuredly on the right side. The latter gentleman expresses much anxiety & betrays some jealousy with respect to the *integrity* of the Southern States in keeping the former one in view for the secondary station. I hope the event will skreen all the parties, particularly Virginia from any imputation on this subject; tho' I am not without fears, that the requisite concert may not sufficiently pervade the several States. You have no doubt seen the late Paris Statement, as well as the comment on it by Observator who is manifestly Hamilton. The two papers throw a blaze of light on the proceedings of our administration, & must I think, cooperate with other causes, in opening thoroughly the eyes of the people. Sincererely yours   Js. MADISON JR.

RC (DLC: Madison Papers); endorsed by TJ as received 23 Oct. and so recorded in SJL.

MR. ALTSON: Joseph Alston.

LETTERS from both Aaron Burr and David Gelston early in October conveyed assurances of strong Republican prospects for the VOTE OF RHO: ISLAND (Madison, *Papers,* 17:418-21).

The LATE PARIS STATEMENT appeared in a French newspaper of 6 Aug. and first ran in the *New-York Gazette and General Advertiser* on 29 Sep. It was reprinted in several American newspapers, including the *Virginia Herald* on 7

Oct. The statement announced the suspension of negotiations in Paris because the powers vested in the American envoys were "too limited to enable them to conclude a treaty" that would afford France the same advantages as England had been given by the Jay Treaty (Madison, *Papers,* 17:420n).

Hamilton's essay, "France and America," was published in the New York *Spectator* on 8 Oct. under the pseudonym OBSERVATOR (Syrett, *Hamilton,* 25:131-9). Hamilton hoped that the two nations would "pass into a state of peace in fact on the basis of the laws of nations" (same, 139).

To George Jefferson

DEAR SIR   Monticello Oct. 24. 1800.

I recieved a letter from mr Callender dated in the jail on the 11th. inst. informing me he was about to publish a volume but was under some difficulty in getting it effected. I will ask the favor of you to call on him *yourself* and to furnish him fifty dollars on my account for which I will request him to send me two copies of his work when out, & the rest to remain till convenience. he mentions in his letter mr Rose's kindnesses to him. mr Rose is a very old acquaintance of mine & was tutor to mrs Jefferson. be so good as to present my respects to him & to assure him I recollect him with esteem

I take for granted mr Barnes remitted you 680. Doll. the first week in this month. I have an offer of 6. D. in Philadelphia for my tobo. if I will send it there. will you be so good as to try what I can get for it with you, on credit till the 1st. of Apr. those who have already known it's quality will be most likely to buy. I will thank you for an answer by return of post, as it is necessary I should give an answer to the application from Philadelphia. I desired mr Barnes also to remit you some money for mrs Key. let me know if you please when you recieve it that I may inform her she may draw on you. I am with esteem Dear Sir

Your's affectionately   TH: JEFFERSON

PrC (MHi); at foot of text: "Mr George Jefferson"; endorsed by TJ in ink on verso.

In his financial records at 23 Oct. TJ noted that he had directed George Jefferson to pay CALLENDER $50 (MB,

2:1028). See also TJ's Statement of Account with Gibson & Jefferson, 15 Jan. 1801.

APPLICATION FROM PHILADELPHIA: Leiper to TJ, 9 Oct. A letter from TJ to Ann KEY of 23 Oct., recorded in SJL, has not been found.

From James Thomson Callender

SIR   Richmond Jail October 27th. 1800

Along with this comes another letter, covering some newspaper pieces. I beg leave to inclose the last half Sheet but one of the pamphlet, being from 136 page to 144; and an uncorrected imperfect half Sheet of the conclusion; wanting the first page, which closed my hints for the conduct of the Assembly in my case. A half Sheet from p 120, to 128, I have never yet been able to get from the printer.

We are all in the highest Spirits here, on the revolutions in Maryland and Rhode Island.

I have the honour to be Sir Your obedt & most obliged servt.

JAS. T. CALLENDER.

P.S. In one end of the lower Story, the blacks are singing psalms. In the other, a boy, who has gone crazed, is shrieking in lunacy. The sailors laughing. *Sic transit Mundus!* chase has sent me a letter that he will beat me; and I have advertised that, in case of an attack, I'll shoot him. The remainder of the piece, with preface &ca, will come next week. Your goodness will forgive the loquacity of joy; but my heart is sick with the pain of gladness at an anticipation of the time, when the herd[1] of federal robbers shall be hunted from their den; when oppression shall feel the pang she has inflicted; and rapine regorge a portion of her prey. A New Jersey Judge in *a Charge*, has advertised Volney, &c. and me, as atheists & blasphemers. I can not get one half of my M.S.S. printed; so that I am ashamed of the comparative ignorance displayed in this piece; and the M.S.S. does not contain $\frac{1}{10}$ of what I know. There certainly never was such another history as ours. Mr. Jones and Mr. Rose have acted like Gentlemen to me. I should have 2 pieces in next Argus, one in the Examiner, and one in the Petersburg Republican.

RC (DLC); addressed: "The Honble. Thomas Jefferson Vice President of the United States Charlottesville"; endorsed by TJ as received 3 Nov. and so recorded in SJL. Enclosures not found.

In a piece from the Richmond jail dated 28 Oct., Callender noted with delight the projections—which proved to be inaccurate—that MARYLAND would give TJ 7 or 8 out of 10 electoral votes and RHODE ISLAND "to the amazement of all mankind" would give TJ the state's 4 votes (Richmond *Examiner*, 31 Oct. 1800).

Reporting that Samuel CHASE had threatened him "with a personal correction," Callender responded that to repel an attack he would "compliment" the Supreme Court justice "with the contents of a pistol" (Richmond *Examiner*, 21 Oct. 1800). In A CHARGE to the grand jury at the New Jersey circuit court meeting in Gloucester County on 7 Oct., Supreme Court Justice Isaac Smith declared that "your Talleyrand's, your Volney's, your

Duane's, your Callender's, and hundreds besides" pollute the presses "with their corruptions and blasphemies." Their principles were "atheistical," and it was

"*contamination* to be near them" (*Philadelphia Gazette*, 14 Oct. 1800).

¹ Interlined in place of "gang."

From Joseph Young

HONORED SIR/ Stamford State of Conecticut Octobr. 29. 1800.

When I sat down to address you, my first intention was to apologize for the liberty I have taken in troubling you with my speculations on Astronomy, Physiology, and Mechanics, at this critical period, when the most important national concerns demand your attention, and doubtless occupies all the faculties of your mind; But when I considered that the great Doctor Franklin, and the celebrated Ritenhouse, had both gone to study Astronomy in the upper regions, and that you, their worthy successor, delighted to patronize and encourage American improvements in arts and Science, I conceived a laboured apology to be unnecessary, because I was convinced, that if the work contained any useful discovery or improvement, you would freely afford a leisure hour to peruse it; But if it contains nothing valuable, all that could be said concerning it, cannot give it any intrinsic worth, or save it from merited oblivion; But if happily it should gain your approbation, either in the whole, or in part, I will thank you for your candid opinion, whenever you can make it most convenient, and in whatever way you may please to convey it. Which favour shall be most gladly received, and gratefully acknowledged

By Your Most Obedient Humble Servt. JOSEPH YOUNG

RC (CtY); at foot of text: "Honble. Thomas Jefferson Esquire"; endorsed by TJ as received 29 Nov. and so recorded in SJL. For enclosure see below.

Joseph Young (1733-1814), New York physician and author of a 1793 treatise on *Calvinism and Universalism* (New York, 1793), forwarded his SPECULATIONS on astronomy and physiology to TJ by a Mr. Davenport. The work most likely was his *A New Physical System of Astronomy; or, an Attempt to Explain the Operations of the Powers which Impel the Planets and Comets to Perform Eliptical Revolutions Round the Sun. . .To Which Is Annexed, a Physiological Treatise* (New York, 1800; see Sowerby, No. 963; TJ to Young, 10 Dec. 1800).

From James Thomson Callender

Sir   Richmond Jail Novr. 1. 1800.

Sir   Richmond Jail Novr. 1. 1800.

I had, some days ago, a visit from Mr. Jefferson of this place. I have just now got the pamphlets stitched, and have sent him 3 copies for you; but under the same parcel, I used the freedom, I almost fear I was in the wrong, of inclosing[1] 9 for Mr. Madison, who is a Subscriber, or was to the first part, for 15 copies, so that I hazard nothing with him in sending him 9. *I did not know his address*; but I understand that his place is not at a considerable distance from Yours.

If health permits, I mean to begin printing the second part, of which a great deal has already been published in the Petersburg Republican, next week.

I sent Mr. Pleasants one long piece he did not put in, on the electioneering prospects of Mr. A.

I have the honour to be, Sir, Your Most obedt. & most humble servt.,   Jas. T. Callender.

RC (DLC); endorsed by TJ as received 6 Nov. and so recorded in SJL.

George W. Erving delivered the copies of part one of the second volume of Callender's *The Prospect Before Us* to Madison (TJ to Madison, 9 Nov. 1800).

[1] MS: "I inclosing."

From Bishop James Madison

Dear Sir,   Novr. 1. 1800 Williamsburg.

Mr. Wilkinson, the late Agent or Steward for Mrs. Paradise, having departed this Life, I have been solicited by a Friend of mine, Mr Coleman, to mention him to you, as a fit Successor; upon the Supposition, that you had, in Conjunction with some other Gentlemen, full Authority to act in such a Case. I have said to Mr Coleman, that I was disposed to beleive, you had declined an Acceptance of the Trust which Mrs. Paradise wished to repose in you. But as it may be otherwise, & he is anxious upon the Subject, I determined to assure you of his perfect Integrity, & Capacity for Business. Mr Coleman is a near Neighbour, has been long Known to me, & is in every Respect a truly worthy Citizen. Should the Appointment be in you, with those other Gentlemen alluded to, I am persuaded you wd. wish to be informed of some meritorious Person for the Office; & it is upon that Ground, I have taken the Liberty of recommending Mr. William Coleman of James City.

What an important *Denoûment* has lately been made! Hamilton's Attack upon Mr. Adams is a perfect Confirmation of all that *that* arch & very clever[1] Fellow Duane has been so long hinting at, or rather affirming.—It will be a Thunderbolt to both. I rejoice with you, that Republicanism is likely to be *completely* triumphant; & particularly, as the Event will prove the great Mass of the People of America not to be so far degenerated, as there was, at one Time, too much Reason to apprehend.—

With sincere Respect & *Esteem*—I am, Dr Sir, Yr. Friend & Sert

J MADISON

Your Letter to Miss Digges was carefully delivered—
Novr 3.
This Moment I am told the Republn Ticket has a Majority of One Third in this County—

RC (DLC); endorsed by TJ as a letter of 3 Nov. received on the 14th and so recorded in SJL.

William WILKINSON had managed the property of Lucy Ludwell PARADISE in Williamsburg (Vol. 15:270n; Vol. 22:28). TJ recorded no correspondence with either Wilkinson or COLEMAN in SJL.

HAMILTON'S ATTACK: *Letter from Alexander Hamilton, Concerning the Public Conduct and Character of John Adams, Esq. President of the United States* (New York, 1800). Hamilton originally intended the tract to have only limited, discreet circulation to induce presidential electors in South Carolina to favor Charles Cotesworth Pinckney over John Adams. Copies came into the hands of Republican publicists, however, and the *Aurora* in Philadelphia began printing extracts of Hamilton's condemnation of Adams on

22 Oct., two days before the authorized publication of the pamphlet in New York. William DUANE, disappointed in obtaining copies for sale, issued his own printing "pro bono publico" on 1 Nov. The original publisher rapidly produced four editions (Syrett, *Hamilton*, 25:169-78; Kline, *Burr*, 1:456-7n; Evans, Nos. 37566-70; Sowerby, No. 3237).

TJ wrote to Maria DIGGES on 11 Sep. 1800, probably enclosing the letter in one he wrote to Bishop Madison that day. Those letters, along with communications from Digges to TJ of 12 Aug. 1800, received from Williamsburg on the 21st of that month, and 22 Oct., received 14 Nov., are recorded in SJL but have not been found; see also Maria Digges to TJ, 25 Oct. 1801.

[1] Preceding two words and ampersand interlined.

From George Jefferson

DEAR SIR,   Richmond 3d. Novr. 1800.

Your favor of the 24th. ultimo should have been answered by last post agreeably to your request but that I did not return home until a few days ago after an absence of several weeks. it was then handed to me by Mr N—

I immediately waited upon Mr. C— and paid him the sum you directed. I desired him to send you two copies of his work immediately, and the balance at his convenience—but he the next day sent me a packet which from its bulk I suppose must have contained a dozen, and which I forwarded by Mr. Randolph.

Mr. N— having informed me that you intended this letter *for me alone* I shall keep it with my private papers, and as I could not with propriety charge you with the money above mentioned in the books of G. & J. without filing the Letter in which its payment is directed, I concluded to pay it out of my private funds. it can therefore remain between you & myself, until I have the pleasure of seeing you at Monticello, which I expect will be in the course of the ensuing summer at furthest; as I regretted much not having it in my power to avail myself of your friendly invitation the last. Mr. N. likewise informs me that you expect occasionally to write confidentionally to me upon the subject of politics, and that you wish for me to point out some mode by which your letters may be opened *by myself only*. The best way which occurs to me at present will be for you to add after the superscription—"for himself"—or to write at the top of the letter "(private)"—and inclose it under a blank cover to G. & J. or perhaps it will be still better if the first letter of this kind which you write is inclosed at a time when you have something to say to G. & J., as it would more certainly be observed.

Your letters never would have been opened except by myself had you not been in the habit of directing to me individually when you wrote upon business which concerned the company. the change however will be soon observed.

I have been endeavouring to get some offer for your tobacco which will be better than shipping it to Philada.—but the most I have been offered is $:5—on a credit 'till the 1st. of Apl—that however I suppose is equal to 6 in Phila. which is as much as could be calculated upon.

I think though that I could get more than 30/ if I were authorised to sell—as most persons expect the offer to be made them. Brown for instance (like himself) refused to make any offer whatever, but observed he would be glad to know what we would take.

I think it probable that 5.$\frac{1}{2}$$: could be had if there were more credit purchasers, but there are very few who are perfectly undoubted. Brown though I think is, his conduct respecting Mr. Shorts claim to the contrary notwithstanding.

What passed between us was by message only as he was sick in bed, or I should have pressed that business—I will see him on it immediately on his recovery.

I am Dear Sir Your Very humble servt.   GEO. JEFFERSON

RC (MHi); addressed: "Thomas Jefferson esquire Monticello"; endorsed by TJ as received 6 Nov. and so recorded in SJL.

MR N: perhaps Philip Norborne Nicholas, who resided in Richmond serving as the state's attorney general. According to SJL, TJ wrote Nicholas on 24 Oct. (a letter now missing), the same day he wrote George Jefferson. MR. C: James T. Callender. Thomas Mann RANDOLPH may have carried both letters to Richmond and then returned home with the package of books from Callender. According to SJL on 24 Oct. TJ also received a letter from his neighbor Wilson Cary Nicholas dated 22 Oct., which has not been found.

G. & J.: Gibson & Jefferson.

From George Jefferson

DEAR SIR,   Richmond 3d. Novr. 1800

It just occurs to me that I have omitted to inform you of the receipt of $:680— of Mr. Barnes on your account & $:296.$\frac{97}{100}$ on account of Mrs. Key.

This information would have been sooner given, but that Mr. B— sent it to us in a dft on the Cashier of the bank—and as it could not be disposed of at the time we sent it to our friend in Phila. to collect & to forward the amount in notes—and which were only received on the 29th.; owing as he says to our letter having been missent.

Yr. Very humble servt.   GEO. JEFFERSON

RC (MHi); addressed: "Thomas Jefferson esquire Monticello"; franked; endorsed by TJ as received 6 Nov. and so recorded in SJL.

From James Monroe

DEAR SIR   Richmond Novr. 3. 1800.

I was very sorry my visit to Albemarle took place when you were in Bedford, especially as the calls of duty here put it out of my power to wait yr. return. Indeed such is the nature of the trust I hold that I can scarcely ever be absent from the seat of govt. I intended leaving Mrs. M. at home and making another visit there before yr. departure, but so delicate is the state of her health at present that I was fearful of the experiment. I have nothing new from any quarter that changes the state of things since the departure of Majr. Randolph, except the arrival of Mr. Irvin from Boston who will probably see you before you sit out for the federal town.

I have yet heard nothing either from Darrelle or Craven. When above I heard the latter had not returned from the neighborhood of Alexa., whence I inferr'd, they were engaged in making provision to purchase my land. I hope they will take it. I think it well worth what I ask, compared with the price of other tracts. If they find difficulty in raising the sum required I am disposed to accomodate as far as I can, but as I sell it to command money, and want all that can be had, I wod. wish you to intimate that only in case of necessity to secure the bargain. sincerely I am

> your friend and servant   JAS. MONROE

RC (DLC); endorsed by TJ as received 6 Nov. and so recorded in SJL.

MR. IRVIN FROM BOSTON: George W. Erving.

To Charles Pinckney

DEAR SIR   Monticello Nov. 4. 1800.

I recieved last night your favor of Oct. 22. and we are so near seeing one another at Washington that I should not have troubled you with an answer (which indeed I have little hope of your recieving at Charleston) but that you mention having written to me frequently, & forwarded all the numbers of the [Republican &] other papers, your speeches &c. I assure you that the letter recieved last night is the only scrip of a pen or paper I have recieved from you since I had the pleasure of seeing you in Philadelphia, except a line of introduction by mr Alston dated before the last session of Congress. I had the pleasure of his company here one day only. he was hurrying on to the affairs of your sta[te. his] information was so full & so recent from all the Northern states that it [is un]necessary for me to do more than supply a few facts of later date than [his] departure. in Delaware the Feds have carried two thirds of their house of representatives. in Philadelphia the republicans carried their member for Congress by a very small majority owing to the refusal of several of the old [quakers] to vote at all. the Federalists carried their member in Lancaster (Barton) but still the elections in that state have been greatly in favor of the republicans. [the Govr.] issued a proclamation convening his legislature, & I am assured from the best authority this state will have a *legal* election. it is said that the Republicans have succeeded in Jersey, but I am uninformed of the particulars. of Maryland I know nothing new since mr Alston [left u]s. the elec[tion of el]ectors took place in this state yesterday: as yet all [. . .] *the* [minority] will be about one sixth of the majority. [. . .] coming session being the last act of the federal tragedy [&] that [. . .] a bloody one? will they yet attempt to [prorate?] things? I rather suppose they [will be forwarded by] [. . .]. I [. . .] respect & esteem.   TH: JEFFERSON

P.S. I [neither post? nor] superscribe in my own hand.

PrC (DLC); faint; at foot of text: "Charles Pinckney esq."

For Pinckney's FAVOR OF 22 Oct., see his letter to TJ at 12 Oct. 1800. Pinckney's communication to TJ of 18 Dec.

1799, a LINE OF INTRODUCTION for Joseph ALSTON, is recorded in SJL as delivered by Alston on 23 Oct. 1800, and has not been found (see Burr to TJ, 9 Oct. 1800).

From Benjamin Hawkins

Creek agency 6 novr. 1800

I wrote you some time past and sent on the Creek and Chickasaw, I now add the Choctaw words required by you. The Cherokee is at best doubtful. The seperate communication requested by you will be made as soon as I can obtain a book or paper to transcribe it on. My residence has been lately changed and is two hundred miles from the frontiers of Georgia and that frontier a great distance from regular supplies: my last order for stationary has been sent three months and I do not expect a supply till the next week.

I request you to accept of my sincere wishes for your health and happiness and to believe me with the truest esteem and regard

My dear sir, yr. obedient servt.   BENJAMIN HAWKINS

RC (DLC); at foot of text: "The Honble Mr. Jefferson"; endorsed by TJ as received 1 Dec. and so recorded in SJL. Enclosures: vocabularies of Choctaw and possibly Cherokee, neither found, presumably incorporated into the "Comparative Vocabulary" described at Hawkins to TJ, 12 July 1800.

Hawkins's letter of SOME TIME PAST was that of 12 July.

RESIDENCE HAS BEEN LATELY CHANGED: Hawkins was probably at Tuckabatchee, a principal town of the Upper Creeks (Upper Muskogees) and

the site of their national councils. It was in the same part of Alabama as the present city of Montgomery, some distance to the west of Hawkins's first permanent agency, which had been on the Chattahoochee River. He subsequently established his agency on the Flint River in Georgia (Joel W. Martin, *Sacred Revolt: The Muskogees' Struggle for a New World* [Boston, 1991], 93-6, 135-6; Thomas McAdory Owen, *History of Alabama and Dictionary of Alabama Biography*, 4 vols. [Chicago, 1921], 2:1332; Hawkins to TJ, 1 Mch. 1801).

From James Monroe

DEAR SIR   Richmond Novr. 6. 1800

Mr. Ervin will present you this, who is already known to you under the honorable testimonial of Saml. Adams. He wishes to visit Mr. Madison on his return to this place, to whom it may be of use for you to give him a line of introduction. The republican ticket has had complete success in this quarter. In Prince George the vote for it was 197. while it was only 9. for the opposit one. In this city it had a majority, and of the 5. or six counties we have heard from, the majority was in the proportion of at least 5. for 1. in each, or rather the most unfavorable one. I send you the letters of Mr. Skipwith and Fenwick wh. support the statment in the paper I gave Mr. R. If they will be of any use retain them; if not inclose them to Mr. Madison to be returned me, by Mr. Ervin. Sincerely I am yr. friend and servant

JAS. MONROE

RC (DLC); endorsed by TJ as received 7 Nov. and recorded in SJL as received 6 Nov. Enclosures not found (see below).

MR. ERVIN WILL PRESENT YOU THIS: one purpose of George W. Erving's visit to Virginia was to warn of the consequences should Burr and TJ receive the same number of electoral votes. Erving advocated giving some of Virginia's votes to a candidate other than Burr, but by the time Erving saw Madison after his visit to Monticello he no longer pressed that view. Madison, and presumably TJ, thought that a tie would be easily resolved by the House of Representatives in TJ's favor (Ammon, *Monroe*, 190-1; Madison, *Papers*, 17:431, 434-5).

For the TESTIMONIAL of Samuel ADAMS, see his letter to TJ of 31 Jan. 1800.

From Fulwar SKIPWITH and Joseph FENWICK Monroe had received commentaries about the prospects and status of the negotiations between the French government and the American envoys. Fenwick, who sailed from Bordeaux for the United States on the first of September, carried a piece that he had written and published in France as well as a letter from Skipwith to Monroe. Skipwith and Fenwick claimed as sources, in some cases indirectly, Volney, Moreau de St. Méry, Pierre Louis Roederer, and Joseph Bonaparte. As expressed by Madison, Skipwith's letter, if "thrown into an unexceptionable form," might "produce reflections suitable to the crisis of our affairs with France." Soon after Monroe sent the communications to TJ for his and Madison's appraisal, word arrived in the United States of the convention completing the negotiations with France (Madison, *Papers*, 17:434; Fenwick to Monroe, 22 Oct., 8, 22 Nov. 1800, in DLC: Monroe Papers).

To George Jefferson

DEAR SIR   Monticello Nov. 7. 1800.

In order to replace the money paid by you to Callender & to carry it into my account with the company, I inclose you an order on the company for the sum paid, 50. D. so that his name will not appear on their books. I wish you could have visited us this summer; however what is only deferred is not lost. I am Dr. Sir

Your's affectionately   TH: JEFFERSON

PrC (MHi); with enclosure pressed below signature; at foot of text: "Mr. George Jefferson"; endorsed by TJ in ink on verso. Enclosure: Order dated 7 Nov. 1800 on Gibson & Jefferson to pay

George Jefferson $50 for value received (PrC in MHi; written and signed by TJ; at foot of text: "Messrs. Gibson & Jefferson").

To George Jefferson

DEAR SIR   Monticello Nov. 7. 1800.

Yours of the 3d. are recieved. if $5\frac{1}{2}$ D can be got for my tobo. in Richmond I would have you sell it at once, unless you see that the market is rising. credit to be given to the 1st. day of deposit. I inclose you the Manifests for the 21. hhds from Poplar Forest. whether you have before recieved those for the 9. hhds made here, or whether they have never been taken out, I am unable to say at the moment of writing this. I will immediately enquire at Milton, & if not yet delivered out, they shall come by the next post. in the mean time you may sell by the weight & marks as stated above.—I have just recieved a letter from mr Short which makes it absolutely necessary to bring mr Brown's account with him to a close. be so good as to mention this to him and remit the money to mr Barnes. I am Dear Sir

Yours affectionately   TH: JEFFERSON

PrC (MHi); with list of weight and marks from tobacco manifests at top of sheet; at foot of text: "Mr. George Jefferson"; endorsed by TJ in ink on verso. Manifests not found.

For the chart of WEIGHTS & MARKS AS STATED ABOVE for TJ's 1799 tobacco crop, see MB, 2:1026. The letter from William SHORT is that of 6 Aug. 1800.

From John Armstrong

DEAR SIR/   Chilicothe 8 November 1800

Agreeably to your riquest I have enterd with the auditer the Lands Located for General Koscuskiosko, and payed the taxes thereon. this track is well situated on the Sioto, if the general does not intend it fore sale perhaps he would do well, to have an agent in this country who would let it out on Lease, improving the Land would inhance its value, and the tenant in possession always be accountable for the taxes

this letter Sir will be handed you by William McMillen Esqr. delegate in congress from this country, who will convey any communications you may have to make on the above subject. he is a gentleman of Talents and integrity. it would be using too much freedom to ask leave of introducing him to your acquaintance. I have the honer to be with much respect your Obd. Servt.   JOHN ARMSTRONG

RC (MHi); at foot of text: "Honorable Thomas Jefferson"; endorsed by TJ as received 5 Dec. and so recorded in SJL.

John Armstrong (1755-1816) had become acquainted with Tadeusz Kosciuszko during the American Revolution, when Armstrong was a young officer of Pennsylvania regiments in Continental service. Armstrong remained with the army, serving in the Ohio Valley, until 1793, when he took up residence near Cincinnati. Three years later he became treasurer of the Northwest Territory. He was also a magistrate and judge (ANB; TJ to Kosciuszko, 7 May 1800).

From Pierre Samuel Du Pont
de Nemours

MONSIEUR,   Good-Stay, near New York 8 9bre. 1800.

C'est vers le 20 d'Aoust que j'ai eu l'honneur de vous envoyer *par la Poste*, selon que vous m'avez marqué que je pouvais le faire, mon Ouvrage—*sur l'Education nationale dans les Etats-unis.*

Je commence à craindre que le service des Postes ne soit pas plus scrupuleux ici qu'en Europe; que votre nom et la grosseur du paquet n'aient piqué la curiosité; et qu'après l'avoir satisfaite, on n'ait jugé convenable de garder ou de bruler le tout: ne fût-ce que parceque l'on est peut-être encore mal-adroit dans cet art du Vieux Monde, et qu'on n'aura pas voulu vous certifier par le désordre de l'envelope ou du cachet qu'on avait violé la foi publique.

Il se peut aussi que vous n'ayiez pas eu le tems de lire un assez long Manuscrit en français, et que vous n'ayiez pas voulu m'en écrire sans l'avoir lu. Je conçois très bien que vous avez plus d'une affaire; et celle de l'Education, qui ne pourra vous occuper que dans votre Présidence, n'est pas au nombre des pressées.

Il se peut encore que vous ayiez confié le livre à quelque ami pour le traduire en anglais: ce qu'au reste je compte faire moi-même cet hiver, si vous n'en avez chargé personne.

Mais dites moi par un mot si vous l'avez reçu.

Voila enfin la Paix.—Votre haute Magistrature n'aura que du bien à faire.

Agreez mon tendre et respectueux attachement.

Du Pont (de Nemours)

Pusy travaille aux reconnaissances et aux projets pour les Fortifications de la Rade de New York.—Il vous présente son hommage

Et mes Enfans leur respect.

E D I T O R S'   T R A N S L A T I O N

Sir   Good-Stay, near New York, 8 Nov. 1800

It was around the 20th of August that I had the honor of sending you *by the mail,* as you indicated I could do, my work—*on National Education in the United States.*

I begin to fear that the postal service may be no more scrupulous here than in Europe; that your name and the size of the packet may have aroused curiosity; that after having satisfied it, they may have judged it appropriate to keep or to burn the whole thing: if only because they are perhaps still clumsy in that art of the Old World, and they may not have wished to prove to you, by the disorder of the wrapping or the seal, that they had violated the public trust.

It is also possible that you may not have had the time to read a rather long manuscript in French, and that you did not care to write me about it without having read it. I very well understand that you have more than one undertaking; and that of education, which you will only be able to do something about when you are president, is not among the most urgent.

It is also possible that you may have entrusted the book to some friend to translate into English, which actually I expect to do myself this winter, if you have not already commissioned someone to do it.

But let me have word if you have received it.

Finally peace is here.—Your High Office will have only to do good.

Accept my affectionate and respectful fondness.

Du Pont (de Nemours)

Pusy is working on reconnoitering the ground and on the projects for the fortifications of the roadstead of New York.—He extends to you his compliments

And my children, their respects.

RC (DLC); at head of text: "Mr. Jefferson"; endorsed by TJ as received 1 Dec. and so recorded in SJL.

Du Pont de Nemours had sent his treatise on education to TJ on 24 Aug.

From James Herry

Sir   New York Nov 8th. 1800

I take this opportunity to let you know that I am verry much in want of alittle money I have heard that you are very good to the nedy

I shall take it favour of you to spare me Some money as my father works very hard to support his famaly—

I your most obeidient Servant JAMES HERRY
Student of Physic

pleas to leave the answer at the post office

RC (MHi); endorsed by TJ as received 1 Dec. and so recorded in SJL.

To James Monroe

TH:J. TO JAS. MONROE Monticello Nov. 8. 1800

Yours by your servant has been delivered as also that by mr Erwin. I think Skipwith's letter contains some paragraphs which would do considerable good in the newspapers. I shall inclose that & the other by mr Erwin to mr Madison, to be returned to you. I shall set out for Washington so as to arrive there as soon as I suppose the answer to the speech is delivered. it is possible some silly things may be put into the latter on the hypothesis of it's being valedictory, & that these may be zealously answered by the federal majority in our house. they shall deliver it themselves therefore. I have not heard from Craven since I wrote to you. I told him I should leave this on the 12th. therefore I think it certain he will be here before that date, as we have some important arrangements to make together. I shall not fail to encourage the purchase of your lands.—I am sincerely sorry I was absent when you were in the neighborhood. I wished to learn something of the excitements, the expectations & extent of this negro conspiracy, not being satisfied with the popular reports. I learnt with concern in Bedford that the important deposit of arms near New London is without even a centinel to guard it. there is said to be much powder in it. we cannot suppose the federal administration takes this method of offering arms to insurgent negroes: yet some in the neighborhood of the place suspect it. would it not be justifiable in you to suggest to them the importance of a guard there? in truth that deposit should be removed to the river. Health, respect & affection.

RC (DLC: Monroe Papers). PrC (DLC); endorsed by TJ in ink on verso.

The letter carried by Monroe's SER-VANT was apparently that of 3 Nov. The other letter acknowledged by TJ above was that of 6 Nov.

Adams gave his SPEECH to both houses of Congress in the Senate chamber of the new Capitol on 22 Nov., five days after the opening of the second session of the Sixth Congress. Uriah Tracy, Abraham Baldwin, and Gouverneur Morris, who had been elected to fill the seat vacated by the resignation of James Watson of New York, drafted the Senate's response, which was adopted with John E. Howard of Maryland presiding pro tem. At noon on the 26th the Senate assembled at the President's House to deliver their address to Adams. TJ arrived in Washington the following day, having left Monticello on 24 Nov. (JS, 3:105-110; MB, 2:1031; *Biog. Dir. Cong.*, 63-4).

On 7 Nov. TJ wrote a letter to John H. CRAVEN that is recorded in SJL but has not been found.

ARMS had been stored and manufactured at NEW LONDON, Virginia, for some years (CVSP, 2:166, 221, 231; 8:363, 419, 420).

From Abraham Labagh

SIR   Nyork Novr. 9 1800

having to contend with the *Author of a pamphlet, who has wrote against what *he wishes to make* your Religious oppinion, and having his authority before me from which *he* endeavours to make you to be a person who disbelieves in what is commonly called Divine Revelation—I would as a favour ask you to answer me (if you think fit) only these two Questions—first do you believe there was a Deluge and do you believe that Mankind Originally Sprang from one pair—I believe you are of my and his oppinion but I would wish to have an answer from you. Since times have altered words may have altered—he says that you would think little of the Man who would endeavour to prove you to be no Infidel, which is one of the reasons I have writen you on this Subject. I disbelieve this, and if I were convinced you were one, (*like he*) I should think it my duty to hear more from you than I have, before I would publickly pronounce you such, and should take the same Liberty in requesting an answer. if you will oblige me you will a number of our Religious friends who are at a loss to determine. a line from you directed to Aaron Burr will be thankfully received by your—

Friend and Wellwisher   ABRM. LABAGH

*Serious Considerations Dr L

RC (ViW); addressed: "Thomas Jefferson Vice President of the United States Washington"; franked and postmarked; endorsed by TJ as received 8 Dec. and so recorded in SJL.

For the pamphlet, SERIOUS CONSIDERATIONS, attributed to William Linn, see George Smith Houston to TJ, 11 Sep.

To James Madison

DEAR SIR   Monticello Nov. 9. 1800.

This will be handed you by mr Erwin, a gentleman of Boston, with whom I became acquainted last winter on a letter of introduction from old Saml. Adams. he is sensible, well informed & strongly republican, wealthy & well allied in his own state & in England. he calls to pay his respects to you. I inclose you two letters which the Govr. sent me by him for perusal. it is a pity that a part of one of them was not put into the papers, to shew the effects our maniac proceedings have had, & were intended to have. when perused, be so good as to re-inclose them to the Governor by the same bearer. I think it possible that mr Adams may put some foolish things into his speech on the possibility of it's being his valedictory one; and that this may give the Senate an opportunity again of shewing their own malice. I propose therefore to give time for the speech & answer to be over before I arrive there. at present I think of being with you on Friday the 21st. on my way. I have a great deal to do however before I can get away. the Republicans in Charleston have lost 11. out of 15 in their city election. the country is said to be firm: but this I imagine cannot be counted on, considering local & personal interests & prejudices. nor do I rely on what Govr. Fenner of R.I. said to mr Alston. you know that 2. of the 3. counties of Delaware elected Fedl. represent. to their legislature. Health & affection.   TH: JEFFERSON

P.S. I send by mr Erwin 9. copies of Callendar's Prospect forwarded me for you.

RC (DLC: Madison Papers, Rives Collection); addressed: "James Madison," with notation "favd. by mr Erwin." PrC (DLC). For enclosures see below.

MR ERWIN: George W. Erving.
The TWO LETTERS enclosed were from Fulwar Skipwith and Joseph Fenwick; see Monroe to TJ, 6 Nov.

From George Jefferson

DEAR SIR,   Richmond 10th. Novr. 1800

Your favor of the 7th. inclosing manifests for 21 Hhds. Tobacco is duly received.

As the Inspectors at Milton are not *over-correct* I think it necessary to inform you that the manifests for that Tobo. have never been forwarded to us.

Although I suppose there would not be the smallest difficulty in obtaining the price you mention for the Tobacco, yet as information was received here last night from Philadelphia that our Envoys have concluded a treaty with France which is perfectly satisfactory to both parties, & which is forwarded on to Washington—I have concluded not to offer it for sale until I again hear from you.

I think however it would be well not to hold it up too long, as I am of opinion that the spirit of speculation will probably run the article up to a price which it cannot hold.

Yr. Very humble servt. GEO. JEFFERSON

RC (MHi); at foot of text: "Thos. Jefferson esqr."; endorsed by TJ as received 14 Nov. and so recorded in SJL.

From George Jefferson

DEAR SIR   Richmond 11th. Novr. 1800

Having been much engaged last night after the arrival of the post I entirely forgot in my hurry to inform you that I received a few days ago of Messrs. Pendleton & Lyons $:1315– on acct. of Mr. Short.   This sum I presume should be remitted to Mr. Barnes in George Town; if so I expect I shall have to send it by post in notes—there being such little intercourse between the two places, that I think there is scarcely any chance of procuring a bill.

I think it probable however that Mr. B. may be able to dispose of one on us to some person who may be coming on from the North to make purchases here.

Knowing of your unwillingness to trust any thing of consequence to the mails (although I should not myself apprehend any danger) I shall wait for your instruction.

I am Dear Sir Your Very humble servt. GEO. JEFFERSON

RC (MHi); at foot of text: "Thos. Jefferson esqr."; on 17 Nov. George Jefferson wrote and signed on verso: "The preceding was written in the hope of meeting with a private opportunity to Albemarle—in which I have been disappointed. The *current* cash price of Tobo. is now 30/. and it is expected to rise still further"; endorsed by TJ as received 20 Nov. and recorded in SJL as a letter of 17 Nov.

From Lafayette

MY DEAR FRIEND   La Grange 20th Brumaire [i.e. 11 Nov.] 1800

As I'll Have By this Opportunity the pleasure to Write to You, I shall Now only Mention the Affair of M. de BeauMarchais Which You Better know than I do—His Claims Have Been InHerited By a former Aid de Camp of Mine Who Married Beau-Marchais's daughter and Whose Sister is a Wife to General Dumas the Chief of the Staff in the Middle Army—My Attachement to My two Companions Makes it a duty for me to Give them the Recommendation Which they Have Requested—The Merits of the Cause Have Been often and are Now, I Unterstand, to be Again debated—Your knowledge of it Leaves Nothing More for me to Say, after I Have Related the friendly Motives of this Letter, than that I am Most Affectionately

Yours   LAFAYETTE

You Have known Mathieu Dumas in the beggining of the french Revolution, and it is probable You Have Seen Delarue, as an Aid de Camp, at My House.

RC (DLC); at foot of text: "Hble Thomas Jefferson Esq."; English date supplied; at head of text in an unidentified hand: "Copd."; endorsed by TJ as a letter of 11 Nov. 1800 received 10 July 1801 and so recorded in SJL. Tr (DLC); in an unknown hand; at head of text: "Exd."; with minor variations.

During the American Revolution Pierre Augustin Caron de BEAUMARCHAIS, by secret arrangement with the French crown, had sent arms and equipment to aid the revolt of Britain's American colonies. After the playwright's death in 1799 his heirs continued to press his claim for the completion of payment. Resolution of the matter met delay after delay because it seemed impossible to ascertain if one million livres tournois paid in 1776, known as the "lost million," had subsidized matériel sent to America. The matter dragged on until the 1830s, when the United States applied part of an indemnification from France to a final settlement of the claim of Beaumarchais's heirs (Syrett, *Hamilton*, 11:207-11; 20:357-60n; Brian N. Morton and Donald C. Spinelli, *Beaumarchais and the American Revolution* [Lanham, Md., 2003], 317-26; Vol. 26:243-7, 277).

From James Madison

DEAR SIR   [ca. 11] Novr. 1800.

Yours by Mr Erwin was delivered by him, safe with the two letters inclosed. I forwarded them by him this morning, as you desired to the Governour. They confirm in substance the state and difficulty of the negociation as presented by the late Statement under the Paris head. The observations on the delays carried out by the Ex. and the favorable moment lost thereby, are interesting, and deserve the public attention, if they could be properly submitted to it. I have suggested the idea to the Govr. The accts. from S. Carolina are rather ominous. but I trust we shall soon be relieved by an overbalance of republicanism in the upper elections. To the most unfavorable suppositions we can as yet oppose the hopes presented by Pennsylva. and the chance that a competency of votes may be obtained in spite of defections in the former State. I inclose a hand bill lately published in Maryland & industriously circulated there & to the Southwd. You will probably be surprized at one of the documents included in it. Mr. Duval expresses considerable fears of its tendency, but I cannot view the danger in so serious a light. I am glad to find you do not mean to postpone your journey to Washington later than the 21st. as I wish much to see you on the way, and shall set out for Richmd. if called thither on the electoral errand as is probable, at least 8 or 9 days before the legal day. The elections as far as I have learned are successful beyond expectation. In this County the votes were 340 odd to 7. and in a number of other Counties in the most commanding[1] majorities. Even in Frederick, I hear the difference was nearly as 3 to 1.

Yrs affy.   Js. Madison Jr

RC (DLC: Madison Papers); endorsed by TJ as received 13 Nov. and so recorded in SJL. For enclosures, see Monroe to TJ, 6 Nov. and TJ to Madison, 9 Nov.

LATE STATEMENT UNDER THE PARIS HEAD: see Madison to TJ, 21 Oct.

HAND BILL LATELY PUBLISHED IN MARYLAND: The Annapolis *Maryland Gazette* of 25 Sep. published a "Certificate of Mr. Peregrine Fitzhugh, a gentleman of unquestionable veracity, honour and integrity," dated 9 Sep., in which Fitzhugh wrote: "In a conversation which took place a few months after the last election for president and vice-president of the United States, Mr. Jefferson expressed to me the great satisfaction he felt at the choice of president having devolved on Mr. Adams instead of himself . . . and that the charge of Mr. Adams's being a monarchist, however it might have served to answer an electioneering purpose, was totally unfounded . . . and that he could with great truth pronounce Mr. Adams to be as *firm* and *decided* a republican as ever lived.—In giving this certificate I derive additional pleasure from the hope that it may tend to rescue Mr. Jefferson from the unmerited charge exhibited against him by some of his friends, that the high encomiums which he passed on Mr. Adams's character in his speech on assuming the office of vice-president, were not his *real* sentiments, but the effect of mere compliment." Gabriel Duvall wrote Madison that he was "fearful" what the effects of the handbill would be (Madison, *Papers*, 17:424). Duvall also published a series of letters in the *Maryland Gazette* from July through October 1800 as a vindication of the conduct and character of TJ.

THE LEGAL DAY: 3 Dec. 1800, when the electors were scheduled to meet in their respective state capitals.

[1] Preceding three words interlined.

To John McDowell

Sir Monticello Nov. 13. 1800.

Being within a few days of my departure for Congress where I shall continue through the winter, & desirous of leaving all my pecuniary affairs settled, I must avail myself of the post rider from your place to Charlottesville for the transmission of the balance which may be in your hands for me. any sum which you may put into his hands for me on return from his present tour, will still find me here and shall be applied to your credit. the nails formerly desired to be forwarded to the late Colo. Bell, may be delivered for me to mr Kelly merchant of Charlottesville. I am Sir

Your very humble servt TH: JEFFERSON

PrC (DLC); at foot of text: "Mr. John Mc.Dowell"; endorsed by TJ in ink on verso.

Thomas BELL died at his home in Charlottesville on 16 Oct. (Richmond *Examiner*, 24 Oct. 1800).

Letters from McDowell to TJ of 3 Oct. and 12 Nov., recorded in SJL as received on 11 Oct. and 20 Nov., respectively, have not been found.

From James Thomson Callender

Sir Richmond Jail Novr. 17th 1800

I inclose some newspapers, and Shall probably use the freedom of sending you by this same post A part of the second part of the 2d volume of *The Prospect*. The whole is written excepting the *first* Chapter. I Could not have gone to press, but for the assistance of a Subscriber, who sent me 14 days since his 50 dollars, as mentd in my last, as I want a great deal of money here, I cannot get.

I mean to Collect the Defence, print 500 Copies, and send 200 of them to mr Leiper and Mr Dallas. I had forsworn pamphlets, as one always loses by them. But in truth I feel a kind of pride, at this moment, to let them see I Can write as well *here*, as any where else.

I am just Come to that ridiculous business the C—n & R—n; wherein, they have been so obliging as to misquote and lie monstrously. I shall therefore make short work with them, and hasten to Hamilton's *glorious pamphlet*!

Begging your pardon, Sir,—for this intrusion,

I have the honour to be Sir Your most obliged & obedient Servt.

JAS. T. CALLENDER.

P.S. I mentioned Mr. Davis, and his Virginia Gazette, by way of anticipating *one* reason, for a republican administration dismissing him; his attacks, or those of his writers upon the Republicans. But there is another reason, which could not so well be brought above board; the possibility of intercepting our newspapers, which gives those who use it so decided an advantage; an advantage sometimes taken.

RC (DLC); addressed in Robert Richardson's hand: "The Honorable Thomas Jefferson Vice President of the United States Charlottesville"; franked and postmarked; endorsed by TJ as received 20 Nov. and so recorded in SJL.

MY LAST: Callender to TJ, 1 Nov. 1800. COLLECT THE DEFENCE: the "Defence of Thomas Jefferson" under Callender's signature, "a Scots Correspondent," began appearing in the Richmond *Examiner* on 11 Nov. and probably concluded on 2 Dec. The "Defence" refuted accusations published in the 4 Nov. *Washington Federalist* against TJ's views on the Constitution and religion (Richmond *Examiner*, 11, 14, 18, 21, 25, 28 Nov. 1800).

On 31 Mch. 1824, Robert Richardson, a native Virginian who had settled in Union Village, Ohio, and was related to Richard Richardson, wrote TJ that he had served as Callender's amanuensis and that all but 15 or 20 lines of "the Defence, under the signature of a Scots correspondent," which extended to 19 columns when it appeared in the *Examiner*, was in his hand. He had also worked with Callender on the second volume of *The Prospect before Us*. Richardson recalled that he broke off his relationship with the writer when Callender began assailing his political friends: "I told him plainly to his face, that I would not in future write any thing with him, or any thing for him" (RC in ViW).

From John Barnes

SIR   GeorgeTown (Potomac) 20th Novr 1800

Your Esteemed favr 5th. addressed to me at Washington (instead of this Place) did not reach me Untill the 15th.—by Your expected Arrival the 17th. I did not think of Answering it, but immediately sent on your several packages—and uncased them at Mr Conrades.— your Accomodations are eligant, and the Other Rooms filled with your particular friends—Messrs: Langdon Baldwin Brown &ca—are every Moment expecting your Arrival.—

This Morning Mr. Randolph informs, you had postponed your setting out, to this very day, and still it may be possible,—you may be detained a few days longer—I could not withhold advising—of these particulars & withal my having already Ordered your 3 Nautical Almanacs—for the pamphlet mentioned, it is, at hand, and would have been sent a week since—but, Mr Langdon, was persuaded you must have recd it ere this—via Philada—it has I believe effectually Answered the very *contrary purpose* intended by the Author—in respect—to Mr C.C. P—

your many friends—are Anxiously wishing your safe & speedy Arrival—as well Sir

your Obedt: & very humle servt: JOHN BARNES

RC (ViU: Edgehill-Randolph Papers); at foot of text: "Thomas Jefferson Esqr: Monticello"; endorsed by TJ as received 1 Jan. 1801 and so recorded in SJL.

TJ's FAVOR of 5 Nov. 1800 and letters from Barnes of 3 and 25 Oct. that TJ received on 12 Oct. and 3 Nov., respectively, are recorded in SJL but have not been found.

PAMPHLET MENTIONED: Hamilton's *Letter*.

From Charles Pinckney

DEAR SIR   November 22: 1800 In Columbia

I have just recieved your favour after an interval since its date of nearly one Month—I am to particularly regret Your not recieving my communications, as I wanted some facts from you to aid me in the very delicate & arduous struggle I have in this state—finding from my intelligence that the Pennsylvania Senate intended to contend for a concurrent vote in the choice of Electors & thus to shield themselves under a pretended affection for the rights of their Branch from the popular odium I very early percieved that the choice of a President would in a great measure depend upon this States Vote—I therefore very assiduously have attended to this Object since June & now wait the Issue which is to be decided on Tuesday next.—my anxiety on this subject is very much increased by a Letter I have recieved from Governour Monroe in answer to one I wrote him on the subject—he seems to think with me that our state must decide it & that Pennsylvania is very uncertain—Since Mr: Monroe's Letter I have seen *that Woods* is elected President of the Senate of that state—this I think is a bad symptom—he is Ross's Brother in law—it would if it was possible make me redouble my Exertions—. I am hopeful we shall succeed & although my situation is truly delicate in being obliged to oppose my own Kinsman, (who does not now on that account speak to me) yet Urged by those principles it is my duty never to forsake & well convinced that the Election depends on this State I have taken post with some valuable friends at Columbia where our legislature meet & are now in Session & here I mean to remain until the thing is settled——I have been told I am to be personally insulted for being here while I ought to be in Washington & that a Motion will be made expressing the opinion of one of the Branches that all their Members ought to be present at the discussion of the French Treaty—But I who know that the President's Election is of more consequence than any Treaty & who feel my presence here to be critically important, mean to remain & my friends with You who know the reason will readily excuse my absence—To weaken the federal Party in our Legislature which is Stronger than I ever knew it an attempt is made to set aside the Charleston Election & I have suggested a new idea to the Petitioners which is to suspend those sitting members[1] immediately from their seats. I inclose You a Petition on this subject which at their request *I have drawn & they are* now debating it. whether they vote or not I think We shall carry the Election & the Moment it is decided I will write you.—my situation here is peculiarly delicate & singular. I am the *only member* of Congress[2] *of either side present* & the federalists view me with a very jealous Eye. I long to see the Business happily & safely over & to personally pay my respects to you being with great respect & regard

    Dear Sir Your's Truly   CHARLES PINCKNEY

We have elected 3 republican Members of Congress

And a 4th. had a narrow Squeeze

December 2: 1800 The Election is just finished & We Have (Thanks to Heaven's Goodness) carried it—We have Had a hard & arduous struggle & I found that as there Were no hopes from Philadelphia & it depended upon our State entirely to secure Your Election & that it would be almost death to our hopes for me to quit Columbia I have remained until it is over & now permit me to congratulate You my dear sir on an Event, which You will find we had an arduous & doubtful struggle to carry & of which I will send You the particulars before I set out—Expect me soon in Washington, But I shall be late. important public arrangements for the republican Interest detaining me here a little longer—As to my own affairs I never think of them— to secure Your Election has employed me Mind Body & Estate since June——

I use the same precaution not to superscribe in my own hand. I trust all this precaution will not long be necessary.[3]

RC (DLC); addressed: "The Honourable Thomas Jefferson At the seat of Government of the United States At Washington In Maryland To go by Post"; franked; postmarked 2 Dec.; endorsed by TJ as a letter of 2 Dec. received on 12 Dec. and so recorded in SJL. Enclosure not found, but see below.

YOUR FAVOUR: see TJ to Pinckney, 4

Nov. The petition drawn by Pinckney, which sought to SUSPEND THE SITTING MEMBERS from Charleston until the question of election fraud in the city could be considered, was presented on 25 Nov., the day after the state legislature convened, but it was referred to the House Committee on Privileges and Elections, which was not due to report until after the presidential electors were chosen on 2

Dec. (Cunningham, *Jeffersonian Republicans*, 233; Charleston *City Gazette and Daily Advertiser*, 2 Dec. 1800).

The three REPUBLICAN MEMBERS elected to Congress were William Butler, the successor to Robert Goodloe Harper, who moved to Maryland and did not stand for reelection; Thomas Moore, who won the seat held by Federalist Abraham Nott; and incumbent Republican Thomas Sumter. Federalist Congressmen Benjamin Huger and John Rutledge retained their seats and Thomas Lowndes, another Federalist, won the seat vacated by Thomas Pinckney (*Biog. Dir. Cong.*; ANB, 10:129; Dauer, *Adams Federalists*, 324-5, 329).

¹ Preceding two words interlined.
² Preceding two words interlined.
³ Preceding two sentences added at foot of text.

From George Jefferson

DEAR SIR   Richmond 24th. Novr. 1800

I am informed by the Treasurer of the James River company that he is directed to make a further reimbursement of the money lent by the individuals of the company, of one fourth.

In looking over the powers for the last reimbursement he cannot find yours in my favor for Mr. Shorts, and cannot therefore ascertain whether or not it was *general.*   he also informs me there is some Interest due Mr. S. and recommends your giving me a general power, as it will save you trouble.

This information he says would have been given you sooner, but he has been much from home of late—having taken a journey to Kentuckey.

Mr. Brown is still confined to his room. I have spoken to Burton upon the subject of the balce. due by him to Mr. Short, but that Gentleman informs me it cannot be settled without Brown.

I am Dear Sir Your Very humble servt.   GEO. JEFFERSON

Tobacco 30/. to 33/. Cash.

RC (MHi); at foot of text: "Thos. Jefferson esqr."; endorsed by TJ as received 19 Dec. and so recorded in SJL.

TREASURER OF THE JAMES RIVER COMPANY: Robert Pollard. A letter from Pollard to TJ of 12 Dec. 1796, recorded in SJL as received on the 16th, and TJ's response dated 18 Dec. have not been found.

LOOKING OVER THE POWERS: for TJ's power of attorney to George Jefferson giving him the right to care for William Short's interest in the James River Company, see George Jefferson to TJ, 11 Nov. 1799.

To Thomas Mann Randolph

TH:J TO TMR. mr Madison's Tuesday morng. [25 Nov. 1800]
I ought to have brought with me my catalogue of books, but forgot it. it is necessary for me in making out a catalogue for Congress at the desire of their joint commee. it is lying I believe either on the table in my book room, or under the window by the red couch in the Cabinet. will you be so good as to send it to me by return of post, well wrapped & sealed up in strong paper. direct it to me at Washington on Patomac.

Mr. Trist's information as to the Pensva legislature was not quite exact. the lower house past a bill, which the upper rejected at once. the two houses are decisively pitted against each other. a majority of two Federalists in the upper. Adieu affectionately

RC (DLC); endorsed by Randolph as a letter of 25 Nov. 1800 received on the 27th. Not recorded in SJL.

CATALOGUE FOR CONGRESS: on 25 Apr. the House of Representatives resolved to establish a joint committee "for the purpose of making out a catalogue of books, and adopting the best mode of procuring a Library, at the City of Washington," as recommended in Section 5 of the law providing for the removal and ac-

commodation of the government, enacted the previous day. A sum of $5,000 was appropriated for the project. Robert Waln of Pennsylvania and Thomas Evans and Levin Powell of Virginia were appointed by the House to serve on the committee. The Senate agreed to the resolution on 28 Apr. and appointed Samuel Dexter, William Bingham, and Wilson Cary Nicholas to serve (*Annals*, 10:684; JHR, 3:682-3; JS, 3:81; U.S. Statutes at Large, 2:55-6).

From Thomas Leiper

DEAR SIR Philada. Novr. 26th. 1800
Inclosed is a copy of a letter I sent you by Post on the 9th Ult: in answer to yours of the 26th of Septr. and the post following I sent you a Note informing I had wrote you an answer to your letter of the 26th and in that beged leave to refer—Since have had no answer and from that circumstance conclude my letters to you or yours to me have miscarried is the reason I again write you on the subject—Notwithstanding the News from France which I believe to be true and the effect the papers say it had on the price of Tobacco at Petersburg I will not give more for your Tobacco than six Dollars per ~~Cwt~~. delivered here this fall for I expect Tobacco will be chapper in the Spring—My opinion is founded on the Large Quantity of Tobacco on the Continent and the want of Funds to purchase it—I am with much esteem Dear Sir

Your most Obedient St. THOMAS LEIPER

RC (MHi); endorsed by TJ as received 1 Dec. and so recorded in SJL. Enclosure: see Leiper to TJ, 9 Oct. 1800.

YOURS OF THE 26TH: TJ to Leiper, 26 Sep. 1800, noted in SJL but not found. Leiper had given TJ the same rate for the PRICE OF TOBACCO in their transaction in New York of 3 Mch. (MB, 2:1015).

Terms for Conrad & McMunn's Boarding House

[ca. 27 Nov. 1800]

pr Week	
Rooms	$25.—
board	10.—
Servant board	5.—
hire of Servant	2.50
fuel & lights	5.—
barber	1.—
	$48.50

The above are the terms on which Mr. Jefferson is to be accommodated at.

To CONRAD S

MS (MHi); on verso: "Honbl Thomas Jefferson Esqr."; endorsed by TJ: "Conrad mr."

Conrad and McMunn's boarding house, belonging to the local proprietary Thomas Law, was at the corner of New Jersey Avenue and C Street, convenient to the Capitol. TJ leased a bedroom as well as a parlor or reception room, but took his meals at the common table. He lodged here from his arrival in Washington on 27 Nov. until after his inauguration, when he moved into the President's House on 19 Mch. 1801 (Malone, *Jefferson*, 3:491-2; MB, 2:1031, 1032, 1034, 1035; Samuel Clagett Busey, "The Centennial of the First Inauguration of a President at the Permanent Seat of the Government," *Records of the Columbia Historical Society*, 5 [1902], 99; Bryan, *National Capital*, 1:379-80).

TJ received a statement of account for his expenses at Conrad & McMunn's for 1-31 Jan. 1801: "To board, rooms &c. &c. from 1st. inst. 'till this day both days included in 4 weeks & 3 days @ 48\frac{50}{100}$ per Week" for £80.10.7$\frac{1}{2}$ and "To keeping a horse 4 weeks & 3 days @ $4 per W." for £6.12.9. Also recorded are charges of 6/7 per day for 24 days for alcoholic beverages, including a bottle of porter at 3/9 and wine at 2/10. TJ's expenses also covered an occasional stage hire at 7/6 as well as 16/10$\frac{1}{2}$ for three friends who dined with him on 31 Jan. His total bill with Conrad & McMunn's for the month was £97.6.3, which TJ calculated to be $259.50 (MS in MHi; in unknown hand, with total figure in dollars and cents in TJ's hand written adjacent to total; endorsed by TJ in ink on verso).

To George Jefferson

DEAR SIR Washington Nov. 29. 1800.

I recieved your favor of the 11th. when too much hurried for my departure to answer it from Monticello. I would wish you to retain awhile the money you recieved from mr Pendleton. it is necessary for me to know from the Secretary of the Treasury whether he chuses to recieve the money or to pass it as a paiment to mr Short. mr Fenwick lately from Bourdeaux does not give me much expectation of a high price for tobo. on opening our communication. he thinks the manufacturers will only buy from hand to mouth of the first supplies which [come?] till such quantities get in as will glut the market. still I think [it] prudent to hold up my tobo. as long as the market rises, and to sell on the first appearance of fall. I am with great esteem Dr Sir

Your's affectionately TH: JEFFERSON

PrC (MHi); faint; at foot of text: "Mr. George Jefferson"; endorsed by TJ in ink on verso.

From James Lyon

SIR, Saturday. Nov. 29. 1800

Some weeks since I received a letter from Mr. Madison, in which he became a subscriber to "*The Cabinet*," and mentioned that he would send the money (4.$.) by you.

Being under strict necessity for every farthing of money that I have a right to ask for, I hope you will excuse the abruptness of this application; I know you will; for altho you may never have experienced the *practice*, you might be acquainted with the *theory* of *poverty*; for the inability to comply with engagements, let it arise from whatsoever cause it may, is in short, *poverty*,—if a man is ever so rich in demands against others: this is exactly my case; and altho' several hundred good men are in arrears to me, the property of their debts will neither pay my journeymen nor carry me to market.

Please to excuse this reverie, and believe me to be with perfect Esteem your &c J LYON.

RC (DNA: RG 59, LAR); addressed: "Thomas Jefferson Esqr."; endorsed by TJ.

James Lyon (1776-1824) was the oldest son of congressman Matthew and Mary Hosford Lyon. At his father's paper works in Fair Haven, Vermont, he began publishing the *Farmers' Library* in 1793, a newspaper that encouraged the formation of Democratic Societies in the state and followed the events of the French

Revolution. He also ran Voltaire's Head, a publishing house. He edited *The Scourge of Aristocracy and Repository of Important Political Truths*, which first appeared during his father's congressional campaign in October 1798. In 1799 he moved to Virginia, where he established the *National Magazine; or, a Political, Historical, Biographical, and Literary Repository*, and in the next year founded several newspapers to disseminate political information for the Republican party. Only Callender received more financial support from TJ than Lyon. He served briefly as a clerk in the Treasury Department. Between 1802 and 1820 he edited and published newspapers in the District of Columbia and several southern states and sought contracts to publish the U.S. laws. He speculated in land and took part in entrepreneurial activities, including the management of the shipyards established by his father when he settled at Eddyville, along the Cumberland River in Kentucky

(Loyal S. Fox, "Colonel Matthew Lyon: Biographical and Genealogical Notes," *Vermont Quarterly*, 12 [1944], 179; Aleine Austin, *Matthew Lyon: "New Man" of the Democratic Revolution, 1749-1822* [University Park, Pa., 1981], 76-83, 121, 133-4; Andrew N. Adams, *A History of the Town of Fair Haven, Vermont* [Fair Haven, Vt., 1870], 96; Pasley, *Tyranny of Printers*, 172-3; Smith, *Freedom's Fetters*, 227; *Terr. Papers*, 6:366-7; Brigham, *American Newspapers*, 1:6, 98; 2:1447; Madison, *Papers, Sec. of State Ser.*, 1:372-5; Jackson, *Papers*, 2:195, 528, 590-1; MB, 2:1002-3; James Lyon to Albert Gallatin, 2 May 1802, in NHi: Gallatin Papers; Gallatin to Nathaniel Macon, 6 Apr. 1802, and enclosure, in DNA: RG 233, House Records, 7th Cong., 1st sess.).

Letters from Lyon to TJ of 12 June 1799 and 1 Jan. 1800, recorded in SJL as received on 14 June 1799 and 25 Jan. 1800, respectively, the last from Richmond, have not been found.

From James Wilkinson

SIR City of Washington Novr. 29th. 1800

I enclose you a series of the Meteorological observations, which, should they be deemed worthy of record, may I hope be ascribed to the Author, the Honble Willm: Dunbar of the Forest near Natchez.—

Some petrifactions, an Indian Knife, & a Sketch of the settled parts of the Mississippi Territory, are also offered for your amusement, but I must request that no copy of the Sketch may be allowed to be taken, as it is intended to publish a correct Map of that & the adjacent Spanish Territory.—With the most respectful consideration I have the Honor to be sir

Your Obliged & Obedt Servant   JA WILKINSON

RC (DLC); at foot of text: "The Honble T. Jefferson Esqr"; endorsed by TJ as received 3 Dec. and so recorded in SJL. Enclosure: "Meteorological Observations For One entire year," made by William Dunbar at "The Forest," near the Mississippi River, from 1 Feb. 1799 to 31 Jan. 1800 (MS in DLC: TJ Papers, 106:18106-13; in an unidentified hand); enclosed in TJ's first letter to Caspar Wistar of 16 Dec. 1800, given to the American Philosophical Society on 16 Jan. 1801, and approved for publication on 6 Feb. (APS, *Proceedings*, 22, pt. 3 [1884], 308-9); printed in APS, *Transactions*, 6 [1809], 9-23. Other enclosure not found.

To Thomas Mann Randolph

TH:J. TO TMR.   Washington. Sunday eveng. Nov. 30. 1800.

Davy will set out in the morning on his return with the horses. I will endeavor before he goes to get one of Hamilton's pamphlets for you, which are to be sold here. Bishop's pamphlet on political delusions has not yet reached the bookstores here. it is making wonderful progress, and is said to be the best Anti-republican eye-water which has ever yet appeared. a great impression of them is making at Philadelphia to be forwarded here. from abroad we have no news. at home the election is the theme of all conversation. setting aside Pensva. Rhode isld. & S. Carolina, the Federal scale will have from the other states 53 votes & the Republican 58. both parties count with equal confidence on Rho. isld & S. Carolina. Pensva. stands little chance for a vote. the majority of 2. in their Senate is immoveable. in that case the issue of the election hangs on S. Carola. it is believed Pinckney will get a complete vote with mr Adams from 4. of the New Engld. states, from Jersey, Delaware & Maryland probably also N. Carolina.—Congress seem conscious they have nothing [to do.] the territorial government here, & the additional judiciary system seem the only things which can be taken up. the Feds do not appear very strong in the H. of R. they divided on the address only 3[6]. against 32. we are better accomodated here than we expected to be; and not a whisper or thought in any mortal of attempting a removal. this evident solidity to the establishment will give a wonderful spri[ng in] buildings here the next season. my warmest affections to my ever dear Martha, kisses to the young ones, and sincere & affectionate attachment to yourself. Adieu.

P.S. mr Brown called on me to-day. the family is well. I forgot to mention to him that Davy could carry letters to Mr. Trist & family.

PrC (MHi); faint; endorsed by TJ in ink on verso. Recorded in SJL as carried by Davy Bowles.

Mathew Carey's Philadelphia printing of Abraham BISHOP'S PAMPHLET entitled *Connecticut Republicanism. An Oration, on the Extent and Power of Political Delusion, Delivered in New-Haven, On the Evening preceding the Public Commencement, September, 1800* was dated 13 Nov. (see Evans, No. 36977).

A letter from Randolph to TJ of 29 Nov., recorded in SJL as received 5 Dec., has not been found.

To Benjamin Ogle

SIR,   United States, In Senate, December the 1st. 1800.

The Senate of the United States, have requested me to notify your Excellency, that the honorable James Lloyd hath resigned his seat in the Senate, as appears by the Journals of the Senate, an authenticated copy whereof I have directed to be made out and herewith transmit for your information and that of the Legislature of the State of Maryland.

I have the honor to be, Sir, Your Excellency's most obedt. and hble. servt. Vice President of the United States and President of the Senate.   TH: JEFFERSON

RC (MHi); signature only in TJ's hand; at foot of text: "His Excellency The Governor of the State of Maryland." Not recorded in SJL. Enclosure: Resolution of U.S. Senate, 1 Dec. 1800 (MS in same; attested by Samuel A. Otis).

JAMES LLOYD, Federalist senator from Maryland, was elected to fill the vacancy created when John Henry resigned to become governor of Maryland. Lloyd served from December 1797 until 1 Dec. 1800 when he also resigned (DAB; *Biog. Dir. Cong.*). Lloyd's letter to TJ of 12 Nov. 1800 written from "Kent county. Maryld." was recorded in SJL as received 1 Dec. but has not been found.

From Benjamin Waterhouse

SIR   Cambridge Massts. Decr. 1st. 1800

Having long regarded Mr. Jefferson as one of our most distinguished patriots & philosophers, I conceived that a work which had for it's end the good of the community, would not be unexceptable to him. — Under that impression I have here sent him "*A prospect of Exterminating the small-pox*," and am with the utmost consideration and respect

his very humble servt.   BENJN. WATERHOUSE

RC (DLC); at foot of text: "Honbl. Thomas Jefferson"; endorsed by TJ as received 24 Dec. and so recorded in SJL. Enclosure: Benjamin Waterhouse, *A Prospect of Exterminating the Small-Pox; Being the History of the Variolæ Vaccinæ, or Kine-Pox, Commonly Called the Cow-Pox* (Cambridge, Mass., 1800); Sowerby, No. 945.

Benjamin Waterhouse (1754-1846) was professor of medicine at Harvard, the first incumbent of that position. In 1799 he learned of Edward Jenner's use of cowpox vaccine in England to protect humans against smallpox. Waterhouse, who began to administer the new vaccine in the United States during the summer of 1800, became a great advocate of the method, with TJ as a prime facilitator. TJ had the vaccine given to members of his Virginia household, encouraged wide use of the technique, and suggested means of protecting the vaccine during shipment. In 1807 TJ appointed Waterhouse chief physician at the U.S. Marine Hospital in

Charlestown, Massachusetts, a position that the doctor lost in 1809, as he later did his position at Harvard, in part due to feuds with rivals in the medical community. Waterhouse, whom the American Philosophical Society elected to membership in 1791, also lectured on natural history and helped to build Harvard's collections of scientific specimens. In TJ's papers at DLC are two printed items associated with Waterhouse, a description of the "Cabinet of Ores and other Minerals, in the University of Cambridge, in New-England," dated 17 May 1796, and "Heads Of a Course of Lectures, Intended as an Introduction to Natural History," without date (ANB; Silvio A. Bedini, *Thomas Jefferson: Statesman of Science* [New York, 1990], 310-14; APS, *Proceedings*, 22, pt. 3 [1884], 195).

From Morgan Brown

SIR   Palmyra Decbr. 2d. 1800

Your letter of the 16th. of Jany. did not come to hand untill the boats from this river had gone down, except one or two which I did not think it would be safe to send the Indian bust in—but the season is now approaching when oppertunities will be frequent; and you may rest assured they shall be carefully packed and sent.

I am Your most Obt. Humble Servt.   MORGAN BROWN.

RC (MHi); endorsed by TJ as received 8 Jan. 1801 and so recorded in SJL.

From Peter Freneau

SIR   Columbia So Carolina Decr 2d. 1800.

I do myself the honor of informing you that at one oClock this day the election for Electors for President and Vice President of the United States was terminated by the Legislature now sitting in this Place. the result is as follows.

Republican		Federal	
John Hunter	87	William Washington	69
Paul Hamilton	87	John Ward	69
Robert Anderson	85	Thomas Roper	67
Theodore Gaillard	85	James Postell	66
Arthur Simkins	84	John Blasingame	66
Wade Hampton	82	John McPherson	66
Andrew Love	82	William Falconer	64
Joseph Blyth	82	Henry Dana Ward	63.

The Vote tomorrow I understand will be Thomas Jefferson 8. Aaron Burr 7. Geo Clinton 1. you will easily discover why the one Vote is varied.—I take the liberty of giving you this information because Mr C. Pinckney is not on the spot, he is at his plantation about five miles distant and will not be in time for the Post of this day. I know that it is his most earnest wish to give you the earliest information of the result of all our labors.

with the most Sincere respect I have the honor to be, Sir, Your Most obedient & Very Huml Servant,   PETER FRENEAU

RC (DLC); at foot of text: "Thomas Jefferson Esqr."; endorsed by TJ as received 12 Dec. and so recorded in SJL.

Peter Freneau (1757-1813) was a printer, publisher, newspaper editor, and translator in South Carolina. With Seth Paine in 1795 he purchased the Charleston *City Gazette and Daily Advertiser* and three years later started a weekly paper, the *Carolina Gazette*. He and Paine were also official printers for the state of South Carolina and, by the late 1790s, for the U.S. government. In 1800 Freneau, a New Jersey native and the brother of Philip Freneau, was a key ally of Charles Pinckney in the consolidation of a strong Republican element in South Carolina. In 1810 he sold his interest in the two newspapers, and during Madison's presidency he received a federal appointment in South Carolina. Although he engaged in a variety of business activities beginning in the 1780s, including shipping, slave trading, and land speculation, he never achieved great financial success (Richard B. Davis and Milledge B. Seigler, "Peter Freneau, Carolina Republican," *Journal of Southern History*, 13 [1947], 395-405).

WHY THE ONE VOTE IS VARIED: on this day Freneau wrote to his partner, Seth Paine, in Charleston: "it is not the wish to risque any person being higher than Jefferson." Freneau's information proved faulty; in balloting by the electors on 3 Dec., TJ and Burr received the same number of votes (Davis and Seigler, "Freneau," 399-400).

From Benjamin Rush

DEAR SIR/   Philadelphia Decemr 2nd. 1800

Herewith you will receive the musk melon seed which I promised to send you by a private hand in my last letter, to which I refer you for an Account of the Method of cultivating it. The Seed came originally from Minorca.

Receive Once more the Assurances of respect and esteem from Dear Sir your sincere Old friend   BENJN: RUSH

RC (NIC); endorsed by TJ as received 9 Dec. and so recorded in SJL.

LAST LETTER: Rush to TJ, 6 Oct. 1800.

From Charles Pinckney

DEAR SIR   [3] December 1800 In Columbia

I wrote you yesterday a short Letter of sincere congratulation on our success in the Election & as it will be some time before I can be at Washington I wish to detail to you the reasons that will inevitably detain me.—When I was two Years since a candidate for the Senate I pledged myself to the republican Interest of this State to use every Exertion in my power to make a peace with France & place You in the chair & told them that from my belief of their principles & some little knowledge of the American Character & people[1] that I believed they only wanted to be properly informed & some Exertions to be used & *persevered in* to do every thing that was right—In a confidence in my Industry at least & perseverance, the upper Members on this occasion gave up in my favour a rule they had always observed, which was to have one senator from the Upper & one from the lower country, & elected me—You know what has since happened with respect to France & my Exertions on that subject & it only remained at the present time to realize our Expectations respecting your Election.—I clearly foresaw that if Pennsylvania did not *vote fully*, the Fortune of America depended in a great Measure on the Vote of this state. I also saw that the nomination of General Pinckney was done with a View to divide us & particularly calculated to place me in a difficult & delicate & perhaps dangerous situation—they supposed I had some influence here & thought that family reasons or the number of, otherwise good republicans who would from private & personal attachment support General Pinckney, would draw me off or at least neutralize me—You must remember I mentioned this to You in Philadelphia & the Event has fully justified the opinion I had at that time formed—I returned in June & immediately commenced my Writings & operations for the Elections that were to take place in October throughout every part of the state.—The particulars of the Charleston Election I transmitted & from the Loss of that (they have 17 Members) I found it was indispensable to redouble my Exertions—the Weight of Talent, Wealth, & personal & family influence Brought against us were so great, that after the Charleston Election was lost many of our most decided friends began to despair—the federal party acquired immense confidence & it was under these circumstances I found it indispensable to come to Columbia myself & remain there until the Election was over.—Most of our friends believe that my Exertions & influence owing to the information of federal affairs I gave them, has in a great measure contributed to the decision & firmly believing myself that they were indispensable to Your Success I did not suppose myself at Liberty to quit Columbia until it was over— —they have insured to me the hatred & persecution of the federal party for ever & the Loss of even the acquaintance or personal civility of many of my relatives, but I rejoice I have done my duty to my country & shall ever consider it as among the most fortunate Events of my Life—. If as Governour Monroe writes me Pennsylvania is uncertain, & South Carolina has decided the Point, I shall doubly rejoice at the honour she has done herself & *"that she is South Carolina still"*——I am uncertain Yet when I shall, from important public reasons, be able to set out or whether by sea or Land.—I am at present better employed here in fixing the republican Interest in this state like a rock against which future federal storms may beat with less probability of success & when this is finished & the Election of a Senator over I mean to set out.—In the interim believe me with affectionate attachment & great respect

Dear Sir Yours Truly   CHARLES PINCKNEY

For fear of accidents to my former Letter I inclose You a Duplicate of the Charleston Petition to shew what Difficulties we had to encounter there & the List of the Votes for Electors here to shew how hard & strongly contested their Election has Been at Columbia——General Pinckney has taken his seat in the senate the first Day & is now in Columbia——

———

I am so occupied here Night & Day in public Business that I have Not one Moment to write to my friends & therefore I will thank You to communicate to my worthy friends General Mason & the Mr Nicholas's & Mr Burr all such intelligence from our state as I send You or may transmit & you think I would wish them to know.—

This will be delivered to You by a Very confidential young man Who carries our eight Votes for Yourself & Mr. Burr & We have been at some pains to get so confidential a [Man] to carry them——

Post Script—

Since writing the within I have some reason to Believe that much unfounded & *pretended friendly information* may be transmitted to promote applications to You & to decieve. I have therefore to request that so far as respects South Carolina, You would be so good as to wait the arrival of a Body of information I am collecting for your use & intend, if nothing prevents, to Bring with me—When I arrive I will submit it to You merely[2] for your information on such subjects as are interesting to the Republican Interest in this State & your own Superior Judgment will afterwards[3] always best & most safely determine what is right or ought to be done—

RC (DLC); partially dated, with day determined from internal evidence; torn; with final paragraph marked "Post Script" written on separate half-sheet and likely sent with this letter; addressed: "To The Honourable Thomas Jefferson At the seat of the Government of the United States at Washington Favoured By Mr George Brown"; endorsed by TJ as received 23 Dec. and recorded in SJL under that date, but as a letter of 6 Dec. Enclosures not found, but see Pinckney to TJ at 22 Nov. for the Charleston petition and Peter Freneau to TJ at 2 Dec. for a list of votes for electors.

Pinckney's SHORT LETTER OF SINCERE CONGRATULATION dated 2 Dec. was written on the same sheet as the letter he began on 22 Nov. and is printed above

under that date. BEFORE I CAN BE AT WASHINGTON: Pinckney did not take his Senate seat until 23 Feb. 1801 (JS, 3:129). CONFIDENTIAL YOUNG MAN: George Brown.

[1] Preceding word and ampersand interlined.
[2] Word interlined.
[3] Pinckney here canceled "dictate" and then continued "always safely determine what is best to be done" before altering it to read as above.

From Dr. John Vaughan

HOND. SIR,   December 3d. 1800

You will please to accept the enclosed pamphlet as a tribute of esteem from its author. The only apology, I have to plead in extenuation of the privilege assumed, is the liberality necessarily attached to your character as a Philosopher.

With anxious solicitude for the (just) result of this auspicious day, I am your most obedient, incognant, hbl Servt.

JNO. VAUGHAN

RC (DLC); at head of text: "Thos. Jefferson"; endorsed by TJ as received 6 Dec. and so recorded in SJL. Enclosure: John Vaughan, *The Valedictory Lecture Delivered Before the Philosophical Society of Delaware* (Wilmington, Del., 1800); Sowerby, Nos. 993, 3773.

John Vaughan (1775-1807) a native of Chester County, Pennsylvania, was the son of Jane Taggert and Joshua Vaughan, a Baptist minister. John Vaughan studied medicine under Dr. William Currie in Philadelphia and at the University of Pennsylvania from 1793 to 1794. In 1795 he set up practice as a physician in Christiana Bridge, Delaware, and moved to Wilmington in 1799, where he was a member of the Delaware Medical and Philosophical Societies. He delivered a series of lectures on chemistry and natural philosophy in 1799 and 1800. Among his publications were *Observations on Animal Electricity, in Explanation of the*

Metallic Operation of Doctor Perkins (Wilmington, Del., 1797); *Chemical Syllabus* (Wilmington, Del., 1799); and an edition of Hugh Smith's *The Female Monitor, Consisting of a Series of Letters to Married Women on Nursing and the Management of Children* (Wilmington, Del., 1801). Vaughan studied the effect of the weather on various diseases, developed a twofold classification system of fevers, and introduced vaccination into the state of Delaware. An active member of several medical associations, Vaughan wrote a pamphlet in 1803 for the American Philosophical Society, *A Concise History of the Autumnal Fever, which prevailed in the Borough of Wilmington in the Year 1802* (Wilmington, Del., 1803; Sowerby, No. 984). He also compiled a history of diseases in Delaware for publication in the New York *Medical Repository*, and, at the urging of David Ramsay of Charleston, South Carolina, kept a medical journal of Wilmington in 1803, which was to be included in a proposed annual medical history of the United States (Dean B. Ivey, ed., "John Vaughan's Wilmington Medical Register for 1803," *Delaware History*, 14 [April 1971], 188-204; J. Thomas Scharf, *History of Delaware. 1609-1888*, 2 vols. [Philadelphia, 1888], 1:492-3; APS, *Proceedings*, 22, pt. 3 [1884], 310).

TJ wrote a brief reply from Washington on 10 Dec.: "Th: Jefferson presents his compliments to Doctr. Vaughan, and his thanks for the pamphlet inclosed to him, which he is assured he shall peruse with pleasure at the first leisure moment. he prays him to accept the assurances of his respect" (PrC in DLC; endorsed by TJ in ink on verso).

From Thomas Law

SIR. Washington Decr 4. 1800.

As you feel an interest in every measure for the amelioration of the condition of man, I will not apologize for submitting to your perusal some Lres which occasioned Security & prosperity to 50 Millions of Asiatics, but I must make my excuses for the trouble I have caused by not being versed in the art of Book making—If you begin at page 38 where I have put some papers, you will perhaps obtain a sufft insight into my plan—

As you are debarred from the agreeable Society of Philadelphia, You may perhaps by these tracts pass away an hour or two not unacceptably in being made acquainted with what cost me many Years of consideration & trouble

I remain With respect yr mt Ob He St THOMAS LAW.

RC (DLC); endorsed by TJ as received 4 Dec. and so recorded in SJL.

Thomas Law (1756-1834), son of the Right Reverend Edmund Law, Lord Bishop of Carlisle, was born in Cambridge, England, to a prosperous family. In 1773 he traveled to India as a writer in the civil service of the East India Company where he was promoted from novice to the collectorship of the Bahar in 1783. Law became a member of the Asiatic Society of Bengal and the Association for Preserving Liberty and Property and wrote several pamphlets on land usage and taxation in India. Declining health prompted Law's departure from India. In 1794 he arrived in New York after suing the East India Company for seizing one-fifth of his fortune acquired in India. Law moved to Washington where, in 1796, he entered into a marriage settlement or in-denture tripartite with Elizabeth Parke Custis (Martha Washington's granddaughter) and James Barry as trustee. The couple gave many grand parties in Washington society. Law traveled to England without his wife, however, in 1802, submitted official separation documents in 1804, and filed a bill for divorce in 1810. Most of Law's money was invested in land and houses in Washington. An avid promoter of a national currency, Law published some of his writings with the Columbian Institute and the *National Intelligencer* under the pseudonym, "Homo" (O. P. Kejariwal, *The Asiatic Society of Bengal and the Discovery of India's Past 1784-1838* [Delhi, 1988], 34, 38; Bryan, *National Capital*, 1:244-7; Allen C. Clark, *Greenleaf and Law in the Federal City* [Washington, D.C., 1901], 237, 285-9).

From John Barnes

SIR   G. Town saturday Morng. 5th. decr.

The Weather is realy too bad, to walk, or I should have waited on you personaly I am almost certain, you must, be in want of some little matters.—If you Approve of these two hankerfs:—I can procure more at same Rate ie, 4/6—and should you think of any Other Article—Mr. Mc.Munn—or his servant—is almost every day in Town, and calls, here—you could be Accomodated without the trouble of sending *Yours*—or, if any thing in particular is wanting I will come—at the first Notice ℔ Coachee,

I am sir most respectfully your Obedt: Hb st.

JOHN BARNES

RC (ViU: Edgehill-Randolph Papers); at foot of text: "Thomas Jefferson Esqr."; endorsed by TJ as received 6 Dec. and so recorded in SJL.

TROUBLE OF SENDING YOURS: TJ's servant during his residence at the boarding house may have been the otherwise unidentified "Thomas" to whom he paid $2 on 31 Dec. and again on 7 Feb. 1801 (MB, 2:1032, 1034).

To Thomas Mann Randolph

TH:J. TO TMR.   Washington. Dec. 5. 1800

You are probably anxious to hear of the election, and indeed it is the only thing of which any thing is said here: and little known even of it. the only actual vote known to us is that of this state. 5. for A. & P. and 5. for J. & B. those who know the Pensva legislature best, agree in the certainty of their having no vote. Rhode isld. has carried the Fedl. ticket of electors by about 200 in the whole state. putting Pensva, S.C. and Pinckney out of view the votes will stand 57. for J. & 58. for A. so that S. Carola will decide between these two. as to Pinckney, it is impossible to foresee how the juggle will work. it is confidently said that Massachusets will withold 7. votes from him. but little credit is due to reports where every man's wishes are so warmly [mis-stated?]. if the Federal electors of the other states go through with the Caucus compact, there is little doubt that S.C. will make him the President. their other vote is very uncertain. this is every thing known to us at present. the post [that] will arrive here on the 15th. inst. will bring us the actual vote of S.C. the members here are generally well accomodated. about a dozen lodge in Georgetown, from choice, there being lodgings to be had here if they preferred it.

every body is well satisfied with the place, and not a thought indulged of ever leaving it. it is therefore solidly established and this being now seen it will take a rapid spring. my tenderest love to my dear Martha & the young ones. affectionate & warm sentiment to yourself. Adieu.

PrC (MHi); faint; endorsed by TJ in ink on verso.

THIS STATE: Maryland. CAUCUS COMPACT: for the strategy designed to elect

Charles C. Pinckney president, reportedly developed at a meeting of Federalist members of Congress in May 1800, see Vol. 31:561-3.

From Alexander White

DEAR SIR   Commissioners Office 5t Decr 1800

I have examined my correspondence with Col: Little and Mr Strode respecting the proposed road; I find Colonel Little only engaged to join with Mr. Strode in tracing the ground, in which he said three other gentlemen one a surveyor and all good Woods men, would assist; but I never heard of anything being done; and unless Mr Strode was on the ground (and of this he would probably have informed), there certainly has not, I am with sentiments of great respect

Dear Sir Your most Obt Servt   ALEX WHITE

RC (DLC); endorsed by TJ as received 5 Dec. and so recorded in SJL.

The PROPOSED ROAD between the Georgetown ferry and Slate Run church was located on TJ's route from Washington to Monticello between his first night's stop at William Brown's tavern in Prince

William County and his stay the second night with John Strode in Culpeper County (MB, 2:834, 975, 1048; Table of Mileages, 30 Sep. 1807 and 21-23 July 1808, in DLC: TJ Papers, 233:41688; TJ to Strode, 25 Mch. 1801; TJ to Charles Little, 31 Mch. 1801).

From Benjamin Williams

SIR   Raleigh December 5th. 1800

Permit me to introduce to your Notice William Tate Esqr. late an Elector to vote for a President & Vice President of the U.S. who goes charged with the Vote of that Body to you, & to assure you of the great Respect & Esteem of

Sir your Obt. Servt.   B WILLIAMS

RC (DLC); at foot of text: "Thomas Jefferson Esquire Vice President of the United States"; endorsed by TJ as received 12 Dec. and so recorded in SJL.

Benjamin Williams (1751-1814), described as a "mild Federalist," served as congressman from North Carolina during the Third Congress and as the state's governor from 1799 to 1802 and again from 1807 to 1808 (*Biog. Dir. Cong.*; Gilpatrick, *Jeffersonian Democracy in North Carolina,* 107, 132).

From Philip Mazzei

a Mr. Jefferson   6 xbre, 1800

Non avendo ricevuto alcuna sua lettera dopo quelle del 31 Genn. e 24 Aprile, 1796, ò avuto più volte sotto gli occhi nelle mie afflizioni quel che Ella mi dice nell'ultima: "I begin to feel the effects of age. My health has suddenly broke down, with symptoms which give me to believe I shall not have much to encounter of the tedium vitæ." Combattuto per molto tempo tra il timore e la speranza, intesi che da varie parti era venuta sulle gazzette la nuova della sua morte. L'intesi casualmente, perché non leggo mai gazzette, e passo il più che posso i miei vecchi giorni lavorando nell'orto. Ero in casa del Dr. Vaccà celebre Professor di medicina in questa Università, dove Ella è tanto conosciuto quanto in qualunque casa di Virginia, e dove me lo avevasi taciuto, benché non ne dubitassero, poiché quello de' suoi figli ch'io ebbi il piacer di presentarle in Parigi e condussi un giorno a pranzo da Lei alla barriera, ne aveva avuto la conferma in una lettera di Francia. Contutto ciò fui consigliato a scriverne al Console degli Stati Uniti in Livorno. Allora fù ch'io seppi, cioè 6 giorni sono, che il Filicchi non lo è più da molto tempo, e che gli è succeduto Mr. Ths. Appleton, che io credevo non aver mai veduto, né sentito nominare. Gli scrissi, e ne ricevei una gentile obbligantissima risposta, della quale trascrivo alcuni passi. "And although you may not recall to mind my name, nevertheless I have frequently had, during some years residence in Paris, the satisfaction of meeting you both at Mr. Jefferson's and the Marquis de la Fayette.—The report of the death of Mr. Jefferson you may rest assured is totally without foundation, he is still officiating as Vicepresident of the United States." Nel tradurre la lettera d'Appleton alla sopraddetta famiglia, remarcabile per il cuore come per i talenti, quando dissi *senza fondamento,* i loro occhi, turgidi per eccesso di tenera gioia, accompagnarono gli effetti che la natura e l'amicizia mi avevan già più volte forzato ad esternare. Prosegue Mr. Appleton, rispondendo alle mie interrogazioni: "Mr. James Madison of Virginia, as I am informed, has been dead, for a considerable time. There is however a Mr. Js. A. Madison, who in 1794 was a member of Congress, still living in a private capacity in Virginia."

La pirateria inglese, la sola cosa forse considerata come Legge costituzionale da quella nazione, e che i suoi nemici sono finalmente stati forzati ad adottare, à probabilmente impedito, che alcuna delle mie tante lettere e copie di lettere Le sia pervenuta, ed ella mi avrà facilmente creduto morto. Non solo son vivo, com'Ella vede, ma ò una figlia di 28 mesi, di figura non dispiacevole, che pare aver talento e buona disposizione, e che sarebbe di mia somma consolazione s'io fossi con lei e colla sua buona madre in Virginia. Ella si ricorderà forse di Mlle. Vuy, la mia buona compagna che avevo in Parigi. Quando ne partii per la Pollonia, se n'andò in Savoia da sua madre. Morta la madre; venne a trovarmi a Pisa. Aveva 17 anni meno di me, ottima salute, e tutte le requisite qualità per tenermi buona compagnia, e farmi un'affettuosa assistenza nel resto de' miei giorni. Ci fù procurata qua per nostro servizio una ragazza di circa 28 anni, di figura piacevole, nata di parenti poveri alle falde degli Apennini, con pochissimo ingegno e senza istruzione, insensibile all'amore, sensibilissima all'amicizia, sommamente affettuosa, e incapace di deviare da quel che chiamasi dovere. Mlle. Vuy assalita da una timpanitide, che passò all'ascite, finalmente all'anasarca, dopo una penosissima malattia di 6 mesi, nel qual tempo subì 2 operazioni della paracentesi, morì stringendomi la mano e congiurandomi di mai abbandonare quella povera ragazza, da cui aveva ricevuto un'assistenza qual potrebbe la più tenera figlia prestare alla cara madre. Per darLe un'idea della mia gran perdita, basta ch'io Le dica che i più grandi amici di Mlle. Vuy erano il Dr. Gemm, Jacob Vanstaphorst, e il Piattoli, dai quali era molto amata e sommamente stimata. Negli ultimi tempi della sua malattia, ragionando meco dell'inevitabil bisogno d'un'assistenza fedele nel resto dei miei giorni, m'assicurò che non potevo sperar nulla di meglio della detta ragazza. In fatti si richiedeva gioventù, amicizia, e anche fedeltà per evitare il ridicolo dovendola prender per moglie, considerata la disparità grande dell'età nostra, poichè tra pochi giorni terminerò il mio settantunesimo anno.* La sposai per tranquillizzar la sua coscienza, e più ancora per conservare il suo onore. Non volevo figli, a motivo delle mie basse circostanze, come dell'improbalità di viver tanto da poter contribuire alla loro educazione. Ma un'affettuosa persecuzione di circa un'anno, fondata principalmente sulla riflessione di dover essa restar sola dopo la mia

---

*oggi siamo il 5 Febb. 1801. Nell'intervallo del tempo, essendo già 2 mesi che scrissi l'originale, mi è venuta fra mano lo fede del Battesimo, dovè ò veduto che nacqui il 25 xbre 1730, e conseguentemente che sono un'anno più giovane che non credevo.

morte, m'indusse a cedere, sulla promessa che si contenterebbe d'un solo. Questa bambina mi serve ora di passatempo, e le mie occupazioni sono quasi affatto divise tra lei e l'orto.

In varie lettere, delle quali non ò mai avuto riscontro, Le parlavo di cose riguardanti l'agricoltura. Verso il fine del 96, o al principio del 97 Le dissi le ragioni, per cui non si posson mandare le veccie di figura rotonda in una lettera, e L'avvisavo d'averlene mandate un sacchettino con bastimento partito da Livorno per Baltimore. Le dissi che avevo intenzione di mandarle alcune piante d'ottima frutte, ma che prima bramavo di sapere, se per l'acquisto di nuove specie Le converrebbe di mandare al porto a prendere la cassa che le conterrà, e a quali porti sarebbe proprio che venissero. Le domandai quale si chiama *Squash* delle 2 specie di zucchettine, delle quali mi mandò i semi. Le richiesi i semi della pianta a cespuglio, perchè non ne avevo potuta rilevare neppur'una. Le dicevo che le piante che fanno i tralci lunghi, avevan prodotto pochissimo in Primavera, nulla nella State, abondantemente nell'Autunno subito che le pioggie ànno rinfrescata l'aria; che ne deduco la causa dalla grande aridità, poichè qui dal principio di Maggio a 7bre piove molto meno che in Virginia, e una lunga esperienza mi à dimostrato che l'innaffiatura, benchè abondante, non serve ad altro (quando l'atmosfera è molto arida) che a mantener le piante in vita.

Quanto ai miei interessi, La ragguagliai d'aver ricevute tutte le rimesse venute per me agli Amici Vanstaphorst, eccettuatane quella su Wm. Anderson di Londra, in £ sterl. 39:17:10$\frac{1}{2}$, data gli 11 Giugno 1794, la quale i detti Amici mi scrissero aver rimandata a Lei col protesto, in conto della quale non ò saputo più nulla.

Edmond Randolph mi scrisse molti anni sono, che i miei military-certificates, lasciati a Foster Webb, avrebbero probabilmente potuto recuperarsi da Alexander, al quale Foster gli aveva ceduti.

Dalla sua dei 31 Genn. 96 intesi, che Mr. Charles Carter of Blenheim aveva assunto il pagamento di Colle.

Se da questi, come dagli altri miei piccoli crediti, e dalla vendita dei miei 2 Lotts in Richmond, dopo saldato [il] suo conto con me e pagato Antonio, si potesse mettere insieme una sommarella, che Ella avesse la bontà di farmi pervenire, o in cambiali, o in contante; o in mercanzia, giungerebbe molto opportunamente, poichè oltre l'accresciuta spesa che mi causa la mia cara figliolina, le spese ordinarie inevitabili, vivendo colla più rigorosa parsimonia, sono qui circa 3 volte maggiori di quel che erano, vivendo con qualche agio quando ci venni a motivo delle truppe mandateci dalle Potenze belligeranti, che ànno fatto della povera Italia un vero scheletro.

Questo disgraziato paese, diviso in piccoli stati, sotto governi di varia natura e d'interessi opposti, non à potuto aver'altro in sua difesa, che ignoranza negli affari, debolezza, e duplicità, ed à solamente sfogata la sua energia nella persecuzione di quei dei suoi figli, che avrebbero voluto sollevarlo, e liberarlo dall'obbrobrio in cui è stato per tanti secoli. Oh quanti degni cittadini acquisterebbero gli Stati Uniti, se i mezzi di pervenirvi fossero meno difficili! E io, non ostante l'età e gl'imbarazzi d'una moglie e d'una figlia, mi farei un piacere e un dovere d'accompagnarvegli. Il destino della Toscana è tuttavia indeciso; io però son portato a credere che ritornerà al suo antico Padrone. Qualunque ne sia la decisione, mi par probabile che basterà per gli Stati Uniti d'averci un Console in Livorno; ma se mai si pensasse di tenerci un'incaricato d'affari, e la mia Assenza non me ne avesse fatta perdere la cittadinanza, io potrei (aggiunto quel poco che ò a £200 st. di salario) essercitarne le fonzioni con sufficiente decenza; e se bisognasse portarsi anche presso qualche altro Governo, mi basterebbe d'essere indennizzato delle spese del viaggio. Questo sarebbe ℔ me un grande e decoroso sollievo nella mia vecchiaia.

Gradirei molto le nuove dei nostri amici viventi, come pure di sapere se quel Madison, che Mr. Appleton mi dice esser morto, fosse quello di Orange County, e il Pres. dell'Università, o qualche altro.

Mr. Jefferson   6 Dec. 1800
As I did not receive any letter from you after those of 31 Jan. and 24 April 1796, several times have I perused, in my afflictions, what you said in the latter: "I begin to feel the effects of age. My health has suddenly broke down, with symptoms which give me to believe I shall not have much to encounter of the tedium vitæ." For a long time torn between fear and hope, I heard that the report of your death had come to the gazettes from several places. I heard about it by chance, for I never read gazettes, and I spend as much as I can of the days of my old age working in my orchard. I was at the home of Dr. Vaccà—a famous Professor of Medicine in this university—where you are as well known as in any Virginia home, and where they kept the report from me, although they did not doubt it, because one of his sons, the one whom I had the pleasure of introducing to you in Paris and whom one day I took for lunch with you at the toll booth, had confirmation by a letter from France. Nevertheless I was advised to write about it to the consul of the United States at Leghorn. It was then, that is, six days ago, that I heard that Feliechy long since ceased to be consul, and that he was succeeded by Mr. Ths. Appleton, whom I thought I had neither seen nor heard of before. I wrote to him and received a kind, most obliging, reply, from which I transcribe a few passages: "And although you may not recall to mind my name, nevertheless I have frequently had, during some years residence in Paris, the satisfaction of meeting you both at Mr. Jefferson's and the Marquis de la Fayette's.—The report

of the death of Mr. Jefferson you may rest assured is totally without foundation, he is still officiating as Vice-president of the United States." As I translated Appleton's letter to the afore-mentioned family, remarkable for their
heart as for their talent, when I said *without foundation*, their eyes, swollen
for the overwhelming tender joy, accompanied the effects that nature and
friendship had already compelled me to manifest several times. Mr. Appleton
goes on, answering my questions: "Mr. James Madison of Virginia, as I am
informed, has been dead for a considerable time. There is however a Mr. Js.
A. Madison, who in 1794 was a member of Congress, still living in a private
capacity in Virginia."

English piracy, perhaps the only thing regarded as a constitutional law by
that nation, and which her enemies have at last been forced to adopt, has
probably prevented some of my many letters and copies of letters from
reaching you, and it is likely that you believed that I was dead. Not only am
I alive, as you see, but I have a daughter who is twenty-eight months old, of
not unpleasant appearance, who seems to have both talent and a good disposition, and who would be my greatest comfort if I were with her and her
good mother in Virginia. You may perhaps remember Mlle Vuy, my good
companion in Paris. When I left for Poland, she went to her mother's in
Savoy. After her mother's death, she visited me at Pisa. She was seventeen
years younger than I, in perfect health, and with all the requisite qualities to
keep me good company, and give me affectionate assistance for my remaining days. Here a servant girl was provided for us. She was about twenty-
eight years old, of pleasant appearance, born of poor parents at the foot of
the Appennines, with very little talent and no education, insensitive to love,
most sensitive to friendship, affectionate in the highest degree, and incapable of deviating from what is called duty. Mlle Vuy, stricken with tympa-
nites, which turned into ascites, and finally into anasarca, after a most
painful illness of almost six months, during which she underwent two para-
centesis operations, died gripping my hand and beseeching me never to forsake that poor girl, from whom she had received such care as the most
tender daughter could take of her dear mother. In order to give you an idea
of my great loss, I will only say that the greatest friends of Mlle Vuy were
Dr. Gemm, Jacob Van Staphorst, and Piatoli, by all of whom she was
greatly loved and esteemed in the highest degree. In the last days of her illness, talking with me of the inevitable need of faithful assistance during the
rest of my days, she assured me that I could hope for nothing better than the
afore-mentioned girl. As a matter of fact, what was required was youth,
friendship, and faithfulness too in order to avoid ridicule, if I had to marry
her, in view of our disparity in age, considering that in a few days I shall
come to the end of my seventy-first year.* I married her in order to settle her
conscience, and even more to preserve her honor. I did not want any children because of my straightened circumstances, as well as the unlikelihood
that I would live long enough to be able to contribute to their education. But
about a year's loving pressure, based mainly on the consideration that she
would remain alone after my death, persuaded me to give in, on her promise that she would content herself with only one child. This young girl is

*Today is 5 Feb. 1801. In the interval of time, as it is already two months since I wrote
the original, I came across my certificate of baptism, which states that I was born on
25 Dec. 1730, and therefore that I am one year younger than I thought.

now my pastime, and my occupations are quite completely divided between her and the orchard.

In various letters, to which I have never had an answer, I spoke to you of things concerning agriculture. Towards the end of '96, or at the beginning of '97, I told you the reason why the round-shaped vetch cannot be sent in a letter, and advised you that I had sent a small bag with a ship which had sailed from Leghorn to Baltimore. I told you that it was my intention to send you a few plants of excellent fruit, but that I wished to know whether for the purchase of new species it would be convenient for you to send someone to the harbor for the collection of the trunk which will contain them, and to which harbors it would be appropriate that they should be sent. I asked you which of the two species of small pumpkins, of which you sent me the seeds, is called *Squash*. Again I asked you for the seeds of the bush-like plant, because I had been unable to raise a single one. I told you that the plants sending out long stems had produced very little in the spring, nothing at all in the summer, abundantly in the fall as soon as the rains cooled off the air; from which I infer that the cause is the great aridity, for here it rains much less than in Virginia from the beginning of May to Sept., and a long experience has shown to me that watering, however abundant, does not effect anything else (when the atmosphere is very arid) than keeping the plants alive.

As for my interests, I informed you that I had received all the remittances sent for me to my friends the Van Staphorsts, except the one on Wm. Anderson of London, of £ 39.17.10½ sterl. dated 11 June 1794, which the aforementioned friends wrote me they had sent back to you with the protest, about which nothing else has been heard since.

Edmund Randolph wrote to me many years ago that my military-certificates left to Foster Webb could probably be recovered from Alexander, to whom Foster had ceded them. From yours of 31 Jan. '96 I understood that Mr. Charles Carter of Blenheim had undertaken the payment for Colle.

If from these, as from my other small credits and the sale of my two lots in Richmond, after settling your account with me and paying Antonio, it were possible to put together a small sum, which you were kind enough as to send me—either by bills of exchange, or in cash, or in merchandise—it would come to me very opportunely, since besides the increased expenditure caused to me by my dear little daughter, the inevitable current expenditures, living in the strictest parsimony, are here three times as high as they used to be, living rather comfortably, when I came here, because of the troops sent here by the belligerent powers, which have reduced poor Italy to a bare skeleton.

This unfortunate country—divided into many small states, under governments of various sorts and of clashing interests—could not muster in self-defense anything but ignorance in public affairs, weakness, and duplicity, and has given vent to her energy in the persecution of those of her sons who wanted to lift her up and deliver her from the opprobrium in which she has remained for many centuries. Oh, how many worthy citizens would the United States secure, if only the means to get there were less difficult! And, despite my age and the encumberment of a wife and a daughter, even I would consider it both a pleasure and a duty to accompany them there. Tuscany's destiny is as yet undecided; however, I am inclined to believe that she will go back to her old master. Whatever the decision, it seems likely to me that it will be sufficient for the United States to have a consul in Leghorn; but if they ever thought to have here a chargé d'affaires and my absence had not caused me to lose my citizenship, I could (having added whatever little I have to a salary of £200 st.) discharge his functions with sufficient decency; and were it also necessary to travel to some other government, I would be content with only reimbursement of my traveling expenses. This would be a great and dignified relief for me in my old age.

I would much appreciate news of our living friends, as well as to know whether the Madison that Mr. Appleton informed me to be dead, was that of Orange County and the president of the university, or someone else.

FC (DLC: Mazzei Papers); in Mazzei's hand; at head of text: "a Mr. Jefferson." Recorded in SJL as received 13 Mch. 1801, from Pisa.

DR. VACCÀ: Francesco Vaccà-Berlinghieri of Pisa was a physician and surgeon (Howard R. Marraro, "Unpublished Mazzei Letters to Jefferson," WMQ, 3d ser., 1 [1944], 383).

FILICCHI: Philip Feliechy was U.S. Consul at Leghorn effective 10 Dec. 1794 until his replacement by Thomas Appleton on 8 Feb. 1798 (same, 383).

UNA FIGLIA DI 28 MESI: Elisabetta, the only child of Philip Mazzei, was born 23 July 1798 and named for her paternal grandmother (Richard Cecil Garlick Jr., *Philip Mazzei: Friend of Jefferson: His*

Life and Letters [Baltimore, 1933], 137-8).

MLLE. VUY: Giuseppina Vuy. See Philip Mazzei, *Memoirs of the Life and Peregrinations of the Florentine, Philip Mazzei, 1730-1816*, trans. Howard R. Marraro (New York, 1942), 292, 335, 377-84.

UNA RAGAZZA DI CIRCA 28 ANNI: Antonia Antoni, whom Mazzei married in late 1796.

PAGATO ANTONIO: for the arbitration with Anthony Giannini, see TJ to Mazzei, 30 May 1795 and 24 Apr. 1796. Letters from Giannini to TJ of 25 Jan., 8 and 24 Feb. 1794, recorded in SJL as received on 26 Jan., 12 and 27 Feb., respectively, have not been found.

From Charles Pinckney

DEAR SIR   December 6: 1800 In Columbia

I wrote you some days since by the Express which carried our Votes & informed You of the necessity there was for my remaining sometime longer here to use my Exertions & those of my friends to fix the republican interest out of the reach of any future federal attack—that the Exertions of the Federalists had been so uncommonly great in the late Election, as to give serious apprehensions to our friends particularly after the loss of the Charleston Election & that all the Talents Wealth & Influence of the Country had been on both sides brought into the Legislature—that believing the fortune of America to depend on our Vote I had thrown every consideration of affinity or Name or local attachment out of View & urged the giving the republican *candidates only*, our unanimous Vote—having carried this point We proceeded & have elected Yesterday a republican Governour & Mr John Ewing Colhoun a staunch republican as

my Colleague in the Senate—there are still some points important to
the republican Interest to be settled & which require my presence—
I then propose to go immediately to Charleston & proceed from
thence to Washington to join You in time for the French Treaty
which I find has not yet arrived nor have We any certain accounts of
its being Signed——. You must recollect that when I saw You in
Philadelphia I told You it would be late before I could see you this
Session—that I considered the carrying Your Election in this State
as the thing to which I ought above every other to attend to, for that
could We but carry that, all subordinate arrangements would follow
of course & I well knew from General Pinckney's public & private
influence the opposition would be formidable & that it would be
dangerous to give him the Vote of this State even if he was upon the
same ticket with You—but this both parties never thought of—both
were so confident of their own Strength & the junction of about a
dozen cautious members who would not declare themselves for
either, that they rejected at the outset, all idea of compromise, &
never I believe has Disappointment been greater than to the
Federalists—or Joy more Sincere than to the Republicans—Our
State has done itself immortal honour & will I trust be considered in
future as one of those firm Pillars of American republicanism which
no private affection or attachment or local interest can ever for a
moment shake—as such I hope We shall have the honour of presenting her to You & I will undertake to promise her warmest support to those republican & liberal measures which We are all sure
will so eminently distinguish Your administration & bless your country——If no accident happens to my health, you will see me as soon
as the public good authorises me to leave this place & state—no private concerns ever detain me—embarked as I am in a great Cause I
have been & am wholly devoted to it & with every sentiment of
respect & affectionate attachment

    I am my dear sir Yours Truly   Charles Pinckney

You very much surprise me by saying you have not recieved my
Book & Numbers—The Book therefore I send again & inclose You
all the Numbers I have—the remaining ten will be sent you—at
present they have all that were here[1] been distributed among the
members—& the new Edition is only finished as far as I send them
now—to the 14 partly. I will send the rest for I wish You very much
to see the 4 Numbers on the Common Law as applicable to the
Courts of the United States & to give me your Opinion of my reasonings on them.—

RC (DLC); addressed: "To The Honourable Thomas Jefferson At the Seat of the Government of the United States at Washington Maryland By the Post"; franked and postmarked; endorsed by TJ as received 17 Dec. and so recorded in SJL. Enclosure: for the numbered essays signed "A Republican," see Pinckney to TJ, 12 Oct. 1800.

Pinckney's letter sent BY THE EXPRESS is printed at 3 Dec. REPUBLICAN GOVERNOUR: John Drayton. JOHN EWING COLHOUN, cousin of John C. Calhoun, was elected senator by a 75 to 73 vote to take the place of the Federalist incumbent Jacob Read (*Biog. Dir. Cong.*; Har-rison, *Princetonians, 1769-1775*, 368-70; Charleston *City Gazette and Daily Advertiser*, 8 Dec. 1800). For accounts emphasizing the desire of some members of the South Carolina legislature to vote for Charles C. Pinckney and TJ on the SAME TICKET, see Marvin R. Zahniser, *Charles Cotesworth Pinckney: Founding Father* (Chapel Hill, 1940), 227-32; Cunningham, *Jeffersonian Republicans*, 232-7; John H. Wolfe, *Jeffersonian Democracy in South Carolina* (Chapel Hill, 1940), 157-61n. MY BOOK: for Pinckney's volume of speeches, see his letter to TJ of 12 Oct.

[1] Preceding three words interlined.

From George Wythe

G'W to T'JEFFERSON   7 decembr, 1800.

Your sollicitations are with me more cogent motives than with his slave are the mandates of a despot.

Page 1, line 9, &c. is not the parliamentary term 'leave out' instead of 'strike out'?

21. the statement seemeth exact.

23. the question is simply, that the committee do agree to it, if amendments be not made, or, if they be, that the committee do agree to it, with the amendments

24. the final question upon the whole i suppose to be in cases where the subjects upon which votes have passed are connected with one another.

26. that they do agree to the address, &c, in the whole. if upon this a negative be put, i suppose the address, &c, which the committee have no power to reject, must be reported to the house, who, if they do not[1] pass it as it is, or recommit, may reject, it.

Page 2. no. 1. i believe the speaker doth not read more of the bill than the parts of it which are amended, first without, and then with, their respective amendments.

2. upon the paragraph amended only.

3. i suppose the bill is not read at all; and the question to be that the bill be engrossed, if it originated in that house, or, if not, that this house concur with the other house &c.

4. i had believed that it is read by the clerk only.

5. i remember nothing of reading them by paragraphs, or putting them to the question by paragraphs.

Page 3, i can conceive nothing more exact than these definitions of questions, nor am i able to add any information, which you can want, on their occasions.

Page 4, paragr 1. the conferees cannot propose, or authorize either house to propose, an amendment in the new part, &c.

2. yea.

3. my opinion, at present, is not before. i might change it, if i knew what had been urged to the contrary.

4. i agree, in believing with you.

5. i think the amendments should all be proposed before the question for leaving out is put.

6. nay.

8. no. 2. i think the motion admissible

3. the same.

last paragr likewise.

Page 5, paragr 2. the exception extends to any other form, to prevent a juncture cervicis equinae capiti humano.

3. i suppose not.[1]

My language is didactic. yet am i confident of nothing that i have writen. i am persuaded the manual of your parliamentary praxis will be more chaste than any extant, and, if you can be persuded to let it go forth, that it will be canonized in all the legislatures of America. farewell

RC (DLC); endorsed by TJ and recorded in SJL as received 12 Dec.

YOUR SOLLICITATIONS: see TJ to Wythe, 28 Feb. and 7 Apr. 1800. TJ once again approached Wythe, in a now missing letter of 29 Nov., that TJ recorded in SJL with the notation that he had not retained a copy of it. In that letter TJ enclosed an updated and abbreviated set of his queries on parliamentary procedures, which Wythe returned with the comments above. NO POWER TO REJECT: for TJ's incorporation of this idea in the 1801 edition of the parliamentary manual, see note to enclosure printed below.

A JUNCTURE CERVICIS EQUINAE CAPITI HUMANO: a juncture of a horse's neck with a human head, or, a centaur (PW, 24).

[1] MS: "not not."

Queries on Parliamentary Procedure

In Committee. The paper before a committee, whether select or of the whole, may be a bill, resolutions, draught of an address &c. and it may either originate with them, or be referred to them. in every case the whole paper is read first by the clerk, & then by the chairman by paragraphs, Scob. 49. pausing at the end of the paragraph, & putting questions for amending if proposed. in the case of distinct resolutions[1] originating with themselves, a question is put on each separately as amended or unamended, & no final question on the whole.[2] if it be a bill, draught of an address or other paper originating with them, they proceed by paragraphs, putting questions for amending,

9. or striking out paragraphs if proposed,[3] but no question on agreeing to them; that is reserved to the close, when a question is put on the whole for agreeing to it as amended, or unamended. but if it be a paper referred to them, they proceed to put questions of amendment if proposed; but no final question on the whole; because all parts of the paper having been adopted by the house stand of course, unless altered or struck out by a vote. even if they are opposed to the whole paper, & think it cannot be made good by amendments, they must report it back to the house without amendments & there make their opposition.

When the committee is through the whole, a member moves that the committee may rise, and that the Chairman may report the paper to the house with or without the amendments agreed to, as the case may be.

———

Queries on the above passage.

21.   Is it's statement exact as to the cases where questions are to be put on agreeing to the paragraph as amended or unamended? or

23.   In what cases is a question put Whether the paragraph is agreed to either as amended, or where no amendment has been made?

24.   And in what cases does he put a final question on the whole?

26.   What is the form of that question? to wit, is it Whether they agree to the address, resolutions or bill in the whole, even where they have already past a vote of agreement on all it's parts? or is it Whether it shall be reported to the house?[4]

In the house.   When the report of a paper originating with a committee is taken up by the house, they proceed exactly as in the Committee.

On the 2d. reading of a bill, if it be taken up in the house without commitment the Speaker reads it by paragraphs, pausing between each to give time for proposing amendments. when through he puts the question Whether it shall be read a 3d. time?

On taking up a bill reported by a committee with amendments, the clerk reads the amendments only. then the Speaker reads the first & puts it to the question, & so on till the whole are adopted or rejected.

[283]

when the amendments of the committee are through, other amendments may be proposed to any part of the bill: but the Speaker does not read the bill over; nor does he when it is reported without amendments; but having waited a convenient time, puts the question for the 3d. reading.

Doubts on this passage.

No. 1. After the amendments of a committee to a bill have been agreed to in the house, does the Speaker then *read* the whole bill over from beginning to end by paragraphs.

2 2. does he put a question on each paragraph as amended, or if unamended?

3 3. if the bill has been reported without amendmts does he read it by paragraphs? does he put questions on agreeing to every paragraph?

4. 4. if the bill be taken up in the house on the 2d. reading, without commitment, does he read it by paragraphs? does he put each paragraph to question?

5 5. on an address, resolution &c reported by a committee, does he read them by paragraphs? & put them to question by paragraphs?[5]

It is proper that every Parliamentary body should have certain forms of question, so adapted, as to enable them fitly to dispose of every proposition which can be made to them. such are 1. the Previous question. 2. to Postpone indefinitely. 3. to adjourn a question to a definite day. 4. to lie on the table. 5. to commit. 6. to amend. the proper occasion for each of these questions should be understood.

1. When a proposition is moved, which it is useless or inexpedient now to express or discuss, the *Previous Question* has been introduced for suppressing *for that time* the motion & it's discussion.

2. But as the Previous question gets rid of it only for that day, it may be *postponed indefinitely*, after which it cannot be moved again during that session.

3. When a motion is made which it will be proper to act on, but information is wanted, or something more pressing claims the present time, it is *adjourned* to such day within the session as will answer the views of the house. sometimes however this has been irregularly used by adjourning it to a day beyond the session, to get rid of it altogether, as would be done by an indefinite postponement.

4. When the house has something else which claims it's present attention, but would be willing to reserve in their power to take up a proposition whenever it shall suit them, they order it to *lie on their table.* it may then be called for at any time.

5. If they are ready to take it up at present, but think it will want more amendment & digestion than the formalities of the house will conveniently admit, they refer it to a *committee.*

6. But if the proposition be well digested, & may need but few & simple amendments, & especially if these be of leading consequence, they then proceed to consider & *amend* it themselves.

———

Qu. the exactness of these definitions of questions & their occasions? and particularly as to *postponement*, the parliamentary use of which I recollect with great uncertainty.[6]

On a disagreement between the houses as to amendments to a bill, & a conference agreed on, can the conferees propose, or authorise either house to propose an amendment in a *new* part of the bill, having no *coherence* with the amendment on which they have disagreed.

When the Previous question is moved, must the debate on the Main question be immediately suspended?   [G.W. yea.]

When a Previous question has been moved & seconded, may the Main question be amended *before* putting the Previous qu.? [G.W. no] we know it cannot afterwards; & that it is a vexata questio whether it may before. what is mr Wythe's opinion?

When a member calls for the execution of an *order* of the house, as for clearing galleries &c. it must be carried into execution by the Speaker without putting any question on it. but when an *order of the day* is called for, I believe a question is put 'Whether the house will *now* proceed to whatever the order of the day is? is it so?

When a motion is made to strike out a paragraph, section, or even the whole bill from the word 'Whereas' have not the friends of the paragraph a right to have all their amendments to it proposed, before the question is put for striking out?

G.W. n   After the question for striking out is negatived, can the section recieve any new amendment? if the equivalent question whether the section as amended shall stand part of the bill, had been put and decided affirmatively, it is apprehended no after-motion to amend could be recieved.

1. A motion is made to amend a bill or other paper by striking out certain words, & inserting others; & the question being divided, & put first on striking out, it is negatived, & the insertion of course falls.

G.W. it 2. After this a motion is made to strike out *the same words* & to insert others, of a different tenor altogether from those before proposed to be inserted. is not this admissible?

do.   3. Suppose the 2d. motion to be negatived; would it not be admissible to move to strike out *the same words*, & to insert nothing in their place?

do.   So if the 1st. motion had been to strike out the words, & to insert nothing; & negatived; might it not then have been moved to strike out *the same words* & insert other words?[7]

When a paper is under the correction of the house, the natural order is to begin at the beginning, & proceed through it with amendments. but there is an exception as to a *bill*, the *preamble* of which is last amended.

G.W. yes Does this exception extend to any other form of paper? e.g. a resolution &c. or would the *preamble* of the resolution be first amended, according to the natural order?

G.W. no. Suppose a paper, e.g. a resolution brought in without a preamble & that a motion be made to prefix a preamble: can such a motion be recieved & acted on before the body of the paper is *acted* on?

[285]

MS (DLC: TJ Papers, 108:18473-5); entirely in TJ's hand, with TJ adding the numerals and words in margin, the responses by "G.W." in the text, which are in brackets supplied by the Editors, and the emendations in pencil after he received, and as a key to, Wythe's letter above; page breaks in the MS are indicated in notes 4-7 below. PrC (DLC: TJ Papers, 108:18246-50); lacks emendations made by TJ after receipt of Wythe's letter above; endorsed by TJ in ink on verso: "Wythe George. Nov. 29. 1800." MS enclosed in TJ to Wythe, 29 Nov. (letter now missing) and returned by Wythe in letter above.

IN COMMITTEE: TJ begins his queries here as he did in the set of questions he sent to Wythe on 28 Feb. But this time his opening paragraph more closely resembles that published in Section 26 of his *Manual of Parliamentary Practice*. In response to Wythe's comments TJ made other emendations to the paragraph. For example TJ modified part of the closing sentence to reflect Wythe's response to his question in line 26 (see letter above) by emending THEY MUST REPORT IT BACK TO THE HOUSE to read "they cannot reject it but must report it back to the house" (*Parliamentary Manual*, 1801, Section 26). For the other changes TJ made to the paragraph after receipt of Wythe's letter, see notes 1 and 2, below.

TJ found support for Wythe's response on limiting the actions of CONFEREES

(see letter above) in the fourth volume of John Hatsell's *Precedents of Proceedings in the House of Commons; with Observations*. The volume was published in London in 1796, but TJ did not consult it for the 1801 edition of the *Parliamentary Manual*. He emended Section 46 on "Conferences" in the second edition in 1812. For this and other emendations in TJ's hand, all with references to Hatsell's fourth volume, see the 1801 edition of the *Manual of Parliamentary Practice* in the TJ Papers at DLC, ser. 7.

VEXATA QUESTIO (quaestio): a vexing question, one often discussed, but not settled.

[1] TJ altered the preceding passage, in pencil, to read "of resolutions on distinct subjects." PrC lacks emendation. The paragraph in Section 26 on "Bills Commitment" in the 1801 edition of the *Parliamentary Manual* reflects the change.

[2] TJ here interlined in pencil "but if the resolns relate to the same subject or" in response to Wythe's answer (see letter above) to page 1, line 24. PrC lacks emendation. The paragraph in Section 26 on "Bills Committment" in the 1801 edition of the *Parliamentary Manual* reflects the change.

[3] Preceding two words interlined.

[4] Page one ends here.

[5] Page two ends here.

[6] Page three ends here.

[7] Page four ends here.

From Thomas Mann Randolph

TH: M. RANDOLPH TO TH: JEFFERSON,   Richd. Dec. 8. 1800

I left home on Tuesday the 2d. at which time all was as we could wish with us; and was so the day before yesterday as I learn from John Henderson, today arrived here.—Passing thro' Goochland I learnt a circumstance which I communicate to you as it may be in your power without trouble to procure redress for those incommoded by it. A man called Nathaniel Perkins (being then a store-keeper at the Court house) was made Post-Master for that place & kept the post office there for some time, but at length finding it his interest to move his goods to a place between Little-creek &

Licking hole, prevailed on the post rider to stop there instead of the Court house and now keeps the office there, to the manifest inconvenience of the people. Samuel Woodson a very respectable freeholder & tavernkeeper at the C: House was desired by all the neighbourhood to apply for the place of P.M. there and did by letter to Habersham, but has received no answer tho very long time has passed.

Yours most affectionately   TH: M. RANDOLPH

RC (ViU: Edgehill-Randolph Papers); endorsed by TJ as received 17 Dec. and so recorded in SJL.

NATHANIEL PERKINS received the appointment as postmaster at the Goochland County courthouse in January 1799. A year later Joseph Habersham allowed him to continue in the position even after he had moved, noting that there was no one to "take charge of it at the Court House." Perkins resigned effective 31 Dec. 1800. With a promise to keep the post office in the vicinity of the courthouse, Anthony Gadsbury was appointed in his place, resigning within a few months. In April 1802 SAMUEL WOODSON was given the post (Stets, *Postmasters*, 258; Habersham to Nathaniel Perkins, 7 Jan., 5 Dec. 1800 and Habersham to Robert Poor, 11 Apr. 1801, all in DNA: RG 28, LPG).

From Hugh Williamson

DEAR SIR   New York 8th Decr 1800.

The inclosed account of the Temperature of the Air in Quebec was given me by a gentleman from that City who had little to do and amused himself with meteorological observations. The circumstance that induced me to copy this Part of the Journal was the remarkable coincidence of the coldest weather with the conjunction of the Sun & Moon during the 4 cold months. Has it been observed in other Years and in other Places that the weather is tempered in the least by the Light of the Moon, or that the Moon has any Effect on the Temperature of the Atmosphere? I do not know that the philosophical Society take any account of meteorological observations.

I propose in the course of this winter, if the rheumatism by which I am confined shall abate, to publish the History of N Carolina. I shall have occasion to speak of the Turkey as a dark coloured bird in America its *native* Country. This fact however, being opposed to the common Opinion, needs proof. You was informed as I think by a Mr Strickland that his family wear a Turkey for the Crest of their Arms. The Petition of their ancestor to the king for Permission to wear that crest, where is it found? Is it in the heralds Office? The head of the family I think is at present a Baronet. Do you know his first Name? I think he lives in Yorkshire.

When I shall have stated the facts will you give me leave to quote my authority? I am

With the utmost Consideration Your most obedt and very hble Servt   HU WILLIAMSON

RC (DLC); at foot of text: "Honble Thos Jefferson"; endorsed by TJ as received 12 Dec. and so recorded in SJL. Enclosure: "A Register of the Temperature of the Air in the City of Quebec in Canada as it was observed at Sun Rise from 1 Decr 1798 to 31 March 1799" (same; in Williamson's hand).

METEOROLOGICAL OBSERVATIONS: Williamson later published *Observations*

on the Climate in Different Parts of America (New York, 1811). His HISTORY of North Carolina did not appear in print until 1812 (ANB).

For the incorporation of the TURKEY into the Strickland family's crest, see Notes on Conversations with William Strickland, May 1795. The HEAD OF THE FAMILY was William Strickland's father, Sir George Strickland of Yorkshire (Vol. 28:371).

From Caspar Wistar

DEAR SIR   Philada. Decr. 8. 1800.

I am not certain that you will have leisure to attend to the subject which follows, but the circumstances appear so interesting that I cannot refrain from communicating them to you, & if you are not able to devote any time to the subject you will still be much interested in the event—

It appears by the Medical Repository (a periodical publication at New York) that there have lately been found, in morasses among the Highlands, the remains of several Sceletons, either of the Mammoth, or of an Animal of equal size—Among other bones, those of the head are mentioned, & also those of the feet, which it is said evince that the Animal was of the Clawed kind—Some hair was also found among the bones—These facts, as well as the enormous size, & the[1] number of the different bones, have interested me so much that I would send a person to endeavour to purchase them, but I am apprehensive that the inquiries of a Stranger would induce the people who are in possession to consider them as worth more than they really are, & of Course, to refuse to part with them—it is also probable that the College & Musæum of New York will engage in the endeavour to procure them, & will necessarily have more influence than any person in a rival City. For these reasons I have not mentioned my intention of trying to procure them to any one, & after reflecting on the subject, can think of no method so likely to succeed, as an application to Chancellor Livingston, whose residence I believe is not very distant from the spot—A request from you would interest him, & would not excite the Competition from New York which I have anticipated, for the prior right to examine the natural productions of our Country, will be readily conceded by every American to the Author of the Notes on Virginia—If therefore you approve of the plan, I hope & beg that you will write very soon to your very respectable friend, & request him to procure *for you* some of these very interesting remains—The whole Sceleton would be best, but if that cannot be had the head & feet will be particularly desireable—we have an Os femoris & an Os Humeri, here, so that, if it should prove to be the Mammoth, we do not stand in need of them, but the other large bones will be very interesting, especially the Ossa Innominata & the Scapula—Some of the last discoveries were made about twelve miles west of Newburgh, I should suppose from the map about 15 or 18 miles North West of New Windsor—they are said to be about three miles east of the town of Shawangunk—Our friend Genl. Van Cortland can probably assist in a more exact specification of the place if it be necessary—I beg leave to repeat my wish that the application may be made early, for I know two instances where most important remains of this nature were long ago sent out of this County & no account of them has as yet been made public—to this request I will venture to add another, that you will favour me with a line of information respecting the measures you may take or think adviseable— Our anxiety is wound up here to the highest pitch possible—returns of the election have only arrived from Maryland & Jersey we all look to South Carolina for the decision (as the people of this State have been maneuvered out of fourteen of their votes) & the accounts here are so very various that they produce perfect suspence—What ever may be the result, the friends of true Republicanism will be Consoled by ascertaining the fact, that their Candidate has the suffrages of a Considerable majority of the American People, & by believing that the maneuvres of this election will not fail to establish the republican principle for the time to come.

With sincere & affectionate esteem I am your obliged friend

C. WISTAR JUNR

RC (DLC); endorsed by TJ as received 12 Dec. and so recorded in SJL.

The appendix to Volume 4 of Samuel L. Mitchill's serial, the MEDICAL REPOSITORY, which bore an 1801 imprint date, contained a letter from Sylvanus Miller of 20 Sep. 1800 describing the discovery of the large bones in the Hudson Valley that were later classified as remains of a mastodon (*Medical Repository*, 4 [1801], 211-13). Wistar may have enclosed the printed version of Miller's account in a letter to TJ, 18 Feb. 1801.

COLLEGE & MUSÆUM OF NEW YORK: Columbia College, where Mitchill taught natural history; and, apparently, the "American Museum," which the Tammany Society had founded in 1790 but after 1795 was a private enterprise of Gardiner Baker, who exhibited, along with objects of natural science, such curiosities as a guillotine (Greene, *American Science*, 94-6; Charles Coleman Sellers, *Mr.*

Peale's Museum: Charles Willson Peale and the First Popular Museum of Natural Science and Art [New York, 1980], 52-3, 98).

[1] Wistar here canceled "variety."

From John Hoomes

DEAR SIR   Bowling Green Decemr. 9th. 1800

I have this moment red. a letter from Colo. Wade Hampton dated Columbia Decer. 2d. 1800, after the electors were chosen for S. Carolina, & I have the *unbounded pleasure* to inform you that yourself & Mr. Burr will get every vote there (so Colo. Hampton writes me) Inclosed is the list of the electors; Mr. Thos. Pinkney is *now here*, has seen the list & he declares them all in the *opposition*. I congratulate you most cordially, & rejoice very heartily with all the friends of liberty every where

I am dear Sir with real respect yr. Hble St   JOHN HOOMES

RC (MHi); endorsed by TJ as received 13 Dec. and so recorded in SJL. Enclosure not found, but for a list of votes for electors, see Peter Freneau to TJ, 2 Dec.

Col. John Hoomes (1749-1805), a wealthy Virginia planter and businessman, was Bowling Green postmaster and contractor for carrying the mail from 1790 to 1796. He represented Caroline County in the Virginia House of Delegates from 1791 to 1795 and Hanover and Caroline counties in the Virginia Senate from 1796 to 1803 (Ralph Emmett Fall,

People, Postoffices and Communities in Caroline County, Virginia, 1727-1969 [Roswell, Ga., 1989], 18, 19, 36; "Will of Col. John Hoomes," VMHB, 38 [1930], 74-9; Latrobe, *Virginia Journals*, 2:543; Ralph Emmett Fall, *Historical Record of Bowling Green [County Seat of Caroline County, Virginia] 1667-1970* [Bowling Green, Va., 1970], 30, 32; Richmond *Enquirer*, 27 Dec. 1805).

A letter from Hoomes to TJ, written at Bowling Green on 25 Mch. 1800 and recorded in SJL as received 4 Apr., has not been found.

From Edward Livingston

SIR   New York Decr. 9. 1800

An arrival here from Charleston brings intelligence which perhaps may not reach the Seat of Government before this letter in which case it may not prove unacceptable—A man of Understanding & by no means of a sanguine disposition writes from Columbia on the 25th. that the Legislature had met. the Republicans in high Spirits that no Question was made of an unanimous republican Vote for P.

& that they Spurned at the idea of a compromise with respect to the Vote for V.P.

We have nothing farther from the East than you must have heard. Vermont will Very probably give us one Vote. On the Whole the business is considered as completely settled with us, at which You will rejoice I am sure more on account of our Country which so much needs a change than for any personal gratifications to yourself.—I may I believe safely congratulate You on an Event Which gives more real Satisfaction to no One than

Your Mo Obdt Friend & Servt   EDW LIVINGSTON

RC (DLC); endorsed by TJ as received 15 Dec. and so recorded in SJL.

Timothy Green, a resident of New York with whom Aaron Burr had business ties, wrote the letter of 25 Nov. 1800 that contained INTELLIGENCE from South Carolina (Kline, *Burr*, 1:188-9, 236-7, 466-7).

From William Short

DEAR SIR   La Rocheguyon Dec. 9th. 1800

The last letters which I had the pleasure of addressing you were of the 6th. of August & 18th. of Septr. This last was sent by our Envoys—Soon after I came to this place where I have remained since; & should not have troubled you at present had it not been for a letter I have recieved from Mr Skipwith requesting one on the subject wch. will be here explained to you.[1]—He desires to resume the functions of Consul General at Paris, which as you know, he exercised from the first establishment & for several years, & indeed as long as they were exercised at all—In consequence of the late treaty they will of course be revived, & the appointment will probably be made as soon as the ratification shall take place—Mr Skipwith concieves that your recommendation may have weight with the President, & that mine will be agreeable to you—He therefore requests of me to write to you on this subject, as he hopes to be able to forward you this letter in time by the French Chargé des affaires who is setting out & expects to have a quick passage, so that he will probably arrive in the next month. As you are well acquainted with Mr Skipwith I am persuaded there is little occasion for my enlarging on his subject—If it were any other than yourself I should begin the recommendation by assuring you (of what is true) that he is most strongly & sincerely attached to you—but I know that with you this consideration has not the same weight in public appointments, which it has with most persons—I will confine myself therefore to the personal merit of Mr. Skipwith in relation to the office he desires.—He is the only person who has hitherto held this office—he exercised it during several years, & for a considerable time under delicate & difficult circumstances, & being the only the accredited agent of the United States here—His exercise was satisfactory to our Government, as I suppose, as he was continued in office not only as long as he chose to remain, but long after he had sollicited to be relieved from the burthen, (& at that time it was really an heavy one)—As Government postponed accepting his resignation, he continued faithfully at his post, notwithstanding, the inconvenience he then experienced therein, & waited thus a considerable time their convenience, until they granted his request to resign—As circumstances have now changed and as he is now desirous to resume those functions which hitherto have not been exercised by any other, I should imagine that these considerations would have weight in the appointment. It appears also that Mr Skipwith has given satisfaction to his countrymen here who are the most immediately concerned in his gestion, as I learn from him, that it is at their request, amongst other circumstances, that he has determined to resume the exercise of this office, if it should meet the approbation of the President. I am persuaded also that he would be agreeable to this Government, & as I learn from him, the Chargé des affaires who is going out & who is well acquainted with Mr Skipwith, will confirm this.—Under a view of all these circumstances I am persuaded you will think that no person can have a better claim to the appointment in question, or be more likely from his experience in the place to give satisfaction to the United States, than Mr. Skipwith—And if as he supposes, your recommendation would have influence with the President, I am equally persuaded that you will take pleasure in recommending a person thus worthy of it. As to myself I need only be the bearer of Mr Skipwith's wishes on this occasion, as I am sure you will have no occasion of any thing further to be favorably disposed to him, & to be useful to him as far as may depend on you.

It is a very pleasing circumstance to see the wonted relations of commerce & friendship about to be established between the U.S. & this country—It is so much better for all parties to be interchanging their superfluous productions, than to be bickering, quarelling & destroying each others property—The advantages of this change will be considerably enhanced, if the war should continue in Europe, & the system of the Northern powers (of which the symptoms have been for some time shewing themselves) be consolidated.—These symptoms so important for the consideration of our Government, have without doubt been carefully observed & successively developed by our foreign agents.[2] There is certainly no subject more worthy of all the attention of the Government of the U.S. than what concerns the protection & security of neutral flags. Time & chance have brought about a crisis in the North which may go further in this way than all the arguments of morality justice &c. &c. which it would be possible to form.—With some of these powers it is a meer matter of circumstance & may pass—with others of them the desire to see such a system consolidated, is permanent—unfortunately they are not the strongest—It is possible they may so employ the present dispositions of their more powerful neighbors as to interweave a system which may bind them in some degree by the ties of honor or dignity.—The moment is an unexpectedly favorable one & rendered so by a variety of circumstances which have combined—The Minister of the U.S. at Berlin is well situated for the observing of this subject, as to the present moment; yet it is to be regretted in my opinion that we have not had a sentinel also at one of the other Northern courts, & particularly that of Denmark. From the moment that the question of neutrality has become so important an one for the U.S. this Court has been one of those the most worthy of their attention—I was for some time during the present war in habits of intimacy with a person enjoying the full confidence & possessing influence with that government, & I am persuaded now that it would have been of advantage to our two countries, if they had then adopted measures of habitual & confidential communication by the interchange of Envoys.—I do not mean by this that they should have concerted measures of force, but I think they would probably have hit on some passive means of rendering their neutral rights more respected; & perhaps might have induced the King of Prussia[3] to have adopted some plan for at least encouraging maritime neutrality, if he could not defend it as efficaciously as he has hitherto done with respect to territorial neutrality in the limits he fixed.—   The time past is of course out of our reach—It is therefore the more reasonable to make use of the present whilst within our power—If I had to advise as to the best means; it would be that an Envoy should be without delay sent to Copenhagen, either on a temporary or permanent mission—& from thence communicate & concert with the Minister at Berlin. Their situation would enable them to judge well of the nature & duration of the present crisis— how far the U.S. might rely on it—whether it would be for their advantage to become a party—(& in that case on what terms)—or whether it would be best to wait & enter the association hereafter as accessory.—The situation of the U.S. is such that they may be sure of being well recieved whenever they may please—They may therefore wait & consult—Their Ministers at Copenhagen & Berlin, would be able to give them the best information & Government might judge on comparing the information recieved from these two sources—The subject will be elucidated during the present winter—the real views & future conduct of the Northern powers will be ascertained & if our Government were immediately to send an Envoy to Copenhagen I think he might in a very short time render the U.S. more real service than from any other point at this moment—That Court has a more permanent disposition to the state of neutrality than any other & therefore in a state the most conformable to that of the U.S.—It is evident that the present dispositions of Berlin & Petersburg, are matters of circumstance, & therefore ought not to be absolutely relied on as to duration—It is at, & in concert with, the Court of Denmark where this matter can be best judged of—& I should think it of importance that no time should be lost in ascertaining how far the present crisis can be relied on as protective of a system of neutrality—or in examining on the spot whether seeds may not be now sewn in that Northern soil, which may hereafter produce this fruit.

I have dwelt longer on this subject as you will see than I have for some years back been accustomed to do on any political matter—I have yielded to it because it is a favorite one with me—& because I think that the procuring a permanent system of neutral maritime rights, should be the polar star of our Government in all their foreign relations—I have always supported the doctrine that they should by all means keep themselves disentangled from European politics—but it is time to see if there be no means of adopting some measure by which foreign powers may cut & slash each other, without our vessels being for that exposed in all the distant quarters of the globe to be ransacked robbed & plundered, by all the scoundrels who may obtain a patent for that purpose from their Sovereign, under pretext of pursuing his enemies. The present combination of affairs in this hemisphere is a very favorable one for this purpose, & I hope our Government will not let it pass without examining well whether any thing & what can be made of it. The only belligerent power which has a real interest to oppose the system of neutral maritime rights, is at this moment in a situation peculiarly embarrassing as to that point—Amongst other circumstances their scarcity of provisions at home, renders their free communication with the North uncommonly necessary—In this crisis the Emperor of Russia has not only excluded them from a great port, but stopped the vessels they had in his ports, of which a great number was loaded with grain—If the affair of Maltha were the only cause of this measure, it would probably be arranged—but it will most likely be complicated with other interests before it can be arranged between these two parties. It is an object of great importance to see how the cabinet of St James will reply to this Russian argument, & whether they will make use of the kind of logic they lately exhibited to the Court of Denmark, with its usual success.

I have not had the pleasure of hearing from you since your letter of April 18th. which I have acknowleged in my two last abovementioned.—I hope the affair of the 9. m. dollars, with our government will have been settled finally before this & that I shall soon hear so from you—I am really ashamed of the trouble I have already given you respecting it.—My two last letters were so prolix, & must have taken up so much of your time, as to all my little private concerns, that I will not touch on them here—My intention of embarking in the spring for the U.S. was there mentioned also—Should nothing interfere to delay it, it will be probably in the month of April. I imagine we shall by that time have a number of our vessels in the ports of this country.

The French gazettes have copied from the British a report of the Negroes having been on the eve of an insurrection at Richmond, & of its having been prevented—no particulars are given—of course we know little or nothing on the subject. Yet it appears to me that whatever relates to those people is a matter of so much importance & delicacy to our Southern States, that I never think on it & cast my view forward without some uneasiness as you will have seen by several of my former letters. I have thought a great deal on it; but I am not sure that I see what is for the best; & if I did, there is no reason to suppose that in this case more than in most others the best possible, be the practicable. I feel that it is a delicate subject to be touched on in the situation of the Southern States, & yet their Legislatures as it seems to me, cannot with prudence abandon the subject entirely to time & chance.

This expression of time & chance brings into my mind a Spanish proverb, & that again recalls a circumstance of the Spanish language although it has no concern with the proverb—but regards the appellation which we give in Virginia to certain objects, borrowed from the Spanish language—I think I mentioned this whilst I was in Spain, but I am not sure of it—For instance the name we give to one of our shrubs which we commonly call *Chinkapin* (I know not how it is written but I suppose somewhat in that way) is evidently taken from the Spaniards & named thus from its resemblance to a fruit which grows on a kind of pine called *pina*—In that language *chica* signifies *little*—The name therefore which we give to the fruit of this shrub, is composed of *chica pina*—The name we give also to the bed bugs, is the same that they have in the Spanish language, & which is unknown in the English language, in wch. I think they are merely called bugs—It seems to me it would be an object of some curiosity to ascertain how these names were derived by us from the Spanish establishments to the south, & whether there be a considerable number of words which we have thus derived from that language instead of our mother tongue—I take it for granted that the States to the south of us make use of the same names borrowed from the Spaniards—I know not how far these names extend to the north—I have always neglected to enquire among the Americans here from the different parts of the U.S.—I take the liberty of inclosing you a letter for my brother for which I ask your friendly care & beg you to be persuaded of the constant & invariable attachment of your friend & servant

W SHORT

My friend coming into my room at this moment insists on my opening my letter to mention her to you & to assure you of her gratitude for your kind remembrance—She hopes you will believe that she has preserved her family's attachment for you & begs you to continue to her your friendship for them—She adds that she desires it *du fond de son coeur.*—

RC (PHi); at foot of first page: "Thomas Jefferson—V.P. of the U.S."; with marginal notations by TJ recorded in notes below; endorsed by TJ as received 18 Mch. 1801 and so recorded in SJL. Enclosure: William Short to Peyton Short, 10 Dec. 1800 (FC in DLC: Short Papers; a summary in Short's epistolary record).

CONSUL GENERAL AT PARIS: in his late-term appointments of February 1801 John Adams nominated James Cole Mountflorence as commercial agent at Paris. The Senate did not confirm that appointment. TJ named Fulwar Skipwith to the post, the Senate agreeing in January 1802 (JEP, 1:384, 403, 405).

Louis André Pichon was the new FRENCH CHARGÉ d'affaires—properly the commissary general for commercial rela-

tions—in the United States. He took up his post in March (Tulard, *Dictionnaire Napoléon*, 1329; Abraham P. Nasatir and Gary E. Monell, *French Consuls in the United States: A Calendar of Their Correspondence in the Archives Nationales* [Washington, D.C., 1967], 550).

John Quincy Adams continued as U.S. minister to the Prussian government at BERLIN (ANB).

AFFAIR OF MALTA: Emperor Paul of Russia felt great affinity for the knights of Malta, and when the French seized the island in 1798 he took the order under his protection, even assuming the title of grand master. After Britain captured Malta in September 1800 but excluded Russia from any role in the occupation, Paul completed the severance of his alliance with the coalition against France. By conventions of 16 and 18 Dec. Russia created a league of armed neutrality with Sweden, Denmark, and Prussia (Roderick E. McGrew, *Paul I of Russia, 1754-1801* [Oxford, 1992], 259, 271-9, 313-16; Ehrman, *Pitt*, 154, 395-7; Francis Piggott and G. W. T. Omond, eds., *Documentary History of the Armed Neutralities, 1780 and 1800* [London, 1919], 439-43, 447-51, 453-7).

LETTER OF APRIL 18TH: TJ to Short, 13 Apr. 1800. Short made the same error in his letter of 6 Aug.

The name of the chinquapin (chincapin) tree came not from SPANISH but from Algonquian languages of American Indians. Short was correct, however, in relating "chinch," a term for a bedbug, to the Spanish word "chinche." "Chinch" was in turn the origin of "chinch bug," used to denote a particular agricultural pest (J. A. Simpson and E. S. C. Weiner, eds., *The Oxford English Dictionary*, 2d ed., 20 vols. [Oxford, 1989], 3:126; Mitford M. Mathews, ed., *A Dictionary of Americanisms: On Historical Principles* [Chicago, Ill., 1951], 314, 315; Vol. 7:402, 409n).

MY FRIEND: the Duchesse de La Rochefoucauld. DU FOND DE SON COEUR: from the bottom of her heart.

[1] Here in margin TJ wrote: "Skipwith Consul."

[2] In margin TJ wrote: "Neutrality."

[3] Short interlined the preceding three words in place of "court of Berlin."

From George Jefferson

DEAR SIR,   Richmond 10th. Decr. 1800.

The price of Tobacco having continued stationary from the date of my last until a few days past, and having then rather declined, on receipt of intelligence that it had become so very dull in Philadelphia & New York that scarcely any sales were made, and of course that the prices in those places were merely nominal; I concluded, in compliance with your instruction, to make sale of yours—which I did accordingly to Macmurdo & Fisher of this place at 6 dollars payable the first of April next.   this information would have been given you some days sooner, but that I was called out of Town *immediately* after making the sale, on a very mournful occasion.

This sale I am rather apprehensive may be somewhat below your expectation, but as the House to whom I made it is *perfectly safe*, and, as *perfectly pointed* in complying with their engagements, I did not think myself justifiable in letting the opportunity slip; and especially when I took into consideration a circumstance with which you are not acquainted: which is this—that in a falling market it is a very rare thing indeed to meet with any one who is considered to be entirely safe, who will give an extra price in consideration of a long credit. indeed *at any time* since the great fall in the price of Tobacco, it has not been a very usual thing for persons of undoubted credit to give more on time, than[1] is barely adequate to the outlay of money.

I am Dear Sir Your Very humble servt.   GEO. JEFFERSON

[297]

I included in the sale the Hhd which was received in lieu of the one which was lost of the former crop. G.J.

RC (MHi); at foot of text: "Thos. Jefferson esqr. Washington"; endorsed by TJ as received 16 Dec. and so recorded in SJL.

DATE OF MY LAST: George Jefferson to TJ, 24 Nov. 1800. For TJ's INSTRUCTION, see his letter to George Jefferson of 29 Nov.

[1] George Jefferson first concluded the sentence "the outlay of money would be worth to the [seller]" before altering it to read as above.

To Robert Patterson

DEAR SIR   Washington Dec. 10. 1800.

The annual period for electing a President of the American Philosophical society being now approaching, and no circumstances rendering it probable that I may be able to attend their sessions in Philadelphia it is become my duty to desire the society to turn their views to some other person, better situated and more capable of discharging the functions of their President. permit me to do this through you, and at the same time to express my grateful thanks for the honor the society has been pleased to do me on several preceding occasions. I recieved it as a mark of their esteem, and valued it as among the most precious testimonies of my life, and shall never cease to be a faithful and zealous associate of the institution. accept assurances yourself of the great personal regard and esteem of Dear Sir

Your most obedt. humble servt.   TH: JEFFERSON

PrC (DLC); at foot of text: "Mr. Patterson"; with one word repeated above the line by TJ in ink for clarity.

Patterson was one of three vice presidents for 1800, along with Caspar Wistar and Benjamin Rush, of the AMERICAN PHILOSOPHICAL SOCIETY. He sometimes presided over meetings in TJ's absence. On 2 Jan. 1801 the society again elected TJ president (APS, Proceedings, 22, pt. 3 [1884], 290, 295, 297, 299-300, 302, 305, 307).

To Joseph Young

SIR   Washington Dec. 10. 1800.

I have to acknolege the receipt of your astronomical & physiological treatises by the hands of mr Davenport and to return you my thanks for this attention. the heads of these works shew them to be interesting, and I shall peruse them with great satisfaction. their nature however requiring serious reflection it is possible that my occupations here may oblige me to delay the pleasure of the perusal till my return home. the Newtonian theory appears to have solved the very complicated phaenomena in astronomy, and so far to call for our assent. but we are commanded to prove all things and hold fast that which is good. I pay you to accept assurances of the respect of Sir Your most obedt. humble servt   TH: JEFFERSON

PrC (DLC); at foot of text: "Doctr Joseph Young—Stamford. Connecticut."

TJ is acknowledging THE RECEIPT of Young's letter of 29 Oct. 1800.

To Pierre Samuel Du Pont de Nemours

Washington Dec. 12. 1800.

I know, my dear friend, that you sent me, so long ago as August, the much desired, and much valued piece on education, which I read with great pleasure, and ought to have acknoleged it's receipt. but when I am at home there are so many delicious occupations of the more active kind that it is as difficult to drag me to my writing table, as to get a horse, broken loose from confinement, to re-enter his stable door. I intended to [have] brought on the piece and left it with my friend mr Madison [who] associates with me in the wish to improve the state of our education. but in the hurry of my departure, I left it at home. you say you propose to get it translated. but I believe it impossible to translate your writings. it would be easier to translate Homer, which yet [has] never been done. several of us tried our hands on the memoir you gave me for the Philosophical society, but after trials, gave it up as desperate and determined to print it in French.—at length our [labor] seems to have a certain issue, notwithstanding the annihilation of the vote of Pennsylvania. when will your affairs lead you to visit this place? you [may] probably find here one friend more than at any preceding period. salutations of respect & esteem to your good family, & to yourself [life, health] & happiness. Adieu.   TH: JEFFERSON

PrC (DLC); faint; at foot of text: "M. Dupont."

PIECE ON EDUCATION: see Du Pont de Nemours to TJ, 24 Aug. 1800. For the

essay by Du Pont that the American PHILOSOPHICAL SOCIETY published in French, "Sur les Végétaux, les Polypes et les Insectes," see TJ's letter of 12 May (Vol. 31:578).

To Thomas Mann Randolph

TH:J. TO TMR.   Dec. 12. 1800.

I believe we may consider the election as now decided. letters recieved from Columbia (S.C.) this morning, & dated Dec. 2. which was the day of appointing their electors, announce that the republican ticket carried it by majorities of from 17. to 18. the characters named are firm, & were to elect on the next day. it was intended that one vote should be thrown away from Colo. Burr. it is believed Georgia will withold from him one or two. the votes will stand probably T.J. 73. Burr about 7[0.] mr Adams 65. Pinckney probably lower than that. it is fortunate that some difference will be made between the two highest candidates; because it is said the Feds here held a Caucus & came to a resolution that in the event of their being equal, they would prevent an election which they could have done, by dividing the H. of R.—my tender love to my dear Martha & the little ones. sincere affection to yourself. [Adieu.]

PrC (MHi); faint; endorsed by TJ in ink on verso.

The correspondence that TJ received from COLUMBIA, South Carolina, on 12 Dec. was from Peter Freneau and Charles Pinckney. For the contents of the letter from Pinckney, see his correspondence at 22 Nov. See the Freneau letter at 2 Dec. for the number of votes by which the RE-PUBLICAN TICKET CARRIED.

To James Currie

DEAR SIR   Washington Dec. 14. 1800.

I recieved your favor covering mr Ross's last observations, some time before I left home. a great deal of business pressing on me at that time, as preparatory to my departure for this place, I was unable to attend to this at all. I have taken the first leisure moment I had here, to consider these last observations. we differ in a fact, no further material than as explanatory of the state of things at a particular moment. that there may be an end to this [dispute?], I am contented the case should proceed to arbitration without further addition on my part.   my thanks to you for the trouble you take in this business, and assurances of all possible esteem & attachment from Dear Sir

Your friend & servt   TH: JEFFERSON

PrC (MHi); blurred; at foot of text: "Doctr. James Currie"; endorsed by TJ in ink on verso.

According to SJL, TJ received Currie's FAVOR of 27 Oct. (now missing) on 3 Nov. For the settlement of TJ's dispute with David Ross, see note to TJ to George Jefferson, 14 Oct. 1799.

A letter from TJ to Currie of 6 Oct., recorded in SJL with the notation "cov-erg. Ross's papers," and Currie's response of the 17th, recorded in SJL as received 24 Oct., are also missing.

To Thomas Leiper

DEAR SIR   Washington Dec. 14. 1800.

Your favors of Oct. 9. & 16. came to hand in due time, as has done that also of Nov. 26. in the country we put off writing letters to a rainy day, and are apt then to take up what is most pressing. your first letter being an answer to mine, and the terms for my tobo[1] inferior to what I was offered in Richmond, the replying to it yielded to some others more immediately urgent. I had been assured that I might have $5\frac{1}{2}$ D. for my crop at Richmond, which was better than your offer of 6. D. at Philadelphia. I am now assured that $6\frac{1}{2}$ D. are given at Richmond for prime crops. mine is still awaiting the spring which our new treaty will give further to the price.

To the offer of a contract there are 3. objections. 1st. you confine it to Albemarle tobo. 2dly. that it should not be smoked, which in some seasons would lose the whole. 3dly. the price. be assured that no man can make tobo. in my part of the country for less than 7. D. delivered at Richmond. I know we are often obliged to take less; but often we get more; and he whose prices do not average 7. D. is wasting his land, that is his capital, without profit. I should have been fond of a fixed price, if I could have had one which was not a losing one.

Tho our information from S. Carolina is not official, yet I suppose one may rely on our success there, and that we shall now have an opportunity of putting the vessel of the Union on her republican tack, and of seeing how she will work on that. I have no fear she will work well. be so good as to present my respects to your neighbor mr Dallas, and to accept yourself my friendly salutations.

TH: JEFFERSON

PrC (DLC); at foot of text: "Thomas Leiper esq."; endorsed by TJ in ink on verso.

[1] Preceding three words interlined.

To Robert R. Livingston

DEAR SIR   Washington Dec. 14. 1800.

Your former communications on the subject of the steam engine, I took the liberty of laying before the American Philosophical society, by whom they will be printed in their volume of the present year. I have heard of the discovery of some large bones, supposed to be of the Mammoth, at about 30. or 40 miles distance from you: and among the ones found are said to be some which we have never yet been able to procure. the 1st. interesting question is Whether they be the bones of the Mammoth? the 2d. what are the particular bones, and could I possibly procure them? the bones I am most anxious to obtain are those of the head & feet, which are said to be among those found in your state, as also the ossa innominata, and the Scapula. others would also be interesting, though similar ones may be possessed, because they would shew by their similarity that the set belongs to the Mammoth. could I so far venture to trouble you on this subject as to engage some of your friends near the place to procure for me the bones abovementioned? if they are to be bought, I will gladly pay for them whatever you shall agree to as reasonable; and will place the money in N. York as instantaneously after it is made known to me as the post can carry it, as I will all expences of package transportation &c to New York, and Philadelphia, where they may be addressed to John Barnes, whose agent (he not being on the spot) will take care of them for me.

But I have still a more important subject whereon to address you. Tho' our information of the votes of the several states be not official,[1] yet they are stated on such evidence as to satisfy both parties that the Republican vote has been successful. we may therefore venture to hazard propositions on that hypothesis without being justly subjected to raillery or ridicule. the constitution, to which we are all attached, was meant to be republican, and we believe it to be republican according to every candid interpretation. yet we have seen it so interpreted and administered, as to be truly, what the French have called it, a *monarchie masquée*. so long however has the vessel run on in this way, and been trimmed to it, that to put her on her republican tack will require all the skill, the firmness & the zeal of her ablest & best friends. it is a crisis which calls on them, to sacrifice all other objects, and repair to her aid in this momentous operation. not only their skill is wanting, but their names also. it is essential to assemble in the outset persons to compose[2] our administration, whose talents, integrity and revolutionary name & principles may inspire the nation

at once with unbounded confidence, impose an awful silence on all
the maligners of republicanism; and suppress in embryo the purpose
avowed by one of their most daring & effective chiefs, of beating
down the administration. these names do not abound at this day. so
few are they, that your's, my friend cannot be spared from among
them without leaving a blank which cannot be filled. if I can obtain
for the public the aid of those I have contemplated, I fear nothing. if
this cannot be done, then are we unfortunate indeed! we shall be
unable to realize the prospects which have been held out to the people, and we must fall back into monarchism, for want of heads, not
hands, to help us out of it. this is a common cause my dear Sir, common to all republicans. tho' I have been too honorably placed in front
of those who are to enter the breach, so happily made, yet the energies of every individual are necessary, & in the very place where his
energies can most serve the enterprize. I can assure you that your
collegues will be most acceptable to you; one of them, whom you
cannot mistake, peculiarly so. the part which circumstances con-
strain me to propose to you is the Secretaryship of the navy. these
circumstances cannot be explained by letter. republicanism is so rare
in those parts which possess nautical skill, that I cannot find it allied
there to the other qualifications. tho you are not nautical by profession, yet your residence, and your mechanical science qualify you as
well as a gentleman can possibly[3] be, and sufficiently to enable you
to chuse under-agents perfectly qualified & to superintend their conduct. come forward then, my dear Sir, and give us the aid of your talents, & the weight of your character, towards the new establishment
of republicanism: I say, for it's new establishment; for hitherto we
have seen only it's travestie. —I have urged thus far, on the belief
that your present office would not be an obstacle to this proposition.
I was informed, and I think it was by your brother, that you wished
to retire from it, & were only restrained by the fear that a successor
of different principles might be appointed. the late change in your
council of appointment will remove this fear. —it will not be improper to say a word on the subject of expence. the gentlemen who
composed Genl. Washington's first administration took up too unadvisedly a practice of general entertainment, which was unnecessary,
obstructive of business, & so oppressive to themselves that it was
among the motives for their retirement. their successors profited
from the experiment, & lived altogether as private individuals, & so
have ever continued to do. here indeed it cannot be otherwise, our
situation being so rural, that during the vacations of the legislature
we shall have no society but of the officers of governmt. and in time

of sessions, the legislature is become & becoming so numerous that for the last half dozen years, nobody but the President has pretended to entertain them.—I have been led to make this application before official knolege of the result of our election, because the return of mr Van Benthuysen one of your electors & neighbors offers me a safe conveyance, at a moment when the post offices will be peculiarly suspicious & prying. your answer may come by post without danger, if directed in some other hand writing than your own: and I will pray you to give me an answer as soon as you can make up your mind. accept assurances of my cordial esteem & respect, & my friendly salutations.   TH: JEFFERSON

P.S. you will be sensible of the necessity of keeping this application entirely secret until the formal declaration in February, of who is President, shall have been made.

RC (NNMus); endorsed by Livingston. PrC (DLC); at foot of text in ink: "Robt. R. Livingston"; lacks postscript.

For Livingston's COMMUNICATIONS on the STEAM ENGINE, see 26 Jan. 1799 and 4 June 1800. The next VOLUME of APS *Transactions* did not include those letters.

MONARCHIE MASQUÉE: disguised monarchy.

ONE OF THEIR MOST DARING & EFFECTIVE CHIEFS: see also TJ's reference to "evil genius" near the end of his letter to Burr, 15 Dec. The *Aurora* had called Alexander Hamilton "the arch-intriguer," "the evil genius of America," "the grand *master*" of mischief." Hamilton himself, in his published letter attacking Adams, sarcastically acknowledged the label "arch juggler." Republicans were unaware that Hamilton would soon urge key Federalists to support the election of TJ over Burr (*Aurora*, 28 Aug., 10 Dec. 1800; Syrett, *Hamilton*, 25:202, 257-60, 269-70, 275-7, 280-1, 286-8).

WHOM YOU CANNOT MISTAKE: see TJ to Madison, 19 Dec. 1800, and Livingston to TJ, 7 Jan. 1801.

For some time Livingston had been determined not to resign from the chancellorship of the state of New York while Federalists dominated the powerful COUNCIL OF APPOINTMENT. The council,

which controlled not just offices in the state government but even many county and local positions, consisted of the governor and four members of the state senate. In November 1800 the assembly gave the council a Republican majority, but when the panel next convened, in February 1801, the Republican members deadlocked with Governor John Jay. Not until August, with George Clinton in the governor's chair, would Republicans have actual control over appointments in the state (George Dangerfield, *Chancellor Robert R. Livingston of New York, 1746-1813* [New York, 1960], 90, 264, 269, 305; Kline, *Burr*, 1:502-4n; Hugh M. Flick, "The Council of Appointment in New York State: The First Attempt to Regulate Political Patronage, 1777-1822," *New York History*, 15 [1934], 265-8).

John VAN BENTHUYSEN of Dutchess County, although not one of New York's ELECTORS, served in the legislature in 1800 and other years (Kline, *Burr*, 1:470, 473).

[1] TJ first wrote "[are] not officially known" before altering the phrase to read as above.

[2] TJ first wrote "such persons for" before altering the phrase to read as above.

[3] Preceding two words interlined in place of "may be expected to."

From James Lyon

Dr. Sir   Georgetown Dec. 14th. 1800.—

After my most sincere congratulations on the event of the election,—I am compelled to open a less pleasing subject.—that of my embarrassments. The manner in which I have come by them emboldens me to speak with more confidence to republicans, than I should, if they had been the result of common speculations. My poverty has arisen from my zeal, and perhaps imprudent zeal, in the republican cause, by distributing presses around the country.

I have however, of late condensed all my business and concerns into this place, where with the *National Magazine* and *Cabinet*, I have a business that is something profitable upon paper, but the difficulty of getting my collections made, renders it rather embarrasing in practice.

This has made me want some assistance from the friends of that cause which I have been serving; I opened this subject, a few days since to general Mason, who rendered me some assistance by the loan of 50$. it was his intention to speak to you upon the business; but he is now out of town, & a circumstance has occurred which will not let me wait for his return: There is against me a debt,[1] which is to pass through the hands of your nephew George Jefferson, of Richmond; some months since, to prevent a prosecution, I procured for him the obligation of a *friend*; and now unless it is paid *he* must suffer, and I must be called a villain; I am suddenly called on to do what is out of my power—to pay the money. The object of this letter is therefore to request of you the loan of *100*.$. to be returned within, or at the end of 6 months. Your compliance will greatly relieve me, and confer an proportionate obligation. I mentioned the name of your nephew, thinking it might, perhaps, be more convenient through him to do me this favor.

With Every respect Sir your obedient Servant   J Lyon.

RC (DNA: RG 59, LAR); at foot of text: "Thomas Jefferson Esqr."; endorsed by TJ as received 14 Dec. and so recorded in SJL.

same name. On receipt of this letter on 14 Dec. TJ gave Lyon an order on Gibson & Jefferson for $50 as a LOAN (MB, 2:975, 1032).

GEORGE JEFFERSON was not TJ's nephew but the son of TJ's cousin of the

[1] Preceding two words and punctuation interlined.

[305]

To Benjamin Rush

Dear Sir   Washington Dec. 14. 1800.

I have duly recieved your favor of the 2d. inst. and the melon seeds accompanying it. I shall certainly cherish them, and try whether the climate of Monticello can preserve them without degeneracy. the arrival of Genl. Davie here with the treaty is our only news. mr Elsworth is gone to England, and returns again to France to pass the winter in it's Southern parts for his health. notwithstanding the annihilation of the Pensylvania vote, the Republicans seem to have obtained a majority of 8. in the late election. if so the vessel of the Union will be put on her republican tack, and shew us how she works on that. my respects to mrs Rush; to yourself friendly & affectionate salutations.   Th: Jefferson

RC (PPAmP); addressed: "Doctr. Benjamin Rush Philadelphia"; franked; postmarked 15 Dec. PrC (DLC); endorsed by TJ in ink on verso.

After landing at Norfolk William R. Davie proceeded to Washington, arriving there on 11 Dec. with the convention with France negotiated by the U.S. envoys (Blackwell P. Robinson, *William R. Davie* [Chapel Hill, 1957], 356).

To Aaron Burr

Dear Sir   Washington Dec. 15. 1800.

Although we have not official information of the votes for President & Vice President and cannot have until the first week in Feb. yet the state of the votes is given on such evidence as satisfies both parties that the two Republican candidates stand highest. from S. Carolina we have not even heard of the actual vote; but we have learnt who were appointed electors, and with sufficient certainty how they would vote. it is said they would withdraw from yourself one vote. it has also been said that a General Smith of Tennesee had declared he would give his 2d. vote to mr Gallatin; not from any indisposition towards you, but extreme reverence to the character of mr G. it is also surmised that the vote of Georgia will not be entire. yet nobody pretends to know these things of a certainty, and we know enough to be certain that what it is surmised to[1] be withheld will still leave you 4. or[2] 5. votes at least above mr A. however it was badly managed not to have arranged with certainty what seems to have been left to hazard. it was the more material because I understand several of the highflying federalists have expressed their hope that the two republican tickets may be equal, &

[306]

their determination in that case to prevent a choice by the H. of R. (which they are strong enough to do) and let the government devolve on a President of the Senate. decency required that I should be so entirely passive during the late contest that I never once asked whether arrangements had been made to prevent so many from dropping votes intentionally as might frustrate half the republican wish; nor did I doubt till lately that such had been made.

While I must congratulate you, my dear Sir, on the issue of this contest, because it is more honourable and doubtless more grateful to you than any station within the competence of the chief magistrate, yet for myself, and for the substantial service of the public, I feel most sensibly the loss we sustain of your aid in our new administration. it leaves a chasm in my arrangements, which cannot be adequately filled up. I had endeavored to compose an administration whose talents, integrity, names & dispositions should at once inspire unbounded confidence in the public mind, and ensure a perfect harmony in the conduct of the public business. I lose you from the list, & am not sure of all the others. should the gentlemen who possess the public confidence decline taking a part in their affairs, and force us to take up persons unknown to the people, the evil genius of this country may realize his avowal that 'he will beat down the administration.'—the return of mr Van Benthuysen, one of your electors, furnishes me a confidential opportunity of writing this much to you, which I should not have ventured through the post office, at this prying[3] season. we shall of course see you before the 4th. of March. accept my respectful & affectionate salutations.

TH: JEFFERSON

RC (MWA: Aaron Burr Papers); at foot of first page: "Colo. Burr." PrC (DLC).

EVIL GENIUS: see TJ to Robert R. Livingston, 14 Dec.

[1] Word apparently written over "will."
[2] Preceding word and numeral interlined.
[3] Word written over a partial erasure, "[. . .] of."

From Thomas McKean

DEAR SIR,   Lancaster Decemr. 15th. 1800.

Long ere this you must have learned, that at the election in behalf of this State of President & Vice-President of the United States, you & Mr; Burr had but eight votes, and Messrs. Adams & Pinckney seven votes each. Three fifths of the[1] citizens of this State, had an opportunity afforded, would unquestionably have voted for the former; and tho' this was a fact known & admitted, yet thirteen Senators, making a majority of only two, in opposition to a majority of thirty two in the House of Representatives, have prevented the public will from being declared. The thirteen are execrated by the Whigs, they will never have the power to perpetrate the like mischief again, and I cannot help using the words of St. Paul to Alexander the Coppersmith, "they have done much wrong, the Lord reward them according to their deeds."

Believe me, Sir, every honorable measure has been exerted to prevent this catastrophy; the principal causes of the event, independent of party-principles, appear to me to have been, as follows; John Woods Esquire, the Speaker of the Senate, has ambition at least equal to his talents, and from the conduct of his brother-in-law James Ross Esquire in your Senate, of his brother Henry in the other House and his own maneuvres in this business, expects (in case of the election of either Mr; Adams or Mr; Pinckney) that himself & Mr; Ross will be preferred to Seats in the judiciary department of the United States, or in the Government of the territory North-West of the Ohio, as Governor St. Clair is not expected to live long; Samuel Postlethwaite, Senator for Cumberland county, is the brother-in-law of Henry Miller, Supervisor for this State, and has been perswaded to believe, that if you were President Miller would be removed; the like circumstance has influenced Dennis Wheelen, a Senator for the county of Chester &c., whose brother Israel is Purveyor &c. at Philadelphia. These men have in a great degree governed their colleagues, all of whom are Anglo-federalists. Indeed, the officers of the customs at Philadelphia and all the officers under the Pres[ident] of the U.S., with scarce an exception, have leagued against you, and evidenced as much malignity[2] as they displayed in my Election: similar arts, calumnies & baseness have been practiced in both cases. Henry Miller, General Hand, Robert Coleman &c. have been in this borough almost const[antly] since the Legislature have been convened, keeping the[3] thirteen firm to the party. In addition to the letters almost daily written to them by a committee at Philadelphia, of which Thomas Fitzsimons, Wm. Lewis, William Rawle & several other Tories were members, a special committee was deputed & sent here by them, fearing the Federalists might waver, near the approach of the election; they gave the thirteen a dinner, to cheer their spirits & keep them steady: Messrs. Henry & Wm. Miller were of the party; the latter is Commissioner of the Revenue, now at Washington.

When all expectations of an election for this State had ceased, Wm.

Findlay Esq. of the Senate, a true Republican, was induced to revive the affair by bringing in a Bill, differing in form tho' in substance the same with a former one, which passed rapidly thro' that House, but with considerable opposition from the Republicans & some of the Tories in the other; however a majority were at length prevailed upon to pass it, as it would prevent the precedent of a dereliction by a State of so important a federal duty, and even one vote might possibly operate favorably to the Republican cause: these considerations had weight with me, and obtained my concurrence. The Federalists are now dissatisfied with the renewal of the business.

It seemed to me proper, that you should have this detail whether we are successful or not in the great event: if South Carolina has not disappointed us, all will yet terminate propitiously; there will be 73, to 71 at the utmost. May God grant it; for the good of my country.

This will be handed to you by General Muhlenberg, to whom it will be inclosed, to prevent the prying curiosity of Postmasters &c.— Permit me to subscribe myself what in great truth & sincerity I am, dear Sir,

Your affectionate friend & most obedient servant

THOS M:KEAN

RC (DLC); at head of text: "Private"; with text in brackets lost at edge of paper supplied from Dft; addressed: "The Honoble. Thomas Jefferson Esquire, Vice-President of the United States, At Washington"; endorsed by TJ as received 19 Dec. and so recorded in SJL. Dft (PHi).

For the WORDS attributed to ST. PAUL, see 2 Timothy 4:14.

JOHN WOODS made an unsuccessful bid for a congressional seat in 1798. Henry Woods, his brother, served in Congress from 1799 to 1803. HENRY MILLER became supervisor for the collection of the internal revenues for the district of Pennsylvania in 1794. He was highly recommended to Hamilton by James Ross. The Senate confirmed Israel Whelen's appointment as PURVEYOR of public supplies on 13 May 1800. Edward HAND was appointed inspector of the revenue in Pennsylvania in 1792 and was confirmed as a major general of the Provisional Army in 1798.

The *Aurora* gave extensive coverage to the meeting of Federalists at Dunwoody's tavern in Philadelphia on 5 Nov., at which

the COMMITTEE of prominent Federalists drew up a resolution emphasizing the importance of selecting presidential electors through a concurrent rather than a joint vote in the Pennsylvania legislature, thus ensuring the dominance of the 13 Federalists in the Senate. In the end a joint vote was taken but on 8 candidates selected by each house. Robert Coleman of Lancaster County, who had cast the only Pennsylvania electoral vote for Adams in 1796, was the candidate on the Senate's list of electors who received only 36 votes and thus was not elected (JEP, 1:102, 111, 164, 292-3, 355; *Biog. Dir. Cong.*; Syrett, *Hamilton*, 16:482-4; Philadelphia *Aurora*, 10, 13 Nov., 6 Dec. 1800; Tinkcom, *Republicans and Federalists*, 151, 170, 172, 185-7, 189, 247-54).

REVIVE THE AFFAIR: the decision of the state's Republican leadership to accept the proposal by which eight Republican and seven Federalist electors would be chosen by the legislature is described in Tinkcom, *Republicans and Federalists*, 251-3. When criticized for accepting the Federalist formula, one Republican state representative wrote: "if our presidential

[309]

Election depended upon a single Vote and we had refused to give it there would have been greater cause for censure" (same, 253).

[1] In Dft McKean here canceled "freemen."

[2] Interlined in Dft in place of "rancour."

[3] In Dft McKean here canceled "treacherous" and then interlined and canceled "ill disposed."

From Pierpont Edwards

SIR,   Rye Decr 16—1800

At the request of the bearer, Major Wm. Munson, I take the liberty to inform you, that he is a very worthy meritorious officer, who served, thro the revolution, in our late army—He always has been a firm, but oppressed republican, of a very fair unblemished character. The character in which he will appear before you, delivering the votes of Connecticutt, might present to your apprehension a different man—Permit me, Sir, to congratulate myself and my Countryman on the success of the efforts of republicans. I am very respectfully

    your Obed Serv   PIERP EDWARDS

RC (DLC); endorsed by TJ as received 23 Dec. and so recorded in SJL.

For the career of William MUNSON as a port officer at New Haven, see Munson to TJ, 22 Feb. 1801.

From James Monroe

DEAR SIR   Richmond 16. Decr. 1800.

We are yet ignorant of the issue of the election that is, whether you are a head of the secondary object. It is believed that every other point is settled. On this however it is best to say but little by post. I shod. not perhaps write you by it, were it not to inquire whether you have seen Craven or heard of him, and what dependance you think I may put in Darrelle as a purchaser of my land above Charlottesville. I wait yr. answer, on rect. of which I immediately sit out for Albemarle to make some disposition of that tract, by lease if not by sale.   Genl. Davie called but sd. nothing of his treaty. What think you of the probable price of tobo. &ca. Do you think my land wod. be an object worthy advertising at the federal town, in Lancaster & York town, specifying the price I wod. take for it. We are tolerably well & all desire to be affecy. remembered to you. Sincerely I am yr. friend & servt   JAS. MONROE

If you wish I will send you a copy of my communication respecting the conspiracy of the Slaves.

RC (DLC); endorsed by TJ as received 19 Dec. and so recorded in SJL.

COMMUNICATION: on 5 Dec. Monroe reported to the Virginia General Assembly on the steps taken against the slave revolt when the legislature was not in session (*Journal of the Senate of the Commonwealth of Virginia. Begun and Held at the Capitol in the City of Richmond, on Monday the First Day of December, One Thousand Eight Hundred* [Richmond, 1801], 11-13; Monroe, *Writings*, 3:234-43).

To Caspar Wistar

DEAR SIR   Washington Dec. 16. 1800.

Having lately recieved from Count Rumford, one of the managers of the Royal institution of Great Britain a prospectus of that institution, with a letter expressing their desire to cultivate a friendly correspondence with the American Philosophical society, I have now the honor of forwarding them for the society. the application of science to objects immediately useful in life, which seems to be the principal end of this establishment must interest in it's favor every friend of human happiness, & I have no doubt the society will meet with cordiality the overture made them, and add their example to the many existing proofs that the votaries of science, however widely dispersed, however separated by religion, by allegiance or vocation, form but one family.

I have recieved from mr Wm. Dunbar, who is settled near the Natchez sundry communications, which I think worthy of being made to the society. though the writer has not expressly authorised the laying them before the society, yet if it should be thought desireable to give any parts of them a place in their transactions, it could not be displeasing to him.   so learned a correspondent, planted a thousand miles off, on the very verge of the great terra incognita of our western continent, is worthy of being cherished. he is easy in his fortune, master of his own time, and employs it in science altogether.

I am with great esteem Dear Sir Your friend & servt.

TH: JEFFERSON

PrC (DLC); at foot of text: "Doctr. Wistar." Enclosures: (1) William Dunbar to TJ, 30 June 1800, and enclosure. (2) Enclosure No. 2 listed at Dunbar to TJ, 14 July 1800. (3) Enclosure listed at James Wilkinson to TJ, 29 Nov. 1800.

For the communication from COUNT RUMFORD, see 1 June 1800.

To Caspar Wistar

Dear Sir   Washington Dec. 16. 1800.

I have written you a letter of this date to be laid before the society. this is for yourself only. I have proposed so many members at different times that I am afraid to add to the number. yet Dunbar ought to be associated to us. I inclose you a letter with some communications of his to a mr Smith of London, which he sent to me open for perusal, desiring me when read to forward them as directed. they will enable you to judge of his degree of science, & therefore I leave them open for your perusal, & will pray you to seal & send them by some vessel bound to London.

I have this day written to Chancr. Livingston, to pray him to procure for me the bones you mention, either for money or favor: and if obtained, to address them to Mr. Barnes, Philadelphia, where his agent mr Richards will recieve & hold them subject to my orders, and of course at your service. accept my respectful & friendly salutations.

Th: Jefferson

PrC (DLC); at foot of text: "Dr. Wistar"; endorsed by TJ in ink on verso. Enclosure: Enclosure No. 1 listed at William Dunbar to TJ, 14 July 1800.

The American Philosophical Society had already made William Dunbar a member in January 1800. TJ was absent from that meeting of the society (APS, *Proceedings*, 22, pt. 3 [1884], 290, 294).

this day written to chancr. livingston: see 14 Dec. above.

From Pierre Samuel Du Pont de Nemours

Good-Stay, near New-York 17 Xbre. 1800.

Vous voila donc à la tête de votre sage Nation. Elle a mis librement son plus Grand-Homme à sa plus grande Place. Vous n'avez conquis que les cœurs.

Je demande à Dieu[1] de bénir votre Gouvernement.

Et j'assure qu'il le bénira. Car il vous a éminemment donné *la Raison, cette lumiere qui éclaire tout homme venant en ce monde*, mais qui ne les éclaire pas tous également.

Vous aurez auprés de Vous *La Fayete*, dont la bonté, la moralité, l'attachement pour ce Pays, font une Compagnie digne de votre âme élevée et patriotique.

Quand mes Enfans, que j'envoie en Europe pour mes affaires,

seront revenus, j'irai m'établir à *Alexandrie*, où j'ai acheté une maison, afin d'être plus à portée *de me réjouir dans vos Oeuvres*.

Un de mes Fils, que *Lavoisier* m'a instruit pendant cinq ans pour la Fabrication et la Régie des Poudres (*Gun-Powder*), et qui est un des meilleurs *Poudriers* de la France, où se font les meilleures Poudres du monde, établira ici une Manufacture excellente de cette matière indispensable à la défense des Etats.

Son voyage en France a pour objet de rapporter diverses machines en Cuivre et en Bronze, qu'il ne pourrait faire exécuter ici, ni aussi vite, ni aussi bien, pour le triple de la valeur.

J'ôse vous répondre qu'il enverra les Boulets à un cinquieme de distance *de plus* que ne vont les Boulets anglais et hollandais.

Et, sur cette promesse, je vous prie de ne faire aucun marché pour les fournitures de Poudre à vos magasins de Guerre, avant d'avoir essayé comparativement aux autres celles que nous vous ferons.

Sous votre Présidence, tout doit être, tout sera *aux meilleurs* et aux plus dignes. Et malgré *vos, nos Principes* extrêmement *démocratiques*, on dira qu'en ce sens *Jefferson penche vers l'Aristocratie.—* Aussi fait le sublime *Président de l'univers*.

Par précaution contre le *Post-office*, j'ai gardé une minute de mon Livre sur l'Education nationale dans les Etats-unis. Et, qu'il vous soit parvenu ou non, j'espere que je pourrai le traduire en anglais cet hiver, avec bien du regret que ce *Patois énergique*, mais incorrect et peu philosophique, soit la langue de votre Pays.

Vous connaissez mon inviolable et respectueux attachement

DU PONT (DE NEMOURS)

Pusy et Madame *Du Pont* me chargent de féliciter l'Amérique en votre Personne sur votre avénement à la Présidence.—Et je crois que l'Europe, les sciences, la Philosophie et la morale doivent avoir leur part du compliment.

Mes Fils vous présentent leur respect.

Je désire que *l'Ainé*, qui a treize ans d'habitation, deux enfans nés en *South-Carolina* (République qui me devient bien chere) et serment d'allégeance en Virginie, soit complettement naturalisé le plus tôt possible.

21 Xbre.

Mon Fils, chargé de mettre ma Lettre à la Poste, me la renvoie avec la vôtre du 12.

Je suis bien aise que vous ayiez joui du bonheur d'un cheval échappé.—Vous ne le retrouverez de longtems aussi complet.—On vient de vous atteler à un *Wagon* qui ne laisse pas d'avoir son poids. Mais Hercule portait le monde.

Vous êtes bien poli sur la difficulté de me traduire. Ce sera donc pour moi une bonne étude d'Anglais.—Imaginez que mon audacieuse ambition va jusqu'à espérer que vous aurez la bonté de corriger mon Thême.

EDITORS' TRANSLATION

Good-Stay, near New York 17 Dec. 1800.

So there you are at the head of your wise nation. She has freely placed its greatest man in her highest place. You have conquered the hearts only [i.e., not by force].

I ask God to bless your Government.

I am sure that He will bless it. For He has eminently given you *Reason*, *that light which enlightens all men coming into this world*, but which does not enlighten them all equally.

You will have at your side *Lafayette*, whose kindness, morality, and affection for this country make him worthy company for your lofty and patriotic soul.

When my children, whom I am sending to Europe for my business affairs, return, I shall go settle in *Alexandria*, where I have bought a house, so as to be in greater proximity *to rejoice in your works*.

One of my sons, whom *Lavoisier* taught for me for five years in the manufacture and control of powders (*gun-powder*), and who is one of the best *powder makers* in France, where the best powders in the world are made, will establish here an excellent factory for this substance that is indispensable for the defense of nations.

The object of his trip to France is to bring back different machines in copper and in bronze that he could not have made here, neither rapidly enough, nor well enough for three times the price.

I make bold to guarantee that he will send cannonballs to a distance one-fifth *farther* than English and Dutch cannonballs go.

And according to that promise, I beg you to make no contract for furnishing powder for your war magazines before having made a comparative assay between the others and the ones we shall make for you.

Under your presidency, everything will go *to the best* and the worthiest. And despite *your*, *our*, extremely *democratic principles*, it will be said that in that sense *Jefferson leans towards the aristocracy*.—So does the sublime *president of the universe*.

As a precaution against the *post-office*, I have kept a draft of my book on national education in the United States. And whether or not it got to you, I hope that I can translate it into English this winter, with great regret that this *forceful*, but incorrect and largely unphilosophical *dialect*, is the language of your country.

You know my inviolable and respectful affection

DU PONT (DE NEMOURS)

Pusy and Madame *Du Pont* have charged me with congratulating America through you upon your accession to the Presidency. And I believe that Europe, the sciences, philosophy, and morality must partake of this compliment.

My sons present their respects to you.

I wish that the *elder*, who has thirteen years of residence, two children born in *South Carolina* (a republic that is becoming very dear to me) and an oath of allegiance in Virginia, may be completely naturalized as soon as possible.

21 Dec.

My son, charged with mailing my letter, has brought it back to me with yours of the 12th.

I am quite happy that you enjoyed the happiness of a runaway horse.—You will not find it again so completely for a long time.—You have just been hitched to a *wagon* that does not lack weight. But Hercules carried the world.

You are very polite about the difficulty of translating me. Hence it will be for me a good English study.—Imagine that my bold ambition extends so far as to hope that you will have the kindness to correct my translation.

RC (DLC); at head of text: "a Mr Jefferson"; endorsed by TJ as a letter of 17 and 21 Dec. received 29 Dec., and so recorded in SJL.

Du Pont's sons Victor and Éleuthère Irénée departed for EUROPE in January 1801. As a young man Éleuthère Irénée du Pont de Nemours had learned about the manufacture of gunpowder by working with Antoine Laurent LAVOISIER at the French powder works at Essonne (Saricks, *Du Pont*, 130, 284).

[1] Du Pont wrote this word larger than the surrounding text.

From Horatio Gates

DEAR SIR   New York 17th: Decem. 1800.—

I have the pleasure to Address this to You by my Friend, and long Companion in the late War, General Armstrong. He is sent to the Senate in Congress, by what I call an Unanimous Vote of this Legislature; (100, against 2;) He will most readily acquaint you with the Struggles of the Whiggs here, to bring about the Total Defeat of their Opponents; I heartily rejoice at the Glorious Event; for I can compare our last four Years to nothing under the Sun, but the last four Years of the Reign of Queen Ann; and allowing for difference of Countrys, circumstances, & Times, they are exactly similar;—The Tories here, hide their diminish'd Heads; but they will be at their dirty Work again, if the Wise Measures of the approaching Administration doth not prevent their Designs—I have that good Opinion of the Bearer as to believe he will coopperate in every Measure to Defeat them; I have many reasons to think I cannot live to the End of your Presidentcy, that I am permitted to see it commence, will rejoice the Old Heart of   Your Faithfull Friend

HORATIO GATES.

RC (DLC); endorsed by TJ as received 8 Jan. 1801 and so recorded in SJL.

John ARMSTRONG, connected through marriage with the Livingston family, was elected to fill the vacancy caused by John

Laurance's resignation (*Biog. Dir. Cong.*; ANB). During the last four years of Queen Anne's reign, the TORIES regained control of Parliament and, in 1714, passed the Schism Act, directed against religious dissenters (DNB).

From Rembrandt Peale

SIR   Philada: Dec 17th: 1800.

My Knowledge of your fondness for the fine Arts, is my only excuse for troubling you with this Letter; prepossessed at the same time with the idea that you are particularly interested in the perfection of American Genius, and must feel Satisfaction in being the Instrument of forwarding it.   Devoted to the practice of my Art, with but poor encouragement & without scarcely having any Models but what Nature placed before me, I have arrived to that State, in which the celebrated Models of Beauty and Perfection in Europe, would be at the same time the most delicious treat and the only mean of determining my stile. Your knowledge of this is sufficiently proved by your generous Conduct to Mr: Trumbull. I shall therefore only add that by this days Post, I have directed a Letter to the President, soliciting some appointment which may enable me to employ a portion of leisure to the Study of my Art. The unremitting Attention bestowed by France to the Arts, has thrown into their possession most valubable acquisitions, and renders a journey into Italy scarcely necessary to the Artist. It may be proper to mention that for some years I have been pretty well acquainted with the French language & may very easily make myself Master of it.

It would be with much reluctance, I should be obliged to give up totally the practice of Painting—and yet very little dependence is to be placed on it as a Profession, at this time in America, one case excepted, in that of Superior Eminence; this of course must be my Ambition. Should my present application fail in Success, much of my object may perhaps be answered without leaving the Country; and there may be found a Situation where I may find a Support for my family & sufficient leisure to persue my desired improvements.

With the presumption that you will lend Your assistance in my project, And a Sincere assurance of my Gratitude, I remain, Sir Respectfully Yours.   REMBRANDT PEALE.

RC (Thomas Jefferson Foundation, on deposit ViU); addressed: "His Excellency Thomas Jefferson Esqr. Washington"; franked and postmarked; endorsed by TJ as received 20 Dec. and so recorded in SJL.

Rembrandt Peale (1778-1860), one of the sons of Charles Willson Peale and Rachel Brewer Peale, identified himself as an artist at an early age and, while still a teenager, made life portraits of famous Americans for his father's museum in Philadelphia. Some months before he wrote the letter above he painted a likeness of TJ that, disseminated in the form of engravings, became one of the defining images of its subject. Peale also, in 1805, painted another of the best-known portraits of TJ. The artist worked in several American cities in the course of his career,

executing portraits and larger works on historical and allegorical themes. He also studied lithography, wrote, lectured, and from 1814 to 1822 kept a museum in Baltimore. Peale first crossed the Atlantic in 1802-3, supervising the exhibition of the mastodon skeleton that his father had recovered in New York State and taking advantage of the opportunity to acquaint himself with British art. On two visits in 1808 and 1809-10 he worked and studied in France. He married Eleanor May Short in 1798 and with her had nine children (ANB; Vol. 31:xli).

LETTER TO THE PRESIDENT: Peale on this day wrote to John Adams asking consideration for an appointment in France, given the renewed American relationship with that country, or secondarily in England or Italy (MHi: Adams Papers).

To Stephen B. Balch

SIR   Washington Dec. 18. 1800
    I took a little time the other day to consider of the application of mr Cathcart, his proposition being new, himself an entire stranger, & no paper communicated which could explain the intentions of the respectable authority under which he stated himself as acting. your presence however, as well as his statement, satisfies me on these points. but having omitted to ask his lodgings, & unable to learn [them], I ask permission to make you the channel of my contribution. I therefore inclose an order which will be paid you on sight, and which you will be so good as to apply to the object explained to me. I have the honor to be with great personal respect & esteem Sir
    Your most obedt.

PrC (MHi); faint; signature omitted in letterpressing; at foot of text in ink: "The revd mr Balch"; endorsed by TJ in ink on verso. Enclosure: Order to John Barnes, this day, for payment of $50 to Balch or his designee "for value recieved" (PrC in same, letterpressed to same sheet as enclosing letter; at foot of text: "Mr. John

Barnes No. 16. High street. Georgetown").

Stephen Bloomer Balch (1747-1833) grew up in Maryland and North Carolina before attending the College of New Jersey in Princeton, from which he received a diploma in 1774. Licensed as a

Presbyterian preacher in 1779, the next year he founded the first church of that denomination in Georgetown, Maryland, serving as its minister until his death. He was also involved in education and philanthropy. In October 1802 TJ asked Barnes to pay the clergyman $75 "in charity." Although TJ recorded no other details in his financial memoranda, apparently that payment was for a subscription to enlarge Balch's church, where non-Presbyterians were made welcome and officers of government sometimes attended services. The letter above is the only correspondence with Balch recorded in SJL (Harrison, *Princetonians, 1769-1775*, 359-62; Richard P. Jackson, *The Chronicles of Georgetown, D.C. from 1751 to 1878* [Washington, D.C., 1878], 145-6; MB, 2:1084).

To Hugh Henry Brackenridge

DEAR SIR   Washington Dec. 18. 1800.

I received while at home the letter you were so kind as to write me. the employments of the country have such irresistable attractions for me, that while I am at home, I am very unpunctual in acknoleging the letters of my friends. having no refuge here from my room & writing table, it is my regular season for fetching up the lee way of my correspondence.

Before you receive this you will have understood that the state of S. Carolina (the only one about which there was uncertainty) has given a republican vote, and saved us from the consequences of the annihilation of Pensylvania. but we are brought into dilemma by the probable equality of the two republican candidates. the federalists in Congress mean to take advantage of this, and either to prevent an election altogether, or reverse what has been understood to have been the wishes of the people as to their President & Vice-president, wishes which the constitution did not permit them specially to designate. the latter alternative still gives us a republican administration; the former a suspension of the federal government for want of a head. this opens upon us an abyss at which every sincere patriot must shudder.—General Davie has arrived here with the treaty formed (under the name of a convention) with France. it is now before the Senate for ratification, and will encounter objections. he believes firmly that a continental peace in Europe will take place, and that England also may be comprehended. accept assurances of the great respect of Dr. Sir

Your most obedt. servt   TH: JEFFERSON

PrC (DLC); at foot of text: "The Honble Judge Breckenridge." PrC (same); a press copy of a signed Dupl in TJ's hand, with some variation of punctuation and abbreviations; at head of text: "Copy" (see TJ to Aaron Burr, 1 Feb. 1801).

Brackenridge's LETTER of 13 Sep., recorded in SJL as received from Pittsburgh on 12 Oct., has not been found.

John Adams submitted the CONVEN-TION with France and the journal of the American envoys to the Senate on 16 Dec. (JEP, 1:359).

From Mathew Carey

SIR,   Philada. Decr. 18. 1800.

With this letter you will receive a copy of a new work intended for Schools, which, if your avocations permit, I request you will be so kind to examine.

I have compiled it with a view to familiarize to the minds of youth, the grand truths of morals and politics, the latter of which particularly has never had sufficient attention paid to it in School Books.

Unless I deceive myself egregiously, the use of Books on this plan, in our Seminaries, wd. give a fairer chance to the very important experiment we are making of the practacability and advantages of republican Government, than that of Books compiled in Countries hostile to the smallest semblance of republicanism. Among those to whom the work has been shewn, this has been the uniform opinion.

The subject of this letter, sir, is to request the Sanction of your approbation, should the work appear to deserve it. I shall try to procure other respectable names, & under their countenance, to have it introduced into Schools.

Nothing but a hope that you will regard this as a probable means of advancing the best interests of the great family of mankind, wd. induce me thus to trespass on your precious time.

With the sincerest respect, I am, Sir, Your obt. hble. Servt.

MATHEW CAREY

RC (DLC); at head of text: "Thomas Jefferson, Esqr."; endorsed by TJ as received 26 Dec. and so recorded in SJL.

Carey sent TJ a COPY OF A NEW WORK INTENDED FOR SCHOOLS entitled *School of Wisdom: or, American Monitor. Containing a Copious Collection of Sublime and Elegant Extracts, from the Most Emi-nent Writers, on Morals, Religion & Government* (Philadelphia, 1800). Carey's preface noted that he had examined the works of such "celebrated writers" as Shakespeare, Milton, Dryden, Pope, Fielding, Montesquieu, and others. A second edition of the work was published in 1803.

To Simon Chaudron

DEAR SIR   Washington Dec. 18. 1800.

I am informed by a gentleman who called on you in Philadelphia that the watch is arrived, which you were so kind as to undertake to import for me. the question is how to procure a safe conveyance of it to this place, which can only be in a gentleman's pocket; as experience has proved to me that no precautions of package can secure a watch brought in a trunk, on the wheels of a carriage, from the effects of the shaking of the carriage. mr Jones, the member of Congress from Georgia, is now in Philadelphia, and perhaps may still be there at the moment of your recieving this. he would be so kind as to bring it to me. if still there he will be found at mrs Wigman's. 67. Vine street. should he be come away, by examining from time to time the books of the stage office within a few doors of you, some person no doubt might be found coming on who would be so kind as to take charge of the watch. the price shall be remitted to you the moment it is made known to Dear Sir

Your most obedt. servt   TH: JEFFERSON

PrC (MHi); at foot of text: "M: Chaudron"; endorsed by TJ in ink on verso.

Jean Simon Chaudron (1758-1846), a native of Vignory, France, learned watchmaking in Switzerland before moving to Saint-Domingue, where he dealt in watches and jewelry and became a planter. Displaced by the island's revolution, he went to Philadelphia and opened a shop at 12 South Third Street. Chaudron cleaned a watch for TJ in March 1797, shortly after TJ paid him for a timepiece for John Randolph of Roanoke. A gold French watch that TJ purchased for one of his granddaughters in 1807 and a fine gold watch chain that he sought a few months later both came from Chaudron's firm. The watchmaker was also a poet and writer, composing odes on events in Europe and songs for the Loge Française l'Aménité, a Philadelphia lodge of émigré French and Saint-Dominguen freemasons of which he was the *orateur* (orator). In that capacity in 1800 he delivered a New Year's Day address on George Washington that Auguste Belin, another of the lodge's officers, sent to TJ. Before June 1817 Chaudron became the editor of *l'Abeille Américaine*, a weekly publication. Joining the Vine and Olive Colony, a settlement of French exiles in Alabama, he left Philadelphia in 1819 for the group's lands on the Tombigbee River. He subsequently moved to Mobile. A selection of his verse, *Poésies Choisies*, was published in Paris in 1841 (Winston Smith, *Days of Exile: The Story of the Vine and Olive Colony in Alabama* [Tuscaloosa, Ala., 1967], 9, 53, 114, 128; *Tableau des F.F. Composant la T. R. Loge Française l'Aménité, No. 73* [Philadelphia, 1803], 3; *Ode sur la Conquète de l'Italie* [Philadelphia, 1799]; *Recueil de Cantiques, de la Loge Française l'Aménité, No. 73* [Philadelphia, 1801], 17-19; A. J. Blocquerst and F. Malicot, *Bureau de l'Abeille Américaine. Les Éditeurs, au Public et aux Anciens Abonnés de l'Abeille* [Philadelphia, 1817]; Stafford, *Philadelphia Directory, for 1800*, 30; MB, 2:955, 956, 1218; Vol. 31:396, 417; bills of Chaudron & Co., 18 Dec. 1807 at MHi and 26 Apr. 1808 at DLC; TJ to Henry Voigt, 3 Dec. 1807; Henry Voigt to TJ, 19 Dec. 1807; William Short to TJ, 28 Apr. 1808; Chaudron to TJ, 7 Feb. 1819; TJ to Chaudron, 3 Mch. 1819).

To Andrew Ellicott

DEAR SIR   Washington Dec. 18. 1800.

I recieved a little before I left home your favor of Oct. 17. as I had in due time the preceding one. the attractive nature of country employments are my apology to my friends for being a very unpunctual correspondent while at home. having no refuge here from my room and writing table, it is here that I fetch up the lee-way of my correspondence. I am glad to hear you are ready for printing your journal. it will be a great gratification to see it. I cannot suppose the administration can have any objections to the publication of the charts &c. my own opinion is that government should by all means in their power deal out the materials of information to the public in order that it may be reflected back on themselves in the various forms into which public ingenuity may throw it. mr Dunbar has been so kind as to pass through my hands a copy of his journal, made for the use of a friend of his in London. he sent it open for my perusal with a request to seal & forward it. I am happy to see that the location of the boundary has been so scientifically executed. he gives a physical account of the country which is interesting.

I think you had it in contemplation to establish an accurate meridian at this place, but whether in one of the public buildings, or where else I do not recollect. was it done? or is there any thing here which will preserve the meridian as found and worked on by you?

The election is under dilemma. the two republican candidates are probably even; and the states in Congress which are federal are disposed to take advantage of that circumstance, to prevent an election by Congress, and permit the government of the Union to be suspended for want of a head. this tells us who are entitled to the appellation of anarchists with which they have so liberally branded others. accept assurances of perfect esteem   TH: JEFFERSON

RC (DLC: Ellicott Papers); addressed: "Andrew Ellicot esq. 16. North 6th. street Philadelphia"; franked and postmarked. PrC (DLC).

Ellicott's letter PRECEDING that of 17 Oct. was the one of 28 May.

To James Madison

                                            Washington Dec. 19. 1800.

Mrs. Brown's departure for Virginia enables me to write confidentially what I would not have ventured by the post at this prying season. the election of S. Carolina has in some measure decided the great contest. tho' as yet we do not know the actual votes of Tenissee, Kentucky & Vermont yet we believe the votes to be on the whole[1] J. 73. B. 73. A. 65. P. 64. Rhode isld. withdrew one from P. there is a possibility that Tenissee may withdraw one from B. and Burr writes that there may be one vote in Vermont for J. but I hold the latter impossible, and the former not probable; and that there will be an absolute parity between the two republican candidates. this has produced great dismay & gloom on the republican gentlemen here, and equal exultation in the federalists, who openly declare they will prevent an election, and will name a President of the Senate pro tem. by what they say would only be a *stretch* of the constitution. the prospect of preventing this is as follows. G. N.C. T. K. V. P. & N.Y. can be counted on for their vote in the H. of R. & it is[2] thought by some that Baer of Maryland & Linn of N.J. will come over. some even count on Morris of Vermont. but you must know the uncertainty of such a dependance under the operation of Caucuses and other federal engines. the month of February therefore will present us storms of a new character. should they have a particular issue, I hope you will be here a day or two at least before the 4th. of March. I know that[3] your appearance on the scene before the departure of Congress, would assuage the minority, & inspire in the majority confidence & joy unbounded, which they would spread far & wide on their journey home. let me beseech you then to come with a view of staying perhaps a couple of weeks, within which time things might be put into such a train as would permit us both to go home for a short time for removal. I wrote to R.R.L. by a confidential hand three days ago. the person proposed for the T. is not come yet.

Davie is here with the Convention as it is called; but it is a real treaty & without limitation of time. it has some disagreeable features, and will endanger the compromitting us with G.B. I am not at liberty to mention it's contents, but I believe it will meet with opposition from both sides of the house. it has been a bungling negociation. Elsworth remains in France for his health. he has resigned his office of C.J. putting these two things together we cannot misconstrue his views. he must have had great confidence in mr A's continuance to risk such a certainty as he held. Jay was yesterday nominated Chief Justice. we were afraid of something worse. a scheme of government for the territory is cooking by a committee of each house under separate authorities but probably a voluntary harmony. they let out no hints. it is believed that the judiciary system will not be pushed as the appointments, if made by the present administration, could not fall on those who create them. but I very much fear the road system will be urged. the mines of Peru could not supply the monies which would be wasted on this object, nor the patience of any people stand the abuses which would be incontroulably committed under it. I propose, as soon as the state of the election is perfectly ascertained, to aim at a candid understanding with mr A. I do not expect that either his feelings, or his views of interest will oppose it. I hope to induce in him dispositions liberal and accomodating. accept my affectionate salutations.

RC (DLC: Madison Papers, Rives Collection); addressed: "James Madison junr. Orange." PrC (DLC).

MRS. BROWN: probably Catherine Brown of Philadelphia whose daughter Mary was the wife of Hore Browse Trist (Jane Flaherty Wells, "Thomas Jefferson's Neighbors: Hore Browse Trist of 'Birdwood' and Dr. William Bache of 'Franklin,'" *Magazine of Albemarle County History*, 47 [1989], 1, 3, 8).

George BAER OF MARYLAND, a Federalist, served in the House of Representatives in the Fifth, Sixth, and Fourteenth Congresses. James LINN OF N.J., a graduate of the College of New Jersey and a lawyer, was elected as a Republican to the Sixth Congress, and was a supporter of TJ's although some of his colleagues in the House considered him a swing vote. Lewis Richard MORRIS OF VERMONT was a Federalist representative in the Fifth, Sixth, and Seventh Congresses (*Biog. Dir. Cong.*; Harrison, *Princetonians, 1769-1775*, 29-30).

R.R.L.: Robert R. Livingston, to whom TJ offered the secretaryship of the navy on 14 Dec. Albert Gallatin, THE PERSON PROPOSED FOR THE T. (treasury), arrived in Washington on 10 Jan. 1801 although TJ did not formally offer him the post until after 17 Feb. 1801 (Raymond Walters, Jr., *Albert Gallatin: Jeffersonian Financier and Diplomat* [New York, 1957], 126, 141-2).

I AM NOT AT LIBERTY TO MENTION IT'S CONTENTS: although the *Journal of the Executive Proceedings* indicates simply that on 17 Dec. the Senate progressed in reading the papers communicated by the president with the Convention of 1800, a motion on a scrap of paper in TJ's hand, "that it be a standing order that all treaties be considered as secret while the question of their ratification is depending before the Senate," is docketed as "Mr Morris motion for injunction of secrecy on consideration of Treaties Decr 17th 1800." The passage, "which shall be hereafter submd to the considn of the Senate," appears in TJ's hand on the verso of the docketing (DNA: RG 46, Senate Records, 6th Cong., 2d sess.). It provides the only official evidence that New York Senator Gouverneur Morris introduced the motion on secrecy on that date. But on 19 Dec. the *National Intelligencer* not only carried an account of Morris's motion, the newspaper also noted that a Senate vote on the measure resulted in an equal division, with TJ casting the tie-breaking vote against it. On 19 Dec. the Senate requested that the president send them the instructions given to the U.S. envoys when they embarked on their mission. The president transmitted the instructions on 22 Dec., with the request that the Senate consider them "in strict confidence" and return them to the executive as quickly as possible. On the same day the Senate passed a resolution "That all confidential communications made by the President of the United States to the Senate, shall be, by the members thereof, kept inviolably secret; and that all treaties which may hereafter be laid before the Senate, shall also be kept secret, until the Senate shall, by their resolution, take off the injunction of secrecy" (JEP, 1:359-61). TJ included this resolution in his parliamentary manual (see TJ to Samuel H. Smith, printed at 6 Jan. 1801).

When William R. Davie returned from France he carried a letter from Oliver Ellsworth indicating he had RESIGNED HIS OFFICE OF chief justice. A painful kidney ailment prompted Ellsworth's decision and prevented him from making the transatlantic journey until the end of March 1801 (ANB; William Garrott Brown, *The Life of Oliver Ellsworth* [New York, 1905], 302-3, 310). John Adams nominated John JAY on 18 Dec. 1800 and the Senate confirmed him the following day. He declined the office because of his health (JEP, 1:360; Syrett, *Hamilton*, 25:264).

For the SCHEME OF GOVERNMENT for the District of Columbia, see TJ to Madison, 26 Dec.

Revision of the JUDICIARY SYSTEM resulted from "An Act to provide for the more convenient organization of the Courts of the United States, " also known as the Judiciary Act of 1801, which expanded and reorganized the federal court system by redefining districts and creating 23 judgeships and court posts (U.S. Statutes at Large, 2:89-100; Vol. 31:261-3, 434n).

ROAD SYSTEM: "An Act further to alter and to establish certain post roads" was signed on 3 Mch. 1801 (U.S. Statutes at Large, 2:125-27).

¹ Preceding three words interlined.
² TJ here canceled "believed" before interlining the following three words.
³ Canceled: "nothing."

To Thomas Mann Randolph

TH:J. TO TMR.   Washington Dec. 19. 1800

Your's from Richmond is recieved. as soon as Colo. Cabell comes, within whose district Goochld. C.H. is, that matter shall be attended to. the French convention is recieved. it will meet objections from both sides of the house; but I am not at liberty to mention it's contents. the event of the election is now pretty well known. the two republican candidates have 73. each, mr A. 65. & P. 64. Rhode island having withdrawn 1. from P. some believe that Tenissee will withhold 1. from Burr. if it does not, we are in a dilemma from which no one can see how we are to be extricated. the [Feds] are determined to prevent an election, which is practicable perhaps as there are but 7. states whose majorities in the H. of R. could be counted on. there are hopes from some individuals of the other representation; but nothing with certainty.—since beginning this letter there is a report that Kentucky has given one vote for mr G. I do not learn the foundation of the report. it would be fortunate if it is so. I am of opinion little will be attempted & less done this session on any subject. we think the less the better, and the other side are not disposed much to press things they are not to [. . .].—interruptions by company oblige me to conclude here. with my tenderest love to my dear Martha & affections to yourself. Adieu.

PrC (MHi); faint and blurred; endorsed by TJ in ink on verso.

See Randolph's letter FROM RICHMOND at 8 Dec.

MR G.: Albert Gallatin. For a similar report from Tennessee, see TJ to Burr, 15 Dec.

From Delamotte

l'inactivité absoluë á laquelle notre port est condamnée depuis trois ans, me laisse le tems de venir ici deux ou trois fois l'an. cette fois-ci, en y arrivant, j'ai appris que toutes les nouvelles, qu'on a d'Amerique, vous proclament président des Etats-unis. Je persiste á ne pas vouloir vous faire de Compliments lá dessus. Je sçais bien qu'en penser pour les Etats-unis, & je ne sçais pas qu'en penser pour votre bonheur personnel, mais je ne peus pas apprendre cette nouvelle sans un grand Interet, ni sans vous le donner á connoetre. Ce n'est qu'en mars que nous aurons la certitude de cet évenement, et j'attends cette époque avec impatience. Une chose dont je crois avoir á vous faire mon Compliment, c'est qu'il y a á esperer que votre gouvernement commencera sous des Auspices favorables, que la paix sera enfin renduë au monde & que le Commerce va renaitre. L'Amerique a beaucoup gagné dans cette guerre, elle a aussi beaucoup perdû, mais, avec la paix, ce qu'elle gagnera, sera gagné solidement. Les seuls produits de votre sol vous enrichiront toujours de plus en plus & je crois que les Americains mettront aussi plus de retenuë dans leurs spéculations qu'ils n'ont fait avant la rupture de nos liaisons avec vous. Je scais, Monsieur, quel interet vous portés au Commerce de votre pays; je prévois qu'il va prosperer & que les moyens de prosperer s'ouvriront en même tems que votre Avenement; ce sont des circonstances heureuses dont je me rejouis pour vous.

J'ai eû l'honneur de vous ecrire par le Navire qui a reporté Mr. Davies en Amere.[1] J'ai aussi écrit au Secretaire d'etat pour demander qu'on me nommât de nouveau Consul au Havre. Si le gouvernement des E.U. regarde comme interessant pour lui, de ne nommer que des Americains, ou croit et veut faire en celá quelque chose qui soit agréable à la france, je ne demande plus rien & je n'en resterai pas moins attaché á lui de Coeur, parceque je lui porte estime & respect, comme font tous ceux qui Ont affaire á lui, mais si rien ne s'oppose a ma demande & que celá dépend de vous, Veuillés Monsieur, me donner cette marque de votre estime. elle me sera précieuse.

Mr. Swan est ici, j'ai eû avec lui des rapports de Commerce trés intimes, qui me mettent à même de le bien connoitre. Je vois qu'il desireroit etre nommé Consul général & je crois qu'il est plus propre que personne á remplir cette place dignement. Il avoit des Comptes importants á régler avec notre gouvernement, ils sont réglés et sa conduite est approuvée audessus d'aucun des autres agens que le gouvernemt. ait employés. Il est en grands rapports avec tous les

Membres du gouvernement & fort estimé, demême que Mr. Dallarde son ancien Associé, qui est aujourdhuy fermier general des Octrois de Paris. Mr. Swan a d'ailleurs une éducation, une représentation et une maniere de vivre, qui sont tous des Accessoires necessaires auprés d'un gouvernement qui reprend tous les jours plus de dignité. En vous parlant de lui, je suis détaché de tout interet personnel, je vous prie d'en etre assuré & ce n'est même que parceque je crois que vous aurés de moi cette bonne opinion, que je me hazarde á vous dire la mienne sur son compte.

Mr. Short est toujours bien portant, bien heureux et il merite de l'etre. J'ai le bonheur d'entretenir avec lui des liaisons d'amitié, dont je fais grand cas.

Recevés, Monsieur, l'assurance de mon dévouement bien sincere & du respect avec lequel j'ai l'honneur d'être

Votre trés humble & trés obeisst. serviteur   DELAMOTTE

SIR   Paris, 20 Dec. 1800

The total inactivity to which our port has been condemned for three years, leaves me the time to come here two or three times a year. This time, as I arrived, I learned that all the news that we have of America proclaims you president of the United States. I persist in not wanting to compliment you thereon. I know well what to think of it with respect to the United States, and I do not know what to think of it for your personal happiness, but I cannot learn that news without great interest or without informing you of it. It will not be until March that we have the certainty of that event, and I am impatiently awaiting that time. One thing about which I think I must compliment you is that there is reason to hope your government will begin under favorable auspices, that peace will finally be returned to the world, and that commerce will be born again. America has gained much in this war; she has also lost much, but, with peace, what she gains will be solidly won. The mere products of your soil will always enrich you more and more, and I believe that Americans will also use more restraint in their speculations than they did before the break in our relations with you. I know, Sir, how much interest you take in your country's commerce; I foresee that it is going to prosper and that the means of prospering will open up at the same time as your taking office; those are happy circumstances about which I rejoice for you.

I have had the honor of writing to you by the same ship that brought back Mr. Davie to America. I have also written to the secretary of state to request that he reappoint me consul at Le Havre. If the U.S. government considers it in its interest to name only Americans, or thinks in this matter to do something agreeable for France, I ask nothing further, and shall remain in my heart no less attached to the U.S., because I bear it esteem and respect, as do all those who have relations with it, but if there is no obstacle to my request and if that should depend on you, kindly, Sir, give me that token of your esteem. It will be precious to me.

Mr. Swan is here; I have had very intimate commercial relations with him, which have enabled me to know him well. I see that he would like to be named consul general, and I believe that he is more suited than anyone else to fulfill that position worthily. He had important accounts to settle with our government, they are settled, and his conduct has been approved more highly than that of any other agents that the government has employed. He is in close relations with all the members of the government and highly esteemed, and the same for Mr. Dallarde, his former associate, who is today the farmer general of the Paris city tolls. Mr. Swan has, moreover, an education, a personal presence, and a manner of life, which are all necessary accessories in the presence of a government that is assuming again each day more dignity. In speaking to you of him, I am devoid of any personal self-interest, I beg you to be assured of that, and it is only because I think that you probably have the same good opinion of me that I risk telling you mine of him.

Mr. Short is still in good health, quite happy, and deserves to be so. I have the good fortune to maintain with him bonds of friendship which I prize highly.

Accept, Sir, the assurance of my very sincere devotion and of the respect with which I have the honor to be

Your very humble and obedient servant   DELAMOTTE

RC (DLC); endorsed by TJ as received 18 Mch. 1801 and so recorded in SJL.

L'HONNEUR DE VOUS ECRIRE: Delamotte's letter of 1 Oct., conveyed by the ship on which William R. Davie returned to the United States.

ME NOMMÂT DE NOUVEAU CONSUL AU HAVRE: on 26 Jan. 1802 the Senate confirmed Delamotte as commercial vice-agent at Havre (JEP, 1:403, 405).

[1] Abbreviated "Amerique."

From Samuel McDowell, Sr.

DEAR SIR/   Jessamin County Kentucky Decr. 20th 1800

I feel my Self happy in the hope that you will Shortly be at the head of the General Government of the United States. And formerly having the honour of an acquaintence with you, Imboldens me to Say a few things on a Subject on which delocasy forbids my Saying much. The Subject is with regard to my Son Samuel who has acted as Marshal in the Kentucky District from the commencement of the General Government of the United States—

When he was first appointed he was in doubts whether to accept of the appointment or not, he asked my Advice I told him as he was appointed he Ought to Act and that for many reasons. One of which was that as the Genl Government was not well approved of in this Country If he refused to Accept it might be an Injury to the Govt in this Country. He Said (And truly) it would be a loss to him for Some years. which I know it has been for the greatest Part of the time he has Acted. And now it is of Some Benefit to him I am told there are Several Persons who either have applyed or are about to apply to Your Excellency to be appointed in his Place [. . .] Present appointment Expiers. I never have heard of any charge against him as to misconduct in his office Even by those who wish to Suplant him. And I am of opinion had he acted Improperly I Should have heard it. The only Reason I have heard of is, he has been long anough in that office: But I assure you Sir that the greatest Part of the time he has held that office, it was an Injury to himself and his Young rising family. he could not hold any office under this State And could not Undertake any other Business, As he was always determined to do his duty in that office So long as he held it. And during Perhaps all the time (Since he was first appointed) that the office was of little or no Value, No Person that I ever heard of made any attempt to Suplant him. But now when the office is making my Son Some compensation for the time he lost when it was not worth any thing, I am Told there are Several who wish to take it out of hand. The danger to his Person as marshal is now over, And the People generally Reconsiled to the Govrnment. And the office of Marshal is now [. . .] not have Acted as Such for any Consideration whatever

I therefore hope Your Excellency will again appoint him, when the Term for which he was last appointed Expiers. Unless You are well Satisfyed that from his Past Conduct he ought not to be again appointed.

I Only wish him to hold the office till he has had Some compensation for the time he in fact lost by it. And beleive me to be with Esteeme Dear Sir Your Excellencys

Most Obedient And Very Humble Sert

SAM'L. MCDOWELL

RC (DNA: RG 59, LAR); bottom of sheet frayed, with one or more lines on recto and verso missing; addressed: "The Honbl. Thomas Jefferson Vice President of the United States"; endorsed by TJ as received 22 Jan. 1801 and so recorded in SJL.

ACQUAINTENCE WITH YOU: before moving to Kentucky, McDowell resided in Virginia and represented Augusta County in the House of Burgesses in 1772 and in the House of Delegates from 1776 until 1778. He served as a delegate for Rockbridge County during assembly sessions in 1778 and 1780-81. McDowell and TJ carried on a brief correspondence while TJ was governor (Leonard, General Assembly, 102, 105, 122, 125, 131, 139; Vol. 3:467; Vol. 5:507-8, 541-2, 621-3).

Samuel McDowell, Jr., MARSHAL IN THE KENTUCKY DISTRICT, received his appointment in 1789 and upon expiration of his term was reappointed in December 1793 and again in January 1798. In a list of appointments and removals compiled in 1803, TJ recorded that on 27 June 1801 he removed McDowell for misconduct, specifically "extortion" (MS in DLC: TJ Papers, 119:20546; JEP, 1:29, 32, 143, 258, 403).

Piano by John Isaac Hawkins

Equivalent questions. these questions are perfectly equivalent
to that the negative of the one amounts to the affirmative of
the other, & leaves no other alternative, the decision of the one
concludes necessarily the other. thus the negative of striking out
amounts to the affirmative of agreeing, & therefore to put a question
on agreeing, after that on striking out, would be to put the same
question in effect twice over; which is contrary to rule.

But on questions on amendments between the two houses,
a motion to recede 'being negatived, does not amount to a
positive vote to insist, because there is another alternative
viz. to adhere. therefore another question is necessary.

Additional queries.
On a disagreement between the houses as to amendments to a bill
and a conference agreed on, can the conferees propose, or can
'thouse either house to propose an amendment in a new
part of the bill, having no coherence with the amendment
on which they have disagreed?

When the Previous Question is moved, must the debate on
the Main Question be immediately suspended?

~~May the main question be amended after the Previous Ques~~
~~tion has been moved & seconded, before it be put?~~

When a Previous Question has been moved & seconded, may the
Main Qu. be amended before putting the Prev. Qu.? we know
it cannot afterwards; and that it is a vexata questio
whether it may before. ~~I do not recollect to have seen~~
~~I remember to have heard discussions on this subject between mr Pendleton, mr Wythe~~
~~& the Speaker Randolph. what were their several opinions?~~
When a member calls for the execution of an order of the
house, as for clearing galleries &c. it must be carried into
execution by the Speaker without putting any question on it.
but when an order of the day is called for, I believe a
question is put 'whether the house will now proceed
to whatever the order of the day is? is it so?

When a motion is made to strike out a paragraph, section, or even the whole bill, from the word 'whereas', and
to insert something else in lieu thereof, it is understood that
the friends of the paragraph, section or bill, have first a

18472

correct. but I suppose a motion
to amend, may be made to a question, after that for striking
out is negatived. you would
retain the substance, but may
change the dress.

I suppose they may, as the
bill is still under the power of
both houses: tho the Joint ~~as that~~
the Senate have agreed to the
~~Bill & Amendmts~~ implying their
approbation ~~again~~ ~~~~ to put
since if the am were not agreed to,
the Senate may reject the bill.
it would seem to follow, that if on
a conference, to accept that passed
another part, will bring the houses
to accord, it may be done by the
Senates receding from the
former, & proposing the new
amendment.

I do not recollect this discussion, nor of course any
opinions on it. nor remember
any part[r] rule for deciding
the qu. Upon principle, I see
no reason for precluding the
previous amendmt, since what
might embarras the thirteen
part of the prop., induce the
withdrawing or negativing
the new. quest?

Yes.

Queries on Parliamentary Procedure

Aaron Burr

Benjamin Rush

James A. Bayard

Napoleon Bonaparte

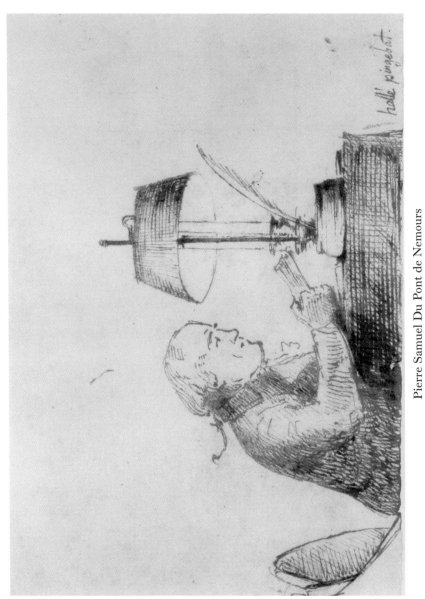

Pierre Samuel Du Pont de Nemours

View of the City of Washington

From James Madison

DEAR SIR Orange Decr. 20. 1800

I did not write to you from Richmond, because I was considerably indisposed during my stay there, & because I could communicate to you nothing that would not reach you with equal speed through other channels. Before I left that place, the choice of electors in S. Carolina, had been recd. by the Govr. in a letter from Col. Hampton, and was understood by all parties to fix the event of a Republican President. The manner in which the Electors have voted in that State, in Va. Maryland, Penna. & N.Y. makes it probable that the V.P. will also be republican. If the States of Georgia N.C. Tene. & Kentucky, should follow these examples it will even devolve on the H. of Reps. to make the discrimination. There can be no danger I presume but that in such an event a proper one will be made; but it is more desireable that it should be precluded by the foresight of some of the Electors. Gilston of N.Y. assures me, that there are two if not three States in which something to this effect may be looked for, but he does not name the States. Govr. Davie passd. thro' Richd. whilst I was there. I happened not to see him however, nor did I learn from others what complexion he seemed disposed to give to the business of his mission. It was my intention to send by you my subscription money for Lyon, as well as Smith, and my memory leaves me at a loss whether I did so or not. I rather suspect that it was not done. Will you be so good as to recollect & let me know; and if it be in no respect out of your way, you will further oblige me by making the advance to him for me. It shall be replaced as soon as possible. He was promised that the sum 5 dollars should be forwarded by you, and the disappt. may be as inconvenient to him as disagreeable to me. I observe an answr. to Hamilton's pamphlet by a Citizen of N. York, as advertized in Washington. If this be not the piece published in the Aurora under the name of *Aristedes*, I would thank you for a Copy. I recd. a copy of H's pamphlet lately under cover from Mr. Steele. My Rheumatic complaint has sensibly increased on me of late. I am trusting for a remedy to temperance & flannel. Wishing you an exemption from the like & all other evils I remain

Dr. Sir. Yrs. affecy. Js. MADISON JR.

RC (DLC: Madison Papers); endorsed by TJ as received 25 Dec. and so recorded in SJL.

GILSTON OF N.Y.: David Gelston wrote to Madison on 21 Nov. that "three States, two at least, will give Mr. J.—3 or more Votes, more than Mr B. will have" (Madison, *Papers,* 17:438).

For the subscription money for James LYON, see Lyon to TJ, 29 Nov. and TJ to Madison, 26 Dec. 1800. TJ recorded in his financial records a payment of $5 to "J. Lyon one year's subscription for the Cabinet" (MB, 2:1031).

ANSWR. TO HAMILTON'S PAMPHLET: *An Answer to Alexander Hamilton's Letter, concerning the Public Conduct and Character of John Adams, Esq., President of the United States* (New York, 1800; Evans, No. 36844) was signed "A Citizen of New York" and attributed to James Cheetham, a hatter from Manchester, England, who was a part-owner of the New York *Argus* and a member of the liberal Constitutional Society (Syrett, *Hamilton,* 25:181; Bishop James Madison to TJ, 1 Nov. 1800).

The PIECE PUBLISHED IN THE AURORA, "A letter to General Hamilton, Occasioned by his letter to President Adams. By a Federalist," which was signed "Aristides" and attributed to Noah Webster, appeared on 5 Nov. It was also published as a pamphlet under the same title in New York in 1800 (see Evans, No. 39045; Syrett, *Hamilton*, 25:179).

To James Monroe

DEAR SIR   Washington Dec. 20. 1800.

Your's of the 16th. came to hand yesterday morning, and in the course of the day it happened that Craven arrived here, so that I had an opportunity of enquiring into what you wished to know. He says that Darrelle failed altogether in the sale of his land so that he was unable to purchase. I asked him if some accomodation as to time, which might give him time to sell, might not induce him to purchase. he said not. I should suppose Alexandria & Lancaster perhaps York would be good places to advertise them in; the papers of this place go little into the country. a specification of the quality & price, & situation (Charlottesville being well known) could not fail to attract notice. I am not able to conjecture as to the price of tobacco. but I hardly expect it to rise after the first shipments for France are over, until the magazines of England are emptied. the Treaty does not please any body. I believe it will be attacked by the Feds; and that a modification of time will be proposed by all. I am not at liberty to speak of it's contents. it is pretty certain that, in the late election, the two republican candidates have prevailed; but probably they are equal, and the Feds in the legislature have expressed dispositions to make all they can of the embarrasment; so that after the most energetic efforts, crowned with success, we remain in the hands of our enemies by the want of foresight in the original arrangement.—I will thank you for any information you can give me on the subject of the conspiracy, as I have never understood it, and perhaps I may be placed in a situation which may render it not amiss that I should understand it. present my respectful attachment to mrs Monroe, & accept cordial & affectionate salutations. Adieu.

RC (DLC: Monroe Papers); at foot of text: "Govr. Monroe." PrC (DLC).

To Thomas Newton

DEAR SIR   Washington Dec. 20. 1800

I ask the protection of your cover to obtain a safe conveyance of the inclosed to it's address, as I understand the person lives in Norfolk. we have recieved the French Treaty, but not being yet ratified, we are not at liberty to specify it's contents. it does not give satisfaction; however I suppose it will be agreed to. the parity of votes between the two republican candidates at the late election, which, tho' not certainly known, is thought probable, is likely to produce an embarrasment, the issue of which is not yet discoverable. Accept assurances of the constant esteem & respect of Dear Sir

Your friend & servt   TH: JEFFERSON

PrC (DLC); at foot of text: "Colo. Thomas Newton"; endorsed by TJ in ink on verso. Enclosure: the following document.

To Patricot

SIR   Washington Dec. 20. 1800.

I have in my possession a letter & power of attorney for you, recieved from France, which I am desired not to forward till I know certainly where you are. if this should find you, be pleased to inform me by what address I may send them to you. I am Sir

Your most obedt. servt   TH: JEFFERSON

PrC (MHi); at foot of text: "M. Patricot. Norfolk"; endorsed by TJ in ink on verso. Enclosed in the preceding document.

Patricot, who lived in New York when TJ located him in January 1801, was evidently one of a number of French refugees from Saint-Domingue who made Norfolk a temporary or permanent home beginning in 1793. His brother, whose first name is also unknown, was the librarian of the La Rochefoucauld estate at La Roche-Guyon, France, and probably served as secretary to the Duc de La Roche-Guyon et de La Rochefoucauld d'Enville. Following the death of the duke in 1792, that Patricot continued in the employ of the Duchesse de La Rochefoucauld, the nobleman's widow and William Short's intimate friend, which explains how TJ became the channel for communication between the two brothers (Thomas J. Wertenbaker, *Norfolk: Historic Southern Port* [Durham, N.C., 1931], 97-8; Doina Pasca Harsanyi, ed., *Lettres de la Duchesse de La Rochefoucauld à William Short* [Paris, 2001], 265; Patricot to TJ, 16 Jan. 1801).

LETTER & POWER OF ATTORNEY: see Enclosure No. 2 listed at William Short to TJ, 18 Sep. 1800, and TJ to Patricot, 24 Jan. 1801.

From Charles Pinckney

DEAR SIR   Winyaw (in South Carolina) December 20: 1800

Having finished the public Business I went to Columbia as I was returning to Charleston to take shipping for Washington & at this place met with a paper which is inclosed & which has surprised me exceedingly—is it possible that the State of Pennsylvania has been deprived of her Vote by a majority of two in the senate? Or, taking the whole number of the federal part of their senate together, by *13 men, & that*, after the public opinion had been expressed by so decided a majority in every way in which their Citizens had an opportunity of doing so—? & what is to be result?—fortunately for the United States South Carolina has by her Vote decided the Election without Pennsylvania but will the people of that state so easily acquiesce in being thus deprived of their constitutional right & of the honour of having participated in the change that is to take place?—I now feel doubly pleased that I remained & went to Columbia to aid with my Exertions the securing the Vote of this State *entire*, for had she Voted otherwise I can scarcely concieve what may have been the consequence—& you must have long before this been convinced that without the Vote of this state the Event might have been doubtful; for that of Rhode Island was a thing scarcely to have been looked for, & I am afraid even now to rely implicitly on it, as we have just heard that some of our intelligence from Maryland is premature & that after all You will not have more than one half their Vote—I wish you to be handsomely elected & to have so many sound votes to spare that no little carpings or cavils at dates or Words or trifles shall vitiate the Election or give to your opponents the most distant right to dispute it's regularity——I trust You & all my friends at Washington have recieved all my letters & therefore are not surprised at not seeing me with You yet—I knew my presence at Columbia to be of more consequence than it could possibly be elsewhere, for I was always afraid Pennsylvania Would not vote—Mr: Monroe's Letter which I inclose you—strengthened this opinion & therefore I gave up the idea of going to Congress & went there—I send You Mr Monroe's Letter to shew You how convinced I was & ought to have been, that Our state was to decide & as I have always made a point of attending my public duties with diligence I wish You & my friends to know the absolute necessity there was for my absence & not to blame it.—I intend, if nothing prevents to be with You sometime in January & until then I remain with great Esteem & regard Dear Sir

    Yours Truly   CHARLES PINCKNEY

I omitted to mention to You that *the Letters* I got from Mr Monroe & you, both shewed marks of having *been opened*

If Colonel Hampton of this State should go to Washington & call upon You I beg to introduce him to You in the most particular manner as one of our best friends & whose communications & services in the republican cause have been very important to us—It is with great concern I have just heard that my fears on the Rhode Island head were too well founded. I was always afraid that much good could not come out of either Nazareth or Galilee & I find I was right—New England is New England *still* & unless an earthquake could remove them & give them about ten degrees more of our southern sun in their constitutions, they will always remain so—You may as well attempt to separate the Barnacle from the Oyster, or a Body of Caledonians as to divide New England—not so our southern Gentry—View Maryland & North Carolina & tell me by what Policy can it be, that We have lost so many Votes from states who ought to cling to the southern republican interest as to the rock of their *earthly* salvation— states too with whom so much pains have been taken to direct them in the right road—

I must request You not to come to any determination with respect to arrangements in this state until You see me, if I live to come on, as I have some information I do not choose to commit to Paper to give You after which, you will be better able to judge what is best to be done here—I have reasons very important to the republican interest for making this request—reasons which our late very arduous contest in this State could alone have developed, but which are very important to You to know—

RC (DLC); addressed: "To The Honourable Thomas Jefferson At the City of Washington in Maryland"; franked; postmarked Georgetown, S.C. on 22 Dec.; endorsed by TJ as received 4 Jan. 1801 and so recorded in SJL. Enclosures not found.

To Matthew L. Davis and William A. Davis

GENTLEMEN   Washington Dec. 21 1800

Your favor of Oct. 14 did not get to my hands till the 3d. of Nov. when the arrangements for my departure to this place engrossed my whole time nor have I been master of the earliest part of it here.

With respect to the Notes on Virginia which you propose to reprint it is not in my power to add to, or alter them at present. the subject would require more time & enquiry than are within my power to [provide.] the most correct edition is the one originally published at Paris. Stockdale's London edition is tolerably correct. I know nothing of the American editions, not possessing any of them. I think it might be of some use to publish with them a Report of mine on Weights & Measures, made to Congress in 1790. it was printed in N. York by Chiles & Swaine. I have no copy of it here or I would have inclosed it. by getting abroad it might prepare the public mind for adopting something more certain & convenient than the present system of weights & measures.

I am Gentlemen Your most obedt. servt   TH: JEFFERSON

PrC (DLC); faint; at foot of text: "Messrs. W. L. & W. A. Davis. N. York" (TJ mistakenly wrote W. L. instead of M. L.); endorsed by TJ in ink on verso.

For TJ's role in the printing of his NOTES ON VIRGINIA and his opinions on the American, Paris, and London editions of the work, see TJ to John Stockdale, 1 Feb. 1787, Stockdale to TJ, 10 July 1787, and TJ to John Riley, 7 Oct. 1809. The printed text based on Stockdale, and including the fourth appendix of 1800, was the version most familiar to TJ's contemporaries (*Notes*, ed. Peden, xviii).

WEIGHTS & MEASURES: Francis Childs and John Swaine published a *Report of the Secretary of State, on the Subject of Establishing a Uniformity in the Weights, Measures and Coins of the United States* in New York in 1790, and with corrections in 1791 (Sowerby, No. 3760; Evans, No. 23910; Vol. 16:615, 674-5). The Davis brothers published, in 1801, a third American edition of the *Notes on the State of Virginia*, which did not include the report on weights and measures despite TJ's suggestion here.

To George Douglas

SIR   Washington Dec. 21. 1800

Your favor covering an Almanac and the Washingtoniana, was recieved in due time, and would have been immediately acknoleged, but that I had [in?] contemplation to suggest to you some additions to your almanac, which without making it dear to the purchaser, might render it useful for some higher purpose than the common almanac. we certainly want such an one. the day of the month, rising of the sun, moon & principal stars, the sun's right ascension & declination, eclipses, & Jupiter's satellites, tables of the equation of time, of refraction of the Latitude & Longitude of principal places, of sines & tangents, of the probabilities of life &c &c might be brought into the compass of a common almanac, by excluding the trash with which they are [usually] crammed. however I never found time to digest the subject, & therefore did not write to you. it is now less likely that I should be able to do it.

Your letter of Oct. 15. came to my hands on the 3d. of Nov. when I was so engaged in preparations and arrangements for my departure to this place that I was only able to put up some notes on the subject of the Capitol that I had made when I gave the plan of it to Monsr. Clarissault. these have enabled me to make out the inclosed account of it. whether the execution conformed to the original plan I do not know. still less can I say anything of the expence: but that I presume might be obtained from mr William Hay who was one of the Directors, & principally attended to it. I think it was in [. . .] or 1796. the directors wrote to me in France for a plan, which was not [being delivered]. they asked at the same time a plan of a prison, & I sent them one by an architect of Lyons reduced to a smaller scale, better adapted to our use by myself, with cells for every prisoner separately. this I believe was the first idea of solitary confinement started in [America]. but it slept for that time, and Pensylva had the honor of first carrying it into execution. the father of it was an architect of Lyons. I am Sir

Your humble servt

TH: JEFFERSON

PrC (DLC); faint and blurred; at foot of text: "Mr. G. Douglass. bookseller. Petersburg." Enclosure: probably "An Account of the Capitol in Virginia" (PrC in DLC: TJ Papers, 17:2956-7), which was later printed under the heading "A Short Description of the Capitol" in Douglas's *Annual Register and Virginian Repository* (Petersburg, Va., 1802; Shaw-Shoemaker, No. 1764).

TJ had conveyed NOTES ON THE SUBJECT OF THE capitol to French architect Charles Louis Clérisseau in January

1786. William Hay wrote to Virginia Governor James Wood in March 1799 that the plans had been sent from France and eventually transmitted to the director of public buildings in the federal city, but that he had not seen them (Vol. 8:368n; Vol. 9:221-3, 602-4; Fiske Kimball, *The Capitol of Virginia: A Landmark of American Architecture*, rev. ed. [Richmond, 2002], xx-xxi).

ARCHITECT OF LYONS: Pierre Gabriel Bugniet.

For TJ's PLAN OF A PRISON, see TJ to James Wood, 31 Mch. 1797.

From Andrew Ellicott

SIR   Philadelphia December 21st. 1800

Among all those who will address you upon the fortunate issue of the late election for President, and V.P. of the U.S. (an event equally propitious, both to liberty, and science,) no one will do it with more sincerity, and friendship than myself,—and with that sincerity, and friendship, I join my fellow citizens in congratulating you, on your being called by the voice of your country to fill the most important office it can bestow.[1]

I intend being at the City of Washington some time next month, and shall take with me the whole of my correspondence, official, and otherwise during my absence to the southward; together with my journal, and astronomical observations: likewise a map of the Mississippi River from the mouth of the Ohio, down to the mouth of Willings bayou, which is a few miles below the line, with the maps of several other rivers of considerable importance to our country,[2] tho at present but little known.

I am sir with all due respect your friend and Hbl. Servt.

ANDW. ELLICOTT.

RC (DLC); at foot of text: "T. Jefferson V.P. U.S. and President of the Senate"; endorsed by TJ as received 25 Dec. and so recorded in SJL. Dft (DLC: Ellicott Papers). Enclosed in Ellicott to TJ, 23 Dec. 1800.

[1] Here in Dft Ellicott continued: "No political event since our revolution has in my opinion been equally important and in no one has my feelings been equally interested—I went to Lancaster (where I met Genl. Irvine) a few days before the commencement of the present session of our Legislature where we continued till the compromise became inevitable using every argument we could suggest with some members of the <opposition> majority in the Senate but to no purpose.—I then returned home and thought the event so doubtful that I <came to a determination to leave the City and retire into the country—and began to make my arrangements> scarcly went out of my house except to carry a paragraph or two once or twice a week for Duane's paper— till the fate of the election for electors in South Carolina was known."

[2] Dft ends here.

To Caesar A. Rodney

DEAR SIR   Washington Dec. 21. 1800.

I recieved in due time your favor of Oct. 13. and, as it did not require a particular answer, I have postponed the acknolegement of it to [this] time and place. it seems tolerably well ascertained (tho' not officially) that the two republican candidates on the late election have a decided majority, probably of 73. to 65. but equally probable that they are even between themselves; and that the Federalists are disposed to make the most of the embarrasment this occasions, by preventing any election by the H. of Representatives. it is far from certain that 9. representations in that body can be got to vote for any candidate. what the issue of such a dilemma would be cannot be estimated.   the French treaty is before the Senate. it is not agreeable in all it's parts to any body, but it is to be hoped it will be ratified with a limitation of time which cannot produce difficulty with the other party. Congress seem hardly disposed to do any thing this session. the judiciary bill, the territorial government, and the taking into their hands the making roads through the union, are the subjects talked of. the last business will be a bottomless abyss for money, the most fruitful field for abuses, and the richest provision for jobs to favorites that has ever yet been proposed. we have been 12. years grasping at all the expences of the Union. I hope a shorter term will suffice to restore them to whom they belong, and who can manage them with so much more correctness & raise them in ways so much less burthensome to the people than we can. foreign relations are our province; domestic regulations & institutions belong, in every state, to itself. I pray you to accept the assurances of my high regard & esteem, & to present my affectionate veneration to mr Dickinson. Adieu

TH: JEFFERSON

RC (Mrs. William S. Hilles, Wilmington, Delaware, 1946); frayed at margin; word in brackets supplied from PrC; addressed: "Caesar Rodney esq. Wilmington Delaware"; franked; postmarked 22 Dec. PrC (DLC).

To Samuel Harrison Smith

Dec. 21. 1800.

Th: Jefferson presents his compliments to mr Smith, and incloses the little book which he wishes to have printed, without subjecting it to any copy-right. he will ask of mr Smith either to print him 100. copies at his own expence, or for mr Smith to print it on his own account & let Th:J. have 75. copies at the selling price. the sooner it is begun, the better.

RC (DLC: J. Henley Smith Papers); addressed: "Mr. Smith"; endorsed by Smith. Not recorded in SJL. Enclosure: MS (now missing) of *A Manual of Parliamentary Practice. For the Use of the Senate of the United States* (Washington, D.C., 1801).

In *Forty Years of Washington Society*, Margaret Bayard Smith recalled her impressions of TJ as he brought the manuscript of the parliamentary manual to her husband for printing. It was her first meeting with the Republican leader. She remembered: "I knew not who he was, but the interest with which he listened to my artless details, induced the idea he was some intimate acquaintance or friend of Mr. Smith's and put me perfectly at my ease; in truth so kind and conciliating were his looks and manners that I forgot he was not a friend of my own, until on the opening of the door, Mr. Smith entered and introduced the stranger to me as *Mr. Jefferson*." Margaret Smith noted that the manuscript was "in his own neat, plain, but elegant hand writing" and was "still preserved by Mr. Smith and valued as a precious relique" (Margaret Bayard Smith, *The First Forty Years of Washington Society*, ed. Gaillard Hunt [New York, 1906], 5-8).

A letter from Smith to TJ of 31 Oct. 1800, recorded in SJL as received 20 Nov., has not been found.

From Amos Alexander

DR SIR   Alexandria 22nd December 1800

    On Mr Peyton And Myself returning from the City of Washington, And Mentioning to Our Fellow Citizens, Your Wish that the Invitation, we were Authorized to give you, to a publick Dinner Might be Suspended for Some time, I find a great Many people dissatisfy.d with Our Answer,—And extremely Anctious to have your Company to a publick Dinner . . .[1] And Many of them, not being possess.d of much reflection, though Worthy Citizens, I am fearfull the delay . . May have the tendency to disunite Us,—which Would be, by no means desireable at this time, . . . The business appearing to be so popular here—I Am Induced from a wish, for the publick good, to solicit your permission—Once More to renew the Invitation . . to Yourself And some few of your Intimate friends. I presume the day before, Or the day after New Years day . . . would Suit the Inhabitants of Our Town,—but Sir, If you can thinck of Honouring us With Your Company at this time, And Will signify to Me, the day that Would be most Convenient for you, I will take Care that Your day Shall be fixt On,—of which you shall have timely Notice . . . I thus far Intrude On your goodness . . In consequence of the, great desire Shewn by your friends, in this Town, And a wish that nothing May happen to weaken Our Interest—

    I have the Honour to be With respect And Esteem Your Obedient Servt.   AMOS ALEXANDER

RC (DLC); at head of text: "Thomas Jefferson Esqr"; endorsed by TJ as received 25 Dec. and so recorded in SJL.

A letter from Alexander to TJ of 20 Oct. 1800, recorded in SJL as received 3 Nov., has not been found.

[1] Here and below, extra periods in MS.

From Joseph Barnes

Messina Sicily Decr. 22. 1800

    If from the then Occurrent Circumstances, as Suggest'd in my Last dat'd Naples Sepr. 1800—Exulting I congratulat'd you, my best friend Mr Jefferson, & felicitat'd myself and fellow citizens on the *presumption* of your election to the presidency of the Unit'd States, I need not Suggest, your own feelings will indicate how *much* more I must Exult from the Several numbers publish'd by the Federalists in the Boston papers to the 6th Sepr. Last purporting your Election beyond a doubt!, And consequently, with how much more *feeling* Satisfaction I again congratulate you, & felicitate my Self & fellow Citizens on the propitious prospect which appears to brighten before us—For my further Sentiments relative to the happy effects, I need only quote them from my Last—

"Adverting to the great influence of the advice and recommendations of the President on the Legislature, what may we not hope? from him who possesses not only Such *Eminently* Superior Abilities but *disposion* to promote the happiness of his fellow Citizens particularly, & of the great family of the human race generally? as far as the Nature of Circumstances will admit; Should the funding System be abolish'd, the *curse* of every Country in which it exists; Should the Army & Navy be disolv'd, & a well regulat'd Militia be effect'd, & one general, uniform & Liberal System of education be establish'd thro' out the Unit'd States on the genuine natural principles of Morality & Virtue, Presided *not* by fanatics, but by the most *eminent Sages*, as the only Sure means of promoting & perpituating the true principles of Republicanism & Virtue in the Unit'd States 'tis *Mr Jefferson* who will have been the *cause*"

Tis with much Satisfaction I Learn from the Florence Gazette, that a treaty has been conclud'd & mutually Sign'd by the French & American Commissioners at Paris, and I hope to the Mutual advantage & happiness of the two great Nations; And, that in consequence the French Commissioners had given a *grand Fete* at Paris, demonstrative of their joy on the Occasion.—

Consequent on which, Should the English recommence their unprovok'd Spoilations on the American commerce, especially under the Presidency of Mr Jefferson, knowing his disposition, I feel confident they will be promptly brot. to their Senses, by *Shutting* the Ports of the Unit'd States against, Sequestering all British property, Laying & continuing an Embargo on, guarrantee the demurrage of all the Merchant Vessels of the U.S. 'till a reconciliation takes place, and permit as many privateers or Letters of Marque as the Merchants might chuse to Sent out to embarrass the British West-India trade: And, meanwhile to complete the Stroke, Authorise an Army of Volenteers to March & take possession of the British Colonies—

This done, the Manufacturers &c of England would effect the rest—for, Should the ports of America, the chief Source of the vent Left for their Manufactures, remain Shut Six Months, they would *down* with the *Minister* & regulate the Matter for themselves.—

Permit me to repeat, as Suggest'd in my Last, that an extensive & Mutually advantageous Commerce might be effect'd betwixt the

Subjects of his Sicilian Majesty and the Unit'd States, provid'd a proper agent with the requisite powers & Abilities, & disposition was Sent for the purpose.—Having paid Some attention Since my residence of near three months in Naples & more than two in Sicily, I consider it an object worthy the immediate attention of the Unit'd States, especially as the number of American Vessels are increasing fast to the Ports of these Countries; *without* even a consul who has either common interest, common feelings with the citizens of the U.S. or common Abilities in this Kingdom.—Having came well introduc'd to the Vice Roi, & a Gentln. to whom the King owes Much at Naples, & who is my particular friend; & being familiariz'd in the Country, add'd to Seven years experience in Europe, & a knowledge of Several Languages, are circumstances which no doubt will receive due consideration & have due weight—Should an Agent be deem'd necessary, or the office of Consul [. . .] to the two Sicilies, or the office of Consul [. . .] or other chief port in France be fill'd

[. . .] being my primary object, & holding *ingratitude* as the only unpardonable crime, Should I be prefer'd to either of the Said offices, to Act worthy the trust repos'd in me, would be the Summit of my wishes.—

With eternal wishes for your prosperity, happiness, & Long preferment—I remain yours most respectfully JOS: BARNES

P.S. Notwithstanding all efforts from the purport of a Letter dat'd Naples 29th Ult. it appears that the French & the Emperor were to recommence hostilities on the preceding day—& that 80.000 Russians have March'd to join the Austrians again—! And, 'tis Said the French are concentring in force in the North of Italy in order to *defeat* the Austrians before the Arrival of the Russians—to ensure which Massina, at the head of 60.000 French is Marching from Dijon to join their fellows in Italy, this effect'd, I have no doubt the *fate* of the Russians will be that which ought ever to be the fate of Slaves who wish to enslave others, destruction, disgrace & contempt.—The report of the day, is, that the Republican Citizens have taken possession of the Citidall & hoist'd the French flag in Venice.

Should circumstances require address to care of Mr E. Noble—Naples—or Msr Appleton Leghorn 'till further advice—Report Since, which circumstances corroborate, Says, that the Russians are Marching,—*not* to join, but to induce or force the Ausstrians to peace; and that the French & Russians have or are about to come to an understanding—if so, judge of the [effect] of the [. . .]!—

RC (DNA: RG 59, LAR); torn; addressed: "Thomas Jefferson Esqr. V.P. of the U.S. Philadelphia pr favor of Capn. Robinson"; franked; endorsed by TJ as received 9 May 1801 and so recorded in SJL; also endorsed by TJ: "to be Consul Genl. of the two Sicilies Consul at Marseilles."

One pseudonymous contributor to a Federalist newspaper in BOSTON during the period mentioned by Barnes thought that the odds in favor of TJ's election were "three to one," and another writer noted that "people whine forth the probability of Mr. Jefferson's being elected President of the United States." But there was no capitulation to the "Jacobins" by early September, despite acknowledgment that divisions among Federalists might cause electors to throw some votes to TJ instead of voting for Adams and Pinckney across the board (*Columbian Centinel*, 16, 30 Aug., 3, 6 Sep. 1800).

TO RECOMMENCE HOSTILITIES: after a period of quiet since June, with the expiration of the most recent armistice Austrian and French armies clashed in Bavaria and Austria beginning the first of December. That fighting lasted three weeks, then ended in another armistice at the Austrians' request. On 25-26 Dec. the French army in Northern ITALY defeated Austrian forces at the Mincio River. General Massena, who had been recalled from Italy in August, commanded no army late in 1800; another officer, Joachim Murat, led the French reserve army from DIJON into Italy (Digby Smith, *The Greenhill Napoleonic Wars Data Book* [London, 1998], 188-92; T. C. W. Blanning, *The French Revolutionary Wars, 1787-1802* [London, 1996], 258; Tulard, *Dictionnaire Napoléon*, 1207; James Marshall-Cornwall, *Marshal Massena* [London, 1965], 128-9).

From Richard Richardson

DR. SIR   Monticello Decmbr 22d 1800

This morning I leave this, and you will Receive this, By the hands of Mr Carr, or his Servent, who Is the Bearrer of it from this place, we are all well at this time and nothing of Importance to write you, that has occured since your departure from this, Mr powel has Been up, he Came some few days after you, left this, to see you Before you left this, But you Being gone he mentioned he was at a loss to know, wheather he was to Come as a maried man or singel, which I told him it was to his own Choice, But that you had Expected him since the death of his wife to come as a single man, which he said he would and went Back to Bord out his Children, and said he would Be Back In ten or fifteen days, which time has a lapsd and he has not arived as yet, I Carryed Mr lilley to the Shop this morning and told the Boys they was to Be under his direction and Joe to say when their nails was made tow Big or too small with this arangement they will go on till I see Mr powel or hear wheather he is a Comeing. if he does not I will Return direcly after Christmas, the prospect of geting of hands for labour another year, is not a veary good one I fear they Cant Be had In this part of the County, Mr lilley has Been to louisa But Cant get But one. since your departure I have Rote to the oners of the ne-groes we have this year and they Informe me that the Estates, will Be setled, this next new years day, and desires that I will Come froward on that day and take In my Bonds as they will Be accountabel for all debts not paid, with Intrust their on from the time of payment, the order you gave me on Th: Carr, Mr Gambell says their is not as much due you, and he Cant advance any money that you must take Chanc as the Rest of the Creaditors which I Inclose to you and would Be glad of about a Hundred dollars, on my own account when you froward on, the sum for the hires the Job mentioned when you left this is not all Compleat, we took down the two Collums, that was to take down, and Raised one and a half of the two that was down, But, I find they was not marked, when taken down, I never Experience so troublesone a Job In my life, and found they must Be put together Before they are put up, to marke them, as they are to stand, the weather proving veary Cold and the morter freesed I thought it, would Be Best to Refur them till Spring as the workmen mentioned they Could find Jobs Enough, with out them You will Be good Enough to write me and direct it to the post office of Richmond a line from you will Be desirable at any time and Believe me to Be sincerly, your friend and Humble servant   RD RICHARDSON

NB you will Be good Enough to mention what pospect for work In the Citey and what a gornaman¹ gets pr day I am yours

RD. RDSON

RC (MHi); addressed: "Honable Thomas Jefferson Vice preasident of the usa, States at the Fediral Citey"; endorsed by TJ as received 31 Dec. and so recorded in SJL. Enclosure not found.

On 23 Nov. TJ gave Richardson an ORDER on Thomas CARR for £30.14.2¾, the balance due TJ from Thomas Bell's estate. TJ noted in his financial records that it was "returned unpaid." Not until October 1805 did Robert Gamble pay TJ $58.80, for the settlement of the account

(MB, 2:1029-30, 1165). JOB MENTIONED WHEN YOU LEFT: for the difficulties Richardson faced in reassembling and erecting the columns for the east portico at Monticello, see Jack McLaughlin, *Jefferson and Monticello: The Biography of a Builder* (New York, 1988), 286-8.

A letter from Richardson to TJ of 15 May 1800, recorded in SJL as received at Mont Blanco six days later, has not been found.

¹ A journeyman.

From Aaron Burr

DEAR SIR   NYork 23 decr. 1800

Yesterday Mr. Van Benthuysen handed me your obliging letter. Govr. Fenner is principally responsible for the unfortunate result of the election in R.I. So late as semptember, he told me personally that you would have every Vote in that State and that A. would certainly have one & probably two: this he confirmed by a Verbal Message to me through a confidential friend in October. He has lately given some plausible reasons for withdrawing his Name from the republican ticket. I do not however apprehend any embarrassment even in Case the Votes should come out alike for us—My personal friends are perfectly informed of my Wishes on the subject and can never think of diverting a single Vote from you. On the Contrary, they will be found among your Most Zealous adherents. I see no reason to doubt of you having at least Nine States if the business shall come before the H— of Reps.

As far forth as my knowledge extends, it is the unanimous determination of the republicans of every grade to support your administration with unremitted Zeal: indeed I should distrust the loyalty of any one professing to be a republican who should refuse his services. There is in fact no such dearth of Talents or of patriotism as ought to inspire a doubt of your being able to fill every office in a Manner that will command public confidence and public approbation—as to myself, I will chearfully abandon the office of V.P. if it shall be thought that I can be more useful in any Active station. In short, my Whole time and attention shall be unceasingly employed to render your administration grateful and honorable to our Country and to yourself—To this I am impelled, as well by the highest Sense of duty as by the most devoted personal attachment   A Burr

RC (DLC); at foot of text: "Th. Jefferson"; endorsed by TJ as received 1 Jan. 1801 and so recorded in SJL. Probably enclosed in Burr to TJ, 26 Dec.

OBLIGING LETTER: TJ to Burr, 15 Dec. Timothy Green was the CONFIDENTIAL FRIEND who conveyed Arthur Fenner's guarantee to Burr (Kline, *Burr*, 1:472-4).

From Nicolas Gouin Dufief

MONSIEUR,   à Philadelphie, ce 23 de decembre. 1800.

Je profite de l'occasion que m'offre Mr. *Jones* l'un des representans de l'état de Géorgie, au Congrès, pour vous adresser les deux ouvrages que vous desiriez avoir, & qui ne se trouvoient pas dans ma collection, lorsque j'eus l'honneur de vous voir à Philadelphie. Je les ai reçus depuis peu, avec plusieurs autres livres. J'attends vers le mois de Mars, un assortiment assez étendu des meilleurs auteurs français dans tous les Genres & des ouvrages nouveaux les plus piquans. Je vous enverrai la liste & la notice litteraire de ceux que je croirai devoir vous intéresser le plus. Ce sera un vrai plaisir pour moi de le faire, & non point une peine, ou une perte de tems; ainsi je serois bien fâché d'en être dispensé.

Je respecte trop les soins importans dont vous étez chargé, pour vous parler d'un ouvrage que je me propose de livrer a l'impression. Le sujet en est entièrément neuf, ce qui ne seroit pas un grand mérite si l'utilité n'y etoit jointe. Je l'ai composé dans la vue de faciliter & d'abréger considérablement le tems que l'on passe ordinairement à apprendre les langues vivan[tes.] L'addresse ci incluse vous donnera une idée de cet ouvrage & de la méthode qui étant analytique, s'applique à tous les Idiom[es.]

Quand il aura acquis toute la maturité, que je suis susceptible de lui donner, je le soumettrai au jugement du premier homme de Lettres des Etats-Unis, du Président de la Societé Philosophique.

Je ne saurais conclure cette lettre que je crains être beaucoup trop longue, sans me joindre, *ex toto corde et animo*, à ceux qui se felicitent de ce que le choix des Citoyens des Etats-Unis vient de vous porter a une place distinguée.

J'aime à voir les Philosophes tenir les rênes du Gouverneme[nt;] cela nous rappelle le beau Siecle de *Pericles* & celui de *Solon*.

Acceptez les assurances de ma haute Estime & de mon respectueux dévoüement. N. G. DUFIEF, Professeur de Lang. Françoise

EDITORS' TRANSLATION

SIR, at Philadelphia, this 23rd of December 1800.
  I am taking advantage of the occasion offered by Mr. *Jones*, one of the representatives of the state of Georgia, in Congress, to forward to you the two works which you wished to have, and which were not in my collection when I had the honor of seeing you in Philadelphia. I received them a short while ago, with several other books. I am expecting, towards the month of March, a rather broad assortment of the best French authors in all genres and some most tempting new works. I will send you the list and the literary review of those that I think most likely to interest you. It will be a real pleasure for me to do so, and not a chore or a waste of time; hence I should be quite sorry to be exempted from it.
  I respect too much the important cares with which you are burdened to speak to you of a work that I propose to hand over to be printed. The subject is completely new, which would not be of great worth if utility were not joined to it. I have composed it with the object of facilitating and considerably abridging the time ordinarily spent in learning living languages. The enclosed prospectus will give you an idea of this work and of the method, which, being analytic, is applicable to all languages.
  When it has attained the full maturity that I am capable of giving it, I shall

[344]

submit it to the judgment of the first man of letters in the United States, the President of the Philosophical Society.

I could not conclude this letter, which I fear is much too long, without joining, *with whole heart and spirit*, those who congratulate themselves that the choice of the citizens of the United States has just borne you to a distinguished position.

I like to see philosophers hold the reins of government; that reminds us of the fine age of *Pericles* and that of *Solon*.

Receive the assurances of my high esteem and my respectful devotion.

N. G. DUFIEF, Professor of the French Language

RC (DLC); damaged; endorsed by TJ as received 1 Jan. 1801 and so recorded in SJL. Enclosure: probably Dufief's address "To the Lovers of the French Language," printed in the *Gazette of the United States*, 1 Sep. 1800, a clipping of which is in DLC (with Dufief's letter to TJ of 27 Feb. 1807); the address, subjoined to an announcement of Dufief's opening of a school in Philadelphia for instruction in French, discussed his approach to the teaching of language and outlined the work that he later published under the title *Nature Displayed* (see below); the address also appeared in the *Aurora* beginning 30 Aug. 1800.

Nicolas Gouin Dufief (1776-1834) became an important source of books for TJ's library. From a French aristocratic family of strong antirevolutionary sympathies—his mother was renowned as the "heroine" of the Vendée—Dufief, while still in his teens, joined a royalist military corps, then sought exile in Britain and the West Indies before finally arriving in Philadelphia. According to his later assertions, he fled the city in the summer of 1793 to escape yellow fever and, finding himself stranded in Princeton without his recently acquired English grammars and dictionaries, taught himself English by concentrating on phrases and conversation rather than the mastery of rules and individual words. He developed that method, of which William Rawle claimed to be the true source, as a teacher of French and a writer on the subject of language instruction. Dufief's two-volume *Nature Displayed, in her Mode of Teaching Language to Man* (Philadelphia, 1804), of which TJ was one of the original subscribers, was reprinted in multiple editions. In 1799 Dufief entered the book trade, and four years later he sold a significant portion of Benjamin Franklin's library. It was Dufief who in 1804 supplied TJ with Greek and English editions of the New Testament for the compilation of TJ's "Philosophy of Jesus." In 1817 Dufief went to Europe, leaving his Universal Book Store under the supervision of John Laval. He returned to the United States at least once, but died in England (Madeleine B. Stern, *Nicholas Gouin Dufief of Philadelphia: Franco-American Bookseller, 1776-1834* [Philadelphia, 1988], 9-32, 35-46, 60-8, 71, 74-5; EG, 27; Sowerby, No. 4819; TJ to Dufief, 20 Jan. 1804).

LES DEUX OUVRAGES: the books that Dufief sent were probably Jean Paul Rabaut Saint Étienne, *An Impartial History of the late Revolution in France, from its Commencement to the Death of the Queen, and the Execution of the Deputies of the Gironde Party* (Philadelphia, 1794), which was Mathew Carey's printing of a translation by Englishman James White of a work first published in Paris in 1792; and *Fragments sur Paris* (Hamburg, 1798), Dumouriez's translation of a work in German by Friedrich Johann Lorenz Meyer (Sowerby, Nos. 229, 3895; TJ to Dufief, 9 Jan. [1801]). For TJ's search for the latter work, see Vol. 31:87, 88n.

From Andrew Ellicott

SIR   Philadelphia December 23d. 1800

After writing, and sealing the enclosed, your favour of the 18th. came to hand.—I am much pleased with Mr. Dunbar's complaisance in giving you the satisfaction of perusing his journal.—he is a gentleman of singular acquirements, and would make a figure in any country.—

It is difficult for me to suppose that any doubt can arise in the house of representatives with respect to the late election, (so fortunate in designating the republican majority of our country,) for it must be known to every person in the U.S. that Col. Bur was intended to be ran as V.P. and not President;—neither did one single elector vote with any other view:—Then why take advantage of an obvious defect in the constitution to embarrass the government? would it not be acting more like good citizens, and friends to their country, to obey the wishes of the people on whom the government rests like a pyramid on its base? A contrary conduct could only arise from an opposition to[1] such parts of our constitution as are periodically carried into effect by the people, and would therefore be at war with the principles of republicanism, and if this war be meditated all the confusion, and consequent mischief, which would ensue from having a government without a head would be brought forward as an argument against free and popular governments; but I trust none of our citizens particularly in the house of Representatives will yet be found so daring as to attempt to stifle the voice of the country.

The Capitol in the City of Washington stands at the intersection of the meridian, and prime vertical,—the center of the north, and south avenue may therefore be taken as the true meridian.—The positions of all the leading avenues were determined by celestial observations, and will be found in the 4th. volume of the transactions of our philosophical society.

I have the honour to be with sincere esteem your friend and Hbl. Servt   ANDW. ELLICOTT.

RC (DLC); at foot of text: "T. Jefferson V.P. U.S. and president of the Senate"; endorsed by TJ as received 25 Dec. and so recorded in SJL. Dft (DLC: Ellicott Papers). Enclosure: Ellicott to TJ, 21 Dec. 1800.

In 1791-93 Ellicott surveyed the boundaries of the Federal District and laid out the courses of several avenues of the CITY OF WASHINGTON. He reported the results with other "Astronomical Observations" he transmitted to the American PHILOSOPHICAL SOCIETY in April 1795 (ANB; APS, *Transactions*, 4 [1799], 49-51).

[1] Here in Dft Ellicott canceled "republican forms of government."

To John Wayles Eppes

DEAR SIR   Washington Dec. 23. 1800.

I arrived here on the 4th. day of my journey without accident, & found myself better provided with lodgings than I expected. in general Congress is comfortably & conveniently lodged; dearer however than at Philadelphia; in my own case considerably so. the French treaty will meet considerable opposition in Senate. the judiciary system is again brought forward, & there is great fear will prevail. a system of territorial government is also on the anvil, which is expected to be highly enough tempered.—the actual votes of Vermont, Kentucky, & Tennissee are not yet known, but it is believed the two republican candidates will have each 73. votes in the whole, mr A. 65. and P. 64. the Feds are determined to avail themselves of the parity of votes between the two highest candidates, & to prevent an election in Congress; which they may do, as there are but 7. states which have republican majorities in the H. of R. & 9. are necessary to make a choice. Colo. Burr behaves with candour in this dilemma, but what is to be the issue of it no mortal can foresee.—I will pray you to attend to mr Powell, & get him on as soon as possible. you may assure him that the first work in the spring shall be to build a good nailery. I hope you will also exert yourself to hire me what good labourers you can, not exceeding 10. I heard of your leaving Edgehill in health, but nothing later. my tenderest affections to my ever dearest Maria; and cordial salutations of esteem & attachment to yourself. Adieu.

TH: JEFFERSON

RC (InMuB); addressed: "John W. Eppes Bermuda Hundred by the Petersburg mail"; franked and postmarked.

Notes on Candidates for Public Office

1800.

Dec. 23. Majr. Wm. Munson, bearer of the Connecticut votes, recommendd. by Pierrept Edwards as a good Whig. he is surveyor of the   of New haven. was a good officer in the revolutionary war.

he says that about a twelvemonth ago, the Marshal of that state turned out his deputy marshal, because he summoned some republicans on the grand jury. it seems the Marshal summons the juries for the Fedl. courts.

———

see a lre from Govr. Mc.Kean on the conduct of Genl. Hand, Robert Coleman & Henry Miller supervisor for Pensylva while their legislature were on the appointmt of electors.

———

Doctr. Jarvis of Boston is a man of abilities, a firm whig, but passionate, hot-headed, obstinate and unpliant.[1]
Doctr. Eustace is of equal abilities, amiable, & almost too accomodating. was once rather a trimmer, & was forced by the Feds to become decided against them. ex relat. Baldwin.
Colo. Hitchburn's acct is different, that Eustis is superficial & Jarvis compleatly profound.[2]

———

N. Hampsh. Sherburne an able lawyer, republican & honest.

———

S. Carola. there is a ⸻ Ramsay, son of Dr. Ramsay, a judge of a state court, a good lawyer, of excellent private character, eminent abilities, much esteemed, & republican. this character from Genl. Sumpter. the father is also republican.

———

Hamilton & DOyley of S. Carola, attached to the state treasury, good republicans

———

Brockhurst Livingston. very able, but ill-tempered, selfish, unpopular.

———

Dewitt Clinton. very able, good, rich & lazy. very firm. does not follow any profession.
married Osgood's daughter in law.

———

Thos. Sumter, son of Genl. Sumter. S. Carolina. a man of solid understanding.
writes correctly. seems discreet & virtuous. follows no profession.

———

Harrison, of Carlisle. Genl. Hanna tells me he is as able a lawyer as any in Pensva, & a zealous republican.

MS (DLC: TJ Papers, 108:18524); entirely in TJ's hand, perhaps written in several sittings; on same sheet and preceding note of 10 Nov. 1801.

President Washington appointed William MUNSON customs surveyor and revenue inspector for the port of New Haven in February 1793 (JEP, 1:129-30). The MARSHAL of Connecticut was Philip B. Bradley, who resigned at the expiration of his term in 1801 (same, 1:258, 397).

For Thomas McKean's letter on Edward HAND and others in Pennsylvania, see 15 Dec. 1800.

Physicians Charles JARVIS and William EUSTIS were both Harvard graduates and supporters of the Republican cause in Massachusetts. Jarvis graduated in 1766 and received medical training in London while Eustis received his degree in 1772 and studied medicine with Boston physician Joseph Warren. In 1795 Jarvis led the protest in Boston against the ratification of the Jay Treaty. He was characterized as "one of the greatest orators that ever controlled the people in Faneuil Hall." At the urging of Samuel Adams, TJ appointed him surgeon of the Marine Hospital at Charlestown. Eustis won election to Congress in 1800 (John L. Sibley and Clifford K. Shipton, *Sibley's Harvard Graduates: Biographical Sketches of Those Who Attended Harvard College*, 17 vols. [Cambridge, Mass., 1873-1975], 16:376-83; ANB, 7:590-1; Paul Goodman, *The Democratic-Republicans of Massachusetts: Politics in a Young Republic* [Cambridge, Mass., 1964], 99; James S. Loring, *The Hundred Boston Orators Appointed by the Municipal Authorities and Other Public Bodies, From 1770 to 1852*, 2d ed. [Boston, 1853], 308-10; Samuel Adams to TJ, 24 April 1801).

John S. SHERBURNE served as a con-

gressman from New Hampshire from 1793 to 1797 (*Biog. Dir. Cong.*).

In December 1799 Ephraim RAMSAY was elected an associate judge of the South Carolina Court of General Sessions and Common Pleas. DR. RAMSAY: Ephraim was the brother of John Ramsay, a Charleston physician who had studied medicine at the University of Pennsylvania and in London. Their father died in 1770. TJ may have thought Ephraim was the son of Dr. David Ramsay, historian of the American Revolution, with whom TJ had last corresponded in 1790. GENL. SUMPTER: Thomas Sumter was serving as a congressman from South Carolina in 1800 (*S.C. Biographical Directory, House of Representatives*, 4:465-7; *Biog. Dir. Cong.*; Vol. 16:332-3, 577).

Paul HAMILTON became South Carolina's comptroller of finance on 5 Mch. 1800 and Daniel D'Oyley was elected treasurer of the Lower Division of South Carolina on 18 Dec. 1799. Hamilton served as one of South Carolina's eight Jefferson-Burr electors (*S.C. Biographical Directory, House of Representatives*, 3:192, 299-300; Peter Freneau to TJ, 2 Dec. 1800).

In 1796 DeWitt CLINTON married Maria Franklin, daughter of Walter and Maria Bowne Franklin. Ten years earlier Samuel Osgood had married Maria Franklin's mother, a wealthy widow (ANB).

[1] MS: "unplian."
[2] Preceding sentence in lighter ink and smaller hand, probably added at a later date.

From Bishop James Madison

DEAR SIR   Decr. 24th. 1800 Williamsburg

As young Munford has returned to America, it is highly probable he will again solicit your Attention in some Way or other. Knowing your Disposition to befriend young Men of Talents, I thought it a Duty to make his Character known to you. He has plunged deeper into Villainy, than any Youth of his Age I have ever heard of. His

History which is now well known, from Norfolk to L'orient; from thence to Paris, & from Paris to Edinburgh, is one Tissue of the most abominable swindling.—Mr Davie knows his History at Paris.—He is now at Col. Burr's in New York; & probably is in his Confidence. How far it might be proper to put Col. Burr on his Guard, with Respect to this young Man, I do not know.

Munford has written to me, since his arrival, & also to one of the Students in College. He expects to conceal himself under his Falsities; but Col. Hamilton the British Consul at Norfolk, who was first cheated out of 40, or 50. Guineas, has developed his whole Conduct.

It gives the real Friends of Republicanism the highest satisfaction to learn, that the Result of the late Election will be conformable to their ardent Wishes.

I am Dr Sir, with the greatest Esteem & Respect Yrs most sincerely

J MADISON

I have just got the Vol. of the Phil. Society, for 99. I am well pleased with it.

RC (DLC); endorsed by TJ as received 30 Dec. and so recorded in SJL.

YOUNG MUNFORD: William G. Munford, who used the surname "Montfort" following his travels mentioned by Bishop Madison above; see Vol. 30:596-7n.

VOL. OF THE PHIL. SOCIETY: Madison's description of three experiments in magnetism appeared in APS, *Transactions*, 4 [1799], 323-8; see Vol. 30:273.

From Samuel Smith

DR. SIR/   Baltimore 24. Decr. 1800

In Consequence of the Conversation we had on the subject of Banks I made application (without saying for what cause) to the President & Directors of the Bank of Maryland & they directed their Cashier to make out A Statement from the Book every day in Use.— Indeed I did not want it farther back as It would only have shown a similar Result—I would only Add that I do not believe any Bank has it more in its power to put its Paper into Circulation than the Bank of Maryland—In addition to its Capital & Loan (the loan forming a part of the Capital) the average Deposit for the time inclosed has been about $360,000, the Deposits being nearly equal to the Capital— By this It appears that on the average Banks have not in Circulation more than two thirds the amount of their Capital.

I have the Honor to be Your Obedt. servt.   S. SMITH

RC (MHi); endorsed by TJ as received 25 Dec. and so recorded in SJL. Enclosure: Statement from the books of the Bank of Maryland dated 24 Dec. 1800, giving the total amount of notes in circulation on a weekly basis from 3 July 1799 to 24 Dec. 1800, ranging from a low on 7 Aug. 1799 of $197,460 to a high of $266,674 on 22 Oct. 1800 (MS in DLC; 2 p.; in Robert Wilson's hand and initialed by him; at head of statement: "The Permanent Capital and the Loan to the Bank of maryland amount to Dls. *380,000*").

Smith was a founding director of the BANK OF MARYLAND, which was incorpo-rated in 1790 with $300,000 in capital to be raised through the sale of shares of $300 each. The bank's president, Baltimore merchant William Patterson, was Smith's brother-in-law. THEIR CASHIER: Robert Wilson (*Laws of Maryland, Made and Passed at a Session of Assembly, Begun and held at the city of Annapolis on Monday the first of November, in the year of our Lord one thousand seven hundred and ninety* [Annapolis, 1791], chap. 5; *The New Baltimore Directory, and Annual Register; for 1800 and 1801* [Baltimore, 1800], 6; Frank A. Cassell, *Merchant Congressman in the Young Republic: Samuel Smith of Maryland, 1752-1839* [Madison, 1971], 42, 72, 166).

To Gouverneur Morris

SIR   Washington Dec. 25. 1800.

I recieved last night from Colo. Wm. S. Smith the inclosed letters & documents with his request to lay them before the Senate, for their satisfaction on the subject of his late nomination. if the Senate had been in the course of daily meeting, it would have been my duty to have done so, that they might have been regularly referred to the committee of which you are chairman. but as you are instructed to seek testimony on this subject, and may perhaps proceed in this during the recess of the Senate, I suppose it regular to hand them to you directly, and that the object which Colo. Smith must naturally have at heart, of having them read in Senate to satisfy their minds can be answered by reading them when your report comes in. I have the honor to be with great respect Sir

Your most obedt. humble servt   TH: JEFFERSON

RC (DNA: RG 46, Senate Records, 6th Cong., 2d sess.); at foot of text: "Gouverneur Morris esq."; endorsed by clerk: "No. 1 Letter of the Vice President of the U.S. to G. Morris Esqr. Decr. 25th. 1800" and designated "F—No. 1." PrC (DLC); endorsed by TJ in ink on verso. Enclosures: (1) William Stephens Smith to TJ, New York, 18 Dec. 1800, requesting a copy of charges against him as well as the opportunity to refute them stating, "I know of no circumstance of my Life, that I should shrink from an investigation of, and I have too great a Veneration for the Characters of the Senators of my Country to suppose, for a Moment, that they would permit a faithful Soldier of the Revolution, and a Gentleman who has Served in various Civil Employments, absolutely uncensured, and never suspected in any public Station, to be stabbed by private Assassins, and his reputation blasted in the dark." (2) Smith to TJ, New York, 20 Dec. 1800, suggesting that the charges against him should be published and, if found false, "that I may have a well earned reputation restored to me brightened by my passage thro' a firey ordeal in which I have been kept Hissing Hot." (3) John Sullivan to Smith, 13 Oct. 1779, testifying to Smith's service under his command. (4) George Washington to Smith, 24 June 1782, testifying to Smith's Revolutionary War record as "a brave and valuable Officer" detailing his "gallantry intelligence and professional knowledge." (5) Benjamin Lincoln to Smith, 2 July 1782, recommending Smith "as a Gallant, Enterprising, and highly meritorious Officer." (6) Robert R. Livingston to Smith, 18 July 1782, recommending Smith to the "patronage and Protection" of the generals and commanders in the West Indies. (7) James McHenry to Smith, 17 Dec. 1798, accepting Smith's provisional appointment as adjutant general to the army. (8) Washington to McHenry, 13 Dec. 1798, reporting that Smith stood charged with "very

serious instances of private misconduct," most notably that of pledging "Property to Major Burrows, by way of Security, which was before conveyed or Mortgaged, for its full Value" to William Constable, thus financially ruining Burrows. (9) Smith to James McHenry, 20 Dec. 1798, stating "I deny the Charge and Defy the informer" (Trs in DNA: RG 46, Senate Records, 6th Cong., 2d sess.; in clerk's hand; docketed and numbered F-2 through 10, respectively; with docketing on cover sheet: "Papers and Documents sent under cover of a letter from the Vice President U.S.").

On 10 Dec. the Senate referred Adams's nomination of his son-in-law William S. SMITH to serve as surveyor and revenue inspector of New York to Morris's committee, which did not REPORT until 16 Feb. The Senate consented by an 18 to 8 vote on 21 Feb. (JEP, 1:357, 380, 384).

Notes on Conversations with Benjamin Hichborn

1800.

Dec. 25. Colo. Hitchburn thinks Dr. Eustis's talents specious & pleasing, but not profound. he thinks Jarvis more solid.

he tells me what Colo. Monroe had before told me of, as coming from Hitchburn. thus he was giving me the characters of persons in Massachusets. speaking of Lowell, he said he was in the beginning of the revolution a timid whig, but, as soon as he found we were likely to prevail he became a great office hunter. and in the very breath of speaking of Lowell, he stopped, says he I will give you a piece of informn which I do not venture to speak of to others. there was a mr Hall in Mass. a reputable worthy man who becoming a little embarrassed in his affairs, I aided him, which made him very friendly to me. he went to Canada on some business. the governor there took great notice of him. on his return he took occasion to mention to me that he was authorised by the Govr. of Canada to give from 3. to 5000 guineas each to himself & some others, to induce them, not to do any thing to the injury of their country, but to befriend a good connection between England & it. Hitchburn said he would think of it, and asked Hall to come & dine with him tomorrow. after dinner he drew

Hall fully out; he told him he had his doubts, but particularly that he should not like to be alone in such a business. on that Hall named to him 4. others who were to be engaged, two of whom said Hitchburn are now dead & two living. Hitchburn, when he had got all he wanted out of Hall, declined in a friendly way. but he observed those 4. men from that moment to espouse the interests of Engld. in every point & on every occasion. tho' he did not name the men to me, yet as the speaking of Lowell was what brought into his head to tell me this anecdote, I concluded he was one. from other circumstances respecting Stephen Higginson of whom he spoke, I conjectured him to be the other living one.

Dec. 26. In another conversn I mentioned to Colo. Hitchburn that tho he had not named names, I had strongly suspected Higginson to be one of Hall's men. he smiled & said if I had strongly suspected any man wrongfully from his information he would undecieve me: that there were no persons he[1] thought more strongly to be suspected himself than Higginson & Lowell! I considered this as saying they were the men. Higginson is employed in an important business about our navy.

MS (DLC: TJ Papers, 108:18534); entirely in TJ's hand; with text between 25 and 26 Dec. clipped out, leaving only one-half inch of sheet at left margin.

Benjamin Hichborn (1746-1817), whose father was a boat builder in Boston, graduated from Harvard in 1768 and became a prominent Boston attorney. He made several trips to France during the 1790s, where he associated with James Swan in business ventures and attempted to sell land that he had purchased in Maine. He also owned shares and served as an agent for the New England Mississippi Land Company that invested heavily in the Yazoo lands. In 1791 and 1792 Hichborn served in the Massachusetts House of Representatives and in 1801 he was elected to the state senate. Citing poor health, he did not stand for reelection in 1803 (Madison, *Papers, Sec. of State Ser.*, 3:171-2; Kline, *Burr*, 2:649; William Stinchcombe, *The XYZ Affair* [Westport, Conn., 1980], 83, 85; John L. Sibley and Clifford K. Shipton, *Sibley's Harvard Graduates: Biographical Sketches of Those Who Attended Harvard College*, 17 vols. [Cambridge, Mass., 1873-1975], 17:36-44).

When Thomas Jefferson Randolph published his four-volume edition of TJ's papers, it caused a stir in New England. It prompted William Sullivan to write a series of letters in defense of the Federalists whom he believed TJ had maligned. In one letter, dated 16 Feb. 1834, Sullivan responded to TJ's notes on the conversations printed above. He noted that TJ made his accusations against John LOW-ELL, a U.S. district court judge until 1801 when he was appointed by Adams to the U.S. circuit court, and Stephen Higginson, a prominent Boston merchant, 25 years after the "supposed and imputed transactions and crimes" took place. Sullivan claimed TJ intentionally left his notes to be "published to the world" a half century after the event. Lowell and Higginson had enjoyed "the entire confidence of the intelligent and astute people of the state of Massachusetts." By putting these posthumous charges on record against them, Sullivan believed, TJ was indulging "his passions, to gratify his own personal hatred towards men who differed from him in political opinions." Although TJ clearly wrote that it was a Mr. HALL who provided Hichborn with the information, Randolph transcribed it as "Hale." Sullivan charged that without a Christian name or any other information, it was impossible to identify the accuser. It is also impossible to identify "Hall" with certainty (William Sullivan, *Familiar Letters on Public Characters, and Public Events; From the Peace of 1783, to the Peace of 1815* [Boston, 1834], iii-iv, 375-80; TJR, 4:514-15; David Hackett Fischer, *The Revolution of American Conservatism: The Federalist Party in the Era of Jeffersonian Democracy* [New York, 1965], 249-51). For Sullivan's full critique of the notes on TJ's conversations with Hichborn, see Sullivan, *Familiar Letters*, 375-82.

BUSINESS ABOUT OUR NAVY: Stephen Higginson, Sr., served as naval agent for the port of Boston at the time the Navy Department was established in 1798 and continued in the position until 1801 (NDQW, Dec. 1800-Dec. 1801, 374; Marshall Smelser, *The Congress Founds the Navy, 1787-1798* [Notre Dame, Ind., 1959], 151, 174, 178).

[1] TJ here canceled "should."

From James Swan

SIR   Paris 25 Decemr. 1800.

Having settled my Accots. with the Government here, and being declared Crediter of more than Two Millions of Livres—as well as recognized a faithfull & intelligent Agent, I presume to present myself to the Executive of the United States for the place of Consul General here. May I hope for your influence in my favor?—The acquaintance I have, with many of the administrators in Government—in the Bureaux & with persons of Credit & influence—the manner & appearance I am enabled to live in from my private fortune—the pecuniary support (in case of need) which I may have from my old partner D'allarde, actually Fermer General of the Octrois at Paris—all enable me to believe, that I realy can serve the interest of the United States, if I be honored with the appointment of Consul General. I flatter myself that no one can be of more service to the Citizens of America, than I can at this place; and I presume the Opinion of Mr. Pichon, the new chargé d'affaires, will coincide with mine.

I am with respect Sir Your mo. obdt st   JAM'S. SWAN

I make this application to you as Vice President: but I hope & expect, it will fall into your hands when President.

RC (DNA: RG 59, LAR); at foot of text: "Thomas Jefferson Esqr.—Vice President of the United States"; endorsed by TJ as received 18 Mch. 1801 and so recorded in SJL.

The French government appointed Swan its financial AGENT in 1795, and he arranged the retirement of the U.S. debt to France (DAB).

A letter from TJ to Swan of 27 May 1797 and two letters from Swan to TJ dated 5 June, both recorded in SJL as received from Boston on the 10th, as well as a letter of 15 Mch. 1798, received from Boston on 3 Apr., have not been found.

To Benjamin Waterhouse

SIR   Washington Dec. 25. 1800.

I recieved last night, and have read with great satisfaction your pamphlet on the subject of the kine-pox, and pray you to accept [my] thanks for the communication of it. I had before attended to your publications on the subject in the newspapers, and took much interest in the result of the experiments you were making. every friend of humanity must look with pleasure on this discovery, by which one evil the [more] is withdrawn from the condition of man: and contemplating the possibility that future improvements & discoveries, may still more & more lessen the catalogue of evils. in this line of proceeding you deserve well of your [country?] and I pray you to accept my portion of the tribute due you, and [assurances] of the high consideration & respect with which I am Sir

Your most obedt. humble servt   TH: JEFFERSON

PrC (DLC); faint; at foot of text: "Dr. Benjamin Waterhouse. Cambridge Mass."   YOUR PAMPHLET: see Waterhouse to TJ, 1 Dec.

To Amos Alexander

DEAR SIR   Washington Dec. 26. 1800.

Your favor of the 22d. did not come to hand till yesterday. I am extremely sensible and thankful for the marks of esteem which I recieve through you from your fellow-citizens & yourself, and should be very uneasy indeed were it possible that my motives could be mistaken for recommending all public manifestation of this [. . .] to be suspended until the actual commencement of a new administration. the more I have reflected on the subject, the more certain it appears to me that till then it would produce effects really injurious to views which we all wish to forward. I had the honor of explaining to you some of the circumstances which recommend this forbearance. since that others have occurred which strengthen the motives for it. it being difficult to enter fully into these by way of letter, my friend Genl. Mason has been so kind as to undertake to do it in person. I have been honored with a like invitation from another quarter. but those by whom it was expressed became entirely sensible of the expediency of postponing it. I pray you to accept for yourself and those to whose friendly dispositions I am so much indebted, assurances of the high consideration and thankfulness of Dear Sir

Your most obedient & most humble servt   TH: JEFFERSON

PrC (DLC); faint and blurred; at foot of text: "Amos Alexander esq."

From Alexandre Charles Louis d'Ambrugeac

MONSIEUR   Washington.—26 Xb 1800

Depuis deux jours je me suis presenté trois fois chez vous, pour avoir lhonneur de vous voir, et de vous demander, Vos ordres et Commissions pour Paris.

Je pars demain matin. et je Vous assure que cest avec un regret bien sincere, et bien senti, que je quitte le pays, sans avoir pu satisfaire Mon intensif Desir, dirai je ma Curiosité, *de Causer*, avec Monsieur Jefferson;

Si je pouvois etre assez heureux pour pouvoir vous étre bon a quelque chose, en france, Ordonnez. je me croirai fort honoré, de cette Circonstance fortuite,—je resterai Deux jours a Baltimore, où je Compte voir le general Samuel Smith.

Je n'ai pas besoin sans doute Monsieur, de vous avouer le plaisir que je vais avoir a Mon arrivée a Paris, d'avoir a leur annoncer les *Esperances* que les republicains Americains, ont relativement a Vôtre Election.

Jai lhonneur d'etre avec profond respect Monsieur Vôtre tres H. et t. O. S.   DAMBRUGEAC

EDITORS' TRANSLATION

SIR   Washington, 26 Dec. 1800

Over the last two days I have presented myself three times at your residence in order to have the honor of seeing you and of asking for your orders and errands in Paris.

I am leaving tomorrow morning, and I assure you that it is with a very sincere and deeply felt regret, that I am leaving the country without having satisfied my intense desire, may I say my curiosity, *to converse* with Mister Jefferson.

If I could be fortunate enough to be useful to you in any way in France, give the order. I should consider myself very honored in that fortuitous circumstance—I shall stay two days in Baltimore, where I expect to see General Samuel Smith.

I certainly have no need, Sir, to confess to you the pleasure I shall have upon my arrival in Paris to be able to announce to them the *hopes* held by American republicans concerning your election.

I have the honor to be with deep respect, Sir, your very humble and very obedient servant   DAMBRUGEAC

RC (MHi); at head of text: "Chr. dambrugeac—a Monsieur Jefferson Vice President des E.U."; endorsed by TJ as received on 27 Dec. and so recorded in SJL.

Alexandre Charles Louis d'Ambrugeac (1770-1834), the Comte de Valon du Boucheron, was en route to France from Saint-Domingue with communications from Toussaint-Louverture, but had no means of reaching Europe. Two days before writing the letter above, d'Ambrugeac had asked the United States government, in a request that John Marshall passed along to John Adams, for passage across the Atlantic. Despite the comte's expectations of a prompt departure, he had to wait to embark with his secretary and a servant until March 1801, when the U.S. government dispatched the sloop *Maryland* to France with the recently ratified Convention of 1800. Of an aristocratic family, the son of a career military officer, d'Ambrugeac had entered the French army as a youth, was an officer of

royalist émigrés during the revolutionary wars, and for his service to the Bourbon princes in exile was made a chevalier of the Order of Saint Louis. Those antirevolutionary credentials notwithstanding, he returned to France by 1799, when he evidently initiated his journey to the West Indies. He married a daughter of the Vicomte de Rochambeau, the Comte de Rochambeau's son. In 1813 d'Ambrugeac resumed his career with the French army (Marshall, *Papers*, 6:43; NDQW, Dec. 1800-Dec. 1801, 141, 147-8, 368; *Dictionnaire*, 2:543-4; *Biographie des hommes vivants, ou Histoire par ordre alphabétique*, 5 vols. [Paris, 1816-19], 1:61-2; *Biographie universelle, ancienne et moderne*, new ed., 45 vols. [Paris, 1843-65], 36:203-5; U.S. House of Representatives Report No. 1071, 27th Cong., 2d sess.).

The only other communication between TJ and d'Ambrugeac recorded in SJL was a "Memoire" from d'Ambrugeac of 9 Mch. 1801 that was received the same day but has not been found.

From Aaron Burr

NYork 26 Dec. 1800

after detaining the enclosed for several days in hopes of a safe private conveyance, I hazard it by Mail under Cover to Captn. Duncanson, a name less calculated to excite curiosity than that of T.J.—The post office in this City is kept by a Man of strict honor and integrity—Nothing is to apprehended here. how you are in Washington I know not—

We still hope that you have the Vote of your friend Col. Dewey of Vermont—He declared openly for J. & A. after he was appointed elector & before the ballots were given—Yet the most profound Secrecy prevails—

faithfully your friend & st.   A;B

RC (DLC); at foot of text: "Th. Jefferson Esqr."; endorsed by TJ as received 1 Jan. 1801 and so recorded in SJL. Enclosure: probably Burr's letter of 23 Dec.

William Mayne DUNCANSON, a friend of Thomas Law and a former business associate of James Greenleaf, had lost a substantial investment in land development in the federal district. Early in TJ's presidency, Duncanson sought appointment as marshal of the district—without success, despite support from Stevens Thomson Mason. Acknowledging Duncanson's loyalty to the Republican cause, in 1807 TJ thought that events in the failed speculator's past, his irritable nature, and perhaps too close an affiliation with Burr hurt his chances for even a modest government position (Allen C. Clark, "William Mayne Duncanson," *Records of the Columbia Historical Society*, 14 [1911], 1-24; Kline, *Burr*, 1:478n; William Mayne Duncanson to TJ, 11 Apr., 15 Dec. 1807; TJ to Henry Dearborn, 21 Apr. 1807; TJ to William Duncanson, 15 Aug. 1816).

MAN OF STRICT HONOR: Sebastian Bauman, postmaster at New York City since 1789. Thomas Munroe was the postmaster at WASHINGTON (Stets, *Postmasters*, 107, 184; Vol. 29:403-4).

Elijah DEWEY, a Federalist, cast his votes for Adams and Pinckney (Kline, *Burr*, 1:471n).

To James Madison

Dec. 26. 1800.

All the votes are now come in except Vermont & Kentuckey, and there is no doubt that the result is a perfect parity between the two republican characters. the Feds appear determined to prevent an election, & to pass a bill giving the government to mr Jay, appointed Chief justice, or to Marshall as Secy. of state. yet I am rather of opinion that Maryland & Jersey will join the 7. republican majorities.

the French treaty will be violently opposed by the Feds. the giving up the vessels is the article they cannot swallow. they have got their judiciary bill forwarded to commitment. I dread this above all the measures meditated, because appointments in the nature of freehold render it difficult to undo what is done. we expect a report for a territorial government which is to pay little respect to the rights of man.—your's of the 20th. came safely to hand. I am almost certain that you sent money by me to Lyon, which he sent to me for & recieved as soon as he heard I was arrived. as I was merely the bearer I did not take a receipt. I will enquire into it, and do what is necessary. no answer yet from R.R.L. cordial & affectionate salutations. Adieu.

RC (DLC: Madison Papers, Rives Collection); at foot of text: "James Madison junr." PrC (DLC).

Article 3 of the FRENCH TREATY stated that "the Public Ships, which have been taken on one part, and the other, or which may be taken before the exchange of ratifications shall be restored" (Miller, *Treaties*, 2:459).

A bill for the TERRITORIAL GOVERNMENT of the District of Columbia was debated in the House of Representatives on 31 Dec. 1800 and recommitted. The act, "An Act concerning the District of Columbia," was passed on 27 Feb. 1801 (*An-* *nals*, 10:868-74; U.S. Statutes at Large, 2:103-8).

R.R.L.: Robert R. Livingston.

From Andrew Alexander

SIR/   Richmond Decr. 27. 1800

The late Genl. Washington having given to Liberty Hall accademy now Washington accademy, one hundred shares in the James river canal company, which do not as yet yield any income, and the trustees being anxious to bring the seminary into useful operation as soon as possible; did authorise Colo. Moore formerly a member of Congress and now a member of the Senate of this state whome I presume you are personally acquainted with, and my self to procure a loan for the purpose of purchasing some necessary books and philosophical apparatus, and discharging some debts heretofore contracted—

I have been informed that a Mr. Short has some money lent to the James river company a part of which they are now ready to pay, and which is under your direction

I have taken the liberty, though a stranger to enquire if this money or a part of it can be continued on loan to the trustees of Washington accademy, on their pledging the future profits of the shares of the accademy in the company—with the addition of good personal security if required, for the repayment of any sum borrowed—

If you think proper to lend on these terms—be so good as to inform me by a line and for what time the money can be lent—and devise a way in which the business can be accomplished.

I expect to continue here during the Session of the Assembly, if you should write after it breaks up direct to Lexington Rockbridge.

It may be unnecessary to inform you that the trustees have by their exertions built a stone house three stories high with four rooms and a passage in each story and a fireplace in each room, and a stone house sufficiently commodious for a Stewards family and the Students to dine in; which they have nearly paid off by the help of donations and some other funds—

Last summer there were about forty students, and the number will in all probability encreas owing to the healthiness of the situation—

I am Sir with respect your &c   ANDREW ALEXANDER

NB. Colo. Moore being indisposed has not as yet attended the Senate

                                      AA

RC (DLC); addressed: "Thomas Jefferson, Esqr Vice President US. Washington"; franked; postmarked at Richmond on 28 Dec.; endorsed by TJ as received 1 Jan. 1801 and so recorded in SJL.

Andrew Alexander of Lexington, Virginia, represented Rockbridge County in the House of Delegates in the General Assembly session of December 1798-January 1799 and in each annual session from that of December 1800-January 1801 to that of 1806-7, when he left the legislature to become the county surveyor. He served again in the House of Delegates, 1818-22. Early in TJ's presidency Alexander was recommended for the position of U.S. marshal for the western district of Virginia. He was a member of the Belles Lettres Society (later Franklin Society) of Lexington, a literary and scientific discussion group that was probably in existence by 1796. Following a fire at Washington Academy in 1803, Alexander exchanged property with the school and sold it some additional land to give the institution—which later evolved into Washington and Lee University—a new home and what would become its permanent site (Leonard, *General Assembly*, 213, 221, 225, 229, 233, 237, 241, 245, 295, 300, 305, 310; Henry Boley, *Lexington in Old Virginia* [Richmond, 1936], 81; Ollinger Crenshaw, *General Lee's College: The Rise and Growth of Washington and Lee University* [New York, 1969], 36-7; TJ to Archibald Stuart, 25 Apr. 1801).

LIBERTY HALL Academy near Lexington, one of a succession of schools that originated with a classical school begun by Robert Alexander in 1759, received a charter from Virginia in 1782. Fourteen years later, when George Washington chose to donate to some educational purpose 100 shares of stock given to him by the James River Company, the trustees of Liberty Hall made a successful proposal for the grant. In recognition of the endowment, the institution's name became Washington Academy. Andrew MOORE, a member of Congress from 1789 to 1797, a former student of the school, and one of the original trustees when the academy was chartered, played a role in obtaining the endowment of Washington's canal shares (Oren F. Morton, *A History of Rockbridge County Virginia* [Staunton, Va., 1920], 188-90, 193, 244; Crenshaw, *General Lee's College*, 26-8; *Biog. Dir. Cong.*, 1523; Vol. 8:3-6; Vol. 28:275-8, 306-8).

From Stephen Thorn

HONOURD SIR   Norfolk Decem 27. 1800

The enclosed letters for you were particularly entrusted to me by the author who is my friend—I have been several Years in Europe on my travels, and returned to this port in the US. frigate Portsmouth, and had not some private concerns (which I was in hopes daily to have finished) prevented, I should err long this have deliverd them in person as requested, and as they are of Consequence I have at length put them in the post Office—I hope you will receive them safe—the two books are also from the author—I shall go from this to Richmond being invited by Gov. Monroe to pass that way, I have the pleasure of his acquaintance, and when I pass Washington, I shall hope to hear all have arived

I am with great respect your very huml: Sert.

STEPN: THORN

RC (MHi); at foot of text: "M. Th Jefferson. V. President of the United States"; endorsed by TJ as received 6 Jan. and so recorded in SJL. Enclosures: Thomas Paine to TJ, 1, 4, 6, and 16 Oct. 1800, all recorded by TJ in SJL as received 6 Jan. 1801.

Stephen Thorn (1771-1813), was a merchant-trader in Granville, Washington County, New York, during the early 1790s. An ardent republican, Thorn in 1794-96 solicited support among officials in France for a plan to retake Canada and encouraged a French attack on Quebec from Vermont. He chartered the *Olive Branch* to carry arms to America for the effort, but it encountered a British naval vessel and was forced to turn back. Thorn eventually abandoned his plans. In December 1796 he went to London to help Thomas Paine with a reprint of an open letter to George Washington. Upon his return to New York, Thorn was an officer in a county and then the state militia and subsequently served in the New York state senate, representing the Eastern District from 1804 to 1808 (T. S. Webster, "A New Yorker in the Era of the French Revolution: Stephen Thorn, Conspirator for a Canadian Revolution," *New-York Historical Society Quarterly*, 53 [1969], 251-72; John J. Duffy and others, eds., *Ethan Allen and His Kin: Correspondence, 1772-1819*, 2 vols. [Hanover, N.H., 1998], 2:502n; *Northern Post* [Salem, N.Y.], 1 Apr. 1813).

A letter from Thorn to TJ from Granville dated 6 Apr. 1792 is recorded in SJL as received 1 May but has not been found.

From Ebenezer Burling

SIR, Peeks Kill 28th Decer. 1800

I am sensible that in addressing a letter to you, as the first *political* Character, in the United States; I might be accused of unjustifiable *Confidince*. But, I have been taught to believe, from your own writings, and Common *fame*; that you, unite the Philosopher with the States-man. And I am the more readely induc'd, to troble you, with the result of my rescearches for obtaining an univercal Standard of Measure; as yourself have employ'd at times, your thoughts on the same subject.

I Confess that on account of the obscurity of my situation in life, I have been able only, to obtain a superfical knowledge of your scheme of the Pendulum. which has incline'd me to raise objections to it. those objections, I have, myself been able, so far to remove, as very much to discorage me in offering mine to the Public. for, I Concider that if the first Philosophical Character, in Our Country, Cannot introduce an improvement, that is a good one; I may well despair of gaining patronage for mine, tho I may think it more iligible.

But I will troble you no farther with tiresom observations. If you have never thought of the same thing yourself; nor read a description of it in the Monthly Magezine, Publish'd in N. york, it will be new to you, and I hope suficently entertaining to plead my excuse for the troble I give you.

I take for granted, that we agree upon the principles of Central forces; that when a body of matter, is made to revolve round its Centre, it is acted upon by two powers opposed to each other. It is an establish'd theorem, that these powers are subject to Certain Laws, of variation; but if I am not mistaken, what is said of Centripetal force is only true in theory, and when reduce'd to practice will be found to be the same in all Cases where there is but one Common Centre; and that the point where the Centrifugal force acts. as supose you suspend a weight, by a line held in your hand, and Cause it to revolve round your hand, in a vertical direction, your hand will be the Centre; and the Centrifugal force incras'd with the velocity, either by increacing the length of the line or the number of periodic movements, or both. but the Centripetal force is neither more nor less than its own specific gravety, notwithstanding different velocities.

If you lay the weight on a whirling table, and Cause it to revolve horizontaly, it will be found in practice to have no Centripetal inclination at all.

But if you hang the weight pendulous and Cause, it to move spiraly, then what is said in theory is also true in practice—I have been the more minute on this subject, as my scheme, has been Condemn'd on account of my asserting that Centripetal force was invariable under the fore-mention'd Circumstances. Least you should anticipate me I will come imediately to the point.

If the Centripetal force is invariable, and the Centrifugal dependant on the velocity; then by fixing the revolutions arbitrary, we Cause the increace of Centrifugal force to depend on the distance from the Centre. And visa versa, if the distance is determinate, the force is as the periodic movements. so that if a distance is giveen, there is (tho yet unknown) a Certain rate of movement, necessary to produce, a Centrofugal power equal to the Centripetal, or gravety of the weight employ'd. This being once assertain'd in all future experiments, the distance will be governed by the number of revolutions. To Conceive a just idea of my scheme, it is necessary to use in imagination, a Common whirling table, in a groove on which, place a weight, at, supose one yard from the Centre; let a line pass from this through the Centre of the table; to this line under the table, suspend another weight equaly pondurous. sit the table in motion and increace the velocity of the weight on the table, untill it acquires Centrifugal force suffcent to preponderate the weight oppos'd to it. then note the times of its movement, to govern the distance in other experiments. I trust that the differance of magnetude in bodies of equal ponderocity, will not vary the result in diferant experiments as the same meterials Cannot be used at all times. but I Confess this is a subject I want advice upon, altho it appears Clear to me that it is no objection, at least it is none to the plan I had first invented. but My favourite scheme, may possebly be affected by it,

This I propose to your better judgement as most worthy attention being more simple. in this I would make use of liquid in stead of solid weights.

But the Machines, for realizeing these theorems, Cannot be explain'd within the Compass of this letter, and my principle object, is to ascertain *if I Can* your opinion, of the theoretical principles of my scheme. And Conclude that if it should be so fortunate as to meet your approbation, you will Condecend to lay your Commands on me, for an explaination of the machanical part.

I feel the impropriety of attempting [to] draw you into a Corespondance, with an obscure *Mill-wright*, but believe, if there is real merit in the discovery, the importance of the subject, will excuse the attempt. for I feel at the same time, that if this is new to you, it will not be me but my proposal you will Contemplate.

I am with unfeigned respect, for you; and sincear happiness, on the fair prospect, that the day is at hand, when the improvement of Arts & Manufactures shall take place of *Political intrigue*

Yours &c.   EBENEZER BURLING,

RC (DLC); torn at seal; on a separate slip in Burling's hand: "Peeks kill is a Post Town in the County Westchester State of N York"; addressed "Tho. Jefferson Esqr. Vice President of the United States City of Washington"; franked; endorsed by TJ as received 7 Jan. 1801 and so recorded in SJL.

Ebenezer Burling may have been an Eastchester, N.Y., resident of that name, 1784-85, who was a Westchester County supervisor and a member of the state assembly (Ernest Freeland Griffin, ed., *Westchester County and Its People*, 3 vols. [New York, 1946], 1:323, 430).

In his July 1790 report to Congress on weights and measures, TJ proposed basing the standard unit of measure on the length of a PENDULUM rod that would travel through its full arc in exactly one second. That year both Britain and France also considered using that method

of fixing a standard of weights and measures. Although TJ resolved OBJECTIONS to the plan himself and asked David Rittenhouse to confirm his reasoning, Congress had not, in the decade since his report, adopted any standard of measure (Silvio A. Bedini, *Thomas Jefferson: Statesman of Science* [New York, 1990], 204-5; Ronald Edward Zupko, *Revolution in Measurement: Western European Weights and Measures Since the Age of Science* [Philadelphia, 1990], 137-41; Vol. 16:279, 510, 542-3, 611, 623, 650-74; Vol. 24:44-5, 64-6; Vol. 27:819-20, 822n).

A DESCRIPTION of Burling's idea, written originally as a letter addressed to Samuel L. Mitchill on 1 June 1800, appeared as "A Project for finding an Universal Standard of Measure" in the September issue of the *Monthly Magazine, and American Review*, 3 (1800), 185-7.

From Mary Jefferson Eppes

Bermuda Hundred December 28th [1800]

I feel very anxious to hear from you my Dear Papa it is a long time since you left us, and it appears still longer from not having heard from you, opportunitys from Eppington to Petersburg so seldom occur that I could not write to you while there, here I hope we shall recieve your letters more regularly, by directing them to City Point (which Mr Eppes thinks will be the best) we can get them the same day that they arrive there & in the expectation of hearing from you a little oftener I shall feel much happier. we have had the finest spell of weather ever known allmost for the season here, fires were uncomfortable till within a day or two past, & it still continues very mild & pleasant, it happen'd fortunately for us, as the house was not in a very comfortable state & everything was to be moved from Mont Blanco here, we have not finish'd yet moving & the carpenters are still at work in the house but we have two rooms that are comfortable & I prefer it infinitely to living on a rented place. we are still in anxious suspence about the election if the event should be as it is expected[1] I shall endeavor to be satisfied in the happiness I know[2] it will give to so many tho I must confess mine would be much greater could I be forever with you & see you happy I could enjoy no greater felicity[3]— but it is very late & I must bid you adieu my dear Papa[4] may every blessing attend you. your affectionate daughter   M EPPES

RC (MHi); partially dated, with year supplied from endorsement; endorsed by TJ as received 4 Jan. and so recorded in SJL.

[1] Preceding nine words interlined in place of "whatever is the event."
[2] Preceding two words interlined.
[3] Eppes here canceled three lines of text, almost entirely illegible.
[4] Previous three words interlined.

From Thomas Herty

SIR   City of Washington Decr. 28th 1800

Having transmitted you a circular letter some time since, relative to the propriety of the Legislature's circulating a Digest of the Laws of the United States published by me; I presented a Memorial to the House of Representatives to that effect—the Committee who were appointed to report thereon, namely, Messrs. Craik, Wadsworth & Grove, have not yet reported and I have reason to believe they trifle therewith, being three weeks tomorrow since the Memorial was presented.

I now take the liberty of soliciting your influence in this business; the only claim I make to your support, is grounded on my having been persecuted for my political opinions and which I apprehend is the motive that induces some of the Committee from acting.—Independent of any other consideration, I think it adequate to the end proposed; every member with whom I conversed on the subject, think the same.

I lived in Talbot County on the Eastern Shore of this State in the capacity of Deputy Clerk of the County Court, under William Stoddert Bond then Clerk; in the Fall of 1798 I had taken an active part in the election of Joshua Seeney a Republican candidate for congress, against the decided interest of my employer and others who professed friendship.—the various disputations which I had with those characters (who were decided Monarchists) relative to the merits and demerits as well of the then candidates, as of your moral and political conduct, which had invariably been the topic, procured me the names Jacobin, disorganizer &c and consequently an immediate discharge from the service. This opposition I made, not from a personal knowledge of the characters I supported, but from a consciousness of supporting principles congenial to my own feelings, and conducive to the happiness of our species; which I aver has since been (tho perhaps more circumspect) and ever shall be my guide, however it may operate against my private interest.

I had then no other alternative but to repair to Baltimore, where I issued proposals for publishing an Abridgment of the Laws of Maryland, which I transcribed and arranged after office hours, during 16 months that I had been Deputy Clk.—By the interference of a friend, I got the attorney general to examine the same, of which he gave a favorable certificate, and without which it must inevitably have fallen thro'.

The great expense attending the publication of that work, and the small circulation which it had contrary to my then sanguine expectations, prevented me from fully discharging the debt contracted for printing—the proceeds of the work now submitted to Congress, has not yet repaid the expenses attending the same.

This brief statement is thus candidly submitted to you, under a presumption that you will be pleased to consider it in its proper light; and being convinced that you are fully disposed to countenance the industrious part of society in laudable undertakings, I flatter myself that you will not consider the present application beneath your notice, but that you will be pleased to give it your influence and support, should you be of opinion that it is worthy of the same.

I shall write to Genl. Smith and Mr. Jos. H. Nicholson, (both members of this State) to the above effect; the latter I believe, knows something of my sufferings, he has been instrumental in getting a Resolution passed in my favor in the State legislature, relative to a distribution of the Laws of that State, and thro' him I got Mr. Craik to present my Memorial as the most likely way of succeeding.

I beg leave to subscribe myself Sir your most respectful and obedt. hble servt.

THOMAS HERTY

RC (DLC); endorsed by TJ as received 28 Dec. 1800 and so recorded in SJL.

Thomas Herty moved his office, where he drew up legal documents such as land conveyances, powers of attorney, wills, petitions, and manumissions "with the utmost punctuality, accuracy, secrecy and dispatch, and on moderate terms," from Baltimore to Washington in late 1800. A few months later he applied to Albert Gallatin for a clerkship in one of the government departments, declaring that he had been a "continual sufferer" for the Republican cause. In 1807 he became a land office clerk in the Treasury Department, a position he continued to hold into 1810 (*National Intelligencer,* 5 Dec. 1800; Thomas Herty, *A Digest of the Laws of the United States of America, Being a Complete System, (Alphabetically arranged) of All the Public Acts of Congress Now in force—From the commencement of the Federal Government, to the end of the third Session of the fifth Congress, which terminated in March 1799, inclusive* [Baltimore, 1800], following p. 562; Gallatin, *Papers,* 4:670; 15:393; 20:344, 481-3, 776). For Herty's role as secretary of the Washington Building Company, see Bryan, *National Capital,* 1:433-4.

The CIRCULAR LETTER Herty conveyed to TJ is not recorded in SJL and has not been found, but on 2 May 1800 TJ paid a subscription of $2.50 for Herty's *Digest of the Laws of the United States of America* (MB, 2:1016-17). The

memorial, in which Herty sought from Congress a resolution authorizing the distribution of his abridgment of the laws, is found in the *National State Papers: Adams,* 21:237. It was presented to the House on 8 Dec. and William Craik of Maryland, who chaired the committee appointed to consider the petition, brought in a report on 5 Feb. 1801, but no action was taken (JHR, 3:735, 787, 842).

Joshua Seney, REPUBLICAN CANDIDATE FOR CONGRESS in Maryland's seventh district in 1798, handily defeated the incumbent William Hindman, but died before he could take his seat. Republican Joseph H. Nicholson was elected in his place (*Biog. Dir. Cong.*; L. Marx Renzulli, Jr., *Maryland: The Federalist Years* [Rutherford, N.J., 1972], 206-7; Dauer, *Adams Federalists,* 312, 318).

ABRIDGMENT: Herty edited *A Digest of the Laws of Maryland, Being an Abridgment, Alphabetically Arranged, of all the Public Acts of Assembly Now in Force, and of General Use* (Baltimore, 1799; Evans, No. 35617). In the certificate dated 6 Nov. 1798, Luther Martin, ATTORNEY GENERAL of Maryland, cited Herty's work as having "very considerable merit" and "public utility." Martin was among 14 subscribers who each contributed $10 to Herty's endeavor. The Maryland legislature appropriated $200 (*Digest of the Laws of Maryland,* preface; *Digest of the Laws of the United States,* following p. 562).

To John Marshall

SIR   Washington Dec. 28. 1800.

I have the honor to inform you that a list of the votes for President & Vice-president of the US. has come to my hands from every state of the union; and consequently that no special messenger to any of them need be provided by the department of state. I have the honor to be with great respect Sir

Your most obedt. humble servt   TH: JEFFERSON

PrC (DLC); at foot of text: "The Secretary of State"; endorsed by TJ in ink on verso.

The first LIST OF THE VOTES that TJ received in his capacity as president of the Senate was from Pennsylvania, which he acknowledged on 8 Dec.: "Received by the hand of George Nauman a packet certified by the electors for the state of Pensylvania to contain a list of the votes given by them for a President and Vice president of the US." (MS in DNA: RG 217, MTA; entirely in TJ's hand and signed by him; at foot of text: "Geo. Nauman. from Lancaster to the Capitol—128 Miles"). The bearer of a state's official vote was entitled to an allowance of 25 cents per mile (U.S. Statutes at Large, 1:240), and TJ's receipt of most of the packets after the one from Pennsylvania is recorded by vouchers prepared with slightly modified wording by clerk Patrick Ferrall of the auditor's office. TJ signed each voucher after filling in the date (in most cases), the name of the messenger, and the state. Ferrall also wrote a separate statement of the payment due to each courier. The vouchers and statements—the dates of which reflect the submission of requests for disbursement, not necessarily receipt of the packets—have the following sequence: Virginia (by William O. Callis, 10 Dec.), New Jersey (Jonathan Rhea, 10 Dec.), Delaware (John Elliot, by 11 Dec.), North Carolina (William Tate, 13 Dec.), New York (John Van Benthuysen, by 13 Dec., TJ first dating the voucher 1800 and later adding 12 Mch.), Maryland (Horatio Gates Munroe, 17 Dec.), Rhode Island (Amos Jenckes, 22 Dec.), Connecticut (William Munson, 23 Dec.), South Carolina (George H. Brown, by 24 Dec., voucher lacking), Tennessee (John Kennedy, 24 Dec.), Kentucky (John Bridges, 28 Dec.), Vermont (Richard Whitney, 30 Dec.), New Hampshire (William Gardner, 30 Dec.), Massachusetts (Salem Town, by 1 Jan., voucher lacking), and Georgia (Moses Speers, by 5 Jan., voucher lacking); all MSS in DNA: RG 217, MTA.

SPECIAL MESSENGER: under the 1792 "Act relative to the Election of a President and Vice President of the United States," the electors for each state were to seal three certificates listing their votes. A person appointed by a majority of the electors would deliver one of the certificates to the president of the Senate at the seat of government before the first Wednesday of January following the election. The second certificate was mailed to the same destination. The third was placed in the care of the federal judge of the district in which the electors had assembled. If the president of the Senate did not receive certification of a state's votes by the first Wednesday of January, the statute required the secretary of state to "send a special messenger" to the district judge for the third certificate (U.S. Statutes at Large, 1:239-40).

From Julian Ursin Niemcewicz

Sir   28 Decr. Elizabeth Town New Jersey

I hope the letter I had the honour of writing you sir three months ago containing information respecting Mr. Littlepage has reached you. I hasten now to communicate you information I received two days since from Poland. My friend writes that Mr. Littlepage is about to set out for this Country and that he only waits for the payment of 9000 pounds sterg. arising from a claim he has upon the late king. the robbers who divided our country are to satisfy his demands. I think Mr. Littlepage may reasonably be expected in the coarse of next summer. Before I close this letter permit me sir (as to one who takes the liveliest share in the wellfare of America) to congratulate you upon the testimony of Confidence & respect the people of the U.S. in choosing you for their first Magistrate, have so conspicuously shown to you.

With great respect I am Sir Your most obedient humble servant

J. U. Niemcewiz

Tr (ViHi: Holladay Family Papers); in an unidentified hand; at foot of text: "Thomas Jefferson Esqe Vice President of the U.S.—City of Washington." Recorded in SJL as received 5 Jan. 1801.

Forwarded to Carter Littlepage (see TJ to Niemcewicz, 11 Jan. 1801).

Niemcewicz's previous LETTER was that of 2 Aug.

From Caesar A. Rodney

Honored & Dear Sir,   Philadelphia Decr. 28th. 1800.

Your esteemed favor of the 21. inst: was transmitted from Wilmington this morning to me at this place, where I generally spend Christmas week ever since my marriage with the daughter of Capt: John Hunn of this City.

I most sincerely regret the situation in which an equality of votes for the Republican candidates is likely to place us, but in case of such an event I should calculate with great confidence on unanimity among the States having Republican majorities in the house of Representatives viz. Georgia. N. Carolina—Tenessee—Virginia, Kentucke, Pennsylvania. N. jersey & N. York—8. I can not indulge for a moment the suspicion that N. York would swerve from principle on so all important an occasion or be swayed by any local considerations on the subject & I cannot even harbour a suspicion of the rest.

If I am correct as to the number of Republican States & as to the patriotic motives by which they will be guided we must have eight states certainly voting for the man whom the voice of the people has proclaimed already as our Chief Magistrate & to all eyes have been turned at this crisis: that altho' I should have much preferred, that the *Federalists* as they style themselves should have had no such opportunity embarassment[1] afforded them, yet I do not contemplate any great difficulty—From all I hear & see with us every man is for a President's being chosen for they say the question is not whether we shall have *this* or *that* administration, but whether we shall have any administration or government at all. Indeed the attempt would be too bold & daring, to deprive us of a head for one year, to ruin the countenance of any but perfect fire-brands of faction & would be veiwed with a degree of horror by every thinking man in the community. It seems very generally I may say allmost universally agreed by those who differ with me in politics, that Col. Burr never having been contemplated as the President, but only as V. President ought not to be appointed but that the Federalists should vote for the man intended by us to fill that office. I do not know what intrigues under various shapes may be going on at head-quarters or what influence, or system already concerted there by the Federal Partizans, may have on the mind of my friend Bayard (I call him my friend, widely as we differ in our political course, with great truth & justice, for in private life I have never met with a better) when he arrives, but I have lately heard him say repeatedly in company, that in case of an equality of votes between yourself & Col. Burr, he should not hesitate to vote for you & he has spoken frequently of the dignified impartiality observed by you in your conduct as President of the Senate with marked approbation.

If his mind be perfectly made up from my knowledge of his disposition & temper I feel great confidence in the path he will pursue. He will not yield up his opinion or bow down to all the low machinations which some less sensible on points of national or personal honor would readily stoop to.

I mention now only what has passed in mixed companies; for altho from habits of personally intimacy & friendship, he frequently converses with me in a confidential manner, I hold every communication of that kind sacred.

As We want therefore according to the preceding statement but one vote from a Federalist State & I do confidently trust that Delaware will act a noble & manly part, that she will rival her former conduct on the great question of independence & shine among the brightest stars in the constellation. What a glorious opportunity will be presented to a man possessed of a spirit of independence, to elevate himself above the low groveling views of prejudice & party & to raise a monument of character "*aere perennius.*"

In throwing my mite into the scale of Republicanism, I am actuated by no desire but that of aiding a good cause & of supporting those principles in which I have been educated from my earliest infancy & the practice of which I hope I shall pursue to my grave. At the moment of my entrance on the theatre of future life, a large estate left me by my Uncle was by legislative grasp destroyed. His accounts which were very extensive & settled in his life time were all rent asunder on his death. The friends of the revolution no longer filled our legislature & the influence of party accomplished the measures necessary to deprive me of his estate. My father Thomas Rodney was persecuted even into the prison where he was confined for 18. Months in the lowest state of health, Notwithstanding he had served his Country in the Councils in the field—had been a member of the Convention of Delaware in 1775. For a great number of years a member of congress and of the assembly the judge of the admiralty during the war a post which he had on the commencement of the Fedl. Government I think rather unadvisedly declined the acceptance of, for I believe Genl. Washington in every instance continued them—He had a Major's command I believe in the battle of Princeton & was in the engagements of Trenton & Brandywine—At the moment however when "not a [wreck?]" of my uncle's estate was to be left behind, the present Governor MKean the old & unshaken friend & associate of my uncle & father (& who has been a second father to me) & in consequence of whose removal from Delaware together with my Uncles death & my fathers circumstances embarassed by the war the tories acquired the ascendancy in Delaware stepped forward & saved me a remnant sufficient to put me forward in the world. My situation in life made me industrious & my progress in business was rapid beyond my most sanguine expectations—I have now arrived at that stage of practice in my profession from whence I can look back on those as benefactors who aided in taking away my property, for I would not exchange places to be put in possession of it all. I have uniformly followed the old rule "that honesty is the best policy" I have been open & firm in my political sentiments without giving offence to those who differ with me & amongst whom are many of my constant companions & sincerest friends. I have long since consigned to the "tomb of the Capulets" every personal resentment, as far as I know myself, against the authors of the destruction of the property which I ought to have inherited, & oppose them on the solid basis of public principle alone. At present with an amiable wife & five children to take care of & a father to maintain I look no farther than to the assiduous practice of the law on which I am solely dependent until I acquire a competence which will not be for a number of years & the little support I have given & shall continue to give[2] yourself (for I shall give every support in my power)—you will believe the declaration I often make to those who oppose you, that I am influenced by no desire of office or appointment but by higher motives that of contributing my share to the support of a system of just & virtuous principles & to arrest a reign of expence taxation & terror. I have troubled you with the preceding sketch as a proof of the sincerity of my declaration & which I trust will be a sufficient excuse for my not opposing Mr. Bayard at our late election. I am not so sanguine as to expect from you Sir, an immediate change of all the bad manners of the late administration to good ones, this must be a work of time, I look however for a stop, to further loans additional taxes & warlike armaments.

The Federalists say the people must now ask us to administer the government without taxes but I always reply if the course of increased taxation be arrested, we have reason to return thanks to the Deity for so great a favor[3] & consider you as worthy the confidence of all good men. Pardon the Author of this letter & believe me to be very sincerly Yours   C A RODNEY

P.S. I forgot to mention, that the canal will come before our legislature again this winter & with a prospect of success as we lost it last year by but one vote. Notwithstanding the opposition of Mr. Ridgely our Attorney Gen. the great leader of the Federal party in our house I carried the resolution in favour of it but he clogged the law so as to render it useless with provisions which he carried by one vote.

Gov. MKean is now here in good health & spirits & I have the honor & pleasure of dining with him to day when I contemplate receiving more useful political information.

CAESAR A. RODNEY

RC (DLC); endorsed by TJ as received 31 Dec. 1800 and so recorded in SJL.

AERE PERENNIUS: "more lasting than bronze."

Juliet feigned death in the TOMB OF THE CAPULETS (Shakespeare, *Romeo and Juliet*, 5.3). The reference is used to indicate that something is forever lost or forgotten.

PERSECUTED EVEN INTO THE PRISON: Thomas Rodney was confined in Dover

from June 1791 until 30 Aug. 1792. He served as a JUDGE OF THE ADMIRALTY court from 1778 to 1785 and acquired political enemies through his condemnation of the brig *Endeavor* (DAB; William B. Hamilton, *Thomas Rodney: Revolutionary & Builder of the West* [Durham, N.C., 1953], 32, 42-6, 51). For the Rodney family's business ventures during the war and Caesar Rodney's estate, see Hamilton, *Thomas Rodney*, 33-6, 50-1.

Rodney supported building a CANAL

between the Delaware River and Chesapeake Bay and introduced a resolution in January 1800 indicating that it would be "very beneficial to the agricultural and commercial interests" of Delaware as well as Pennsylvania and Maryland. As Rodney predicted in January 1801 the Delaware assembly passed the act to incorporate the Chesapeake and Delaware Canal Company (*Journal of the House of Representatives of the State of Delaware,*

7-25 Jan. 1800 [New Castle, Del., 1800], 27-8; *Laws of the State of Delaware, Passed at A Session of the General Assembly,* 6-30 Jan. 1801 [Dover, Del., 1801], 170-88).

[1] Word interlined.
[2] Passage interlined from this point to dash.
[3] Remainder of sentence interlined.

From Thomas Newton

DR SIR   Norfolk Decr. 29th—1800

I Received your favor of the 20th Mr Patricot is not here at present, he is at New York the letter shall be deliverd him or Doctr Toret his friend, in case I leave this before he arives, to assure you that it will give me pleasure to execute any of your commands, I hope is not wanting, beleive me I shall with pleasure obey—we have the French treaty at length from Brittain here, *wch* is not so disagreeable as expected from reports;—my wish is that it may be agreed to, war above all things if to be avoided, (without giving up the most desireable object independance of our Country) is my utmost wish. I still hope that no embarasmts. may happen to the Candidates for Prisedincy & that all will[1] be right & that we shall have you at our head, which appears to be the desire of the people. things are in our favor I belive in Europe, an Arival here, in 38 days brings intelligenge, that Brittain is excluded the Congress at Lunenville, which is removed to Paris; you can best Judge the Effects of this movement. I pray you present my best wish to Mr. W C Nicholas, & accept the same from

Yrs. most respectfully   THOS NEWTON

RC (DLC); endorsed by TJ as received 6 Jan. 1801 and so recorded in SJL.

On 4 Jan. 1801 Newton wrote TJ a brief communication from Richmond, returning TJ's letter to PATRICOT of 20 Dec. and stating that its intended recipient had become a resident of New York City, where Patricot could be reached through the firm of merchant Stephen Jumel. Newton also advised TJ that he would remain in Richmond through the session of the General Assembly (RC in

DLC; endorsed by TJ as received 10 Jan. and so recorded in SJL).

CONGRESS AT LUNENVILLE: in October as the talks between Austria and France were about to open, Bonaparte attempted to relocate the negotiation to Paris and exclude the British. The Austrians insisted on returning the discussions to Lunéville, but the British, their coalition against France crumbling, never sent a representative. In the aftermath of the French victories and Austrian capitulation of December, Austria and France concluded the Treaty of Lunéville on 9 Feb. 1801. In addition to affirming peace between the two countries, the pact guaranteed certain provisions of the Treaty of Campoformio and made additional territorial changes, including the cession of the left bank of the Rhine to France (Roider, *Thugut*, 354-9; Ehrman, *Pitt*, 388-90; Clive Parry, ed., *The Consolidated Treaty Series*, 231 vols. [Dobbs Ferry, N.Y., 1969-81], 55:475-82).

[1] MS: "will Will."

From James Monroe

DEAR SIR   Richmond Decr. 30. 1800.

In case you shod. have recd. the enclosed already, permit me to request you will be so kind, as forward them to Mr. Beckley; to whom I promised a copy of both papers: but you will retain them if you have not. It is mortifying the election shod. be attended with any circumstance, wh. checks or delays the expression of the publick will: but I consider the affair as plac'd beyond all doubt. It was natural to expect in the first moment of disappointment, that the party ousted wod. indulge itself in the expression of sentiments that were most likely to irritate their opponents. but I am inclined to think as soon as the passions attendant on disappointment subside that a different train of sentiment, and more correct views will succeed. It is certain they cannot defeat the object, altho' they may possibly occasion embarrassment, unless indeed our friends, or rather the friends of republican govt., shod. yield the ground after gaining the victory. This is surely impossible.   I lament that Darrelle does not take my land. I must however endeavor to do the best with it I can. we are in tolerable health; Mrs. M. in a more delicate state than the rest of the family. Mrs. Trist who is with us unites in best wishes for yr. health & welfare. Sincerely I am yr. friend & servt.   JAS. MONROE

RC (DLC). Enclosures not identified.

From Oliver Wolcott, Jr.

SIR,   Treasury Department December 30. 1800.

I have the honor to acknowledge having received from you a statement of the claim of William Short Esquire, for salary, as Minister Plenipotentiary of the United States to Spain.—It was my expectation that the question upon which this Demand has so long unfortunately been suspended, would have been determined during my continuance in Office—I have however been informed within a few days, that the suit against Mr Randolph has been again continued by the Circuit Court, and this event, must for reasons heretofore explained, still further prolong a final Decision on Mr Shorts claim against the United States

I have however taken measures for drawing into the Treasury, through the Agency of John Hopkins Esquire Commissioner of Loans the sum of 1315 dollars, which you have been pleased to notify as being in the hands of Mes[srs.] Gibson and Jefferson subject to my order; which sum, when paid, will be passed to the credit of Mr Randolph or Mr Short, according as one or the other course, shall be rendered proper by the Decision hereafter to be made by the Circuit Court

I have the honor to be with perfect respect Sir, Your Obedt Servant.   OLIV. WOLCOTT.

RC (DLC: Short Papers); in a clerk's hand, signed by Wolcott; at foot of text: "The Honble Thomas Jefferson Esquire"; torn, with missing text supplied in brackets from FC; endorsed by TJ as received on the same date as written and so recorded in SJL. FC (CtHi: Wolcott Papers).

Richmond merchant John Hopkins had been appointed COMMISSIONER of the continental loan office for Virginia in 1780 (Madison, *Papers*, 3:325-6n). On 5 Jan. 1801 Gibson & Jefferson informed TJ that they had paid Hopkins $1,315 as directed by Wolcott (RC in MHi; in George Jefferson's hand, including firm's signature; at foot of text: "Thos. Jefferson esqr. Washington"; endorsed by TJ as received 9 Jan. and so recorded in SJL).

From John James Barralet

SIR   Philadelphia Decr 31st. 1800

I am sorry that it was not in my power to send to you the likeness of Mr Volney at the time promissd Mr Groombridge in mooving had mislayd it amongst other Drawings, only found it last week, took the first opportunity in forwarding it to You, with Respect give me leave to be

Your Most Humble and Obedient Servant

JOHN JAMES BARRALET

RC (DLC); at foot of text: "Eleventh Street The Corner of philbert St"; endorsed by TJ as received 30 Jan. 1801 and so recorded in SJL.

Irish-born artist John James Barralet (ca. 1747-1815) studied painting in his native Dublin and worked there and in London as a portrait and landscape painter, book illustrator, and drawing master. By December 1794 he moved to Philadelphia, where he remained until his death. There he was acquainted with Robert Field, who painted a watercolor portrait of TJ, David Edwin, the engraver of two images of TJ, and George

Isham Parkyns, for whom TJ wrote a letter of recommendation in 1800. Finding it difficult to earn a living in the United States by painting and drawing, Barralet devoted much of his attention to engraving, illustration, and making improvements to the engraving process (Henry A. Boorse, "Barralet's 'The Dunlap House, 1807,' and Its Associations," PMHB, 99 [1975], 145-55; George C. Groce and David H. Wallace, *The New-York Historical Society's Dictionary of Artists in America, 1564-1860* [New Haven, 1957], 30-1; Henry Boylan, *A Dictionary of Irish Biography*, 3d ed. [Dublin, 1998], 12; Peale, *Papers*, v. 2, pt. 1:103-11; Vol. 30:xxxix; Vol. 31:xli, xlv, 446-7).

TJ offered Barralet five guineas for the artist's ink and black chalk drawing of VOLNEY, which was perhaps the original of an engraving published in 1796. TJ hung the work among the portraits displayed on the walls of the parlor at Monticello (Susan R. Stein, *The Worlds of Thomas Jefferson at Monticello* [New York, 1993], 75-6; Gilbert Chinard, *Volney et l'Amérique d'après des documents inédits et sa correspondance avec Jefferson*, The Johns Hopkins Studies in Romance Literatures and Languages, 1 [Baltimore, 1923], frontispiece, 108; TJ to Barralet, 12 Mch. 1801; Barralet to TJ, 17 Mch.).

Originally of Kent, England, William GROOMBRIDGE, a painter of portraits, landscapes, and miniatures who had also written a set of sonnets, emigrated to the United States about the same time as Barralet (Groce and Wallace, *Dictionary of Artists*, 277; DNB).

To Tench Coxe

[31 Dec. 1800]

I shall neither frank nor subscribe my letter, because I do not chuse to commit myself to the fidelity of the post office. for the same reason I have avoided putting pen to paper through the whole summer, except on mere business, because I knew it was a prying season. I recieved from time to time papers under your superscription which shewed that our friends were not inattentive to the great operation which was agitating the nation. you are by this time apprised of the embarrasment produced by the parity of votes between the two republican candidates. the contrivance in the constitution for marking the votes works badly, because it does not enounce precisely the true[1] expression of the public will. we do not see what is to be the [result?] of the present difficulty. the Federalists, among whom those of the republican section are not the strongest, propose to prevent an election in Congress, & to transfer the government by an act to the C.J. (Jay) or Secretary of state or to let it devolve on the Pres. pro tem. of the Senate till next December, which gives them another year's predominance, and the chances of future [ascendancy?] the Republicans propose to press forward to an election. if they fail [in] this, a concert between the two higher candidates may prevent the [diso]lution of the government & danger of anarchy, by an operation, bungling indeed & imperfect, but better than letting the legislature take the nomination of the Executive entirely from the people. excuse the infrequency of my acknolegements of your kind attentions. the danger of interception makes it prudent for me not to indulge my personal wishes in that way. I pray you to accept assurances of my great esteem.

PrC (DLC); frayed and torn; dateline supplied from SJL; at foot of text: "Tench Coxe esq."

UNDER YOUR SUPERSCRIPTION: a letter from Coxe to TJ, recorded in SJL as having "no date" but as received 3 Nov. 1800, has not been found.

[1] Preceding two words interlined in place of "an."

To Henry Remsen

DEAR SIR   Washington Dec. 31. 1800.

I see advertised by Campbell 124. Pearl street, Scatcherd's pocket bible, bound in Marocco. it is an edition which I have long been wishing to get, to make part of a portable library which the course of my life has rendered convenient. will you be so good as to get a copy for me and forward by post, sending a note of the price which shall be immediately remitted with the annual subscription for the Republican watchtower. I expect the book is dear for it's size. cover it securely if you please with strong paper to save it from rubbing. mr Denniston has more frequently latterly sent me his daily paper instead of the Repub. Watch T. it is not as agreeable on account of it's volume, and as I bind up my papers at the end of the year—indeed I am obliged to abandon all daily papers on account of their bulk. we have nothing new here except that Congress are resting on their oars. there appears to be a suspension of the public will and councils, until they recieve their permanent impulse. accept assurances of my constant esteem.   TH: JEFFERSON

RC (E. Garfield Gifford, Jr., Short Hills, New Jersey, 1955); at foot of text: "Mr. Remsen." PrC (ViW); endorsed by TJ in ink on verso.

The advertisement for SCATCHERD'S POCKET BIBLE available at Samuel Campbell's bookstore began appearing in the New York *American Citizen* on 30 Oct. 1800.

David DENNISTON began publishing the semiweekly *Republican Watch-Tower* in March 1800, and in 1801 James Cheetham joined him in the enterprise. In 1803 Cheetham became the sole publisher of the newspaper to which TJ subscribed throughout his presidency. Denniston's daily newspaper was the *American Citizen and General Advertiser*, which he established after purchasing the New York *Argus* and its semiweekly publication, *Greenleaf's New York Journal* (Brigham, *American Newspapers*, 1:608, 610, 684; Sowerby, No. 588).

From William Thornton

Dear Sir   City of Washington Decr: 31st: 1800

I have been too long acquainted with your Goodness and Benevolence to hesitate in making to you an Application in behalf of one of the most worthy Men of my Acquaintance.—I informed you of the Death of my much esteemed Friend and Colleague Mr: Scott, and I doubt not that many Applications will be made to succeed him. I have not heard of any, nor have I received any Application direct or indirect from the Gentleman in whose favour I take the liberty of addressing you.—Mr: William Cranch is a very near relative to the amiable Consort of our worthy President. He is a Gentleman of integrity & Ability, & would do honor to any Family. He has long been an Inhabitant of, and is well acquainted with the Affairs of, this City, and I recommend him as a Gentleman worthy of public Confidence & patronage.—Mr: Cranch's Connection in the President's Family may, perhaps, from Delicacy be an obstacle to his Appointment, unless recommended from a high Source. Your mention of him to the President, would, from your intimate Acquaintance & mutual regard, have great weight. If, in requesting this favour, I have presumed too much, I will rest my Apology on a desire to advance modest merit, which Apology I know you will at once admit.—

Accept, dear Sir, my most sincere Assurances of respectful Attachment.   WILLIAM THORNTON

RC (DNA: RG 59, LAR); endorsed by TJ as received 31 Dec. 1800 and so recorded in SJL; endorsed by a clerk: "William Cranch."

The death of Gustavus SCOTT on 25 Dec. had created a vacancy on the board of commissioners of the federal district. John Adams appointed attorney WILLIAM CRANCH, who was a nephew of Abigail Adams, to the commission on 8 Jan. 1801, but Cranch only occupied the position until early March, when on Adams's nomination he became a judge of the district (C. M. Harris, ed., *Papers of William Thornton: Volume One, 1781-1802* [Charlottesville, 1995], 550n; JEP, 1:387, 389; ANB).

Bill for Settling Disputed Presidential Elections

[1800]

Whereas on an election of President or V. President of the US. questions may arise

whether an elector has been appointed in such manner as the

[377]

legislature of his state may have
directed?

whether the time at which he was chosen, & the day on which he
gave his vote, were those
determined by Congress?

whether he were not at the time, a Senator or Representative of the
US. or held an office of trust
or profit under the US.?

whether one at least of the persons he has voted for is an inhabitant
of a state other than his own?

whether the electors voted by ballot, & have signed certified & transmitted to the President of the
Senate a list of all of the persons voted for, & of the number of votes
for each?

whether the persons voted for are natural born citizens, or were citizens of the US. at the time of
the adoption of the constitution, were 35 years old, & had been 14.
years resident within the
US.?

And the constitution of the US. having directed that 'the President of
the Senate shall in the presence of the Senate & H. of Representatives, open all the certificates & that the votes shall then be counted.'
from which is most reasonably inferred that they are to be counted by
the members composing the said houses & brought there for that
office, no other being assigned them; & inferred the more reasonably,
as thereby the constitutional weight of each state in the election of
those high officers is exactly preserved in the tribunal which is to
judge of it's validity, the number of Senators & Representatives from
each state composing the said tribunal being exactly that of the electors of the same state:

Be it therefore enacted &c [here insert the former clause.]

Provided that the certificate of the Executive of any state shall be
conclusive evidence that the requisite number of votes has been given
for each elector named by him as such. [here add all other limitations
on the preceding questions which may be thought proper; stating
what the two houses shall not decide.]

And be it further enacted that whensoever the vote of one or more
of the electors of any state shall for any cause whatever be adjudged
invalid, it shall be lawful for the Senators & Representatives of the
said state, either in the presence of the two houses, or separately &
withdrawn from them to decide by their own votes to which of the
persons voted for by any of the electors of their state [or to what per-

son] the invalid vote or votes shall be given; for which purpose they shall be allowed the term of [one hour] and no longer, during which no other certificate shall be opened or proceeded on.

MS (facsimile in New York *World*, 15 Aug. 1877); undated; entirely in TJ's hand, including brackets, with closing bracket of first set supplied by the Editors. PrC (MHi).

In 1877 Sarah Nicholas Randolph, TJ's great-granddaughter, found this manuscript in the papers of another of her great-grandfathers, Wilson Cary Nicholas, and had it photographed and published in the New York *World*. In a cover letter to the newspaper, she described Nicholas as TJ's "intimate friend and his mouthpiece in Congress." As a senator from Virginia in 1800, Nicholas used the first part of TJ's document—that preceding BE IT THEREFORE ENACTED— in his effort to modify James Ross's election bill, the legislation which sought to give a committee consisting of six members from each house of Congress and the Chief Justice of the Supreme Court the

right to decide on disputed electors. On 24 Mch. Nicholas laid his amendment before the Senate (MS in DNA: RG 46, Senate Records, 6th Cong., 1st sess.; in Nicholas's hand; endorsed by clerk: "Amendments to bill Supplemental to the act, entitled 'An Act prescribing the mode of deciding disputed elections of President & V. Prest. March 24th. 1800' "). It gave all the senators and representatives present during the counting of the votes the power to decide on the qualification of electors instead of giving only the SENATORS & REPRESENTATIVES OF THE SAID STATE the decision-making power, as called for in TJ's plan. Nicholas's amendment was considered by the Senate on 25 Mch., printed, and ultimately defeated. While TJ informed Madison of Nicholas's amendment to the Ross bill, he did not indicate his active interest in the measure (JS, 3:57-8; Vol. 31: 381-2, 455-6, 605).

Extracts from Beeke's *Observations*

[1800?]

Extracts from Beeke's Observns on the produce of the Income tax

	mr Pitt.	Beeke	
Landlord's rents	25,000,000£	20,000,000£	
fa[rm]ing profits	19,000,000	15,000,000	
t[it]hes	5,000,000	2,500,000	
mines &c	3,000,000	4,500,000	
houses	6,000,000	10,000,000	
professions	2,000,000	*	*this included
proportion for Scotld.	5,000,000	8,500,000	below in labour.
Foreign income	5,000,000	4,000,000	
Int. on funds.	15,000,000		
profit on forn. trade	12,000,000	8,000,000	
shipping		2,000,000	
home trade		18,000,000	
labour.		*110,000,000	

Private property. productive of income.

		£
1. cultivated lands S. Britain 600,000,000£ 　　　　　　　 N. Britain 120,000,000	}	720,000,000
2. tithes		75,000,000
3. houses not included in the rent of lands		200,000,000
4. mines, canals, timber, tolls &c		100,000,000
5. present value of income from public debt		300,000,000
6. farming capital, equal at present to not less than 　　5. clear rents, viz. pasture 2. to 3. arable 5. to 　　7. rents		125,000,000
7. home trade		120,000,000
8. foreign trade & shipping		80,000,000
		1,720,000,000

Unproductive of income.

9. waste lands, (excludg all incapable of improvemt 　　adequate to the expence, about 　　10,000,000 acres	30,000,000
10. houshold furniture	160,000,000.
11. plate, jewels & other useful & ornamentl 　　articles nt considd as furniture	50,000,000
12. Specie	40,000,000
	2,000,000,000

Public property.

value of permanent income, applicable to annual 　expenditure	160,000,000
value of income appropriated to extinguish the 　public debt	90,000,000
value of shipping, arsenals, national buildings, stores, 　credits, & all other assets after deducting all 　unfunded debt	15,000,000
value of provincial & municipal buildings, as 　churches, hospitals, bridges, prisons &c with the 　effects belonging to them	25,000,000

MS (DLC: TJ Papers 108:18555); entirely in TJ's hand; torn and probably incomplete; letters in brackets conjectured by Editors from context.

Reverend Henry Beeke first published his *Observations on the Produce of the In-* *come Tax, and on its Proportion to the Whole Income of Great Britain including Important Facts Respecting the Extent, Wealth, and Population of this Kingdom* in London in 1799. It is likely, however that TJ referred to the "new and corrected edition, with considerable additions" published also in London in 1800. TJ's second table above ("Private property. productive of income") was copied, with some omissions, from pp. 183-4 of this 1800 edition.

Notes on Potential Changes to the Constitution

[1800?]

war to require ⅔ of Congress.

power over the purse expressly declared a check

impeachmt.

all laws void after   years

no foreign ministers.

no foreign-armed vessels in our ports during war.

no protection out of our limits

a declaratory part as to all former breaches of constn

states make citizens—bankrupts.

council of appointment.

no appmt. to member of Congress.

electors to be chosen by people not by legislatures

     by district & not by a general vote.

quota—all taxes according to numbers.

exercise no power but relative to war

Senate new modeled.

MS (DLC: TJ Papers, 234:41909); entirely in TJ's hand, undated.

TJ asserted to Edmund Pendleton early in 1799 that "the fate of this country" depended on "whether it shall be irretrievably plunged into a form of government rejected by the makers of the constitution or shall get back to the true principles of that instrument" (Vol. 31:36). If the document printed above constitutes a list of potential revisions to the Constitution, it probably originated no earlier than the spring of 1798, when Madison corrected TJ's misconception that a declaration of WAR already required a two-thirds vote of Congress (Vol. 30:190-1, 239-40, 279-80). The attempt to block appropriations for the Jay Treaty had brought out the prospect of using the POWER OVER THE PURSE as a CHECK on the executive, but Federalists argued in

1798 that Congress was obliged to fund certain measures (Vol. 29:4, 70-1, 94-5; Vol. 30:155, 471-3). Constitutional issues related to impeachment had come up during William Blount's case (Vol. 30:58-61, 91, 163, 614-15). In a letter to Philip Norborne Nicholas on 7 Apr. 1800 TJ stated that once Republicans had sufficient strength in Congress they should promulgate a DECLARATORY statement of "the principles of the constitution," which could take the form of "a Declaration of rights, in all the points in which it has been violated" (Vol. 31:485). Protesting the Alien Friends Act, TJ in the Kentucky Resolutions of 1798 avowed that only the STATES, and not the federal government, had any say about CITIZENS, and he lamented the passage of a federal bankruptcy act in the spring of 1800 (Vol. 30:537, 545, 551; Vol. 31:443, 573). The state of New York, as he was aware before

14 Dec. 1800, when he mentioned the subject to Robert R. Livingston, provided an example of a COUNCIL OF APPOINTMENT. Problems with the selection of presidential ELECTORS, Madison and his Virginia colleagues said early in 1800, required constitutional, rather than statutory, remedy (Vol. 31:300n, 439-40). QUOTA as an issue in apportionment of taxes had arisen with the Direct Tax (Vol. 30:394).

Although in February 1801 TJ made reference to the possibility of a constitutional convention—see his letters to Benjamin Smith Barton and Monroe at 14 and 15 Feb.—the notes above, which do not address constitutional issues associated with a tied electoral vote, would appear to be of a somewhat earlier date.

According to memorandums filed with the facsimile of this document in the editorial offices, in March 1948 the Editors—specifically Julian P. Boyd and Lyman H. Butterfield—queried at least

four scholars to conjecture a probable date for the manuscript. Adrienne Koch posited that the notes dated from the last eight or nine months of 1800, citing TJ's letters to Nicholas on 7 Apr., Gideon Granger on 13 Aug., and Livingston on 14 Dec. She also related the notes to TJ's expectations of Republican success in that period. Douglass Adair, unaware of the details of Koch's response, affirmed that she would be the most capable person to infer a date for the document. By his own somewhat more limited analysis Adair tied it to the 1798-1800 period. Constitutional scholar Edward S. Corwin found that the document dated no earlier than the spring of 1798 and thought that the reference to citizenship related it to that year. Unaware of the specific evidence used particularly by Koch and Corwin, Charles A. Beard could not determine whether TJ made the notes before the ratification of the Constitution or perhaps as late as circa 1800.

Bill on Intercourse with Nations at War

[before 1801]

Whensoever war shall take place between two foreign nations, all the citizens or subjects of those nations within the US. shall withdraw from the US. within—months after the commencement of the war. on failure they shall be out of the protection of the law, shall be emprisoned in some convenient sea-port, and sent by such conveyance as shall occur to any foreign country which the Executive shall find convenient, excepting always that of their enemy.

No citizen or subject of either belligerent nation shall during the war, enter the ports or territories of the US. except as navigators of vessels in commerce, nor then shall be permitted to remain for a longer time than the bonâ fide necessities of their commerce shall in the opinion of the Executive require, nor to be on shore but between sunrise & sunset, under the penalties beforementioned.

No armed vessel nor armed men, either public or private, no prize vessel of either party before her condemnation or the effects taken in her, shall enter the harbours or territories of the US. in any case, not even in that of distress. vessels or armed men contravening this prohibition shall be obliged immediately to depart & in the mean time shall be so guarded as that no person may come from or go to the same. persons communicating with them shall be banished from the US. during the war; & pilots conducting any such vessels into our ports shall forfeit their piloting vessel & be imprisoned one year.

If any armed vessel public or private of either belligerent party, or in their employ, shall enter the American seas, that is to say, shall approach within 100. leagues of any part of the islands or continent of America, on the Atlantic side, between the Equator & the 45th. degree of North latitude, all supplies of provisions from the US. to the possessions of that power in America shall be suspended instanter, & so shall continue until the Executive shall be satisfied, & shall so declare by proclamation, that such vessel is departed out of the said American seas; and if during such suspension there shall be reason to apprehend that it's effect will be defeated through the channel of neutral ports, it shall be lawful for the Executive either to suspend or restrain supplies of provisions to any neutral places in America, according to the exigency of the case:

After the 1st day of the year 1801. no agent of any foreign power, whether diplomatic, consular, commercial, or special, shall be allowed to reside within the US. and if any one shall come on any special mission he shall not be permitted to remain longer than two months: after which term he shall be dealt with as is herein before directed as to citizens or subjects of a belligerent nation failing to withdraw. nor shall any such agent on the part of the US. reside or remain a longer term in any foreign country.

2d Dft (DLC: TJ Papers, 108:18560); undated; entirely in TJ's hand; with brackets added around final paragraph by TJ, probably at the same time he emended Dft; at head of text: "A Bill concerning intercourse with nations at war." Dft (same, 106:18115); undated; entirely in TJ's hand, written on both sides of narrow strip of paper; paragraphs numbered one through five in left margin, with unnumbered final paragraph added by TJ at a later date, which reads: "[qu. if this last clause would be valid under the constitution? and whether it's object might not be effected indirectly by 1. resolving that no money should be allowed for foreign intercourse. 2. disallowg. by law the indemnity of the L. of nations to the domicil of the minister? &c.]," with closing bracket supplied by Editors.

No evidence has been found to indicate that this bill was ever introduced in the House or Senate. It was certainly completed by TJ before 1 Jan. 1801 and he may have worked on it during the summer of 1798 at the height of the XYZ affair when legislation was being passed to abrogate the U.S. treaties with France and to suspend commercial intercourse. Debate on the punitive alien friends bill and Adams's refusal to accept the appointment of Victor Marie du Pont as the French consul general led du Pont, Volney, and other French citizens to leave the U.S. in early June 1798. At the same time Republicans believed that British minister Robert Liston continued to influence U.S. policy and encourage anti-French sentiment. In his correspondence in 1798 TJ noted that France had "given just cause of war" but so had Great Britain, capturing as many U.S. vessels as the French. In August TJ wrote Samuel Smith, "I have thought it would have been better for us to have continued to bear from France through the present summer, what we have been bearing both from Her & England these four years and still continue to bear from England, and to have required indemnification in the hour of peace." TJ here sought to establish equal treatment for both combatants through a position of neutrality and withdrawal (Vol. 30:223n, 227, 299-302, 360-4, 378-80, 395n, 397, 408-9, 418-19, 440-1, 443n, 448, 485; Vol. 31:151, 153n).

From Joseph Mathias Gérard de Rayneval

MONSIEUR, À St. germain en laye ce 1. Janvier 1801.

J'ai apris par M. Dupont, que Votre Excellence a reçu avec bonté et intérêt la lettre qu'il lui presentée de ma part: je n'en attendois pas moins des sentiments d'estime et d'amitié que vous m'avez constamment temoignés, Monsieur, durant votre séjour en france.

Par une suite de la confiance que ces mêmes sentiments m'ont inspirée, je prends la liberté d'écrire de nouveau à Votre Excellence sur l'objet de mes reclamations. M. Pichon, porteur de ma lettre, est chargé par notre gouvernement de les suivre auprès du Congrès. j'ose espérer, Monsieur, qu'il trouvera un appui en Vous. Vous connoissez par vous-même mes titres personnels (comme ceux de feu mon frere) à l'acte d'équité que je sollicite; et si je juge bien de vos principes, j'ose me flatter, qu'ils vous porteront a faire prévaloir la convenance de prendre ma demande en considération, sur la convenance de laisser intacte la révocation du titre primordial. Je vous prie d'avance, Monsieur, d'être bien convaincu de toute l'étendue de ma reconnoissance; elle sera égale au parfait et respectueux attachement avec lequel j'ai l'honneur d'être,

Monsieur, De Votre Excellence Le trés-humble et très-obéissant serviteur GERARD DE RAYNEVAL

E D I T O R S' T R A N S L A T I O N

SIR St. Germain-en-Laye, 1 January 1801.

I have learned from M. Dupont that Your Excellency received with kindness and interest the letter that he presented on my behalf: I expected nothing less from the sentiments of esteem and friendship that you had continually shown me during your stay in France.

As a result of the confidence that those same sentiments inspired in me, I am taking the liberty of writing again to Your Excellency on the subject of my claims. M. Pichon, the bearer of my letter, is charged by our government to follow them up with the Congress. I dare to hope, Sir, that he will find support from you. You know yourself my personal entitlement (as well as that of my late brother) to the act of equity that I am requesting; and if I judge your principles rightly, I dare to feel assured that they will bring you to make prevail the propriety of taking my request under consideration, on the propriety of leaving intact the revocation of the original title. I beg you in advance, Sir, to be fully convinced of the full extent of my gratitude; it will equal the perfect and respectful devotion with which I have the honor to be,

Sir, the most humble and obedient servant of Your Excellency

GERARD DE RAYNEVAL

RC (ViW); endorsed by TJ as received 18 Mch. and so recorded in SJL. LA LETTRE: Gérard de Rayneval to TJ, 24 Aug. 1799.

To Thomas Mann Randolph

TH:J. TO TMR. Washington Jan. 1. 1801.

I wrote you last on the 19th. acknoleging yours of Dec. 8. from Richmond which is the last come to hand. we have nothing from Europe more than you see in the newspapers. Congress seem to be resting on their oars, uncertain what to do. we think the less they do the better, and therefore concur in all adjournments, postponements & whatever else will rid of time. the election is still problematical. the Feds of the Essex school who muster strong in Congress, propose to prevent an election in the H. of R. by a division & to transfer the government by a law to the Chief justice or the Secretary of state, which will give them predominance for another [year] & the chapter of chances for further time. we have 8. states certain for election, and as two or three other States depend on the votes of a single ind[ividual] we believe we shall carry it. but if we fail in this [we] have it in [our] power, as a [dernier] resort, to prevent their plan by my undertaking the government in the character of Vicepresident.— we are extremely apprehensive they will press and carry their judiciary bill. it's effect will be very mischievous, as it would be so difficult hereafter to undo it. it is probable the Mausoleum and territory of Columbia may [whither] away a great deal of time for us, which is our best resource. we have [a] surplus of 2. or 3. millions in the treasury which they will be very much puzzled how to get rid of, while in their power. tenderest love to my dearest Martha, kisses to the little ones and sincere affection to yourself. Adieu.

PrC (MHi); faint and blurred; endorsed by TJ in ink on verso.

Later in 1801 TJ described the FEDS OF THE ESSEX SCHOOL or the Essex Junto as those Federalists who wished "to sap the republic by fraud" if they could not "destroy it by force" and "erect an English monarchy in it's place" (TJ to Levi Lincoln, 11 July). For a profile of the "Essexmen," named for the leaders who, for the most part, came from Essex County, Massachusetts, and included Timothy Pickering, Stephen Higginson, Sr., and John Lowell, see David H. Fischer, "The Myth of the Essex Junto," in WMQ, 3d ser., 21 (1964), 191-235. Harrison Gray Otis and Theodore Sedgwick, Massachusetts representatives in the Sixth Congress, were often identified with the Essex Junto (same, 195; *Biog. Dir. Cong.*).

During the closing days of the previous session of Congress, the House passed a bill calling for the erection of a MAUSOLEUM to the memory of George Washington in the city of Washington, but the Senate decided to postpone action on it until the next session. After much debate the House passed a revised bill on 1 Jan. 1801 and appropriated $200,000 for the project. The Senate amended the bill and when the two bodies could not agree, the measure was once again postponed, this time until December 1801 (*Annals*, 10:711-12, 799-800, 817-20, 837-8, 855-65, 874-5; JS, 3:94, 116-17, 119-20, 139).

From Joseph Moss White

SIR   Danbury in Connecticut Janry. 1st. AD 1801

Having had the Care of the Post Office in this Place, as an assistant to my Brother who is the Post Master, here, I have observed that Samuel Morse the Printer, so long as he continued printing a New Paper in this Town was wont weekly to send one to You, which if received by you I doubt not you must have noticed Several Numbers Entitled, The Inquirer   All upon the Subject of Religious Liberty, which appeared to me not only well, and pertinantly wrote: but also perfectly agreable to what it is said has been wrote by You in Your Notes on Virginia, as I have seen the same published in several New Papers, (for I have never had the Pleasure of seeing any of Your writings, except such extracts in News Papers &c lately made, on the one side to prove your being a Deist, and on the other to clear you from the Stigma:) as there appears such an agreement between what you & the inquires have wrote on this subject, and so perfectly consonant to my own thoughts on the same subject for more than 30 years past: I have for some Time been wishing you might see the same Persons thoughts on Religion itself: as it stands opposed to the reigning Religion not only of this: but of other Countries called Christian.

I have therefore at length ventured to send you herewith a Pamphlet wrote by him entitled The Bible needs no Apology &c which please to accept off, as a small Present, as well as token of my high esteem of your Person and Character: notwithstand all the calumny and reproach where with many have lately been endeavoring to load You, on account of what has been wrote by you on religious Liberty.

Whether you may approve of the peculiar Tenets maintained in the Pamphlet, or not; or whether a Deist, or not, I consider as unimportant Questions to me as they relate to You, in the high Station Providence seems to be alloting you for several Years yet to Come.   In which I have the highest Confidence in you (from the acceptable Services which you have heretofore rendered in the several Publick offices you have sustained) that you will gain the approbation of not only the wise & Good but even of those who now seem inveterate enemies, by that wise, and Prudent Administration which I am perswaded will be pursued by you.

That this may be the Case, and that Harmony and amity thereby, may banish from the union those Feuds and Discords which of late seem to threaten such serious and fatal Evils to these heretofore Happy and flourishing States is the hearty wish, and prayer of your most obedient Humble Servant   JOSEPH MOSS WHITE

P.S. The Author of the Pamphlet I send you &c is Daniel Humphreys Esqr of Portsmouth N.H. —Brother to David; with whom I presume you must have had an acquantance.

RC (CSmH); at foot of text: "Honble Thomas Jefferson Esqr."; endorsed by TJ as received 7 Jan. and so recorded in SJL. Enclosure: Daniel Humphreys, *The Bible Needs No Apology: or Watson's System of Religion Refuted; and the Advocate Proved an Unfaithful One, by the Bible Itself: of Which a Short View Is Given, and Which Itself Gives, a Short Answer to Paine: in Four Letters, on Watson's Apology for the Bible, and Paine's Age of Reason, Part the Second* (Portsmouth, N.H., 1796); see Sowerby, No. 1653.

Joseph Moss White (1741-1822), a lifelong resident of Danbury, Connecticut, studied divinity at Yale and was licensed to preach in 1761. Shortly thereafter he established a Sandemanian society, advocating the tenets of Robert Sandeman, who had broken with the Church of Scotland. Sandeman, a correspondent of Ebenezer White, Joseph's father, came to America in 1764, settling permanently in Danbury three years later. The Sandemanians, who met vigorous opposition from the established clergy in New England, asserted the independence of church and state and believed that one was justified and found peace with God by doing nothing but obtaining "a just notion of the

person and work of Christ." White voted for the ratification of the Constitution at the Connecticut convention in 1788 and served in the Connecticut House of Representatives in 1786, 1788, and 1794 (Dexter, *Yale*, 2:681; DAB, 16:329; Sowerby, No. 1653 in vol. 5; Merrill Jensen, John P. Kaminski, Gaspare J. Saladino, and others, eds., *The Documentary History of the Ratification of the Constitution*, 20 vols. [Madison, Wis., 1976-], 3:538).

MY BROTHER: Ebenezer Russell White, also a Yale graduate who belonged to the Sandemanian society. He served as the postmaster at Danbury until 1808 (Dexter, *Yale*, 2:679-80; Stets, *Postmasters*, 98). For the publication of the *Sun of Liberty* by SAMUEL MORSE, see his letter to TJ of 26 June 1800.

DANIEL HUMPHREYS, a Yale graduate admitted to the bar in New Haven in 1762, was also a Sandemanian and reportedly never stayed in the courtroom while the minister delivered the opening prayer. After the Revolution, he settled and practiced law in Portsmouth, New Hampshire, and in 1804 became the U.S. district attorney (Dexter, *Yale*, 2:471-4; JEP, 1:471, 473).

From Robert Patterson

Sir Philada. Jany 2d. 1801—

I duly received your favour of the 10th. of last month, and communicated your desire to the Society at their meeting on the 19th. I perceived, however, among the members, an universal wish of continuing you at the head of their Institution: For though they would highly prize the advantage of your personal presence at their sessions, yet they considered this as but of secondary importance—and, accordingly, at their meeting this afternoon, you were unanimously elected President of the Society for the ensuing year—Of this, however, you will be officially acquainted, immediately after the next meeting of the Society; when a report of the election of officers will be made—I am, Sir, with sentiments of the highest respect—Your Most Obedt. Servant   R. PATTERSON

RC (DLC); endorsed by TJ as received 6 Jan. and so recorded in SJL.

From James Lyle

DEAR SIR   Manchester January 3d. 1801

I wrote you a considerable time ago and then enclosed a state, how accounts stood between us at that time, in order that you might see the credits and examine, the charges of Interest, and the mode adopted which I beleive to be right.

I hope that letter got safe to your hands; your not writing me, I imputed to your having business of more consequence to attend to, and so many calculations &c might require more time to examine than you could at that time spare.

I am happy at the prospect of your being chosen to the highest office in the United States; I think, and hope there is no doubt now remaining.   I am with sincere Esteem

Dear Sir Your Most humle Servt.   JAMES LYLE

I shall expect to hear from you if the state mentioned got safe to you.

RC (MHi); endorsed by TJ as received 9 Jan. and so recorded in SJL. WROTE YOU A CONSIDERABLE TIME AGO: Lyle to TJ, 18 Aug. 1800, enclosing a statement of their account.

From Thomas McKean

Sir,   Lancaster. Janry. 3d. 1801.

This will be handed to you by Captain Thomas Mendenhall of the borough of Wilmington in the State of Delaware, he purposes to make a visit to the city of Washington and is desirous to have the honor of being introduced to you. Some of my friends in Wilmington have recommended him to me as a young Gentleman of integrity, of good information and genuine republican principles, and from my knowledge of him personally I have not been misinformed, and conceive him not unworthy of the notice & countenance of the friends of American Independence & of our present happy form of government.

I present you with the compliments of the season, and sincerely pray that the present century as well as the present year may terminate as propitiously for the happiness of the United States and of mankind as the last.

I have the honor to be Sir, with great regard, Your most obedient and most humble servant   Tho M:Kean

RC (MHi); at foot of text: "The Honoble. Thomas Jefferson"; endorsed by TJ as received 19 Jan. and so recorded in SJL.

From James Monroe

Dear Sir   Richmond 3. Jany. 1801.

Mr. Tyler a nephew of the Judge will present you this. He is a young man of respectable talents, sound in his political principles, and of perfect integrity. He visits the federal city from a zeal to be present on the interesting occasion which is at hand, and I forward his wishes by making him personally known to you. Being a member of our assembly, and having attended the last session, you will obtain from him information on every thing which occurred here that deserves attention.

I promised and shall send a copy, if I get one in time, of the communication to the genl. assembly respecting the late conspiracy of the negroes. But shod. I fail by this opportunity, will send it, by the next mail. yrs. affecy.   Jas. Monroe

RC (DLC); endorsed by TJ as received 12 Feb. and so recorded in SJL. PROMISED: see Monroe to TJ, 16 Dec.

From Thomas Mann Randolph

TH:M.R. TO TH: JEFFERSON,   Edgehill Jan: 3. 1801.

Your letters of the 30th. ult. 12th. & 19th. inst. arrived giving us the joyfull news of your continued health &c. each thirteen days after date: which surprizes us much being several days longer even than from Philad'a. — We are all perfectly well & have been so without interruption: not one cold has happened in the family this winter except a slight one to myself from rain: the habit of being in the open air which our gallery produces fortifies the children completely against colds and gives them all the appearance and reality of health.

Lillie has failed in hiring, except one single laborer; they could not be had under 25.£ any where & difficultly for that: his exertions were what might have been expected of him but the great price in our neighbourhood & the impossibility of persuading them to come up from below, which the facility of hiring every where makes allways a condition, have rendered them vain. — Craven arrived on the 31. Dec. with his family servants & farming stock. He found the house quite unfinished & was much dissatisfied, but the exertions the Carpenter & all of us have made to render him comfortable make him now tolerably contented. His family passed one night & a day without window or door & the walls even not completely filled in; but his wife has a cheerfull temper and bears every thing with the greatest good humor. They passed E.hill in the night without our knowledge and she would neither come back or go to Mont'o. next day lest she might draw off her husband too much from the scene of their affairs. I went next day on purpose to bring her back, her situation (a much advanced pregnancy) being entirely unfit for hardship, but she was positive tho perfectly good humored. He thinks more of the backwardness of the clearing you undertook to make for him than any thing else now; nothing but some grubing having been done; from what cause I know not as I was out of the County most of December; the one assigned is, the detention of the able hands by Richardson about the Columns.* Knowing your anxiety that Craven should be satisfied and succeed in his under taking, being convinced *that* depended wholly on the land opened, not confiding much in Powels engagement & having abandoned all hope of Lillies hiring hands I directed him to take the lads from the shop, leaving 3 full fires of the boys with Burwell at their head. If Powell does come they can be returned in a moment; untill he does, they will be better employed,

---

*One is entirely up but not perpendicular I suppose from the wrong placing the pieces of the Shaft, another half up.

such as are fit for it, at the axe than, wholly without control, in idleness & mischief, about the Shop. They will soon make excellent Axemen and the work undertaken for Craven will be advancing with the Winter. I have directed Lillie to look himself to those who remain at the nailery, for their work; Dinsmore keeps account of the nail rod and nails. It was absolutely necessary to do something without waiting to consult you for the Nailery was all in confusion, Lillie without a hand and Craven in despair because the work to be done for him was standing still. I have done the best possible in the case and do not doubt you will be satisfied tho you may make other arrangements when you write again.

With the warmest affection   Th: M. Randolph

RC (ViU); endorsed by TJ as received 8 Jan. and so recorded in SJL.

To Mary Jefferson Eppes

Washington Jan. 4. 1800. [i.e., 1801]

Your letter, my dear Maria, of Dec. 28. is just now recieved, and shall be instantly answered, as shall all others recieved from yourself or mr Eppes. this will keep our accounts even, and shew by the comparative promptness of reply which is most anxious to hear from the other. I wrote to mr Eppes Dec. 23. but directed it to Petersburg. hereafter it shall be to City point. I went yesterday to Mount Vernon, where mrs Washington & mrs Lewis enquired very kindly after you. mrs Lewis looks thin, & thinks herself not healthy; but it seems to be more in opinion than any thing else. she has a child of very uncertain health.—the election is understood to stand 73. 73. 65. 64. the Federalists were confident at first they could debauch Colo. B. from his good faith by offering him their vote to be President, and have seriously proposed it to him. his conduct has been honorable & decisive, and greatly embarrasses them. time seems to familiarise them more & more to acquiescence, and to render it daily more probable they will yield to the known will of the people, and that some one state will join the eight already decided as to their vote. the victory of the republicans in N. Jersey, lately obtained, by carrying their whole congressional members on an election by general ticket, has had weight on their spirits. should I be destined to remain here, I shall count on meeting you & mr Eppes at Monticello the first week in April, where I shall not have above three weeks to stay. we shall there be able to consider how far it will be practicable to prevent this new destination from shortening the time of our being together. for be assured that no considerations in this world would compensate to me a separation from yourself & your sister. but the distance is so moderate that I should hope a journey to this place would be scarcely more inconvenient than one to Monticello. but of this we will talk when we meet there, which will be to me a joyful moment. remember me affectionately to mr Eppes; and accept yourself the effusions of my tenderest love. Adieu my dearest Maria.

RC (ViU); addressed: "Mrs. Maria Eppes Bermuda hundred near City point"; franked and postmarked.

TJ began his trip to MOUNT VERNON on 2 Jan. and returned the next day, dining and spending the night at Gadsby's tavern at Alexandria, for which he paid $5.50, plus 75 cents as a tip for the servants. He crossed the Potomac by ferry at Georgetown, paying 50 cents each way. New Hampshire Senator John Langdon, another boarder at Conrad and McMunn's, probably accompanied the vice president (MB, 2:1032). For the journey TJ hired a horse from William Tunnicliff, paying him $3 for the two days (MS in

MoSHi: Jefferson Papers, undated, in Tunnicliff's hand and signed by him, on small scrap of paper, endorsed by TJ on verso; with payment noted in TJ's financial records on 7 Jan., see MB, 2:1033). Tunnicliff operated the Washington City Hotel located near the Capitol (Bryan, *National Capital*, 1:310, 519).

MRS. LEWIS: Eleanor (Nelly) Parke Custis, Martha Washington's granddaughter who grew up at Mount Vernon, married Lawrence Lewis, George Washington's nephew, in February 1799. Frances Parke Lewis, the couple's first child, was born at Mount Vernon on 27 Nov. 1799 (Washington, *Papers, Ret. Ser.*, 4:445, 508).

From Madame de La Marche

MONSIEUR [on or before 4 Jan. 1801]

La reputation que vous vous etes acquis sur un grand nombre d'esprit par votre naturel honnête et bienfésant etant parvenue Jusqu'a nous, qui sommes trois dames française de famille distingués autrefois dans la France, savoir de la rochefoucault et de la Marche que les malheurs de la guèrre et de la revolution ont obligée de se refugier dans ces pays ci, pour y attendre la tranquilitée à renaitre dans notre patrie. A cet effet nous avions il y à près de trois ans elevé une academie pour léducation des Jeunes demoiselles dans la ville de georgetown tant a dessein de nous rendre utiles au publiques, que dans l'espoir de nous procurer une existances, et dans cette vue nous avons depansé tous nos fonds pour faire batire deux maisons sur un meme terrain qui fussent convenables a cette entreprise qui avoit trés bien reussi près d'un an, Jusqu'a ce que des personnes de ce meme pays qui ont esperés s'etablir sur nos ruines ont renversé par de mauvais et faux propos notre pansion que nous avons etés obligées d'abandonner depuis dix huit mois, et n'ayant point encore trouvé a vandre notre proprieté qui est belle et qui nous passe 5000 dollars de dépanse, et que nous sommes toutes prêtes de donner a 5000 et meme quatre mils huit cens si on vouloit nous les donner comptant, ou au moins à moitié, et un bon pour payer le reste en six ou huit mois de terme afin de pouvoir assurer notre existance, qui par toutes ses circonstances est depourvue, est trés incertaine. hè quoi Monsieur par un trait de bienfésance & d'humanité qui vous est comme naturele, vous qui etes riche ne pouriez vous pas nous avancer cette somme, et vous charger de cette proprieté que vous trouverez à revendre avec avantage bien mieux que nous, qui n'avons point la langue englaise, vous adoucirai les malheurs de personnes honnêtes qui sont à la veille et au moment de manquer des choses les plus necessaires a leur existances vous acquererez un droit a leur reconnoissance qui sera eternel et qu'elles feront connoitre à tous cœurs sensibles et capable deterniser votre memoire telles sont les dispositions de celle qui à l'honneur de se dire dans les sentimens de la plus haute estime et de la plus parfaite consideration

Monsieur Votre trés humble servante   DE LA MARCHE

honorez moi Je vous prie Monsieur de deux mots de reponse par le present porteur qui doit en meme tems vous remettre un prospectus de la maison dont il vous enseignera la place si vous desiré venir la voire

E D I T O R S '   T R A N S L A T I O N

SIR
The reputation that you have acquired over a large number of minds by your honest and beneficent nature having come to us, who are three French ladies of families formerly distinguished in France, namely de La Rochefoucauld and de La Marche, whom the misfortunes of the war and the revolution have obliged to take refuge in this country, to await the rebirth of tranquility in our fatherland. For this purpose we had, about three years ago, founded an academy for the education of young ladies in the city of Georgetown, as much for the purpose of rendering ourselves useful to the public as in the hope of procuring for ourselves a living, and, to that effect we had spent all of our funds for the construction of two houses on the same site that were suitable for the undertaking, which had succeeded very well for almost a year, until some persons of this very country who hoped to establish themselves on our ruins, overthrew by evil and false rumors our boarding school, which we were forced to abandon eighteen months ago, and not yet having been able to find a buyer for our property, which is beautiful and has required of us an expenditure of more than 5,000 dollars, and which we are ready to give up for 5,000, and even 4,800 if someone were willing to give it in cash, or at least half, plus a bond to pay the remainder in a term of six or eight months

[393]

in order to secure our existence, which from all these circumstances is destitute, is very uncertain. Look here, Sir, by an act of beneficence and humanity, which is quite natural to you, you who are rich, could you not advance us that sum and take over that property, which you would be able to resell advantageously much better than we, who do not possess the English language, you would relieve the misfortunes of honorable people who are on the brink and at the very moment of lacking the things most necessary for their existence, you will acquire a right to their gratitude which will be eternal and which they will make known to all sensitive hearts capable of perpetuating your memory, such are the intentions of one who has the honor of saying that she has feelings of the highest esteem and the most consummate regard

Sir your very humble servant   DE LA MARCHE

Do me the honor, I beg you, Sir, of two words of reply by the present bearer, who will, at the same time, remit to you a prospectus of the house, whose location he will indicate to you if you wish to come to see it.

RC (ViW); undated; endorsed by TJ as received 4 Jan. 1801 and so recorded in SJL, where he also noted that he received it from Georgetown; he recorded the letter's author as "March Mde. de la."

Madame de La Marche (1746-1804) was Sister (sometimes Mother) Geneviève de Saint Théodose, a Roman Catholic nun belonging to the Franciscan order called the Poor Clares. Born Geneviève Marie Abert in Beaufort-en-Vallée, France, she made her religious profession at the age of 22 and entered the convent at Tours, which she left for Amiens in 1790. Two years later she and two other Poor Clare sisters, displaced by the government's measures against church establishments, left France for the United States. Landing at Charleston early in 1793, they traveled to Baltimore, which was the diocese of John Carroll, the country's only Roman Catholic bishop at the time. The three nuns hoped to establish a school but knew no English and left Baltimore for Ste. Genevieve on the Mississippi River. From there the governor of Louisiana summoned them to New Orleans. Geneviève by that time represented herself as the former abbess of the convent at Tours, a position that she never held. The governor obtained a modest pension for them from Spain. They stayed at the Ursuline convent in New Orleans for two years, then in October 1796 left for Cuba, where there was a Poor Clare convent. The following spring they returned to Baltimore and set about

establishing a convent. They relocated to Georgetown and opened a school there in September 1798. Geneviève's health failing in 1801, she moved to Frederick, Maryland. Recovering sufficiently to return to Georgetown, she died there in November 1804. In the United States she used the name Madame de La Marche (see below) and made her will, drawn up in 1801, as Marie de La Marche. She had no apparent tie to the couple named La Marche from whom TJ purchased linens in Paris in 1784, for at that time Sister Geneviève was in the convent at Tours, and the letter above, which was her only correspondence with TJ, gives no indication of any previous acquaintance with him (Abbé Jean Desobry, *Un Aspect Peu Connu de la Révolution Française de 1789 a Amiens: Le Monastère des Clarisses*, vol. 54 of *Mémoires de la Société des Antiquaires de Picardie* [Amiens, 1986], 84, 111-33, 175-6; Gabriel J. Naughten, "The Poor Clares in Georgetown: Second Convent of Women in the United States," *Franciscan Studies*, new ser., 3 [1943], 63-72; ANB, s.v. "Carroll, John"; MB, 1:564, 565, 568).

DE FAMILLE DISTINGUÉS: during their sojourn from France, Sister Geneviève and her two Poor Clare companions all used secular names. Two of the nuns appear to have appropriated family names to which they had no claim. Geneviève's baptismal record gave her surname and that of her father, who was a captain of the brigade at Beaufort-en-Vallée, as Abert. When she made her religious profession she called herself Marie Abert La Marche and gave her father's surname as Abert La Marche. When she reached New Orleans in 1794 the governor there understood her family name to be Bourbon de La Marche. One of her companions, Sister Marie des Anges, was born Marguerite Scholastique Céleste Le Blond in La Rochelle, France, but called herself, by the time of her arrival in New Orleans, Céleste Le Blond de La Rochefoucauld. After returning to Europe in 1806 she defrauded the Poor Clare sisters of Amiens of their property and subsequently appeared in various locales, drawing the attention of the police, as the Comtesse Le Blond de La Rochefoucauld. When confronted by a genuine member of the La Rochefoucauld family she claimed that she had been born in Saint-Domingue and no longer had proof of her lineage. She died in 1827. The third of the Poor Clares in Georgetown, Mother Marie Agnès de Saint Hugues, was the abbess of Amiens but played the least noticeable role during the nuns' residence in North America. During her absence from France, to which she returned in 1804, she used her recorded baptismal name, Marie Françoise Chevalier (Desobry, *Un Aspect*, 30, 61, 84, 111, 113, 114n, 126n, 132-3, 149, 175-84).

UNE ACADEMIE: a March 1799 advertisement for the academy of Madame de La Marche, like her letter to TJ above, said nothing of any religious affiliation. The advertisement, in fact, referred to Leonard Neale, who was Carroll's vicar general, the head of Georgetown College, and a future bishop, simply as a helpful "Mr. Leonard Neall." Although Madame de La Marche promised the addition of an English-educated lady to the school's faculty to teach grammar and embroidery and a "French Clergyman, very eminent in science, who will teach the French Languages, Geography, Writing and Arithmetic," evidence of students is lacking and the advertisement for the school also promoted La Marche's sale of salves and eye wash. The Poor Clares rented the property they used for the school from John Threlkeld, who in June 1799 offered the three and a half adjoining lots, with two "handsome" dwelling houses, a fish pond, an orchard, and assorted outbuildings, for sale. The Poor Clares, who had a $300 subvention from St. Mary's Seminary in Baltimore, apparently some money provided by the convent in Havana, and perhaps some resources they had brought from France, purchased the property in August 1800. Title was in Geneviève's name as Madame de La Marche, and she subsequently willed her assets to Le Blond. The reputedly English-educated woman expected to join the academy's staff in 1799 was likely one of three women from Ireland who intended to become nuns. Neale temporarily assigned them to work with the Poor Clares. As the academy failed to thrive the "Pious Ladies," as the Irish women were called, assumed the leading role in the Catholic church's efforts toward female education in Georgetown. They purchased the Poor Clares' academy site and it became the Convent of the Visitation (Georgetown *Centinel of Liberty*, 8 Mch., 25 June 1799; Desobry, *Un Aspect*, 126n, 128, 129-131, 133; Naughten, "Poor Clares," 67-70; George Parsons Lathrop and Rose Hawthorne Lathrop, *A Story of Courage: Annals of the Georgetown Convent of the Visitation of the Blessed Virgin Mary* [Boston, 1894], 146-53; ANB, s.v. "Neale, Leonard").

From Joseph Yznardi, Sr.

RESPECTED SIR,   Philadelphia 4th January 1801

I had this honor on the 21. of october last, since which I have continued a convalesents, depriving me the pleasure of personally paying you my respects, as I have long wished and continue to do so, when the inclemency of the season moderates in mean time I am happy to avail myself of the goodness of General Smith, now in this City, to express to you the satisfaction I have in the current report that you will be elected to the Presidency of this Government, for their public good and other Nations in amity with them.

The inclosed Copy manifests the charge that the Minister of State of HCM placed under my care from the disopinion arising to Mr. Yrujo, by Mr. Pickerings representation, in my view without proper foundation, for he certainly merits to the contrary, from the knowledge I now have of the motives that caused this misunderstanding, and my particular acquaintance with this Gentleman and his personal talents, and not having it in my power to reveal the Secrecy of my Commission, I have represented to HCM, what I thought in justice since my arrival to this Continent

I have communicated with Mr. Marshall, and delivered him a Copy of my Credential, assuring him also of the best wishes from HCM towards a good understanding with the US—and have referred him to the new Minister appointed Mr. Orosco with whom I am to confer on different points, which I think proper to communicate to you, for your private government, until the arrival of said Gentleman, Conceiving it my duty to do so, in Consequence of my said Commission, as I have wrote to Mr. Urquijo, HCM, Secretary of State of the tranquility good understanding &ca. existing in this Government towards that, as far as I could learn by my Conference with Mr. Marshall, from whom I expect an Official acknowledgment of my presentation, to manifest to HCM. Minister that I have complied with his wishes.

Having read the treaty concluded between this Country and France and hearing thro' some public opinions that it possibly would not be ratified, which I shall feel for from the alliance existing between Spain and that Country, and fearing the disagreeable consequences that probably might be the result, desirous to see in Amity the three Nations, that in a body could defend their just rights—the general benefit of which, If I possessed a public power I think I could easily explain: I hope for your Excuse touching on this subject while I have the honor to be with Great respect and veneration

Sir Your most obedient and very humble Servant

JOSEF YZNARDY

RC (DLC); in an unidentified hand, signed by Yznardi; at foot of text: "Rt. Honble Thomas Jefferson"; endorsed by TJ, on enclosure, as received 8 Jan. 1801 and so recorded in SJL. Enclosure: Mariano Luis de Urquijo to Yznardi, 13 Jan. 1800, noting that Spain wished to maintain good harmony with the United

States and authorizing Yznardi to assure the government that any difficulties would be resolved "on the best terms of friendship"; to obtain better intelligence from the United States, as had previously been the case through David Humphreys, the Spanish government was sending a person who would "expressly carry proper instructions, more Enlarged" (Tr in DLC in TJ Papers, 106:18128-9; in Spanish with English translation, both in the same hand as the letter above).

Yznardi had acted as deputy to his son, who received the appointment as U.S. consul at Cadiz in 1793 (Vol. 27:60n). The letter of the 21st of OCTOBER LAST was probably one of October 1800 recorded in SJL as received from Philadelphia on 3 Nov. along with another from Yznardi dated 1 Oct.; neither letter has been found. On 22 Sep. TJ acknowledged receipt of Yznardi's communication of 20 Aug.—probably a letter, not found, recorded in SJL as written 24 Aug. and received from Baltimore on 5 Sep.—and noted that he had received no other correspondence from him since a letter of 5 Sep. 1799 that he had received when he was about to leave Philadelphia—again, not found but recorded in SJL as received from Cadiz on 14 May 1800. TJ assured Yznardi that the charges against him in the newspapers had made no impression, for rumors in the press merited little confidence (Tr in AHN: Papeles de Estado, Legajo 3891 bis, expediente 1, no. 109, in Spanish, possibly only an extract, recipient identified as "J.Y."; Miguel Gómez del Campillo, comp., *Relaciones Diplomáticas entre España y los Estados Unidos*, 2 vols. [Madrid, 1944-46], 1:121-2; 2:490). Yznardi had come to the United States to answer charges made by several people, including Joseph Israel, master of the *Trial*, and John M. Pintard, U.S. consul at Madeira, who owned the vessel, that he had failed to protect the rights of American ships at Cadiz. Timothy Pickering wrote to John Marshall in Yznardi's defense, saying that American captains were "too apt to expect & demand unreasonable attentions and indulgences" and noting that any consul resisting "their demands, would not fail to incur their displeasure" (Marshall, *Papers*, 6:55-6; Yznardi to John Marshall, 10 Nov. 1800, enclosing "Vindication to the charges," in DNA: RG 59, CD; see also Sowerby, No. 3267, a printed set of documents that TJ catalogued for his library as Yznardi's "Letter in vindication of his conduct as pro-consul at Cadiz," p. 23; Vol. 27:60n).

Yznardi had previously sent the secretary of state a copy of the letter from Urquijo, who was Spain's MINISTER OF STATE for foreign affairs until late in 1800. On 27 Aug. Marshall forwarded it to President Adams with the observation that it "merits some attention. The conduct of the spanish government towards that of the United States has furnished cause for complaints much more serious & extensive than have ever been made. To me it seems that compensation for every American vessel condemnd by the french consular courts in the dominions of spain is justly demandable from the spanish government & that it is not yet too late to make the demand" (Marshall, *Papers*, 4:247-8; Germán Bleiberg, ed., *Diccionario de Historia de España*, 2d ed., 3 vols. [1968-69], 3:851-2; Salvador Bermúdez de Castro y O'Lawlor, Marqués de Lema, *Antecedentes Políticos y Diplomáticos de los Sucesos de 1808*, 2d ed. [Madrid, 1912], 13).

HCM: His Catholic Majesty. For the disagreement between Spanish diplomat Carlos Fernando Martínez de Irujo (YRUJO) and Timothy Pickering over implementation of Pinckney's Treaty, see Vol. 30:53-5. Adams requested Irujo's recall, so in 1800 the Spanish government named Nicolás Blasco de Orozco as the NEW MINISTER to the United States, appointing Irujo minister to the Cisalpine Republic. Irujo, however, elected to stay in America until his replacement arrived. That did not occur before TJ's inauguration, and at TJ's request the Spanish retained Irujo as minister to the U.S. (Samuel F. Bemis, *Pinckney's Treaty: America's Advantage from Europe's Distress, 1783-1800* [New Haven, 1960], 309n; Gómez del Campillo, *Relaciones Diplomáticas*, 1:120, 251; 2:481, 496; Vol. 30:194n; TJ to Yznardi, 26 Mch. 1801).

In Spanish the name of the Yznardi family, which was of Italian origin, is usually spelled Iznardi (sometimes Iznardí), and Joseph or Josef generally appears as José. However, for consistency despite variations in signatures and contemporary usage, we have continued to employ for both father and son the form used by the younger man in his earlier correspondence with TJ: Joseph Yznardi (Alberto García Carraffa and Arturo García Carraffa, *Enciclopedia Heráldica y Genealógica Hispano-Americana*, 88 vols. [Madrid, 1952-63], 46:175; Julián B. Ruiz Rivera, *El Consulado de Cádiz: Matrícula de Comerciantes, 1730-1823* [Cadiz, 1988], 172; Gómez del Campillo, *Relaciones Diplomáticas*, 1:114-15; 2:501-2; Vol. 27:499).

To Andrew Alexander

[SIR]   Washington Jan. 5. 1801.

[Your] favor of Dec. 27. is duly recieved. I am sorry that mr Short's instructions do not permit the disposing of the money now payable by the James river company in the manner you propose. he has directed it to be invested in a particular way for which arrangements are already made [or] I should have been happy to have been authorised to accomodate the academy at Lexington, as no one wishes more sincerely than I do to see education in our state put on a better footing: and especially to see that our youth [are not] put under the tuition of persons hostile to the republican principles of our government; of persons who wish to transfer all the powers of the states to [the general] government & all the powers of that government to it's [executive] [. . .] the depositories of the public authority as far removed as possible [from] the controul of the people. with such principles, the more learned, the [. . .] [ingenious] a tutor is, the more able is he to [debauch] the political [prin]ciples of his pupils, and the most unlettered ignorance will make a better citizen than his perverted learning. I hazard these sentiments, not with a view to the seminary in which yourself & Colo. Moore have a direction, [which] I have no doubt you have duly attended to there, but with a view to the [. . .]ation of the United States in this respect, wherein it will be found [that] with a few exceptions only, the public institutions of science are in the hands [of] men unfriendly to those principles the establishment & the recovery of [which] have cost us so much. it is labor lost, if the rising generation, to whom we are to deliver over the government, are prepared by ourselves to pervert it's principles. I ask pardon for permitting myself to go into these [. . .] in truth [no] circumstance in our situation gives me [so] much [pain] [. . .] [the neglect?] of principles in the public [. . .] give me the education of your

youth & I will [. . .] whatever [. . .] of government you please [. . .]
you can [. . .] [of the majority]
    accept [. . .]   TH: JEFFERSON

PrC (DLC); torn, with several phrases of two or more words lost; at foot of text:
"[Andrew Alexander]."

From James Thomson Callender

SIR   Richmond Jail January 5th. 1800 [i.e. 1801]
An uncommon alarm has been spread here that congress were to
annul the Presidential election. I had sent to the Examiner a piece on
that business, when upon the arrival of *this* news, I was advised to
withdraw it, untill I should see if it was true!

my answer was: "it is a part of my constitution, it is interwoven
with my intellectual existence, that the greater opposition is, I become the more perfectly determined to Strike it in the face; and I
shall let the world see that if I were to stay here for thirty years, I
shall not be moved by one hair's breadth from the prosecution of my
purpose." and so I sent up a postscript. The whole is five columns.
Excuse the freedom of this letter.

Wishing You many happy returns of the season I have the honour
to be Sir Your most obedt. & humble servant
                    JAS. T. CALLENDER.

RC (DLC). Recorded in SJL as received 9 Jan. 1801.

From Benjamin Hichborn

MY DEAR SIR,   Philadelphia Janury 5, 1801
I coud not leave this place without intimating to you a Circumstance, which gives me some little uneasiness—Colo: Burr is in the
house with me & Genl: Smith from Baltimore has been here—I am
convinced that some of our Friends, as they call themselves are willing to join the other party in Case they shoud unite in favor of Colo:
Burr——I was informed as I passed thro' Willmington[1] that Mr Bayard their Representative was decidedly in favor of your Election, if so
I think the question is settled—God grant it may be so!—

I am yours with esteem   B HICHBORN

RC (DLC); endorsed by TJ as received 8 Jan. and so recorded in SJL.

Aaron BURR met with Samuel SMITH in Philadelphia during the first weekend in January. Smith was surprised to learn that Burr no longer disclaimed "all competition" to the presidency or shunned the Federalist overtures as he had previously done in his widely publicized letter of 16 Dec. to Smith. He now informed Smith that he had decided to accept the presidency if he won the vote in the House (Kline, *Burr*, 1:471, 483). On 5 Jan. the *Philadelphia Gazette* reported that Burr "was heard to insinuate that he felt as competent to the exercise of the Presidential functions as Mr. Jefferson." The report continued: "In this case, his appearing to decline the election, resembles the modesty of Caesar, who refused the crown *merely to have it the more pressed upon him!*"

[1] Preceding five words interlined.

From John Hoomes

DEAR SIR   Richmond Jany 5th 1801

I saw Mr. Eppes a few days ago who informed me you were in want of an elegant saddle horse, I have one to dispose of, that I purchased for a friend in Philadelphia; my anziety to get that gentleman a very fine horse prevented my making a purchase for him *so soon* as he wished, & he has supplyed himself there, for which reason this horse is for sale. I think him the finest horse *I Know* in the state, he is 7 years old, near 16 hands high, a very fine presence, gay, but perfectly gentle, & his colour bay. If I *rightly* recollect the roan horse you formerly rode, this is his equal if not his superior. I gave 81£ this currency for him, have been at some expence, in sending for, & keeping him, & suppose he stands me about $300 for which sum you may have him; before I was authorized to sell him a gentleman from S. Carolina who called at my house offered me $400 for him I have rode him but a very small distance never more (perhaps) than half a mile on a good road, that I can only say he trotted & galloped that distance, extreamly well, all who see him are delighted with the horse, & suppose he would answer *well* your purpose, any derections that you think proper to give shall be attended to by

Dear Sir Yr Hble Sevt   JOHN HOOMES

RC (MHi); endorsed by TJ as received 9 Jan. and so recorded in SJL.

TJ authorized John Wayles EPPES to purchase a horse for him with bills on Gibson & Jefferson at ninety days (TJ to George Jefferson, 7 June 1800). TJ replied to Hoomes on 12 Jan. that he relied completely on Hoomes's judgment that the horse proposed was "equal in form to old Tarquin (the roan)" and that he acceded to the proposition of taking him at $300 if the terms suited. TJ's need was "not at all pressing." TJ also added: "Our political horizon here is like a March day, changing from dry to cloudy, stormy & clear again from hour to hour. nobody knows today what will be the measure of tomorrow, much less of the 11th. of Febr[uary]" (PrC in DLC; at foot of text: "Colo. John Hoomes"; endorsed by TJ in ink on verso). Hoomes responded on 16 Jan. 1801 agreeing to the terms of payment for the horse that TJ proposed and remarking, "from appearance he is a very fine horse indeed & I think will suit you well, his size, shape & figure is equal (if not superior) to any horse I ever saw." Because of the poor condition of the roads, Hoomes promised to have a servant rather than a stage deliver the animal. He also expressed concern about the election, exclaiming in exasperation: "have I lived to see the day that there are a party in this Infant Country who wish to usurp the Government, can they be so lost to shame, can they be so base & wicked & so regardless of their own real interest & safety as not to fear the vengeance of an enraged & neglected people" (RC in MHi; endorsed by TJ as received 21 Jan. and so recorded in SJL).

To George Jefferson

DEAR SIR   Washington Jan. 5. 1801.

I now inclose you a power of attorney respecting mr Short's canal shares to supply the place of the former one supposed to be mislaid. this will authorise you to recieve the money now paiable, and to act for him in every thing respecting his canal interest. the money is immediately to be transferred to this place to mr Barnes who is instructed to make a peculiar investment of it. I happen at the same time to have occasion to remit to you through mr Barnes the sum of 920.26 D for purposes hereafter to be mentioned. whether mr Short's whole reimbursement & interest now to be recieved from the Canal be more or less, I know not. if more, be pleased to remit the surplus to mr Barnes on account of W.S. if less, let me know immediately the deficiency & it shall go to you by return of the same post. in the mean time I wish you to pay for me the following sums.

Samuel Dyer	176.67	mr Dyer has my note and will apply with that. I send by this post orders on you to Colo. F. Walker and Richard Richardson, who will soon apply. the three last persons live in Albemarle & I send thither orders on you. mr Brand will re-
Francis Walker	47.30	
Richd. Richardson	550.16	
Joseph Brand	57.	
John Rogers	57.83	
Gabriel Lilly	31.30	
	920.26	

cieve his in Richmond, but Rogers and Lilly have no means of doing that. I must pray you therefore to contrive their sums for them to David Higginbotham in Milton if possible. in the mean time if they find opportunities by any of their neighbors they may send their orders to you, & if you should have made the remittance to Higginbotham, certify that on the back of the order & return it. should there be any delay in recieving mr Short's money, let me know it by post, and by it's return the money shall go on in bank bills, and in that case inform those who present the orders of the cause of the delay & that it will be remedied in a few days. be so good as to debit the sum so exchanged between W.S. & myself as paid to J.B. for him: as I wish to transact his money business through other hands so as to keep it out of my accounts. I must pray you at the same time to close with mr Brown and forward on that money to mr Barnes that it may go into the same investment. if any further delay be proposed, tell mr Brown that mr Short's instructions will permit no further delay, and that he must not impute to me what is to follow. in a case of my own I should shew my respect to mr Brown by waiting his convenience: but in that of another & in the face of instructions I have no right to indulge personal attachments. if he continues sick, as mentioned in yours of Nov. 24. certainly he must not be disturbed with this application till he is well enough to resume business.

I am glad you sold my tobacco as you did. as most of that money is destined for mr Lyle and mr Tazewell, you must give me leave *for their satisfaction* to draw on you for 1000. D. to each payable the first week in April. you can, on their application, satisfy them of the certain foundation of the order. I am Dear Sir

Your's affectionately   TH: JEFFERSON

P.S. I desired the Secretary of the Treasury to give orders for you for the monies last recieved from Messrs. Pendleton & Lyon, as they belong now to the US. and not to mr Short, who looks to them for his money.

PrC (MHi); at foot of first page: "George Jefferson." Enclosure: Power of attorney, dated 5 Jan. 1801, in TJ's hand and signed by him, giving George Jefferson "full power and authority to act" for William Short in all matters concerning his interests in the James River canal, that is, to receive all monies due on his account, to represent and vote for him at meetings, and to have all powers confided by Short in TJ, as his attorney in fact, except that of "alienating or hypothecating" the shares (PrC in MHi; endorsed by TJ in ink on verso).

For the previous POWER OF ATTORNEY, see George Jefferson to TJ, 11 Nov. 1799.

SAMUEL DYER operated a general store about 20 miles south of Monticello. MY

NOTE: on 20 Nov. 1800 TJ gave a note to John Perry to pay Dyer £53 or $176.67 in Richmond by 15 Jan. In his financial accounts on 7 Jan., TJ noted the payment to Dyer was for Perry (MB, 2:915, 1030, 1032). A letter from TJ to Dyer, recorded in SJL at 7 Jan. 1801, has not been found. A letter from Dyer of the same date, recorded in SJL as received 15 Jan. 1801, is also missing.

A letter from TJ to JOSEPH BRAND, recorded in SJL at 7 Jan. 1801, has not been found. For a missing letter from TJ to JOHN ROGERS of 7 Jan., see TJ to George Jefferson, 14 Jan. 1798. According to TJ's financial records the payment to GABRIEL LILLY was for "leather &c." (MB, 2:1032).

From James Kyle, Jr.

SIR   Lycoiming County januery the 5th 1801;

I do Congratuelate you; As Preasedant of the united States in avance; to despotssem; you do fill the chair; of the Brave General Washington, May you be found in virtues; far to Exseed; But at the filling of his Sate I was greatley afraid; that another; would Preside; The united-States, in concord is under your Command; I hope by virtues; conduct you will Rul; in Hieroglyphicks bright; from a true freind to my Cuntrey; and your Humble Survant—

JAMES KYLE JUNR

RC (DLC); at head of text: "His Excellency Thomas Jefferson Presedant"; endorsed by TJ as received 6 Mch. and so recorded in SJL.

The *Lycoming Gazette* of 14 Mch. 1810 advertised the land of a James Kyle, Jr., for sale: "a valuable farm on which he lives, situate on Lycoming creek, twelve miles from Williamsport, containing 260 acres, between thirty and forty of which are cleared, with six acres of meadow, a thriving young orchard of apple trees, and a nice peach orchard. A square log house and kitchen, a good log barn, one of the best mill seats on Lycoming, on which there is a grist mill. In a word, the place is fit for almost any public business, as the great road [Williamson] leading to the State of New York passes through it" (John F. Meginness, *History of Lycoming County, Pennsylvania* [Chicago, 1892], 631).

From James Monroe

DEAR SIR   Richmond Jany 6. 1801.

Some strange reports are circulating here of the views of the federal party in the present desperate state of its affrs. It is said they are resolved to prevent the designation by the H. of Reps. of the person to be president, and that they mean to commit the power by a legislative act to John Marshall, Saml. A. Otis or some other person till another election. I cannot believe any such project is seriously entertained, because it wod. argue a degree of boldness as well as wickedness in that party wh. I do not think it possessed of. The report however has excited a strong sensation here. Some of the legislative body think it wod. be proper to pass resolutions declaratory of the light in which they wod. view such a measure, and that they wod. not submit to it; others for continuing the Session till after the 2d. Wednesday in Feby. to be on the ground to take such steps as might be deemed proper to defeat it. It is generally agreed that shod. the Assembly not be sitting at the time, it ought to be convoked as soon as it was known such an attempt was made. If that party wish to disorganize *that* is the way to do it. If the union cod. be broken, that wod. do it. but independant of the other motives for preserving it, it wod. be wrong to let these gentry escape in that mode the just reward of their merit. I think such an attempt, wod. not ultimately weaken the union, but be sure to expose the usurpers to exemplary punishment. The Eastern people have no thoughts of breaking the union, & giving up the hold they have on the valuable productions of the south. They only mean to bully us, thereby preserve their ascendancy, and improve their profits. My only anxiety is respecting the firmness of the republicans. If they shew themselves equal to the crisis the danger passes in a moment. Indeed there will be none. But we have been so long accustomed to recede & they to conquer, that I fear the same result even in the present case. As it is possible no election or decision may be made before the 4th. of March, ought not our election to take place before that period, that our reps. may then be on the ground? It is said that other States will also then be unrepresented; if so the motive for a change, unless it be general is less urgent; especially as it is known the fedl. party cannot have a majority of all the States. If any thing can be done here that may be useful, we ought to know it in time. I write this by Mr. Erwin & therefore omit details he will be able to give. Sincerely I am

dear Sir your friend & servant

Jas. Monroe

RC (DLC); endorsed by TJ as received 10 Jan. and so recorded in SJL.

STRANGE REPORTS: expecting "*danger and persecution to follow this Publication*," the *Aurora* on 10 Jan. stated that during a weeklong holiday break in the congressional session "a *few desperate characters* well known" had held a caucus—a "Conspiracy"—at Samuel Chase's residence in Baltimore. The schemers' plan, according to the newspaper, was to introduce a bill giving the Senate power to choose a president of the U.S. "under certain circumstances," to use consideration of the convention with France as a pretext to extend the sitting of the Senate beyond 4 Mch., and to rely on TJ's withdrawal, as was customary, from Senate proceedings near the end of the current session. Rumors reached St. George Tucker in Williamsburg approximately the same time that Monroe heard them in Richmond. Tucker urged Monroe not only to keep the legislature on hand but also to ready the militia and, among other steps, promote formation of a state bank that could have funds available should access to the Bank of Alexandria, which lay within the District of Columbia, be cut off. Apparently by 18 Jan. Monroe could assuage Tucker to a degree. Reporting from Washington on the 25th, however, George W. Erving—MR. ERWIN in the letter above—feared that the "*federal* project of a legislative provision" still threatened (Tucker to Monroe, 7, 23 Jan., Erving to Monroe, 25 Jan., all in DLC: Monroe Papers).

To Samuel Harrison Smith

[6 Jan. 1801]

Th: Jefferson sends mr Smith Cobbett's 1st. number of his Porcupine, in which he may find some matters worth publication. his address will convince those, who were duped by him here, what his true character was.

there are two important rules of order past by the Senate which must be inserted in the Manual under the head of treaties. Th:J. must therefore borrow the M.S. a little while.

MS (DLC: J. Henley Smith Papers); undated; addressed: "Mr. S. H. Smith"; endorsed by Smith with note "attended to." Not recorded in SJL.

On 7 Jan. 1801 Smith published extracts from the first number of the POR-CUPINE, the daily newspaper William Cobbett began publishing in London in October 1800. According to Smith they revealed insight into Cobbett's "present sentiments, and may be considered as an elucidation of his late views, in relation to this country." HIS ADDRESS: the extracts were taken from Cobbett's prospectus for the newspaper, a seven-page piece which he also published separately (William

Cobbett, *Prospectus of a Daily Paper, Called The Porcupine* [Wincester, 1800], 1-2, 5-7; *National Intelligencer*, 7 Jan. 1801). For Cobbett's return to England, see Vol. 31:322n.

In the end TJ added three RULES OF ORDER to Section 52 on "Treaties," the second-to-the-last section in his parliamentary manual. The first was passed by the Senate on 22 Dec. 1800, the day after TJ submitted the manuscript to Smith for publication, the second on 6 Jan., and the third on 3 Feb. 1801. The first two rules were published in the 12 Jan. issue of the *National Intelligencer* (JEP, 1:361, 365, 376; *Parliamentary Manual*, 1801; TJ to Smith, 21 Dec. 1800).

From John Barnes

SIR   Geo: Town 7nd: Jany: 1801—

The inclosed 3, Cks. Amt $243.50 I hope will meet your wishes— I could Value my self on my Correspondt. Mr John Richards—as—I have more than the Above Amt still in his hands—

your watch is already—with the Watch Maker—I have sent to you ℔ the bearer, five dollar, in small change not very readily—to be had. here—

I am sir your Obedt. H. svt   JOHN BARNES

RC (ViU: Edgehill-Randolph Papers); at foot of text: "Thomas Jefferson Esqr."; endorsed by TJ as received on 8 Jan. and so recorded in SJL.

The CHECKS drawn on the Bank of the United States were for Joseph Roberts,

Jr., who received $73 for stoves, Dr. David Jackson, and N. G. Dufief (MB, 2:1033). For the two latter payments, see 9 Jan. below. A letter from TJ to Roberts of that date is recorded in SJL but has not been found.

In a statement of account of 13 Dec.

Barnes recorded $100 paid to Stevens Thomson Mason under the date of 12 Sep. 1800 (see Mason to TJ, 5 Sep.); on 8 Oct., $1,241.02 for sundry drafts on the Bank of the United States noted by TJ in his financial memoranda as payments of $406.62 to Roberts & Jones "for nail rod &c. of July," $154.70 to Henry Sheaff for wine, and $680 to Gibson & Jefferson on account, for a total of $1,241.32 (see TJ to Barnes, 26 Sep.); $200 paid to Gibson & Jefferson on 13 Oct. (see TJ to George Jefferson, 5 Sep.); and, on 22 Nov., payments of $4.50 for three nautical almanacs (see Barnes to TJ, 20 Nov.), $1.20 for two handkerchiefs, and a half dollar for ointment. Barnes's statement also recorded payments of: $32.62½ in cash, $5 to an unidentified "Carrol" (possibly a farrier recorded as John Carrol in TJ's memoranda of household and stable accounts, 26 Feb.-12 May 1801, in CSmH), and $100 to Conrad & McMunn (MB, 2:1032), all recorded under 8 Dec.; on the 16th of that month, $4 paid in change (same); and on 19 Dec., $50 to Stephen B. Balch (see TJ to Balch, 18 Dec.) and $8 to Anthony Reintzel, probably for storage (see below). Barnes credited TJ with a balance of $193.51 in TJ's favor brought forward on 18 Sep. 1800; with $1,243.75 recorded under 7 Oct. as the net proceeds of TJ's quarterly salary (see statement of account described at

Barnes to TJ, 15 Jan. 1801); and with $13.06 credit "By 3 pr Gold" on 8 Dec. Dated 15 Nov. but appearing below the 8 Dec. entry were credits of $463.58½ and $307.46½ representing Thomas Leiper's fifth and final payments to TJ and Thomas Mann Randolph, respectively, for their tobacco (see Barnes to TJ, 28 Aug. 1800). To close the statement Barnes credited TJ with a balance of $474.52½ to be carried forward (MS in ViU; in a clerk's hand, signed and endorsed by Barnes; in two places the date of carrying the new balance forward was apparently changed from 13 Jan. to 13 Dec.; some dates of transactions differ from those that TJ recorded in his financial memoranda).

In another statement of account Barnes recorded charges against TJ of $65 for bank notes, $1 for a penknife, $5 in silver for TJ, and a payment of $1.50 to the Georgetown jewelry firm of Burnett & Rigden for repairing a watch, all under the date 26 Dec. 1800. Those debits were balanced by the $474.52½ carried over to TJ's credit under the date 13 Dec., plus an undated abatement of $1 from Reintzel on the storage of seven packages and a new balance of $403.02½ in TJ's favor carried forward on 31 Dec. (MS in ViU, in a clerk's hand, signed by Barnes; *Records of the Columbia Historical Society*, 33-4 [1932], 248).

From Robert R. Livingston

DEAR SIR   ClerMont 7th. Jany 1801.

Mr Van Benthuysens solicited that I should receive your favor of the 12th. by a safe conveyance, & some of his domestic arrangments prevented its reaching me till yesterday, just as I was preparing to answer your former letter which I delayed till I could with certainty offer you my congratulations on the happy effects of the republican exertion, & my wishes for your happiness for such a portion of the new century, as you may chuse to add to the years & the honours of the last. Life will acquire new charms from the hope we may now entertain that the labours which occupied the best part of yours & mine will not be thrown away, but terminate ultimately in the freedom &

happiness of our country, an issue which we have not long since had well grounded reasons to doubt.

I have paid the earliest attention to your request relative to the bones found at Shawangun, & have this day written to a very intelligent friend in that neighbourhood, who will think himself honoured by your request, & take a pleasure in serving me. I fear however that till they have finished their search, there will be some difficulty in procuring any part of the bones, because when I first heard of the discovery I made some attempts to possess myself of them, but found they were a kind of common property the whole town having joined in diging for them till they were stoped by the autumnal rains. They entertain well grounded hopes of discovering the whole skelleton since these bones are not, like all others that they have hitherto found in that county, placed within the vegetable mould, but are covered with a stratum of clay, so that being better sheltered from the air & water they are more perfectly preserved.

Among the bones I have heard mentioned, are the vertebræ, part of the jaw with two of the grinders, the tusks which some have called the hornes. The Sternum, the scapula, the tibia & fibula, the tarsus, & metatarsus. Whether any of the phalanges, or the ossa innominata are found I have not heard. A part of the head containing the socket of the tusks is also discovered. From the bones of the foot it is evidently a claw footed animal, & from such parts of the shoulder bones as have been discovered, it appears that the arm or fore leg had a greater motion than can possibly belong to the Elephant, or any of the large quadrupedes with which we are acquainted. This would seem to contradict Mr. Daubenton's theory; which as ever seems to be adopted by Buffon, & other European naturalists. Whatever it was, I can hardly think it was carniverous, from the great number that must have existed judging by the bones that are found in a small space of country. Since bog earth has been used by the farmers of Ulster county as a manure, which is subsequent to the war, fragments of at least eight or ten have been found; but in a very decayed state, in the same bog. But if, as Daubenton & Buffon suppose, they were Elephants, besides the obvious objection arising from the climate, how are we to account for their being constantly found in Low grounds both here, & in [Siberia?].

If I might venture a conjecture it would be that they were amphibious & that the bogs in which they are found are the last remains of the great lakes they formerly freequented. there are many reasons to conclude that the whole country above the highlands &

below the Cohoes falls on the Mohawk river has formed a large lake, whose eastern boundary was the Mountains that seperate the waters that fall into the connecticut from those that empty into Hudsons river & its western one the blue mountains. Stones evidently formed from indurated clay, & containing impressions of shells of a species that not now found in our rivers, together with large quaries of slate are freequently seen on our high ground. When the waters had broken thro' the mountains of the high lands & the large lake was drained, amphibious animals would naturally retire to the river & the lakes that would be found for a time in every deep & extensive vale. here from the drying up of the waters & the want of food they would die—those that perished in the river would be [car]ryed into the ocean, while the carcasses of those that inhabited the lakes would be placed under the vegetable substances, when the lakes were filled by the wash of the adjoining mountains. The distant period of these events accounts for the total ignorance of the natives as to the existence of this animal.

The political part of your letter gives me great pleasure, since it at once assures me of your friendship & of what, indeed I should not have doubted, your determination to preserve your administration from being degraded by attempting to work with the tools you have on hand. Nothing proves more fully the influence of Hamilton on the late president than his last appointment of Secretaries from men totally undistinguished by talents and political character, doubtless by Hamiltons advice, who expected thereby to continue to govern tho he had quited the administration.

You can not doubt Sir the sincerity of my wishes for your happy administration, I see the arduous task you will have to go thro' before you can bring us back to the point from which we set out. but I firmly hope, that you will not want the means, as you possess the will, to effect this desirable object. Every firm republican will contribute his aid where he has reason to think that he can usefully assist. For my own part, I feel that your friendship for me has esstimated my talents at too high a rate, when you propose to me the department you mention, I have never turned my attention to nautical objects, I have never been engaged in any species of commerce, nor viewed it in detail, or in any other way than generally as a political object. nor ever examined a ship, except as an ingenious & useful invention, A perfect conviction of my own unfitness for the duties of this department compels me to decline, (while I thankfully acknowledge the partiality that dictated) the obliging offer. But sir independant of this consideration, I am satisfied that in the present disposition of the country they will not add to their navy, & it is by no means improbable, that, among the plans of œconomy that may be adopted, will be the suppression of the naval department, & the anexing it to that of war which will be thought competent to the discharge of both duties. And as I am myself rather inclined to that sentiment I should feel some reluctance in filling a station that might be deemed unnecessary, either by myself, or others.

I pray you however my dear Sir to accept my assurances of every kind of support that any little influence I may have, or any station that I may occupy can give to the administration that you may esstablish. The Gent. you propose to place at the head of the department of State too fully merrits, not to receive the public confidence. The voice of the nation will concur with yours in the appointment. The treasury (if my conjectures are right as to the person) will be alike distinguished for talents and industry. And who ever you may chuse for the department of war (for on this subject I have formed no distinct idea) will I dare say fully justify your choice. I intended to have proceeded to answer your former favor, in [. . .] & to accompany it with some drawings which I have just finished. but I have already extended my letter to so unreasonable a length that I will postpone it to another opportunity which will better œconomize your patience, without subjecting you to any other inconvenience than that of reading my letters, (like the witches prayers) backward, while it will afford me another opportunity of declaring the sincerity of the attatchment, & respect with which I have the honor to be Dear Sir

Your Most Obt hum: Servt   Robt R Livingston

RC (DLC); torn; at foot of text: "His Excellency Thomas Jefferson Esqr Vice pres: U.S:"; endorsed by TJ as received 21 Jan. and so recorded in SJL.

your favor of the 12th: TJ to Livingston, 14 Dec. The former letter was that of 2 [Sep.] 1800.

TJ had disputed DAUBENTON's THEORY that American mammoths (mastodons) were the same species as ELEPHANTS (*Notes*, ed. Peden, 45-7, 53-4, 269; Vol. 13:593).

To Francis Walker

Dear Sir   Washington Jan. 7. 1801.

I took before I left home a note of the amount of your nail-account, which was £33–16–3. but omitted to draw off a copy of it that I might now furnish it to you. this shall be done on my return. in the mean time I inclose you an order on Gibson & Jefferson for 47. D. 30. C.

say £14–3–9 making with the above nail account the sum of £48. which I was to pay you for mr Randolph.

We have little news but what the public papers give you. it is certainly true that Lord Grenville expressed himself to mr King contented with our treaty with France. it is not equally certain that it will escape opposition here, but from all the trading towns we learn it has given general content.—the election to take place in the H. of R. is in dubio. but of this you may be more properly informed by others than myself.　　　　I am with great esteem, Dear Sir

Your friend & servt　　　　　　　　　　　　　　Th: Jefferson

PrC (DLC); at foot of text: "Colo. Francis Walker"; endorsed by TJ in ink on verso. Enclosure not found.

On 31 Oct. 1800 Rufus King informed Secretary of State John Marshall that he had had a conference with lord grenville that morning to determine the British government's views on the U.S. convention with France. He reported that the British foreign secretary saw nothing in the convention that conflicted with the Jay Treaty or gave his government any grounds for complaint (King, Life, 3:324).

From William Arthur

Sir,　　　　　　　　　　　　　　　　　　Pequea 8th Jany 1801.

Be not offended (though you may be surprised) when you receive this from an individual whom you do not know, & of whom, perhaps, you never would have heard, had he not, after much hesitation, & with almost invincible reluctance, resolved to write to you; An individual, who has no ambition to be regarded in any other view than as a minister of the gospel, & can plead no excuse for his present officiousness, except the motive, which this is intended to develop.—As the writer is unfeignedly impressed with a deep veneration for your character, this address, even if it should betray great weakness, or inconsiderateness, cannot be viewed as an intended insult, or imputed to want of due respect. Your enlightened mind will, therefore, excuse what may appear to you to be the effect of Zeal, not sufficiently tempered with judgment.

Your election, Sir, no man wished more ardently than the writer of these lines, & to none does it afford more sensible pleasure. He has, often congratulated others, as well as himself, upon an event, which he cannot but consider as highly auspicious to America.

It is not unknown to you that one of the artifices, which those, who arrogate to themselves an exclusive claim to Federalism, employed to prevent your election, was a report of your hostility to the christian religion; A report, which, he believes, is as groundless as it was industriously propagated, & must have originated either in malignity of passion, or the predominance of party-principle. In your writings there is no foundation for it that he can perceive. Of religious toleration you are the friend & the advocate. This, Sir, is alike honourable to your head & heart. Persecution, whatever ignorance or fanaticism may say to the contrary, is a diabolical [work]. Penal laws & compulsory measures [on] religion, or even legal inabilities imposed upon one Sect more than [others] are equally antiscriptural & irrational.

Had you condescended to contradict the report, previous to your election, malevolence (the writer is convinced) would have imputed it to motives, which are beneath you. But now, Sir, the case is materially altered; & a publick avowal of your belief in the christian religion at the time, & in the manner, which may seem to you the most proper; would be a signal triumph to religion & religious [pens].

—It would add as much weight, as the influence of any one can give, to a religion, which is the best system of philosophy, & which, while it cements the bonds of civil Society, brightens the hopes of man for an endless hereafter, & is verily of God.—Besides, it would stop, the mouths of many gainsayers, who, there is too much reason to believe, regard the honour of religion no farther than the pretence is subservient to party-purposes. Such an avowal, Sir, would not lessen your dignity. It would have a contrary effect; & give to thousands, who love & highly esteem you, infinite joy.

Do not imagine that the writer presumes to *dictate* to you. He has not vanity sufficient to prompt him to any thing of this kind. Your good sense is the Security, on which he relies, that you will not take this address ill; & all the notice he wishes you to take of it, is, after reading it, to consign it to the flames.   WM. ARTHUR

RC (MHi); torn; at foot of text: "The Honorable Thomas Jefferson"; endorsed by TJ as received 14 Jan. and so recorded in SJL.

Reverend William Arthur (1769-1827), a native of Peebles, Scotland, received a classical education at Edinburgh, and was ordained a Presbyterian minister at Paisley before immigrating to the U.S. in 1793 where he preached in New York, Albany, and Pennsylvania. In 1794 he delivered a sermon in Philadelphia and New York that was subsequently published as *Family Religion Recommended. A Sermon Preached from Joshua XXIV.15* ([Philadelphia, 1794]; Evans, No. 26576). On 5 Jan. 1796, he was installed as pastor of Pequea and served there until 1 May 1818 after which he moved to Ohio (W. U. Hensel, *Presbyterianism in the Pequea Valley: Memorial Address at the Dedication of the Founders' Windows Bellevue Presbyterian Church, Gap, Pa., September 8, 1912 And Other Historical Addresses* [Lancaster, Pa., n.d.], 24; William B. Sprague, *Annals of the American Pulpit; or Commemorative*

Notices of Distinguished American Clergymen of Various Denominations, 9 vols. [New York, 1857-69], 3:207-8; W. C. Alexander, *History of the Pequea Presbyterian Church, Delivered September 8, 1876* [Lancaster, Pa., 1878], 33-4).

From James Currie

DR SIR   Richmond Jany. 8th. 1801

I recd. your last communication in regard to Mr Ross's last remarks, in due course of post, & forthwith, communicated to Mr Ross your wish, he closed immediately with it, & requested the papers might be submitted—without farther Observations from him. my having been very much indisposed prevented My—laying the papers—before the gentlemen till the day before yesterday—they are apprised that they are to Consider the business,—decide upon the principle of adjustment; & procure some Accurate Accomptant, to do that part of the business, which, as well as their own agency in it, will be recompensed by the parties. the same as if it had been litigated in Court. Mr Nicholas is gone to Baltimore today. at his return it will be proceeded upon without delay—

I have only to add, with great truth, that with best wishes for your health & happiness that I Ever Am

Dr Sir—your Very H Serv.   JAMES CURRIE

RC (MHi); endorsed by TJ as received 13 Jan. and so recorded in SJL.   LAST COMMUNICATION: TJ to Currie, 14 Dec. 1800.

From Charles Pinckney

DEAR SIR   January 8: 1801 Winyaw

I wrote you some weeks since informing you that after the finishing some indispensable public Business important to the continuance & increase of the republican interest in this state I should go to Charleston & proceed from thence by Water either to Baltimore or to Washington as passages offered—Since this I am concerned to inform You that in my way down from Columbia stopping at this place I have been siezed with a most violent cold & sore throat occasioned by the severe cold weather we have had & my being exposed to it—it has confined me to my chamber & continues to oppress me very much—I am afraid it will be some time before I can go on to Charleston, where I left my little ones & to which place I have written to my friends to look out for a passage from thence to Baltimore that I may be with you as soon as possible after I am better—I wish I was with you now but my absence was inevitable, as I am sure I did more good by going up to our Legislature at Columbia than I could have done by going to any other Part of the Globe at that time— Whenever I see you & recount to You *my situation* at Columbia & what passed there you will be not a little astonished—it has unravelled mysteries which I wish to explain to You & is the reason for my requesting you not to think of any arrangements for this state until You recieve the information I have collected & prepared for you— after which You will be fully able to judge for yourself & know what is best to be done——

the feds have had some hopes of creating confusion by their being an equality of Votes but I find by the inclosed Extract that Tenesee has made a difference of one Vote—& as Your Majority over the federal candidates is so great[1] there can be no cavil—I am hopeful to be with You before the Votes are opened & counted & am with affectionate respect & attachment

Dear Sir Your's Truly   CHARLES PINCKNEY

I am glad the French convention is ratified By Sen—it was feared the payment for Captures might have been a clog by the disappointed federalists But I suppose the public opinion has over awed them & that it passed as a matter of course—they would not venture to stop it.—

RC (DLC); endorsed by TJ as received 25 Jan. and so recorded in SJL. Enclosure not found.

Eleanor Laurens Pinckney, died in October 1794 (*S.C. Biographical Directory, House of Representatives*, 3:558).

I WROTE YOU: see Pinckney to TJ, 20 Dec. 1800. MY LITTLE ONES: Frances Henrietta, Mary Eleanor, and Henry Laurens Pinckney. Pinckney's wife, Mary

[1] Pinckney first wrote "your majority is so great" before revising it to read as above.

To Richard Richardson

SIR   Washington Jan. 8. 1801.

I recieved a few days ago your letter of Dec. 22. and on the 5th. inst. I wrote to mr Jefferson, and now inclose you an order on him for 550.16 D say £165–1. to be applied as follows.

for Henry Duke for	Simon	£ 21–10
	Stepney	20–10
Edmd. Goodwin admr.	John	16–16
of Dickeson's estate	Isaac	16– 1

the widow Duke for	Mat	20– 0
Hendrick's estate for	Moses	20– 0
yourself for	Joe	19– 0
do. on account		31– 4
		165– 1 = 550.16 D

the last sum was intended to have been £30. exact as you desired: but a mistake in addition made me state £165–1 to mr Jefferson so that your part became £31–4 to be credited in our account. I do not recollect whether I was to pay you or not for mr Duke. so you can either recieve & pay him the £42. or give him an order for it on mr Jefferson. as it is hasardous to send money by the post, I procured an exchange of money here with a person who was to recieve money there. tho I believe there is no doubt of it's being paid on demand, yet I have desired mr Jefferson if there is any delay to let me know by return of post, and I will instantly send [on] bank bills to him. this would occasion a delay of 10. days, which however I am confident will not be necessary. I am very sorry indeed to hear of so poor a chance for hiring laborers. it will be a serious embarrasment to me. I am in hopes you will have been able to procure me some. I have not yet heard of Powell's going up to stay: but have written to mr Eppes to press him off. I am not yet able to give you information as to Journey work here. I am Sir

Your humble servt   TH: JEFFERSON

RC (R. M. Smythe & Co., New York City, 2002); torn at folds; with word in brackets supplied from PrC. PrC (MHi); endorsed by TJ in ink on verso.

TO BE APPLIED AS FOLLOWS: TJ recorded the same information in his financial accounts on 7 Jan. (MB, 2:1032-3). For TJ's letter to John Wayles EPPES, see 23 Dec. 1800.

From James Thomson Callender

SIR   Richmond Jail January 9th. 1801

I hope you will pardon my having sent you revises, instead of clean Sheets of the thing now printing; a freedom inexcusable in any circumstances but mine. I Cannot get my printer to work, although I am actually paying him *ready money*, as he goes on. So that the whole Sale of the Season will be lost, by the delay of *revising the Sheets*! I mention this, Sir, that You may not think me addicted to freedoms I would not assume.

I am Sir Your most obed Servt   JAS. T. CALLENDER

RC (DLC); endorsed by TJ as received 14 Jan. and so recorded in SJL.

To Nicolas Gouin Dufief

SIR   Washington Jan. 9. 1800. [i.e. 1801]

I am much obliged to you for thinking of me when you got the copies of Rabaut & Meyer, and I now inclose you John Barnes's check on the bank of the US. for four dollars, the sum noted. should you possess Dumourier's account of his campaigns, Carnot's or Madame Roland's books, I will thank you for them, by the stage, noting their cost which shall be remitted in the same way.—you will render a great service if you can abridge the acquisition of a new language. it would greatly facilitate our progress in science, if we could shorten the time necessary for learning the languages in which it is deposited. accept assurances of my respect.   TH: JEFFERSON

PrC (DLC); at foot of text: "Mr. N. G. Dufief"; endorsed by TJ in ink on verso as a letter of 9 Jan. 1801 and recorded under that date in SJL. In a prospectus for his book on language instruction, Dufief in 1803 quoted as an endorsement from TJ the passage from "you will render" through "deposited," with variations in capitalization and punctuation and the substitution of "if you could" for "if we could"; the extract, with the one phrase changed again to "if one could," appeared also in at least one later edition of Dufief's book (*Gazette of the United States*, 21 Dec. 1803; N. G. Dufief, *Nature Dis-*

played, in her Mode of Teaching Language to Man, 16th ed. [London, 1836], iv).

RABAUT & MEYER: see Dufief to TJ, 23 Dec. The books requested by TJ were Charles François Du Périer Dumouriez's *Mémoires*, published in Hamburg and Leipzig in 1794; the *Réponse de L. N. M. Carnot, Citoyen Français . . . au Rapport fait sur La Conjuration du 18 Fructidor . . . par J. Ch. Bailleul* (London, 1799); and the *Appel à l'Impartiale Postérité* of Marie Jeanne Phlipon Roland de la Platière (Paris, 1795). See Sowerby, Nos. 233, 235-6.

To David Jackson

DEAR SIR   Washington Jan. 9. 1801.

I promised Doctr. Wardlaw to pay you for him in the beginning of this month one hundred and sixty dollars & a half, for which I now inclose you John Barnes's check on the bank of the US. a line of acknolegement will probably be satisfactory to Dr. Wardlaw. I am with much esteem Dear Sir

Your most obedt. servt   TH: JEFFERSON

PrC (MHi); at foot of text: "Doctr David Jackson"; endorsed by TJ in ink on verso.

David Jackson (ca. 1730-1801), a graduate of the University of Pennsylvania, was a physician and apothecary in

Philadelphia. During the Revolution, he served as surgeon of the Pennsylvania militia, Continental Line, quarter-master general of the Pennsylvania militia, and senior surgeon of the military hospital. He was a delegate to the Continental Congress from April to November 1785, became a trustee of the University of Pennsylvania in 1791, and was elected to membership in the American Philosophical Society (*Biog. Dir. Cong.*; DAB; Philadelphia *Aurora*, 3 Nov. 1798; MB, 2:935). His letter to TJ of 3 Jan. 1798 is recorded in SJL as received the same day, but has not been found.

ONE HUNDRED AND SIXTY DOLLARS & A HALF: on 9 Jan. 1801, TJ recorded in his financial records that he enclosed $166.50 to Dr. Jackson on the account of Dr. Wardlaw and William Davenport "ante Nov. 21." An entry for 21 Nov. noted that of this sum "100 D. is for W. Davenport, & the balance I may draw on him for" (MB, 2:1030, 1033).

On 13 Jan. Jackson acknowledged receipt of this letter and of John Barnes's CHECK for $166.50, "which agreeable to your directions I have passed to Doctr. Wardlaw's credit." He added: "With the highest pleasure I congratulate you on the triumph of republicanism in the late Presidential Election—I am however truly sorry that the result is such, as to make it necessary for the House of Representatives to have any agency in the business— I hope no federal trick may be attempted by that body, whereby the people of the United States may be deprived of the men of their choice" (RC in MHi; endorsed by TJ as received 16 Jan. and so recorded in SJL.).

From George Jefferson

DEAR SIR   Richmond 9th. Janr. 1801.

Your favor of the 5th. is but this moment received.   I hasten to inform you that it will be *perfectly* agreeable to me for you to draw in favor of Mr. Lyle, & of Mr. Tazewell, for the 2000$: you mention; indeed I hope you will not have waited for this permission.

There *certainly* can be no delay in the receipt of the money from the James River company. the amount I cannot ascertain to night, but will inform you of it in a post or two.

I am Dear Sir Your Very humble servt.   GEO. JEFFERSON

RC (MHi); at foot of text: "Thos. Jefferson esqr. Washington"; endorsed by TJ as received 14 Jan. and so recorded in SJL.

From James Monroe

DEAR SIR   Richmond 9. Jany. 1801.

I recd. sometime since a letter from P. Carr intimating a desire to act as yr. private Secry. in case you were elected President, provided you were willing to accept his service, approved it as an eligible measure on his part, and other circumstances suited. I declined writing you on the subject in expectation of seeing him first and dissuading him from it, from a persuasion as he has a family it wod. not suit him; but being detain longer from Albemarle than I expected, and knowing that many applications will be made you from every quarter, I have thought it best to communicate what he has intimated on the subject. I sit out in the morning for Albemarle where I shall see him, and on my return which will be on thursday next, will inform you what passes between us respecting it. very sincerely

I am your friend & servant   JAS. MONROE

RC (DLC); endorsed by TJ as received 28 Jan. and so recorded in SJL.

Letters from Peter CARR to TJ of 22 Oct. and 11 Nov., recorded in SJL as received from Mt. Warren on 24 Oct. and 11 Nov., respectively, have not been found. A letter from TJ to Carr, recorded in SJL under 13 Nov., is also missing.

To Thomas Mann Randolph

DEAR SIR   Washington Jan. 9. 1801.

Your favor of the 3d. came to hand yesterday. I suspect that I mistook our post day when I first arrived here, and put the letters you mention into the post office a day too late. I shall be glad if you will mention when that of the 1st. instant gets to you, as well as the present & future letters, that if there be any thing wrong in the post I may get it rectified. the mail for Milton is made up here on Friday at 5. P.M.   that Craven's house should not have been in readiness surprises me. I left J. Perry's people putting up the last course of shingles, & the plank for the floor & loft planed, & they assured me they could finish every thing in a week. they must have quit immediately.   but the most extraordinary of all things is that there should have been no clearing done. I left Monticello on Monday the 24th. Nov. from which time there were 4. weeks to Christmas, and the hands ordered to be with Lilly that morning (except I think two) and according to his calculation & mine 3. or 4. acres a week should have been cleared. but the misunderstanding between him & Richardson had before cost me as good as all the labour of the hired hands from Jany. to June when I got home. the question now however is as to the remedy. you have done exactly what I would have wished, and as I place the compliance with my contract with mr Craven before any other object, we must take every person from the nailery able to cut and keep them at it till the clearing is completed. the following therefore must be so employed. Davy, John, Abram, Shepherd, Moses, Joe, Wormly, Jame Hubard, with the one hired by Lilly making 9. besides these, if Barnaby, Ben, Cary, & Isabel's Davy are able to cut, as I suppose they are, let them also join: shoemaker Phill also if he can cut. I doubt it, & that he had better continue to be

[417]

hired. these make 13. or 14. with whom the clearing which I was to do this year, ought not to be a long job.   there will remain for the nailery Burwell, Jamy, Bedf. John. Bedf. Davy. Phill Hub. Lewis, Bartlet & Brown, enough for two fires; this course I would have pursued even after Powell's arrival, as I had rather derange his department where the loss concerns myself only than one which affects another. I wrote pressingly to mr Eppes to hire some hands for me, and am not without hopes he may have done it. if they arrive, I would still not draw off the nailers till the clearing is completed. I wrote to Lilly yesterday covering an order for some money. I had not then received your letter, so the one to him says nothing on this subject. I must therefore get the favor of you to deliver him the orders.

Nothing further can be said or discovered on the subject of the election. we have 8. votes in the H. of R. certain, & there are 3. other states Maryld. Delaware & Vermont from either of which if a single individual comes over, it settles the matter. but I am far from confiding that a single one will come over. Pensylvania has shewn what men are when party takes place of principle. the Jersey election has been a great event. but nothing seems to bend the spirit of our opponents. I believe they will carry their judiciary bill. as to the treaty I must give no opinion. but it must not be imagined that any thing is too bold for them. I had expected that some respect to the palpable change in public opinion would have produced moderation. but it does not seem so. a commee reported that the Sedition law ought to be continued, and the first question on the subject in the house has been carried by 47. against 33.—we have a host of republicans absent. Gallatin, Livingston, Nicholson, Tazewell, Cabell cum multis aliis. the mercantile towns are almost unanimous in favour of the treaty. yet it seems not to soften their friends in the Senate.   I recieved notices from Dick Johnson to attend the taking depositions in Milton on the 2d. Saturday in Feb. & 2d. Saturday in March, at mr Price's. I do not expect his witnesses have any thing material to say. however if it should not be inconvenient to you to ride there at the hour of 12. and to ask any questions which may be necessary to produce the whole truth, I shall be obliged to you. my unchangeable and tenderest love to my ever dear Martha, and to the little ones: affectionate attachment to yourself. Adieu.   TH: JEFFERSON

RC (DLC); at foot of first page: "T M Randolph"; endorsed by Randolph as received 22 Jan. PrC (MHi); endorsed by TJ in ink on verso.

I WROTE PRESSINGLY TO MR EPPES:

TJ to John Wayles Eppes, 23 Dec. 1800. The letter that TJ WROTE TO Gabriel LILLY on 8 Jan. is recorded in SJL but has not been found. It is the first of 122 letters, which according to SJL, TJ exchanged with Lilly between January 1801 and September 1806, all of which are missing. For the order for payment in the first letter, see TJ to George Jefferson, 5 Jan.

IF A SINGLE INDIVIDUAL COMES OVER, IT SETTLES THE MATTER: George Baer was evidently the Federalist in Maryland whom some Republicans believed would carry the state for TJ by joining Republicans Gabriel Christie, Joseph H. Nicholson, Samuel Smith, and George Dent, who was elected as a Federalist but voted with the Republicans a majority of the time. As Delaware's only congressman, James A. Bayard controlled the vote of that state. While correspondents such as Caesar A. Rodney and Benjamin Hichborn assured TJ that Bayard favored his election, Bayard on 7 Jan. informed Alexander Hamilton: "I am by no means decided as to the object of preference." He noted that he would "wait the approach of the crisis" before making his decision. On 16 Jan. Hamilton wrote Bayard a long letter in which he tried, but without success, to persuade him to vote for TJ. With only two congressmen, Vermont was the other divided state. Some thought Lewis R. Morris, nephew of Senator Gouverneur Morris, would join Matthew Lyon in casting the state's vote for TJ. On 5 Feb. Edward Livingston confidently predicted that TJ would be quickly elected: "A member from the opposite side of one of the divided States has already pledged himself to decide the vote of his State in our favor — there is great probability that another from the remaining divided State will follow his example, and as I can not learn that the Representative from Delaware has firmly entered into the views of his party, I think it probable that he too will join our ballot." Albert Gallatin more than 40 years later recalled that on the day the voting began he "knew positively" that Baer would cast his vote for TJ and decide the election. He thought Morris would bring Vermont into TJ's column as well (Syrett, *Hamilton,* 25:299-302, 319-24; Henry Adams, *The Life of Albert Gallatin* [Philadelphia, 1879], 248-50; *Proceedings of the American Antiquarian Society,* new ser., 29 [1919], 103-4; Dauer, *Adams Federalists,* 323; Rodney to TJ, 28 Dec. 1800; Hichborn to TJ, 5 Jan. 1801).

On 31 Dec. the House Committee of Revisal and Unfinished Business recommended that a bill be brought in to continue the SEDITION LAW, which was to expire on 3 Mch. 1801, and the House on 2 Jan. voted 47 to 33 in favor of considering the resolution. After extended debates from 21 to 23 Jan., Speaker of the House Theodore Sedgwick cast the tie-breaking vote in favor of bringing in a bill. Gallatin and Joseph H. Nicholson were present for the vote on 23 Jan., but the other Republicans singled out by TJ were still absent. Jonas Platt brought in the bill on 19 Feb. and it passed to a second reading but was defeated by a 49 to 53 vote two days later (*Annals,* 10:876-7, 916-40, 946-58, 960-76; JHR, 3:751-2, 771-3, 808-9, 816-17).

NOTICES FROM DICK JOHNSON: several years earlier Richard Johnson had initiated a suit against TJ, contesting his ownership of a portion of the land called Pouncey's tract. TJ responded by bringing his own suit. In August 1800 TJ paid Francis Taliaferro, Albemarle County deputy sheriff, for serving writs and the next month he paid for the attendance of a witness in the case. Dabney Carr and James Barbour were serving as TJ's attorneys (TJ to George Jefferson, 12 July 1799; MB, 2:1003, 1024, 1027).

From Simon Chaudron

MONSIEUR   Philadelphie 10 Janvier 1801

J'attendais pour repondre a L'honneur de Votre lettre, qu'une occasion de Vous envoyer Votre Montre se presentat. J'ai manqué d'une heure celle que Vous m'aviez indiquée, et depuis ce tems Mr Letombe consul de france m'en fait esperer une, dont le retard s'accorde mal avec L'impatience que j'ai de Vous servir

Je joindrai a la montre un dessein dont Mr Barralet Vous fait Lhommage, et peut être aussi, les montres de Messieurs Sumpter & McClay

M'onsr. Barralet á ouvert une souscription pour L'Apothéose de Washington. La composition de cette planche est ingenieuse & touchante, et L'auteur ose esperer de Voir a la tête de ses souscripteurs, L'ami & le protecteur des arts

J'ai L'honneur dêtre avec le plus profond Respect

Monsieur Votre trés humble & trés obeissant Serviteur

CHAUDRON

EDITORS' TRANSLATION

SIR   Philadelphia 10 January 1801

I was waiting to answer the honor of your letter until an opportunity to send you your watch should occur. I missed by one hour the one that you had indicated to me, and since that time Mr. Létombe, the French consul, has kept me hoping for one, delaying in a way that ill suits my impatience to serve you.

I shall send with the watch a drawing that Mr. Barralet dedicates to you, and perhaps also send the watches of Messrs. Sumter and McClay.

Mr. Barralet has opened a subscription for the Apotheosis of Washington. The composition of this plate is ingenious and moving, and the author dares hope to see at the head of its subscribers, the friend and protector of the arts.

I have the honor of being with the deepest respect

Sir Your very humble and very obedient Servant   CHAUDRON

RC (MHi); endorsed by TJ as received 14 Jan. and so recorded in SJL.

VOTRE LETTRE: TJ to Chaudron, 18 Dec.

Chaudron was co-publisher of an engraving by John James Barralet that depicted George WASHINGTON, his arms outstretched, lofted toward heaven amid an assortment of symbolic visual references. Although Barralet and Chaudron opened subscriptions for the "Apotheosis of Washington" by late 1800 and had a proof print available then for viewing, the image was not ready for delivery until February 1802. In March 1801 the artist asked TJ to become a subscriber, without charge, so that his name could stand at the top of the subscription list. There is no evidence of a reply. Barralet's "Apotheosis" was enormously popular in the nineteenth century, appearing on ceramic pitchers, in Chinese paintings on glass for the American export trade, and later in an 1865 print that substituted Abraham Lincoln's head for Washington's (Patricia A. Anderson, *Promoted to Glory: The Apotheosis of George Washington* [Northampton, Mass., 1980], 17-18, 23, 31-3; Phoebe Lloyd Jacobs, "John James Barralet and the Apotheosis of George Washington," *Winterthur Portfolio*, 12 [1977], 115-37; Noble E. Cunningham, Jr., *Popular Images of the Presidency: From Washington to Lincoln* [Columbia, Mo., 1991], 13-16; *Aurora*, 19 Dec. 1800, 8 Feb. 1802; Barralet to TJ, 17 Mch. 1801).

To Charles Copland

SIR   Washington Jan. 10. 1801.

As I have occasion to write soon to mrs Randolph, I would ask the favor of you to take the trouble of informing me by a line what sum you have received from mr Grymes for her, what sum you have remitted, and whether she may expect soon any further & what remittance? which will oblige Sir

Your humble servt   TH: JEFFERSON

PrC (MHi); at foot of text: "Mr Charles Copeland"; endorsed by TJ in ink on verso.

Charles Copland (ca. 1756-1836) was probably born in Charles City County but moved to Richmond in 1788 where he became a leading member of the Virginia bar. He represented Richmond in the House of Delegates from 1799 to 1801 and had previously served as court-appointed defense counsel for the slave Gabriel. With his wife Rebecca Nicholson, Copland had nine children. After her death he married Hennengham C. Bernard in 1808 (*Richmond Whig & Public Advertiser*, 29 Nov. 1836; Anna Melissa Graves, "Extracts from Diary of Charles Copland," WMQ, 1st ser., 14 [1905], 45, 46; [1906], 229-30).

For the efforts of MRS Ariana RANDOLPH in collecting her annuity, see Mortgage of Slaves and Goods from Edmund Randolph, 19 May 1800; TJ to Philip Ludwell Grymes, 24 July and 30 Aug. 1800.

Copland and TJ corresponded with some regularity between 1797 and 1800. Recorded in SJL, but missing, are letters that TJ wrote to Copland on 16 Apr. 1797, 4 Dec. 1798, 15 Oct. 1799, 30 Aug. 1800, and 17 Sep. 1800. Also recorded in SJL, but missing, are letters that Copland wrote to TJ at Richmond on 16 May 1797 (received 25 May 1797), 20 Dec. 1798 (received 1 Jan. 1799), 22 Nov. 1799 (received 30 Dec. 1799), 24 Feb. 1800 (received 3 Mch. 1800), 21 Aug. 1800 (received 28 Aug. 1800), and 10 Sep. 1800 (received 17 Sep. 1800).

From Tench Coxe

SIR   Jany 10. 1801.

I had the honor to learn from the person, who left you on the 31st. instant that you were then well.

The Situation of our post office is a great evil. It has occasioned me to be very guarded in my correspondence for some time. I have missed two letters, one of which related to private business of very great consequence to myself, and others.

The republican interest of the United States have been thrown for a few years past into an unjust and dangerous situation. The struggle however from the beginning of 1798 has been wisely, undauntedly, and upon the whole, I think, very temperately made. It does not yet appear whether it is with complete success. We have so far prevailed as to secure republicans in a number of the state governments—we have procured a republican representative House of Congress—we shall make a deep impression on the other branch—we have defeated the army and volunteer plans—we have prevented the success of a dangerous projector against the present and the *elected* chief Magistrate—we have effected a rotation in the Presidency upon principles favorable to our republican constitutions: we have resuscitated the Militia—avoided antirepublican alliances and an antirepublican war—brought the evils of the British treaty into full view—awakened the public mind to a sense of the dangers of a judiciary complaisance to the executive power—we have proved that respectable circles of men and even individuals cannot be compelled to yield their independence of opinion, language or conduct for honors, emoluments or even the bread of their families—and we have proved, that public mind, whenever fairly and fully informed abandons favorites, turns to the wise and good, relieves itself from deception, and inclines to measures favorable to liberty, œconomy, and peace.

We seem to have our judgments pretty well corrected and settled upon the subject of regular hired armies—whether we call them standing armies or permit their friends to bring them forward as necessary defenders. But it seems difficult to establish as correct ideas upon the subject of navy. It is plain that there is no grand naval power upon earth but G Britain, and if her expences in that line in the 18th. century be taken from her public accounts they will prove her vainglorious navy to have rendered her a splendid ruin—The maximum of her commerce is an export of less than 28. millions in the year, and her navy has cost her 24 millions in the period. It is a great trading country that neats $12\frac{1}{2}$ ℔cent upon it's exports clear of losses and deductions of all kinds. In this country, where agricultural preponderance is increasing, the advantages of navy are still less worth paying for. In 1793 this commercial state had nearly as many taxable inhabitants in its commercial district as now; but it has gained more than twenty thousand agricultural citizens—by the same lists of taxables. Our increase in seven years is about 25 cent, but the commercial population is little enlarged. But our trade is much increased. This is by foreigners then, and their vessels and cargoes are not objects for our navy to defend—The proper resource to defray the various branches of the public expenditure would seem, at first view, to be the property and citizens benefited by those branches of expence respectively. If Merchants, Mariners, ships and cargoes were to pay all contributions for the navy, we should be less profuse in that way. Perhaps our produce would not be lower nor our supplies higher, if all foreign ships might bring in and carry away cargoes on as good terms as our own. If so the carrying trade would appear to be the principal object for a navy. We should find the cost of our small fleet cut deeply into *the profits* of the carrying trade, and even into the amount of our freights. It seems to be a subject for prudence then. Our navy department should execute with Spirit, judgment and effect the plans of the Legislative and executive powers, but that department should be prudent, reflecting, disposed to examine into results, the good produced and the cost of it. British naval plans and views should be examined and considered with great prudence and candor. Her insular character, and our vast territorial extent. Her having foreign Colonies—we none. Her concessions to domestic defence, and to naval pride. Her vast increase of her naval expences, being one month—one or two hundred thousand dollars ₩ week. The multiplication of the chances of war is no small consideration in respect to a navy.

I do not mean to say any thing in opposition to the present System or to invite to new plan, or new principles. Tho I am of opinion that this complicated subject requires much consideration and a past œconomy of the state. In England Ideas of safety, glory, and trade have banished all attempts to estimate the benefits of the navy to that Country. It behoves America to consider first a reference to trade. I have good reason to believe it has not been viewed heretofore with out any eye to great & numerous colonial acquisitions—We have colonized 20,000 taxable inhabitants (perhaps 100. to 120,000 of all ages & races) to our country West of the Allegeny Mountains since 1782. I prefer this to a sugar colony keeping up the slave system. Humanity, justice & policy all forbid any new Scheme involving the use of Slaves.

In our department of state, we seem, of late entirely to have neglected the domestic section. It is the least expensive, the most interesting, the most at our own command, the most universally connected with individual interest, the most sure and permanent in its beneficial results, the most favorable to the promotion and preservation of the Union, the most moralizing and promotive of internal energy and industry, the most favorable to the expansion of the public mind. The improvement of the post roads, the power of uniting waters in different states by canals, a complete map, a complete chart and book of topographical description of the U.S, a legislative library, a board of agriculture and arts favorable to the production and consumption of its fruits, the incessant amelioration of the militia and the increase of the means of their sudden equipment, the fulfillment of *the promise* of a guarranty of a republican form of government to the States, the timely preparation of a system of free

Government for the federal territory, the imposition of a duty on the importation of slaves to the whole amount of the constitutional limit, the publication of a german edition of the laws, and many other small, considerable or great Objects could have been executed for the fruitless sums, which the plans of some persons have caused to be expended. The cultivation of the interior is the first object in a country so capable, and whose capacities have been so little drawn forth. The foreign division of the department of State seems to have occasioned the domestic department of it to have been much neglected. It is of great consequence to our prosperity, and future honor as a government that we prove more attentive to that Object than heretofore —at least if we continue as expensive as we have been for three or four years past.

The foreign division of our department of State presents to my mind some very singular appearances. The supplying, trading with, negociating about, and maintaining the independence de facto of the greatest of those Colonies, and all those colonies whose defence we engaged for seems much to do, and much to be allowed to do. The formation of a treaty with new privileges of trade in war, with a contraband favorable to one enemy power and injurious to the other and to our own agriculture, trade & navigation, the provision orders of the British Council, and our treaty on that point, the direction of our diplomatic affairs by the Treasury, and by a person in private life, the unresented proposition to have the provision orders revoked in 1795 till the treaty should be ratified with the avowed intention to renew them, the employment of that very minister to carry home the ratified treaty, the discontinuance of proceedings in the Case of Blount when the world saw that he was [a criminal?], the unnoticed appeal to the people by the British Commissioners in the case of the debts &ca., the readiness to cure all that is too open and too bad to bear on the British side, and the disposition to make heat, embarrassment, and impatience out of all that is unpleasant on the side of Holland, Spain and France, the alienation from France, the alienation from France from the Moment of her becoming a republic and the attachment to England which was displayed at the same time, the persecution of those who shewed or expressed a sense of these things, these and too many like circumstances run in our annals since 1792 are historical romance. To adopt a correct and practicable proceedure, which shall prevent the increase and continuance of such evils and substitute a just and wise course in their stead without producing an instigation and open unfriendliness of those powers, which are cut off those improper indulgences, sufferances &

preferences will require much wisdom, temper, firmness and conciliation. It will be seen that a cessation of devotion to the Monarchical states, and impartiality to the republican states will be to cease to war for one and against the other. On this subject much might be said and written, but it would amount to a respectful suggestion that a return to impartiality, justice, and the general interests of free government are no less difficult, than necessary.

The treasury department has been the source of action of a man of powers with certain attentions to Character, who was responsible while in place, but was followed by a man of a contracted mind & who was not bred under circumstances that give that cast to feeling and judgment, which generate a proper sense of Character. The eastern states have kept that department, its plans, its benefits in the hands of a devoted friend or a worse hand for the Union from the beginning. It is plain that much injustice has arisen from it, by preferences of New England views and interests, but they will never be ascertained or cured until the incumbents are removed—I say incumbents because I am satisfied, that the same persons do & will govern the treasury under any set of men, but one, that are predominate in the Government. On this department much is to be said, but it would be too extensive for a letter.

When I reflect upon the subjects at which I have hinted, the interest the party have to keep our friends out, the interests they have to desire themselves to be in, I cannot doubt their using every effort and hazarding every consequence to defeat our republican candidate. They will not suffer it, if they can avoid it. They leave too much to hazard, too much to suffer, too much to lose, too much to gain by success or disappointment. Every prudence therefore should be observed. Every effort made. Every contingency thought of & provided for. I hope the Virginia representatives will be chosen before the 4th. March—the Senators from the Republican interest chosen—the state legislatures kept in Session, the attendance of the Republican Senators & representatives at Washington on the 4th. March be at least considered—if not at once requested—Unfriendly foreign ministers should be observed. The professions of federalists should not be too hastily credited. Any real criminals among the federalists should be put into a state of formal Accusation. I mean such as are *important*, whose cases are capable of *proof*, and whose misconduct will commit the heads of their party—Honest and prudent men in the House may thus have their eyes opened; and bad men of timid minds may be placed under too serious reflexion to co-operate in defeating the continuance of the Government. The real fairness of

our views will be truly inferred from the manifestation of a dangerous and real criminality in our accusers and opponents—Nothing of
this kind should be hastily, lightly, or inconsiderately hazarded, but
nothing of the kind that can be supported should be neglected, when
proof is ready.

I am not at all alarmed at the dispositions or conduct of our opponents. But I have no confidence in them—I mean their leaders. I
would therefore neither believe nor trust in any thing. They will
make a plea of necessity. They will go any length on that plea. They
will justify it from analogies and precedants drawn from unwritten
constitutions—undefined principles. They will disregard the limitations of federal power, and the reversion of all lawfull authority to the
states, in failure of the general system. It is a case wherein we cannot
fear too far, if we preserve our firmness, and temper. The original
solemn obligations and engagements of the confederation appear to
me worthy of consideration, with the [confederation?] of the [. . .] or
virtually [repealing law.] On this point however, I have fully expressed myself before in communications to another from whom I
may hear this evening. I intended to have pursued those speculations,
but uncommon urgency of Business has prevented me—

This goes through a particular channel—With perfect respect, I
have the honor to be, Sir,

yr. most obedt. and hble servant   TENCH COXE

RC (DNA: RG 59, LAR); frayed, torn at folds; endorsed by TJ as received 19 Jan. and so recorded in SJL.

DIRECTION OF OUR DIPLOMATIC AF-FAIRS BY THE TREASURY: Oliver Wol-cott, Jr., became secretary of the Treasury upon Alexander Hamilton's resignation and return to private life in January 1795. During the summer of that year Hamilton wrote articles signed "Camillus" in sup-port of the Jay Treaty, which the Senate consented to on 24 June, but with a reser-vation. Secretary of State Edmund Ran-dolph recommended that Washington not sign the treaty until the British revoked their order in council of 25 Apr. 1795. Washington agreed and Randolph met with British Minister George Hammond on 13 July. Randolph reported: "Mr. Hammond asked me, if it would not be sufficient to remove the order out of the way; and after the ratification to renew it? I replied, perhaps with some warmth,

that this would be a mere shift, as the principle was the important thing. He then asked me, if the President was irrev-ocably determined not to ratify; if the pro-vision-order was not removed?" Wash-ington left for Mount Vernon on 15 July without signing the treaty. On 28 July the British minister supplied Wolcott with what appeared to be incriminating evi-dence against Randolph in an intercepted dispatch from French minister Jean An-toine Joseph Fauchet. Wolcott and Secre-tary of War Pickering, who both avidly supported the treaty, presented the evi-dence against Randolph to Washington upon his return to Philadelphia on 11 Aug. The president signed the treaty on 14 Aug., the day before Hammond's scheduled departure for England, allow-ing the British minister TO CARRY HOME THE RATIFIED TREATY. On 19 Aug. Washington confronted Randolph with the controversial dispatch and Randolph, protesting his innocence but realizing he had lost the confidence of the president, immediately resigned (Syrett, *Hamilton*, 18:475-9, 526-32; [Edmund Randolph], *A Vindication of Mr. Randolph's Resignation* [Philadelphia, 1795], 31-2; Vol. 28:392, 450-1n).

For the dismissal of the impeachment charges against William BLOUNT on the grounds that the Senate lacked jurisdiction, see Vol. 30:614-16, 618-19.

The PARTICULAR CHANNEL may have been Thomas Mendenhall, who carried a letter of introduction from Thomas McKean at Lancaster to TJ in Washington. According to SJL, TJ received both letters on 19 Jan.

From George Jefferson

DEAR SIR,   Richmond 10th. Janr. 1801.

I have to day received of the Treasurer of the James River company £160–15—as at foot, & which I have applied to the credit of Mr. Barnes.

I will by next post forward your account to the end of the year & am

Dear Sir Your Very humble servt.   GEO. JEFFERSON

Reimbursement of *two* fourths of the principal lent the company—(a further proportion of one fourth having been determined to be reimbursed since my last letter upon the subject)   £ 148–10–
Interest to 1st. Janr.   12– 5–
℞ statement herewith   £ 160–15–

RC (MHI); at foot of text: "Thos. Jefferson esqr."; endorsed by TJ as received 15 Jan. and so recorded in SJL.

From Lafayette

La Grange—20th Nivose.
MY DEAR FRIEND   feb. the 10h 1800 (o.s.) [i.e. 10 Jan. 1801?]

I Have Not, this Long While, Had the Satisfaction of a Line from You—it Was on My Emerging from Captivity that I Received Your Last Letter, dated Six Years Before, when You Heard of My Leaving the Mountains of Auvergne for the Command of an Army—You were foretelling the Successes which the European Revolution, the Institution of The National Guards, and My personal Situation Seemed to Have Reserved for Me—the Crop was Ready—it Has Not Been Reaped By Your friend—But By His Country Men, His Comrades, Many of Whom Raised By Him, and At the Expence of

His Ennemies Who Had Become His Geolers—so that in Spite of
Both persecutions, the Military Result with Respect to Me Has Been
Very Good.

far Was it from Being the Case in Civil Matters. Not for My pride,
Was I Capable to prefer it to Liberty, Humanity, justice, and to the
friends I Have Lost—But this Justification of My Conduct, When I
Opposed those pretenders to Republicanism By Whom our Republican Institutions Have Been Ruined, was writen with the purest the
Most Virtuous Blood of france—the Girondine Leaders Unable to
Improve the Revolution of the [10 Aug.] they Had Not Meant, Unfitted to Assert the principles of Legal Order, fell Victims to their
Own Success and their own Instruments, and While the Best Citizens Were Murdered, disarmed, Hunted out, whilc the Late Royal
family paid with their life a Repugnancy to Have Been Saved By patriotic Measures and By a friend of freedom, the Common Wealth
Became a prey to the Most Diabolical tyranny that Ever disgraced
and distracted Human Nature—Numberless Assassinations, pityless
pillage, Vexations of Every kind, and upon Almost Every Body were
Exercised in the Name of freedom, for the Honour of the Rights of
Men, and Amidst the Vociferations of Health to the Republic! So that
their principal Aim Seems to Have Been to Vitiate Every Liberal Notion, to destroy the New Raised Respect for Every patriotic Expression, and to Leave, as their Inheritance, an Horror for the principles
and the Very Name of liberty—The Constitution of the third Year
Could Have Restored it, Had it Not Been framed in the Convention,
Weaved With a Selfish Law, entrusted to Unpopular directors who
Had, in their Own defense, destroyed it two years Before it Received
from Sieyes and Bonaparte a Last and Avowed Blow—it is Evident
that the Common Wealth was on the 18th Brumaire Saved from the
paws of Returning Jacobinical tyranny—Sieyes Made out His System of Representation and Election as you Now See it—Bonaparte
Engrafted Upon it the Authority He thought proper to Exercise—
and So Was Made the Constitution of the Eight Year for the Execution of Which You May See Magistrates and Agents of principles,
and a Conduct in the past years totally different, But Among Whom,
Associated as they are, a decided Majority of Numbers is Given to
Men of Honesty and Good Morals—As to Liberty, My dear Jefferson, the Sufficiency of What We Now Have is Aknowledged By
those Who In 92 defended Constitutional freedom, By those Who
found at that time there was not freedom enough in the Constitution,
as well as By the people at large Who Are tired of and disgusted with
political Concerns—So that Active Opposition is Confined to a few

Counter Revolutionary and Jacobine people, the Extremes of parties, Whose Ways and Means Never Were So distant as they Appeared to Be, Who Ever Have Been Instruments to foreign Intrigues, and Who Have from the Beggining United in their Exertions, However different the Mode, to diffame the Good Cause, and to Stop, at Home and Abroad, the Love and the progress of the Revolution.

You know that on the 18th Brumaire I Was in Holland Among My old friends the patriots of 87—The delivery was obvious—the Engagements formal—it was a proper time for me to Arrive, and Insure the Recall of My friends Who Had Not like Me, an American Country to Resort to—So I did—But with a determination to live in Rural Retirement, without Any Connection with public Affairs—I feel every day more and more Confirmed in this plan—My Son Serves in the Army as an Officer of Huzzards—I am with the Rest of My family in A Country place, forty Miles from paris, wholly addicted to farming Occupations, and preserving in My Solitary Abode the principles and the Sentiments which No Vicissitudes in the public or personal times Have Ever Been able to Alter.

I Need Not telling You How Happy I Have Been Made By a Reconciliation Between the United States and france—I Have Every Reason to Believe that the Dispositions of this Governement Are in that Respect Very Good—You Will, I think, Be Satisfied With Cen pichon, Whose Acquaintance Has Been Very Agreeable to Me, Who Has the Confidence of those Who Send Him, and Deserves it the More, as He Has during the Negociation Been Well Meaning towards the United States, and Expresses Himself with Respect to them and their Citizens, in a Manner Which Has Greatly pleased me.

You will See in the papers our late Victories Every Where—particularly those of Moreau—a Continental peace is Insured—Great Britain is Coming to a Negociation—with what Sincerity I do not know—there is Nothing More Immoral than Her present Rulers—the Mischief to be Imputed to them, in the Revolution, passes description—we are However Under Obligations to them for the preservation of Egypt into our Hands—while the first Consul occupies the former Lodgings of the Elder Branch of Bourbon—You will See that with the Southern part of the family He is on Very Good terms.

The public prints Assert Your Nomination to the presidency as Being Almost Certain—My feelings, on the Occasion You do Not Question—it Has Been Said I Was Going to America as an Ambassador—the Health of My Wife Would Not Admit Her Crossing the Atlantic—I think Myself Unfit to Act a foreign part, However friendly, in the United States—it Would not at All Suit me—when I Go it Must Be on a Visit, as a fellow Citizen, a fellow Soldier, nor shall I Give up those titles for Any Other—Indeed it Behoves me to Remain Quiete, to See my family Enjoy Some tranquillity and Happiness, to Adjust My Affairs so as to keep, My debts Being paid, Some thing to Live Upon, and to Addict Myself Wholly to farming Studies and Occupations of Which I Now am Extremely fond—the distance from paris permits My friends Visiting me—I Go But Seldom to the Capital, and for a Short time—I am on proper terms with Bonaparte, My deliverer from Olmutz—The Last Attempt, Against His Life Endears Him to the people as it Was to Have Been followed with a Bloody Confusion—I Hope He May Consecrate His Glory By a final Establishement of freedom—My Civil and Military Companions Have Reentered the public Carrier—I am pleased to See Honest Men Help to the Repair of Many Injuries, to the doing of Many Good things—But I Had no Hand in the New Constitutional Settlement— I am totally a Stranger to the Governing and Legislating Business— a private, independant farmer I am and Shall Remain—The fourth part of a Century, in My life, Has Been, Either Actively, or passively devoted to public Concerns—Now I Have a Right, as a Veteran, to be Quiete, and Am determined Not to Give it Up, and to Cherish in My Rural Solitude the doctrine and the feelings to which my life in Both Hemispheres Has Been devoted. I know, My dear friend, those details are Not Uninteresting to You—of Yourself I Have Said Very Little, But think and feel a Great deal—Be so kind as to Give me Every particular Concerning you—They Will Not Be Misplaced.

I Beg You to present My Respects to Your Amiable daughters— My Best Compliments wait on our friends, particularly the Good doctor Logan to whom I Have Had the Obligation to Hear of You at Hamburg—My Wife and family Beg to Be Most Affectionately Remembered—Georges Has Been lately Employed in passing the Italian Rivers Under General dupont—His friend Who Had Also the Honor to See You is *Sous préfét* to our district—Mde de tessé and Her Husband are in paris—So is Mde de la Rochefoucauld—You Have, No doubt, Letters from Short—adieu My Dear Sir, Most Affectionately and respectfully I am

Your Constant friend   LAFAYETTE

Mrs Pichon a Very Amiable Young Lady Accompagnies Her Husband—She is a daughter to the Celebrated Architect, Brognard— She is Much Regretted by Her Relations and friends, and I am persuaded She Will be Both pleased and Beloved in America.

RC (DLC); internal evidence contradicts any date early in 1800; 20 Nivose of the Year 9 was 10 Jan. 1801, perhaps the most plausible date (10 Feb. 1801 was 21 Pluviose); addressed: "Thomas Jefferson Esq. favour'd By Cen Pichon Consul gal &c." (that is, "Citoyen Pichon Consul general &c."); at head of text in an unidentified hand: "Copd."; endorsed by TJ as a letter of 20 Nivose 1800 received 18 Mch. 1801 and so recorded in SJL (see also TJ to Lafayette, 13 Mch. 1801). Tr (same); in an unknown hand; dated 20 Nov. 1800; at head of text: "Exd."; with minor variations.

The LAST LETTER that Lafayette had from TJ was dated 16 June 1792; see Vol. 24:85-6. The Austrians freed Lafayette from confinement at Olmütz, Moravia, in September 1797. BONAPARTE, on instructions from the Directory, had presented the formal demand for the release of the marquis and other prisoners, and it was with Bonaparte in 1799 that Lafayette's wife, the Marquise de Lafayette, negotiated for her husband's return to France. In the disruption of the coup of 18 Brumaire the marquise hastily summoned her husband to Paris, where Bonaparte initially demanded that Lafayette stay in RURAL RETIREMENT at La Grange, an estate of his wife's family. The government restored the marquis's citizenship in March 1800, and in October he was a guest at the great festival staged at Môrtefontaine to celebrate the convention between France and the United States (Harlow Giles Unger, *Lafayette* [Hoboken, N.J., 2002], 315-17, 326-30).

FIRST CONSUL OCCUPIES THE FORMER LODGINGS: in February 1800 Bonaparte and the other consuls had taken up residence at the Tuileries, a former royal palace (Tulard, *Dictionnaire Napoléon*, 1661).

According to Lafayette's memoirs, when Talleyrand asked him to be AMBASSADOR he replied that he was too much of an American—"trop Américain"—to represent his native country in the United States. To Louis André Pichon, Lafayette explained his refusal by citing his wife's health, his desire to remain a quiet farmer with close ties to

family, and a reluctance to visit the U.S. in any official capacity. When Talleyrand pressed him to take a seat in the national senate, Lafayette expressed distrust for Bonaparte's regime and declared that remaining out of the public eye would be the extent of his deference to the government (George Washington Louis Gilbert du Motier de Lafayette, ed., *Mémoires, Correspondance et Manuscrits du Général Lafayette, Publiés par sa Famille*, 6 vols. [Paris, 1838], 5:173-4).

LAST ATTEMPT, AGAINST HIS LIFE: on 24 Dec. 1800 a bomb concealed on a Paris street exploded not long after Bonaparte passed by in his carriage. The "machine infernale," as the device was called, killed a dozen people and seriously injured several others. Although Bonaparte initially blamed Jacobins, prompting the execution of several of their leaders and the deportation of 130 people, further investigation by the police determined that the explosion was the work of royalist Chouans (Tulard, *Dictionnaire Napoléon*, 1107-8; Jean Tulard, *Napoleon: The Myth of the Saviour*, trans. by Teresa Waugh [London, 1984], 96-9).

GEORGES: the Lafayettes' son, George Washington du Motier de Lafayette, who had joined the army of the Batavian Republic and then transferred to the French hussars. He went to northern Italy in 1800 as a staff officer with Bonaparte's army and was for a time aide-de-camp to General Pierre DUPONT de l'Étang. HIS FRIEND WHO HAD ALSO THE HONOR TO SEE YOU: Félix Frestel, the younger Lafayette's tutor and a faithful helper to the young man's mother during her husband's imprisonment, had accompanied George to the United States in 1795-97 and was a member of the family's household at La Grange (Arnaud Chaffanjon, *La Fayette et sa descendance* [Paris, 1976], 167-9; Tulard, *Dictionnaire Napoléon*, 631-2; Unger, *Lafayette*, 277, 292, 301-2, 307, 319-20, 331, 347; Vol. 29:126-7).

Émilie Brongniart, a daughter of ARCHITECT Alexandre Théodore Brongniart, married Pichon shortly before the couple's departure for the United States. In Washington, Madame Pichon became a close friend of Margaret Bayard Smith

(Jacques Silvestre de Sacy, *Alexandre-Théodore Brongniart, 1739-1813, Sa Vie—Son Œuvre* [Paris, 1940], 62n, 124; Margaret Bayard Smith, *The First Forty Years of Washington Society*, ed. Gaillard Hunt [New York, 1906], 34, 213-18).

From Thomas McKean

DEAR SIR,   Lancaster, January 10th. 1801.

The important election has been so far favorable for the Republicans; you & Mr; Burr have 73 votes each, and the House of Representatives must, on the second Wednesday in the next month, chuse one of *you two* for President. As it appears from the explicit & honorable conduct of Mr; Burr there will be no competition on his part, it is reasonably to be expected that there can be no difficulty in the ballot. Interest, character, duty, love of country all conspire to insure this event; but I have been told that envy, malice, despair and a delight in doing mischief will prompt the Anglo-Federalists to set all other considerations at nought, and that it is intended to so manage as to keep the States equally divided, in order that Congress may in the form of a law appoint a President for us until a new election shall take place. This however seems very improbable, for it can scarcely be credited that the virtuous part of the Federalists will unite in so nefarious & dangerous a measure: Mr; Linn of New-Jersey, I have heard, and Mr; Bayard of Delaware, I am certain, have declared publicly, they will vote for Mr; Jefferson; the same has been reported of a majority of the members for Maryland.

But should it be possible that Gentlemen will act the desperate part that has been suggested by the partizans of anarchy & civil war, by what constitutional authority can the Congress assume the power of appointing any person President for the people of the Union, who has not been elected by the Electors, and in the place of two citizens who have been duly elected, and when both are in full health & capacity to act?   By the 2d. Article & 6th. paragraph of the 1st. sect. of the Constitution such a power is only given in four cases, removal of the President & Vice-President from office, their deaths, resignations or inability to discharge the duties of the office; neither of which has occurred on the present occasion, so that the case contemplated is a casus omissus, & within neither the letter nor spirit of the instrument, at least such a power in such a case is no where expressly delegated to them: but if the Congress can *agree in such an Act,* (law I will not call it) why not appoint one of the two candidates elect, or why cannot a majority of the States in the House of Representatives make an election of one of them by ballot?

On the other hand it may be asked what is to be done, must we have an interregnum? I answer no. The people of the United States having fairly & duly chosen two Gentlemen for President & Vice-President, by an equal number of votes, the conclusion would seem to be, that they are content with either as President. It is the unbounden duty of the majority of the States in the House of Representatives to determine between them by ballot, under an implication that the two candidates may not agree [in][1] the matter themselves; but suppose there shall be an equal division of the States, what is then to be done? The answer is let the two candidates agree between themselves by an instrument in writing, executed under their respective hands & seals before two or more subscribing witnesses, acknowledged before the Senate, recorded in the office of the Secretary of State or elsewhere and published to the world, designating which of them shall act as President & which as Vice-President. Thus the constitutional choice of the people will be substantially carried into effect, and all good men will support the measure: The people of Pennsylvania will, I rest assured, do it at all events, and I pledge myself as their Governor & Commander in chief to support them. If bad men will dare traitorously to destroy or embarass our general Government & the Union of the States, I shall conceive it my duty to oppose them at every hazard of life & fortune; for I should deem it less inglorious to submit to foreign than domestic tyranny. I can readily conceive a case that might occur, wherein no remedy can be constitutionally applied, and an interregnum for a year must necessarily ensue; such are the imperfections of human institutions. The evil will no doubt be redressed by an amendment of the Constitution.

But avaunt all these gloomy apprehensions, for, sure I am, that the States represented in the larger House will give an unanimous vote for the Gentleman, whom the people intended for their future President, and for whom the general wish was & is unequivocal, tho' not expressly declared in form, owing to a want of proper concert.

You will in a few weeks be wearied with applications and recommendations for office. How it may be in other States I know not, but in Pennsylvania & Delaware I do not hesitate to declare, that a great many officers are unworthy of their stations in any but particularly in a Republican government. I have already resisted several sollicitations for introductions to you, but importunity of friends has prevailed on me to name Stephen Sayre Esquire of the city of Philadia.

formerly a Sheriff of London, and William Irvine Esquire of Carlisle, an old General in our Revolutionary war, sometime a member of the old & also new Congress and now first Major General of our Militia, as Gentlemen worthy of your notice. Their wishes, I conjecture, are, the latter for supervisor of the excise, the former for a place in the customs: I think you must have seen and known them. I must beg your excuse for this liberty, it is one I am determined sparingly to take; but I have a son named Robert, who has had a liberal education tho' brought up a merchant; he is now an Auctioneer for the city of Philadelphia, it was all I could do for him, and yet he merits a better office; if a vacancy should happen in the custom-house or any other department I think him qualified to fill, I shall beg your permission to interfere for him; he is the only person I am anxious about.

I sincerely pray for your health & happiness, and am with great attachment and regard, dear Sir, Your most obedient & devoted humble servant   THO M:KEAN

Lancaster, January 27th. 1801.

P.S.

Knowing that the Chevalier de Yrujo intended soon to pass thro' this place on a visit to the city of Washington, and considering the flagrant practices of some persons familiar in the Post-offices, I have detained the inclosed letter for this conveyance: The Chevalier has at length arrived here.

I have nothing material to add, unless that I have heard, several officers of the U.S., conscious of their violent & reproachful conduct respecting the late Election and fearful of the consequences, have held caucuses in different places to consult, whether it would be expedient to resign, or force a removal, and that finally they had determined on the latter. This is a repetition of the measure adopted on my being chosen Governor.

My principle in this particular was, to give a preference to a real Republican or Whig, having equal talents & integrity, and to a friend before an Enemy: it is at least imprudent to foster spies continually about oneself. In Pennsylvania this conduct has been so generally approved, that at our last general election the Republicans obtained a majority of thirty two in the House of Representatives out of seventy eight members, whereas they had but two the year preceding; and in the Senate out of seven new members they succeeded in six; and this notwithstanding three of the most influential of the displaced officers were candidates for the Congress, several for the State Senate and many for the House of Representatives: not a single person of them succeeded, nor indeed had any chance. I am only sorry that I did not displace ten or eleven more, for it is not right [to] put a dagger into the hands of an Assassin.

The burning of the war-office last month and now the treasury have probably been accidental, but as these events were predicted in Philadelphia and subjects of conversation in July last, suspicions of design will be entertained by many. The circumstance is at any rate unfortunate for the present administration; it seems to me adviseable that vigilance & enquiry should take place.

With impatience do I wait the result of the eleventh of next month. I cannot conceive it possible, that the members of the House of Represent[atives] will risque the termination of all offices under the United States, whose tenure is during the pleasure of the President; and not at all probable that the Congress will hazard so bold a stroke as to usurp the power of mak[ing] a President for us, in the face of the constitution & against the choice & w[ill] of the people.

My next to you will, I trust, be in a different stile: in the mean[time] Adieu, dear Sir,

Your most obedient humble   THOS M:KEAN

RC (DLC); at head of text: "(Private)"; with letters and words obscured by tape supplied in brackets from FC; at foot of text: "The Honoble. Thomas Jefferson"; endorsed by TJ as a letter of 10 Jan., received 6 Feb., and so recorded in SJL. FC (Lb in PHi); in a clerk's hand, except for last full paragraph, closing, and signature in McKean's hand; with same postscript as in RC but with postscript dated 22 Jan. in a clerk's hand; endorsed: "Copy of a Lre. to the Honoble. T. Jefferson V.P. of the U.States Jany. 10th. 1801."

In March 1801 TJ appointed WILLIAM IRVINE superintendent of military stores in Philadelphia in place of Samuel Hodgdon, who had held the position since its establishment in June 1794. As secretary of state TJ had corresponded with Irvine, who served on the commission to settle the accounts between the states and the federal government. He was a congressman from 1793 to 1795 and a Pennsylvania elector in 1796, casting his vote for TJ and Burr. He worked closely with John Beckley, a Republican campaign manager in Pennsylvania, in the 1800 presidential campaign (ANB; Syrett,

Hamilton, 16:503-4; Notes on a Cabinet Meeting, printed at 8 Mch. 1801; Vol. 20:608, 621; Vol. 26:343n). Robert McKean was appointed an AUCTIONEER FOR THE CITY OF PHILADELPHIA in March 1800, a position he held until February 1801. He died in June 1802 without receiving a federal appointment (G. S. Rowe, *Thomas McKean: The Shaping of an American Republicanism* [Boulder, Colo., 1978], 321-2; Philadelphia *Aurora*, 13 Oct. 1800). For Thomas McKean's patronage practices, see Rowe, *McKean*, 318-27, and Tinkcom, *Republicans and Federalists*, 263-8.

CHEVALIER DE YRUJO: recalled Spanish minister Carlos Martínez de Irujo, McKean's son-in-law (Vol. 30:194n).

Fire broke out in the WAR-OFFICE on 8 Nov. 1800 and in an office of the TREASURY on 20 Jan. 1801. After the first fire the *Aurora* charged: "The *federal fireworks* at Washington will be found to have made a very rueful chasm in our *war history*; Alexander Hamilton's projects and Timothy Pickering's transactions, while secretary, will have had a *partial sweep*, to avoid the scrutinizing research of a Jeffersonian administration." An excerpt from a letter printed in the *Aurora* observed that no man was "free from suspicion" and that "many of different politics" declared "that this fire was not an accidental one." Virginia congressman John Nicholas chaired the committee appointed in early February to investigate the fires, which were probably caused by faulty chimneys (Philadelphia *Aurora*, 18 Nov. 1800, 26, 27 Jan. 1801; *Annals*, 10:1357-76; Bryan, *National Capital*, 1:384-5).

[1] Word missing in RC.

From James Madison

Dear Sir   Jany. 10. 1801.

Mrs Browne having been detained at Fredg for some time, I did not receive your favor of the 19th. in time to be conveniently acknowledged by the last mail. The succeeding one of the 26th. came to hand on the 7th. instant only, a delay that fixes blame on the post office either in Washington or Fredg. In all the letters & most of the newspapers which I have lately recd. thro' the post office, there is equal ground for complaint.

I find that the vote of Kentucky establishes the tie between the Repub: characters, and consequently throws the result into the hands of the H. of R. Desperate as some of the adverse party there may be, I can scarcely allow myself to believe that enough will not be found to frustrate the attempt to strangle the election of the people, and smuggle into the chief Magistracy the creature of a faction. It would seem that every individual member, who has any standing or stake in society, or any portion of virtue or sober understandg must revolt at the tendency of such a manouvre. Is it possible that Mr. A. shd give his sanction to it if that should be made a necessary ingredient? or that he would not hold it his duty or his policy, in case the present House should obstinately refuse to give effect to the Constn. to appoint, which he certainly may do before his office expires[1] as early a day as possible, after that event, for the succeeding House to meet, and supply the omission. Should he disappt. a just expectation in either instance, it will be an omen, I think, forbidding the steps towards him which you seem to be meditating. I would not wish to discourage any attentions which friendship, prudence, or benevolence may suggest in his behalf, but I think it not improper to remark, that I find him infinitely sunk in the estimation of all parties. The follies of his administration, the oblique stroke at his Predecessor in the letter to Coxe, and the crooked character of that to T. Pinkney, are working powerfully agst. him, added to these causes is the pamphlet of H[2] which, tho' its recoil has perhaps more deeply wounded the author, than the object it was discharged at, has contributed not a little to overthrow the latter staggering as he before was in the public esteem.

On the supposition of either event, whether of the interregnum in the Executive, or of a surreptitious intrusion into it, it becomes a question of the first order, what is the course demanded by the crisis. will it be best to acquiesce in a suspension or usurpation of the Executive authority till the meeting of Congs. in Decr. next, or for Congs. to be summoned by a joint proclamation or recommendation of the two characters havg a majority of votes for President. My present judgment favors the latter expedient. The prerogative of convening the Legislature must reside in one or other of them, and if both concur, must substantially include the requisite will. The intentions of the people would undoubtedly be pursued. And if, in reference to the Constn: the proceeding be not strictly regular, the irregularity will be less in form than any other adequate to the emergency; and will lie in form only rather than substance; whereas the other remedies proposed are substantial violations of the will of the people, of the scope of the Constitution, and of the public order & interest. It is to be hoped however that all such questions will be precluded by a proper decision of nine states in the H. of R.

I observe that the French Convention is represented as highly obnoxious to the Senate. I should not have supposed that the opposition would be hinged on the article surrendering public vessels. As the stipulation is mutual it certainly spares our pride, sufficiently to leave us free to calculate our interest, and on this point there cannot be a difference of opinion. I was less surprized at the obstacle discovered in the British Treaty, the latter of which combined with the repeal of the French Treaty, begat a suspicion that in some quarters at least the present posture of things has been long anticipated. It is certain[3] however that the convention leaves G.B. on a better footing than the B. Treaty placed her, and it is remarkable that E. D. & Murray, should have concurred in the arrangement, if it have any real interference with bona fide engagements to G.B. It may be recollected that the privilege given to British prizes was not purchased like that to French prizes, by any peculiar services to us; and never had any other pretext, than the alledged policy of putting the two great rival nations of Europe as nearly as possible on an equal footing. Notwithstanding this pretext for the measure, H. in his late pamphlet acknowledges the error of it. It would be truly extraordinary if a measure intended for this equalizing purpose, should be construable into an insuperable barrier to the equality proposed. It is of vast moment both in a domestic & foreign view, that the Senate should come to a right decision. The public mind is already sore & jealous of that body, and particularly so of the insidious & mischeivous policy of the British Treaty. It is strongly averse also to war, and would feel abhorrence of an unjust or unnecessary war with any nation. It is much to be wished that these facts may not be disregarded in the question before the Senate. If there be any thing fairly inadmissible in the Convn. it would be better to follow the example of a qualified ratification, than rush into a provoking rejection. If there be any thing likely, however unjustly, to beget complaints or discontents on the part of G.B. early & conciliatory explanations ought not to be omitted. However difficult our situation has been made, justice & prudence will it is hoped, steer us through it peacefully. In some respects the task is facilitated by the present moment. France has sufficiently manifested her friendly disposition, and what is more, seems to be duly impressed with the interest she has in being at peace with us. G.B. however intoxicated with her maritime ascendancy, is more dependent every day on our commerce for her resources, must for a considerable length of time look in a great degree[4] to this Country, for bread for herself, and absolutely for all the necessaries for her islands. The prospect of a Northern confederacy of Neutrals cannot fail, in several views, to inspire caution & management towards the U.S., especially as in the event of war or interruption of commerce with the Baltic, the essential article of naval stores can be sought here only. Beside these cogent motives to peace and moderation, her subjects will not fail to remind her of the great pecuniary pledge they have in this Country, and which under any interruption of peace of commerce with it, must fall under great embarrassments, if nothing worse.—As I have not restrained my pen from this hasty effusion, I will add for your consideration one other remark on the subject. Should it be found: that G.B. means to oppose pretentions drawn from her Treaty, to any part of the late one with F. may she not be diverted from it, by the idea of driving us into the necessity of soothing France, by stipulations to take effect at the expiration of the Treaty with G.B. and that wd. be a bar to the renewal of the latter, or in case the pretensions of G.B. should defeat the Treaty now, before the Senate, might not such an expedient be made a plaister for the wound given to F!

My health still suffers from several complaints, and I am much afraid that any changes that may take place are not likely to be for the better. The age and very declining state of my father are making also daily claims on my attention; and, from appearances it may not be long before these claims may acquire their full force. All these considerations mingle themselves very seriously with one of the eventual arrangements contemplated. It is not my purpose however to retract what has passed in conversation between us on that head. But I cannot see the necessity, and I extremely doubt the propriety, should the contest in hand issue as is most probable, of my anticipating the relinquishment of my home. I cannot but think, & feel that there will be an awkwardness to use the softest term, in appearing on the political Theatre before I could be considered as regularly called to it, and even before the commencement of the authority from which the call would proceed. Were any solid advantage at stake, this scruple might be the less applicable, but it does not occur that the difference of not very many days, can be at all material. As little can I admit that the circumstance of my participation in the Ex. business could have any such effect on either the majority or minority as has occurred; or if a partiality in any particular friends would be gratified by a knowledge of such an arrangement, that the end would not be as well attained by its being otherwise made known to them that it was to take place, as by its being announced by my appearance on the spot. I only add that I am sensible of the obligation of respecting your conclusion whatever it may finally be; but I can not but hope that it may be influenced by the considerations which I have taken the liberty to hint. very affecly. & respectfully I am Dr. Sir Yrs.

You may recollect a difficulty suggested in makg. appts. witht. a Senate, in case of resignations *prior to March 4.* How have you solved it?

RC (DLC: Madison Papers); endorsed by TJ as received 15 Jan. and so recorded in SJL.

Madison referred to John Adams's May 1792 LETTER TO COXE in which the then vice president criticized the appointment of Thomas Pinckney as U.S. minister to England. The letter was published in the Philadelphia *Aurora* on 26 April 1799 and republished by Duane on 28 Aug. 1800 and several times in the fall of 1800 for which seditious libel charges were leveled against him and then dropped (Cooke, *Coxe*, 358-60, 378).

E. D.: Oliver Ellsworth and William R. Davie.

For the shortage of oak and NAVAL STORES, see Madison, *Papers*, 17:457n.

AGE AND VERY DECLINING STATE OF MY FATHER: Madison's father, James Madison, Sr., died on 27 Feb. 1801 after a lengthy illness at his Montpelier home.

EVENTUAL ARRANGEMENTS CONTEMPLATED: TJ planned to nominate Madison as his secretary of state. Madison, who was recuperating from an illness, decided against going to Washington until after TJ's inauguration and did not arrive there until 1 May (Brant, *Madison*, 4:41, 42).

[1] Preceding eleven words interlined in place of "[. . .] to fix."

[2] Preceding word and "H" interlined.

[3] Word interlined in place of "remarkable."

[4] Preceding four words interlined.

To Thomas Mann Randolph

DEAR SIR   Washington Jan. 10. 1801.

I promised to procure for the Chevalier de Freire, minister of Portugal an account of our manner of cultivating tobacco so detailed as that a person might, by it's instruction, pursue the culture with exactness. I always intended to have got two or three judicious planters to state to me their methods, which I should have noted down, and out of the whole have made out one. I now see that it will not be in my power to do this; and yet if I fail it will be ascribed to jealousy or illiberality. I must therefore pray you to pay this debt for me. it will be the more easy for you as you possess the subject within yourself which I did not. the principal division of the kinds into Sweet scented & Oronoko, with only a partial specification of the principal varieties & their qualities will be sufficient. I have to write to the Chevalr. on another subject, and will delay it till you can with convenience enable me to fulfill my promise to him. I wrote to you two days ago. but the present subject now occurring, I commit it to a special letter. tender love to the family. health & affection to yourself.

TH: JEFFERSON

RC (DLC); at foot of text: "T M Randolph"; endorsed by Randolph as received 22 Jan. PrC (MHi); endorsed by TJ in ink on verso.

Cipriano Ribeiro FREIRE made his request in a letter to TJ of 22 Feb. 1799. I HAVE TO WRITE: no further correspondence between Freire and TJ is recorded in SJL. I WROTE TO YOU: for TJ's last letter to Randolph, see 9 Jan.

From Thomas Mann Randolph

TH: M. RANDOLPH TO TH: JEFFERSON: Jan. 10. 1801.

We are all well except Martha: she has frequent slight indispositions which she attributes to incipient pregnancy and yet has not resolution to wean Cornelia alltho' she is so robust as to have got her mouth set with teeth without our notice. Martha will yield to our persuasions and separate her shortly I am satisfied.

I have nothing to say on your affairs unless that Lillie is likely to make up a gang at last, an occasion luckily offering in our own neighbourhood in some arrangement between Hancock Allen & his mother by which he gets her hands & hires them: they will average 21.£. I expect.

Will you oblige me so far as to include five bushels for me in your order for Clover seed this year? I am greatly pleased with Clover hay: what I thought worth little, from the rain in making, has proved fine food by the effect on my animals. I can think of no preparation for turneps, which have become a necessary crop with me, so good as the Albany peas. Altho' it failed in the large old fields destined for Wheat it may pay well upon land intended for turneps & will certainly keep the land free of weeds and mellow: it comes off full early for turneps. Can you procure a few bushels for me from New York in time to plant the coming Spring? it is worth introducing even if the fly should make it proper to feed it away green. *We* must have sheep; sheep must have turnep & turnep must have some plant to keep the manure laid down for it in Spring moist till July, without stocking the ground with seeds; as oats do and thereby choak the young turneps.

Our anxiety about the election is now removed by a certainty that the house of Representatives is to chuse. I cannot think *myself* that the Feds mean to obstruct the choice as unless they can bring Hamilton immediately into the Senate I do not see what they are to gain by it: perhaps Ross might be able to confound, subvert & embroil suffi-ciently, (to produce the only state of things in which they now can gain), in one year, by the advice and direction of our Catiline. Unless *that* can be done it matters little I conceive whether there be a year of interregnum, thro their malice, or not: if there should be, it will place every honest man of their party on the republican side; it will draw the line between the worthy citizens who have been cheated & duped and the small band of Villains who have acted allways from motives of mischief. Even if it can be done & is done it will only drive Catiline & his band into the field, at the end of the year; where the virtuous young citizens may rush upon them and give them that death they deserve to meet in a more ignoble manner.

    With truest affection y'r. &c   TH. M. RANDOLPH

RC (ViU: Edgehill-Randolph Papers); endorsed by TJ as received 15 Jan. and so recorded in SJL.

TJ paid HANCOCK ALLEN of Albemarle County £40, or $133.33, for the hire of two slaves, Myntas and Ben (MB, 2:1037, 1063).

From Dr. John Vaughan

DR. SIR   Wilmington Jany. 10th 1801
    The friendly manner in which you received my late communication induces me to resume the privilege of addressing you, to mention a

few incidents respecting the unfortunate dilemma in which we are placed.

Mr. Bayard, our representative, has lately written to a friend here, that "the Federalists in Congress talk of supporting Mr. Burr, & that it is in his power to give the casting vote": & surely our political destiny is suspended by a slender thread, while dependant on the integrity of Mr. Bayard. But, notwithstanding he has frequently canted on the importance of his vote, I am authorised to say—that he will take advantage of existing circumstances, to retrieve his reputation. The manner in which he has acted, since the result of the election was known, is truly characteristic of the time serving partizan. I lately heard him declare in a large company, that he should not hesitate a moment in voting for the voice of the people; & on several occasions he has appeared ambitious to toast a name that he, his friend Stockton & others[1] rejected in public company, on the 4th. July 1799. These circumstances, together with many others literally coincident, confirm me in the belief, that he is determined to turn with the current of public sentiment: and if he does act right, for once, we shall give him credit for the *deed* without scrutinizing the motives of action.

The state of Delaware, tho the least, will doubtless be the last to join in the political reformation, which is pervading our country. Church & State are here connected by the rigid ties of interest & superstition; but our short-sighted demagogues have fallen into the general error, of *Governing too much.* The people are beginning to feel—feeling will excite inquiry, & the latter must necessarily lead to a discovery of their political depravity. We are making arrangements for an honorable effort in the ensuing election for Governor.

If you, my dear sir, were informed of the interest I feel, in the existing state of things, you would readily pardon this assumption of privilege. I have passed thro the whole catalogue of Federal persecutions, attempted persecutions under the, *ignoble,* Sedition law not excepted, & have the satisfaction of recounting them in the fortunate incidints of my life. They are honors, purchased rather[2] dearly, but they will serve to sweeten future days, & become useful lessons of instruction to a rising family:—they, at least, authorize me to say

that, I have the honor to be, with sincere respect, your obedt. humble Servt.   JOHN VAUGHAN

RC (DLC); at head of text: "Thomas Jefferson Esqr"; endorsed by TJ as received 12 Jan. and so recorded in SJL.

The ENSUING ELECTION FOR GOVERNOR, not held until October 1801, was decided in favor of Republican David Hall.

James Sykes served as acting governor and filled the remainder of the three-year term after Richard Bassett resigned in February 1801 when John Adams appointed him a judge of the Third District (John A. Munroe, *Federalist Delaware*

1775-1815 [New Brunswick, N.J., 1954], 196, 210, 265; JEP, 1:381).

[1] Word and ampersand interlined.
[2] Vaughan first wrote "too," then canceled it.

To Hugh Williamson

[Dear Sir]   Washington Jan. 10. 1801.

I should sooner have acknoleged your favor of Dec. 8. but for a growing and pressing correspondence which I can scarcely manage. I was particularly happy to recieve the diary of Quebec, as about the same time I happened to recieve one from the Natchez, so as to be able to make a comparison of them. the result was a wonder that any human being should remain in a cold country who could find room in a warm one, should prefer -32. to +55. Harry Hill has told me that the temperature of Madeira is generally from [58]. to [63]. it's extreme about [50. to 70]. If I ever change my climate for health, it shall be for that island. I do not know that the coincidence has ever been remarked between the new moon & the greater degrees of cold, or the full moon & the lesser degrees; or that the reflected beams of the moon attemper the weather at all. on the contrary I think I have understood that the most powerful [concave] mirror presented to the moon, & throwing it's focus on the bulb of a thermometer, does not in the least affect it.—I suppose the opinion to be universal that the Turkey is a native of America. nobody, as far as I know, has ever contra[dicted] it but Daines Barrington: and the arguments he produces are such as none [but] a head, entangled & kinked as his is, would ever have urged. before the discovery of America, no such bird is mentioned in a single author. all those quoted by Barrington by description refering to the Guinea hen, the pheasant, or the Peac[ock.] but the [book] of every traveller who came to America soon after it's discovery is [full] of accounts of the Turkey and of it's abundance: and immediately after that discovery we find the Turkey served up at the feasts of Europe as their most extraordin[ary] rarity. Mr. William Strickland, eldest son of Sr. George Strickland of York in England told me this anecdote. some ancestor of his commanded a vessel in the navigations of Cabot. having occasion to consult the Herald's office concerning his family he found a petition from that ancestor to the crown, stating that Cabot's circumstances being slender, he had been rewarded by the bounties he needed [from] the crown; that as to himself, he asked nothing in that way, but that as a considera[tion] for his services in the same way, he might be permitted to assume for the crest of his family arms, the Turkey an American bird: and mr Strickland observed that their crest [. . .] actually a turkey. you ask whether we may be quoted. in the first place, I now state the thing from memory, and may be inexact in some small circumstances. mr Strickland too stated it to me in a conversation, and not considering it of importance, might be inexact too. we should both [dislike] to be questioned before the publick for any little inaccuracy of [. . .] or recollection. I think if you were to say that the herald's office may be referred to in proof of the fact, it would be authority sufficient, without naming [us]. I have at home a note of mr Strickland's information, which I then committed to paper. my situation does not allow me to refresh my memory from that.—I shall be glad to see your book make it's appearance: and I am sure it will be well recieved by the Philosophical part of the world. for I still dare to use the word philosophy, notwithstanding the war waged against it by bigotry & despotism. Health, respect and friendly salutations.   TH: JEFFERSON

PrC (DLC); blurred, faint, and torn; at foot of first page: "Doctr. Williamson."

ONE FROM THE NATCHEZ: see James Wilkinson to TJ, 29 Nov. 1800.

What TJ COMMITTED TO PAPER is printed in Vol. 28:371-3 as Notes on Conversations with William Strickland, May 1795.

To Ebenezer Burling

SIR   Jan. 11. 1801. Washington.

    I should with great delight deliver myself up to the investigation of the subject proposed in your letter of Dec. 28. had I a right to my own time. but that belongs to the public and is fully engaged in objects far less agreeable to me than those I am obliged to abandon. you seem however so well acquainted with the object on which you are engaged that I dare say you will attain it without difficulty. as to the method I proposed for establishing a standard of weights, measures & coins, by a reference to the pendulum, it has been taught in the schools for a century, with very general approbation so that I did not propose it as a thought of my own, but as the best of those which had been proposed within my knowledge. I still prefer it to a portion of a great circle of the earth, which the French have adopted. I am however candidly open to any other new proposition, and shall be greatly gratified if you should devise something more certain and convenient than has hitherto been thought of. I am Sir

Your very humble servt   TH: JEFFERSON

PrC (DLC); at foot of text: "Mr. Ebenezer Burling. Peekskill"; endorsed by TJ in ink on verso.

TAUGHT IN THE SCHOOLS FOR A CENTURY: TJ and others looked to Isaac Newton's *Principia* as the starting point

for the use of a pendulum to define a unit of measure (Vol. 16:510, 542-3, 567-70, 602, 652, 669-70n).

For the decision by the FRENCH to base their system upon actual measurement of a portion of the earth's circumference, see Vol. 27:818-19, 822n.

To Julian Ursin Niemcewicz

DEAR SIR   Washington Jan. 11. 1801.

I am favoured with yours of Dec. 28. and shall forward it to mr Littlepage's brother, for the satisfaction of the family. it is I believe a twelvemonth since I have had a letter from Genl. Kosciuzko. but I had an opportunity of hearing some particulars of him from General Davie, one of our envoys lately returned from Paris. he says the General is in tolerable health, is considered as the head of the Polish corps in the service of France, keeps a table as such, and is the regular organ between them & the government of France. he is able to walk about.   I thank you for your congratulations on the subject of the late election. it is not however yet decided. the vanquished party have still the resource of some maneuvres to shew their spirit and adroitness. accept assurances of my high esteem & respect, & my friendly salutations.   TH: JEFFERSON

PrC (DLC); at foot of text: "M. Niemcewicz"; endorsed by TJ in ink on verso.

SHALL FORWARD IT: on this day TJ wrote a note to Carter Littlepage: "The inclosed letter from mr Niemcewicz containing some later accounts of your brother I have the pleasure to inclose it to you, and to assure you of the sentiments of esteem with which I am Dear Sir Your most

obedt. sert" (PrC in MHi; at foot of text: "Mr. Littlepage"; endorsed by TJ in ink on verso). A letter from TJ to Carter Littlepage, 20 Aug. 1800, is recorded in SJL but has not been found.

A TWELVEMONTH: TJ's last letter in hand from Tadeusz Kosciuszko was that of 15 Sep. [1799], received on 12 Feb. 1800 (Vol. 31:184).

To Joseph Moss White

Sir   Washington Jan. 11. 1801.

I recieved a few only of mr Morse's papers from Danbury, not more I believe than 2. or 3. and do not recollect to have seen the pieces signed the Enquirer to which you allude in your letter of the 1st. inst. I shall with pleasure read the pamphlet you send me, and I pray you to accept my thanks for it. if I can be instrumental in extinguishing the feuds which some late occurrences have excited among my fellow citizens, it will be to me a circumstance of great consolation. to carry certain measures which the proposers thought for the public good, they concieved it would be expedient to calumniate me, who did not think them for the public good. when these questions shall have past away, I am in hopes my fellow citizens who have given ear to the calumnies, will be disposed to make a juster estimate of my character. it will certainly be my endeavor to merit a better opinion than that which they have been made to entertain. I am Sir

Your very humble servt   Th: Jefferson

PrC (DLC); at foot of text: "Mr. Joseph Moss White. Danbury."

To Joseph Anthony

Sir   Washington Jan. 12. 1801.

I promised that on my return home I would examine & see what paiment I had made to mr Trumbull for the double pair of prints for which I paid you a moiety of the price. I found that on the 17th. Apr. 1790. I gave him an order on Leroy & Bayard, (we were then in New York) for six guineas which was paid & the order returned to me with his reciept & now in my possession. I presume therefore that the paiment I made you was the exact balance. I am Sir

Your humble servt   Th: Jefferson

RC (ViU). PrC (MHi); at foot of text: "Mr. Joseph Anthony 94 Market str."; endorsed by TJ in ink on verso.

For the payment TJ made for the first half of his subscription to the engravings by John Trumbull, see TJ to Anthony, 6 May 1800, and mb, 1:756.

To Mathew Carey

SIR   Washington Jan. 12. 1801.

I recieved some time ago your favor by Doctr. Carey together with the American Monitor, for which be pleased to accept my thanks. I have no doubt of it's utility as a school-book as soon as the pupil is so far advanced as to reflect on what he reads, and that I believe is in an earlier stage than is generally imagined. I concur with you in the importance of inculcating into the minds of young people the great moral & political truths, and that it is better to put into their hands books which while they teach them to read, teach them to think also, and to think soundly. I have always believed that Tacitus would be one of the best school books, even while children are learning to read. they could never forget the hatred of vice and tyranny which that author inspires. you often quote a book under the title of the Spirit of despotism. I never before heard of it: but it is written with great strength of feeling & conception. I am with great esteem Sir

Your most obedt. servt   TH: JEFFERSON

RC (NHC); addressed: "Mr. Matthew Carey 118. Market street Philadelphia"; franked and postmarked. PrC (DLC). Tr (PHi); in unknown hand; at head of text: "Recd. Jany 15."

YOUR FAVOR BY DOCTR. CAREY TO-GETHER WITH THE AMERICAN MONITOR: see Carey to TJ, 18 Dec. 1800.

Vicesimus Knox's SPIRIT OF DESPOTISM was published in London and reprinted in Philadelphia by John Lang and Stephen Clegg Ustick for Mathew Carey, 28 Nov. 1795 (Evans, No. 28936).

From Claudine Cenas

Lyons, France, 12 Jan. 1801. TJ's great reputation prompts her to write in regard to the estate of Gaspard Cenas, who died in Philadelphia about two and a half years ago. Gaspard's father François Cenas, who lives in a home for elderly people in Lyons, is unable to pursue inquiries with regard to the estate. The writer, the Widow Durand, is François Cenas's daughter and has taken up the matter. One Pierre Cenas, a relation, learned of Gaspard Cenas's death and, misrepresenting the amount of the estate, obtained a power of attorney. Going to Philadelphia, he took possession of the estate and has squandered a portion of it. On receiving a statement from him she consulted with a notary whom she trusts. She then revoked the power of attorney and sought to appoint a new representative in the United States through the channel of Monsieur Bosquet, a merchant upholsterer of Lyons who has connections in Philadelphia. Pierre Cenas, whom she has seen in France, claims that in Philadelphia her brother was a dancing instructor of modest means who lived in a furnished room. She knows that Pierre is lying and that he has resources now that he did not have prior to his trip to settle her brother's estate, including merchandise purchased from proceeds of the estate. She can do nothing until she knows that a new agent has been appointed. She implores TJ to assist her and provides the names of Pierre Cenas's contact and attorneys in Philadelphia.

RC (DLC); 3 p., in French; addressed: "Au Citoyen presidant des Etats unis— a phidalphi dans lorient par la Ville denante En Betagne"; in another hand: "Par Bordeaux"; "a phidalphi" struck through, with "The President of the United States Washington City" added in another hand; postmarked at Lyons, Nantes, and Philadelphia; franked; endorsed by TJ as received 8 Apr. 1802 and so recorded in SJL.

Another letter from Claudine Cenas, dated 9 Sep. 1801 and received from Lyons on 13 Feb. 1802, is recorded in SJL but has not been found.

To William Dunbar

DEAR SIR   Washington Jan. 12. 1801.

Your favor of July 14. with the papers accompanying it came safely to hand about the last of October. that containing remarks on the line of demarcation I perused according to your permission, and with great satisfaction, and then inclosed to a friend in Philadelphia to be forwarded to it's address. the papers addressed to me, I took the liberty of communicating to the Philosophical society. that on the language by signs is quite new. soon after recieving your meteorological diary, I recieved one of Quebec: and was struck with the comparison between -32. & +19¾ the lowest depressions of the thermometer at Quebec & the Natchez. I have often wondered that any human being should live in a cold country who can find room in a warm one. I have no doubt but that cold is the source of more sufferance to all animal nature than hunger, thirst, sickness & all the other pains of life & of death itself put together. I live in a temperate climate, and under circumstances which do not expose me often to cold. yet when I recollect on one hand all the sufferings I have had from cold, & on the other all my other pains, the former preponderate greatly. what then must be the sum of that evil if we take in the vast proportion of men who are obliged to be out in all weather, by land & by sea; all the families of beasts, birds, reptiles, & even the vegetable kingdom? for that too has life, and where there is life there may be sensation.—I remark a rainbow of a[1] great portion of the circle observed by you when on the line of demarcation. I live in a situation which has given me an opportunity of seeing more than the semicircle often. I am on a hill 500. f. perpendicular high. on the east side it breaks down abruptly to the base where a river passes through. a rainbow therefore about sunset plunges one of it's legs down to the river, 500. f. below the level of the eye on the top of the hill. I have twice seen bows formed by the moon. they were of the colour of the common circle round the moon, and were very near, being within a few paces of me in both instances.—I thank you for the little vocabularies of Bedaïs, Tankawis & Teghas. I have it much at heart to make as extensive a collection as possible of the Indian tongues. I have at present about 30. tolerably full, among which the number radically different, is truly wonderful. it is curious to consider how such handfuls of men, came by different languages, & how they have preserved them so distinct. I at first thought of reducing them all to one orthography. but I soon became sensible that this would occasion two sources of error instead of one. I therefore think it best to keep them in the form of orthography in which they were taken, only noting whether that were English, French, German or what.—I have never been a very punctual correspondent, and it is possible that new duties may make me less so. I hope I shall not on that account lose the benefit of your communications. a Philosophical vedette at the distance of 1000. miles, and on the verge of the terra incognita of our continent is precious to us here. I pray you to accept assurances of my high consideration & esteem, and friendly salutations.   TH: JEFFERSON

RC (NhHi); addressed: "William Dunbar esquire at the Natchez"; franked; postmarked 17 Jan.; endorsed. PrC (DLC).

In addition to Dunbar's letter of 14 July 1800, see, for the various PAPERS from him, his letter of 30 June and TJ's correspondence with Caspar Wister, the FRIEND IN PHILADELPHIA, on 16 Dec. For the METEOROLOGICAL DIARY, see James Wilkinson to TJ, 29 Nov.

It is likely that the LITTLE VOCABULARIES, which have not been located, were among TJ's collected research on languages that was vandalized, and most of the papers lost or destroyed, in 1809 (see Vol. 20:451-2; Vol. 30:81-2n). The words on the lists from Dunbar may have been from the unrelated languages of the Bidais, the Tonkawas, and the Caddo Indians who were known to the Spanish as the Tejas. Since those groups lived in Texas and were involved in the region's trade networks, Dunbar's source may have been Philip Nolan or his unidentified associate from horse-gathering expeditions who provided information about sign language (Donald E. Chipman, *Spanish Texas, 1519-1821* [Austin, Tex., 1992], 18-21; Jean Louis Berlandier, *The Indians of Texas in 1830*, ed. John C. Ewers, trans. Patricia Reading Leclercq [Washington, 1969], 23, 105-6, 146-7, 149-50; David La Vere, *The Caddo Chiefdoms: Caddo Economics and Politics, 700-1835* [Lincoln, Neb., 1998], 63-9, 80-1, 90-1, 104, 106-7, 120-1; William C. Sturtevant, gen. ed., *Handbook of North American Indians*, 13 vols. to date [Washington, 1978-   ], 17:8, 299, 308; Vol. 30:425-6n; Vol. 31:203, 237, 311; Dunbar to TJ, 30 June 1800).

[1] Here TJ evidently began to write, then canceled, "complete."

From George Jefferson

DEAR SIR,   Richmond 12th. Janr. 1801.

You will receive your account inclosed, made up to the end of the year; from which you will observe there was then an apparent balance in your favor of £1147–19–3. from this deduct £813–19–9 not due from M. & F. until the 1st. of April next, and the *real* balance which was then in our hands will be found to have been £333–19–6.

I have heard of a small draught of yours in favor of James Lyon, but which has not as yet been presented for payment.

I am Dear Sir Your Very humble servt.   GEO. JEFFERSON

RC (MHi); at foot of text: "Thos. Jefferson esqr. Washington"; endorsed by TJ as received 16 Jan. and so recorded in SJL. Enclosure not found, but see Statement of Account with Gibson & Jefferson at 15 Jan. 1801.

M. & F.: McMurdo & Fisher purchased TJ's tobacco (MB, 2:1033; George Jefferson to TJ, 10 Dec. 1800). For the draft IN FAVOR OF JAMES LYON, see note to Lyon to TJ, 14 Dec. 1800.

From George Jefferson

DEAR SIR   Richmond 12th. Janr. 1801.

You will observe from your acct which I forward herewith, that you are not charged with the 50$: which I some time ago paid for you; this I omitted because I did not like there should be any appearance of mystery in pecuniary matters betwixt us. The order therefore I return inclosed.

If you do not choose it should remain until I have the pleasure of seeing you—it will not *now* be inconvenient to you to remit *me* the amount in a bank bill, as heretofore.

I am Dear Sir Your Very humble servt.   GEO. JEFFERSON

RC (MHi); at foot of text: "Thos. Jefferson esqr. Washington"; endorsed by TJ as received 16 Jan. and so recorded in SJL.

George Jefferson OMITTED the $50 he paid to James T. Callender in October 1800 (see TJ to George Jefferson, 24 Oct. and George Jefferson to TJ, 3 Nov. 1800).

From John Jouett, Jr.

SIR.   Kintucky Jany. 12th. 1801

I am an old inhabitant of this Country and have been the Greater part of 17 years employd in the publick service and I flatter myself I have Dischard my Duty to the satisfaction of my Country and With Credit to myself & I niver did Ask or Except any off[ice] to which any pecuniary emolument has been annexed. I do [now] sir solicit the appointment of Marshall for the Kintucky District having good Reason to believe the presant marshall will go out of office Very shortly. sir I ask for this office with some Degree of Confidence you having Known me all my life. and Knowing you have no object in Viw but to have the office well filld. and in this Case I hope you Can have no Doubt as you have the best security this state Can give for my fidelity or ability in as much as their will accompany this, letters of recommendation from a number of the first and most respectable men [of] this state, and was promisd a similar one by our late Governor shelby but he lives to far from me to get his Letter to send on at this time. I hope you will not think it Strange if I should meet with no support from our members in Congress. in the first place I do not Know that they are any particular friends of mine in the second When they left this Country the thing was not talkd of and in all probability made up their Mindes another Way I now Conclude by saying if this meets with your Approbation independent of Every other Consideration I shall think it a great and lasting favour &c

I am Sir. Your Most Ob[t] Servant   J JOUETT

RC (DNA: RG 59, LAR); damaged; addressed: "The Honble Thomas Jefferson City of Washington"; endorsed by TJ as received 23 Feb. and so recorded in SJL, where TJ connected the letter and its enclosures by a bracket labeled with Jouett's name. Enclosures: (1) Samuel Hopkins to TJ, December 1800, writing from Frankfort, Ky., to say that Jouett is "in all respects Qualified" and would perform the marshal's duties with "reputation to himself & justice & integrity towards his Country" (RC in same; at foot of text: "T. Jefferson Esqr."; endorsed by TJ as received 23 Feb. and so recorded in SJL; also endorsed by an unidentified hand). (2) Thomas Todd to TJ, 11 Jan. 1801, recorded in SJL but not found; Todd wrote to John Breckinridge on the same day urging him to use his "personal acquaintance & influence with Mr. Jefferson" in Jouett's behalf (RC in DLC: Breckinridge Family Papers). (3) Harry Innes to TJ, 12 Jan. 1801, noting that "from your personal acquaintance" with Jouett "it will be unnecessary to add any thing relative to his personal merits"; that

Jouett "will do credit to the appointment & himself" in performing the duties of the office, which "are not difficult—industry & punctuality are the essential requisites to make a good Marshal"; and that "it is but justice to the present Marshal Mr. McDowell that I should declare, as far as his own official conduct hath come within my own observation it has been unexceptionable," Innes noting that he expects McDowell to "request a certificate relative to his official conduct" in the hope of continuing as marshal (RC in DNA: RG 59, LAR; written in "State of Kentucky"; at foot of text: "Thomas Jefferson Esqr."; endorsed by TJ as received 23 Feb. and so recorded in SJL). (4) John Breckinridge to TJ, 13 Jan. 1801.

John Jouett, Jr. (1754-1822) of Woodford County, Kentucky, was born in Albemarle County, Virginia, and moved to Kentucky, which was then still part of his native state, in 1782. He sat in the Virginia House of Delegates, 1786-88 and 1790, formed amicable relationships with prominent political families, was a leading advocate for Kentucky statehood, and served three terms in the legislature of the new state. He is best known for his actions in June 1781, when Jouett, a Virginia militia captain, learned that Banastre Tarleton's dragoons were racing toward Albemarle County to capture TJ and members of the Virginia General Assembly. From the Cuckoo Tavern, Jouett rode 40 miles at night to give warning at Monticello and Charlottesville, a feat that helped TJ escape Tarleton and for which the legislature voted to award Jouett two pistols and a sword. Late in life Jouett promoted the importation of foreign cattle breeds to improve Kentucky stock. His son, Matthew Harris Jouett, studied with Gilbert Stuart and became a successful portrait painter. John Jouett's father, John Jouett, Sr., continued to reside in Albemarle County after his son's removal to Kentucky (DAB; Malone, *Jefferson*, 1:355-7; Leonard, *General Assembly*, 161, 165, 180; Vol. 4:261, 265, 277, 278n; Vol. 6:89n; Vol. 31:187).

Innes wrote to TJ again on 11 July 1801 enclosing a letter he had received from John Watkins, who, being a stranger to TJ, was directed by Jouett to address his communication to Innes. Innes had known Watkins since 1788 and vouched for Watkins's service in public office. Innes closed: "I have nothing more to add on this subject except it be to assure you that Mr. Joüett has for 8 months past repeatedly declared to me he had ceased to gamble & never would again,

and I am induced to beleive he has strictly adhered to his declarations" (RC in DNA: RG 59, LAR; at foot of page: "Mr. Jefferson"; endorsed by TJ with Jouett's name and the office he sought; also endorsed by him as received on 5 Aug. 1801 and so recorded in SJL). In his letter to Innes, dated 7 July, Watkins asserted that he had been Jouett's neighbor for several years and could attest to his fitness for the office of marshal. The one element of Jouett's character that could harm him was "his former Attachment to that Accursed practice of gambling," but Watkins believed that Jouett had "forever quted this Abominable practice" (RC in same; endorsed by TJ).

Charles Scott of Kentucky wrote TJ a brief letter on 14 July 1801, stating that it would be handed to him by Jouett, who had renounced his former behavior, and that Scott recommended Jouett "in the highest terms" (RC in same; at foot of text: "The President of the United States"; endorsed by TJ with Jouett's name and the office sought; endorsed by TJ as received on 5 Aug. and so recorded in SJL, where TJ connected Scott's letter and Innes's of 11 July 1801 by a bracket and notation).

On his list of candidates for office printed at 5 Mch. 1801 TJ noted Jouett's name, residence, the office he sought, and Innes, Todd, Breckinridge, and Hopkins as the names of those who recommended him (DLC: TJ Papers, 108:18557).

From Stephen Sayre

SIR   Philada. 12th Jan. 1801. No 31 north 8th Street

I address you this Letter, upon a presumption, that you must, in a short time, become our chief Majestrate. I cannot believe the faction, who wish to disappoint the nation, are hardy enough, to make the attempt.

It is on a subject, which must, I concieve, appear important to you, because, it is, highly so, to our country—therefore, I trust, you will not deem it premature, to offer it, thus early, to your consideration, that you may be prepared, to embrace it, the moment you come into office.

Vanity, does not, so far, lead me out of the path of propriety, as to suppose myself capable of communicating, any thing, to Mr Jefferson, as information, on this, or any other subject—I shall be satisfied, if fortunate enough, to persuade you, that, I am also sensible, as to the importance, & weight of the proposition, I now offer—

If we may judge, from present appearances, there will be a Congress, representing the powers of Europe, the moment, they think seriously of peace—or, the meeting of one, might be effected, by an able Minister, representing a neutral nation, during war.

I conceive, this, a moment, to do somthing more than give temporary rest, to the world—the time is now come, when by a wise, & honest policy, the universe, may, probably, be united, in peace, & progress in happiness.

The arm'd neutrality, of 1780, was a wise, & happy expedient—It was all that could be done, at the time—was attended, with the best consequences, so far, as it respected our country—but there was a bond of union wanting—nations, like families, are liable to change their attachments—nothing, but a weighty, & superlative interest, making a common centre of attraction, ever did, or ever will, prevent it.

I, proposed, when that measure was in its progress, that the combining powers, should get the Island, of Porto Reco—to be interested, in its lands—its commerce—its security—its revenues—and, that it should be guaranteed, like the hanstowns—standing, on the broad basis, of united Europe. Application was made, to Spain, by Prussia & Sweedon—It might have been obtaind, for one tenth of its intrinsic value—but the Count de Vergennes was advised, to prevent it going into other hands, lest, the British might make it a place of rendesvous, in time of war; being so near, & just to windward, of St Domingo—of this, I was inform'd, some time after, by the Marquis De la Fayette.

Had this Island been so acquired, at the time, the planters of the British Islands, would have bought up the greatest share of the lands—all the european nations, would have resorted there—& so circumstanced—it would have been of more value to us, than the possession of all, the other Islands.

I have ardently wish'd for the opportunity, & have long contemplated, an improvement on the arm'd neutrality—*I want to see an unarm'd neutrality*; when the innocent, & enterprising—merchant, may traverse the globe, & find the friend of man, in every sea, & every port—the moment draws nigh, when this may probably, be accomplish'd—it ought to be attempted.

[453]

The great Interests of the world will soon be in a train of settlement. It must be unnecessary to tell you, that we are so immediately, & eventually, interested in the arrangement, that it would be criminal to neglect such a crisis.

There are difficulties to be expected—so there are, in all parties or families, at variance—I see no more, in settling the disputes of nations, than of neibours.

If you employ a Minister, well acquainted with the Interests of Europe, who can discover, the springs, of negotiation, & the means, by which a great & extensive principle, may be wrought, out of petty contentions; the universe will never cease to thank, & honor you.

This is not a fresh subject of my meditation—I have ballanced, every imaginable objection, that can impede its progress, or prevent its accomplishment—and, I am persuaded, that if there should be a Congress, either at Luneville, Paris, or any other convenient place; this object may be effected, on a great, & extensive plan, or a limited one.

A serious, well directed negotiation, press'd with vigour, to gain it, on the large scale, would secure it, on a more contracted one.

Did Great Britain but perceive her true interests, she would advocate the measure—because, the excellence of her manufactures, would now, & may perhaps always, command a great share in all foreign markets—her good sense, is not to be rely'd on—her weakness gives better ground for hope.

One thing however, must assuredly, take place. Spain & Portugal will find all the rest of Europe, & the united states, in a division against them, pressing the dissolution of their colonial Monopoly.

What must be done? who must give way?—experience says, the weakest—but suppose, some unforeseen difficulties, finally embarrass the great object—cannot the parties, so deeply interested, in the greater, accept the other, as a compromise—condescending, to accept Porto Rico, Trinidad, & the Phillipines; leaving them their continental Monopoly?

Supposing, the parties divided thus, or otherwise; you must feel the propriety, & necessity, of taking an early, & active part that, the congress may be form'd, & organized, to settle this point—some fix'd rules—some modes of decision, must be adopted, & practised, on, other subjects, & become sacred, by practice, before this object is brought into question—many other, matters, more pressing, as to time must take up the consideration of this assembly, for many months—or several years—the great question, now apparently under contemplation, among the powers of Europe is first to be decided—

I presume, it will not be expected, that I should, in this letter, enter into a detail, on the proposition. I will therefore conclude, by stating, the grounds, on which, I claim your patronage, in this great work.

I grant—It is a high, & important office—an enviable situation—but it is *arduous*—It requires, an active mind, unabated zeal, quick discernment, extensive knowledge, & long experience, in the affairs of the world, & the Interests of nations, to bring it forward, at the seasonable moment, & combine all its parts.

It would look like vanity in me to claim all those accomplishments—I therefore, shall only say—that I have had opportunities, to acquire them. I submit the following statement of facts, to your consideration, by which, you may form an opinion, how far I have improved those opportunities.

In the early stages of our Revolution—having married into a noble family, and form'd friendships, with some of the greatest men in England—I became the most active agent, in all the measures, & movements of those, either in, or out of parliament, who opposed the american war—the people were, by our exertions, kept in the scale of opposition—troops were sent over in small numbers—time was given to prepare for resistance—we succeeded—I was sacrifised—but our country was saved.

In january 1777. I resolved to leave the country, & all those, whose friendships, & connections, must, under other circumstances, have been invaluable.

In some few months, after my arrival at Paris, the Commissioners all agree'd, that I should go with Mr Arthur Lee, then one of them, to Berlin, to obtain supplies, then offer'd by Frederic.

He left me there to ratify such contracts, as might be agree'd to, by them all—and, to send out the articles. I continued there, some months—nothing was done by the Comrs—they were employ'd only, in disputes—they would not, even answer my letters, keep their promises, or pay my bills—notwithstanding these untoward disappointments—finding, an ardent disposition, in that great monarch, & his ministers, to open a free trade—& having his positive promise, to join other powers, who had navies to support the project—I repair'd to Copenhagen—and after assurances, by my Agent at Stockholm that the king was, irritated, by the loss of his ships, & well disposed; I made a journey, in the midst of winter of 1779. and, in one single interview, he not only agree'd, to every part I had proposed; but, agreed, also, to send off an express, to Russia, pressing the Empress, to take the lead—this was done—the Court of Great Britain, were duped, & paid dearly for the—deception—the arm'd neutrality was made public, about 12 months after—the king, by my ardent request, conceal'd the object, from his Ministers—what they suspected, they betray'd to the British Resident. You will allow me some merit—when I inform you, that, tho the king knew, from the loss of our papers, at Berlin, I must be a public agent—for my name was announced in the Courier de la Europe—he was astonish'd that, I should be some 20. or 30 days, at Court: but had neither waited on, or sought after his Ministers—his impatience urged him at last to send a secret messenger—my answer, that I should trust nothing to a public office caused an interview, immediately—had I done otherwise, the object would have been lost. I did not, in the mean time, neglect lesser objects—I had persuaded Denmark, to send us supplies, and open St. Thomas's a free port for 20 years, where we might meet their Ships, & exchange our articles.

Fortunately, my situation, enabled me, to do these services—and I improved it, tho, at my own expence—I have never yet been lifted up, & supported, by a nation's wealth, to figure on the public stage. Hence I am lead to conclude, under the advantages of your name, & patronage, I should do my country no dishonor.

But, if you can find any other citizen, better fitted for the situation, I shall neither murmur, or complain, at his appointment.

I can, easily account, for the injustice I have hitherto received from my country.

Arthur Lee, began to intrigue against me, to get his brother William placed over my head, the moment, he found that a Minister would be received at Berlin—he had two brothers, then in Congress, and succeeded—otherwise, I must have been an elder brother, in diplomacy.

When I returnd to America, early in 1783. Congress, were driven out of this city, by an arm'd force, insulting their poverty—they had nothing to offer, but the treaty with Algiers—and that, by New England cunning, was given to a sott'd Mule-carrier

While I lived in New York, in 1783. 1784. & 1785. Hamilton courted the Tories—my resentments, were yet alive—I cussed them. As he became the secret adviser, of Washington, I could have nothing to expect, under his administration—and the best freinds of our country have had but few favours from his successor.

All the above facts, I could prove, to your satisfaction, if required, by papers in my possession.

Mr McKean, who bears this, has promised to deliver it into your hands—

Be not offended, if I express a wish to be honor'd with your reply, when he returns; for I have a son now in Europe, who must return immediately unless inform'd, that I may probably go there

I am most respectfully STEPHEN SAYRE

RC (DNA: RG 59, LAR); at foot of text: "To Thomas Jefferson Esqr Vice President &c"; endorsed by TJ as received 6 Feb. and so recorded in SJL.

THE GROUNDS, ON WHICH, I CLAIM YOUR PATRONAGE: TJ and the merchant and adventurer Stephen Sayre (1736-1818) of Southampton, Long Island, N.Y., had met in Paris and last corresponded in the summer of 1793 (Julian P. Boyd, "The Remarkable Adventures of Stephen Sayre," *Princeton Univ. Lib. Chronicle*, 2 [Feb. 1941], 51-64; John R. Alden, *Stephen Sayre: American Revolutionary Adventurer* [Baton Rouge, La., 1983], 2, 3, 49-50, 162-3, 167, 186-91, 198; Vol. 24:346-7, 615-16; Vol. 26:517).

Sayre's SON NOW IN EUROPE was Samuel William Sayre (Alden, *Stephen Sayre*, 191).

Sayre wrote to TJ again on 5 Feb., sending that letter by means of William Duane and noting that although Thomas McKean had intended to convey his earlier letter (i.e., the letter above), the Chevalier Irujo was actually the bearer. Sayre, doubting whether the Senate would approve of the nomination he "hinted at" on 12 Jan., asked TJ "to reserve for me, some respectable employment, at home, if you cannot do me the honor of sending me to Europe." McKean promised to recommend him to TJ for the office of the collector of the port of Philadelphia, now that Sayre had fixed his residence in Pennsylvania. The present collector "has set the laws of the union at defiance—he possesses, neither civility, impartiality, dignity, or justice," Sayre noted of George Latimer. He added that Duane would confirm his assessment of the collector as "an insufferable tyrant" (RC in DNA: RG 59, LAR; endorsed by TJ as received 9 Feb. 1801 and so recorded in SJL).

From John Breckinridge

DEAR SIR   Lexington 13th. Jany. 1801.

Indulge me in congratulating you, and felicitating my country, in your election to the presidential chair. Few events, if any, have given this remote, but republican portion of Amea., such real & universal pleasure. To myself, who am now consigned by my country to a six years Service in an office, many of the important duties of which are so intimately connected with this high and important Department, & independant of all personal attachment & regard, it is highly gratifying indeed.

Mr. John Jouitt who has just called upon me, informs me, that the office of Marshall for this State will become vacant next Spring; that he expects the present Marshall will not be continued, & that he is desireous of the Appointt.—I am unacquainted with the merits of the present Marshall Mr. McDowell, in the discharge of his office, having very seldom attended the fœderal Court, & living at some distance from him.

As you have I presume a pretty good acquaintance with Mr. Jouitt,

& of long standing, I think little from me, in his behalf, can be necessary. Should you deem it inexpedient to reappoint Mr. Mc.Dowell, I hesitate not to declare, that I have no doubt Mr. Jouitt would execute the trust, with great credit to himself, & which is more important, to the satisfaction & quiet of the community.—He is independant in his circumstances, a popular public Character, and a decided Republican.[1] If inducements, other than his duty, were necessary to ensure the most faithful discharge of the trust, his long attachment to your person & character, and his anxiety for the success & popularity of your administration, would alone be sufficient. These considerations, with some others, I confess attach me to his interests in the present application, & I shall of consequence be highly gratified should he meet with success.

With great respect & esteem I am dear sir Your friend & Servt.

JOHN BRECKINRIDGE

RC (DNA: RG 59, LAR); at foot of text: "The Honble Th. Jefferson Esqr"; endorsement by TJ torn. Recorded in SJL as received 23 Feb. Dft (DLC: Breckinridge Family Papers); dated 12 Jan. Enclosed in John Jouett, Jr., to TJ, 12 Jan. 1801.

[1] Preceding two words underlined in Dft.

To James Lyle

DEAR SIR   Washington Jan. 13. 1801.

Your favor of the 3d. inst. is at hand. that also of Aug. 18 was recieved in September. I deferred answering it in expectation of recieving & remitting the paiment of the year, but the instalments for my tobacco were not paid up till I came here, at which time a new circumstance was coming on the preparatory expences of which obliged me to throw the paiment which should have been made to you (agreeably to my letter from Philadelphia) on a fund which was not to come in till April. I therefore now inclose you an order on Messrs. Gibson & Jefferson of Richmond for 1000. D. payable the 1st. week in April. this paiment shall be soon followed by an equal one, which I presume will enable me to settle and take in all the bonds but the last, which shall not be much longer out. on my return home I will compare your statement with my papers, and settle our matters so far. from the view I took of my affairs in 1797. I thought I could have paid off your debt by the end of 1800. it will run on a year beyond that time, or perhaps it may enter 1802. if any thing could [keep me easy?] under it your delicate forbearance would do it, and I deem it great good fortune that you have been spared to close the business with me. I am with unchangeable sentiments of esteem & affection Dear Sir

Your most obedt. servt

PrC (MHi); signature omitted in letterpressing; endorsed by TJ in ink on verso. Enclosure: Order to Gibson & Jefferson, same day, to pay James Lyle $1,000 during the first week of April "for value received"; recorded in TJ's financial memoranda on 13 Jan. as payable to Lyle "agent of Kippen & co." the first week in April "when the money for my tobo. of 99. becomes due" (PrC in same, signed by TJ, letterpressed to same sheet as enclosing letter; MB, 2:1033).

From Richard Brent

Dr Sir   Richmond Jany 14 1801

some days since I received a letter from Mr Wm. Brent, a young Gentleman resident in the City of Washington who is a much esteemed and near relation of mine requesting that my solicitations might be added to those of his other friends in order to obtain for him the honor of being appointed your private Secretary in the event of your succeeding to the Presidency of the Union (of which every honest emotion of the heart induces me to hope there is little doubt)[1] this young Man has for some time past acted as Clerk to the Commissioners of Washington to whom I am told he has given perfect satisfaction. he has inherited a very small patrimony yet notwithstanding this circumstance and the opposite sentiments in relation to public affairs of those on whom he was in some measure dependant for his support notwithstanding the opposite political opinions of all his connections into whose society from his late place of residence he has been principally thrown he has with steadiness and decision on all occasions from the first clawings of Manhood, des[. . .]ded himself— firm Democratic Republican—I do not believe that he possesses much literary information. he is however polite in his manners diligent in his habits discreet intelligent and converses and writes with facility and distinctness in his native language his disposition I coud pledge myself under the heaviest penalties will be found as ameable as coud be wished for—if these qualities will suffice for the Office which it is his wish to attain I am assured he will not be found unworthy of the Character which is here given of him—when I reflect that I have not the happiness to possess more than a limitted acquaintance with you Sir I am fearful that my anxiety to serve a deserving young Man may have carried me beyond the bounds of a

[459]

proper decorum when but little known myself I presume to become pledged for the worth of an other however as my young kinsman is pretty generally known in the Neighbourhood where you now are the means by which you may obtain more satisfactory information respecting his qualifications are obvious and immediately at hand and indeed it is my wish that these may be resorted to lest the seal of friendship or the partiallities of consanguinity may have induced me to view this a prejudicial Medium the subject of the present recommendation. I have D Sir the honor to be with Sentiments of the most profound respect and regard Your Ob. sevt.   RICH'D BRENT

RC (DNA: RG 59, LAR); addressed: "The honble Thomas Jefferson Esqr City of Washington"; franked and postmarked; endorsed by TJ as received 17 Jan. and so recorded in SJL; also endorsed by TJ: "Brent Wm. to be my secretary."

Richard Brent (1757-1814), born and buried at "Richland" on the Potomac at Aquia Creek, was trained as a lawyer. His legislative experience included serving as a delegate in the Virginia General Assembly from Stafford County in 1788 and from Prince William County in 1793,

1794, 1800, and 1801. He was elected to the Fourth, Fifth, and Seventh Congresses, was a member of the state senate from 1808 to 1810, and was elected to the U.S. Senate, serving from 4 Mch. 1809 until his death (*Biog. Dir. Cong.*; Richmond *Enquirer*, 3 Jan. 1815).

Neither TJ's reply to Brent, recorded in SJL on 18 Jan. 1801, nor Brent's subsequent letter, written from "Dumfries" on 24 Feb. and recorded in SJL as received 26 Feb., has been found.

[1] Closing parenthesis supplied by Editors.

From Samuel Brown

SIR   Lexington Jany. 14th 1801

It is expected by a great majority of the Citizens of Kentucky that Mr Samuel McDowell, who is Marshall for this District will not continue to hold that important & lucrative Office. Whether the Marshall himself has been guilty of improper conduct, as an Officer or not, remains doubtful; but it is most unquestionable that his Brothers, who were his Deputies, have repeatedly exacted large sums of money for the performance of those duties which they alone could execute & for which they were allowed, by law, a very liberal compensation. As it is confidently asserted that Evidence will be procured to substantiate these charges & as it is strongly suspected that the Marshall has not been wholly ignorant of the profitable Game which his Brothers are playing, his removal from Office is considered as almost certain. In consequence of this general expectation several Gentlemen have declared themselves anxious to succeed him. In this number I am happy to find Mr Charles Wilkins whose honesty, honor, industry & capacity for business are universally acknowledged by all who have the pleasure of being associated with him—Conscious that any expression of my personal regard & affection for Mr Wilkins ought to have no weight with you in giving him the appointment I beg leave to observe that an intimate freindship existes between him & Major Morrison the Supervisor & I might add between him & Judge Innes which in case of his appointment would promise the restoration of that harmony & confidence among the Officers of the Genl Govt which alone can ensure the faithful Execution of the Laws—

With sentiments of the highest esteem & consideration I have the honor to be Yo Mo Obt.   SAM BROWN

RC (DNA: RG 59, LAR); endorsed by TJ as received 21 Feb. and so recorded in SJL, where by a notation and bracket TJ marked the association of this letter with those of Innes and Peyton Short described below; also endorsed by TJ: "Wilkins Charles. recommdns."

Harry INNES wrote on 12 Jan., giving his location as "State of Kentucky." Believing that information about job seekers whom TJ did not know "would not be unacceptable" and that "in all your appointments you can have no other object, than that of the public good," Innes had "concluded to state my opinion respecting the characters of such Gentlemen as may apply to me on this head, without giving either a preference, leaving the question on its proper ground-merit." On the basis of personal acquaintaince of Charles Wilkins of about ten years, Innes affirmed that there was no doubt of Wilkins's ability to perform the duties of the marshal's office, nor any question about his character. Innes also noted that insofar as he was acquainted with the present marshal, that officer's conduct was "unexceptionable" (RC in same, at foot of text: "Thomas Jefferson Esqr.," endorsed by TJ as received 21 Feb. and so recorded in SJL; see also Enclosure No. 3 listed at John Jouett, Jr., to TJ, 12 Jan.). Peyton Short wrote to TJ from Wood-

ford, Kentucky, on 16 Jan. to recommend Wilkins, his friend and brother-in-law. "Principles of Delicacy forbid my dilating on Mr. Wilkins' Merits," noted Short, who wrote only to help Wilkins and not because of any personal motives against the incumbent of the marshal's office. Short also wrote that "I had it not in my power to go to Virginia, last Fall, agreable to Promise on my Brother's Business with Col: Skipwith, but shall endeavor to do so in the course of the ensuing summer" (RC in same; endorsed by TJ as received 21 Feb. and so recorded in SJL). On 2 Mch. 1801 John Breckinridge drafted a brief letter to TJ from Fayette, Kentucky, stating that Wilkins was qualified for the marshal's position and would demonstrate "sufficient responsibility" in the office. Wilkins was aware, Breckinridge noted, that Breckinridge had written other letters in behalf of other candidates. Breckinridge probably never sent the letter, which is not recorded in SJL or acknowledged with other correspondence in TJ to Breckinridge, 29 July (Dft in DLC: Breckinridge Family Papers; at foot of text: "Thos. Jefferson Esqr.").

On a list of candidates for office TJ noted Wilkins's name, residence, and office sought, along with the names of Innes, Peyton Short, Samuel Brown, and John Brown as Wilkins's references (DLC: TJ Papers, 108:18557).

From Samuel Lewis, Sr.

Sɪʀ,   Debtors apartment, Philadelphia, Jany: 14: 1801

Was I not well convinced of the goodness of your heart, and the commisseration you feel for the distressed, in every Situation of life; but more especially when importuned from such dreary mansions, I would not have presumed to intrude upon your time, to read the Story of misfortune, or dwell upon my unfortunate lot; not mine alone; but with it is involved the miseries (constantly poured out, for fourteen months past) of a Wife and six helpless children, who look up to me, now in vain! for bread.   During the long and irksome confinement I have undergone, several of my Children have been afflicted with Sickness: my Wife, soon after my loss of liberty, was delivered of an infant; and myself, almost continually subject to variety of complicated ills, rendered incapable of alleviating either their troubles, or my own misfortunes.   Nights of Grief and Anxiety, have passed on; and Days of keenest Sorrow, nearly sunk me under their oppressive weight: Silence has often been succeeded by tears; my bodily faculties decaying fast; and want of natural liberty, exercise, wholesome and free Air, have weakened me almost beyond description.   My natural and acquired Abilities are now lost to Society; wherein I have gained reputation, both as an instructor of Youth in the useful and ornamental Arts of Penmanship; and as a Geographer and Draughtsman. This last branch I must be allowed to say, I am master of, and equal to any undertaking. During my existence in this scene of distress, debarred performing those duties by which I might have earned bread for my helpless little ones, we have been obliged to depend upon the bounty of others (and precarious are such expectations,) and selling part of such small remains of necessary household furniture, as produced for the last three months an average of about three dollars per Week, for eight persons—poor pittance, when Clothing, Victuals, Wood, &c: are considered—and certain expences, unavoidable, for myself, in a Prison—

I am thus led, imperceptibly, to unfold to your feeling heart, the misery of an Individual, who has seen better days; and humbly hopes the humanity and liberality of Congress, to whom he has applied, by Petition, for relief, will restore him to his family and the Community.   I am fondly led to believe, that, from the tenor of my Petition and the statement of my extra Services, whilst I was a Clerk in the War Office, accompanying the same, that the Committee will make a favorable Report: should it be acquiesced in by the house of Representatives, and a special law pass, to the

Senate, I am constrained to use every endeavour to hope for relief from your honorable house; this urges me to strain every nerve, to embrace every opportunity of imploring friends, intreating their assistance towards my enlargement.

I was employed in the War Office as a Clerk, from Novr: 1793, to Otobr: 1799. My actual duties were important, and confidential: for several Years the business of two Clerks, were assigned to me, tho' I received only a Salary equal to one: These employments had added to them, the whole official duties of the Indian Factory trade, without any additional Salary.   My extra Services, were as an Agent for the War Department, in paying demands against the United States in the military department—paying other demands as contingencies of the War Office; also receiving considerable Sums and transmitting the same to Officers, Paymasters, Superintendants, Contractors, Indian Agents, &c. &c. To particularize these Services would occupy too much of your time—At the final Settlement of my Account, which exceeded three hundred thousand dollars, a balance was found against me, agreeably to the Report of the Secy of War, of $2711\frac{78}{100}$ Dols: There has since my confinement, been passed to my Credit, a balance of Salary, Expences, and for Maps compiled and drawn by directions of the Secy, amounting to $547\frac{48}{100}$ Dollars leaving a balance to the United States of $2164\frac{30}{100}$ Dols: not making me any allowance for Commission as Agent: my commission, on transmitting Monies, I charged as the Supervisors were empowered, viz: One perCent: and on paying Accounts, and receiving Monies therefor, agreeably to usage, viz $2\frac{1}{2}$ perCent: I leave it to the Justice and Humanity of Congress to grant me such relief, as they may please to grant: With a balance in my favor, and Years of faithful Service; Toil and Labour, I am now, and have been suffering months of misery, pain and anguish; sepcrated from my family, debarred the pleasing prattle of smiling babes, domestic felicity at home, and the means of gaining support for their helpless frames: instead of enjoying these Comforts, I am doomed to be the associate of every description of Character; to drag on a life, amidst, noise, vulgarity, dissipation and excess: subject to the taunts and sneers of ignorance, impudence and low bred beings.

Should a Bill be presented, in my favor, from the house of Representatives, to the honorable the Senate, permit me to hope, I may find a friend in your bosom; and that you may extend your benevolence toward the unhappy Suitor for liberation.

I have taken the liberty to enclose, for your inspection, and as a specimen of my Abilities, a few drawings, of part of a series of Maps, to form a Pocket atlas, of the United States: I had intended them for publication, a few years ago, but the expence was too much—I have compleated near two thirds of the whole number.   When you think proper to return them, please to Address them to me "care of the Postman, Phila:"

I have the honor to be, Sir, with the greatest respect, Your obedient Servant   SAMUEL LEWIS SENR.

RC (DLC); addressed: "Thomas Jefferson Esqr: Vice President of the United States City of Washington"; endorsed by TJ as received 19 Jan. and so recorded in SJL. Enclosure not found, but see Lewis to TJ, 11 Feb. 1801.

Samuel Lewis, Sr. (ca. 1754-1822), worked as a mapmaker and engraver for Aaron Arrowsmith, an English cartographer, who in 1790 started his own mapmaking firm. Lewis's first published map of Virginia was included in Mathew Carey's 1795 edition of William Guthrie's *Geography Improved* and in Carey's 1795

American Atlas. Lewis drew all the American maps that Arrowsmith used and together they produced *A New and Elegant General Atlas, Comprising All the New Discoveries to the Present Time* ([Philadelphia, 1804]; Sowerby, No. 3836; Guy Meriwether Benson and others, *Lewis and Clark: The Maps of Exploration 1507-1814* [Charlottesville, 2002], 78; Ben A. Smith and James W. Vining, *American Geographers, 1784-1812* [Westport, Conn., 2003], 122-4).

For the relief BILL, see TJ to Lewis, 11 Feb.

From John Barnes

SIR   Geo: Town 15th Jany: 1801

I have already by this Eveng Mail remitted Messs: G & J. $384.43, and Credited Mr Shorts a/c   535.83

is $920.26. to your debit, which presume will meet your wishes.—On the 12th. Inst: I, remitted said Gent: $148.48½ Mrs Keys 5th. and last installmt:—

with great Esteem—I am sir your Obedt: H st:

JOHN BARNES

RC (ViU); written on a scrap of paper bearing faint impressions of other text, probably in TJ's hand; at foot of text: "Thomas Jefferson Esquire"; endorsed by TJ.

CREDITED MR SHORTS A/C: in a letter of this day that is recorded in SJL but has not been found, TJ authorized Barnes to transfer $535.83 from TJ's account to Short's (MB, 2:1033). The transfer was in exchange for Short's payment from the

James River Company that was used to cover TJ's drafts in Richmond; see TJ to George Jefferson, 5 Jan. 1801.

Barnes included the transfer of funds to Short's account and the associated remittance to Gibson & Jefferson in a statement of his account with TJ through this day. The statement also recorded $218.90 paid to Conrad & McMunn on 1 Jan.; $20.50 in cash conveyed to TJ by a servant on the 4th; the three checks and $5 in small change mentioned by Barnes in his letter of 7 Jan.; $1.20 for two pocket handkerchiefs on the 10th; and $2.75 on 12 Jan. for two items of horse equipment, a surcingle and a curb. Barnes credited TJ with the $403.02½ carried forward from the previous statement of the account between them on 31 Dec. and, on 3 Jan., with $1,243.75 for TJ's salary compensation for the quarter ending 31 Dec. ($1,250 less $6.25 for Barnes's commis-sion of one half of one percent). Barnes carried forward, as of 15 Jan., a balance of $234.66½ in TJ's favor (MS in ViU, in Barnes's hand, unsigned, endorsed by him as a copy, and endorsed by TJ, probably as a wrapper for other statements of account also: "Barnes John. Series of accounts for 1800"; see MB, 2:1032-3, for some of the transactions).

From Elbridge Gerry

Cambridge 15th Jany 1801

By Judge Lincoln, my dear Sir, I embrace a favorable opportunity of acknowledging your very friendly letter of the 26th of Janry. 1799; but permit me previously to give you some information in regard to this gentleman. Mr. Lincoln is an eminent lawyer in this State, & his professional talents, are accompanied with a humane & benevolent disposition, pure integrity, great liberality, & unsullied honor & morality: he is moreover a rational consistent, & thorough republican. if you do not find that his character corresponds with this description, & that he is a real acquisition to Congress, I will readily relinquish all pretensions to any knowledge of mankind.

I congratulate you, my friend, very sincerely, that we have reason to hope never again "to see the day, when, breathing nothing but sentiments of love to our country, & it's freedom & happiness, our correspondence must be as secret as if we were hatching it's destruction." I have long wished to express the great obligation I felt, for your free & full communication by the letter mentioned; but to do it by the corrupt channel of a post office, or by any one, who betraying his trust, might consider perfidy as a meritorious act of federalism, was less elegible than to delay it till an interview or safe conveyance should present itself. as to my political sentiments, they are not secret, but I wish not to have them promulged by the base means of interception; because one seldom writes to a friend with that precision, which is necessary in expressing, during the reign of faction, political opinions: indeed, before the receipt of your letter, I had every reason to suspect, that a certain disgraced & disgraceful ex-secretary opened a letter which I wrote to President Adams, & fabricated with his coadjutors, a report in regard to my communications which the President was under the necessity of rejecting, as containing, "misrepresentations, calumnies & falsehoods." But that tool & scapegoat of faction after having done more mischief than ever before was effected by a man of such mean & rude abilities, has retired to the woods, the proper situation for savage manners. could you conceive, Sir, after seeing his report on my communications, that he was in possession of a proposition which I made to my collegues, at the very commencement of our disgraceful conferences with X & Y, which would have put an end to them, & which President Adams acknowledged to me, was a full answer to every thing that could be urged against me. it is in these words "To the question, whether the propositions informally & confidentially communicated to us as private citizens, at the request, as is stated of Mr Tallyrand in his private capacity, will be adopted as the basis of a treaty? this answer is given, that it is highly probable some of the propositions communicated on the evenings of the 19th & 20 of october (being the 28th & 29th vendimaire) will be considered as the basis of the project of a treaty, & others as inadmissible; but that it is impossible to discuss, or come to a decision on them, untill they are presented to us in our official character." I have the original proposition by me, & at the bottom of it this note in General Pinckney's hand writing, "intended to be given Saturday the 21st of october." I have in a number of remarks, pointed out to the President, the illiberality, partiallity & injustice of that officious[1] report, & but for the President's request to avoid a public discussion of that extraordinary mission, would have, long e'er this, done justice to my conduct & character. I trust however he will eventually do it.

I am extremely anxious to hear the result of the presidential election. the insidious plan of the *feudalists*, to place Mr Burr in the chair, is the acme of their perfidy & enmity to this country. he himself considers it in this light; well knowing, that the measure does not proceed from any respect or attachment to him, whom they abhor as well as yourself, on account of your mutual predilection for republicanism, but from a desire to promote that division among the people, which they have excited & nourished as the germ of a civil war. I must candidly acknowledge, that I tho't it the best policy to re-elect Mr Adams & yourself; because in that event, you would have united your exertions & respective parties, in suppressing the feudalists, & at the next choice there was little reason in my mind to doubt, that Mr Adams would retire, &, with his friends, support your election to the chair & administration: whereas there is danger now, that many of his adherents will again unite with the Hamiltonians & embarass your administration if you should succeed him, to avenge what they consider as an act of ingratitude to the object of their choice. but every friend to this country, in this event, will double his exertions to support You, as a measure of the last importance to the foreign & domestic peace, & general welfare of the Union.

The silent & dignified contempt, with which you have treated the unparallelled abuse, which to the eternal disgrace of the United States, has been circulated in their gazettes, will be a distinguished trait in your character: I wish the venerable Doctor Priestly, whose reputation, in the opinions of liberal men was invulnerable, had not condescended to notice anonymous calumnies, for the measure, being unnecessary, was of no service to him. to confound slanderers it is sufficient not to merit the slander

Your assurance, in regard to your not having intermeddled with the affairs of our mission, by means of Doctor Logan, was unnecessary: I knew you too well to listen to such a calumny. You have been pleased to make to me "a profession of your political faith," & to add, "these my friend are my principles, they are unquestionably the principles of the great body of our fellow citizens, & I know there is not one of them which is not yours also." in this last expression you do me great honor & justice likewise, & the principles are such as I ever have been, & hope in this country where I mean to spend the residue of my life, I ever shall be free to avow. & altho "we differed on one ground, the funding system," yet was I sure that "from the moment of it's being adopted by the constituted authorities, you became religiously principled in the sacred discharge of it, to the uttermost farthing." your declaration to this effect therefore, was not requisite to confirm my belief.

The corrupt propositions made by X & Y did not appear to me to have been sanctioned by the directory, of whose integrity or justice I had however no great opinion: indeed there was no positive evedence that they proceeded from Mr Tallyrand, but I have no doubt of the fact. £50,000 sterling, which as a douceur to be divided amongst the directory, would at that time have been spurned at by them, might have answered the purposes of Mr Tallyrand &[2] of the principal officers of his bureau, & his general character will warrant the belief, that this was his object: but be this as it may, you would never have seen those dispatches, had I been alone on the mission, untill all hopes of peace were at at end, & their communication had become necessary to unite the nation in a declaration of war. I was apprehensive of their publication, & suggested to one at least of the other Envoys, General Marshal, the propriety of confirming the communication to the President, & frequently to both, the extraordinary light, if published, in which it must be viewed by men of sense. indeed it is wonderful that the promulgation of our dispatches had not proved fatal to me, for the directory were so exasperated at it, as immediately to agitate the question of war, & there was a bare majority against it, on the principle only, that it would be a measure, which however provoked by the United States, was a favorite object of G Britain, & if adopted, would make France a dupe of the policy of that nation & of its own resentment. the great exertions of the british cabinet to circulate thro'out Europe, our dispatches, served to convince the directory of the impolicy of a war with us, at least on that occasion. Mr Tallyrand had early in the spring declared to me in the name of the Directory, that my departure from Paris would bring on an immediate rupture, & as there had been no instance of an official declaration made by the directory which had not been carried into effect, I had no doubt of it in this instance: but when they saw how eager their most inveterate enemy was to attain the object, they did not think so lightly of it, as they before had been wont to consider it. the war party here have pretended, that the martial attitude of the U States prevented a war, but that was not known in France at the time of the declaration made to me in the name of the directory, neither was a war viewed by it then, as an acquisition of such importance to G.B. if however there exists the least doubt, that france would have declared War, or that a suggestion of X & Y to this effect, disavowed as it was by the directory & french minister, was different from the official declaration made to me by Mr Tallyrand, yet I think there can be no doubt, that had all the Envoys have left France at that critical period, the US on their arrival here would have been so hurried away by passion & influenced by faction, as to have rendered the act very popular, if not indispensable on the part of Congress. . . . Mr Pickering in his report has mentioned the threat of X & Y, as a measure proceeding from the directory, & comparing it with the declaration made to me says they both merited contempt, but the one was unofficial & has been disavowed, the other was official & by my correspondence, has been confirmed: judge then of his want of either discernment or candor, & whether it was not my indispensable duty to have remained in France, after the departure of the other Envoys. You appeal to me to say whether peace might not have been attained, if either of my collegues had been of the same sentiment with myself. I have no hesitation to answer in the affirmative, & to assure you candidly, that your opinion that one of them at least possessed this qualification, was the point on which my determination, then held in suspence, turned for accepting the appointment to that embassy. without such a persuasion nothing could have induced me to the measure. but you was unfortunately for me, tho perhaps fortunately for the publick, mistaken,

& the late events have proved, that peace as we both supposed, was attainable. Judge Lincoln has called on rathar soon than I expected, & is in too much haste to wait untill I can answer the other parts of your letter: I must therefore reserve this for another opportunity.

I have thus far communicated without reserve & in the fullest confidence, my sentiments on our important national concerns, & if they are too much tinged with severity, the unmerited provocation which I have had must be my apology. permit me now my dear Sir to renew my assurances of the most sincere attachment & that I remain with the highest respect your affectionate friend   E GERRY

excuse errors for I cannot revise or correct this letter.

RC (DLC); at foot of text: "His Excellency Mr Jefferson"; ellipsis in original; superfluous marginal quotation marks omitted; endorsed by TJ as received 5 Feb. and so recorded in SJL.

AS IF WE WERE HATCHING IT'S DE-STRUCTION: the quotation is from the conclusion to TJ's letter of 26 Jan. 1799 (Vol. 30:650).

Timothy Pickering was the DIS-GRACEFUL EX-SECRETARY. John Adams expurgated passages damning to Gerry before he let Pickering's REPORT on Gerry's dispatches from France go to Congress (George Athan Billias, *Elbridge Gerry: Founding Father and Republican Statesman* [New York, 1976],

296; Vol. 30:636). RETIRED TO THE WOODS: following his dismissal from the cabinet Pickering moved to western Pennsylvania to develop lands he owned there (ANB).

X & Y: Jean Conrad Hottinguer and Pierre Bellamy; Vol. 30:251n.

VENERABLE DOCTOR PRIESTLY: after initially forbearing to reply to attacks on him by William Cobbett, Joseph Priestley responded in his *Letters to the Inhabitants of Northumberland* (F. W. Gibbs, *Joseph Priestley: Adventurer in Science and Champion of Truth* [London, 1965], 233-7).

¹ Word interlined.
² Gerry here canceled "of a few."

To Craven Peyton

DEAR SIR   Washington Feb. [i.e. Jan.] 15. 1801

Your favor of the 6th. came to hand this day, and I am much obliged to you for thinking of me on the occasion. you mention that in [91.] you purchased a share of one of the Hendersons as valued by mr Watson & Snelson and that two others have offered you their shares on the same terms. I will very gladly be the purchaser if you will be so good as to negociate it for me, but in your own name. I could not with convenience pay the money till April or May: but as you say [you] can accomodate that it will add to the obligation. I will thank you to conclude it without delay & to inform me of the particulars.

Tho' I never followed my line which [runs] back of M[. . .]'s from [one] end to the other, yet I have pursued it from the corner—next to

M[. . .] so far towards Colle as to be under no apprehension that any part of my plantation has crossed it. mr Henderson had cut down so many of the line trees that when I attended the processioners in it 4. years ago, it took us so long to find the trees that they gave it up. but I went on it a great way; and when I return home, which will be early in April, I will run it with accuracy.—the equality of vote between the two republican candidates has threatened a good deal of embarrasment & [often] danger: the case of a [new] election by the House of Representatives not having foreseen & provided against by the Constitution. some possible consequences were very alarming. however there is reason to believe at this time that some gentlemen of sincere patriotism, who have not been with us on former occasions, will join us on this, and save their country from the desperate crisis to which some others were willing to risk it, rather than part with their ascendancy in it. I am with great esteem Dear Sir

Your friend & servt   TH: JEFFERSON

PrC (ViU); at foot of text: "Mr Craven Peyton"; endorsed by TJ in ink on verso. According to SJL, TJ wrote to Peyton on 15 Jan. 1801 but not on 15 Feb.

Peyton's FAVOR OF THE 6TH. has not been found but was recorded in SJL as received by TJ on 15 Jan. from "Shadwell." For Peyton's purchase on TJ's behalf of Henderson property, see Vol. 31:199-200n.

Statement of Account with Gibson & Jefferson

Messrs. Gibson & Jefferson in acct. with Th: Jefferson

1800.   Dt.

			£
Feb.	5.	By cash on Barnes's ord. on Heth	240. 0. 0
May.	31.	do. W. C. Nicholas's ord. on	
		Pick. Pol. & Johnson	135. 0. 0
Sep.	18.	do. from G. Nicholson for nail rod recovy.	20.19. 3
	24.	do. remitted by J. Barnes.	60.
Nov.	7.	do. do.	204. 0. 0
Dec.	11.	balance due G. & J. this day	60.10. 6
			720. 9. 9

1801. Jan. 15. To remittance for me from J. Barnes   276. 1. 7

351.12. 1

balance due G & J   75.10. 6

+ Callendar 50. D

[470]

1800.   Cr.

			£	s	d
Jan.		By balance as pr acct. rendd.	60.	15.	7
	23.	By pd. to P. P. & Johnson	2.	3.	0
	29.	By do. to Gordon for Minzies	28.	9.	7
	31	By drayage & toll on nail rod	1.	19.	9
		do. on 28. bundles downwards		6.	6
Feb.	10.	By pd. my ord. to Watson	34.	17.	0
	14.	do. R. Richardson	98.	14.	0
	28.	do. Jas. Lyon	3.	0.	0
Mar.	12.	By pd. Shomaker for portage of nuts	0.	6.	0
	21.	drayage & toll on 41. bundles rod from Milton	0.	11.	10
		cabbage seeds for R. Richardson	0.	9.	0
	24.	for Randolph's abr.	0.	18.	0
	29.	T M Randolph my ord. in favr. W. Page	24.	0.	0
Apr.	11.	freight 5. bar. 2 box. frm. Philada	1.	5.	6
		drayage & toll of do. from Rocket's	0.	13.	9
May.	1.	freight & drayage 2. casks. 1. box frm Phila	0.	14.	6
		toll & drayage on do.	0.	2.	6
	24.	Darmsdat for 16. bar. Herrings	24.	0.	0
		6. loaves sugar 39. lb 10 oz @ 1/10	3.	12.	8
		toll & drayage of herrings	0.	17.	10
June	6.	1 doz. Center	4.	4.	0
	9.	my ord. in favr. Aldridge	4.	4.	7
	12.	freight sundries from Phila	6.	7.	0
		toll and drayage do.	1.	7.	0
		30 galls. molasses @ 4/6 & cask	7.	2.	6
	18.	toll & drayage of 30. hhds tobo.	5.	15.	3
	30.	Gamble & Temple old balance	1.	10.	0
		commn on 32. hhds tobo. shipd N.Y. & Phila 869.13.6	21.	14.	6
July	1.	1 hhd lime £2.14. drayage & toll 3/9	2.	17.	9
		freight & drayage cask fish frm. Boston	0.	7.	6
	5.	repackg 1 hhd tobo. at Shockoe	0.	6.	3
	12.	ord. in favr John Watson	44.	9.	8
	21.	155. lb bacon @ 7½ d	4.	16.	10
		1. doz. center	4.	4.	0
		6. bunches sash cord	0.	15.	0
		toll & drayage	0.	2.	0

	23.	ord. in favr. W. Aldridge	24.11. 0
	31.	freight 4. bar. porter frm Phila	0.12. 0
		do. 3 ton nail rod, 7. bundles hoop	2. 2. 0
Aug.	8.	drayage from Rocket's	1. 4. 0
		toll, wharfage, labor	1. 9. 3
Sep.	3.	ord. in favr. H. Duke	90. 0. 0
	26.	4. boxes ointment	0.18. 0
	27.	ord. in favr. Joel Yancy	79. 5.10
		A. Garrett	48. 3. 3
Oct.	2.	Mat. Rhodes	50.11. 9
	23.	freight 4. stoves from Phila	1.16. 0
		drayage & toll	0. 5. 5
Dec.	11.	Shockoe inspectors diffce. 2. hhds tobo.	1. 3. 5
		commn. on 31. hhds. tobo.	
		£813.19.9 @ 2½ p.c.	20. 7. 0
			720. 9. 9

		By balance [acontra?]	60.10. 6
Dec.	14.	ord. in favr. Jas. Lyon	15. 0. 0
1801.			
Jan.	7.	do. Roger £17.7.–Lilly 9.7.10–	
		Brand £17.2 Walker 14.3.9– }	276. 1. 7
		Dyer 53.0–Richdson 165.1	
			351.12. 1

MS (MHi); entirely in TJ's hand; arranged by TJ with the debit column on the left and without aligning dates in the two columns; with last three lines in the debit column and final total in the credit column added by TJ in pencil; endorsed by TJ on verso "George Jefferson."

TJ's financial records indicate that he received a "post note" from John Barnes ON HETH for $800 on 9 Jan. 1800 and enclosed it to George Jefferson three days later (see MB, 2:1013, and TJ to George Jefferson & Co., 13 Jan. 1800). PICK. POL. & JOHNSON: Pickett, Pollard, & Johnston. On 20 May TJ recorded in his accounts that he gave Wilson Cary Nicholas's draft for $450 on the Richmond firm to Gibson & Jefferson for collection (MB, 2:1019). Letters from Pickett, Pollard, & Johnston to TJ of 10 Oct. and 1 Nov. 1797, recorded in SJL as received on 14 Oct. and 3 Nov., respectively, have not been found.

For the payment of the old debt TJ owed Ninian MINZIES, see TJ to George Jefferson, 12 Jan. 1800. TJ discussed the February payments to John WATSON and Richard RICHARDSON in his letter to George Jefferson & Co. of 13 Jan. 1800. TJ referred to the 12 July payment to Watson in a letter to George Jefferson of 7 June. For the February payment to James LYON for newspapers, see TJ to George Jefferson, 21 Feb. 1800.

PORTAGE OF NUTS: this payment is probably for the pecans sent by Daniel Clark (TJ to Clark, 16 Jan. 1800; TJ to Richard Richardson, 10 Feb. 1800). George Jefferson purchased Edmund RANDOLPH's Abridgment of the Public Permanent Laws of Virginia for TJ (Vol. 31:406-7, 520). TJ recorded the settlement of his account with overseer

William PAGE, who had leased land at Shadwell, at 20 Dec. 1799 (MB, 2:1010-11, 1024). For the purchase and shipment of herring from Joseph Darmsdatt (DARMSDAT), see Gibson & Jefferson to TJ, 27 May 1800. On 3 June TJ noted in his financial accounts that £4.4.7 of his payment to William J. ALDRIDGE, recorded here on the 9th, was for gro-ceries (MB, 2:1021). For the payment to Aldridge in July, see TJ to George Jefferson, 9 July 1800. GAMBLE & TEMPLE: TJ sold nails and purchased groceries and nailrod from this Richmond firm in 1795 and 1796 (Vol. 28:335-6, 431-2). For the old balance, see TJ to George Jefferson, 7 June 1800.

From Charles Copland

SIR   Richmond 16 Jany 1801

Your favor of the 10th instant is recd in answer to which, I have to inform you—that I reced of Mr Grymes (by the sale of Tobacco placed by him in my hands) Eight hundred and fifty two pounds 9/9 this Currency for Mrs Randolph—and on the 7th of October I remitted her a bill of Exchange for five hundred and sixty six pounds 7/2 Sterling at 35 PCt. Exchange which was the lowest exchange that good bills could then be got for—That remittance was the Nett balance of the 852-9-9 after deducting my Commission and the expences of the Suit. In stating my account I charged Mrs Randolph with Commission on one half the amount of the Judgment and mentioned to her that when Mr. Grymes paid me the balance of the moiety of the Judgment, I should remit it to her without any additional charge of Commission, I informed her that you had agreed with Mr Grymes to release him on his paying a moiety of the Judgt—I have recd a letter from Mr. Grymes dated the 5th of this Month, he informs me that he can give me a bill on London for the balance of the moiety of the Judgt—I have replyed to his letter and requested him to send me the bill—which I shall remit to Mrs Randolph without delay—

I am Sir your obt Servt   CHS COPLAND

RC (MHi); at foot of text: "Tho: Jefferson Esqr"; endorsed by TJ as received 21 Jan. and so recorded in SJL.

To George Jefferson

DEAR SIR   Washington Jan. 16. 1801.

I recieved yesterday your's of the 10th. and immediately wrote to mr Barnes at Georgetown to remit you 3[84.]43 D which with the

535.83 D exchanged with mr Short will make up 920.26 the amount of my draughts on you, and be recieved I am in hopes before more of those draughts are presented than the 535.83 will answer. I am with great esteem Dear Sir

Your's affectionately   TH: JEFFERSON

PrC (MHi); blurred; at foot of text: "Mr. Jefferson"; endorsed by TJ in ink on verso.

For TJ's request of John BARNES OF GEORGETOWN to have $384.43 in bank

bills remitted to George Jefferson, see Barnes to TJ, 15 Jan.

MY DRAUGHTS ON YOU: see TJ to George Jefferson, 5 Jan. The largest payment of $550.16 to Richard Richardson was for the hire of slaves (see TJ to Richardson, 8 Jan. 1801; MB, 2:1032-3).

From Patricot

MONSIEUR   New-yorck 16 Jer 1801

Depuis trois mois ayant quitté Norfolk, Je n'ai reçu qu'hier la lettre que vous mavés fait l'honneur de m'écrire pour m'informer que vous aviés en vos mains un paquet de france pour moi. Veuillés avoir la complaisance de me l'envoyer à New-york, chez Mr. Guynemer Mulberry Street No 21, mais Monsieur comme le pacquet doit être volumineux, et que les fraix de poste Sont considérables, s'il est possible de me l'envoyer par une occasion Sure, vous m'obligerés infiniment, Si c'était trop long, Je vous prie de le Jetter tout uniment à la poste. Je vous demande mille pardons d'avance de la peine que cela vous donne, et recevés en mes Sincéres remercimens.

J'ai l'honneur d'être avec la plus haute considération Monsieur Votre trés humble trés obéissant Serviteur   PATRICOT

EDITORS' TRANSLATION

SIR   New York 16 Jan. 1801

Having left Norfolk three months ago, I received only yesterday the letter with which you honored me to advise me that you had in your hands a package from France for me. Please be so kind as to send it to me in New York, care of Mr. Guynemer, 21 Mulberry Street, but Sir, as the package must be voluminous and the post expenses considerable, if it is possible to send it to me by a favorable secure occasion, I shall be very obliged to you. If that should take too long, simply throw it into the post. I beg of you in advance a thousand pardons for the trouble that this is giving you, and accept my sincere thanks for it.

I have the honor to be with the highest esteem Sir your very humble very obedient servant   PATRICOT

RC (MHi); endorsed by TJ as received 22 Jan. 1801 and so recorded in SJL, TJ initially noting the month of the letter as "Feb." in both places and subsequently correcting the endorsement but not SJL.

LA LETTRE: TJ to Patricot, 20 Dec. 1800. John GUYNEMER was a teacher of English and French (*Longworth's American Almanac, New-York Register, and City-Directory, for the Twenty Seventh Year of American Independence* [New York, 1802], 216).

To Martha Jefferson Randolph

MY DEAR MARTHA   Washington Jan. 16. 1801.

I wrote to mr Randolph on the 9th. & 10th. inst. and yesterday recieved his letter of the 10th. it gave me real joy to learn that Lilly had got a recruit of hands from mr Allen; tho' still I would not have that prevent the taking all from the nailery who are able to cut, as I desired in mine of the 9th. as I wish Craven's ground to be got ready for him without any delay. mr Randolph writes me you are about to wean Cornelia.[1] this must be right & proper. I long to be in the midst of the children, and have more pleasure in their little follies than in the wisdom of the wise. here too there is such a mixture of the bad passions of the heart that one feels themselves in an enemy's country. it is an unpleasant circumstance, if I am destined to stay here, that the great proportion of those of the place who figure, are federalists, and most of them of the violent kind. some have been so personally bitter that they can never forgive me, tho' I do them with sincerity. perhaps in time they will get tamed. our prospect as to the election has been alarming: as a strong disposition exists to prevent an election, & that case not being provided for by the constitution, a dissolution of the government seemed possible. at present there is a prospect that some, tho' federalists, will prefer yielding to the wishes of the people rather than have no government. if I am fixed here, it will be but three easy days journey from you: so that I should hope you & the family could pay an annual visit here at least; which with mine to Monticello of the spring & fall, might enable us to be together 4. or 5. months of the year. on this subject however we may hereafter converse, lest we should be counting chickens before they are hatched. I inclose for Anne a story, too long to be got by heart, but worth reading. kiss them all for me; and keep them in mind of me. tell Ellen I am afraid she has forgotten me. I shall probably be with you the first week in April, as I shall endeavor to be at our court for that month. continue to love me my dear Martha and be assured of my unalterable and tenderest love to you. Adieu.   TH: JEFFERSON

P.S. Hamilton is using his uttermost influence to procure my election rather than Colo. Burr's.

RC (NNPM). PrC (MHi); endorsed by TJ in ink on verso. Enclosure not found.

[1] Word interlined in place of "Ellen."

To John Adams

Jan. 17. 1801.

Th: Jefferson presents his respects to the President of the US. and will have the honor of waiting on him to dinner on Thursday next

RC (Gary Hendershott, Little Rock, Arkansas, 1992); addressed: "The President of the US." Not recorded in SJL.

From John Garland Jefferson

MY DEAR SIR,   Amelia Jany. 17th. 1801

It is with pleasure that I resume my pen to write to you after a silence of some years. It has not been from a want of respect, or from the smallest diminution of that affectionate regard I have ever had for you that I have thus long been silent. There are but few circumstances that coud have restrained me till this period, but a conviction that nothing which I coud communicate on my part was of sufficient consequence to render it fit that I shoud divert your attention from more serious, and important subjects. A matter of business is now added to the strong inclination which I exclusively felt to write to you. I have for some time thought that the vicinity of Lynchburg was in many respects a more desireable situation than my present place of residence, and I was informed last fall when in that quarter, that you had a tract of land in the neighbourhood which you had some time before offered for sale. If you are still inclined to dispose of it, and I shoud like it on examination, I woud become the purchaser if we coud agree on the terms. Let me beg of you my dear Sir to deal with me as you woud with a stranger. I have too strong a sense of the many obligations I am under, to wish the number to be increased by any thing like a pecuniary sacrafice. I feel already a stronger sense of gratitude towards you than if you were in reality my father. The one is actuated by the mere benevolence of his nature, the other by those impressive and indelible sensations which bind the father to the son.

The result of the late elections has filled the minds of the people here with sincere and heart-felt joy. I have heard some of your best friends express surprise, at a vote which you are said lately to have given. It is reported that a bankrupt soninlaw of Mr. Adams was nominated as stamp master general, and that the senate being equally divided you gave a casting vote in his favor. This has been a topic of much conversation. You will not I trust consider me guilty of impertinence in having informed you of this rumor. You must be convinced of my high esteem, and friendship for you, and that this is the only motive which actuates me. I am persuaded also that you are too much of a republican in principle, to dislike to hear at any time the opinions or wishes of the people, either directly or indirectly. I have been insensibly led to say much more than I at first intended, I will now therefore conclude, and hope that you will believe what I have always declared, and shall be proud to acknowledge, that I am with sentiments of grateful esteem,

Your most obliged and devoted kinsman

JNO G: JEFFERSON

RC (ViU: Carr-Cary Papers); addressed: "The Honourable Thomas Jefferson Vice President of the United States"; franked; postmarked Richmond; endorsed by TJ as received 24 Jan. and so recorded in SJL.

SILENCE OF SOME YEARS: TJ's last letter to John Garland Jefferson, a lawyer in Amelia County, Virginia, and George Jefferson's brother, is printed at 17 Dec. 1796 (MB, 1:768; 2:975).

On 5 May 1800 TJ cast the tie-breaking VOTE, which led to the confirmation of Joshua Johnson as superintendent of stamps at the newly established General Stamp Office. Republican Senators, along with several Federalists, voted against the appointment. In 1790 TJ had informed Johnson of his appointment as U.S. consul in London, and during the next four years the secretary of state found him assiduous in carrying out his duties. In July 1797 Johnson's daughter Louisa Catherine married John Quincy Adams in London. Facing financial difficulties, Johnson resigned his position as consul, returned to the United States, and settled in Washington (JEP, 1:253, 350-1; Stewart Mitchell, ed., New Letters of Abigail Adams, 1788-1801 [Boston, 1947], 110, 115; Washington, Papers, Pres. Ser., 6:183-4; Vol. 17:119-20; TJ to John Garland Jefferson, 1 Feb. 1801).

From Lewis Littlepage

DEAR SIR,   Altona 17th. January. 1801.

The vicissitudes of fortune which I have experienced, and continual uncertainty of my place of residence, have prevented for several years past my writing to you, or any of my friends in America.— My reason for importuning you at present is this.—I am informed by a letter from Virginia, that *upon the supposition of my Death,* a scandalous litigious dispute has arisen between some persons related to me, respecting my small property in Virginia. I therefore most earnestly entreat you, upon recieving this letter, to cause to be inserted in the Richmond gazette, a short advertisement, importing, "*that you know me to be alive in the town of Altona in Holstein, and only waiting the approach of Spring to return to my native Country.*—" Such is my intention.—I have the satisfaction to inform you that after having been separated by express order of the Empress Catherine II, from the King of Poland, for the part I took in the revolution of 1794, even after her death having been brought into a sort of squabble with her Successor Paul 1st., I at last settled matters with him, and he paid me very nobly the sum assigned to me by the King of Poland for my long and dangerous services.—I arrived in Hamburgh in October last, intending to have gone to France, but an attempt was made to embroil me with the Government of that Country, as you will see by the enclosed printed paper.—That business is settled to my entire satisfaction, but another political episode of a more extraordinary nature has arisen!—I am in a scrape *with England*, because, forsooth, the Emperor of Russia chuses to go to loggerheads with the King of England!—what the devil is all that to me?—Do I direct Paul 1st.? By the bye this Northern business is becoming serious.—Denmark has answered in such a spirited manner the peremptory demand of England, that hostilities seem inevitable.—Moreau is almost at the gates of Vienna, and a Continental Peace cannot be distant.—I am curious to see how Mr. Pitt will manage this Baltic Confederation.—

In the hope of soon saluting you in person in our native, beloved Country, I have the honor to be with the highest esteem and respect,

Dear Sir, your most obedient servant and faithful friend

LEWIS LITTLEPAGE

P.S. Should any accident happen to me before I reach America, I have a will deposited in England, of which you are Executor in America and Lord Wycomb in England.—The sum to be disposed of is between nine and ten thousand pounds sterling.—

RC (DLC); at foot of first page: "Thomas Jefferson Esquire"; endorsed by TJ as received 24 Apr. and so recorded in SJL. Enclosure: for the broadside of 18 Oct. 1800, see note below.

The LETTER FROM VIRGINIA was probably that of his stepfather, Lewis Holladay, to Littlepage of 22 Aug. 1800, which Littlepage received 9 Jan. 1801. Littlepage responded on the same day with an outline of his life and whereabouts in Europe from 1785 to 1801. For the LITIGIOUS DISPUTE, see TJ to Waller Holladay, 4 July 1800.

An ATTEMPT WAS MADE TO EMBROIL or blackmail Littlepage shortly after he moved to Hamburg in late 1800 when one

Forhegger, whom Littlepage had formerly employed in Warsaw to copy his correspondence with Emperor Paul, claimed he had not been paid for his services. Forhegger threatened to publish some of these letters unless Littlepage made a deposit of fifty ducats for him. The latter responded with the ENCLOSED PRINTED PAPER, a broadside in French offering proof that he had given his creditors adequate time to settle their accounts before he left Warsaw. Littlepage also requested that the local police and the first consul in France destroy whatever instruments of the plot came into their hands by Forheg-

ger and his conspirators. Later attempts on his life prompted him to move to Altona, where he stayed until his return voyage to America in 1801 (Boand, *Lewis Littlepage*, 268-69, 277).

ANOTHER POLITICAL EPISODE: in the fall of 1800 Paul I declared an embargo on British shipping, detained thousands of British seamen in Russian ports, and recalled the Russian ambassador in London (Nina N. Bashkina and others, eds., *The United States and Russia: The Beginning of Relations, 1765-1815* [Washington, D.C., 1980], 346).

From Andrew Ellicott

DEAR SIR   Philadelphia Jany. 18th. 1801

The first part of the fifth volume of the transactions of our Philosophical Society is now with the printer.—more than one half of it will consist of the astronomical journal kept on our southern boundary.—The charts, and plans, are yet with our executive, and I do not expect to obtain them till after the 4th. of March next.—I have been told by Mr. Pickering and others, that the work done on our North eastern boundary, has been executed in a truly scientifick manner, that the astronomical observations, and mathematical deductions, are very important, some of which will doubtless be found in the report.—If so, and there should be no impropriety in it, it would be a desirable object to have them for our next volume. The journal with an account, and discription of the instruments made use of, if it could be had, would be preferable to the report, or the observations extracted from it.—It appears to me that publicity ought to be given to all papers of that kind, perticularly such as have a tendency to improve the geography of our own extensive country.—A contrary policy can only originate in a narrowness of mind, and be defended by persons, who would prefer a conclusion drawn from one of Aristotle's syllogisms, to a deduction from Euclids elements.—The observations made by Mason, and Dixon, on the boundary between Pennsylvania, and Maryland, are published in the transactions of the Royal Society at London.—Those on the boundary between Virginia, and Pennsylvania, and Pennsylvania and New York, are published in the 4th. volume of the transactions of our Philosophical Society. From which it appears that publicity has been given, to important national records by institutions, which it has lately been fashionable to treat with redicule, and contempt!—

We had a very full meeting of the members of the Philosophical Society on friday evening last.—My friend Mr. Dunbar's interesting communications which accompanied your letter of the 16th. ultimo to Doctr. Wister, were read, and referred to that gentleman and myself to report on.—

Whilst I resided in the Missisippi Territory, I proposed Mr. Dunbar as a member of the Society, and he was accordingly elected; but had no intimation of it till since my return, when I forwarded his Diploma which he received last July.—He furnished the whole of the mathematical, and astronomical apparatus, on behalf of his Catholick Majesty, for determining our southern boundary.—Since that time, he has imported a valuable collection of instruments, and I have no doubt but we shall, (from his singular industery,) shortly receive a number of important astronomical observations from him.—His meteorological journal, is interesting, and does him great credit.—I presume you observed in perusing it, that the changes of the Thermometer in 24 hours during the winter months, frequently exceeded 30 degrees, which is common in that country, but with us it is generally less.—the greatest change in 24 hours in December 1770, and January, and February, 1771 in this City, was 17 degrees.—

Our friend Doctr. Priestly is now in this City, he arrived on wednesday last and intends staying but two or three weeks:—he has just left me, and requested that if I intended writing to you shortly, not to fail presenting you with his respects, and assuring you of the satisfaction he feels in contemplating the present political prospects of our country.

I have the honour to be with great respect, and sincere esteem, Your friend &c. ANDW; ELLICOTT.

RC (DLC); at foot of text: "Hnble. Thos. Jefferson. V.P.-U.S and President of the Senate"; endorsed by TJ as received 21 Jan. and so recorded in SJL. Dft (DLC: Ellicott Papers).

As secretary of state in 1798 Timothy PICKERING involved himself in research on the boundary between Maine and adjoining British territory (Vol. 30:284). Astronomical observations made by Charles MASON and Jeremiah DIXON as they ran the Pennsylvania-Maryland boundary, including their calculation of the length of a degree of latitude, appeared in Royal Society of London, *Philosophical Transactions*, 58 (1768), 270-335. In a report to the American Philosophical Society that took the form of a letter of 2 Apr. 1795 to Robert Patterson, Ellicott reported observations associated with the extension of the Mason-Dixon line, the running of the western boundary of Pennsylvania, which with the extended southern boundary marked the state's limits with VIRGINIA, and the determination of Pennsylvania's northern boundary, all of which was done in the mid-1780s (APS, *Transactions*, 4 [1799], 32-48).

HAD A VERY FULL MEETING: Ellicott,

who with Caspar Wistar and Robert Patterson was a vice president of the APS for the year 1801, presided over the society's meeting on 16 Jan. (APS, *Proceedings*, 22, pt. 3 [1884], 307).

Before writing the letter above, Ellicott began but did not complete the undated draft of another letter, apparently to TJ, that touched some of the same subjects but with different phrasing. Ellicott began that aborted draft by noting that the finishing work on the southern boundary of the U.S. had given him "leisure to undertake that from the Lake of the Woods to the source of the Mississippi." He had "almost determined never to undertake another piece of business of a similar nature" but found his mind "only sufficiently active when engaged in scientific enterprises." He mentioned the probable delay in publication of the volume of *Transactions* caused by the government's continuing possession of charts and maps needed for his report. And in the final paragraph before breaking off the draft Ellicott wrote: "The prospect of you being shortly elevated to the most

dignified, and important station, our country can bestow, is a subject highly pleasing both to men of Science, as well as to the friends of liberty, and good order.—Philosophy has for some years past been a subject of redicule, it has been artfully coupelled with the enormities committed during the revolution in france, for the purpose of introducing arbitrary measures in our own government" (Dft in DLC: Ellicott Papers).

Writing at Philadelphia on 25 Dec., Ellicott sent TJ a brief letter: "To amuse you a few minutes I have taken the liberty of sending the following extract from my journal." Ellicott subjoined a description of a spectacular meteor shower he witnessed at sea off the coast of Florida on 12 Nov. 1799. He sent the same extract to Robert Patterson, and from that copy, submitted to the APS on 16 Jan. 1801, it was published (RC in DLC, alongside signature: "Thos. Jefferson V.P. U.S. and President of the Senate," endorsed by TJ as received 1 Jan. and so recorded in SJL; APS, *Proceedings*, 22, pt. 3 [1884], 307-8; APS, *Transactions*, 6 [1809], 28-9).

From James Monroe

DEAR SIR   Richmond 18. Jany. 1801.

I returned here lately from Albemarle to which quarter I made a visit of two days last week. While there I saw P. Carr and conferr'd with him on the subject of my last to you. The idea suggested in my last respecting him, was not originally his own but that of some of his friends who thought a change of scene might be useful to him, and some step of a political kind, the means of his future advancement in the county or district where he lives. He yeilded to my objections to it, and indeed seems rather inclined to remain in respose at home than embark in any political pursuit whatever.

It is said here that Marshall has given an opinion in conversation with Stoddard, that in case 9. States shod. not unite in favor of one of the persons chosen, the legislature may appoint a Presidt. till another election is made, & that intrigues are carrying on to place us in that situation. This is stated in a letter from one of our reps. (I think Randolph) & has excited the utmost indignation in the legislature. Some talk of keeping it in session till after the[1] 2d. wednesday in

Feby: others of adjourning to meet then. There has been much alarm at the intimation of such a projected usurpation, much consultation, and a spirit fully manifested not to submit to it. My opinion is they shod. take no step founded on the expectation of such an event, as it might produce an ill effect even with our friends, and the more especially as the Executive wod. not fail in case it occurred to convene the legislature without delay. While up the second carpenter, who has a father in law in Georgeton, a clerk in some office, fell from some part of your building & expired in a few hours in consequence of the contusions he recd. Our assembly has done little business since its meeting. They made a series of experiments to unite in some measure to prevent or suppress future negro conspiracies, without effect. I think it will adjourn in a few days. Sincerely I am Dear Sir your friend & servant

JAS. MONROE

RC (DLC); endorsed by TJ as received 23 Jan. and so recorded in SJL.

TAKE NO STEP FOUNDED ON THE EX-PECTATION OF SUCH AN EVENT: at some point Monroe drafted for a public meeting an undated resolution expressing confidence that the U.S. House of Representatives would resolve the election and declaring that it was not necessary to petition the General Assembly to stay in session beyond the second Wednesday of February (DLC: Monroe Papers).

SECOND CARPENTER: John Holmes. James Stuart, a CLERK in the Register's Office, was Holmes's stepfather (ASP, *Miscellaneous*, 1:58; Philadelphia *Aurora*, 31 Jan.; TJ to Stuart, 12 May 1801).

A bill "To prohibit free negroes and mulattoes from residing in or near certain towns," which the Virginia House of Delegates dropped on 16 Jan., may have been part of the legislature's SERIES OF EX-PERIMENTS. The General Assembly had passed, in the days just before Monroe wrote the letter above, an act for the transportation of convicted slaves (see Monroe to TJ, 15 Sep. 1800) and another that empowered justices of the peace to call out patrols, provided for reorganization of the militia and patrol in Petersburg, and allowed a tax to pay for the guard in Fredericksburg. A few days after Monroe

wrote, the assembly passed an act "to amend the act, intituled 'An act, to reduce into one the several acts, concerning slaves, free negroes and mulattoes.'" Along with measures to prevent slaves from hiring themselves out, the statute contained provisions allowing the testimony of blacks in some court cases, restricting the bringing of slaves into Virginia from elsewhere, requiring each commissioner of the revenue to make an annual registry of "all free negroes or mulattoes within his district, together with their names, sex, places of abode, and particular trades, occupation or calling," and allowing magistrates to declare as a vagrant any free person of color who moved from one county to another without having employment in the new location. As the legislative session waned during January the General Assembly also passed acts to arm the militia of towns and establish a guard force in Richmond (*Acts Passed at a General Assembly of the Commonwealth of Virginia. Begun and Held at the Capitol, in the City of Richmond, on Monday the First Day of December One Thousand Eight Hundred* [Richmond, 1801], 21, 24, 34-5, 37-9; JHD, Dec. 1800-Jan. 1801, 70).

[1] Monroe here canceled "3d."

From Hugh Henry Brackenridge

S<small>IR</small>,   Pittsburg January 19th. 1801.

Did not expect an answer to my note, not meaning to draw a person engaged in affairs into a correspondence:

Cum tot sustineas, et tanta negotia—

—In publica commoda peccem,

Si longo sermone morer—

But it may be useful to you in your present and approaching responsible situation to have hints, or indicia of the public mind on occasional subjects. With a view to inform and from a zeal for the credit of your administration I may occasionally communicate such hints as do not reach the Gazettes or are proper to be inserted in them. A draw-back upon me is that I do not write myself, but use an amanuensis. My hand writing is not easily legible, and it cramps my fingers, and hurts my nerves to write. Hence it is that I have avoided all correspondence not absolutely necessary: a loss no doubt in the course of my life, both of honor and profit, but it has saved time; I have had leisure to read the more. But am sensible of the want of that confirmation in actions, or incitement to improvement which communication with philosophic men gives. "As iron sharpeneth iron, so doth the face of a man his friend."

It is with this view, however slight the assistance, that I subjoin this note on a hint contained in your letter to me, the opening abyss of a probable suspension of the federal government, from the non-election of a President in the present case of an equality of votes for two persons. In the Capital of this state (Philadelphia) from which I have just returned, and in the Villages of Lancaster, Carlisle &ca. the more violent of the ex-federalists protest against an election at all, or declare for Burr as President. The moderate and discerning reprobate both ideas, and say should such a conduct prevail they will no longer class themselves with such federalists. The ex-federal enrageé give us a reason for their declaration, that it will spite the republicans. Some of them have been heard to use the language that they wished to do all the mischief in their power. Thomas Duncan, a lawyer of eminence in the mid-land counties used this language as reported to me by the Governor, and this law character is considered as an organ of the party.

The more strenuous of the republicans affect to declare themselves for Burr, and tell these ex-federalists, that if Jefferson will err it will be on the side of moderation, and for their part they will prefer Burr made, perhaps, of sterner stuff, & from his long Wars personal and political at New-York more habituated to controversy, and if from no other principle, yet to rebutt all suspicion of conciliation will act with double rigor, and sweep from office every individual of the preceding administration.

An idea by the ex-federalists has been thrown out that the present case will come within that section of the constitution enabling Congress to declare what officer shall act as President in case of the removal of a President, and within a subsequent act of Congress March 1st. 1792 Sec. 9. that in the case of removal "the president of the Senate pro tempore, and in case there shall be no President of the Senate, then the Speaker of the House of Representatives, for the time being shall act as President of the United States" &ca. But the term removal carries with it the idea of impeachment, and the expiration of the term of Presidency is no removal. But a President pro tempore by the constitution can be chosen only in the absence of the Vice-President, or when he shall exercise the office of President. There will be no absence in this case, or exercise of office of Presidency, and so no President pro tempore can be chosen. But should it have been done, or should it be done the present case is not that of a removal, and there is no room under the Act of Congress for the President pro tempore to act. The Constitution supports the construction by Art. 2. Sec. IV. stating a removal from office to be an impeachment &ca. But great liberty has been taken with the constitution on what Lawyers call a liberal or equitable construction, and a President pro tempore may be made and that officer as he will be called may usurp the Government. It was announced to me on my way at Bedford the residence of the family of Woods into which James Ross has married, that he had passed down some weeks ago, and was chosen President pro tempore the day of his arrival. At this place (Pittsburg) it is understood that letters had arrived from Senator Tracy to James Ross, wishing his immediate presence with the Senate for the express purpose of being chosen Vice-President, with a view to take upon himself the office of President on the event of a non election by the Legislature.

In this case what ought to be the measure with the Republicans? The Governor of Pennsylvania stated to me as his opinion and of other men of legal knowledge with whom he had conversed, that it was in the power of the two persons equal in vote to settle this among themselves by writing under hand and seal. This would seem to receive countenance from the Act March 1st. 1792 Section 11. "that the only evidence of a refusal to accept of the office of President or Vice-President shall be an instrument in writing declaring the same, and subscribed by the person refusing to accept, and delivered into the office of secretary of State." It would seem therefore in the power of one to refuse the acceptance of the higher office. But doubtless the section contemplates a refusal to accept after a special designation by election to the particular office. There cannot be a refusal to accept until there is an offer. A majority of nine states can alone offer the presidency.

It may be said an individual may wave his right of choice where there is equality of votes, under the maxim, Juri pro se introducto quisquis renunciari potest. But this is not a right of the individual exclusive and independent. It is the right of the people to dispose to the office. This proceeding cannot therefore be strictly regular and legally justifiable. It must savor of usurpation. yet well knowing the public mind on this subject it would be a safe usurpation and from the complection of the next Congress, there can be no doubt but that the irregularity would be purged by a subsequent choice of President sanctioning the intermediate acts as necessary and unavoidable to preserve the Government. Ratification is equivalent to original authority. The Maxim is, Omnis rati-habitio retrotrahitur, atque mandato equiparatur.

In the case of President pro tempore usurping the Presidency there is a trespass upon substance as well as form. It is without foundation or color of authority, and on the succession of the legitimate powers of government this officer so called might be liable on a charge of treason; but under the present judicial authority of the United States the prosecution could not be carried into effect. But in the mean time I have no manner of doubt before the legitimate powers of government could come into exercise the usurpers would fortify themselves by an armed power, and attempt the retaining the sovereignty by force. It would be a fairer opportunity than Cromwell had. An army under the name of Volunteers consisting of ex-federalists with Alexander Hamilton at their head could get possession of Forts, Arsenals, Stores and Arms in a short time. I am confident James Ross has boldness enough, ambition and want of principle, with chagrin of disappointment to attempt this in a moment.

Were I in the place of President designate, in my present mind I would not hesitate one moment, to announce myself on the fourth day of March next President, and to convene the legitimate authorities instantly to ratify that annunciation. The consent of the rival candidate if he might be so called, having in the mean time been obtained in Writing, and filed in the Secretary's office by analogy to the form of proceeding under the Act of March 1st. 1792 in the case of refusal to accept or resignation. In a case of this nature all depends on the decision and rapidity of the movement, the hadrepebalon or fortunate boldness of the Greeks, the coup de main of military men.

But we hope better things, and I think the rascals will tremble at the extremes which they meditate. They will dread the opinion of ex-federalists at home, the more wise and moderate whose opinions will begin to reach them. Should they dare the bayonet, or provoke hostilities by their conduct, they will know that valor, virtue and numbers are against them and they must go down on a contest by arms. I cannot but believe that on the approaching day of election there will not only be nine States, but a unanimous vote in favor of Thomas Jefferson President and Aaron Burr Vice-President; but should they elect Burr president, it will give Jefferson afterwards the presidency an amendment to the Constitution having in the mean time taken place, or the designation of President and Vice President ascertained by consent of dropping votes or vote for one or other of the Republican Candidates in some State or States.

John Israel printer and editor of the tree of liberty at this place informs me that he has occasionally transmitted you some numbers. The patronage of this paper has drawn upon me personally much abuse, and ribaldry in the ex-federal prints. They are aware of the great importance of the post which has been seized, and have felt the effects of it. But the republicans are poor in this extreme of the State and but for considerable pecuniary assistance on my part, it could not have been set up or supported. The adversary press of John Scull is supported by private contributions from the party, and has the advantage of support from Government by the publication of the laws of the United States an emolument which we hope to see soon transfered to the Herald and Tree of Liberty.

Having put this Western house so to speak in order as far as can be done by arrangements and support of mine, I mean to withdraw to a more mid-land situation in the State as necessary to the convenient discharge of the duties of the office which I hold, & my being more in the neighborhood of the sea-coast cities, and the seat of the federal government which I might sometimes incline to visit.

Excuse the trouble I have given in this writing and accept of my gratulation on the testimony which America has given of the high respect they entertain for your talents and virtues, and believe me to be an admirer of your simplicity of manners, your science, political demerit and services and irreproachable moral character and liberallity in religious opinions

Your Most Obedient Humble Servant   H H BRACKENRIDGE

P.S. Writing for Israel's paper with a view to assist it, occasionally while at home I have been noting down this morning some lines, I will not say dictated to me by Urania or any other of the Muses,

"Which Nightly me revisits"

But which I meditated, not altogether in my slumbers, but on my bed in the course of the night, and which entitle

       Jefferson

in imitation of Virgil's

       Pollio

"Sicelides Musæ paulo majora canamus."

Should I finish it I will send it to the press and enclose a copy

I have finished the poem and enclose a copy, though possibly it may be extracted and you may see it in other papers.

In the Aurora of January 10th. by this post I observe the idea which had occurred to me of a seizure of the government by a president pro tempore; and if it is seized, I engage it will be retained. They will not be such fools as to give it up and subject themselves to be called to account for the usurpation, at least if the spirit and counsels of James Ross should prevail. I have known him in law practice capable of every thing short of a falsification of the record and to manage officers. In contracts his character is that of doing any thing that the rigor of law can screen or support. In his canvassing for the election of Governor, and management of it I saw him capable of every thing from general arrangements in the face of the law to the detail of acting on the ground.

It is understood here that he declared before his departure that from the letters of Senator Tracy to himself it was expected that Matthew Lyon of Vermont could be taken off and that State gained, that Lyon could be bribed; farther that it was fixed and he was secured in favor of Burr.

RC (DLC); in a clerk's hand, signed by Brackenridge; endorsed by TJ as received 30 Jan. and so recorded in SJL. Enclosure: Hugh Henry Brackenridge, *Jefferson, in Imitation of Virgil's Pollio*; MS not found, printed in the Pittsburgh *Tree of Liberty*, 24 Jan. 1801, and reprinted in Claude Milton Newlin, *The Life and Writings of Hugh Henry Brackenridge* (Princeton, 1932), 232-4; see below.

ANSWER TO MY NOTE: TJ to Brackenridge, 18 Dec. 1800, replying to Brackenridge's now-missing letter of 13 Sep.

CUM TOT SUSTINEAS ... MORER: an extract from the first four lines of Horace's *Epistulae*, book 2, letter 1, meaning "with your burden of so many great public affairs, I should sin against the public good if I delayed you with long talk."

AS IRON SHARPENETH IRON: Proverbs 27:17.

See TJ to John Marshall, 28 Dec. 1800, for the ACT OF CONGRESS of 1 Mch. 1792.

The Senate had no occasion to name a PRESIDENT PRO TEMPORE between 28 Nov., when TJ took the chair, and 28 Feb. 1801, when he bade farewell to the chamber. James Ross took his seat on 12 Jan. (JS, 3:110, 115, 134-5).

In the law of contracts, the MAXIM "quilibet (or cuilibet) potest renunciare juri pro se introducto" stated that an individual could waive a right that existed only for his own benefit. The maxim concerning RATIFICATION, often rendered "omnis ratihabitio retrotrahitur et mandato priori æquiparatur," declared that ratification of an action was retrospective in effect and equal to the original authorization (Herbert Broom, *Selection of Legal Maxims, Classified and Illustrated* [Philadelphia, 1845], 200-202; *Latin for Lawyers* [London, 1915], 215, 228-9; Henry Campbell Black, *Black's Law Dictionary: Definitions of the Terms and Phrases of American and English Jurisprudence, Ancient and Modern*, rev. 4th ed. [St. Paul, Minn., 1968], 453, 1239).

HADREPEBALON: translated literally from the Greek, "the power of forming great conceptions."

John Israel established the TREE OF LIBERTY in Pittsburgh in 1800 and the *Herald of Liberty* two years earlier in Washington, Pennsylvania (Vol. 30:286n). The ADVERSARY PRESS OF JOHN SCULL was the *Pittsburgh Gazette*, founded in 1786 (Brigham, *American Newspapers*, 2:965).

IN IMITATION OF VIRGIL'S POLLIO: Brackenridge's title mimicked that of Alexander Pope's poem *Messiah*, which first appeared in the *Spectator* in 1712. Inspired by messianic prophecies he saw both in the book of Isaiah and in Virgil's fourth *Eclogue*, which was addressed to Gaius Asinius Pollio, Pope called *Messiah* "A Sacred Eclogue / In Imitation of Virgil's Pollio." The first line of Virgil's work, quoted above by Brackenridge, translates, "Sicilian muses, let us sing in a loftier strain," echoed by Brackenridge in the opening of his poem to TJ as "Begin O muse, begin a loftier strain." Pope's verse opened, "Ye Nymphs of Solyma! begin the song" (Alexander Pope, *Poetical Works*, ed. Herbert Davis [London, 1966], 31-2; Paul Baines, *The Complete Critical Guide to Alexander Pope* [London, 2000], 13-14).

For the report in the AURORA of 10 Jan., see Monroe to TJ, 6 Jan. 1801.

To John Wayles Eppes

DEAR SIR   Washington Jan. 19. 1801.

I wrote to you Dec. 23. via Petersburg, and to Maria Jan. 4. via City point. neither seems to have reached you Jan. 12. the date of your letter which came to hand yesterday. I answer it immediately according to my promise to Maria. and if mine be acknoleged as soon as you recieve it, we may hear from each other regularly every fortnight, as a letter is but 6 days going hence to Richmond, and 1. I presume thence to City point. but does the post go every day from Richmond to City point?—I am sorry you were disappointed in getting the negroes. Lilly hired but a single one. Richardson not one: and [I] have consequently been obliged to take from the nail-shop all able to cut in order to make the stipulated clearing for Craven. since that mr Randolph has by a great accident procured some, I know not how many. Powell was not at Monticello Jan. 10. the necessity of taking away half the nailers makes it indifferent to me whether he goes till the first week of April. this may be as he chuses. but if he puts it off till then he must not fail a single day, as I shall be at home by our April court, & shall make a very short stay. this on the supposition that the issue of the election should fix me here. if such should be the issue, as soon as it is fixed, I shall write to you on the subject of the horses, to wit, Dr. Walker's, Shore's, and those of the [. . .] particularly the carriage horse. as to the saddle horse, Colo. Hoomes has offered me one for 300. D. which he assures me is equal to Tarquin, and I believe I shall take him. I should still wish [for Haxall's] if to be had at a [reasonable] price. I mention this subject now that you may keep your eye on those horses, or any others equal to them, in case I should want them. it will now be known in 3. weeks. time seems to operate in our favor by the manifestation of the public opinion [&] it's influence on those of the Representatives whose minds are not as embittered by party passions as to lose sight of every thing else.—the Northern confederacy will I hope make England tractable towards us, and ease a part of the administration which gives more anxiety than all the rest.—my love to my dearest Maria. oh! for Fortunatus's cap, that I might drop into your hermitage, and sweeten some of the comfortless moments of life. Health and sincere affection. Adieu.

TH: JEFFERSON

PrC (MHi); faint; at foot of text: "J. W. Eppes"; endorsed by TJ in ink on verso.

YOUR LETTER: Eppes's letter of 12 Jan., recorded in SJL as received from Bermuda on 18 Jan., has not been found.

TJ explained his reference to FORTU-NATUS'S CAP in a letter to Maria Cosway, 24 Dec. 1786.

From Elbridge Gerry

MY DEAR SIR   Cambridge 20th Jany 1801

I now propose to finish my letter of the 15th, which was hastily concluded, to prevent inconvenience to my friend Lincoln.

In revising your political faith, I am not clear, that we perfectly agree in regard to a navy. I wish sincerely, with yourself, to avoid the evils pointed out, as the result of a powerful navy. the expence & extensive operation of an imense naval establishment, if our resources would admit of it, might make us more haughty & enterprizing than wise, an object of the envy, jealousy, & hatred of some or of all the maritime powers, &, finally, the victim of our own "autocrasy": &

every one is left to judge from his own observations, whether this is not the natural tendency of an overgrown navy: but at the same time it appears to me expedient, if not necessary, to extend our views to such a naval establishment, as will furnish convoys to our valuable commerce, & place us, at least, above the depredations & insults of small maritime powers.—with this qualification, I readily confirm the avowal of your political faith, as my own.

Indulge me with some observations on the war party's adroitness, to take the credit to themselves of events, which they have laboured abundantly to prevent, & to ascribe these, when popular, to measures which they had adopted to promote a contrary effect. the martial attitude of the US, which is said to have prevented a war, & which I have before stated was not known in France at the time of the official declaration made to me, "that my departure from France would bring on an immediate rupture," did not then exist, as will appear by attending to facts. On the 18th of March 1798, the french minister, in his letter to the Envoys of that date, signified the determination of the directory not to treat with two of them, & their readiness to open a negotiation with me. on the 23d of march Mr Pickering enclosed to the envoys the President's instructions directing them, under certain circumstances, to put an end to the negotiation, & to demand their passports; & those instructions were delivered to me on the 12th of may. it must therefore be evident, that at the period of my resolution to remain in France, the martial attitude, so much boasted of, could not have been known there; because it did not then exist in the U. States. indeed if it had existed, it could not possibly have appalled France, in the Zenith of her power; altho, as an evidence of her contempt, it might have prompted her to a declaration of War. but it is very curious, that when the congretional declaimers, wish'd to make the war party popular, they held up the martial attitude, as the chef d'Œuvre, which prevented war; & when the principals wish'd to point the indignation of that party against the person whom they supposed to have merited it, they then affirmed, that he committed the unpardonable crime, & thus prevented the US from rising to the highest pitch of national glory, by joining the coalition against France. this I am informed is stated in a late pamphlet, issued from a prostituted press of that party at New York—peace with France was a measure of the last importance, in my mind, to the U States: a war wontonly provoked with her, would have made her vindictive & implacable, to the last degree against this country; would have divided, & thus have weakened the nation; would have been immediately followed by a treaty, offensive & defensive, with G Britain; would have made us compleatly dependent on her; would on her part have promoted an hauteur & insolence, proportionate to that dependence; & would finally have left us the alternative only, of being reunited to her government, or of being left by a seperate treaty of peace between her & France, victims to the vengeance of that exasperated & powerful republick. it is evident then, that if in efforts for preventing war there has been any merit, the war party are so far from a claim to it, as to be justly chargeable with having made every exertion to promote that fatal event.

The delicate situation in which I was placed, by the rejection of the other envoys, & by the declaration of the directory in regard to my departure, induced me to consider in every point of View, the effects of every measure which suggested itself; & that which was adopted, a proposition that the french government should come forward with the project of a treaty, & by the joint efforts of their minister & myself should accomodate it to the veiws & interests of the two nations, & that a french minister should be sent to our government to compleat the business, will appear, I think, to have been the best, and would in a short time have been carried into effect, had not the Sophia arrived, or other measures intervened to defeat the proposition. but what, at that time, would have been the fate of the french minister & his project, even if the latter had contained provissions, exceeding the most sanguine expectations of the U States? or in what manner would similar provissions, presented by myself to the government in any form of a treaty been received, at a time when revenge for real, or supposed injuries took place of a principle of accomodation, & when, with many, not to be mad, was to be a traitor?—it was indeed fortunate, all circumstances considered, that measures were not so matured, as to have been presented in any form to our government, either by a french minister or by myself, as their rejection must have increased the irritation on both sides, & have rendered more difficult a reconciliation: and it was not less fortunate, that my communications had a tendency to, & with the operation of other causes really did, produce the effects you predicted.

That in the first instance I was abused, in some measure, by republicans, was to me evident; for I had seen at paris, in the american news-papers severe strictures on my first conference with Mr Tallyrand: but I agree with you, that they did not proceed far in their censures, & that the war party were malignant to excess. the "report" of Mr Pickering I saw, his letters & conversations, I knew nothing of, or even the Presidents last instructions, untill published;[1] but the former produced such an indignation & ineffable contempt for the man, as determined me at once to expose his partiality, malignity, & injustice; & disagreable as it always is to the publick, to see ministers of the same embassy contending with each other, I nevertheless determined to enter the list with either or both of the other Envoys, if they had come forward as Pickering's coadjutors. decency & propriety required, that after the request of the President, stated in my last, I should wait till his return, & till he could have an opportunity to explain matters. this he did without reserve, & communicated the breach, between himself & Pickering, produced in the first instance by the rejection of the most virulent parts of his report on my communications; and evidencd by the Presidents nomination of new Envoys to France. this information changed the complection of affairs, & as the plan of the war faction, of which Pickering was prime agent, was to bring on me the whole of Mr Adams' as well as their own adherents, it was incumbent on me to defeat its purpose. I therefore communicated my remarks & strictures on Pickering's report to the President, & confided in him to do me justice. at that time the President had probably[2] determined to dismiss Pickering, & Whether he (the President) tho't that this disgrace of itself, altho the result of intrigues against himself was full satisfaction for the intrigues against me, or Whether he tho't that a direct vindication of me would be trampling on a fallen foe, & perhaps implicate himself in some degree for having passed the report, no publick notice has been taken of the injustice sustained by me. indeed there was one consideration, in regard to a publick discussion of the affairs of the mission, which, independent of the disgrace generally attending public disputes & attaching itself to all parties, had great weight in my mind. immediately after the publication of my communications, & the nomination of new envoys, such a calm took place of the tempest which had before agitated the publick mind, as to promise a change of publick opinion; & the promise has been fulfilled to an extraordinary degree: insomuch, as that the war faction, who by means of their presses & their general arrangements, had in most of the states, & in this in particular the controul of the public opinion, at that time, are now generally execrated, if that happy state of tranquillity, at the moment of it's return had been again interrupted by a discussion, which must inevitably have engaged the warmest passions of all parties, it was impossible to ascertain whether it could again be restored: & the greater the flame which might have been produced, the more would it have served the purposes of the War party: for their success depended on influencing the passions, & the republicans' success on influencing the reason, of the people at large. but before a war should have been

declared, & thereby our independance have been placed, as it inevitably must have been, on a precarious footing, I would have stated
minutely every circumstance of the embassy, without regard to or
considerations of delicacy, or of the feelings of any man. this I would
have done, at the risk of personal destruction, for whilst the war
party, faithfully rewarded the other envoys for declaring explicitly in
favour of war, & "beamed" as you well express it, "meridian splendor" on them; not a solitary line was drawn in my favor: whilst
"homage" was paid to a molten calf, whilst the continent was alive as
the other envoys pass'd to their homes, the land ransacked for dain-
ties to enrich the tables every where spread for them, & the imagination racked to invent toasts & publish eulogies in their praise, for
having pursued measures, ruinous as we conceived to their country:
the most profound silence in every respect was observed by the real
federalists & true republicans towards me, altho at every hazard of
my property, life & reputation, & even of the welfare of my family, I
had stood in the gap, on a forlorn hope, to repel a desperate enemy.
indeed, a few days after my arrival, the branch faction[3] at Boston, signified that they wished to take publick notice of me, & only waited for
me to come out in the papers, as the other envoys have done, in favor
of a war. my answer which undoubtedly exasperated them, was, that
I did not consider myself as the minister of any one State, county, or
town, much less of a few individuals of the latter; that I was accountable to the governmt: only of the U States; that I had rendered to it a
statement of my whole conduct, & the government may make what
use it pleased of my communications; but that I should take no other
measures, & wanted not any notice, as it was called, taken of me, on
that or any occasion. indeed the rediculous folly of the epicurean
clubs & their toasts, reflected in my mind dishonor on the persons,
who to attain such an Eclat would submit to be managed & played off
as political puppets: & to sell their birth rights, for a mess of potage.
that I was "secretly condemned to oblivion," by that party, that they
wished to have had me "guilotined, sent to Cayenne," or the temple,
to be sunk in the sea, or been sacrificed by a mob that they stood
ready to write me down, as they expressed it, to attack me by all the
vile & vulgar means of ribaldry, caricatures, & effigies, I had no
doubt; & on my arrival had certain information that the mine was
charged & train layed: yet the apprehension of this, disagreable as it
must be to anyone, did not deter me from discharging my duty to the
public. but when the friends of the revolution & independence of this
country appeared by their silence to be overawed on this occasion,
how could they expect, that I would "come forward," take, as you are

pleased to term it "the high ground of my own character, disregard calumny," & depending on the meer presumption of being "borne above it, on the shoulders of my grateful countrymen," take a step, which in regard to it's effect, was at least problematical, &, if unsuccessful would have been condemned probably by the republicans as rash & impolitic, & most assuredly by the war party, as vindictive & inflammatory. this party, long before my mission to France, gave unequivocal proof, that they wished to place & keep me in the back ground: that "I was never to be honored or trusted by them & that they waited to crush me forever, only, till they could do it without danger to themselves"; but this gave me no concern, I was above their favors, not being in quest of public office, or disposed to receive it at their hands, & above their frowns, veiwing with indifference their impotent malice, whilst the country was free from the system of thraldom they were plotting against it. to prevent this, I shall be ever ready to encounter any danger.

I recollect to have seen the expression you allude to of a member of Congress, unknown to me, that "to have acted such a part, I must have been a fool or madman." if his conduct on that occasion did not, in the public opinion, prove him to be both, it must have been for this reason only, that he was below publick consideration & contempt.

I have been prolix, & could not avoid it, because you desired me to be explicit. my mind revolted at the idea of burning your 2d & 3d leaves, but rather than have exposed my friend, I would, after answering your letter, have promptly complied with your wish.—the danger being now past, I shall defer it, untill I have the pleasure of again hearing from you.

I will now, my dear Sir, bid you adieu for the present, with an assurance of the highest respect & sincerest attachment, & that I remain Your affectionate friend   E GERRY

RC (DLC); at foot of text: "His Excellency Mr Jefferson"; endorsed by TJ as received 5 Feb. and so recorded in SJL.

YOUR POLITICAL FAITH: TJ to Gerry, 26 Jan. 1799.

FROM RISING TO THE HIGHEST PITCH OF NATIONAL GLORY: *Desultory Reflections on the New Political Aspects of Public Affairs in the United States of America, Since the Commencement of the Year 1799* (Evans, No. 37417), which appeared in New York at the end of June 1800 and was attributed to John Ward

Fenno, despaired over Adams's decision to reopen negotiations with France. The pamphlet lamented that the "principles, under which the nation soared towards the temple of glory, with an eagle's flight," had been "totally abandoned, exploded, and reversed" by the president's policies (p. 6).

In the spring of 1798 Talleyrand made the DECLARATION to Gerry that his return to the United States would cause an IMMEDIATE RUPTURE between the two countries (ASP, *Foreign Relations*, 2:205, 214). For Talleyrand's message to the

American envoys on the 18TH OF MARCH 1798 and Timothy Pickering's communication of the 23d of that month, see same, 188-91, 200-201.

"BEAMED" AS YOU WELL EXPRESS IT: in this paragraph Gerry quoted and paraphrased passages of TJ's letter to him of 26 Jan. 1799.

The member of the Fifth Congress who depicted Gerry as a FOOL OR MADMAN was John Allen of Connecticut. In the House of Representatives on 21 Jan. 1799 Allen argued that Congress should print Pickering's report on Gerry's correspondence because Gerry's communications contained "gross and stupid errors" that

"one would think no man in his senses could commit." As characterized by Joseph B. Varnum speaking in opposition, Allen said of Gerry "that the man who could write this, must either have been insane, or known he was writing a falsehood" (*Annals*, 9:2730, 2734).

BURNING YOUR 2D & 3D LEAVES: at the conclusion of his letter of 26 Jan. 1799 TJ urged Gerry to destroy at least a portion of that epistle (Vol. 30:650, 651n).

¹ Preceding eight words interlined.
² Word interlined.
³ Gerry here canceled "of their party."

From William Hylton, Sr.

DEAR SIR   Mr. J. Peters Geo Town 20th Jany 1801

Since I came to Town on Thursday last and had the honor to call on you, I have been laid up with a violent and *new* attack of Gout; which has denied me the pleasure of repeating my visit.

I am endeavoring to make arrangements to go to Europe in the Spring to dispose of my Jamaica property. Should you have any commands I will be happy to take charge of them.

My second son, John, has for a long time past, desired to get into the American Army, and has got some friends to make application for an appointment. his Talents and choise are directed to the artillery.

If Sir there be no impropriety in the request; and you can without difficulty, do me the singular favor to further his views you will greatly oblige Dear Sir

Your very obt. hu Sevt.   WM HYLTON

RC (DLC); at foot of text: "Honble. Thomas Jefferson Esqr."; endorsed by TJ as received 20 Jan. and so recorded in SJL.

John Adams nominated JOHN Hylton of Maryland to be a second lieutenant in the third regiment of infantry on 4 Feb.

1801 and the Senate confirmed him on 16 Feb. 1801 (JEP, 1:379, 380; Heitman, *Dictionary*, 1:561; William Hylton, Sr. to TJ, 27 Mch. 1801). William Hylton, Sr., stopped at Monticello in the summer of 1796 on his way to the springs and gave TJ a report on the use of the threshing machine (Vol. 29:170).

From John Barnes

Sir George Town 21 Jany: 1801

As I ought not, any longer, defer, writing to Mr Short, in Answer, to his last favr: 1st: Octr: I have subjoined a statemt. of his a/c copy of which I submit to you, for your perusal and Amendment (if necessary.)—Should it meet your Approbation, you will please retain it—I have the Original before me.—to correct, if needfull—I shall then prepare two setts to forward Mr Short.—first, ℔ the English packet, via Hamburg—as He directs, & Copy, by some Other Conveyance—

I am Sir your very huml servt: JOHN BARNES

PS my young Man—is gone to Baltimore—or I should have waited on you personally—

RC (ViU: Edgehill-Randolph Papers); at foot of text: Thomas Jefferson Esqr:"; endorsed by TJ as received 22 Jan. and so recorded in SJL. Enclosure: John Barnes to William Short, 21 Jan. 1801, incorporating in the letter a statement of account between them from 1 Apr. 1800 through 15 Jan. 1801; with modification in TJ's hand of the entry for the $535.83 credit on 15 Jan., changing "By Thomas Jefferson Esqr. for so much recd. from Messrs. Gibson & Jefferson at Richmd. on yr. a/c" to "By Messrs. Gibson & Jefferson for so much recd. from Jas. river canal co. for interest & principal of loan to them" (Dupl in DLC: Short Papers; in Barnes's hand, with emendation by TJ; at head of text: "Copy"; endorsed by TJ); see Barnes to TJ, 24 Jan.

From Thomas Mendenhall

Sir Wednesday Morning Jany 21st 1801

after I had the pleasure of seeing you last evening I reproached Myself severely, for having omited to offer my servises in case you had any Commands to Wilmington or Philadelphia; more especialy, when it occured to me, that you had enquired "whether I was going on to the City," I was Astonished at my own Stupidity and remisness, & determined, that in some Measure to Atone for this dereliction of politeness, that I would stay till Tomorrow Morning and inform You thereof as early as posible, Assuring You sir at the same time, that if you have any Commands for Wilmington, Philadelphia, or elsewhere, I will with pleasure wait on You this evening to receive them and deliver them with my own hand—

& beleve me Sir, Sincerely & respectfully your real friend & obedient Servant THOMAS MENDENHALL

RC (DLC); at foot of text: "The Hon: Thomas Jefferson"; endorsed by TJ as received 21 Jan. and so recorded in SJL.

Thomas Mendenhall (1759-1843) was a Delaware merchant who engaged in the West Indian shipping trade with the schooner *Pratt*. A major landholder in Wilmington, by the beginning of the nineteenth century Mendenhall owned several houses, two storehouses, and a half-dozen undeveloped parcels of city land. Mendenhall also owned a wharf in Wilmington from which he dispatched his packets with flour cargo to Philadelphia. He was active in the Delaware abolitionist movement, the establishment of the Philosophical Society of Delaware, and the founding of the National Bank of Delaware. Mendenhall wrote *An Entire New Plan for a National Currency, Suited to the Demands of this Great, Improving, Agricultural, Manufacturing, & Commercial Republic*, which was published in Philadelphia in 1834 (Wilmington *Mirror of the Times, & General Advertiser*, 12 Mch., 1 Oct. 1800; Bernard L. Herman, "Multiple Materials, Multiple Meanings: The Fortunes of Thomas Mendenhall," *Winterthur Portfolio*, 19 [1984], 83-5; J. Thomas Scharf, *History of Delaware, 1609-1888*, 2 vols. [Philadelphia, 1888], 2:732, 749-50; Munroe, *Federalist Delaware*, 132n, 217n; Elizabeth Montgomery, *Reminiscences of Wilmington, in Familiar Village Tales, Ancient and New* [Philadelphia, 1851], 177, 218).

From Simon Chaudron

MONSIEUR   Philadie 22 Janvr 1801—

Je remets a Monsieur Richard qui part par le même Courrier que la presente, Votre montre renfermée dans une boîte a Votre adresse—

Je prends la liberté de me reserver l'avantage de La reparer dans le Cas ou elle en auroit besoin

Son prix avec les fraix monte a Cent soixante quinze dollars que Vous voudrez bien ne me faire Compter qu'aprés l'essai de la dte. montre

Je suis avec le plus profond respect

Monsieur Votre trés humble & trés obeissant serviteur

CHAUDRON

EDITORS' TRANSLATION

SIR   Philadelphia 22 Jan. 1801

I am turning over to Mr. Richard, who is leaving by the same post as this letter, your watch enclosed in a box addressed to you.

I take the liberty of reserving to myself the advantage of repairing it, in case it should need it.

Its cost, with expenses, comes to one hundred seventy-five dollars, which you will kindly not pay me without trying out the said watch.

I am with the deepest respect

Sir Your very humble & very obedient servant   CHAUDRON

RC (MHi); endorsed by TJ as received 26 Jan. and so recorded in SJL.

To Joseph Habersham

SIR   Washington Jan. 23. 1801.

I am sorry to add to the numberless application's which a system as extensive & ramified as that of our posts must occasion you. but I am in hopes the interference, I shall ask, will be inconsiderable, to [re]store [order] in the line, in which I am particularly interested, that which goes from here to Orange, Milton, Charlottesville, & Warren. letters put into the mail here by 5. aclock P.M. on Friday, should arrive at Milton the Thu[rsday] morning following. but for two months past (& how much longer I kn[ow not]) they have not arrived there till the 2d. Thursday, losing a week somew[here.] in returning from Milton &c. here, no time is lost. I suspect Fred[ericksburg] to be the place (not on the grounds which some do, that the P.M. or under [. . .] [being] a printer finds an interest in detaining the Northern mail) but [. . .] the rider's not waiting the stated hour. but this is mere conjecture: [and I] am in hopes you will be able to set it to rights. it is not [. . .] trials & proofs of the fact between this & Milton, and good information of the same thing from Orange, that I have ventured to trouble you on [the] subject. I am with great esteem Dear Sir

Your most obedt. servt   TH: JEFFERSON

PrC (DLC); faint; at foot of text: "Colo. Habersham"; endorsed by TJ in ink on verso.

Joseph Habersham (1751-1815), a merchant from Savannah, Georgia, served as postmaster general from 25 Feb. 1795 to 31 Oct. 1801. He resigned under pressure, disagreeing with the president over appointment policies. Habersham re-

turned to Savannah and served as head of the local branch of the Bank of the United States from 1802 to 1815 (ANB; *Biog. Dir. Cong.*; TJ to Gideon Granger, 31 Oct. 1801).

P.M.: Timothy Green served as the postmaster at Fredericksburg in 1801. He also printed the *Virginia Herald* (see Vol. 30:11).

From George Jefferson

DEAR SIR   Richmond 23d. Janr. 1801

Your favor of the 16th. came duly to hand. Mr. Barnes had, previous to its receipt, remitted us the $:384.43 you mention; and which came before it was wanted.

I received, a few days ago (only) two small casks of wine shipped by Messrs. S. Smith & Buchanan[1] of Balto. for you so long ago as the 18th. ultimo—they are forwarded to Milton.

I have at length seen Brown—he promises very shortly to have Mr. Shorts a/c adjusted; he has but lately left his room & is still far from being well. I think there will not be much more delay in this business, as he did not appear at all to relish the heat of a suit; and begged of me to assure you that it was not with the view of keeping the money in his hands that the delay was occasioned.

Not having heard from Moseby I have put his note into the hands of an Atty—Mr. Creed Taylor, who appears to be positive he will not be compelled to institute a suit.

Yr. Very humble servt.   GEO. JEFFERSON

RC (MHi); at foot of text: "Thos. Jefferson esqr."; endorsed by TJ as received 28 Jan. and so recorded in SJL.

Samuel Smith forward to TJ, see Smith to TJ, 8 Oct., and TJ's response of 17 Oct. 1800.

For the TWO SMALL CASKS OF WINE which Joseph Yznardi, Sr., requested that

[1] MS: "Buchananan."

To Thomas Mann Randolph

TH:J. TO TMR.   Washington Jan. 23. 1801.

Your's of the 17th. reached this on the 21st. from Saturday to Wednesday. this will leave this place tomorrow (Saturday the 24th.) and ought to be with you on Thursday the 29th. but it seems that a week is lost somewhere. I suspect the Fredsbg rider leaves that place an hour or two before the Northern post reaches it. on this subject I will this day write to the Postmaster genl. I am sincerely concerned for the misfortune to poor Holmes. I have not yet seen his father on the subject, who is a clerk in the register's office here. Lewis must continue under mr Dinsmore, in order to expedite that work. I will very willingly undertake to pay Gibson & Jefferson for you £135. but I must take from 40. to 70. days for it, having nothing at my disposal sooner. I am not sure of being able to do it at the 1st. term (March 1.) but possibly may. at the 2d. (Apr. 1.) they will have the money in their own hands for my tobo. sold & payable then. but do not consider this as engaging your hands. if you can employ them more advantageously for yourself than by hiring, do it. if not, we will take any which you had rather[1] hire than employ at what we are to pay for others. my former letter will have conveyed to you my wish that the nailers able to cut should be so employed: and I have written to mr Eppes that I am indifferent whether Powell comes till the 1st. of April. I shall then be at home, and shall engage Whateley to undertake to build the new shop, out & out, on his own terms immediately. I forgot to ask the favor of you to speak to Lilly as to the treatment of the nailers. it would destroy their value in my estimation to degrade them in their own eyes by the whip. this therefore must not be resorted to but in extremities. as they will be again under my government, I would chuse they should retain the stimulus of character. after Lilly shall have compleated the clearing necessary for this year for mr Craven, I would have him go on with what will be wanting for him the next year, that being my most important object. the building of the negro houses should be done whenever mr Craven prefers it; as all the work is for him, he may arrange it. I will thank you to continue noting the day of the reciept of my letters, that I may know whether the postmaster corrects the mismanagement.—we continue as uncertain as ever as to the event of an election by the H. of R. some appearances are favorable. but they may be meant to throw us off our guard. mr Adams is entirely for their complying with the will of the people. Hamilton the same. the mercantile or paper interest also. still, the individuals who are to decide, will decide according to their own desires. the Jersey election damps them. so does the European intelligence. but their main body is still firm & compact.—my tenderest love to my dear Martha. I wrote to her the last week. kisses to all the little ones, and affectionate attachments to yourself. Adieu.

P.S. when I come home I shall lay off the canal, if Lilly's gang can undertake it. I had directed Lilly to make a dividing fence between Craven's fields at Monticello, & those I retain. the object was to give me the benefit of the latter for pasture. if I stay here, the yard will be pasture enough, and may spare, or at least delay this great & perishable work of the dividing fence. at least it may lie for further consideration.—I hope Lilly keeps the small nailers engaged so as to supply our customers in the neighborhood, so that we may not lose them during this interregnum. mr Higginbotham particularly & mr Kelly should be attended to.

RC (DLC); endorsed by Randolph as received on the 29th. PrC (MHi); endorsed by TJ in ink on verso.

Randolph's letter OF THE 17TH, recorded in SJL as received 22 Jan., has not been found.

MY FORMER LETTER: TJ to Randolph, 9 Jan. 1801. TJ wrote John Wayles EPPES on 19 Jan. WHATELEY: that is, Thomas Whitlaw (see TJ to Whitlaw, 19 Feb. and Whitlaw to TJ, 28 Feb. 1801). A letter from John H. CRAVEN to TJ of 15 Jan., recorded in SJL as received seven days later, and TJ's response of 23 Jan. have not been found. According to SJL, TJ wrote letters to John Craven on 8 Nov. 1799, 15 Jan. 1800, and 9 Jan. 1801, which were undoubtedly meant for John H. Craven. All are missing.

[1] TJ here canceled "spare."

From John Barnes

Sir   George Town. 24th Jany: 1801

Inclosed I return you Copy of my a/c & letter to Mr Short, the Original, & duplicate of which, shall be, as you have Corrected.—I have also sent ℔ Mr Dunn—2 pair Black silk Stockings—the largest & Best, of the Merchandize—Mr Pickford—my Assistant brought me from Baltimore—Mr. Latimore had a pair of them, Yesterday, in lieu of a former pair (smaller—p 34ƒ)—these are Only 28ƒ a pair— and I think dear enough at that; but we have no Choice—of them at present—the first fair day, I purpose paying my Respects to you

I am—with great Esteem Sir—Your most Obedt Servt:

JOHN BARNES

if not large enough or too Coarse please leave for me,

RC (ViU: Edgehill-Randolph Papers); at foot of text: "The Honble: Thomas Jefferson Esqr—"; endorsed by TJ as received 24 Jan. and so recorded in SJL. Enclosure: see Barnes to TJ, 21 Jan.

A letter of this day from TJ to Barnes is recorded in SJL but has not been found.

From Isaac Briggs

RESPECTED FRIEND,   Sharon, 24th. of the 1st. Month 1801.

As a member of the American Philosophical Society I take the liberty of addressing its President. Although I feel much diffidence when, from an obscure and private station, I look up to that eminence upon which abilities and honors have placed thee; yet when I consider thee as the known friend and patron of useful Arts and Science, I am encouraged to solicit thy attention to some hints on a plan for the improvement of Agriculture in the United States.

It is my opinion that the real prosperity of our common Country is virtually founded upon Agriculture, and I feel a strong persuasion that any subject of such a nature and tendency will not, by thee, be treated with indifference. For a considerable time, I have believed that were details of the practice of individuals collected from different parts, or districts, of the United States; thrown into a general digest; and this again diffused to the extremities; it would, probably, more than any other means, tend to the improvement of Agriculture: This noble Art would derive almost as great advantages from such a circulation of knowledge, as the Animal System does from the circulation of the blood.

Such a method would, I conceive, have a powerful tendency to excite a spirit of laudable emulation—to dissipate inveterate prejudice—to give a spur to *industry*—to increase domestic economy—and consequently to promote sound *morality*. Perhaps th[ere] would be scarcely an individual who would not see himself surpassed by others in some point, wherein his interest might obviously consist in adopting the improvement:—"Il faut gagner les cœurs, et faire trouver aux hommes leur avantage dans les choses, où l'on veut se servir de leur industrie."

My idea is, to form, in each State, a society of the best Farmers, Planters and Graziers; to such an association let each member report his practice and the state of his farm, or plantations; let these State-societies communicate with each other by means of a Convention, of delegates from each, to meet annually at the City of Washington. The State-societies might report to the Convention the information collected from individuals; and the Convention might form these reports into a general digest, for publication. Occasional recommendations and advice from the Convention to the state-societies might also be very useful.

Having now offered but a crude sketch—an imperfect outline—of my favorite plan, I hope that the eminent abilities of the personage I am addressing will deign to give it the finishing hand—make it such as will be most agreeable to himself, and beneficial to his country—and support it with his influence.

Permit me to add, in the words of the great Linnæus, by way of excuse for my ambition in casting in my mite;—"Multum adhuc restat operis, multumque restabit, nec *ulli* nato post mille secula precludetur occasio aliquid adjiciendi."

I am, with profound respect For thy Virtues and For thy Talents, Thy fellow-citizen,   ISAAC BRIGGS

RC (DLC); torn; addressed: "Thomas Jefferson City of Washington"; endorsed by TJ as received 1 Feb. and so recorded in SJL.

Isaac Briggs (1763-1825) grew up in a Quaker household in Haverford, Pennsylvania, where he worked in the shop of his father, Samuel Briggs, who invented and later patented a machine for making nails. In 1783 Isaac Briggs received an undergraduate degree and a master's degree three years later from the University of Pennsylvania. He edited and published *Isaac Briggs's Almanac; for the Year of our Lord,—1799* (Baltimore, 1798; see Evans, No. 33454) and made astronomical calculations for many other almanacs. In 1803 TJ appointed Briggs surveyor of the lands south of Tennessee. At the time TJ praised Briggs, noting that "in astronomy, geometry & mathematics he stands in a line with mr Ellicott, & second to no man in the US." In 1804 the president asked Briggs to lay out a post road from Washington, D.C. to New Orleans. For that work TJ personally paid Briggs $400 because Congress refused to reimburse the surveyor for his expenses, arguing that it had not authorized the survey. Finally in 1818 Briggs received some compensation from Congress. Briggs worked as chief engineer on the section of the Erie Canal from Rome to Utica, New York, which was finished in 1819, and he completed the James River and Kanawha Canal in 1823. He also supported domestic manufactures, sending a statement on agriculture, manufactures, and commerce to Congress in 1816. The next year his address before the Oneida Society for the Promotion of American Manufactures was published (Ella Kent Barnard, "Isaac Briggs, A.M., F.A.P.S.," *Maryland Historical Magazine*, 7 [1912], 409-19; Isaac Briggs, *An Address Delivered before the Oneida Society for the Promotion of American Manufactures in Their Annual Meeting in Whitesboro on the 21st of October, 1817* [Utica, N.Y., 1817]; MB, 2:1130, 1205-6; TJ to William C. C. Claiborne, 24 May 1803). For a critical assessment of Briggs's work as land office surveyor for the district south of Tennessee, see Malcolm J. Rohrbough, *The Land Office Business: The Settlement and Administration of American Public Lands, 1789-1837* (New York, 1968), 35-7, 253-4.

Briggs was elected a MEMBER of the American Philosophical Society in 1796 (APS, *Proceedings*, 22, pt. 3 [1884], 236). PLAN FOR THE IMPROVEMENT OF AGRICULTURE: the American Board of Agriculture, designed to gather and disseminate information, was established early in 1803. In February, James Madison was elected president and Briggs secretary of the board (Madison, *Papers, Sec. of State Ser.*, 4:343, 462-3; TJ to John Sinclair, 30 June 1803).

IL FAUT GAGNER LES CŒURS . . . INDUSTRIE: "It is necessary to gain hearts, and to find in men their advantage in things, through which one seeks to avail oneself of their industry," a quotation from François de Salignac de La Mothe-Fénelon's *Les aventures de Télémaque*, book 3. For TJ's inquiry about a two-volume English translation of this work, see Vol. 30:83n.

MULTUM ADHUC RESTAT OPERIS . . . ADJICIENDI: that is, "Much still remains to do, and much will always remain, and he who shall be born a thousand ages hence will not be barred from his opportunity of adding something further," a quotation from Seneca, *Ad Lucilium Epistulae Morales*, trans. Richard M. Gummere, 3 vols. (New York, 1917), 1:440-1.

From Joseph Habersham

SIR/   Washington 24th. Jany 1801

The delay of a week in receiving the Northern Mails at the Post. Offices on the route from Fredericksburg to Charlottesville was occasioned by making them up at this office, which is the distributing office for the State of Virginia, on *Saturday* instead of Friday—the Mails for those offices are now made up on *Friday* and I am in hopes will be received in future without any delay

I have reason to think that the Post Master of Fredericksburg has in no instance detained the Mails from interested Motives.

As soon as the obstacle to the regular conveyance of the Mails for that route was known it was removed, and I have only to regret that it existed so long   I have the Honor to be with great respect.

Sir Yr mo. obedt. svt   JOS HABERSHAM

RC (DLC); at foot of text: "The Honble Thomas Jefferson esqr Vice President of the United States"; endorsed by TJ as received 25 Jan. and so recorded in SJL. FC (Lb in DNA: RG 28, LPG).

Virginia congressman John Dawson had already informed the postmaster general of the OBSTACLE with the Virginia mail. On 22 Jan., Habersham wrote him that the mails for Fredericksburg would leave Washington on Friday to make the connection with the Charlottesville rider (FC in Lb in DNA: RG 28, LPG).

To John Hoomes

DEAR SIR   Washington Jan. 24. 1801.

Your favor of the 16th. has been duly recieved. I am not in immediate want of the horse; and if your stay at Richmond should be longer than expected, or my want of him should become urging, I could send some person from this place for him. it is more likely that your return may be quite early enough for my want, and your then sending him on at my expence will be sufficient.

There is no change in our prospects as to the election, the party opposed to the public sentiment, keeping their purposes very much to themselves. a vote passed the H. of R. yesterday for the continuance of the Sedition law. it was by the casting voice of the Speaker, and not in it's final stage.   The Senate had annexed several modifications to the Convention with France. yesterday came on the final question, which being divided into as many parts as there were modifications, the whole of them were struck out except one limiting it's duration to 8. years. and on the question to ratify with this single modification it was rejected by 14. out of 30. votes. tho, according to former usage, this would close the proceedings, I am told there will be a proposition to ratify it without any modification, as being a question which has not yet been decided. it's success may be doubted. some say the President will not on this rejection send back the treaty, but will call the new Senate to meet after the 3d. of March and reconsider it. of those who voted against it, 4. will then go out, & would leave them only 10. but we must have a Senate of 30. at least convened to overweigh them, which we can hardly count upon.

Accept assurances of my high esteem & respect.

TH: JEFFERSON

PrC (DLC); at foot of text: "Colo. John Hoomes."

For Hoome's FAVOR OF THE 16TH., see Hoomes to TJ, 5 Jan. 1801.

To Patricot

SIR   Washington Jan. 24. 1801.

The letter which I wrote you on the 20th. of Dec. I inclosed to
Colo. Newton at Norfolk merely to know if you were there. he returned it to me with information that you were in New-York. I then
directed it to New York, and being in consequence assured of your
address by your's of the 16th. inst. I have now the pleasure to forward
you a letter and an open paper which I recieved from mr Short, and
pray you to accept my friendly salutations.   TH: JEFFERSON

PrC (MHi); at foot of text: "M. Patricot"; endorsed by TJ in ink on verso. Enclosures: see Enclosure No. 2 listed at
William Short to TJ, 18 Sep. 1800.

A letter from Patricot to TJ of 1 Feb.
1801, received from New York on the 5th
of that month, is recorded in SJL but has
not been found.

From Charles Pinckney

DEAR SIR   January 24: 1801 In Charleston

Although not sufficiently recovered from the effects of my late fall
from my carriage to venture it I propose embarking on Sunday to join
you at Washington having taken my passage for that purpose & as I
cannot travel by land, again venture a Winter Voyage by sea—I write
this Line to inform you of it & to mention that having seen in the
Northern papers an account that a compromise was offered & rejected by the Federalists I do positively deny that any such compromise was offered by the body of the republican interest or ever
intended by them.—if any thing ever was said on that subject it must
have been by some one or two of our friends who might have been
very anxious to secure Your Election & would rather compromise
than risque it, but if even one did whisper such a thing it was wholly
unknown to me, or to the great Body of the republican interest—for
they were determined from the Jump never to hear of any compromise—& so far from thinking of it they met at the academy hall in Columbia the very first night of the Session & near seventy of them
signed a Paper & determined not to compromise but to support the
ticket of the republican interest as it was run & carried. Ten members
from the Lower Country were absent—out of these Ten three federalists three of the republican interest & four Ties or Equalities common to both—the average Majority to be relied upon on the joint
Vote was 19 & I mention this to You to shew that there is never the
least Danger of the South Carolina Legislature.—

The last Election was the most federal I ever knew in our state owing to Charleston & obvious reasons—the Wind having changed, certain influences will change also & under *a proper* Management I do not doubt Charleston may be made one of *the Strongholds of* republicanism as it possesses most excellent Materials——Health, affectionate respect & Esteem conclude me Dear Sir Your's Truly

CHARLES PINCKNEY

RC (DLC); endorsed by TJ as received 8 Feb. and so recorded in SJL.

For Pinckney's earlier denial that the

Republicans offered to COMPROMISE and place native son Charles C. Pinckney on the Republican ticket, see his letter to TJ of 6 Dec. 1800.

From Anonymous

SIR,   District of Columbia 25th Jany 1801

I have Opposed your Election with all the little power & Influence I had, believeing as I did, and still do, that your Election to the chief Magistracy of the US. wou'd not promote the Interest and happiness of this Country, but that the Riverse wou'd happen, not from any personal Enmity to you Sir, for I can have none, as I have not the Honor of your Acquaintance, but for the following Reasons Vizt, Your modern Philosophy and Deistical principals,—Your Letter to Maza, in my Oppinion Disapproving of the Govermint of the US. and your desire to Assimilate it to the French Goverment, if it can be called a Goverment—

I have heard that you shou'd say as to Testamentary Affairs, that the Children shou'd Inherit from their parents in Opposition to thier Will, making the Child Independant of the Father, as in France the Child prefered the Ruleing power to his Parint, & Carried the heads of thier parents on poles through the Streets,—I have also heard that it is your Oppinion that no Law of the US. ought to be binding for Longer than one year and that Congress (not only have the power) but the Right to Repeal Laws at any time, let them be of ever so sacred a Nature, this certainly wou'd distroy all kind of Confidence between the people and the Goverment,—I have also heard Lately that you are Opposed to the Navy & Commerse, your Notes when you wrote them Contradict this Report—

I have also heard that you will carry on the Govermint, in a most parsimonious manner, that you will Recall all our Embasidors and send Consuls which in the Oppinion of many will Render us Contimptible a Broad and not Respected at home, that you will turn out a great many Officers of Govermint & not Appoint others. that you may have the Character of Œconomising, which may be popular with a great many, but in the end it will be saveing a penny, and Sacrificing Millions, in such a govermint as ours, it is not a Drop in the Bucket; I beleive it to be necessary in our Goverment, to have as many Officers at least as we now have, and Good Policy as well as Justice, wou'd Dictate, that they ought to be *Americans*, and as Equally Dispersed through the US. as the nature of the case will admit, those Officers, if they are Respectable, and I presume they ought to be so, will have Influence. Interest is the Governing passion, and every one who wishes to Support our Excellent Goverment must admit, that we cannot love it too well, or do too much to preserve it,—I am a plain planter and farmer, I never held (or any of my Connections) any Office of profit or Trust, under the Goverment of the US. I never Expect or wish any, so that I can have no Interest more than the publick Good,—I am a Federalist, not what is called a high Toned one I Assure you, and if it is understood to mean Aristocracy, I disclaim it, for in my Oppinion there is no Difference between a great Big Aristocrat, and a great Big Democrat; they are the same thing, fond of power, Haughty, proud, Imperious, Insolent, and Overbearing.—

As Mr. Jefferson I Respect your character, you are certainly a Great man, and I am told by those who know you, that you are a kind neighbour, a Good master, a Charitable, Generous, Hospitable Man;

But Sir I Confess Candidly and Honestly, that, I am afraid of your Religion & your Politicks,—

As there is every probability of your being Elected President of the US, I hope for the sake of America for your sake, and all our sakes, all those things are not True, Dreadfull Indeed will be our Situation if they are, Numbers of the people are alarmed, and some of your Friends think as I do. wou'd it not be better, to Explain your self Candidly on those Subjects.—I was not long since talking with a Gentleman of a Good Deale of understanding, & Influence, and I was Objecting to you on Acct. of your Religion. why said he I am a Deist, (a Sentiment tho Long asquainted with him I never heard before), so that I am a fraid it will become fashionable,—I am not over Religious my self, but what will be the Consequence suppose Religion is done away, and nothing but the Laws to Govern us, Oaths will be nothing, and no one will be safe in his person or property. I have allways understood that there never was an Instance, that where the people Lost their Religion, but what they lost their Liberties,—It appears to me that there is two parties in Congress, and let any thing be proposed by either partie, be it ever so Right and proper, the other partie will Oppose it Right or Rong, Is there no way to do away this kind of Conduct, and to Reconsile,—A House Divided against it self can never Stand,—The Democrats are certainly more Blamable than the Federalists, they will propose nothing, and have proposed nothing for these 3 or four years past, Except in three or four Instances, and if it was necessary for Congress to meet, it was surely necessary for thim to do something. any man or set of men can find fault. but surely that is not Sufficient, they ought to propose something better.—

I am told that the Jurisdiction of the District of Columbia, is now under Consideration, wou'd it not be wise and proper to Assume it at this time, it certainly wou'd be better for all those who live in the District and it wou'd be better for Congress, it wou'd give the City Consequence, and numbers of people wou'd (that otherwise wou'd not) come build Houses and Reside amongst us, so that Congress wou'd be much better Accomodated, the Roads from Alexandria to the City both on the Virginia & Maryland side are Dreadfull, and they might be made Excellent, & that on the Maryland Side two miles nearer than it now is, the Streets in the City are also very bad, if Congress was to Assume the Jurisdiction those things might & I have no Doubt wou'd be Remedied.—

I am a Federalist as I Observed before, and let who will be Elected President of the US, whether a Democrat, Aristocrat, or any other Crat, I Hold it my Duty as well as my Inclination, as I ever have done to Support the first Magistrate of the US, with all my might, and all my power, for the Term of his Election—I hope Sir if you shou'd be Elected you will not meet with the Fate of Mr. Adams, Traduced, Insulted and Abused, from one end of the US to the other, (Indeed Genl. Washington did not Escape it himself) and for what, for being an Honest Man and for doing, what I believe in my Conscience, he thought, wou'd best promote, the Interest & Happiness of this Country, and Reconsile the Different parties, who took the Lead in this Abuse, Foreigners, who followed thim, let it be blotted out forever, Sir, these are a Restless set of beings nothing but Anarchy & Confusion will suit thim, and if there was an Angel to come from Heaven, he wou'd not Satisfy thim, those are your fast Friends now. how long they will Continue so time only will Determine, and if I was to Judge of the future by the past, I shou'd pridict that will not be long, as I think it Impossible you can ever come up to their Ideas of Goverment—This Letter is not wrote with a View to Insult or Affront you, be Assured Sir. but for the purpose of Informing [you], what the Oppinion of the world is of you, [tha]t if you choose you may have an Oppty of Disavowing of it,—I am a poor politician haveing neither ability or Information, to form a proper Oppinion of Goverment, and the Number of things practised under it, but I know this, that no man Loves this Goverment, more than I do, or will do more to preserve it, and I can with Truth Lay my hand on my Heart, and Declare with the Poet,—That I have no wish above,

My Countrys wellfare & my Countrys Love,

I wou'd have put my name to this letter, but as it cannot be of any Consequence to you, and the end proposed by my self will be Answered, I have Declined it—I am very Respectfully

Sir Yr. Obd Svt   AB.

RC (DLC); torn; addressed: "The Honble Thomas Jefferson Esqr. Presidint of the Senate of the United States"; franked and postmarked; endorsed by TJ as received 5 Feb. and so recorded in SJL.

YOUR NOTES: in *Notes on the State of Virginia*, TJ commented: "A small naval force then is sufficient for us, and a small one is necessary. What this should be, I will not undertake to say. I will only say, it should by no means be so great as we are able to make it" (*Notes*, ed. Peden, 176).

DECLARE WITH THE POET: see Charles Churchill's "The Conference," lines 239-40 (Douglas Grant, ed., *The Poetical Works of Charles Churchill* [London, 1956], 239).

To John Redman Coxe

SIR   Washington Jan. 25. 1801.

I have recieved your favor of the 17th. inst. informing me that the American Philosophical Society had been pleased again to appoint me to the Presidency of that institution, and by an unanimous vote. for this mark of the confidence of the society, as dear to me as it is honorable, I pray you to convey to them my humble acknolegements, and a renewal of the assurances of my devotion to their service. I had believed the interests of the society would have been better consulted by the appointment of a President more at hand to perform the duties of his station, and had taken the liberty to express that opinion in a letter to one of the respectable Vice presidents. they have decided on a different course, and have imposed on me a higher obligation, by an attention to such services as may be rendered in absence, to make up for those which that absence prevents.

I pray you, Sir, to accept my thanks for the politeness of your communication, and assurances of my high consideration & respect.

TH: JEFFERSON

RC (PPAmP); addressed: "Doctr. John Redman Coxe Philadelphia. 80 North Front street"; franked; postmarked 27 Jan.; endorsed for the American Philosophical Society. PrC (DLC).

The physician John Redman Coxe

(1773-1864) was born in Trenton, New Jersey. His father, a staunch Loyalist during the American Revolution, was Tench Coxe's first cousin. John Redman Coxe, who completed his general education in London and Edinburgh, was later acknowledged to be a fine scholar of classical languages and culture. He began his medical training in London, then returned to the U.S. to study under Benjamin Rush and receive an M.D. degree from the University of Pennsylvania. He began the practice of medicine in Philadelphia in 1796. He taught chemistry in the medical school of the University of Pennsylvania for several years beginning in 1809 and published several reference works and other medical books, some of which contained only limited original material. Although early in his career he had been an innovative proponent of vaccination, as time went on he was criticized for the backwardness of his medical views. Elected a member of the American Philosophical Society in July 1799, he was made a councillor the following year and in 1801 was one of four secretaries of the society. During his life he amassed a personal library of several thousand volumes with particular emphasis on medicine and theology (ANB; DAB; Cooke, *Coxe*, 10; APS, *Proceedings*, 22, pt. 3 [1884], 283, 290, 307).

The FAVOR of 17 Jan. from Coxe, in his capacity as a secretary of the APS, formally notified TJ of his unanimous reelection as president in the society's balloting on 2 Jan. 1801 (RC in DLC; addressed: "The Honble Ths. Jefferson Vice President of the U. States City of Washington"; endorsed by TJ as received 21 Jan. and so recorded in SJL).

PRAY YOU TO CONVEY TO THEM: TJ's letter above was read at a meeting of the APS on 6 Feb. (APS, *Proceedings*, 22, pt. 3 [1884], 309).

The letter to one of the VICE PRESIDENTS of the APS was TJ to Robert Patterson, 10 Dec. 1800.

From Tench Coxe

January 25th. 1801

My notice of your health on the 31st. Ultimo, Sir, was intended to shew, that I knew what you had written on that day. It was regularly received by the person whom you honored with the communication. None of his letters between the place of his residence and the dated place of that, have ever miscarried, but one, from a southern state in October, upon private business[1] is said to have been destroyed. He believes it now to have been produced by an interested person. It is however certain that great delays, and, it is believed, that actual suppressions of letters have taken place. Innocence therefore requires caution, because its intentions may be known to the criminal; and *prevented*.

It was my intention in my last letter, to have been a little fuller in the statement and to have applied it more particularly and explicitly to the present state of things and to the future course of our public Affairs. But very urgent calls of office duty prevented me, nor are my engagements at this moment such as to admit of further attention to the Subject. Our country has certainly been injured, disordered, *and eminently jeopardized*. To limit the evils, as far even as has been done, has cost great sacrafices of pecuniary advantages, of peace of mind, of domestic connexion, of friendly and social intercourse. To apply future remedies will require great reflexion and judgment, moderation of temper and felicity of manner, but firmness and energy with all. To replace this _____ under a course of rep____ n execution of its government, and to restore to certain diseased quarters a constitutional soundness in politics, will require of more than the principal, much good sense and much good disposition. If the people can be convinced that public good is sought, that even public good will not be pursued but in the manner admitted by the laws, that local interests and favoritism produce no excessive bias, it will be impossible to detach the friends of the administration, or to keep its opponents in a state of alienation.

It has been my aim, since I was first called into public service by my venerable departed friend, the inestimable Franklin, to content myself with those benefits from public station, which the laws admit, and to render to the public in return all the services, which the nature of the station required, or the requests of other members of the government pointed out. It will be very agreeable to me that it should be believed, that I remain in the same state of mind. If it should be thought, that I have suffered deeply from principle—that there has been no honorable service or fearful risk, necessary to maintain public right, which I have refused or avoided on the call of the friends of *good government*, if it should be admitted that I have made, on my own motion, useful and temperate exertions in that half blessed cause, I submit the public prudence and virtue of a proportionate remembrance.

I have the honor to subscribe myself—with perfect respect—Sir, your most obedt & hum Servt.   Tench Coxe

RC (DNA: RG 59, LAR); endorsed by TJ as received 31 Jan. and so recorded in SJL.

MY NOTICE OF YOUR HEALTH: see Coxe to TJ, 10 Jan. 1801.

[1] Remainder of sentence interlined.

From James Monroe

Dear Sir   Richmond 27. Jany. 1801.

The assembly adjourned on friday last in confidence shod. any plan of usurpation be attempted at the federal town, the Executive wod. convene it without delay; a confidence which was not misplac'd. yr. friend & servt   Jas. Monroe

RC (DLC); endorsed by TJ as received 31 Jan. and so recorded in SJL.

From Joseph H. Nicholson

SIR   Tuesday Morning [27 Jan. 1801]

I take the Liberty of enclosing you a Letter which I received last Evening from a man of some Talent for Mechanics, who is desirous of laying before you the Draught of a Machine which he has invented; and which he thinks will be extensively useful in leading to the great *Desideratum*, "Perpetual Motion"—I have felt some Reluctance in making this Application to you, as I confess I have not much Confidence in his Discovery; for although he is the Author of some useful Inventions, and is a man of much personal worth, I have always placed Perpetual Motion in the same Class with the Philosopher's Stone; however as he feels much Solicitude on the Subject and is an acquaintance of my early Life, I could not, consistently with my Desire to serve him, refuse to comply with his Request, which I hope you will consider as a sufficient Apology for this Intrusion—

If therefore it will not tresspass too much on your time, and you will let me know when you will be at Leisure, I will introduce him that he may have an Opportunity of spending half an Hour with you—I have never seen his Machine and know nothing of the Principles on which it is constructed, as he has always been particularly cautious in keeping, what he deems, an invaluable Secret—

I am Sir with due Respect Yr. Ob. Servt.

JOSEPH H. NICHOLSON

RC (DLC); partially dated; endorsed by TJ as written and received on 27 Jan. and so recorded in SJL. Enclosure: Thomas Bruff to Nicholson, 23 Jan. 1801, soliciting Nicholson's aid in obtaining an interview with TJ to present his plan (RC in DLC).

Joseph Hopper Nicholson (1770-1817) was the son of Joseph Nicholson, Jr., and Elizabeth Hopper Nicholson of Maryland. He studied law and served in the Maryland House of Delegates from 1796 to 1798, when he was elected to Congress. He became a close friend of John Randolph of Roanoke, who also began his congressional career in 1799, and Nicholson, along with Randolph and Nathaniel Macon, became a Republican leader in the House of Representatives. Nicholson, a cousin of Albert Gallatin's wife, Hannah, socialized and worked closely with the Treasury secretary. In 1806 Nicholson left Congress to become chief justice of Maryland's sixth judicial district and an associate justice of the Maryland court of appeals, positions he held until his death. He became the first president of the Commercial and Farmers' Bank of Baltimore in 1810. During the War of 1812, Nicholson raised and commanded an artillery company and was present at the battles of Bladensburg and Fort McHenry. He married Rebecca Lloyd in 1793 and is buried on the Lloyd family estate at Wye House (DAB; Noble E. Cunningham, Jr., *The Process of Government under Jefferson* [Princeton, 1978], 190-2, 194, 198-200; Raymond Walters, Jr., *Albert Gallatin: Jeffersonian Financier and Diplomat* [New York, 1957], 119, 148-9, 192).

TJ immediately replied to this letter on 27 Jan. and invited Nicholson and "any person recommended by him" to visit. The vice president noted that he was "at home always when not in Senate," and thus left "the hour to mr Nicholson. perhaps between 10. & 11. may suit mr N. best, as he comes then to Congress, but any other hour or day will be equally agreeable to Th:J" (RC owned by Rosalie S. Magruder, Cambridge, Massachusetts, 1961; not recorded in SJL).

AUTHOR OF SOME USEFUL INVENTIONS: in 1797 Thomas Bruff received a patent for an "improvement in extracting teeth" and the next year Thomas Bruff, Sr., received a patent for an "improvement in grinding coffee." When TJ met with Bruff he advised him to build an operating model of the "machine for perpetual time" as described in his plan if he wished to receive patronage (*List of Patents*, 15-16; MB, 2:1093; Bruff to TJ, 16 Dec. 1801).

From Robert Leslie

SIR   Philadelphia Janry. 28th 1801

As I am confident you must at the time you receive this, have a variety of subjects to engage your attention, of much more consequence than any thing contained in it, I tharefore hope if you are not perfectly disengaged for a few minuts, you will lay it aside.

When you have time to look at it, I beg leave to observe, that the interview I had the honour to have with you, the day after my arival in Philadelphia, was so short, that I had not time to inform you, of a variety of useful arts, with which I had made myself acquainted, while in England, Maney of which, I thought might be of adventage to the United States.

In addition to what relates to my own business I have acquired the best, and most approved, methods of manufacturing, Plate of all kinds: Jewelry, and every useful article of metle, (from a Cannon, down to a sewing needle) and Perticularly Edgetools.

The reason Sir which induces me to trouble you with this information, is from a conviction that no person is a better able to judge of the benefits (if any) which may[1] arise from the introduction of any of the above arts in America.

But as I am convinced that you have not leisure at present, to go into any kind of investigation of those subjects, I shall wave all farther observations on that head,   the main object of this letter, being to request the favour of your opinion, on the most suitable place for the residence of such a person as you may suppose me to be.

You will perhaps recolect, that when I had the honour of seeing you last, I took the liberty of asking your opinion of the City of Washington, to which you very justly observed, that until congress had once met thare, it would be impossible to give an opinion, as it was probable, if thay found on trial, that thay could not be well accommodated thare, they would remove the Seate of government to some other place.

Perhaps the time that Congress have been at that place (tho short) has been sufficent to deside that point, if so, I shall esteem it a particular favour, if you will be so good as to drop me a line on the subject, if it is only three words, to say it will, or will not, be a suitable place for my residence, as I have since my return to America, determined to be governed in that point, intierly by your opinion, in consequence of which, I have not commenced business any whare, but have employ'd my time, in settling the accompts of my late partnership, which I have nearly compleated, and am ready to begin the world a new, in what ever way may seem most adventageous, to the public and myself.

Tho I am well convinced that you at present, have no right to retain that favourable opinion of my abilitys, you ware once pleased to express, as few of the inventions and improvements, I have proposed have been compleated, you must naturally suppose me like maney of my Country men, who have been either too vain, or too sanguine, to refrain from boasting of their inventions, till thay had underwent a proper Course of experiments.

For me at present to detail all the various circumstances which prevented me from compleating the several things I have proposed, would be gratifying myself, at the expence of your time, which I know I have trespassed too much on already, but hope I shall yet regain your good opinion, by exhibiting not only all I have proposed, but more,

I am Sir your most obedient Ser   ROBERT LESLIE

PS Thare are two other branches of business, the machanical operations of which, I made myself acquainted with in England, thay are the Stamp Office, and the Mint, but thay are now perhaps as well performed in America, as is necessary, if not, I could probably give some useful information, to those engaged in the business

RC (DNA: RG 59, LAR); addressed: "Hon Thos Jefferson Vice President of the United States"; franked and postmarked; endorsed by TJ as received 3 Feb. and so recorded in SJL.

Leslie and his family went to London in April 1793 with TJ's recommendation and did not RETURN TO AMERICA, arriving in Philadelphia, until 11 May 1800 (Tom Taylor, *Autobiographical Recollections. By the Late Charles Robert Leslie*, 2 vols. [London, 1860], 1:2-3, 19; Vol. 25:585-7).

A letter of 8 Feb. 1801 from TJ to Leslie is recorded in SJL but has not been found. Also recorded in SJL, but missing, are letters that Leslie wrote to TJ from London on 26 Mch. 1799 (received 20 June 1799) and 5 July 1799 (received 5 Oct. 1799).

[1] MS: "my."

To Littleton W. Tazewell

DEAR SIR   Washington Jan. 28. 1801.

The instalments for my tobacco, sold the last spring, did not come in finally till my arrival here, when a new circumstance appeared to be arising which called indispensably for some preliminary expences, and obliged me to throw the paiment which should have been made to you agreeably to my letter of the last summer, on a fund which does not come in till April. I now inclose you an order on Gibson & Jefferson of Richmond for a thousand dollars paiable the first week of April. this paiment shall soon be followed by that of the 3d. bond so as to close my part of mr Wayles's debt to the house for which you act. I am aware that the article of interest makes the present order not a complete paiment of the two first bonds. accept assurances of the esteem and respect of Dear Sir

Your most obedt. & most humble servt   TH: JEFFERSON

RC (PWacD: Feinstone Collection, on deposit PPAmP); addressed: "Lyttleton W. Tazewell esq. of the Virginia representation in Congress"; endorsed by Tazewell. PrC (MHi); endorsed by TJ in ink on verso. Enclosure: Order on Gibson & Jefferson, dated 28 Jan. 1801, to pay Tazewell $1,000 the first week in April (PrC in MHi; signed by TJ; letterpressed on same sheet as letter above).

MY LETTER OF THE LAST SUMMER: according to SJL, TJ's last letter to Tazewell was of 10 Apr. 1800.

From John Hoomes

DEAR SIR   Bowling Green Jany 29th. 1801

Your esteemed favor of the 24th. Inst. came duly to hand, & on Saturday morning next, one of my servants shall set out with your horse, for the City of Washington. It is with great pain that I hear, congress seem determined to irretate the public mind as much as possible, if they had sumed up there whole powers of recollection, they could not have found three Subjects more irratable than those that have been lately & still are[1] before them, (to witt) the attempt to defeat the election of President, the continuation of the Sedition law, & the rejection of the French Convention; what are we to expect from such representatives, & what do they deserve from their constituents, The people cannot long bear such neglect & contempt. I am dear Sir,

with great Esteem yr H obdt   JOHN HOOMES

RC (MHi); endorsed by TJ as received 1 Feb. and so recorded in SJL.

In a letter to TJ of 30 Jan., Hoomes indicated that his servant James would deliver the HORSE and then return by stage. Hoomes added his wish to "Know whether the horse comes up to your expectation of him, & shall be very sorry if I am deceived in him. . . . The horse was not in good order when I got him he has mended much since but not fatt yet" (RC in MHi; endorsed by TJ as received 3 Feb. and so recorded in SJL).

[1] Preceding three words and ampersand interlined.

From George Jefferson

DEAR SIR   Richmond 29th. Janr. 1801

I am very sorry to inform you that Messrs. M & F. have received a very unfavourable account indeed of your Tobacco; as the subjoined extract of a letter from Jackson & Wharton of Philada., for whom they purchased it, will shew.

This is so very contrary to my expectation that I could scarcely have believed it, if M & F. had not shewn me samples from several Hhds, the heads of which were out when they were about to ship it, and which appeared to be of a very inferior quality. I however represented to them that they could not form a correct judgment from samples taken from the very outside of a Hhd, and particularly when it had been exposed: but this letter confirms them in their first impression—indeed makes it much worse.

I am apprehensive that this will operate much against the sale of your crops in future—& especially as these are persons who will be very fond of making a noise about it.

I am Dear Sir Your Very humble servt.   GEO. JEFFERSON

RC (MHi); at foot of text: "Thos. Jefferson esqr."; endorsed by TJ as received 3 Feb. and so recorded in SJL. Enclosure not found, but see enclosure at TJ to Thomas Leiper, 4 Feb.

M & F.: McMurdo & Fisher.

To Thomas Mann Randolph

TH:J. TO TMR.   Washington Jan. 29. [1801]

Your's of the 24th. came to hand last night. on application to the Postmaster Genl. it seems that I should have put my letters into the office here on the Thursday, instead of Friday. this accordingly goes to the office this day, which is Thursday, and therefore ought to get to you on Thursday next. it may very likely therefore go with my letter of the 23d.

I am very glad indeed to find that Lilly has got so strong a gang, independant of yours & the nailers. with respect to yours I wish you to do exactly what is most for your own interest, either keeping them yourself, or putting any of them with mine as best suits your own convenience. I still think it will be better that such of the nailers as may be able to handle the axe should be employed with it till April, that is to say till Powell comes. it will be useful to them morally and physically, and I have work enough of that kind, with the canal & road to give them full employment. perhaps, as the blowing to be done in the canal will be tedious, it might be worth while to keep Joe & Wormely employed on that in all good weather. if you think so, they should work separately, as I think that one hand to hold the auger & one to strike, is throwing away the labour of one. there should be force enough kept in the nailery to supply our standing customers. there is another reason for employing only the weaker hands in the nailery. I do not believe there is rod to employ the whole any length of time; and none can be got to them till April. I should be glad mr Lilly or mr Dinsmore would count the faggots on hand, & inform me of the quantity by return of post; as I have forgotten the state of the supplies on hand, when I left home.—mr Wilson Nicholas and myself[1] have this day joined in ordering clover seed from New York, where it is to be had, it is said, at 12 dollars. I have ordered 5. bushels for you. I believe I have none to sow myself. mr Jefferson informs me two small casks of wine are forwarded for me to Milton. out of this I wish you to take what I borrowed of you: and I will be thankful to you to inform me as soon as you can of the size of the casks, that I may know how to proportion the equivalent to mr Yznardi. it should be stored in the Dining room cellar, & that secured by double locks, as I presume it is.—with respect to the election, there is no change of appearance since my last. the main body of the Federalists are determined to elect B. or to prevent an election. we have 8. states certain, they 6. and two divided. there are 6. individuals, of moderate dispositions, any one of which coming over to us, will make a 9th. vote. I dare not trust more through the post. my tender love to my ever dear Martha, and to the little ones. I believe I must ask her to give directions to Goliah & his senile corps to prepare what they can in the garden; as it is very possible I may want it. accept assurances of my sincere affection. Adieu.

RC (DLC); partially dated; endorsed by Randolph. PrC (MHi); endorsed by TJ in ink on verso as "Jan. 29. 1801."

Randolph's letter OF THE 24TH, recorded in SJL as received on 29 Jan., has not been found.

A letter from TJ to James DINSMORE, recorded in SJL at this date, has not been found. Letters from Dinsmore to TJ of 11

Apr. 1800 and 15 and 23 Jan. 1801, recorded in SJL as received 18 Apr. 1800, 22 and 29 Jan. 1801, respectively, the first and the last from Monticello, are missing, as is a letter from TJ to Dinsmore, 16 Mch. 1800.

MR JEFFERSON INFORMS ME: George Jefferson to TJ, 23 Jan. 1801.

TJ's slave GOLIAH was born in 1731 (Betts, *Farm Book*, 60).

[1] Preceding two words interlined.

From Hugh Henry Brackenridge

SIR,   Pittsburg 30th. January 1801.

In my absence, your letter acknowledging the receipt of mine relative to the Appendix to your Notes on Virginia, came to hand, and was opened by Mrs. Brackenridge, as directed with regard to all letters, that should any of them require it, they might be forwarded to me, or laid by till my return. The letter containing nothing of a private nature, she permitted a Gentleman the Physician of the family who was present to read it. Information had arrived by the same post to many persons of the only political fact which the letter mentioned, the probable equality of votes for President and Vice President. The Gentleman had not thought it of any consequence his mentioning that the same information had come to me in a letter from Mr. Jefferson himself. I should not have thought it improper had I been at home to have mentioned the contents. For so far from discovering any concern at the equality of votes, it is observed that in the choice of either there will be a republican President. But you see the discoloring that it has received here and at the seat of government. It will be a proof of the indelicacy of the ex-federalists of this place to seize upon so trivial a circumstance and their disingenuity and want of candor in misrepresenting. Ex his disce omnia. I have taken notice of the paragraph in the federal gazette, and have observed upon it with a view to explain and repel what may have been intended.

It was considered by the adversaries as an object of great moment to prevent confidence or correspondence on your part with me lest my representations might affect arrangements of office in this country under your administration having found to their cost the effect of it with the Governor of the State in his arrangements in the Western Country. They were apprehensive that I would be more active in this respect than I had intended to be, & counted more upon what I might be able to do than I myself had ever supposed in my power. The fact is I had sufficiently seen and felt the weight of a knot or junto of persons at this place in the late and present administration, in the appointment of officers for the State and for the Union, and with the great mass of the people wished to see it diminished, and unless in the case of an usurpation of power, that, without me, will be done. I had said in my last that I did not wish to solicit any thing like a correspondence, though I might on my part give occasional information, yet as my wife has been hurt at the use that has been made of opening the letter, and as the malignity of others would be gratified by supposing the object accomplished, it might not be amiss should you think it proper or have leisure, after the matter of presidency is settled to address a letter to me, should it contain but a News Paper. It will have the effect of giving me consequence and power to support myself and my friends in this Country.

It had been my intention ere this time to have removed to a midland situation in Pennsylvania. But it is thought that the republican cause in the State requires my residence here some time longer, at least until after the next election of Governor. It is a post of danger to me and to my family from active and vigilant calumny, but I feel a fortitude to encounter it. The giving the paper at this place a footing is a great object.

James Ross is said to have written by the last mail that Jefferson will be president. It would therefore seem the usurpation is abandoned, and the conspiracy to spite the republicans as they term it by making Mr. Burr President whom they only meant as Vice President.

I am with the greatest respect Your Most Obedient Humble Servant.   H H BRACKENRIDGE

RC (DLC); in a clerk's hand, signed by Brackenridge; addressed: "Thomas Jefferson, Vice-President of the U. States, City of Washington"; endorsed by TJ as received 7 Feb. and so recorded in SJL.

YOUR LETTER ACKNOWLEDGING THE RECEIPT OF MINE: TJ to Brackenridge, 18 Dec. 1800. On 13 Jan. the *Washington Federalist* printed a contribution from "A Federalist." Dated 9 Jan. and addressed "To all to whom it may concern," the piece began: "Know ye, that it is rumoured about this Federal city, that Thomas Jefferson, Esq. Vice President of the United States, did write a letter, very lately, to one Breckenridge of Pittsburg, (who has lately received from Governor McKean the appointment of Judge of the Supreme Court of Pennsylvania) that the electors had given an equal number of votes for him (the said Jefferson) and one Aaron Burr: that he (the said Jefferson) did verily believe, or fear; or expect, or doubt, the present House of Representatives, had a most unreasonable leaning, or squinting, in favor of him the said Aaron, &c. &c. and that the wife of the said Judge Breckenridge did receive this same epistle (*absente Judice,*) and having opened it, divulged the contents." The writer went on to say that anyone acquainted with Brackenridge or others of "the group of *virtuous opposers,* as they call themselves, to all government, in this country," including Gallatin, Mazzei, Callender, Duane, and others, "will probably know the confidential friends of Tom Jefferson, that's all!" The piece concluded with the question, "could any man believe, that Mr. Jefferson was in habits of friendly and confidential correspondence with such people?"

With the Latin comment EX HIS DISCE OMNIA—"from this, you can discern everything"—Brackenridge modified a more common expression, "ex uno disce omnes," which means "from one, you can know everyone."

WITH A VIEW TO EXPLAIN: on 31 Jan.

the Pittsburgh *Tree of Liberty* reprinted the piece from the *Washington Federalist* with an explanation from Brackenridge, who stated that his wife had authority to open his mail in his absence. Brackenridge also declared that saying even "a single word" about the misrepresentation of the contents of TJ's letter would give credence to the slander and "be *an indelicacy towards Mr. Jefferson*" (Claude Milton Newlin, *The Life and Writings of Hugh Henry Brackenridge* [Princeton, 1932], 229-30).

From James Sloan

ESTEEMED FREIND   January 30. 1801

I trust I may with propriety Congratulate thee upon the Resurrection of that Spirit, that once Stimulated the Inhabitants of the Colonies of North America, to Assert the Inherent, and Unallienable Right of all mankind to freedom: Who animated by the Irresistable power thereof, Succesfully opposed the mercenaries of Great Brittain, and thereby Laid a foundation for the Establishment of a Government, upon the only Just principle that Ever did, or Ever can Exist amongst Mankind (Viz) the Consent, and Choice of the Governed—this principle transported across the Atlantic from the new, to the Old world, breaking forth with an unparrallelled Impetuosity, and Irresistible force, in one of the most powerful Europian Nations, Alarmed both the Ecclesiastical, and Civil deceivers, and tyrannical Usurpers of the above mentioned Rights of their fellow Citizens— they, like the preists of Dianna in days of old, foresaw, that if the human mind was permitted the free Exercise of Reasoning upon the nature of things, it would by Virtue of that perceptive power with which it is Endowed by the Creator, discover their base deception, in Imposing upon others as Some thing Supernatural, the workmanship of their own wicked hands, and that nothing could be more diametrically opposite to, or derogatary of the Attributes of a Just, and mercifull God, than to Suppose it consistent with his will, that a Small part of the human Species, should Live in a State of Indolence, Riot, and Luxery, Upon the property produced by the Care, and labour, of the other, and, greater part, of the same kind of beings, by Creation perfectly Equal to themselves—Convinced that Like causes produce Like Effects, and that if free Enquiry was permitted in Europe, Reason and truth, would Soon predominate over falsehood and

Error, as it had [done] in America, by which means their great Dianna, would not basely be consigned to oblivion, but to Eternal Infamy, their Source of Wealth be cut of, and they Reduced to that
State of contempt, which their deception, Injustice, and tyranny, had
long deserved—thus Situated, it was Reasonable to Expect that those
deceivers, Should Stigmatise the genuine promulgaters of Justice,
truth, and the Unallienable Rights of Man, with being blasphemers
of their Goddess, and convene together the whole Infernal phalanx to
Exterminate them; but that any in the United States of America,
Should be found willing to Join in a war of Extermination, or Even
to Countenance their diabolical plans, is as Unaccountable, and contrary to Reason, as the Conduct of the Galations, who haveing Em-
braced the doctrine of Christianity, by which they were freed from
the Greivous burthens Imposed upon them by the Mosaic Law, Soon
turned back again Choosing Slavery, Rather than freedom.—In Reflecting upon the Strange and Unaccountable Retrograde movements
of many of my fellow Citizens, I have Exclaimed in the Language of
the Apostle ([Reavising?] the name) Oh foolish Americans, who
hath bewitched you?—I have said, is it possible, that whilst orphans
yet mourn the Loss of their honoured parents, whilst the Lonely
Widow, weeps for the Absence of her bosom freind, of whose En-
dearing company, and tender Embraces, She finds herself forever deprived, by the Murderous hands of the mercenaries of Brittain, that
any in this Land, can be so callous to the tender feelings of the human
mind, so Lost to a Sense of Universal Justice, and Lastly, to the genuine Spirit of that holy Religion they are makeing profession of,
which breathes peace on Earth, and Good will to men, and Enjoins
all to do unto others as they would be done unto, as to favour the
principles, or Rejoice at the Success of that Government, whose oppression, tyranny, and murder of the human Species, is Unparallelled
in modern history? Yet so it hath been! that Very Government, whose
deception, Usurpation, and tyranny, was so generally, and Justly
Reprobated, may I not say Execrated by the Citizens of the United
States, from the Commencement, to the End of the Late Revolutionary war hath for divers years past, been held up to the public, by that
party who have assumed to themselves the Exclusive title of Supporters of Religion, Order, and good Government, as the most Excellent production of human wisdom, the most perfect System in the
Universe! Our Eyes, Our Ears, Our outward Senses, hath forced conviction upon our minds, that this Diabolical principle, had arose to a
dangerous, and Alarming height in this once free, and happy Land!
we have Seen the Countenances of that party, Evince their heart felt

Satisfaction, in hearing of the Success of the despots of Europe, while Endeavouring to Annihilate a Sister Republic! we have Seen that party, Supporting a base British, hireling printer, in the Metropolis of the United States, who Unequivocally manifested his design to promote a war with Said Republic, and an Alliance with his own Government! they Even Stigmatized as Enemies to Religion, order, and Good Government, those who opposed the principles promulgated by that Obscene, and Infamous Incendiary of a forreign Court, who publickly Avowed his Implacable hatred to Republican Governments! and Lastly, Oh Shocking to Relate! we have beheld their Joyous Exultations, upon hearing of the Success, of British Mercenaries, barbarously murdering thousands of the Citizens of a Long, and Greivously oppressed Nation, for no other cause than Asserting their Inherent Right to freedom, as the Colonists of North America heretofore did, when their Congress (Consistent with the principle of Universal Justice) in a tender and Sympathetic Stile Addressed them, Requesting them to Unite in the Sacred cause of Liberty.—to Investigate the cause of so dreadfull a Relapse, would Exceed the bounds of a Letter, it is also time methinks to Quit those Cyprus Shades, those Dreary Regions of despotic tyranny, where bands of men armed with deadly weapons, Stand Ready at the Nod of a petty tyrant to plunge them into the Vitals of their fellow men, or, as Executioners of Alien or Sedition Laws, Rend assunded the most near, and dear Connections in Life, Immureing in bastiles and Noisome Dungeons, those who Exercise the Inherent Right of all mankind, in Investigateing the Conduct of their Agents! With those horrid Engines of tyranny we have not only been threatened, but Actually began to feell their dire Effects but thanks be to God, who hath in all Ages, Animated, and Influenced, the hearts of Individuals, with a spark of the divine Essence, for the purpose of discovering the Intentions of those hypocritical deceivers, those Wolves in Sheeps Cloathing! and in the fullness of time to kindle that Sacred flame of Liberty, that must Eventually pervade the Universe: the Effulgence of whose beams Shall cause all Despots, Monarchs, and Arristocrats, to fly precipitately (as doth nocturnal birds, and beasts of prey, when the Sun Ariseth) to dens and desolate places, there to be consigned to Eternal Infamy, never to prey upon the Innocent again! My dear freind, this Sacred flame is kindled, this blessed and happy day hath dawned, and Ere Long the Glorious Sun of Liberty will arise, and Advancing to meredian height, dispell not only the mist of Ignorance, but the dark, and Gloomy Clouds of Monarchy, and Arristocracy, that Lately threatened to Envelope this Land in Stygian darkness! that thou mayest Live to Enjoy, and Rejoice, in this Glorious day to Assist, and [. . .]ated, that Blessed work of freedom, and Justice, so nobly begun in the morning of thy days, to Confirm thy freinds, and Convince thine Enemies to Enjoy the Remainder of thy life, that Calm Serenity and peace of mind which the Virtuous only Experience, and finally, to Smile at the approach of Death, Saying with one formerly Come Lord for thy Servant is Ready is the Sincere desire, and fervent prayer of thy Affectionate freind

JAMES SLOAN

P.S. my Eldest Son James I Expect will present these Lines, who can give thee a more particular account of the present circumstance of parties in our State, and will also present thee with some of our feeble productions in support of the cause of Liberty which will give thee Some Idea of the base misrepresentation and false assertions of our opponants, whose Conduct cannot be better described than by Refferring to Miltons Description of Lucifer and his party contending for that Kingdom which their demerits had Justly forfeited—if Leaisure permits a few Lines would be Gratefully Received from the pen of one whose cause has not been more Zealously Supported by any, than by the Committee of Correspondence of the County of Gloucester— J.S.

RC (MoSHi: Jefferson Papers); stained, torn at seal; addressed: "Thomas Jefferson Esqr. Vice President of the United States City of Washington"; endorsed by TJ as received 10 Feb. and so recorded in SJL.

Quaker farmer James Sloan (d. 1811) presided over a meeting in Gloucester County, New Jersey, on 15 Dec. 1800 that published an address attacking Federalists, including both Adams and Hamilton, and affirming a slate of congressional candidates that a state Republican convention at Trenton had selected earlier in the month. As president of the Democratic Association of Gloucester County, Sloan addressed meetings in August 1801 and March 1802. He presided in the spring of 1803 when the association adopted a constitution that included an agreement to settle differences by arbitration. He served in Congress, 1803-1809, and also held local office (*County of Gloucester, New-Jersey. Friends and Fellow-Citizens* [n.p., 1800], Evans, No.

36767; James Sloan, *An Address, Delivered at a Meeting of the Democratic Association of the County of Gloucester* [Trenton, 1801]; James Sloan, *An Oration, Delivered at a Meeting of the Democratic Association, of the County of Gloucester* [Trenton, 1802]; *Constitution of the Democratic Association of the County of Gloucester, in the State of New-Jersey, to Watch Over and Defend the Liberty of the People on the True Principles of Democracy* [Trenton, 1803], 5-6, 12; *Biog. Dir. Cong.*, 1823; Charles Lanman, *Biographical Annals of the Civil Government of the United States, During its First Century* [Washington, 1876], 388).

LANGUAGE OF THE APOSTLE: "O foolish Galatians, who hath bewitched you, that ye should not obey the truth" (Galatians 3:1).

HIRELING PRINTER: William Cobbett.

The only other correspondence with Sloan that TJ recorded in SJL was a letter from Sloan of 18 Oct. 1807. Having learned that Charles Kilgore, register of the land office at Cincinnati, had died,

Sloan hoped that a son of his living there might be considered for the position and that he might be able to speak to TJ about it in Washington within a few days. In a postscript to that 1807 letter, Sloan mentioned unofficial election results that appeared more favorable for the Republicans "than at any former period." Sloan wrote from Newton, a community then in Gloucester County, where a Friends meeting house was located (RC in DNA: RG 59, LAR, endorsed by TJ as received on 21 Oct. 1807 and so recorded in SJL, where he also noted that the letter dealt with Sloan's request for an office for his son; George R. Prowell, *The History of Camden County, New Jersey* [Philadelphia, 1886], 179-80, 650).

From John Tyler

SIR;   Green-Way Jany 30th 1801

I beg leave to recommend to your Notice Mr Saml Tyler my Nephew who anxious as I am and as all true Republicans are to witness the change of sentiment in the people by your promotion to the high and responsible office of President has visited the Fœderal City to join in the Genl. Joy.   I have not the vanity to suppose you bestow a thought on me while engaged in the great duties of your public office; Yet I can not but believe from the knowledge I have of your philanthropy but that you will condescend to receive this Letter as an indubitable evidence of my great regard for your person and character, and therefore will readily excuse the liberty I have taken in obtruding it on you.

Circumstanced as our Country is, I feel how very painful a Preeminence you are exalted to—The envy and bitter malice of an aristocratic Junto and the inveteracy of an English Faction you will no doubt experience, but you will have the heart of Philosophers and Men of Science, and above all the confidence and respect (short of Idolatry) of the republican World, which I hope will always afford you consolation in the most trying exigencies. That you may long live the ornament of our Country, the Friend to Liberty, and the firm supporter of our great Charter is the ardent wish and prayer of Your most obedient,

Huml: Sevt.   JOHN TYLER

RC (DLC); endorsed by TJ as received 12 Feb. and so recorded in SJL.

John Tyler (1747-1813) was born in York County, Virginia, to Anne Contesse and John Tyler, marshal of the vice-admiralty court of Virginia. After attending the College of William and Mary, Tyler read law with Robert Carter Nicholas, became friendly with TJ, and practiced law in Charles City County. In 1776 he married Mary Marot Armistead with whom he had at least seven children, including the future President John Tyler. They established the family home at Greenway near the Charles City County courthouse. Tyler was elected to the Virginia House of Delegates in 1778 and served as its speaker from 1781 until 1785 when Benjamin Harrison defeated him for the position. Elected vice president of the Virginia convention of 1788, Tyler opposed adoption of the federal Constitution. He later became a judge of the General Court of Virginia. He was governor of Virginia from 1808 to 1811, when he was appointed judge of the federal court for the district of Virginia (DAB; Leonard, *General Assembly*, 129, 141, 145, 149, 153, 156; "Will and Inventory of Hon. John Tyler," WMQ, 1st ser., 17 [1909], 231-5).

From Lucy Ludwell Paradise

London

MY DEAR AND RESPECTABLE FRIEND;   January the 31st: 1801

I take up my pen to thank you for the trouble you have taken in all my affairs and to assure you I am greatly obliged to you for the liberty I took in using your Name in the Power of Attorney I sent to you. In consiquence of the Great Distance you live from Williamsburg I have sent out a Power of Attorney to My Nephew Mr. Wm Ludwell Lee Mr. Ambler and Mr P. Harriss to Act for Me and to call in all the Debts due to Me Since the Death of My late Husband without respect of Persons. I have not written thus to Mr. Corbin as I have nothing to trouble that Gentelman with. I have appointed Mr John Rennolds a Native of Virginia an honest and respectable Merchant to be my Merchant he lives in Charlotte Street Bedford Square London and Mr. Reeves No. 1 New Court Old Broad Street near the Royal Exchange London to be My Merchant. All the letters my friends write to Me I desire they will send them with a letter to My Merchants to take care they send them safe to me. Dr. Bancroft often talks of going to America this Summer. I shall be sorry to loose my old friend if it is but for a day. On August the Second My only child Died at Her artful wicked husbands house at venice after loosing half her Nose and the roof of her Mouth. I shall come sooner or later and live in Virginia. Take care what you write to Mr. C.

Accept My Sincere wishes for a long and happy life. Be My Steady friend and let My Interest prevale. My affectionate Compliments to your Daughters. Dear Sir

I have the Honourr to be With Great respect Your Excellencies Most Obedient Friend   LUCY PARADISE

I have written to Mr Ambler I shall come home

RC (MHi); at foot of text: "His Excellency Thoms. Jeffersons."; endorsed by TJ as received 16 May and so recorded in SJL.

Lucy Ludwell Paradise (1751-1814) was the youngest daughter of Frances Grymes Ludwell and Philip Ludwell III of Green Spring, near Williamsburg,

Virginia. In 1760 she sailed for England with her family and did not return permanently to Virginia until 1805. In London in 1769 she married John Paradise of Rathbone-place, the son of an English father who became esteemed in London literary circles, and a Greek-English mother. Known in Virginia circles as "Madam Paradise," Lucy Ludwell Paradise was renowned for her pride, stubbornness, personality, charm, and sometimes violent temper. The litigation over Lucy Ludwell Paradise's estate lasted twenty-three years (Archibald Bolling Shepperson, *John Paradise and Lucy Ludwell of London and Williamsburg* [Richmond, Va., 1942], 6, 11, 18, 25, 293, 439, 440, 442-3, 446, 455, 456; Lothrop Withington, "Virginia Gleanings in England," vmhb, 19 [1911], 289; Lucy Paradise to TJ, 27 Aug. 1805).

TJ begged to be excused of the POWER OF ATTORNEY and when Lucy Paradise's manager William Wilkinson died in 1800, she turned to her nephew William Ludwell Lee who by his authority named William Coleman her new manager (Shepperson, *John Paradise and Lucy Ludwell*, 440).

DEATH OF MY LATE HUSBAND: John Paradise died on 12 Dec. 1795 in London (same, 431).

ONLY CHILD: Lucy Ludwell Paradise's younger daughter died in 1787, leaving Lucy Paradise her only surviving child. She married the Venetian Count Antonio Barziza in 1787, much to her father's displeasure.

Correspondence consisting of eighteen letters from 3 April 1793 to 30 July 1800 between TJ and Lucy Paradise are recorded in SJL but have not been found.

From Martha Jefferson Randolph and Thomas Mann Randolph

January 31 1801

I should not have waited for your letter my Dearest Father had it been in my power to have written sooner but incredible as it may appear, that in period of 2 months not one day could have been found to discharge so sacred and pleasing a duty, it is litterally true that the first fort night of your absence excepted and 3 or 4 days of the last week, I have not been one day capable of attending even to my common domestic affairs. I am again getting into the old way with regard to my stomack, totally unable to digest any thing but a few particular vegetables; harrassed to death by little fevers, for 6 week I scarcely ever missed a night having one untill by recurring to my accustomed remedy in such cases, giving up meat milk coffee and a large proportion of the vegetable tribe that have allways been inimical to my constitution I have at last found some relief. it requires some self denial but I find my self so much recruited both in health and spirits, and every transgression so severely punished, that I shall rigorously adhere to it as long as my health requires it. Cornelia shows the necessity there was for weaning her by her surprising change for the better since that time. the children are all well except Jefferson who cought (that filthiest of all disorders) the itch from a little aprentice boy in the family. he was 6 or seven weeks in constant and familar intercourse with us before we suspected what was the matter with him, the moment it was discovered that the other little boy had it, we were no longer at a loss to account for Jefferson's irruption which had been attributed all along to his covering too warm at night. I am delighted that your return will happen at a season when we shall be able to enjoy your company without interuption. I was at Monticello Last spring 1 day before the arrival of any one, and one day more of interval between the departure of one family and the arrival of another, after which time I never had the pleasure of passing one sociable moment with you. allways in a croud, taken from every useful and pleasing duty to be worried with a multiplicity of disagreable ones which the entertaining of such crouds of company subjects one to in the country, I suffered more in seeing you all ways at a distance than if you had still been in Philadelphia, for then at least I should have enjoyed in anticipation those pleasures which we were deprived of by the concourse of strangers which continually crouded the house when you were with us. I find my self every day becoming more averse to company I have lost my relish for what is usually deemed pleasure, and duties incompatible with it have surplanted all other enjoyments in my breast—the education of my Children to which I have long devoted every moment that I could command, but which is attended with more anxiety now as they increase in age without making those acquirements which other children do. my 2 eldest are uncommonly backward in every thing much more so than many others who have not had half the pains taken with them. Ellen is wonderfully apt. I shall have no trouble with her, but the two others excite serious anxiety with regard to their intellect. of Jefferson my hopes were so little sanguine that I discovered with some surprise & pleasure that he was quicker than I had ever thought it possible for him to be, but he has Lost so much time and will necesarily lose so much more before he can be placed at a good school that I am very unhappy about him. Anne does not want memory but she does not improve. she appears to me to Learn absolutely without profit. adieu my Dear Father we all are painfully anxious to see you. Ellen counts the weeks and continues scoring up complaints against Cornelia whom she is perpetually threatning with *your* displeasure. long is the list of misdemeanors which is to be comunicated to you, amongst which the stealing of 2 potatoes carefully preserved 2 whole days for you but at last Stolen by Cornelia, forms a weighty article. adieu again dearest best beloved Father 2 long months still before we shall see you in the mean time rest assured of the first Place in the heart of your affectionate Child   M. RANDOLPH

P.S. by Th:M.R.
Every thing goes on well at Mont'o.—the Nailers all returned to work & executing well some heavy orders, as one from D. Higinb.m for 30.000. Xd. Moses, Jam Hubbard Davy & Shephard still out & to remain till you order otherwise—Joe cuting nails—I had given a charge of lenity respecting all: (Burwell absolutely excepted from the whip alltogether) before you wrote: none have incurred it but the small ones for truancy & yet the work proceeds better than since George. such is the sound sense cleverness & energy of Lillie.

RC (MHi); endorsed by TJ as received 5 Feb. and so recorded in SJL.

To Aaron Burr

DEAR SIR   Washington Feb. 1. 1801.
It was to be expected that the enemy would endeavor to sow tares between us, that they might divide us and our friends. every consideration satisfies me you will be on your guard against this, as I assure you I am strongly. I hear of one stratagem so imposing & so base that it is proper I should notice it to you. mr Munford, who is here, says he saw at N. York before he left it, an original letter of mine to Judge Breckenridge in which are sentiments highly injurious to you. he knows my handwriting and did not doubt that to be genuine. I inclose you a copy taken from the press copy of the only letter I ever wrote to Judge Breckenridge in my life: the press copy itself has been shewn to several of our mutual friends here. of consequence the letter seen by mr Munford must be a forgery, and if it contains a sentiment unfriendly or disrespectful to you I affirm it solemnly to be a forgery: as also if it varies from the copy inclosed. with the common trash of slander I should not think of troubling you: but the forgery of one's handwriting is too imposing to be neglected. a mutual knolege of each other furnishes us with the best test of the contrivances which will be practised by the enemies of both. accept assurances of my high respect and esteem.   TH: JEFFERSON

PrC (DLC); at foot of text: "Colo. A. Burr." Enclosure: Dupl of TJ to Hugh Henry Brackenridge, 18 Dec. 1800.

According to James Cheetham, who by the time he made the charge was passionately opposed to Burr, William G.

MUNFORD resided at Conrad and Mc-Munn's boardinghouse during his stay in Washington and energetically urged congressmen to support Burr in the presidential voting. Munford denied the accusation. According to Cheetham the young Virginian claimed to have been the author, under Burr's supervision, of the series of essays signed "Epaminondas," which first appeared in the *New-York Gazette and General Advertiser* and constituted "a philippic against Mr. Jefferson; a prodigal eulogium on Mr. Burr" (James Cheetham, *A View of the Political conduct of Aaron Burr, Esq. Vice-President of the United States* [New York, 1802], 66-9; Kline, *Burr*, 1:494n; DAB, 4:47). The *Washington Federalist* reprinted the "Epaminondas" essays beginning 15 Jan. 1801. For Munford's career and relations with Burr, see also Vol. 30:596-7n.

From John James Dufour

TRES HONNORÉ MONSIEUR

First vineyard Kentucky
ce 1r. Fevrier 1801

La renommée qui de bouche en bouche annonce vos vertus et le Zele que vous mettez au bonheur de votre patrie m'enhardy a vous incommoder de cette lettre, et me fait esperer que vous en trouverez le but digne de votre indulgence.

Dans lEté de 1796 je debarquai sur les bords de ce continent dans le dessein de voir par moi même sil étoit impossible de cultiver avec succes la vigne dans les Etats Unis; Etant parti dans ce seul but du Païs de Vaud en Suisse, ou pendant passé vingt ans la Culture de la Vigne a fait mon unique occupation et gagne pain; des lors pendant deux ans jai voyagé sur une tres grande Partie des Etats Unis, et me suis particulierement apliqué a étudier le Climat et à visiter les Essais qu'on avoit deja fait dans ce dessein; Le resultat de mes voyages m'assura que la vigne pouvoit être cultivée avec profit dans tous les endroits que javois vu en choisissant les emplacements, mais que lendroit qui ma paru être le premier en choix, est sur les bords de l'Ohio dans les terres que le Congres possede et qui doivent se vendre ce printems ensuite d'une loi de la Session passée, mais que je ne puis acheter aux termes de la loi faute de moyen que la guerre, la revolution dans ma patrie et mes grands voyages, ont presque anihilé, ainsi que d'empeché ma famille de venir me joindre comme cetoit convenu, cest pourquoi javois presque renoncé a un etablissemt sur l'Ohio et pour netre pas tout a fait venu pour rien, jai planté il y a deux ans sous les auspices dune Souscription une vigne sur les bords du Kentucky qui promet un entier succes, le bruit duquel etant parvenu jusqu'en Suisse a engagé quatre grandes familles tres respectables a se joindre à la mienne pour venir faire la vigne dans ce païs ci, et mordonnent de leur acheter des terres, ne sachant pas que je n'en ai plus les moyens ayant mis le peu de fonds qui me restoient a soutenir l'etablissement ou je suis que le manque de payement des Souscripteurs aloit faire avorter. Cest pourquoi jai cru que le Congres dont la Sagesse tent continuellement au bien du païs voudroit en faveur d'un établissement si consequent à la richesse future du païs faire une petite éxception a leur loi relativement à la vente des terres north west de la Riviere Ohio et me vendre avec un credit de 10 ou 12 ans l'emplacement que je desire depuis long tems et que je crois tres favorable à la vigne, et dans ce dessein j'ose implorer le Congres par une Petition que M. Galatin est prie de présenter, et dont vous trouverez la copie ci jointe à laquelle je vous prie tres humblement de vouloir accorder votre influence; La faveur que je demande au Congres est tres peu de chose pour lui mais tres consequente pour moi, la Culture de la vigne demande de si grandes avances et ne rend que si tard qu'il m'est impossible d'etablir cette Culture sur les terres du Congres, si je suis obligé d'acheter au terme de la loi, cependant le terrein mentionné dans la petition est cellui qui me parois le mieu adapté a cette entreprise de tous ceux que jai vu dans cette Latitude et ne sauroit etre habité avec avantage que par des vigneronts, car éxcepte une lisiere de bottom imediatement le long de la Riviere tout le reste a plusieurs milles en arriere n'est que valées et coteaux rapides insignifiants pour toute autre culture: D'un autre Cotte la grande quantité de terre que le Congres a a vendre, rend la vente de toutes impossible avant douze ans, ainsi si je choisissois un autre quartier pour placer la Collonie qui va arriver, comme le Kentucky ou le Cumberland ou je pourois avoir des terres a un quart de celle du Congres, il est evidant que le mas de terre invendues sera augmenté de la quantite de celles que je demande outre de toutes celles que notre établissement fera vendre ce qui ne sera pas peu Consequent car il est certain que tous les emigrants qui partiront du Païs de Vaud, pour venir en Amerique viendront droit au vignoble qui sera commence ou qu'il soye fut il de l'autre cotte du Mississipi et s'etabliront a nos environs; de maniere que sous ce point de vue la faveur que je demande sera imédiatement autant profitable au Congres qu'a moi. Daignez recevoir lassurance de mes respects et les voeux sinceres que fera toujours au Ciel pour la prosperité du Païs en general et pour la votre en particulier, cellui qui ose se dire

Tres honnoré Monsieur Votre tres humble et affectioné Serviteur

JEAN JAQUES DUFOUR

P.S. Comme des accidents imprevus ont retardé le depart de mes lettres, je crains quelles n'arrivent trop tard pour la Session presente du

Congres; Oserois je dans ce cas esperer de vos bontes votre opinion en reponce a celle ci, si joserois conter sur quelques Succes a ma Petition pour la Session prochaine; dans le cas afirmatif je pourois achetter lors de la vendue en Avril prochain, deux ou trois fractions de Sections qui se trouvent etre dans le terrein que je demande capable de Culture Ordinaire, et par consequent en danger d'etre achetée par dautre (le reste ne courant aucun danger étant trop Montagneux)

Mes moyens me permettrois en me gehenant d'en payer le $\frac{1}{4}$ comme lordonne la Loi et a la prochaine Session du Congres je ferai présenter derechef mon Humble petition: Sous de tells auspices cette colonie pouroit s'etablir en arrivant sur ce terrein pour ne pas perdre de tems, [ceci étant?] tres consequent pour eux, car ils aportent avec eux d'Europe [une provision?] de Vigne et d'Arbres. Monsieur Galatin est prie de vous comuniquer les papiers qui accompagnent la Pétition

EDITORS' TRANSLATION

VERY HONORED SIR   First Vineyard Kentucky 1st February 1801
The renown that from mouth to mouth proclaims your virtues and the zeal that you deploy for the good fortune of your fatherland emboldens me to disturb you with this letter, and makes me hope that you will find its goal worthy of your indulgence.

In the summer of 1796 I landed on the shores of this continent with the plan of seeing for myself whether it was impossible to cultivate vines successfully in the United States; having left with that single goal the region of Vaud in Switzerland, where for over twenty years viticulture was my sole occupation and means of livelihood. Since that time I have traveled for two years over a very large part of the United States, and I have especially applied myself to studying the climate and to visiting the trials that had already been made of this plan. The result of my travels convinced me that vines could profitably be cultivated in all the places that I had seen by choosing the locations, but the place that seemed to me to be the first choice is on the banks of the Ohio in the lands that the Congress possesses and that are to be sold this spring consequent to a law of the past session. But I cannot buy these lands under the terms of the law for lack of means, which the war, the revolution in my own country, and my great travels have practically annihilated, as well as having prevented my family from coming to join me as had been agreed. That is why I had almost renounced a foundation on the Ohio, and, so as not to have come for nothing at all, two years ago I planted a vineyard on the banks of the Kentucky, which promises to be a complete success, and the reputation of which having reached as far as Switzerland, I engaged four great respectable families to join mine to import vines into this country. They order me to buy them some land, not knowing that I no longer have the means, having placed the small funds that remained to me to maintain the establishment where I am, which was going to fail due to the failure of the subscribers to pay. That is why I thought that the Congress, whose wisdom continually aims for the good of the country, would wish, in favor of an establishment so important to the future wealth of the country, to make a small exception to their law relating to the sale of lands northwest of the Ohio River and sell me, with a credit of 10 to 12 years, the location that I have been desiring for a long time and which I believe very favorable for a vineyard. With this in view I dare implore Congress by a petition that Mr. Gallatin is requested to present, and a copy of which you will find attached, to which I very humbly beg you kindly to lend your influence. The favor I request of Congress is a very small thing for it but very important for me. Viticulture requires so much in advance and only pays back so late that it is impossible for me to establish that cultivation on the congressional lands if I am required to buy under the time limit of the law. The plot mentioned in the petition is the one that appears to me the best adapted to this enterprise of all those I have seen in this latitude and could not be inhabited advantageously except by vine-growers, for except for a strip of bottom-land right next to the length of the river, all the rest for several miles inland is only valleys and steep hillsides useless for any other cultivation. On the other hand, the great amount of land that Congress has to sell makes the sale of all of them impossible within 12 years. Thus, if I chose another location to place the colony that is going to arrive, such as Kentucky or the Cumberland, where I could have lands for a quarter of those from Congress, it is obvious that the mass of unsold land will be increased by the quantity of those that I am requesting, besides all those that our colony will cause to be sold, which will not be of small importance, for it is certain that all the emigrants who will leave the region of Vaud to come to America will come straight to the vineyard that has begun, wherever it may be, even if it were on the other side of the Mississippi, and settle in our neighborhood; so that the favor I am requesting will be immediately as profitable to the Congress as to me. Kindly accept the assurance of my respects and the sincere good wishes which will be perpetually made to Heaven for the prosperity of the country in general and for yours in particular, by the one who makes bold to call himself

Very honored Sir Your very humble and affectionate Servant

JEAN JAQUES DUFOUR

P.S. As unforeseen accidents delayed the departure of my letters, I fear that they may arrive too late for the present session of Congress; would I dare hope in that case for your kindness in giving your opinion in replying to this one, and could I dare count on some success in my petition for the coming session; if the answer is yes I could buy at the sale next April two or three fractions of sections that are located in the land I am requesting and are fit for ordinary farming, hence in danger of being bought by others (the rest running no danger, being too mountainous).

My means would allow me by squeezing myself to pay $\frac{1}{4}$ as the law requires, and at the next session of Congress I will immediately have my humble petition presented. Under such auspices, this colony could be established upon arrival on that land so as not to lose any time, which is very important for them, for they are bringing with them a supply of vines and trees from Europe. Mr. Gallatin is requested to communicate to you the papers that accompany the petition.

RC (DLC); addressed: "His Excellency Thomas Jefferson Vice President of the United States City of Washington Eastern mail"; postmarked at Lexington, Kentucky; torn at seal and other text lost at edge; endorsed by TJ as received 6 Mch. 1801 and so recorded in SJL. Enclosure: Petition of John James Dufour to United States Senate and House of Representatives, explaining his situation and noting that "five large families" of experienced vinedressers were moving to the U.S. but lacked the resources to meet the terms of land sales in the Northwest Territory; specifying the desired tract; pledging to plant ten acres in vines within two years of the settlement of the colony and to expand the cultivation thereafter; and noting that the colony would not only help to establish an important branch of agriculture but would utilize a tract that otherwise would not sell promptly (Dupl in same; in English, in Dufour's hand and endorsed by him).

John James Dufour (d. 1827) was the son of a Swiss vinedresser. After immigrating to the U.S. he formed a vineyard association and laid out what he called the First Vineyard, on the Kentucky River about 25 miles from Lexington. Several relatives and friends with their families joined him from Switzerland in the summer of 1801. The vines of the First Vineyard were later devastated by disease. Receiving dispensation from Congress in 1802 for their land purchase, Dufour's group established the Second Vineyard at what became Vevay, Indiana, named for Dufour's native district in the Canton of Vaud. Dufour was in Europe from 1806 to 1816 but returned to the U.S. and wrote *The American Vine-Dresser's Guide: Being a Treatise on the Cultivation of the Vine, and the Process of Wine Making; Adapted to the Soil and Climate of the United States*, which was published at Cincinnati in 1826 (DAB; Dufour to TJ, 15 Jan. 1802).

From Benjamin Hichborn

SIR   Boston 1 Feby 1801

The Bearer of this Mr: Israel Hatch of this town has discovered, as he thinks, a new method to give effect to chaind Shot when directed against Ships of War in defence of forts Towns &c—in this view, it appears to me important & induced me to yeald a ready complyance with his request, to recommend it to your patronage, shoud it be found upon examination to deserve attention—I have a Stronger motive for writing you by him, on account of the Safety of Conveyance, as I am very much inclined to beleive that all Letters addressed to, or known to be from you are liable to be opened—The Suspicion which occasion'd the hint I dropped you in a line from Philadelphia has not been at all diminished by Subsequent Circumstances, I had many Conversations with Colo Burr on the Subject of the approaching Election of President, & am convinced, shoud the first attempt in your favor fail, that he & some of his Friends will consent, that a few Republicans shall joine the aristocratical party in giving him the preference. I am sure I speak the Sentiments of 19 twentieths of the People, in saying, that I had rather have no Presid. till one can be obtained by a new choice—the rejection of the Convention with France must produce incalculable injury; & proportionate discontent—we can only say "quos deus vult perdere, prius dementat"—I am at this moment made happy by a visit from Genl. Knox who tells me there is information in Town, that you will certainly have a great majority of the States on the question which will decide the unmanly Controversy about the President elect—

The Cause of Republicanism begins to be respected even by its Enemies—I hope it will never be injured by the Zeal of its Friends—we scarcely know what to beleive about the Treaty or Convention with france, one hour we are it has been adopted in toto, the next, we hear it is accepted with Conditions amendments &c we are then told it will be rejected in toto—the Cond. of our Governor Strong is so cautious that few people feel any great zeal in opposing him on that ground; but while he holds his place, under the supposed auspices of an aristocratical & royalistical party, the Friends of civil liberty are disgusted—I beleive a strong effort will be made at the next Election, in favor of Gerry[1] but the issue must be doubtful—when any thing occurs which I think you may wish to be acquainted with I shall trouble you with a line—I am with great esteem

Yours   BENJA HICH[BORN]

RC (DLC); signature torn at seal; addressed: "Thos: Jefferson Esqr Vice President of the United States Washington," with "Mr: Hatch" written perpendicularly on address sheet; endorsed by TJ as received 17 Feb. and so recorded in SJL.

In March 1801 ISRAEL HATCH received a patent for "Making and discharging chain and cleaver shot" (*List of Patents,*

24). Hichborn's LINE FROM PHILADELPHIA is at 5 Jan.

QUOS DEUS VULT PERDERE, PRIUS DEMENTAT: "whom God wishes to destroy he first deprives of reason," a form of the adage, often attributed to Euripides, "those whom the gods wish to destroy, they first make mad."

[1] Preceding four words interlined.

To George Jefferson

DEAR SIR   Washington Feb. 1. 1801.

My last to you was of Jan. 16. since which I have recieved your two of Jan. 12. and that of Jan. 23. I inclose you one for your brother, not knowing what is his correct post office, so as to send it to him by post directly.   mr T. M. Randolph states to me that he shall fall in your debt £135 at the end of the year's account, & being at a loss to provide it has asked me to do it. I have informed him I will with pleasure, if it will be convenient to you to recieve it the 1st. of April, before which it would not be in my power to advance it. if this will suit you, you shall be free to take it of the sum recievable by you on that day for my tobacco. I have before drawn on you for 1000. D. payable to mr Lyle, 1000. D. payable to mr Tazewell, & this additional sum of 458. D. will still be more than covered by the whole amount of my tobacco.—I must pray you to procure & send to Monticello a hogshead of molasses for me. it is essential that it be double cased, or it will be half water before it gets there. I am with great esteem Dear Sir

    Yours affectionately   TH: JEFFERSON

PrC (MHi); at foot of text: "Mr. George Jefferson"; endorsed by TJ in ink on verso. Enclosure: TJ to John Garland Jefferson, 1 Feb. 1801.

RANDOLPH STATES TO ME: see TJ to Thomas Mann Randolph, 23 Jan.

To John Garland Jefferson

DEAR SIR   Washington Feb. 1. 1801.

Your's of Jan. 17. 1801. has been duly recieved. about 7. years ago a judgment for about £2000. was obtained against mr Wayles's estate, and came on me at such short notice that I was much embarrassed to raise suddenly my proportion of it. while under that embarrasment I offered for sale the tract of land in Bedford which is the subject of your letter, as also a part of my lands in Albemarle. neither [resource] availed me, and I found other means of answering the demand. since that I have had many applications for the tract in Bedford, which I have declined because nothing but the circumstance abovementioned could ever induce me to think for a moment of selling land. nor do I believe it would suit you. it is 4. or 5. miles from [. . .], [broken?] & not good. it's value is in it's timber, which may some day sell well. I should have imagined that Lynchburg itself must be greatly preferable as a seat for business to any place at a distance from it. on the top of the hill too, one would be withdrawn from intrusion, while near enough to be applied to by those who come to Lynchburg on other business. but of this you can best judge.

with respect to mr Johnson's case, those who censure my vote have been but partially informed. mr Johnson is brother of the gentleman of the same name formerly governor of Maryland. he established himself in London in commerce before the revolutionary war. when that broke out he did not discontinue his trade, but remained in London, & signalised himself by his attentions & aids to distressed Americans carried in there. he was agent also for Maryland in procuring &

sending her arms and ammunition. after the war he continued in the course of constant service to his countrymen, in consideration of which Genl. Washington appointed him our Consul in London about 1790. I corresponded with him while Secy. of State for four years in the line of mutual office, & found him faithful & assiduous. he afterwards became unfortunate in his trade, and came over to America with the consent and at the request of his creditors, as was affirmed in Senate, & that they preferred leaving him to wind up his own affairs for their benefit, rather than put them into the hands of any other person. in this situation mr Adams who had lived in intimacy with him in London 5. or 6. years, named him Stampmaster. a great majority of the Senate were for him, but the question came on in the evening, just as the house was breaking up, when many members had already departed, and it happened that those remaining who greatly disliked the question came to me. every thing I heard on the occasion, every thing I had known of him, and mr Adams's nomination which was a testimony in his favor after an acquaintance of several years satisfied me that that nomination ought not to be rejected. I have now lately heard it suggested by one gentleman that mr Johnson did not come away from Europe so honorably as had been mentioned. but of this he acknoleged he had recieved no proof. I acknolege that bankruptcy is a strong objection to appointing a man to an office, because such men are unusually pressed to make the most of their office. but at the same time I do not think it should be an inseperable bar, and overweigh all other qualifications whatsoever. the division of the Senate shewed that the reasons in his favor were at least equal to those against him, solely derived from his circumstances. it could not then be so palpable a case as to make the siding with either moiety of the members [. . .]. I have never seen mr Johnson in my life, tho' he lives here. this shews there could be no personal partiality to him on my part. I thank you for mentioning the subject, being always desirous of explaining whatsoever I may have occasion to do on a public question. accept assurances of sincere esteem & attachment from Dear Sir
Your's affectionately   TH: JEFFERSON

PrC (ViU: Carr-Cary Papers); blurred; at foot of first page: "Mr. J. G. Jefferson"; endorsed by TJ in ink on verso. Enclosed in TJ to George Jefferson, 1 Feb.

The JUDGMENT in the suit brought by James Bivins, Jr., held the Wayles execu-

tors responsible for the debt incurred when TJ's father-in-law served as security for Richard Randolph (Vol. 28:98-100, 614-16).

FORMERLY GOVERNOR OF MARYLAND: Thomas Johnson.

To James Madison

Feb. 1. 1801.

I have not written to you since the letter by mrs B. your's of Jan. 10. is recieved, and your own wishes are entirely acquiesced in as to time. Clermont has refused. I think to adopt your idea at Baltimore. I dare not through the channel of the post hazard a word to you on the subject of the election. indeed the interception & publication of my letters exposes the republican cause as well as myself personally to so much obloquy that I have come to a resolution never to write another sentence of politics in a letter.—the inclosed came under a blank cover to me, & I broke it open & read it through, and till I was folding it up to put away, I did not discover your name on the back of it, & consequently that it was destined for you. I hope your health is getting better. I think nothing more possible than that a change of climate, even from a better to a worse, and a change in the habits & mode of life, might have a favorable effect on your system. I shall be happy to hear that your father is rallying. the approaching season will be favorable for that. present my respectful attachments to mrs Madison, and accept affectionate assurances of friendship to yourself. Adieu.

TH: JEFFERSON

RC (DLC: Madison Papers). PrC (DLC). For enclosure, see below.

MRS B: Mrs. Catherine Brown; see Madison to TJ, 10 Jan. 1801.

Robert R. Livingston, whose family estate was CLERMONT, declined TJ's request to serve as secretary of the navy. YOUR IDEA AT BALTIMORE: on 9 Mch.

TJ would offer the post to Congressman Samuel Smith of Baltimore (Livingston to TJ, 7 Jan. 1801; TJ to Smith, 9 Mch. 1801).

TJ enclosed a letter from James Thomson Callender to Madison, dated 23 Jan. 1801, which TJ endorsed as received on 28 Jan. and recorded on that date in SJL. See Madison, *Papers*, 17:457-8.

From Mary Jefferson Eppes

DEAR PAPA   Bermuda hundred Febry 2nd [1801]

Your letter to Mr Eppes arrived yesterday from City Point where I imagine from the date it had been some time, the river had been & is often so rough that a canoe could not venture over, tho' it is the most certain way of hearing from you I am afraid it will not be a very regular one which I lament[1] as in your absence it is the greatest pleasure I recieve nor have I any thing so valuable as your letters.[2] sensible of the distance which Nature has placed between my sister & myself the tender affection I feel for her—makes me judge what yours must be, and I rejoice that you have in her so great a source of comfort & one who is in every way so worthy of you, satisfied if my dear papa is only assured that in the most tender love to him I yeild to no one. you mention'd in your letter your intention of being at Monticello in april & I shall then enjoy the heartfelt happiness of being with you & my dear Sister tho' only for a short time after which I suppose you will not be there again till the fall. nothing can be more retired than the life we lead here, it has its pleasures tho', as it leaves us perfect Masters of our own time, & the different occupations we have I hope will prevent our ever feeling ennui. will you be so good as to keep the little sum which the tobacco Mr Eppes gave me will amount to & lay it out for me I will let you know in what way when you recieve it. if you have not engaged the harpsichord to Aunt Bolling or any one else I will if you please put off chusing between them till april as I fear the Piano will not hold in tune long & I shall be able to judge by that time. Adieu My dear Papa. Mr Eppes will write to you a few days hence beleive me with the sincerest affection yours   M Eppes

RC (MHi); partially dated; endorsed by TJ as received 8 Feb. 1801 and so recorded in SJL.

your letter to mr eppes: probably TJ's letter of 19 Jan. you mention'd in

your letter: TJ's letter to his daughter of 4 Jan. 1801.

[1] Interlined in place of "regret."
[2] Eppes here canceled two or three indecipherable words.

To Thomas McKean

Dear Sir   Washington Feb. 2. 1801.

I have long waited for an opportunity to acknolege the reciept of your favor of Dec. 15. as well as of that by Doctr. Mendenhall. none occurring I shall either deliver the present to Genl. Muhlenburg or put it under cover to Doctr. Wistar to whom I happen to be writing, to be sent to your house in Philadelphia or forwarded confidentially to Lancaster.

The event of the election is still in dubio. a strong portion in the H. of R. will prevent an election if they can. I rather believe they will not be able to do it, as there are six individuals, of moderate character, any one of whom coming over to the republican vote, will make a ninth state. till this is known it is too soon for me to say what should be done in such atrocious cases as those you mention of federal officers obstructing the operation of the state governments. one thing I will say that as to the future, interferences with elections, whether of the state or general governments, by officers of the latter will be deemed cause of removal. because the constitutional remedy by the elective principle, becomes nothing, if it may be smothered by the enormous patronage of the General govmt. how far it may be practicable, prudent, or proper to look back is too great a question to be decided but by the united wisdom of the whole administration when formed. our situation is so different from yours that it may render proper some difference in the practice. your state is a simple body, the majority clearly one way. ours is of 16. integral parts, some of them all one way; some all the other: some divided. whatever may be decided as to the past, they shall give no trouble to the state governments in future, if it shall depend on me: and be assured particularly as to yourself, that I should consider the most perfect harmony & interchange of accomodations & good offices with yourself as among the first objects. accept assurances of my high consideration, respect and esteem.   TH: JEFFERSON

RC (PHi); addressed: "His Excellency Governor Mc.Kean Lancaster"; endorsed by McKean as "Private." PrC (DLC).

For McKean's letter to TJ introducing Captain Thomas MENDENHALL, see 3 Jan. 1801.

Notes on Convention of 1800

[before 3 Feb. 1801]

G. Morris's construction of the 6th. & 24th. articles.

By the old treaty with France they had a right to bring in their prizes call that right A.

By the treaty with England we grant them a right with the exeption of that granted to France, to wit A.

our dissolution of the treaty with France does not convey A. to England

it does not give her a right to bring in French prizes

then when we put the French on the footing[1] of the most favored nation it follows that they cannot bring in British prizes, any more than the British can French. but both may those of other nations

this is probably the view the French negotiators had of it & perhaps our own. when the former insisted, that on the dissoln of a treaty between A. & B. no right could be transferred to a 3d person

MS (DLC: TJ Papers, 102:17543); undated fragment; entirely in TJ's hand.

MORRIS'S CONSTRUCTION: New York

Senator Gouverneur Morris, former minister to France, took an active part in the Senate's consideration of the Convention of 1800, first heading the committee formed to obtain translations of the documents in French and then, on 15 Jan., chairing the committee ordered "to reduce the several votes on this treaty into the form of a ratification." The Senate records do not indicate, however, when debate on Articles 6 and 24 took place. Article 6 provided that commerce between the parties should be free, their privateers and their prizes being treated in their respective ports as of the most favored nation, and that in general the two parties should enjoy most favored nation status "in regard to commerce, and navigation." Article 24 provided for ships of war entering port with prizes and stipulated that the article did not extend beyond the privileges of the most favored nation. In the end Morris voted against ratification of the convention (*Biog. Dir. Cong.*; JEP, 1:360-77; Miller, *Treaties*, 2:462, 477).

[1] TJ first wrote "then when we gave the French the rights" before altering the passage to read as above.

To John Hoomes

DEAR SIR   Washington Feb. 3. 1801.

Your servant arrived here this afternoon with the horse, [and I] have only this moment been able to go and see him. I am quite satisfied with his first appearances, & have no doubt I shall continue [to be?] so. the servant wishing to go immediately to Georgetown to take [. . .] passage for tomorrow morning, I give him   dollars to cover your [advances] for his expences, & those of his return & trouble.—I have the pleasure to inform you that the Senate this day determined to reconsider their vote rejecting the French convention, & have ratified it on condition of striking out the 2d. article & adding a limitation of 8. years for it's duration; modifications which I hope will pr[. . .] no difficulty with France; and I trust we are now placed on [smoother] water with that country. it puts an end to the proposition [of the?] H. of R. to continue the non-intercourse law.—I shall [take] care to have the sum of 300. Dollars paid to your order in Richmond according to the [tenor] of my former letter. I am with great esteem Dear Sir

Your most obedt. servt   TH: JEFFERSON

PrC (DLC); faint; at foot of text: "Colo. John Hoomes"; endorsed by TJ in ink on verso.

TJ recorded in his financial records on this date payment for a HORSE: "Recieved from Colo. John Hoomes of the Bowling green a bay horse, Wildair, 7 y. old, 16. hands high, for which I am to pay him 300. D. May 1" (MB, 2:1034).

The vote in the SENATE THIS DAY on modifications to the French convention was 30 to 1 to expunge the second article and 18 to 13 against expunging the third article. The final vote for ratification was 22-9. For the progress of the convention in the Senate, see JEP, 1:372-7; DeConde, *Quasi-War*, 291-3; TJ to Hoomes, 24 Jan.

From William Jackson

Sir,   Philadelphia, February 3rd. 1801.

Should the spirit, by which this letter is dictated, be duly accredited the result anxiously wished by the Writer, a degree of public utility, may be realised, and the Person to whom it is addressed will not deem it an intrusion.

Actuated by the purest public motives, and influenced by no other personal consideration than that of reflecting on the personal kindness and approbation, which, at different times, it has been my good fortune to receive from you, I pray permission to communicate certain opinions relative to the present crisis of public affairs, which interested adherents would not, and which illiberal opponents could not express.

To remove from your mind every idea unfavorable to the reception of these opinions, as being a candid statement of facts, I will introduce them by a declaration of my own political sentiments, whereby it may be seen that nothing, which could impeach my consistency, has governed in the resolution now taken to address you.

a Federalist in the full meaning of the term, if that term intends a strenuous supporter of the federal constitution, my belief of the advantages, which the people of America have derived from their general government, as administered by the illustrious Washington, will remain unchanged and unimpaired to the closing hour of my Existence—My belief, that the principles, on which his administration proceeded are now and always will be cherished by a vast majority of the virtuous and enlightened Citizens of the United-States, is no less firm and unalterable.

That the systems, which it was his policy to institute and to countenance, are eminently calculated to promote the prosperity, the happiness, and the honor of our nation is no less a part of my political creed—That, under these impressions, I have fervently wished their continuance is true, and that to preserve them I would devote the last years of my life (as the first that could be so employed, from the age of sixteen to twenty four, were devoted) to military toil and privation.

This, Sir, is my political faith.—With the impressions, which I trust you have received of my character and conduct, it was, perhaps, unnecessary to have prefaced the communication, which is the object of this letter, with such a declaration; But, under the possibility, however remote, that a regard to the very secondary office, of which I am the Incumbent, might have been considered in any degree to have influenced me, I believed the declaration proper—as I do the avowal that whenever a person more deserving to serve the public in any office that I may happen to hold shall be appointed to supersede me, I shall express no other sentiment than that of the Spartan Candidate.

Regarding you, then, Sir, as the legitimate choice of the American People to be their chief Magistrate, and impelled by a personal attachment, which I have never ceased to entertain, I am desirous to express, in advance, my confidence in the equity of your administration—I shall, therefor, endeavor by a fair exposition of those facts, which, as a citizen mingling in general society, I am acquainted with, to do that service to the community which it is my duty to render, and which it may be no less your inclination to learn.

The various speculations entertained on what will be the conduct of the ensuing Administration are too multiplied to be detailed or reasoned upon—There is one point, however, in which the best judgments appear to be entirely agreed: It has been announced by sanguine Expectants that the changes to be effected will extend to every principle which has, heretofore, governed the Executive, and will embrace every description of Officers, heretofore appointed.

Wise and discreet men are highly alarmed at this suggestion—Warm friends to their country and the constitution are moved to unqualified reprehension of such intentions—While the less prudent are prepared to regard such change as the signal for dissolving the federal compact, and tossing the brand of war.

That wise and discreet men should be alarmed by this intimation is of rational and irresistible conclusion—In such innovation they behold, as in an exact mirror, every consequence which the sanguine, the exasperated, and the desperate are prepared to hasten and render unavoidable—They behold the basis of public confidence about to be removed—They behold those systems, which it had been the policy of the revered Washington in a series of years to establish, destroyed in a day—They behold the fortunes and the actual prosperity of their country committed to the hazard of experiments and placed at the mercy of events.

To do away these rumors of ruinous innovation (to which conviction alone shall force me to subscribe) I have offered the reasonings which flow from my acquaintance with your character—I have stated my belief (and I have called it knowledge for such I thought it) of your respect for General Washington's opinions, which I had occasion to remark during my residence in his family—In addition to this deference for his opinions, I have said, with confidence, that the discernment of a justly discriminating mind would lead you to view the attainment of individual wishes as best connected with the internal tranquillity, and external respectability of the United States—and that as both must depend on the stability of such measures as had hitherto been found promotive of public good, it was utterly impossible that such change would be made, or that such innovation had ever been contemplated.

With reflecting minds these arguments have had an influence; and, in reply to a direct enquiry made from the Seat of Government on the subject, it has been stated that, in the expected parity of votes, the preference to be given by the House of Representatives ought to be in favor of the present Vice President of the United States.

The Men, Sir, who have thus declared themselves will be found among the firmest supporters of an administration proceeding on the principles of President Washington—and to you, Sir, in such a result, they will cheerfully transfer the attachment and support, which they yielded to him.

They confide in your ability—they respect your private virtues— and from both they infer such a course of policy as will command their approbation, receive their assistance, and render your administration as satisfactory to yourself, as they hope it will be beneficial to our country.

Thus far, Sir, had I written when the reflection that this letter might either be deemed impertinent or interested again crossed my mind, and nearly decided me to suppress it—The consideration, however, of the relations in which I stand to the community has prevailed—and to exonerate me from the charges of intrusion or interest I enclose, for your perusal, three letters:

One of them, you will observe, has imposed, as a debt of gratitude, the task which I now perform—(It was not delivered to its address as when I was last in Europe I did not visit Spain) The others will serve to shew that the man, who, at the close of eight years military service, in which he had expended his little patrimony, cou'd embark in a laborious pursuit to replace it—and who, at another time, could leave the bosom of General Washington's family to encounter the uncertainty of professional expectations, is not the Slave of official dependence. No, Sir, the same resort of industry will, in every event, remain to him. He, therefore, prays that his only motive in this address may be truly appreciated—and that you will believe him to be, with unfeigned respect, Sir, Your obliged and faithful Servant

W JACKSON

P.S. Considering the three letters which are enclosed as testimonials of the highest value, and such as my Children may peruse with pride, I pray that they may be returned to me.   W.J.

RC (DLC); at head of text: "(Private)"; below signature: "Thomas Jefferson Esquire"; endorsed by TJ as received 7 Feb. and so recorded in SJL. Enclosures not found.

After appealing to George WASHING-

TON for employment, Jackson, a former Revolutionary War officer, served as one of the president's secretaries, 1789-1791. VERY SECONDARY OFFICE: since early 1796 Jackson had been surveyor and inspector of the revenue at Philadelphia (ANB).

From John Morton

Geo-Town, Tuesday-morning 3. feb. 1801.

Mr Morton's respectful Compliments wait upon the V. President.

Mr. M. takes the Liberty of requesting that if the V. Presidt. has perused the Notes Mr. M. had the Honor to leave with him yesterday, he will do him the favor to return them by the bearer:—but, if the reading thereof has not been completed, M. Morton is also desirous that they may be retained for that purpose untill tomorrow.

RC (DLC); endorsed by TJ as received 3 Feb. and so recorded in SJL; also endorsed by TJ: "(Consul at Hava.)."

John Morton of New York, a brother of prominent Federalist Col. Jacob Morton, was named consul for the port of Havana as of 29 June 1799. In the fall of 1800, after charges of self-interest and improper conduct surfaced against Morton, he returned to the U.S., first to Boston and then to Washington to explain and defend his actions. He had retained, he claimed, "the Confidence & favor of the President

and his confidential officers" and desired "to satisfy the present administration" about his "character, & qualifications for the office which I am desirous of retaining" (John Morton to James Madison, 4 June 1801 [DNA: RG 59, Dispatches from U.S. Consuls in Havana]; JEP, 1:326; Madison, *Papers, Sec. of State Ser.*, 1:108, 263; Roy F. Nichols, "Trade Relations and the Establishment of the United States Consulates in Spanish America, 1779-1809," *Hispanic American Historical Review*, 13 [1933], 300-301).

To Caspar Wistar

DEAR SIR   Washington Feb. 3. 1801.

According to your desire I wrote to Chancellor Livingston on the subject of the bones. the following is an extract from his letter dated Jan. 7. 'I have paid the earliest attention to your request relative to the bones found at Shawangun, & have this day written to a very intelligent friend in that neighborhood. I fear however that till they have finished their search there will be some difficulty in procuring any part of the bones, because when I first heard of the discovery I made some attempts to possess myself of them, but found they were a kind of common property, the whole town having joined in digging for them, till they were stopped by the autumnal rains. they entertain well grounded hopes of discovering the whole skeleton, since these bones are not, like all others that they have hitherto found in that county, placed within the vegetable mould, but are covered with a stratum of clay, so that being better sheltered from the air and water, they are more perfectly preserved.—Among the bones I have heard mentioned, are the vertebrae, part of the jaw, with two of the grinders, the tusks which some have called the horns, the sternum, the scapula, the tibia & fibula, the tarsus & metatarsus. whether any of the phalanges or the ossa innominata are found, I have not heard. a part of the head containing the sockets of the tusks is also discovered. from the bones of the feet, it is evidently a claw-footed animal, & from such parts of the shoulder bones as have been discovered, it appears that the arm or fore-leg, had a greater motion than can possibly belong to the elephant or any of the large quadrupeds with which we are acquainted.—Since bog-earth has been used by the farmers of Ulster county for a manure which is subsequent to the war, fragments of at least 8. or 10. have been found, but in a very decayed state in the same bog.'

From this extract, & the circumstance that the bones belong to the town you will be sensible of the difficulty of obtaining any considerable portion of them. I refer to yourself to consider whether it would not be better to select such only of which we have no specimens, and to ask them only. it is not unlikely they would with common consent yeild a particular bone or bones, provided they may keep the mass, for their own town. if you will make the selection & communicate it to me I will forward it to the Chancellor, & the sooner the better.

Accept assurances of my high consideration & attachment

TH: JEFFERSON

PrC (DLC); at foot of first page: "Dr. Wistar."

To Thomas Leiper

DEAR SIR   Washington. Feb. 4. 1801.

A circumstance has arisen in Philadelphia in which I must ask your friendly aid, because nobody in the world is so able to judge of it as yourself. Messrs. Gibson & Jefferson, as my agents in Richmond, sold my crop of Bedford & Albemarle tobo. of the growth of 1799. to McMurdo & Fisher of Richmond for 6. D. a hundred payable Apr. 1. this sale was made about the latter part of Nov. last of course on a credit of more than 4. months. yesterday I recieved a letter from Gibson & Jefferson, inclosing one from messrs. Jackson & Wharton of Philadelphia to McMurdo and Fisher, by which it appears the tobaccoes were sent to them and you will see by the letter which I inclose what they say of them. you know the qualities of those tobaccos [. . .] having often purchased them. the Bedford, inspected at Lynchburg is made by the same manager who has overlooked the place for 15. years. the Albemarle tobco have been for 50. years in the hands of my father & myself been considered as of the very first made in the state. they were shipped by our merchant for 2[8?]. years to Glasgow who has often told me they were admitted to be the very best ever landed there. you have witnessed to me their character in Philadelphia, and it is well established in Richmond. the letter says that much of the Lynchburg tobo. has been wet before prizing. that is impossible. it could not have been so unknown to Clarke the manager, who is as honest a man as ever breathed, and for whom I would pledge myself without hesitation. he knows too my anxiety to maintain the character of the crop. one thing is possible, that the batteaumen may have [. . .] the tobacco on it's way from Lynchburg to Richmond, & have said nothing of it either to Clarke or Gibson & Jefferson. the tobaccoes of the upper inspections are liable to this [. . .]: & it is very common for the purchaser to guard himself against it by offering a higher price on condition of reviewing the tobo. no objection would have been made to this on my part. when this is not done, the purchaser is always understood to take on himself the risks and loss of weight &c subsequent to inspection. however this right on my part I abandon, if the tobo. was not at the time of the sale what both the seller & purchaser believed it be, in sound condition. I consent to a proper deduction of price. but it may have been injured on it's passage to Philadelphia. this you & I know from experience. with this I can have no more to do than with what may happen to it in going to London. the favor I ask of you is to call upon these gentlemen, to satisfy yourself of the probable condition of the tobo. at the time of the sale, and to make any deduction from the price which you think reasonable. observe that 6. D. was no extra price. it was what was currently given at Richmond at the time for good crops. whatever you agree to do in this I confirm before hand & will abide by. your knolege of the qualities of the tobo. heretofore, your experience in matters of this kind, and your disinterestedness render you the best judge that can be established between us, & I wish you to do for me what liberality and my own dispositions would induce me to do were I there. I might complain of the insinuation in the close of their letter. if the gentlemen had known me of themselves instead of through the medium of party hatred, they would not have said it. however of those things I say nothing. to you indeed I ought to say much in apology for the trouble I propose to you. it is on your friendship I rely for that apology, and the necessity of an interchange of such kind office among men. accept assurances of the sincere esteem & attachment of Dear Sir Your friend & servt

Th: JEFFERSON

PrC (MHi); blurred; endorsed by TJ in ink on verso.

For the LETTER FROM GIBSON & JEFFERSON, see George Jefferson to TJ, 29 Jan. 1801.

ENCLOSURE

Jackson & Wharton to McMurdo & Fisher.

'the weather proving very unfavorable, we have had it in our power to examine but about one third of the parcel, which so far as respects the crop of mr Jefferson we have no hesitation in saying is *very mean*. of about 10. or 11. hhds. we have opened, not one is good. there are of two inspections, of which Lynchburg has originally been the best; but much of it has been wet before prizing and some appears to have been lying some considerable time in the water, so much so as to penetrate nearly through the hogshead—the other inspection is very light quality, much worm eaten, and sunburnt, but it is sound & of good flavor, which is the only thing in it's favor.—this serves to convince us that little confidence is to be placed in great names, so far as respects tobacco.'

Tr (MHi); undated; in TJ's hand; closing quotation mark supplied.

From Andrew Ellicott

DEAR SIR   Philadelphia Feby. 5th. 1801

With this you will receive a Map of the western part of the State of New York which I am requested by my brothers who reside near Niagara to present to you,—it is all laid down from actual survey.—I have accompanied it with a small tract which I drew up while congress had the act for establishing a land office under consideration, and agreeably to which the surveys were directed to be made; but I have been informed that the plan has not been attended to in the execution of the work. —The tract was drawn up at the request of our friend John Page, and it was but seven days after I began it, till each member of both houses was furnished with a printed copy. —This expedition will account for a few errors, the most material are corrected with a pen. As I suspect you will not have leisure to attend to the mathematical part, I have marked a few paragraphs at the beginning, and end of the work, by which you will see the propriety of the method proposed, or the necessity of a better one, if it can be had.

Ever since I heard of the burning of the treasury department, I have been alarmed on account of the maps, charts, and plans annexed to the report respecting our southern boundary, as I had not the privilege of taking copies, and they could not be replaced but by sending to Madrid. —The report by the third article of the late treaty between the U.S. and C.M. was "to become a part of the original compact, and be equally binding on both nations," and therefore equally entitled to publicity; but I do not see that the President has taken notice of it in any of his messages to the two houses. —Neither do I find that publicity has been given to the account of the British taking our provision, (which was publick property,) tho the particulars respecting that unwarrantable business were drawn up by me at St. Mary's last month was a year and received by Mr. Pickering more than one year ago. —On my return home I intended making that communication, together with an account of Mr. Bowles's plans verbally to the President, tho perticularly detailed to Mr. Pickering in a lengthy communication dated at Appalachy October 9th. 1799 and received by him the December following, but Mr. Lee who then acted in the place of Mr. Pickering, and to whom I mentioned my desire of having the interview, told me, that he "did not see any thing, I could have to say to the President beyond the report,"—from that hint I declined pushing it any further.

The whole of my correspondence during my absence, both publick, and private, which makes three large volumes in manuscript, together with my journal, maps of rivers &c. have been open to the inspection of any man, or body of men almost ever since my return.

I should have been in the City of Washington some time[1] ago, but on account of my pay being yet withheld I could not make it convenient.

A few weeks ago I handed to the Philosophical Society an easy, and expeditious method of calculating the equation for the change of the sun's declination, when his equal Altitudes are used to regulate a Clock, or other time keeper,—it will appear in our next volume.

I have the honour to be with due respect, and sincere esteem your friend and Hbl. Servt.   ANDW. ELLICOTT

RC (DLC); at foot of text: "Thomas Jefferson Esqr. V.P. of the U.S. and President of the Senate"; endorsed by TJ as received 9 Feb. and so recorded in SJL. Dft (DLC: Ellicott Papers). Enclosures: (1) An early state, not found, of the map printed in 1804 and in later editions as a "Map of Morris's Purchase or West Geneseo in the State of New York" by Joseph and Benjamin Ellicott for the Holland Land Company; see also Sowerby, No. 3852. (2) Andrew Ellicott, *Several Methods by Which Meridional Lines May be Found with Ease and Accuracy: Recommended to the Attention of the Surveyors in the United States* (Philadelphia, 1796); Sowerby, No. 3779; Vol. 30:162n.

From 1798 to 1800 Ellicott's BROTHERS Benjamin and Joseph surveyed the large tract of the Holland Land Company in western New York. Both brothers remained in the region, Joseph, beginning in 1800, as the company's land agent (William Chazanof, *Joseph Ellicott and the Holland Land Company: The Opening of Western New York* [Syracuse, N.Y.,

1970], 25-33; DAB; *Biog. Dir. Cong.*, 959).

ACT FOR ESTABLISHING A LAND OFFICE: the May 1796 "Act providing for the Sale of the Lands of the United States, in the territory northwest of the river Ohio, and above the mouth of Kentucky river" (U.S. Statutes at Large, 1:464-9).

C.M.: Catholic Majesty; that is, King Carlos of Spain.

BRITISH TAKING OUR PROVISION: in Florida in November 1799 the crew of a wrecked Royal Navy schooner intercepted and made off with a vessel that carried supplies for Ellicott and the party surveying the boundary (Catharine Van Cortlandt Mathews, *Andrew Ellicott: His Life and Letters* [New York, 1908], 172-3, 183-4).

Ellicott's brief paper relating to THE SUN'S DECLINATION, which he submitted to the American Philosophical Society on 16 Jan., appeared in APS, *Transactions*, 6 [1809], 26-8.

[1] Word interlined in place of "weeks."

To George Jefferson

DEAR SIR   Washington Feb. 5. 1801.

I recieved yesterday your favor of Jan. 29 and instantly wrote to mr Lieper in Philadelphia, with full powers to call on Jackson & Wharton, examine the tobacco, and deduct whatever he should think reasonable from the price of any of it which might appear to have [been] damaged before the sale: for I have nothing to do[1] with damages in going to Philadelphia. [it] is possible the batteau-men may have ducked a load & said nothing a[bout] it either to you or Clarke. I will answer for Clarke that he was as uninformed as we were. their [pretence] that it had been wet before [prizing,] we may, on the ground of Clarke's honesty, affirm to be unfounded. however mr Lieper, who has often bought these crops, will be able to do [what] is right between us. I am with great esteem Dear Sir

Your's affectionately   TH: JEFFERSON

PrC (MHi); faint and blurred; at foot of text: "Mr George Jefferson"; endorsed by TJ in ink on verso.

YESTERDAY: according to SJL, TJ received the letter on 3, not 4, Feb.

¹ Preceding five words interlined.

From Edward Livingston

SIR   [5 Feb. 1801]

The enclosed will Shew the use I am making of your Horace. The only good image it contains having been Stolen I only comply with a precept of the civil law in rendering the whole composition to the original proprietor, if he should not find it too much disfigured for his acceptance it will be highly flattering to his Friend & Mo Obd Sev.

EDW LIVINGSTON

RC (DLC); undated; endorsed by TJ as a letter of 5 Feb. received on that day and so recorded in SJL.

THE ONLY GOOD IMAGE IT CONTAINS HAVING BEEN STOLEN: see below.

ENCLOSURE

Verses to Daniel McKinnen

To Daniel McKinnen Esqr

The man whom the muses have markd as their own
On whose birth they benignant have smild
His name on the turf or on 'change is unknown
He looks with contempt on that bauble a crown
Nor searches for glory in fields of renown
Where pity still weeps & horror stalks wild.

At the bar amid cunning contention & noise
No brawling attorney is he
In Assembly or Senate he never enjoys
The rewards which a profligate party employs
As shackles to fetter the free.

But where Hudson his high lands has *torn from their base*
And rolls on majestic between
There the muses have found for McKinnen a place
Where embodied by fancy those forms he may trace
Which by none but the poet are Seen

Yes happy are those Whom the Muses inspire
with their fancy their numbers divine
For me while thus rudely I snatch at the Lyre
If one Spark should elicit of poetrys fire
Tho transient that Spark Shall be thine

MS (same); in Livingston's hand; above title: "Quem tu Melpomene &c.," the opening of ode 3, book 4, of Horace's *Odes*; an endorsement by TJ, also at head of text, identifies the ode.

DANIEL MCKINNEN was a lawyer in New York State (Syrett, *Hamilton*, 22:266n; Kline, *Burr*, 1:295n).

TORN FROM THEIR BASE ... MAJESTIC BETWEEN: the words underlined in the MS, apparently by Livingston to call at-

tention to his "stolen" imagery, echo a passage in the *Notes on the State of Virginia* in which TJ described the passage of the Potomac and Shenandoah Rivers through the Blue Ridge: "In the moment of their junction they rush together against the mountain, rend it asunder, and pass off to the sea." The rivers "have torn the mountain down from its summit to its base," leaving it "cloven asunder" (*Notes*, ed. Peden, 19).

From Thomas Lomax

DEAR SIR   Pt. Tobago Feb. 5th. 1801.

A Mind placed, where Materials can not be found to strike out a Spark to vivify it, must become cold & torpid: for collision I think as necessary to the excitment, and increase of Ideas, as Flint and Steel are to fire, or friction by the Winds, a healthy exercise to Plants. I receive no information of the Political System of my Country, but what I can collect from News Papers, which come very irregularly but from which, I think I can discover under the present and assumed Term Federalism (which I call Toryism) every attempt is made to cheat, and deprive us of the Rights we supposed we had obtained by the Revolution. Daring and self-conceited, as its adherents are, I conceive it to be almost impossible, that they can be hardy enough to attempt to take from the People their constitutional Right of choosing, and thereby risk the Union, with all the Horrors and dreadful consequences that will probably issue from its dissolution. Yet I have my Fears upon this occasion, and sincerely wish they may prove to be groundless. I well remember my Sentiments at the close of the Revolutionary War, were to bury in oblivion the distinction of Whig & Tory, in hopes that Harmony, the most desirable Thing in Society might be effected, and that the Tories having been disappointed in their Expectations, and the omnipotency of their Deity, would, from gratitude, have coalesced with us, and become useful Citizens under a Popular Representative Governmt. I think now it was an erroneous Opinion, and that I might as well have supposed, that Milton's, Out-Casts, from Heaven, taken into its Bosom again, would become honest & useful Members in its Councils. There are political, as well as religious Jesuits; both pursuing the same secret means, for the deception of Mankind, and to draw them off from the Ways; which would lead to Truth & Light, into Darkness and Error. I am not in the least surprised when I see a Man quit his bad Habits and put on better; but it is a matter of the greatest astonishment to me, when I see Saints turn Sinners. But such I beleive have been the Effects, in this Country, of political Jesuitism, and its principal Instrument Sophistry. It appears to me that the last malevolent Effort of the Federalists, is to confuse entangle the Affairs of Governmt. in such a manner, that their Successors will not be able, or have patience to undo it. In this I hope they will be deceived. I sincerely congratulate you in the favorable Opinion; which the virtuous Part of your Countrymen have evinced, by the confidence they wish to repose in you. Knowing the preciousness of your Time, and the important Duties you are engaged in, I must beg that you will pardon this Intrusion, from one who feels the most sincere Esteem and Friendship for you, and who is with due Respect Dear Sir Yor. Mot. Obdt. Hmbl. Servt. THO. LOMAX

RC (DLC); endorsed by TJ as received 20 Feb. and so recorded in SJL.

From Philip Mazzei

5 Febb., 1801

Siccome il bastimento che deve portar la mia lettera non partirà si presto come si credeva, mi determino a dirle qualche cosa dei mali della povera Italia, che nella precedente ò solamente accennati. Le devastazioni ed i bisogni delle armate di tutte le Potenze guerreggianti sul continente, l'ànno ridotta ad una penosissima scarsezza di tutti i generi d'uso, soprattutto di quei di prima necessità, e la pirateria inglese impedisce che le ne vengano d'oltre mare. Alle frequenti eccessive contribuzioni forzate si aggiunge il ladroneccio dei Generali, Commissari, Comandanti di piazza, e di tutti quei che ànno potuto e possono direttamente o indirettamente rubare. I complicati mezzi d'estorsione inventati per un tal ladroneccio giungono fino ad interrompere le necessarie giornaliere operazioni del commercio interno. L'esser l'Italia quasi affatto spogliata di denaro e d'ogni altra cosa di pregio non è il peggior dei mali. Non si parla più della perdita delle sublimi opere di Pittura e Scultura, tanto son fisse le menti nella contemplazione di mali più prossimi e più sensibili. Questi mali vanno giornalmente crescendo e potrebbero ben condurci ad una fame delle più terribili, nell'aspettativa di conseguenze più funeste ancora. . . Parlerò adesso di mali d'un'altra specie.

Le rivoluzioni del nuovo e del vecchio mondo ànno dovuto necessariamente dar luogo a delle riflessioni e a dei ragionamenti su i diritti dell'uomo. I Governi d'Italia, per timore e-o per orgoglio, crederon proprio di sostituire alle leggi la violenza, ed estesero la persecuzione a tutti quei che per il più leggiero e [. . .] indizio supposero nemici del dispotismo. L'aver talenti superiori al comune degli uomini divenne un delitto. Io non m'impegnerei di trovarci in Italia 30 persone tali, che non siano state perseguitate. Il Governo di Napoli ne diede l'esempio, ed è stato il più feroce. Par che abbia voluto immolar delle vittime all'ombre dell'Ar. e Mon. francesi. Ella ne avrà probabilmente veduto qualcosa sulle gazzette. Ci saranno in Italia 300,000 famiglie almeno in varie guise straziate senz'aver'offeso in verun conto le leggi. Nell'incluso stampato si à un saggio della condotta di chi prese in Toscana le redini del governo dopo la partenza delle truppe Francesi il 17 Luglio 1799, e le lasciò fuggendo al ritorno delle medesime il 16 d'8bre 1800. Mediante l'assenza del Granduca il Ministro inglese Windham brigò, il Senato fiorentino si fece reggente sotto i suoi auspicii, e ne ottenne poi da Vienna l'approvazione con espressioni molto lusinghevoli. Uno dei primi decreti di quel Corpo composto di fanatismo, d'ignoranza, e di viltà, fù che si processassero tutti quei che il popolo indicasse come sospetti di giacobinismo. Lo voce popolo era prostituita, poiché bastava l'indicazione di 2, o 3 furfanti, e i processi si facevano coll'istesse regole del defunto tribunale inquisitorio. Questo era dunque un coltello di vendetta posto in mano a qualunque scellerato, e conseguentemente gli uomini più soggetti all'invidia erano in maggior pericolo degli altri. Tre Senatori, non meno portati per la persona del Granduca e per il governo granducale di chiunque del loro ceto, essendo dotati di probità, e conoscendo e valutando la giustizia e la ragione, furono indicati come giacobini, e in 15 mesi non si venne a veruna decisione sul loro conto, per tenergli lontani dal Senato; perché si suppose con molta probabilità, che si sarebbero opposti a tutto ciò che è stato fatto. In questa Città, dopo 6, o 7 mesi di continove persecuzioni e incarcerazioni, si vedde affissa da mano ignota una lista di circa 20 soggetti indicati come giacobini, senza darne ragione alcuna. La detta lista fù rinnuovata più volte, e sempre coll'aggiunta di nuovi soggetti. Finalmente, dopo qualche mese, volendo i Reggenti dello Stato aderire al desiderio, probabilmente d'un solo e anonimo, e che non ardiva neppur di presentarsi ai loro tribunali dove ogni furfante era molto ben accolto, purché si presentasse come accusatore, ordinarono che se ne facesse processo. Io fui del numero dei processati; le accuse furono 4, e terminarono con un'interrogazione. 1.° *d'aver frequentata la bottega del Migliaresi.*

Questi era un libraio, la cui bottega, non frequentavo, perché la maggior parte di quei che vi si trattenevano mi dispiaceva. 2do. *d'essere stato Amico del Castinelli, del Vaccà, e del Lazzerini.* Soggetti di molto merito, veri amici miei, che avevano emigrato, e che son rimpatriati dopo il ritorno dei Francesi. 3.° *d'essere stato nominato come uno dei più zelanti attori nella revoluzione Americana.* 4.° *d'essere stato amico di Condorcet, del Duca de la Rochefoucauld, del Marchese de la Fayette, e di tutti i più illustri rivoluzionarii francesi.* La domanda fù: *Qual condotta io tenni durante il soggiorno dei francesi in Toscana?*

Troppo ci vorrebbe a scrivere le mie risposte. Le dirò solamente, che non possono dispiacere né ai miei amici Europei, né ai miei Concittadini Americani, e che non mancai d'indicare il mio sommo disprezzo della frivolità delle accuse e di chi ne aveva ordinato il processo. Feci ancor più. In una lettera ostensibile a quel Paoletti nominato nell'incluso stampato, mio antico amico, e uno dei più stimati criminalisti esistenti, dopo d'aver parlato dell'irregolarità del mio processo, detto che niuno qui à diritto sulla mia persona mentre rispetto le Leggi, e dichiarato che a suo tempo saprò farmi render conto della temeraria impertinenza di chiamarmi *ad pedes*: soggiunsi: "Per altro ne son contentissimo, perché in questa generale esaltazion dei furfanti, e quasi general persecuzione dei galantuomini, mi sarei creduto umiliato vedendomi negletto."

5 Feb., 1801

As the ship which is to carry my letter will not leave as early as it was believed, I have decided to tell you something about the evils of poor Italy, to which in my previous letter I simply alluded. The devastations and the needs of the armies of all the powers at war on the Continent have reduced her to a most painful scarcity of all articles of general use, especially those of first necessity, and English piracy prevents their importation from overseas. To the frequent, excessive forced contributions, there is added the robbery by generals, commissaries, fortress commanders, and all those who have been or are able to steal directly or indirectly. The complicated means of extortion invented for such robbery go as far as disrupting the necessary daily operations of internal trade. The fact that Italy is almost completely despoiled of both money and any other valuable thing is not the worst of her woes. No longer do we talk of the loss of sublime paintings and sculptures, so much do our minds concentrate upon the contemplation of more immediate and sensible evils. These evils are daily growing, and could throw us into a most terrible famine, with the prospect of even more baleful consequences—I will now speak of evils of another kind.

The revolutions of the new and the old world have inevitably stimulated reflections and discussions concerning the rights of man. The governments of Italy, out of fear and/or pride, deemed it appropriate to replace the law by violence, and extended persecution to all those who for the slightest [. . .] suspicion they believed to be enemies of despotism. To have talents superior to those of the common man became a crime. I would not undertake to find thirty such men in Italy who have not been persecuted. The government of Naples set the example and has been the most ferocious. It seems that it wanted to sacrifice victims to the ghosts of the French aristocracy and monarchy. You will probably have read something about it in the gazettes. There must be in Italy 300,000 families at least racked one way or another without having infringed any law at all. The enclosed printed sheet gives a sample of the behaviour of those who seized the reins of government in Tuscany after the departure of the French troops on 17 July 1799, and then gave them up as they took flight when the French soldiers came back on 15 Oct. Owing to the absence of the Grand Duke, the English minister, Wind-ham, intrigued, and the Florentine Senate, under his auspices, assumed the regency, and later they obtained Vienna's approval in very flattering terms. One of the earliest decrees of that body made up of fanatics, ignoramuses, and cowards was to put on trial all those whom the people pointed out as suspects of Jacobinism. The word "people" was prostituted, since the evi-dence of two or three rogues was enough, and trials took place under rules similar to those as under the late Inquisition tribunal. Therefore this was a knife of revenge in the hands of any scoundrel, and as a consequence the men who were most likely to be envied were the ones in greater danger than anyone else. Three senators, no less loyal to the person of the Grand Duke and the Grand Duke's government than any other person in their rank, being upright, and knowing and valuing justice and reason, were pointed out as Jacobins, and for fifteen months no decision was taken about their case in order to keep them away from the Senate; for it was assumed that most likely they would have opposed all that was done. In this city, after six or seven months of uninterrupted persecutions and imprisonments, a list appeared, posted up by unknown hands, of twenty people said to be Jacobins, without any reason being given. The said list was renewed several times, each time new names being added to it. At last, after a few months, as the regents of the state wished to adhere to the desire probably of one single and anonymous man, who did not dare even to appear in their courts where any rogue was most welcome, provided he appeared as an accuser, ordered them to be put on trial. I was one of those tried; the charges were four, and they were followed by a question. 1st. *That I frequented Migliaresi's shop.* He was a bookseller whose shop I did not frequent, because I did not like most of the people who spent time there. 2nd. *That I was a friend of Castinelli, Vaccà, and Lazzerini,* men of great merit, true friends of mine, who had emigrated, and who have come back after the return of the French. 3rd. *That I have been named as one of the most zealous activists in the American Revolution.* 4th. *That I had been a friend of Condorcet, of the Duke de la Rochefoucauld, of the Marquis de la Fayette, and of all the most illustrious French revolutionists.* The question was: *What was my behaviour during the stay of the French in Tuscany?*

It would be too long to write my answers. I will say only that they cannot displease either my European friends, or my American fellow-citizens, and that I did not miss the opportunity of showing my utmost contempt for the frivolity of the charges and of those who had ordered the trial. I did even more. In an open letter to the Paoletti named in the enclosed printed sheet, an old friend of mine, and one of the most esteemed criminologists in existence, after speaking of the irregularities of my trial, saying that no one has a right to my person so long as I keep the law and declaring that in due course I shall make sure to bring them to account for the temerarious impertinence of summoning me *ad pedes*, I added: "Otherwise I am very glad of it, for in this general exaltation of rogues, and almost general persecution of men of honor, I would have felt humiliated had I found myself neglected."

FC (DLC: Mazzei Papers); in Mazzei's hand. Recorded in SJL as received from Pisa on 23 May. Enclosure not found.

To Martha Jefferson Randolph

My dear Martha   Washington Feb. 5. 1801.

Yours of Jan. 31. is this moment put into my hands, and the departure of the post obliges an answer on the same day. I am much afflicted to learn that your health is not good, and the particular derangement of your stomach. this last is the parent of many ills, and if any degree of abstinence will relieve you from them it ought to be practised. perhaps in time it may be brought to by beginning with a single one of the hostile articles; taking a very little of it at first, & more & more as the stomach habituates itself to it. in this way the catalogue may perhaps be enlarged by article after article. I have formed a different judgment of both Anne & Jefferson from what you do; of Anne positively, of Jefferson possibly. I think her apt, intelligent, good humored & of soft & affectionate dispositions, & that she will make a pleasant, amiable and respectable woman. of Jefferson's dispositions I have formed a good opinion, & have not suffered myself to form any either good or bad of his genius. it is not every heavy-seeming boy which makes a man of judgment, but I never yet saw a man of judgment who had not been a heavy seeming boy, nor knew a boy of what are called sprightly parts become a man of judgment. but I set much less store by talents than good dispositions: and shall be perfectly happy to see Jefferson a good man, industrious farmer, & kind & beloved among all his neighbors: by cultivating these dispositions in him, and they may be immensely strengthened by culture, we may ensure his & our happiness: and genius itself can propose no other object.—nobody can ever have felt so severely as myself the prostration of family society from the circumstance you mention. worn down here with pursuits in which I take no delight, surrounded by enemies & spies catching & perverting every word which falls from my lips or flows from my pen, and inventing where facts fail them, I pant for that society where all is peace and harmony, where we love & are beloved by every object we see. and to have that intercourse of soft affections hushed & suppressed by the eternal presence of strangers goes very hard indeed; & the harder as we see that the candle of life is burning out, so that the pleasures we lose are lost forever. but there is no remedy. the present manners & usages of our country are laws we cannot repeal. they are altering by degrees; & you will live to see the hospitality of the country reduced to the visiting hours of the day, & the family left to tranquility in the evening. it is wise therefore under the necessity of our present situation to view the pleasing side of the medal: and to consider that these visits are evidences of the general esteem which we have been all our lives trying to merit. the character of those we recieve is very different from the loungers who infest the houses of the wealthy in general: nor can it be relieved in our case but by a revolting conduct which would undo the whole labor of our lives. it is a valuable circumstance that it is only thro' a particular portion of the year that these inconveniences arise.—the election by the H. of R. being on Wednesday next, & the next our post day, I shall be able to tell you something certain of it by my next letter. I believe it will be as the people have wished; but this depends on the will of a few moderate men; and they may be controuled by their party. I long to see the time approach when I can be returning to you, tho' it may be for a short time only. these are the only times that existence is of any value to me. continue then to love me my ever dear Martha, and to be assured that to yourself, your sister & those dear to you, every thing in my life is devoted. ambition has no hold on me but thro' you. my personal affections would fix me for ever with you. present me affectionately to mr Randolph. kiss the dear little objects of our mutual love, and be assured of the constancy & tenderness of mine to you. Adieu.   Th: Jefferson

RC (DLC); at foot of first page: "Mrs. Randolph." PrC (ViU: Edgehill-Randolph Papers).

From George Jefferson

Dear Sir   Richmond 6th. Febr. 1801.

I am duly favor'd with yours of the 1st. and have in reply to inform you, that the mode by which you propose to pay us the balance which

Mr. Randolph falls in our debt, is perfectly agreeable to me; as any other would have been, which had been so to you, or to himself.

I will attend to your direction respecting the molasses, as it may now be cased with safety.

I am Dear Sir Your Very humble servt.　　　Geo. Jefferson

RC (MHi); at foot of text: "Thomas Jefferson esqr."; endorsed by TJ as received 11 Feb. and so recorded in SJL.

From Craven Peyton

Dear Sir　　　　　　　　　　　　　　Shadwell 6th Feby 1801

In consequence of James Hendersons being absent it has prevented my Answering yours of the 16 Jany. sooner. immediately on his return I informd him I woud purchase the two shears of Land on the turms which he had offard me he then informd of his purchasing them of Two of his Brothars of the Ages of 20½ & 19½ years but he woud. Oblige him self to make a good title & I shoud have them on the turms which Mr. Kerr soald me, to which I exceeded to On Friday next we are to Close finally, & I shall push him to get John Henderson to Join in the Obligation with him, was I acting for myself I shoud suppose him sufficient. Watson & Snelson valud. the flat Land at 60/ the Arrible fields at 30/ & forrest Lands at 8/ 10/ ℔ Acre including the Widows dower Lands & improvements, it makes each share Worth £102.2s0d the improvements I beliave were valued by your self, which Are the House the Widow lives in & the House above, I made application to Tucker Woodson whom James Henderson soald One share to, he Observd his Cost him five Hundred Dollars therefore he coud not take less, & was there to be an opinion that you wishd to purchase they Coud. not be had I think for near that money. J. Henderson is Anxious to have division. On a supposition that you might wish to be present, I have as yet prevented it. he is fully impressd with An idea that his dam is to come down this summar, by removeing the Mill a few Hundred yards below Nature has done so much for the situation that it will require no dam, On a division shoud that spot fall to him Or some of the Legatees that are quite young he woud. remove the Mill instantly at A very small expence, you will please let me hear from you, Any thing furthar which I can do will give me pleasure. As to Money I hope you will consult your Own Convenience, we are all exceedingly Anxious to no the decision of Congress on the ensuing Election. shoud they not Act in conformity to the wish of three fourths of the People the consequences might become very alarming

I Am with much Respt. Yr Mst. Ob st.   C Peyton

RC (MHi); endorsed by TJ as received 12 Feb. and so recorded in SJL; also endorsed by TJ: "date of purchase from Jas. L. Hend."

the widow: Elizabeth Lewis Henderson, widow of Bennett Henderson (d. 1793). For TJ's transactions and the contested Henderson property, see MB, 2:1047n and Vol. 31:197-200.

yours of the 16 jany: TJ actually wrote to Peyton on 15 Jan., above.

From Thomas Mann Randolph

Th:M.R. to Th: Jefferson,   Feb. 7. 1801

The approach of the 11th. Feb. makes the people here *breath long* with suspence their axiety is so great. I cannot yet have the least apprehension: I had sometime since made the reasoning that when one only was wanting & that one might be either of Many there could be no ground to fear: the least possible *chance* of immeasurable evil will however naturally produce more alarm than the *certainty* of small Misfortune.

We are all well but impatient for the fine season and your return. Lillies industry has benefited our worthy & beloved neighbour Dr. Bache: he could not hire a hand: last night two additional came to Lillie which, not wanting, I have made him refuse as the lateness gave him a right to do; and of course being to hire to another Dr. Bache gets them. Dinsmore sends the acc't. of the nail rod this post: the wine has not come but shall be well recieved when it does. Your directions are followed exactly by Lillie except as to the dividing fence which circumstances make proper to finish now & the two hands to blowing when he does not like to separate from him. with warmest attachment   Th: M. Randolph

RC (ViU: Edgehill-Randolph Papers); endorsed by TJ as received 20 Feb. and so recorded in SJL.

DINSMORE SENDS THE ACC'T.: the let-ter from James Dinsmore of 6 Feb., recorded in SJL as received from Monticello on the 12th, has not been found. A letter TJ wrote to Dinsmore on 18 Feb. is also missing.

To Isaac Briggs

SIR   Washington Feb. 8. 1801.

I have to acknolege the reciept of your favor of Jan. 24. on the subject of the establishment of Agricultural societies, a subject which had formerly occupied my attention to a certain degree, and had been recently called up again by a proposition from the President of the board of agriculture in England. the difficulty in this country is to call into activity some principle which will command the services of the lovers of agriculture here. if money be resorted to, we are hardly rich enough to do much by private contributions, and had the general government authority by the constitution to apply the money of the union to this purpose, it would probably end in providing resources for a few idle favorites & in little further. how far it may be practicable to get the agricultural societies now existing in the different states, to unite in a general committee at the seat of government, and by this means produce an union of effort, which might be communicated to the other states not yet having such societies, is worthy consideration. that central committee might be formed by each state conferring membership on such of it's representatives or Senators in Congress, or on such officers of the genl. government residing here, as possess zeal, for this first of all human callings, and the basis of all others. the ideas expressed in your letter, as well as some parts of the English plan, might perhaps be pursued in this way. I do not know that I can individually do much towards the promotion of such an establishment: however I have for some time past had in contemplation to make the proposition to the existing societies. the members from the different states being necessarily called here once a year, might be able to devise & to pursue some plan effectual for the object. certainly no endeavors of mine would be spared to forward it. I am Sir with respect

Your most obedt. servt   TH: JEFFERSON

PrC (DLC); at foot of text: "Mr. Isaac Briggs. Sharon"; endorsed by TJ in ink on verso.

RECENTLY CALLED UP AGAIN: see Sir John Sinclair to TJ, 6 June 1800.

To Simon Chaudron

                                       Washington Feb. 8. 1801.

Th: Jefferson presents his compliments to M. Chaudron. he has safely recieved the watch by mr Richards, and in good order. he waits his return to Philadelphia, which will be some days hence, to remit him the price, as he finds it impracticable to get bills here on Philadelphia. he supposes the second hand has been omitted because the wheel on which it would have been put would have shewn irregularly on the plate. however, in a machine whose utility is chiefly consulted, he would have sacrificed appearance to that. he prays M. Chaudron to accept his respectful salutations.

PrC (MHi); endorsed by TJ in ink on verso.

From William McDowell

Sir,   Kentucky Feby 8th. 1801

From a sence of the duty I owe to you as well for your instruction and friendship, whilst I [lived] at Colo. Nichs. Lewes's as a student of the Law, as for the use of your books, and other Political considerations, I feel happy in having it in my power to congratulate you on your election, to the *Presidential Chair*; you have had the united suffrage of this state, and will (I flatter myself) long continue to deserve well of your country—

From a confidence, that it will be your wish to do Justice, & Support harmony & Concord throughout our government; I trust no change will be made in this state without good cause.

An attempt it is whispered, will be made to *Oust* my Brother Saml McDowell jr. from the office of *Marshal*,   In consequence of this I have taken the liberty of enclosing the Certificate of the Judge of the District Court of the United States for the Kentucky District, & of the Clerk & principal Attornies, who practice in sd Court, stating the charactor my Brother is entitled to; and the manner in which he has transacted the business of his office; in addition to those certificates I can assure you no complaint has ever within my knowledge been alledged agt him—

At the time he first accepted the office, it was by no means profitable, but in fact from the exposed situation of this country to the incursions of the savages, and the opposition to the excise Law, it was extremely hazardous to execute a great share of the process—The Office for about 18 months past has been profitable, this will induce a number no doubt to aim at the office as soon as you qualify, and the hopes of some of those offering will probably be founded on a desire to have a change of the officers, under the govt. at this time that they may derive some advantage there from—

[561]

A Mr. Jas Brown who has been long an enemy to a Young brother of mine who has in some instances acted as a Deputy Marshal, has I am told sent forward the affedavit of a trifling Charactor by the name of *Stephenson*, which has been taken *ex parte*, to prove that my young Brother had demanded extra fees, the truth is, a Mr. Trotter the party ordering writs offered extra fees, as the writs could not be executed without riding in the night &c and the afsd Brown who was requested to fill up blank writs, Antedated the writs a month; my Brother found fault with this, as he would not probably have time to execute, & then from the date it would be Supposed he had not done his duty, there then being but three or four days before return day and more than 150 miles to ride, Brown told him not to be a *fool*, a quarrel ensued and now I am told Brown means to hand this agt. the *Marshal*, & by this means if possible get a friend of his appointed— My young Brother, would now have Obtained the Certificate of Mr Trotter a Mercht of Charactor, but he is gone to Philadelphia but I consider this as foreign to the continuance of my Brother Saml McDowell jr in office, or his reappointment, he stands now commissioned untill the first of March 1802—& from the certificates will be equal if not Superior in Charactor to any that offer, and as those most concerned can find no fault, I trust the meddling Interested conduct of those aiming at the office will be treated with contempt

I have the honor to be with every consideration your Obt H St

Wm Mc.Dowell

RC (DNA: RG 59, LAR); torn; addressed: "The Honble. Thomas Jefferson Vice President City of Washington"; franked; postmarked Danville, Ky., 10 Feb.; endorsed by TJ as received 13 Mch. and so recorded in SJL. Enclosures: (1) Certificate of Joseph Hamilton Daveiss, 21 Jan. 1801, stating that he has served in the District Court of the U.S. for Kentucky for two or three years and "had very full and continual opportunity of seeing, and being concerned" with Samuel McDowell's official conduct as marshal; that he has always "remarked the punctuallity vigilance, and industry of Mr McDowell and his deputies" and that he has "known no ministerial office of such a nature, executed in a manner so examplery"; that although he has recently heard that his deputies requested extra fees, as far as he knows, McDowell has "given public satisfaction." (2) Certificate of James Hughes, Lexington, 23 Jan. 1801, stating that in his several years of practice before the court he has always believed "that Samuel McDowell has faithfully discharged the duties of his office" and knows "of no cause of complaint against him." (3) Certificate of William Murray, Frankfort, 24 Jan. 1801, stating that he has served in the District Court of the U.S. for the Kentucky district since its establishment and during this time McDowell has always conducted his office with "Punctuality and Fidelity" and has done nothing to warrant his removal or prevent his reappointment. (4) Certificate of Thomas Todd, Frankfort, 26 Jan. 1801, stating that he has practiced several years in the U.S. district court and "observed great punctuality vigilance & attention" in the marshal and that McDowell's conduct, as far as he knows, is "unexceptionable" in every respect. (5) Certificate of Isham Talbot, 31 Jan. 1801, stating that during the one or two years he has practiced law before the U.S. district court for Kentucky, he has observed no "impropriety or misconduct" in McDowell's official capacity. (6) Certificate of Thomas Tunstall, undated, stating that as clerk of the District Court of the U.S. for the Kentucky District since 1795, he has found McDowell's conduct as marshal "strictly conformable" to his duties, "And as to his private character it is unquestionably fair." (7) Certificate of Harry Innes, 31 Jan. 1801, stating that as far as he has observed, McDowell's conduct as marshall "has ever been consistant with the important duties of the office"; that if anything improper had occurred in his business routine "no information has ever been made to the Court respecting it"; and that in his opinion, "founded on an acquaintance of sixteen years," McDowell's moral character stood "unimpeached" (MSS in DNA: RG 59, LAR, on four sheets; Trs in same, endorsed: "Certificates in favor of S. Mc.Dowell," attested by William McDowell).

Born in Rockbridge County, Virginia, William McDowell (1762-1821), lawyer and judge, moved with his parents Samuel and Mary McClung McDowell and siblings to Danville, Kentucky, in 1783. William served as a representative from Mercer County in the Virginia House of Delegates during the 1787-88 term. On 26 May 1787 he was elected a member of "The Political Club," a debating society founded in Danville a few months earlier, the first meeting being held at his father's house. The participants discussed the new Constitution and separation from Virginia, and formulated ideas that would be contained in the first Kentucky constitution. After the state's admittance to the union, McDowell served as Kentucky's first auditor and in the state legislature. He married Margaretta Madison (Thomas Speed, *The Political Club, Danville, Kentucky, 1786-1790, Being an Account of an Early Kentucky Society from the Original Papers Recently Found* [Louisville, 1894], vii, 58-62, 100-2, 111, 136, 144-51; Lewis Collins, *Collins' Historical Sketches of Kentucky. History of Kentucky*, 2 vols. [Covington, Ky., 1878], 1:508, 2:92; DAB, 2:291-3; Leonard, *General Assembly*, 165).

William Clarke, appointed U.S. attorney for the district of Kentucky in December 1796, also provided a certificate in favor of Samuel McDowell, at the marshal's request, dated 2 June 1801, at Bourbon, Kentucky, in which he stated that McDowell had requested advice respecting fees for mileage and that he had informed him "that in my opinion, he was entitled to mileage in these cases." Clarke stated that as far as he had "discovered" the marshal had the "character of a good Officer." He continued: "His character in private life is amiable, and I do not think that the said Office of Marshal could be filled with a more suitable person." In December 1800 Adams appointed Clarke to the chief justiceship of the Indiana Territory and Joseph Hamilton Daveiss, author of the first enclosed certificate described above, U.S. attorney for the Kentucky district (MS in DNA: RG 59, LAR, endorsed: "Wm. Clarke in fav. of Saml. Mc.Dowell as marshal of Kentucky"; JEP, 1:217, 357).

YOUNG BROTHER OF MINE: a deposition by Thomas Stevenson (Stephenson), dated 28 Feb. 1801, identified Joseph McDowell as the deputy marshal who demanded extra fees (MS in DNA: RG 59, LAR). James Brown specified the charges against Samuel McDowell, Jr., in a letter to his brother Senator John Brown on 24 Feb. 1801, by which he forwarded "some documents procured after a few hours examination in the Clerks Office which will throw light on some parts of the Marshalls conduct and convince every impartial mind that he has not discharged his duty with that integrity which should mark the transactions of one who fills so important a Station" (same).

From James Barbour of Kentucky

Kentucky Garrard County
near Danville February 9th [1801]

I heartily & Sincearly Congratulate on the triumph of Republicanism over the Administration party it gives Pleasure to nearly all the people of this Country (those holding offices under the General Government & a few others excepted) it is said that many complaints will be made against the Marshall of this State, should he be removed as it is a pecuniary office no doubt many applications will be made, shoud it be given as a reward for past Services I think none can apply with more propriety than my self, & I can the more freely say so to you as you were personally Acquainted with part of my Services when you were Governor of Virginia & my self County Lieut. of Culpeper, in which Capacity I served all the eight years of the War, I was employ'd nearly half my time in Raising Minutemen Regulars eighteen months men & drafting the Militia providing Cloathing provisions Arms Blanketts & & all this was by law put upon the Commanding Officers of the Militia & Superintended the Collection of [his?] Taxes. All this I did do Chearfully & never received one Shilling for my Services & Culpeper being one of the [larg]est County in the State have[ing] [. . .] made it so much the more troublesome. surely eight years [. . .] [some unpaid], tho I shou'd not Ask it only that it can be given without burthening the People, you will have applications from some of the officers of the Army lately disbanded who has been receiving our Countrys money for a considerable time for which they have not render'd one hours Service

I am Sir with much respect your most Obedt Servt

JAS. BARBOUR

RC (DNA: RG 59, LAR); faint; endorsed by TJ. Recorded in SJL as received 13 Mch. 1801.

James Barbour (1734-1804) served in the Virginia House of Burgesses from 1761 to 1765 representing Culpeper and in 1775 was county lieutenant and an officer in the revolutionary army. He served as a judge in the first court held in Kentucky, where he headed a commission, appointed by the Virginia legislature, to settle disputed land titles. An owner of property north of Madison Court House, Barbour was involved as an agent for James Madison, Sr., in a Kentucky land claim dispute (Raleigh Travers Green, *Genealogical and Historical Notes on Culpeper County, Virginia. Embracing a Revised and Enlarged Edition of Dr. Philip Slaughter's History of St. Mark's Parish* [Culpeper, Va., 1900], 136; Daughters of the American Revolution, *DAR Patriot Index* [Washington, D.C., 1966], 34; Madison, *Papers, Sec. of State Ser.*, 2:223-5, 273, 402-3; Leonard, *General Assembly*, 91).

MARSHALL OF THIS STATE: Samuel McDowell, Jr.

From John Barnes

Geo: Town, 9th feby, 1801—

It Occurs, to J Barnes, that the salaries or Compensations are all regularly Accounted for—and Warrants issued therefor, immediately After, 31st. Mar: 30th June. 30th sepr & 31st decr. And that, in Case any One Office, is closed—or Vacated—by death, resignation—or removal, &c. each Accot. is made up, to the day it happens—but the Accot. is not Usually passed—untill the expiration of the Quarterage.

In like Manner, when an Office—commencing—viz—As that of the 4th: March—By removal from another the former a/c will be made up—at the End of the Qr. viz from 31st. Decr: to 3d. March—the Other a/c commencing—4th March, will be made Up—to 31st Mar: seperately, and the two Warrts. issued immediately After—

in Manner following viz. for 2 Mos: & 3 days,

Compensation, from 31st. decr to 3d. Mar a $5000. is   875.

And from the 3d, Mar to 31st: do is 28 days 25,000   <u>1875.</u>

$2750.

J Barnes beg leave to Assure you—his resources—are Amply. sufft: for any present demands you may have Occasion for—exclusive of Mr Sts: $1700—lodged in Bank of Columbia and Genl K— 600 & upwds. as well P.Ms: $567. in Bank US.—at your Order.

Under these circumstances, JB. intreat you wd: not hesitate a moment—in addressing any Order, you may Occasionaly require—as no possible inconveniency can intervene. in preference to any other expedient—unless you may, please—to direct Otherwise—

RC (ViU: Edgehill-Randolph Papers); in Barnes's hand. Recorded in SJL as a letter of 9-10 Feb. received 11 Feb. 1801.

The funds in the BANK OF COLUMBIA and the Bank of the United States belonged to William Short, Tadeusz Kosciuszko, and Philip Mazzei.

From Horatio Gates

DEAR SIR   New York 9th: February 1801.

When Men, like Women, go astray—there is no knowing where they will Stop. One act of folly, or Wickedness, brings another after it and down right Prostitution is the Consequence.—Our Feds: began with the Project of putting up Burr against You, and this on the Hollow principle with respect to him, that he would be lost to the

Republican Party, and that at another Election he could be set aside without Difficulty or Danger. This project was however quite as fool-ish as that of the Cardinals who made Sixtus Quintus Pope, because they believed him to be Old, & Decrepid, and short Lived;—for Burr like Sixtus, were he once in the Chair, might shew them that it was more easy to make a Chief than to unmake him.—as far as their pol-icy can be gathered from their Friends here, they seem to have given Burr Up, except only to Use him, as an Instrument in defeating your Election.—the regular consequence of which is that we are to be blessed with an Experiment, either of an Interregnum, or an Usurpa-tion! this is however so Abominable in itself, and so mischievous to All, that no Man of Honour, or Conscience, can join them in it. Some of their Leaders may be fit for Murders, Stratagems, and Spoils, but they are not all Leaders, and if your Phalanx is but kept in good order, and good Countenance you have nothing to fear—there is a wide difference between "Speaking Daggers, & using them"; should we however be brought to such a Crisis, there is enough of Spirit & Patriotism in the Country to save it, and the sooner Col: Pride's Purge is administered to the Usurpers the better.—The Public Mind is a good deal agitated on the Subject of the French Treaty, nor is there any difference of Opinion on the Subject—we Unite in thinking it ought to have been Adopted.—

My Old acquaintance John Adams seems determined to close his Administration as he began it; Improper appointments to Office, makes one of the Characters of his Reign. We have lately heard that he has appointed a Boy of the Name of Stockton, to be Secretary at War, who if he knows anything of his business must have acquired it, from Coke upon Littleton, or some other great Law Warrior. When a Ministry in England made Lord Winchelsea first Lord of The Ad-miralty,—Admiral Vernon said in Parliament, "He was like a Mon-key in a China Shop, where he did much Mischief without knowing it"—I know no department where œconomy and Success are more in-separably connected with Knowledge, than that of War; and just by the Way—if when you are Seated, where you unquestionably ought to be, you should want a Secretary at War, who knows his Duty, and is every way Qualified to do it, cast your Eyes upon Armstrong: there you will find Abilities, Honour, and Integrity:—I know not how far it might suit his Family circumstances &c, to Accept an Appointment of this Sort, but this I do know, that no Man of the Old Army would better Suit the Office.

I have Blunder'd in writing this page the wrong way of the Paper, but you will excuse an Error of that sort in one of 73; who is scarcely steaddy in any thing, but his Republican Principles, and in being your faithfull Friend, & Servant   HORATIO GATES.

RC (DLC); endorsed by TJ as received 15 Feb. and so recorded in SJL.

Felice Peretti, a Franciscan, was 64 years old when he became Pope SIXTUS QUINTUS (V) in 1585. Described as "energetic, violent, and inflexible," he was called "the iron pope," and when he died in 1590, the people of Rome tore down his statue (J. N. D. Kelly, *The Oxford Dictionary of Popes* [New York, 1986], 271-3).

COL: PRIDE'S PURGE: on 6 Dec. 1648 Colonel Thomas Pride and his soldiers kept Presbyterian moderates, who had a majority, from entering the House of Commons. The purged parliament was then controlled by those who called for the execution of King Charles I, the abolition of the monarchy, and the establishment of a Puritan Commonwealth (David Underdown, *Pride's Purge: Politics in the Puritan Revolution* [Oxford, 1971], 1-2).

On 15 Jan. President Adams nominat-

ed ardent Federalist Lucius Horatio STOCKTON, who was 32 years old and the U.S. attorney for the district of New Jersey, to serve as secretary of war in place of Samuel Dexter, who had become secretary of the Treasury. When the Senate held up the confirmation, Stockton had Adams withdraw his nomination (Ruth L. Woodward and Wesley F. Craven, *Princetonians—1784-1790—A Biographical Dictionary* [Princeton, 1991], 237-44; JEP, 1:363-4, 367-8, 370, 375, 389).

COKE UPON LITTLETON: the first part of Sir Edward Coke's *Institutes* consisted of a reprint, translation, and commentary on Sir Thomas Littleton's *Les tenures* (Coke, *The First Part of the Institutes of the Lawes of England: or a Commentary upon Littleton, not the name of the author only but of the law it selfe*, 4th ed. [London, 1639]; see Sowerby, No. 1781).

WRITING THIS PAGE THE WRONG WAY: when Gates turned the sheet over, what should have been the bottom of the verso became the top.

From Carlos Martínez de Irujo

[9 Feb. 1801]

Le Chevalier d'Yrujo presents his compliments to Mr. Jefferson, & takes the liberty to inform him that when in Philadelphia the both Houses of congress used to meet on some solemn occassion, the Speaker of the House of Representatives was in the habit of inviting him by the Sergeant at Arms & a chair was provided for him on the right side of the Speaker—He understand congress is to meet the day after to morrow in the Senate room with an object, whose result cannot but be highly pleasant to the Chevalier, & in consequence, he addresses himself to Mr. Jefferson to Know if he could flatter himself to enjoie in the Senate the same distinction he has enjoied heretofore in the House of Representatives?

RC (MoSHi: Jefferson Papers); undated; accent marks that Irujo placed over some vowels have been omitted; endorsed by TJ as a letter of 9 Feb. 1801 received on that day.

CONGRESS IS TO MEET: on this day, a Monday, the Senate declared that it would "receive the House of Representatives in the Senate Chamber, on Wednesday next, at twelve o'clock, for the purpose of being present at the opening and counting of the votes for President of the United States." The House then agreed to the rules it would follow in the event of the expected tie in electoral votes. Before adjourning on 10 Feb. the House resolved to attend the next day in the Senate chamber and appointed John Rutledge, Jr., and John Nicholas its tellers for the count, to act with one named by the Senate, William H. Wells of Delaware (JHR, 3:789-92, 796, 798).

From George Jefferson

DEAR SIR   Richmond 9th. Febr. 1801.

I have at length effected a settlement of Mr. Shorts account with Mr. Brown; the balce. of £112.1.5. which was found to be due by Mr. B. ℔ his account which you will find inclosed, I have received.   I was surprised to find that the fees which have caused a delay of 9 or 10 months in the adjustment of this account, amount only to 47/.

I shall wait for Mr. Barnes to draw for this money, or for him to direct us to forward it in notes, as we cannot procure a bill. of this be pleased to inform him.

I am Dear Sir Your Very humble servt.   GEO. JEFFERSON

RC (MHi); at foot of text: "Thos. Jefferson esqr."; endorsed by TJ as received 14 Feb. and so recorded in SJL. Enclosure not found.

From Charles Pinckney

DEAR SIR   Monday Morning [9 Feb. 1801] New York

I am this moment arrived in New York on my way to the seat of Government, it Being the only Port to which I could procure a passage at this rough Season & my arm is too lame from the accident to it to travel by land, unless very slow & with care.—I was anxious to have been with You by the 11th. & set out for that purpose but a long passage & contrary winds prevented—it now snows very much & the moment it stops & clears I propose setting out for Washington—. all the republicans in New York are anxious about Your Election & fear the Federalists are trying to defeat it—such is the report here & it makes me so anxious on the subject that I shall risque my arm to be on with you as quick as possible, for after all we have done & suffered, to be tricked out of our choice by unworthy means would be what Patience itself could scarcely endure—

I am hopeful to be in Philadelphia on Thursday & with You by to morrow week by which time I trust the Voice of our country Be attended to & its Wishes gratified in seeing you their President——I am with regard & attachment Dear sir Yours truly

CHARLES PINCKNEY

RC (DLC); partially dated; endorsed by TJ as a letter of 9 Feb. 1801, received on the 13th, and so recorded in SJL.

From Harry Innes

DEAR SIR,   Kentucky Feby. 10th. 1801

It is with extreme reluctance that I request one moment of your attention to the reading of this letter, yet the information this moment received from a friend in Lexington, relative to the probable change in the Judiciary of the U. States, which would create an additional Judge in this State & if so, that Wm. McClung would certainly be nominated to that office, compels me to write.

From a long acquaintance with Mr. McClung & a decided opportunity of becoming well acquainted with his abilities as a Lawyer I do not hesitate to declare that he is not qualified to fill that office & that there are 20 or more Attornies in Kentucky capable of filling the office with more propriety in every respect. Add to this, he is a mere creature to party & faction—as a Lawyer he was void of candour & was not able to make his way good either in the late Supreme Court for Kentucky whilst a part of Virginia, nor since in the Qr. Session Courts of this State. In case of a change, whither he took precedence of me or not I could have no confidence in him.

My situation would be extremely painful in another point of view— H. Marshall & myself are not on speaking terms—that family have imbibed all his dislikes & are my avowed enemies & have been for several years spies on my conduct, & altho' there never has been any thing personal between Mr. McClung & myself yet I fear if he meets with the appointment he will be governed by the family influence as he is married to a Sister of Genl. Marshall's & of Mrs. H.M.

My decissions on questions respecting the Excise have not been favorable to the views of the Government—as to their propriety, the candid are to determine; however, conscious of my rectitude I have furnished the Supervisor with copies of my opinions—yet no reversal has been attempted & the late Secy. of that department has considered me as hostile to the views of that party—from some circumstances I have reason to suspect the candour of the Secy. of State.

Should any change in the Judiciary take place & my information have any influence on your mind respecting the appointment of Mr.

McClung, permit me to request your influential aid in preventing it.

Was I asked to recommend upon the occasion Buckner Thruston one of the State Dist. Judges & son of Colo. Thruston of Frederick would meet my preference.

Pardon me for this intrusion, my wish to see the public good promoted is my appology—. Wishing you every happiness I am with sentiments of respect & esteem Dr Sir your friend & servt.

HARRY INNES

The appointment of H.M. would not be more unpopular

RC (DLC); at foot of text: "Thomas Jefferson Esqr."; endorsed by TJ as received 6 Mch. and so recorded in SJL.

The Judiciary Act of 13 Feb. 1801 grouped the judicial district of Kentucky with the districts of East Tennessee, West Tennessee, and Ohio to form a sixth circuit. On 24 Feb. the Senate approved John Adams's nomination, made the day before, of William MCCLUNG to be the circuit judge. McClung, a native of Rockbridge County, Virginia, lost that position in 1802 following the repeal of the Judiciary Act (JEP, 1:383, 385; U.S. Statutes at Large, 2:89-91; *Biographical Directory of the Federal Judiciary, 1789-2000* [Lanham, Md., 2001], 648).

SISTER OF GENL. MARSHALL'S & OF MRS. H.M.: Humphrey Marshall's wife was his first cousin, Anna Maria (Mary) Marshall. She was John Marshall's sister, and McClung had married their sibling,

Susan Tarleton Marshall, in 1793. Beginning in 1791 Thomas Marshall, the father of John, Anna Maria, and Susan, had been U.S. revenue inspector for Kentucky, responsible for collection of the liquor EXCISE, and from late 1794 to mid-1797 he was also a SUPERVISOR of the revenue. McClung had been named U.S. attorney for the Kentucky district in 1794, but that position, tied to enforcement of the whiskey tax, was so unpopular that McClung, like some other attorneys at the time, declined the commission. LATE SECY. OF THE DEPARTMENT: Alexander Hamilton. SECY. OF STATE: John Marshall, who by the time Innes wrote the letter above was chief justice (Marshall, *Papers*, 1:132n, 3:45n; Syrett, *Hamilton*, 9:35, 17:418, 461; Mary K. Bonsteel Tachau, *Federal Courts in the Early Republic: Kentucky, 1789-1816* [Princeton, 1978], 35-6, 69-72, 98-107; JEP, 1:160; DAB).

From Caesar A. Rodney

HONORED & DEAR SIR,   Wilmington Feby. 10th. 1801.

I had the pleasure of writing to you some time since from Philada. in answer to a letter I had the honor to receive from you whilst on a visit there.

Our legislature have adjourned after passing the canal law on such terms I hope, as will secure the execution of the design. It was not done however without a great struggle. We did not appoint any senator in the place of Dr. Latimer & I entertain considerable imputations that the next legislature will be sufficiently Republican to send a firm & zealous supporter of your administration.

We wait with a great degree of anxiety the issue of next wenesday tho' I feel confident in my own mind that it will meet the wishes of every genuine friend to American liberty. I cannot believe that any set of men will be weak or wicked enough to attempt to defeat the election of a President altogether or even to disappoint the wishes of this free nation who desire so earnestly to see you at the helm of affairs.

There is perhaps in the united States no place that will display more spontanious joy than Wilmington so much abused for its un-shaken attachment to the cause of virtue & republicanism—It will not be the mere forced effect of interested activity & exertions by sysophants & office hunters, but will flow from hearts capable of feeling a change in system which would enable us once more to hail each other "as brothers." What a happy state for this country, already we are very sensible of the beneficial effects, those who but the other day were mere firebrands are now moderate. It seems as if

"Magnus ab integro sæclorum nascitur ordo."

I suppose as the last efforts of an expiring faction some of their desparate leaders will perhaps make some faint[1] efforts to produce a little confusion but I rely on the firmness of the Republicans who at this crisis like the band of Leonidas will not desert their posts, for an easy conquest over a few desperadoes. With great esteem I remain Dr. Sir

Yours Very Sincerely   C. A. RODNEY

RC (DLC); endorsed by TJ as received 12 Feb. but mistakenly recorded in SJL as a letter of "7" not 10 Feb., received on the 12th.

FROM PHILADA.: Rodney's letter, printed at 28 Dec. 1800, was in response to TJ's letter of the 21st.

In February 1801 Governor Richard Bassett appointed Samuel White, a Federalist, as SENATOR IN THE PLACE OF

Henry LATIMER who resigned (*Biog. Dir. Cong.*; DAB, 20:114-15). A letter from Latimer to TJ of 10 Aug. 1796, recorded in SJL as received on the 26th, has not been found.

MAGNUS AB INTEGRO SÆCLORUM NASCITUR ORDO: "Time has conceived and the great Sequence of the Ages starts afresh," from Virgil's *Eclogues*, 4.5.

[1] Word added by Rodney in margin.

To Tench Coxe

DEAR SIR   Washington Feb. 11. 1801.

Your favor of Jan. 25. came to hand some days ago, and yesterday a gentleman put into my hand, at the door of the Senate chamber, the vol. of the Amer. Museum for 1798. as no letter accompanied it I took it for granted it was to bring under my eye some of it's contents. I have gone over it with satisfaction. this is the morning of the election by the H. of R. for some time past a single individual [had] declared he would by his vote make up the 9th. state. on Saturday last he changed, and it stands at present 8. one way; 6 the other & 2. divided. which of the two will be elected & whether either I deem perfectly problematical: and my mind has long been equally made up for either of the three events. if I can find out the person who brought me the volume from you I shall return it by him, because I presume it makes one of a set. if not by him, I will find some other person who may carry it to Philadelphia if not to Lancaster. very possibly it may go by a different conveyance from this letter. very probably you will learn before the reciept of either the result, or the progress at least of the election. we see already at the threshold, that if it falls on me, I shall be embarrassed by finding the offices vacant, which cannot be even temporarily filled but with advice of Senate, and that body is called on the 4th. of March, when it is impossible for the new members of Kentucky, Georgia & S. Carolina to recieve notice in time to be here. the Summons for Kentucky dated as all were Jan. 31.[1] could not go hence till the 5th. & that for Georgia did not go till the 6th. if the difficulties of the election therefore are got over, these are more & more behind, until new elections shall have regenerated the constituted authorities. the defects of our constitution under circumstances like the present, appear very great. accept assurances of the esteem & respect of Dear Sir

Your most obedt. servt   TH: JEFFERSON

RC (Carl H. Pforzheimer, Purchase, New York, 1944); stained, with word in brackets supplied from PrC; at foot of text: "Tench Coxe esq."; endorsed by Coxe. PrC (DLC).

AMER. MUSEUM: an essay by Coxe appeared in the first volume of the *American Museum*, published by Mathew Carey in 1787, and his articles continued to appear in subsequent volumes. In 1798 Carey's publication included eight numbers by Coxe. Under the signature "An American

Merchant" and dated between the 1st and 28th of March, the pieces examined neutral spoliations. When the series initially appeared in the *Philadelphia Gazette* and *Aurora*, TJ called the early numbers "excellent pieces" (*The American Museum: or, Annual Register of Fugitive Pieces, Ancient and Modern. For the Year 1798* [Philadelphia, 1799], 226-60; Cooke, *Coxe*, 99, 202, 227-8; Vol. 30:125, 168-9).

[1] Passage from "dated" to this point interlined by TJ.

From Thomas Leiper

SIR   Philada. Febry. 11th 1801

I duely received yours of the 4th. inclosing a Copy of a letter from Jackson & Wharton to Murdo and Fisher—

This day was appointed by Jackson & Wharton for a reinspecting of
your Tobacco but the snow of yesterday and to day has prevented it
but when-ever the weather will permit we have agreed it shall be
done—
I have seen some 7 or 8 sample's which is all they have opened of your
Tobacco and out of those seven or eight Hhds they have sold three—
The Tobacco is good but it is not equal in quality to what I purchased
of you last year but perhaps these Hhds may be the very worst in the
whole Crop—They are by no means pleased with their bargain and
offered the Tobacco to me at Cost and Charges which will be some
where about 7 $\frac{25}{100}$ Dollars pr. Ct.—Jackson & Wharton mentioned
to me a very singular circumstance that two of the Hhds they sold one
of them fell short in the weight 234 ℔ and the other 95 they also
shew'd me their invoice where most of the Hhds were of the same
Tare viz. 150. Ct. This by the bye is much in your favor for it is certainly a Large weight for a Tobacco Hogshead Those I had of you
were most of them about 130 Ct.

I enformed them I had full powers from you to do what was right
and should make every reasonable allowence—I was shewen one or
Two Hands which they had drawn from that Hhd it did appear to
me as if it had been hung upon a Nail for there was the mark & nail
of the head set to one side—If there should be any thing like unto
Tobacco being wet and dried again I can certainly ascertain it by
examining it and should I find there is much in that way I will certainly close with them and take the Tobacco at Cost and charges for
it will never do for them to have any thing that they can make a
Storry of—Jackson was one of McPhersons Blue's and Wharton if
possible is more on the other side than Jackson he sued me sometime ago for £17.5— I know he had nothing in View but to have to
say with his party that he had done such a thing—How ever the
Temper of mind is much subsided but in case they should make a
storry of it I wish you to write Gibson & Jefferson and Clark for a
true account of the matter for I am affraid the Tobacco falling so far
short of the weight that the Boat men perhaps has been playing
tricks for I know they cannot put so Tobacco that been wet an dried
again into a Hhd as if it had been in its original state with all its
substance and oil about it—My neighbour Mr Dallas returned this
evening very much hurt by the Waggon upsetting 5 Miles on this
side of Baltimore—it was reported yesterday that he had brock some
of his Ribbs but I am informed there is no bones brock but not with-
standing he is much hurt for he went to bed immediately and none
but the Doctor and his own family has seen him—I trust in God he

will soon get better for he is the life and soul of his family and I may add with great Justice he is the Life and Soul of the Republican cause of Pennsylvania—As far Back as the 7th. of Janry. General Mason informed me the Presidential Election was in Safety. All the Town has beleived it for some days, so from these circumstances I run no risk in wishing you Joy of the appointment and I wish you more comfort than you Two Predecessors—General Washington was too prudent John Adams too imprudent Do what is just and right and have no reference to consequences and you will most certainly succeed This I am certain off you will have every Honest man in the country with you and his last drop of Blood and his last Shilling into the Bargain I am with as much esteem as any man ought to have for another Dear Sir

    your most Obedient St.   THOMAS LEIPER

RC (DLC); endorsed by TJ as received 15 Feb. and so recorded in SJL.

For the association of William JACK-SON with the Federalist volunteer militia unit known as McPherson's Blues, see William Duane to TJ, 12 Nov. 1801. See also PMHB, 47 [1923], 174n.

From Samuel Lewis, Sr.

SIR,   Debtors apartment, Philadelphia Feby: 11, 1801

I think it my duty to acknowledge the receipt of your letter, enclosing the small Maps.   Your favorable Opinion of my Abilities, merits my most sincere thanks: and, approbation coming from so respectable a source, and from one, so capable of ascertaining true worth, adds not a little to my Vanity.   Geographical drawings have been my eager pursuit and ambition to excel, almost from my infancy: and in which branch I am warranted in saying, I am perfectly competent.

The Sentiments of humanity you express towards my unfortunate Situation, I know not how to return Gratitude for: but by a constant wish for your future health and happiness.

Permit me to add, that the Bill, which has passed the house of Representatives, for my relief, and is now before the honorable the Senate, may meet with support from you, and may I presume to hope, your influence, in restoring me to my afflicted and distressed family, who daily languish at my seperation from them.

I have the honor to be, Sir, with the greatest respect, Your most obedient Servant   SAMUEL LEWIS SENR:

RC (DLC); at foot of text: "Thomas Jefferson Esqr:"; endorsed by TJ as received 15 Feb. 1801 and so recorded in SJL.

YOUR LETTER: TJ wrote to Lewis on 24 Jan. and returned Lewis's MAPS, which TJ called "specimens of as exquisite penmanship as I have ever seen, and if they could have been compleated and engraved, would probably have been useful to yourself as well as the public." TJ also pledged that he would "with great pleasure see any act of justice" enacted by Congress "and every remission of useless severities which may place you in a situa-tion to accomodate the public by the employment of your talents, or leave them free for the support of your family" (PrC in DLC).

A petition for the relief of the former War Department clerk was first introduced in Congress on 11 Feb. 1800 and was referred to the secretary of war. A BILL for Lewis's discharge became law on 25 Feb. 1801 (JHR, 3:587, 774; JS, 3:131; U.S. Statutes at Large, 6:43).

Lewis also wrote letters to TJ on 15 Apr. and 23 May 1801, recorded in SJL as received 6 and 26 May, respectively, which have not been found.

From Frederick Muhlenberg

SIR,   Lancaster Feby. 11th. 1801.

It being the prevailing Opinion, whether well or ill founded, I do not presume to judge, that a Change will be made in the Revenue officers of this State, acting for the United States; permit me in the most respectful Manner to offer myself as a Candidate for the Office of Collector at the Port of Philadelphia. Tho' I humbly hoped I had some small Claim on the Public, after a Life of Toil & Industry, 21 Years of which were devoted to the public in honourable but unprofitable Stations, yet seeing how things went, I had concluded to retire from public Life and public Affairs, but just at this Period a Son in Law of mine who was deeply engaged in Trade suffered a Series of Misfortunes occasioned entirely by french & british Captures, which was attended with the most serious Consequences to myself, & that at a time of Life, when Misfortunes have double Weight. Thus circumstanced, & the Business I was engaged in, vizt. Refining of Sugar having been rendered unprofitable by the Exise or duty on it, unless carried on more extensively than my Capital would admit, I was again obliged to seek for public Employment, & accordingly made Application for the Office of Treasurer of the Mint, but met with no Success. Some time afterwards, when the Office of Collector became vacant by the Resignation of Mr. Delany, I was advised by my friends to apply for it, & from their Information as well as some Hints given to me, I had reason expect Success. But whatever good Wishes may have been entertained for me, Mr. Wolcotts Influence prevailed. This Gentleman I had offended by taking the active part I had in discovering his friend

[575]

Hamiltons Affair of Gallantry, & thus I had once more to lament my fate & sing with Ovid. Cur aliquid vidi &c. Mr. Latimer, who never had served the State or U. States in any Capacity, except that of Member of Assembly 4 Years 2 of which he was Speaker, was appointed, tho' I had served the State 2 Years as a Member of the old Congress vizt. 1779 & 1780—3 Years as Speaker of the Assembly—one Year as President of the Council of Censors—one Year as President of the ratifying Convention & four Years as a Member & four Years as Speaker of the House of Representatives of the U. States.

During the whole of my political Career, no one, even of my Enemies, if any I have, has ever laid any thing improper to my Charge unless it be the unfortunate Vote on making Provision for carrying the british Treaty into Effect, which I gave at that time from a Conviction that it was choosing the least of two Evils, & which I trust has not deprived me of the Confidence of my fellow Citizens.

From a long Residence in the City & having heretofore been extensively engaged in Business myself, I have a general Knowledge of, and intimate Acquaintance with the principal Merchants of that Place, and can obtain any Recommendations that may be deemed necessary, having also very frequently transacted Business at the Custom house myself, and assisted in framing the present Revenue Laws, I trust I understand them fully, & am capable of performing the Duties required by them to Your & the Publics Satisfaction.

To Your Wisdom & Goodness I submit my Application, with the most solemn Engagement on my part, that I shall, if appointed, endeavour to the utmost of my Abilites, to perform the Duties of the Station with Industry fidelity & Accuracy, and that nothing will ever alter or diminish that cordial Attachment & high Respect with which I have the Honor to be

 Sir Your most obedient humble Servant

FRDK MUHLENBERG

RC (DNA: RG 59, LAR); at foot of text: "Thos. Jefferson Esqr. Presidt. elect"; endorsed by TJ as received 23 Feb. and so recorded in SJL.

Frederick Augustus Conrad Muhlenberg (1750-1801), a younger brother of John Peter Gabriel Muhlenberg and a native of Trappe, Pa., was educated in Germany and for nine years served as a Lutheran minister in New York and Pennsylvania. He was a member of the Continental Congress from 1779 to 1780 and a member of the Pennsylvania House of Representatives and eventually its speaker in November 1780. Elected to the first four federal congresses, Muhlenberg also served as speaker for the First and Third Congresses. He was president of the Pennsylvania council of censors and was appointed collector general of the Pennsylvania Land Office on 8 Jan. 1800. He and Jacob L. Lawersweiler maintained a sugar refinery in Philadelphia from about 1791 until 1800 (Oswald Seidensticker, "Frederick Augustus Conrad

Muhlenberg, Speaker of the House of Representatives in the First Congress, 1789," PMHB, 13 [1889], 185, 192, 198, 203, 204; Paul A. W. Wallace, *The Muhlenbergs of Pennsylvania* [Philadelphia, 1950], 248, 282, 284-7, 291).

SON IN LAW OF MINE: Muhlenberg's sons-in-law were John S. Hiester, son of Pennsylvania governor Joseph Hiester (married Maria or Mary Catharine), John H. Irwin (married Elizabeth), Jacob Sperry (married Margareth). It is not clear which son-in-law is referred to in this letter (Seidensticker, "Frederick Augustus Conrad Muhlenberg," 206; Wallace, *Muhlenbergs of Pennsylvania*, 290).

The office of revenue collector for the district of Pennsylvania became vacant with the resignation of Sharp DELANY. On 28 June 1798 John Adams nominated George Latimer to the post (JEP, 1:282).

Muhlenberg's involvement in the 1792 investigation of Alexander Hamilton's AFFAIR OF GALLANTRY with Maria Reynolds disturbed Oliver Wolcott, Jr., the comptroller of the treasury, who initiated suits against James Reynolds, John Delabar, and Jacob Clingman. The latter was a former clerk for Muhlenberg and sought his employer's aid in extricating himself from the suits by offering the information that Reynolds and Wolcott had been partners in illegal speculation. Muhlenberg shared the allegation with Virginia congressmen James Monroe and Abraham B. Venable, who confirmed it (Jacob Ernest Cooke, *Alexander Hamilton* [New York, 1982], 177-83; Vol. 29:479n).

CUR ALIQUID VIDI &C.: roughly translated "Alas, why did I see anything" (Ovid, *Tristia*, 2.103).

Muhlenberg's tie-breaking UNFORTUNATE VOTE for the Jay Treaty resulted in his being stabbed by his brother-in-law, Bernard Schaeffer, two days after the final House resolution to implement the treaty. Muhlenberg recovered from his wounds but was not re-elected to Congress in the fall of 1796. Schaeffer was charged with assault and battery and imprisoned for a year (Elaine Forman Crane, ed., *The Diary of Elizabeth Drinker*, 3 vols. [Boston, 1991], 2:800; Wallace, *Muhlenbergs of Pennsylvania*, 291; Vol. 29:95).

From Aaron Burr

DEAR SIR   Albany 12 Feb. 1801

It was so obvious that the most malignant spirit of slander and intrigue would be busy that, without any enquiry, I set down as calumny every tale calculated to disturb our harmony. My friends are often more irritable and more credulous: fortunately I am the depository of all their Cares and anxieties, and I invariably pronounce to be a lie, every thing which ought not to be true—my former letter should have assured you of all this by anticipation—Montfort never told me what you relate & if he had, it would have made no impression on me—Your Solicitude on this occasion, though groundless, is friendly & obliging. Continue to believe in the very Great Respect & Esteem with which I am

Your friend & st   A. BURR

RC (DLC); at foot of text: "Hon. Thos. Jefferson"; endorsed by TJ as received 20 Feb. 1801 and so recorded in SJL.

MY FORMER LETTER: 23 Dec. 1800.

Jefferson's Reports of Balloting in the House of Representatives

EDITORIAL NOTE

On 12 Feb. Jefferson sent copies of Thomas Paine's *Compact Maritime*, newly printed from manuscripts received in January, to eleven of his friends in Virginia. He accompanied at least some, and presumably all, of the pamphlets with brief letters, written at 7:00 A.M. and updated in a postscript at 1:00 P.M., in which he gave a succinct account of the progress of voting in the House of Representatives to choose the president of the United States. After the two houses of Congress had witnessed the counting of the electoral votes in the Senate chamber on Wednesday, 11 Feb., and the tie between Jefferson and Burr became official, the members of the House withdrew to their chamber and, in accordance with the rules they had adopted on 9 Feb., postponed all other business to proceed with voting by states to break the tie. After seven votes, each yielding eight states for Jefferson, six for Burr, and two divided, the House stopped for an hour, then balloted eight more times in succession. Resuming with the sixteenth tally at 9:00 P.M., the representatives then voted at one-hour intervals through the night except for the 22d canvass, which was taken at 2:30 in the morning of 12 Feb. rather than 3:00, giving a longer respite before the resumption of balloting at 4:00 A.M. The 26th ballot came at 7:00 A.M. and the 27th an hour later. The House voted for the 28th time, still with the same results, at noon, then broke until 11:00 A.M. on Friday, 13 Feb., as Jefferson reported in the postscript to his early-morning letters. Subsequently the House voted once on Friday without breaking the impasse, four times at hourly intervals on Saturday afternoon, and once at noon on Monday. Gathering again at noon on Tuesday, 17 Feb., the House took another ballot with no change in the result. An hour later, on the 36th ballot, the votes of ten states went to Jefferson and the balloting was over (JHR, 3:796-803; Carlos Martínez de Irujo to TJ, at 9 Feb. above).

Jefferson pressed a copy of one of the short letters he wrote early on the 12th, one addressed to Philip Norborne Nicholas (Document I). On that copy and in his epistolary record in SJL he listed the people to whom he sent the letters and the pamphlet. Although the pressed copy lacks the postscript that appears, with slight variation, on each of four extant recipients' copies (see below), Jefferson most likely added the P.S. to all the letters, including the one to Nicholas that he had already pressed for his files. He may have penned the batch of letters before designating their recipients: in the surviving examples, including the press copy, spacing in the salutation lines suggests that he inserted each addressee's name after writing the letter, and for Madison, Monroe, and Thomas Mann Randolph he added personalized good wishes to a sentence that had previously ended with a full stop (Documents II-IV). For the enclosure to the letters, *Compact Maritime*, see Paine's letters of 1, 6, and [16] Oct. 1800.

I. To Philip Norborne Nicholas

TH:J. TO P. N. NICHOLAS.   Washington Feb. 12. 1801. 7. A.M.

The H. of R. has been in conclave ever since 2. aclock yesterday. 25. balots have been taken at intervals of from half an hour to an hour. they were invariably 8. 6. & 2. divided. I can venture nothing mo[re by] the post but my affectionate salutations.

PrC (DLC); faint, text in brackets supplied from Documents II-V; in ink at foot of text TJ wrote the names of Mann Page, John Page, James Monroe, Nicholas, John Wayles Eppes, Thomas Mann Randolph, Col. Nicholas Lewis, Peter Carr, William Bache, James Madison, and Archibald Stuart; he used a brace to connect that list to a notation also in his hand: "with a copy of Payne's Compact Maritime"; he also entered those names in SJL as letters sent on this day, again setting the group off with a brace and adding the note about the enclosure.

II. To James Madison

TH:J. TO JAS. MADISON.   Washington Feb. 12. 1801. 7. A.M.

The H. of R. has been in conclave ever since 2. aclock yesterday. at 10. P.M. 17 ballots had been tried, & were invariably 8. 6. & 2 divided. I have not heard from the Capitol this morning.[1] I can venture nothing more by the post but my affectionate salutations,[2] to yourself & mrs Madison.

P.S. 1. P.M. the H. of R. suspended the balloting from 7. to 12. this morning, & after trying a few more balots with the same effect, suspended it again till 11. A.M. tomorrow.

RC (DLC: Madison Papers, Rives Collection); addressed: "James Madison junr. near Orange C.H"; franked and postmarked.

[1] Sentence interlined.
[2] TJ originally ended the sentence here with a period.

III. To James Monroe

TH:J. TO GOVR. MONROE.   Washington Feb. 12. 1801. 7. A.M.

The H. of R. has been in conclave ever since 2. aclock yesterday. 25. ballots have been taken at intervals of from half an hour to an hour. they were invariably 8. 6. & 2 divided. I can venture nothing more by post but my affectionate salutations[1] to yourself & mrs Monroe.

P.S. 1. P.M. the H. of R. suspended the balloting from 7. to 12. this morning & after trying a few balots with the same effect, have suspended it till 11. A.M. tomorrow

RC (DLC: Monroe Papers).   [1] Remainder of sentence added.

IV. To Thomas Mann Randolph

TH:J. TO TMR.   Washington Feb. 12. 1801. 7. A.M.

The H. of R. has been in conclave ever since 2. aclock yesterday. 25. balots have been taken at intervals of from half an hour to an hour. they were invariably 8. 6. & 2. divided. I can venture nothing more by the post but my affectionate salutations,[1] to yourself & my dear Martha.

P.S. 1. P.M. the H. of R. suspended the balloting from 7. to 12. this morning & after trying a few balots with the same effect have suspended it till 11. A.M. tomorrow

RC (DLC); addressed: "Thomas Mann Randolph Edgehill near Milton"; franked and postmarked; endorsed by Randolph.   [1] Remainder of sentence added.

V. To Archibald Stuart

TH:J. TO A. STUART.   Washington Feb. 12. 1801. 7. A.M.

The H. of R. has been in conclave ever since 2 aclock yesterday. 25. ballots have been taken, & were invariably 8. 6. & 2. divided. the intervals of balloting were from half an hour to an hour. I can venture nothing more by post but my affectionate salutations.

P.S. 1. P.M. the H. of R. suspended the balloting from 7. to 12. this morning, & after trying a few balots again with the same effect suspended it till 11. A.M. tomorrow.

RC (ViHi); addressed: "Archibald Stuart Staunton Virga"; franked and postmarked.

From Nathaniel Niles

SIR,   West Fairlee (Vermont) Feb. 12th. 1801—

Permit me to indulge a very sensible pleasure in congratulating my Country on the prospect, which I hope is this moment realized at the seat of Government, that you are elected President of the United States. In times so strongly marked as the present are, by the virulence of faction at home, & by the rage of nations abroad, a friendly heart can hardly congratulate its respected object upon his elevation to any place distinguished by its eminence, not even though it be to the supreme magistracy of a great nation; since it will be no less distinguished, if nature shall still pursue her usual course, by its attending care, solicitude, and vexation. We have had different accounts, and formed different conjectures concerning the probable object of the house of Representatives in the election. But whether they have adopted measures, to tranquilize the public mind, or to produce still further, and greater agitations, I firmly beleive all must result in the increased felicity of the Nation, and the disapointment of those who would prepare means for the Erection of A monarchy upon the ruins of the Republic.

Altho a state of war necessarily lets loose incalculable evils upon multitudes of Individuals, yet benevolence itself cannot regret, that Russia is at war with Great Brittain, when she considers the intolerable and still growing tyranny of the naval system the latter. When will mankind submit to the maxims of moderations and justice!

I duly received, and am much obliged by the apendix to the Notes on Virginea, altho the strictures of Mr. Martin, had not, so far as I know, reached this part of the country. I have not learned how he received, nor how he treated the apendix, but presume he must have been silent.

The current of political opinion among us, has ceased its unnatural flow, and is full rapidly enough returning in its natural channel, for sudden revolutions, are liable to as sudden reversions. I cannot but hope that two years hence the party, which fondly and proudly, but falsly denominates itself federal, will have shrunk to a mere skelleton, forsaken of its flesh and its sinews.

I am told, sir, that the Marshal of this district has often declared that, if there should be a change of the administration he would resign his office, and if he should not I presume he will not long hold it, as I expect such complaints will be exhibited & supported against him as will cause him to be displaced. Should this be the case, will you permit me to recommend for that office, Dr. John Willard. I have not an intimate acquaintance with him, personally, but from what I have, and from his character among the republicans in the State, and especially those in the western district where he resides, I beleve he will discharge the duties of that office with wisdom and fidelity.

I should ask for some moderate, but decent appointment for myself, did any such occur to my mind which I beleve you could *consistently* give *me*, but I think of none. But, Sir, the little all I can do to support, that administration which I believe will be yours, may be unequivocally expected, from me whether in or out of office. It is not therefore in mere formality, I assure you that

I am with great esteem, your much obliged & Hml Sevt.

NATHL: NILES

RC (MoSHi: Jefferson Papers); addressed: "Thos. Jefferson Vice President of the United States Washington"; endorsed by TJ as received 2 Mch. and so recorded in SJL.

Nathaniel Niles (1741-1828) received a bachelor's and a master's degree from the College of New Jersey at Princeton, where he was noted for his theological debates. After graduation he studied medicine and law. In 1774 he married Elizabeth Lothrop of Norwich, Connecticut. During the Revolution he worked in the Lothrop mills, inventing a method for making wire—needed for wool cards—from iron bar to avoid having to import from Great Britain. In 1782 Niles purchased land and settled in West Fairlee, Vermont. He served as a lawyer and physician in the frontier community and although he was never ordained, he was a prominent leader among the local clergy. He served as speaker of Vermont's House of Representatives in 1784, as a judge in the supreme court from 1784 to 1788, and as a member of the Vermont council and the council of censors. A supporter of the

Federal Constitution, Niles became one of the state's first congressmen in 1791. He was defeated for reelection in 1794 by Federalist Daniel Buck, but remained active in state politics as a Jeffersonian Republican, serving again in the House of Representatives and the governor's council. He spoke out against banks, slavery, and the Hartford Convention of 1814. He was a trustee of Dartmouth College from 1794 to 1820. In 1787, a few years after the death of his first wife, Niles married Elizabeth Marston Watson, who was noted for her literary and theological attainments (James McLachlan, *Princetonians, 1748-1768: A Biographical Dictionary* [Princeton, 1976], 585-7; *Biog. Dir. Cong.*; DAB).

In a list of appointments and removals compiled in 1803, TJ recorded that on 5 Mch. 1801 he decided to remove Jabez G. Fitch "for cruel conduct" and appointed DR. JOHN WILLARD as U.S. marshal for the district of Vermont in his place (MS in DLC: TJ Papers, 119:20546; JEP, 1:403). See also Matthew Lyon to TJ, 1 Mch. 1801.

Notes on a Conversation with Edward Livingston

1801. Feb. 12. Edwd. Livingston tells me that Bayard applied to-day or last night to Genl. Sam. Smith & represented to him the expediency of his coming over to the states who vote for Burr, that there was nothing in the way of appointmt. which he might not command, & particularly mentioned the Secretaryship of the navy. Smith asked him if he was authorised to make the offer. he said he was authorised. Smith told this to Livingston & to W. C. Nicholas who confirms it to me. Bayard in like manner tempted Livingston, not by offering any particular office, but by representing to him his L's intimacy & connexion with Burr, that from him he had every thing to expect if he would come over to him. to Dr. Linn of N. Jersey they have offered the government of N. Jersey. see a paragraph in Martin's Baltimore paper of Feb. 10. signed a Looker on, stating an intimacy of views between Harper & Burr.

MS (DLC: TJ Papers, 108:18534); entirely in TJ's hand; on verso of sheet with Notes on Conversations with Benjamin Hichborn, 25 and 26 Dec. 1800.

MARTIN'S BALTIMORE PAPER: the avowedly Republican Baltimore *American*, edited by Alexander Martin (Cunningham, *Jeffersonian Republicans*, 168; Brigham, *American Newspapers*, 1:223).

From Diodati

MONSIEUR   BrunsWic le 13 février 1801

Les Sentiments pleins d'estime & d'Attachement que je Vous avois Voués à Paris, étoient de nature a deVoir Vous Suivre par tout, avec mes Voeux & c'est avec un grand plaisir & un grand intérêt que j'ay appris a la continue, les postes éminents dont l'estime & la confiance de Vos Concitoyens vous avoient d'abord revetu, des Votre retour en Amérique, & enfin a présent, de celui de Président des Etats Unis; Puissent les Connoissances, les Talents & l'Expérience de Votre Excellence contribuer a augmenter encore la Prospérité déjà grande, des etats unis de l'Amérique & Puissent ils, même, influer en Europe, Ou Cela Seroit bien nécessaire, pour y dissiper les troubles, dont le nombre & les malheurs augmentent a un tel point, Que l'on ne Voit plus, Quand & comment l'On pourra en Sortir.

Votre Excellence Sçait qu'apres avoir quitté Paris en May 1792 je m'etois rendu en Suisse Ou je Suis resté jusques au moment de Son invasion, Que je me décidai a Venir en Allemagne Ou j'ay préféré le

Séjour de BrunsWic a tout autre, & jy resterai (& toujours en Connexion avec le Duc de Mecklembourg) jusques apres la paix de l'Empire, la quelle déterminera ma derniére Résidence, pour y passer la reste de mes jours, déja tres avancez.

BrunsWic étant dans la proximité d'Hambourg. J'y envoye cette lettre, que l'on priera le Consul des Etats unis d'envoyer a Votre Excellence, Qui daignera j'Espére me dire, Qu'Elle me conserve dans Son SouVenir & dans Son amitié, Que j'ose dire je mérite aussi par tous mes Sentiments pour Elle.

Je Vous Supplie Monsieur d'agréer tous mes Voeux, pour Votre précieuse Santé Si nécessaire au milieu de tant d'importantes Occupations, de même que ceux de ma femme & croire Qu'on ne peut étre avec plus d'Estime d'Attachement & de Respect

Monsieur de Votre Excellence le tres Humble & tres Obéissant Serviteur   LE COMTE DIODATI

Mon Parent Mr Tronchin de Genéve dont j'ay reçu récemment des lettres apprendra Surement avec bien du plaisir la Nomination de Votre Excellence a son Eminent Poste.

SIR   Brunswick, 13 February 1801
The sentiments full of esteem and devotion that I dedicated to you in Paris were of a kind as to follow you everywhere with my wishes, and it is with a great pleasure and a great interest that I learned in sequence of the eminent posts with which the esteem and the confidence of your fellow citizens immediately bestowed upon you right after your return to America, and finally at present with the presidency of the United States of America. May Your Excellency's knowledge, talents and experience contribute to increasing the prosperity, already great, of the United States of America, and may they even be influential in Europe, where it would be quite necessary to dissipate its disorders, of which the number and the misfortunes are growing to such a point that one can no longer see when and how one may come out of them.

Your Excellency knows that after leaving Paris in May 1792 I went to Switzerland, where I remained up until the moment of its invasion, when I decided to come into Germany, where I preferred to stay in Brunswick rather than anywhere else, and I shall stay here (still in relations with the Duke of Mecklenburg) up until the peace of the Empire, which will determine my final residence where I shall spend the rest of my days, already quite advanced.

Brunswick being near to Hamburg, I shall send this letter there, requesting the United States consul to send it to Your Excellency, who will, I hope, tell me that he keeps me in memory and friendship, which I dare say I also deserve through all my sentiments for him.

I beg you, Sir, to accept all my wishes for your precious health so necessary in the midst of so many important occupations, as well as my wife's, and believe that no one could be, Sir, with more esteem, devotion, and respect

Sir, Your Excellency's very humble and very obedient servant

COUNT DIODATI

My relative, Mr. Tronchin of Geneva, from whom I have recently received letters, will certainly learn with much pleasure the appointment of Your Excellency to such an eminent post.

RC (DLC); endorsed by TJ as received 23 May 1801 and so recorded in SJL. Dupl (same); in unidentified hand; at head of text: "Copie de ma lettre à Monsieur Jefferson Président des Etats Unis de L'amérique, Remise à Mr Pittkern Consul Genéral des Etats Unis de L'amérique"; enclosed in Diodati to TJ, 29 Aug. 1806.

Diodati and TJ had known each other in PARIS when TJ represented the United States there and Diodati was minister plenipotentiary of the Duke of Mecklenburg-Schwerin. Although TJ's endorsement and his entry in SJL confirm that he received the above letter in May 1801, when Diodati sent the duplicate five years later TJ replied that he had "never received, or had notice of," the original letter. TJ declared to Diodati, "I often pass in review the many happy hours I spent with Made. Diodati & yourself on the banks of the Seine, as well as at Paris, and I count them among the most pleasing I enjoyed in France" (TJ to Diodati, 29 Mch. 1807; Vol. 9:86; Vol. 13:439; Vol. 16:295).

TRONCHIN DE GENÉVE: Diodati was related to the Tronchin family through his mother and was also connected to them through his wife, the former Marie Élisabeth Tronchin. She was the daughter of a noted Geneva physician, Théodore Tronchin, who had died in 1781. Diodati's extended family was part of a small but influential group of Italian Protestants who took up residence in Geneva during the Reformation. The family figured prominently in the early silk industry in Geneva and produced a Protestant theologian and translator of the Bible into Italian and French, Giovanni Diodati. Count Diodati, writer of the letter above, had received his title from the Holy Roman Empire (Jacques Augustin Galiffe and others, *Notices Généalogiques sur les Familles Genevoises, Depuis les Premiers Temps jusqu'a Nos Jours*, 7 vols. [Geneva, 1829-95], 2:732, 742-3; Paul Guichonnet, ed., *Histoire de Genève* [Toulouse, 1974], 178-80; René Guerdan, *Histoire de Genève* [Paris, 1981], 138; *Encyclopédie de Genève*, 11 vols. [1982-96], 8:24-5, 27; 9:236).

From Joseph Barnes

Messina. Sicily Feb. 14th 1801

When I had last the pleasure of addressing you, my best friend Mr. Jefferson, from this place Decemr. 22nd 1800—I Suggest'd in the Postscript, that hostilities had recommenc'd between the French and imperialists; and that report said, tho' I reced. it confidentially thro' a private channel, the French & Russians were about to come to an understanding, that if So, you would judge of the effect of the Campaign—

Which Occurrant circumstances have fully verifi'd; for, it appears from the Bouletin publish'd at the French head quarters in Italy, and the Vienna Account of the Battles in Germany, the French have been so *completely triumphant*, in Italy, as to have driven the imperialists entirely out of Italy (except those in Mantua) And on the Danube, as to have, 'tis Said, *forc'd* the emperor of Germany to terms—

A Letter I reced. from my worthy friend Mr Noble in Naples dat'd the 30th Ult. purports, that the Emperor had *made* his *peace*, on the principles of the Convention of Campo Formo, with some additional articles in favor of the French—The loss on both Sides has been enormous, and the Battles *Sanguinary* beyond parallel.—

Had the emperor in this instance *refus'd* peace, 'tis Suppos'd the *views* of the French were, to *dethrone* him, re-organize Germany into Free States, & constitute the King of Prussia Limitt'd Emperor and dissolve the Ottoman empire—All of which is in their power, Should they keep the Tyrant of the East, Paul the Ist. if *not* actively, inactively of their Side; which the presumption is, they have & will, he is *very Avaricious*, & has so *Little* to hope from adherence to the Allies, and So *much* to expect from favoring the French—especially as the Russians have *Sequestr'd* upwards of 300 English Vessels, and all the British Manufactures in Russia—in fine, 'tis Said and appears that a Serious League is form'd between Russia, Prussia &c with the influence of the French, to *Shut all* the ports of Europe against the English!! indeed, they Suggest fears in the House of Commons, as the King of Prussia has taken Possession of Cuxhaven, which Commands the Elbe, that *all* except Lisbon and Constantinople *will* be Shut— Should this be the case, the American Markets will be almost the *only vent* Left for the British Manufactures, consequently we become So *essential* to the English, that the presumption is, they will *respect us as we merit*—but should they be So *presumptive* as to commit any further *Spoilations* on the Property of the Citizens of the Unit'd States, they may Soon be made *Sensible* of their *error* & *promptly* brot. to *our own terms,*— *not* by Arms, but by *Shutting* the ports of the Unit'd States against them, & *Sequestring* all the British debts &c as formerly Suggest'd.

It Seems Paul has refus'd to take off the embargo, unless the English will give him joint possession of Malta, conformably to an existing Convention, which the presumption is, will be refused.

Tis Some time Since the English Expedition Sail'd from Malta for Egypt; and advice is reced. of their having arriv'd in Asia near Rhodes; but, in consequence of the French having *preced'd* them in a Small expedition, which is Suppos'd to have arriv'd at Alexandria; & being So firmly establish'd & incorporat'd with the Natives, which I have from a confidential person who is from that Country, the presumption is, the english will be *too Late*, & the result as *usual abortive*—this however, tho' yet to be prov'd, is clearly my opinion from all circumstances.—

One report of the day is, that in Some of the Fortresses of Italy there are French, Russians and Italians!! a Singular association, if so. Naples must be includ'd in the Convention with the Emperor; and another, that a body of French are advancing Southward, Suppos'd for Naples—which I conceive most probable; for the double object of keeping possession & Shuting that port against the english, 'till a general Peace—Indeed the People Seem alarm'd even here.

I expect Shortly to Set for Malta, & from thence most probable to Barcelony in Spain or Marseilles in France, but Mean to return & reside Some-time at Malta—Mean while Should you have occasion, Address for me to care of Mr J. Broadbent, Merchant Messina Sicily—or to Governer Ball, Malta—

I need not remind you of the *object Solicit'd* in my Last, your own disposition to promote merit & the interest & happiness of your fellow Citizens especially, will *prompt* you Sufficiently to *Serve me* therein when ever in your power—and this will be, the presumption is, after the fourth of March ensuing, as there is no doubt in my mind[1] of your being prefer'd to the presidincy—

With constant Solicitude for your health & happiness & long preferment—Mr Jefferson I remain yours most respectfully

JOS: BARNES

P.S. command me on all occasions & be assur'd nothing can afford me more pleasure than to serve you

P.S.   Feb. 22nd 1801

Advice is reced. that *war* has been declar'd by England, against Danemark Sweden & I believe Russia—& report yesterday Said, that the two former have Sent out 45 Sail & the Latter 49 Sail of Vessels agait. England—And an American who arriv'd this morning in two days from Naples, reports, that from an order of the English Consul, & Lord William Stuart Commander of an English Frigate, all the English Vessels had withdrawn out into the Road & all the english were Sending their property on Board—tho' it was not known whether in consequence of the approach of the French, or of a Treaty between them & Naples—Tis also Said that Mantua has been given up as the purchase of an Armstice—or prelude to a Treaty—

As a Protest will be prefer'd to the Unit'd States against Mr Matheu, who holds the office of Consul general of the U.S. at Naples, for his highly improper conduct towards an American Captain from the *false* allegations of an Englishman at Leghorn, I need not, your own disposition will remind you of my repeat'd Solicitations— Should he be displac'd—health & happiness— J. B—

RC (DLC); addressed: "Thomas Jefferson Esqr. V.P. of the Unit'd States City of Washington"; franked; postmarked 20 June; endorsed by TJ as received 24 June 1801 and so recorded in SJL.

A British expeditionary force, organized in the autumn of 1800 and intended to oust the French from EGYPT, landed at Aboukir Bay in March 1801 (Ehrman, *Pitt,* 409, 411; William Laird Clowes, *The Royal Navy: A History from the Earliest Times to the Present,* 7 vols. [London, 1897-1903; repr. 1996-97], 4:455-6).

SUPPOS'D FOR NAPLES: although Bonaparte canceled orders for the occupation of Naples, in February the kingdom's Bourbon rulers agreed to an armistice under which they would retain the throne but, among other concessions,

close their ports to the British. Naples and France signed a formal peace in March (John D. Grainger, *The Amiens Truce: Britain and Bonaparte, 1801-1803* [Woodbridge, Suffolk, 2004], 22; Desmond Gregory, *Napoleon's Italy* [Madison, N.J., 2001], 53-4; Tulard, *Dictionnaire Napoléon,* 1207, 1225).

WAR HAS BEEN DECLAR'D BY ENGLAND: during January the British government prohibited commerce with Denmark, Sweden, and Russia, placed those nations' ships under embargo, planned the capture of Danish and Swedish islands in the West Indies, and prepared for naval operations in the Baltic (Ehrman, *Pitt,* 399).

[1] MS: "miny."

To Benjamin Smith Barton

DEAR SIR Washington Feb. 14. 1801.

Your favor of Jan. 18. is duly recieved. the subject of it did not need apology. on the contrary should I be placed in office, nothing would be more desireable to me than the recommendations of those in whom I have confidence, of persons fit for office. for if the good withold their testimony, we shall be at the mercy of the bad. if the question relative to mr Zantzinger had been merely that of remaining in office, your letter would have placed him on very safe[1] ground. besides that no man who has conducted himself according to his duties would have any thing to fear from me, as those who have done ill would have nothing to hope, be their political principles what they might. the obtaining an appointment presents more difficulties. the republicans have been excluded from all offices from the first origin of the division into Republican & federalist. they have a reasonable claim to vacancies till they occupy their due share. my hope however is that the distinction will be soon lost, or at most that it will be only of republican & monarchist: that the body of the nation, even that part which French excesses forced over to the Federal side, will rejoin the republicans, leaving only those who were pure monarchists, and who will be too few to form a sect.—this is the 4th. day of the balot, and nothing done: nor do I see any reason to suppose the 6½ states here will be less firm, as they call it, than your 13. Senators. if so, and the government should[2] expire on the 3d. of March by the loss of it's head, there is no regular provision for reorganising it, nor any authority but in the people themselves. they may authorize a convention to reorganize & even to amend the machine. there are 10. individuals in the H. of R. any one of whom changing his vote may save us this troublesome operation. be pleased to present my friendly respects to mrs Barton, mrs Sarjeant & mrs Waters, and to accept yourself my affectionate salutations.   TH: JEFFERSON

RC (PHi: Benjamin Smith Barton Papers); addressed: "Doctr. Benjamin S. Barton Philadelphia 44. N. 5th."; franked and postmarked; endorsed by Barton as received 18 Feb. PrC (DLC).

Barton's FAVOR OF JAN. 18 was a plea in behalf of a brother-in-law, merchant Paul ZANTZINGER of Lancaster, Pennsylvania, who had held a place in the U.S. revenue system that had come to an end. With 11 children to support, he was in need of another position. Barton praised Zantzinger's accounting abilities and dedication to the Whig cause during the Revolution, but confessed his brother-in-law's commitment to Federalist politics since about 1794. Without recommending Zantzinger for a specific position, Barton hoped that TJ would keep him in mind (Dft in PPAmP: Barton Collection; recorded in SJL as received 11 Feb.). Zantzinger had received his appointment as a commissioner of the Direct Tax in July 1798 (JEP, 1:288-9). In

an undated list of people recommended for office, TJ recorded Zantzinger's name, residence, the date of Barton's letter above, and "in the revenue &c" as the office sought by the applicant (DLC: TJ Papers, 108:18557).

MRS BARTON, MRS SARJEANT & MRS WATERS: Barton had wed Mary Pennington in 1797 (ANB). His cousins Elizabeth Rittenhouse Sergeant, the widow of attorney Jonathan Dickinson Sergeant, and her sister Esther (Hetty), widow of Dr. Nicholas B. Waters, were the daughters of David Rittenhouse and his first wife, Eleanor Coulston Rittenhouse, and acquaintances of TJ and his daughters (Brooke Hindle, *David Rittenhouse* [Princeton, 1964], 24-5, 304-5, 316, 344, 350-1; DAB, 2:17, 16:589-90; Vol. 22:294; Vol. 23:159).

[1] Preceding two words interlined in place of "high."

[2] TJ here canceled "run out."

To Andrew Ellicott

DEAR SIR   Washington Feb. 14. 1801.

I have to acknolege the reciept of your favors of Feb. 5. & 9. and to thank you for the pamphlet contained in the former one which was a desideratum to me. I will forward the diplomas to Chr. Livingston & mr Stewart. the latter is almost out of date. I am Dear Sir

Your most obedt. servt   TH: JEFFERSON

PrC (DLC); at foot of text: "Mr. Andrew Ellicot"; endorsed by TJ in ink on verso.

Ellicott's letter of 9 Feb. enclosed two DIPLOMAS for TJ to forward: "It being the practice of the American Philosophical Society, for that member, who nominates a person, and who is in consequence of that nomination elected a member, to furnish him with his diploma" (RC in DLC; at foot of text: "Thos. Jefferson Esqr. V.P. of the U.S and President of the Senate"; endorsed by TJ as received 11 Feb. 1801 and so recorded in SJL).

Notes on a Conversation with Gen. John Armstrong

Feb. 14 Genl Armstrong tells me that Gouvernr. Morris in conversation with him today on the scene which is passing expressd himself thus. how come it, sais he, that Burr who is 400. miles off (at Albany) has agents here at work with great activity, while mr Jefferson, who is on the spot, does nothing?' this explains the ambiguous conduct of himself & his nephew Lewis Morris, and that they were holding themselves free for a price, i.e. some office, either to the uncle or nephew.

MS (DLC: TJ Papers, 108:18534); entirely in TJ's hand; on same sheet as Notes on a Conversation with Edward Livingston, 12 Feb. 1801.

To Stephen Sayre

SIR   Washington Feb. 14. 1801

I have to acknolege the reciept of your favors of Jan 12. & Feb. 5. it is far from being certain at this date that I shall have any thing to do with the executive councils of the country. yet as you make the movements of your son to depend in some measure on the circumstance stated in your letter of Jan. 12. I will hazard an observation which will merit no more weight than would have that of any other individual. it is that the public opinion in this country is so unequivocally understood to be that we shall haul off from European politics, have no political engagements with them, nor intermeddle in the smallest degree with any thing which may entangle us in their quarrels, that whatever administration may come into place, I am persuaded it will take no part in the combinations of Europe. commerce with all is desireable, but no other connection.—we are now at the 4th day of the balot of the H. of R. & not a single vote changed.

I am Sir Your most obedt. sert   TH: JEFFERSON

[590]

PrC (DLC); at foot of text in ink: "Stephen Sayre esq."

This is the only response TJ ever sent to Sayre, who continued to write letters throughout TJ's presidency.

YOUR SON: Samuel William Sayre.

To John Stuart

SIR   Washington Feb. 14. 1801.

You were chosen a member of the American philosophical society so long ago as 1797. and as I lived at a distance from Philadelphia, the Secretaries were advised how to address your diploma when it should be filled up. by some accident unexplained to me it seems it has never been forwarded. I did not know this till I recieved it a few days ago. I have the honour now to inclose it. the bones you were so kind as to forward to me, with some supplementary ones I luckily obtained from another gentleman are considered as a valuable deposit in the collection of the society. there are two papers on their subject in their last volume. I am with much respect Sir

Your most obedt. servt   TH: JEFFERSON

RC (WvLe); at foot of text: "Colo. John Stewart." PrC (MHi); endorsed by TJ in ink on verso.

Stuart, who in 1796 had sent TJ newly discovered BONES of the megalonyx, was elected to membership in the APS in April 1797. TJ obtained SUPPLEMENTARY specimens of the prehistoric

sloth from Samuel Hopkins of New York (APS, *Proceedings*, 22, pt. 3 [1884], 256; Vol. 29:64, 152, 291).

TWO PAPERS: TJ's report on the megalonyx and Caspar Wistar's technical description of the bones (APS, *Transactions*, 4 [1799], 246-60, 526-31; Vol. 29:299-300n).

To William Thornton

Feb. 14. 1801.

Th: Jefferson presents his compliments to Doctr. Thornton. he has recieved his friendly invitation to pass the evening on Monday next; but for 10. years past he has been in the habit, from considerations of health, of never going out in the evening. his friends have been so kind as to indulge this habit, & he is sure Dr. Thornton will accept it as an apology.

RC (DLC: William Thornton Papers); addressed: "Doctr. Thornton." Not recorded in SJL.

From Joseph Crockett

Jessamene County Kentucky Febry 15th 1801

By the law establishing federal Courts I beleve it is provided there shall be a reappointment to the Office of Marshal to that Court once in four years. If that is the case applications I Suppose will be numerous to you for the Office; That Supposition is founded on its being generally beleved that Some one will succeed Saml McDowell Junr the present Marshal, I flatter my self that I hold an equal rank in your esteem with any other person who may be a candidate, and Should I be so successfull as to meet with it, I hope I will give general Satisfaction to the people, and it will confer a Singlar favour on Sir your Most Obedt and very Hble Servt.

JOSEPH CROCKETT

PS It is thought this State will be laid off in Two Districts and a federal Court in each if so I expect Kentucky River will divide the two I live on the North Side J C

RC (DNA: RG 59, LAR); endorsed by TJ as received 12 Mch. and so recorded in SJL.

Colonel Joseph Crockett (1742-1829), a native of Virginia, served on the frontier prior to and during the American Revolution. In 1776 he enlisted in a company of minutemen of the Continental Army, was later a lieutenant colonel of the Illinois regiment, and continued in military service until February 1781. An acquaintance of TJ's, Crockett surveyed most of the land around Monticello. In May 1782, Crockett wed Elizabeth Moore Woodson, the widow of TJ's relative Tucker Woodson. They moved to Kentucky in 1784, where they established a farm on 1,900 acres on Hickman Creek in Jessamine County. Crockett was a representative to the Virginia Assembly in 1786 and 1790 and served in the newly formed Kentucky House until 1795. From 1800 to 1804, he was a member of the Kentucky Senate. TJ appointed him on 26 June 1801 as marshal for the district of Kentucky to succeed Samuel McDowell, Jr. When informed of the applicants for the marshalcy and of Crockett's candidacy, TJ is said to have exclaimed to his secretary, "You need not read any more. I will appoint honest Joe, for I know him personally to be true, and faithful, and honest." In his capacity as marshal, Crockett was most known for his arrest of Aaron Burr in 1806 (ASP, *Miscellaneous*, 1:303; G. Glenn Clift, *Kentucky Obituaries, 1787-1854* [Baltimore, 1977], 59; John E. Kleber, ed., *The Kentucky Encyclopedia* [Lexington, Ky., 1992], 242; Kline, *Burr*, 1:571; Samuel W. Price, *Biographical Sketch of Colonel Joseph Crockett*, [Louisville, Ky., 1909], 4, 7, 9-10, 17-19, 26-29; Vol. 4:303-4; Vol. 5:142-3).

The LAW ESTABLISHING FEDERAL COURTS, An Act to Establish the Judicial Courts of the United States, or the Judiciary Act of 1789, stipulated that "a marshal shall be appointed in and for each district for the term of four years, but shall be removable from office at pleasure" (U.S. Statutes at Large, 1:87).

To Mary Jefferson Eppes

Washington Feb. 15. 1801.

Your letter, my dear Maria, of the 2d. inst. came to hand on the 8th. I should have answered it instantly according to our arrangement, but that I thought, by waiting till the 11th. I might possibly be able to communicate something on the subject of the election. however, after 4. days of balloting, they are exactly where they were on the first. there is a strong expectation in some that they will coalesce tomorrow: but I know no foundation for it. whatever event happens, I think I shall be at Monticello earlier than I formerly mentioned to you. I think it more likely I may be able to leave this place by the middle of March. I hope I shall find you at Monticello. the scene passing here makes me pant to be away from it: to fly from the circle of cabal, intrigue & hatred, to one where all is love and peace. tho' I never doubted of your affections, my dear, yet the expressions of them in your letter give me ineffable pleasure. no, never imagine that there can be a difference with me between yourself & your sister. you have both such dispositions as engross my whole love, and each so entirely that there can be no greater degree of it than each possesses. whatever absences I may be led into for a while, I look for happiness to the moment when we can all be settled together, no more to separate. I feel no impulse from personal ambition to the office now proposed to me, but on account of yourself & your sister, and those dear to you. I feel a sincere wish indeed to see our government brought back to it's republican principles, to see that kind of government firmly fixed; to which my whole life has been devoted. I hope we shall now see it so established, as that when I retire, it may be under full security that we are to continue free & happy. as soon as the fate of the election is over, I will drop a line to mr Eppes. I hope one of you will always write the moment you recieve a letter from me. continue to love me my dear as you ever have done, and ever have been & will be by your's affectionately   TH: JEFFERSON

RC (ViU); addressed: "Mrs. Maria Eppes Bermuda Hundred near City point"; franked.

FORMERLY MENTIONED TO YOU: in the letter to his daughter of 4 Jan., TJ indicated that he would be at Monticello the first week in April.

To James Monroe

DEAR SIR   Washington Feb. 15. 1801.

I have recieved several letters from you which have not been acknoleged. by the post I dare not, and one or two confidential opportunities have past me by surprise. I have regretted it the less, because
I knew you could be more safely and fully informed by others. mr
Tyler, the bearer of this, will give you a great deal more information
personally than can be done by letter. four days of ballotting have
produced not a single change of a vote. yet it is confidently believed
by most that tomorrow there is to be a coalition. I know of no foundation for this belief. however as mr Tyler waits the event of it he will
communicate it to you. if they could have been permitted to pass a
law for putting the government into the hands of an officer, they
would certainly have prevented an election. but we thought it best to
declare openly & firmly, one & all, that the day such an act passed the
middle states would arm, & that no such usurpation even for a single
day should be submitted to. this first shook them; and they were
completely alarmed at the resource for which we declared, to wit, a
convention to reorganize the government, & to amend it. the very
word Convention, gives them the horrors, as in the present democrat-
ical spirit of America, they fear they should lose some of the favorite
morsels of the constitution. many attempts have been made to obtain
terms & promises from me. I have declared to them unequivocally,
that I would not recieve the government on capitulation, that I would
not go into it with my hands tied. should they yield the election, I
have reason to expect in the outset the greatest difficulties as to nom-
inations. the late incumbents running away from their offices & leaving them vacant, will prevent my filling them without the *previous*
advice of Senate. how this difficulty is to be got over I know not. accept for mrs Monroe & yourself my affectionate salutations. Adieu.

TH: JEFFERSON

RC (DLC: Monroe Papers); ad-   MR TYLER, THE BEARER: Samuel
dressed: "Governor Monroe Richmond";   Tyler. See the following document.
endorsed by Monroe. PrC (DLC).

To John Tyler

DEAR SIR   Washington Feb. 15. 1801.

Your favor of Jan. 30. by mr Tyler your nephew has been duly recieved, and I read in it with great satisfaction the expression of

friendly regard which I can with truth reciprocate. we have had a long course together, and in the moments of trial, I have seen you always at your post. our political vessel has rode very uneasily under the gales of monarchy: I hope, when put on her republican tack, she will shew herself built for that. the old rigging may for a while perhaps disorder her motion. perhaps too we are counting too fast, for after 4 days of balloting not a single vote has been changed. a strong idea is abroad at present that tomorrow there is to be a coalition but on what grounds it is suggested I know not. your nephew however has determined to stay a day longer to see the issue. he will consequently be able to supply what is not known at the date of this letter. I pray you to accept assurances of the sincere esteem & respect of Dear Sir

Your friend & servt   TH: JEFFERSON

PrC (DLC); at foot of text: "The honble John Tyler." Tr (MHi).

From John Breckinridge

DEAR SIR   Fayette (Kentucky) 16th. Feby. 1801.

The general beleif, which prevails here, that the present Marshall for this State, will not be reappointed, has induced Colo. Joseph Crockett to come forward as a candidate. I was not informed by him of his intentions untill this day.

His character, was, I presume, well known to you during his residence in the neighbourhood of Charottesville. It has suffered no diminution here.—In the exercise of all those virtues & good qualities, which constitute an upright & valuable citizen, he stands here, with estimation of all his acquaintances, second to no man. His public character is equally spotless. He fellow citizens have hitherto refused him nothing within gift which he has asked for; & he is now in the Senate of this State. He hitherto has been, & still is, a decided republican.—This much I feel myself bound to say in behalf of a man who on account of his modesty may be too backward in placing himself before you in that point of view in which he ought to stand.

We are still in a state of anxious solicitude here, respecting the election of president; but I confess I have charity enough still left to believe, that the representatives of the People have yet so much public virtue, & such a regard for character, as not to act directly counter to the sense & wishes of *all*[1] the people of America

With the greatest respect & Esteem I am dear Sir Your friend & Ob St.   JOHN BRECKINRIDGE

RC (DNA: RG 59, LAR); at foot of text: "The Honble Thomas Jefferson"; endorsed by TJ. Dft (DLC: Breckinridge Family Papers). Recorded in SJL as received 6 Mch. 1801.

[1] Word interlined in Dft in place of "those who [expect] a majority."

To Robert R. Livingston

DEAR SIR   Washington Feb. 16. 1801.

Your favor of Jan. 7. came duly to hand. a part of it gave me that kind of concern which I fear I am destined often to meet. men professing minds of the first order, and who have had opportunities of being known & of acquiring the general confidence, do not abound in any country beyond the wants of the country. in your case however it is a subject of regret rather than of complaint, as you are in fact serving the public in a very important station.

It is some two or three or four years since I enquired of the members of the A. Phil. society whether you were a member. the answer was that they were pretty sure you were, & had been for a long time. after acquiescing awhile on that authority I expressed a wish to the Secretaries that they would ascertain the fact, which they promised. my absences from Philadelphia prevented a repetition of the enquiry as often as I wished, and the members names being to be sought through the whole minutes of our proceedings, obstructed the search. at length I nominated you, & at the next election you were chosen a member. whether you were one before, you probably know: and if already of the elect, you are now doubly so. I inclose the diploma.

I have on several occasions been led to think on some means of uniting the State Agricultural societies into a central society: and lately it has been pressed from England with a view to a cooperation with their board of agriculture. you know some have proposed to Congress to incorporate such a society. I am against that, because I think Congress cannot find in all the enumerated powers any one which authorises the act, much less the giving the public money to that use. I believe too if they had the power, it would soon be used for no other purpose than to buy with sinecures useful partisans. I believe it will thrive best if left to itself as the Philosophical societies are. there is certainly a much greater abundance of materials for Agricultural societies than Philosophical. but what should be the plan of union? would it do for the state societies to agree to meet in a central society by a special deputation of members? if this should present difficulties, might they not be lessened by their adopting into their society some one or more of their delegates in Congress or of the members of the Executive residing here, who assembling necessarily for other purposes, could occasionally meet on the business of their societies? your Agricultural society standing undoubtedly on the highest ground, might set the thing a going by uniting to such state societies as already exist, and these once meeting centrally might induce the other states to establish societies & thus compleat the institution. this is a mere idea of mine, not sufficiently considered or digested, & hazarded merely to set you to thinking on the subject, & to propose something better or to improve this. will you be so good as to consider it at your leisure, and give me your thoughts on the subject? Accept my affectionate salutations.   TH: JEFFERSON

RC (NNMus); addressed: "The honble Chancellor Livingston Clermont"; endorsed by Livingston. PrC (DLC).

Livingston was CHOSEN A MEMBER of the American Philosophical Society on 16 Jan. 1801 (APS, *Proceedings*, 22, pt. 3 [1884], 308).

PRESSED FROM ENGLAND: see Sir John Sinclair to TJ, 6 June 1800.

Notes on a Newspaper Article

Feb. 16. see the Wilmington Mirror of Feb. 14. mr Bayard's elaborate argument to prove that the common law, as[1] modified by the laws of the respective[2] states at the epoch of the ratificn of the constn, attached to the courts of the US.

MS (DLC: TJ Papers, 108:18534); entirely in TJ's hand; on same sheet as Notes on a Conversation with Gen. John Armstrong, 14 Feb.

WILMINGTON MIRROR: *Mirror of the Times, & General Advertiser*, a semiweekly Republican newspaper established in Delaware in November 1799, with James J. Wilson serving as writer and printer. The newspaper printed James A. Bayard's arguments in defense of the common law delivered on 22 Jan.

during the debate in the House of Representatives on renewal of the Sedition Act. The account in the *Mirror* varied slightly from that printed in the *Annals of Congress* (Wilmington *Mirror of the Times*, 14 Feb. 1801; *Annals*, 10:946-50; Pasley, *Tyranny of Printers*, 320-2; Brigham, *American Newspapers*, 1:84). For Bayard's previous remarks on the subject, see Vol. 31:357n.

[1] TJ here canceled "existing."
[2] Word interlined in place of "several."

From Richard Richardson

DR SIR   Richmond fabuary 16th 1801

having Received yours of January the 8th I now have the pleasure of answering it with pleasure. I am sorry to have omited it so long—

nor would I have done it on any other provisor a tall But not having of my helth so as to admit of my going from home till now has ocasioned it my not writing to you Before now I was at your place since I wrote you or as I may say since new years day to know why Mr lilley did not Come down as he told me he would. his Reply was he depend on Mr [paiton] for Eight hands In which he disappointed him In they Could have Been got By me if he had of Come froward as I Requested of him to do But his not Comeing I Relide on his Being furneshed and did not get any for him when I was up he was gone to Bedford to Mr Randolph place on Request of Business for him I have not Ingage any Business as yet nor neither shall I till I get answer from you I Cant tell wheather Mr powel has gone froward or not you will Be good Enough to Informe me wheather you feel disposed for me to Return to Continue anothre year for you or not as it is my wish so to do or any thing you would Confur on me will Be gladly Receivd and Beleve me to Be Sincearly yours with astem

RD. RICHARDSON

If you will Be good Enough to answer this as soon as be in your power

RD RDSON

RC (MHi); endorsed by TJ as received 21 Feb. and so recorded in SJL.

Appendix
Notations by Jefferson on Senate Documents

E D I T O R I A L   N O T E

As vice president of the United States, Jefferson's primary responsibility was to preside over the Senate (see Vol. 29:633) and rule on procedural issues. Jefferson did not take an active legislative role in the Senate's proceedings, but he often did make notes on documents that came before that body. These markings, which reflect less his own thought or opinion than his recording of the deliberations of the senators, give some indication of Jefferson's involvement in day-to-day proceedings of the Senate. Several documents, as noted in the list below, are entirely in Jefferson's hand. The resolution of 21 Jan. 1801 directing the secretary of the Senate "to inform the Commissrs. of the City of Washington that the Senate consent to the accomodation of the Supreme court in one of the Commee rooms as proposed in their letter" is one in the vice president's hand, as is the order of 10 Feb. 1801 "that when the two houses shall proceed to opening & counting the votes for Presidt. of the US. <*the doors of the gallery*> no persons be admitted into the gallery" with the notation "agreed to by Y. & N." (MSS in DNA: RG 46, Senate Records, 6th Cong., 2d sess.).

Between 16 Dec. 1800 and 3 Feb. 1801 the Senate considered the ratification of the Convention of 1800 with France. Shortly after the Senate received the convention, the vice president noted that it had "some disagreeable features" and predicted that it would "meet objections from both sides of the house" (TJ to Madison and TJ to Thomas Mann Randolph, both at 19 Dec. 1800). Many procedural questions arose while the convention was considered, and Jefferson took an active role in addressing them. In a document endorsed "Form of Entry on French Treaty," 6 Jan. 1800, he recorded the language to be used by the Senate when voting on articles of a convention or treaty: "The 2d. article being under consideration a question was moved & put 'Will the Senate advise and consent to the ratification of this article'? and the yeas & nays being taken were as follows." Jefferson left space and then directed that the vote be recorded as carried in the affirmative or negative. On the same sheet, he added: "Note. if two thirds be found on the yeas & Nays to have voted affirmatively, then the question is carried in the affirmative; but if two thirds have not voted affirmatively, then the question is carried in the negative." On 15 Jan. in a document endorsed "Report of VP Committee of the whole Convention," Jefferson reported "that the Senate as in a commee of the whole had had under their consideration the Convention &c had gone through the same, & had agreed to sundry modifications which he proceeded to state to the house, and again to put questions thereon severally for confirmation as follows. on the question whether the Senate would advise & consent to the ratification of the 2d. article the yeas and nays being taken were as follows." He then added: "so it passed in the negative." The report, entirely in the vice president's hand, also included a second paragraph, which concerned the Senate's action on the third article, including the motion "to amend the same by adding to the end of the article these words 'or paid for', and the question on that amendment being put & the yeas and Nays taken, they were as follows." He recorded: "so the amendmt was *not* agreed to." Below the docketing or endorsement on the verso of the sheet there appears a query in Samuel A. Otis's hand: "Sir Do you intend to take the yeas & Nays on the several articles? If so how enter vote on 1st Article?" This query and the report; amendments to the convention considered on 15 Jan., which are in the vice president's hand; procedures, in Jefferson's hand, for dividing the question into four parts, dated 23 Jan., when the convention was rejected; and Jefferson's emendations to the 3 Feb. draft of the minutes when the convention was reconsidered and ratified, indicate that the vice president was responsible for formulating the language for the rules and procedures to be followed in ratifying treaties (MSS in DNA: RG 46, Senate Records, 6th Cong., 2d sess.; JEP, 1:359, 365-77). Finally, TJ retrieved the manuscript of his parliamentary manual that he had submitted to Samuel H. Smith on 21 Dec. to add the rules adopted by the Senate regarding the consideration of treaties (TJ to Smith, printed at 6 Jan. 1801).

The following list enumerates bills, motions, committee reports, and petitions that came before the Sixth Congress during the second session and received some written comment by the vice president, who took his seat as president of the Senate on 28 Nov. 1800 (JEP, 3:110). The Editors have grouped Jefferson's markings on the documents into three categories: (1) "emendation" indicates that Jefferson recorded changes to a bill or motion, from a word or two to several sentences, often incorporating amendments passed; (2) "notation" means that information on action taken by the Senate appears in Jefferson's hand, most often in a brief entry such as "disagreed" or "agreed" in the margin of the text of the document, but sometimes with other information such as that found on the bill for the organization of the U.S. courts, where the vice president noted "Mr. Nich's. amdmt. disagreed to by Y. & N."; and (3) "endorsement" indicates that Jefferson provided one or more entries in the docketing or clerical record of the history of the document. On the documents listed below, Jefferson often provided the title as well as all of the entries on the panel. This was the case with the bill concerning the District of Columbia, where Jefferson recorded the action taken by the Senate between 17 Dec. 1800 and 25 Feb. 1801, ten entries in all.

The endorsement panel provides inclusive dates for a document; in the absence of such endorsements we have derived the dates from the printed *Journal of the Senate* and they are supplied in brackets. If the document marked by Jefferson was a motion or bill printed for the Senate's consideration, that fact is also noted in the description below. Motions are rendered as they appear on the endorsement panel unless clarification requires substituting the language of the motion itself.

All the documents listed below are from Senate Records, DNA: RG 46, 6th Cong., 2d sess.

Bill Extending the privilege of franking letters to the delegate from the territory of the United States north-west of the river Ohio, and making provision for his compensation, 2-5 Dec. 1800; printed; emendation and endorsement by TJ.

Motion in respect to local powers over the District of Columbia, 4-5 Dec. 1800; endorsement by TJ. Printed in JS, 3:111.

APPENDIX

Bill For the relief of Robert Hooper, 16 Dec. 1800-19 Jan. 1801; printed; endorsement by TJ.

Bill and Report of Comt. concerning the District of Columbia, 17 Dec. 1800-7 Jan. 1801; emendation and endorsement by TJ.

Mr Morris motion for injunction of secrecy on consideration of Treaties, 17 Dec. 1800; entirely in TJ's hand.

Order of Senate for erection of two Stoves for Senate chamber order to the doorkeeper, 17 Dec. 1800; notation by TJ. Printed in JS, 3:113.

Bill Concerning the District of Columbia, 17 Dec. 1800-25 Feb. 1801; printed; notation, emendations, and endorsement by TJ.

Motion for Instructions given to the Envoys to the French Republic, 18-19 Dec. 1800; endorsement by TJ. Variant text printed in JEP, 1:359.

Mr Tracys motion on the subject of Secrecy, 22 Dec. 1800; endorsement by TJ. Variant text printed in JEP, 1:361.

Motion to have the cession of Columbia district &c. by the states Maryland & Virginia to U.S. printed, 30 Dec. 1800; entirely in TJ's hand. Printed in JS, 3:114.

Motion for an additional Rule [on the consideration of treaties], 5 Jan. 1801; endorsement by TJ. Printed in JEP, 1:365.

Bill To erect a Mausoleum for George Washington, 5 Jan.-4 Feb. 1801; printed; notation, emendations, and endorsement by TJ.

Form of Entry on French Treaty, 6 Jan. 1801; entirely in TJ's hand. Variant text printed in JEP, 1:365.

Convention Between the French Republic and the United States of America, 6-19 Jan. 1801; printed; notations and endorsement by TJ.

Report (In Part) of the Committee to Whom was Referred on the 28th Ultimo, so much of the Speech of the President, as Respects the District of Columbia, 7 Jan. 1801; printed; notation by TJ.

Additional Article to Convention with France, limiting its duration, 12 Jan. 1801; entirely in TJ's hand; notation by TJ. Printed in JEP, 1:367.

Motion, resolving that the Senate will attend the funeral of James Jones, a member of the House of Reps., 14 Jan. 1801; notation by TJ. Printed in JS, 3:115.

Additional article to Convention with France stating that nothing shall be construed or operate contrary to former and existing treaties, 15 Jan. 1801; entirely in TJ's hand; notation (with date) by TJ. Printed in JEP, 1:366.

Additional article to Convention with France limiting its duration, 15 Jan. 1801; entirely in TJ's hand; notation (with date) and emendations by TJ. Printed in JEP, 1:367, 370.

Report of VP to Committee of the whole on Convention, 15 Jan. 1801; entirely in TJ's hand. Variant text printed in JEP, 1:368.

Mr Hill[house]'s motion to amend amendt 2d [i.e. 3d] Article, French Convention, 15 Jan. 1801; notation by TJ. Printed in JEP, 1:368.

Report of Committee appointed to reduce the votes, on the Convention with France into the form of Ratification, 19-23 Jan. 1801; notations, emendations, and endorsement by TJ. Printed in JEP, 1:372.

Resolution requesting of the President of the United States to communicate such information (if any such there be) as may have been received respecting Convention with France, 20 Jan. 1801, notation by TJ. Printed in JEP, 1:371.

Resolution, to authorize the accommodation of the Supreme Court in the Capitol, 21 Jan. 1801; resolution entirely in TJ's hand, with dateline in Otis's hand. Printed in JS, 3:116.

Bill For the relief of Solomon Boston, 21-28 Jan. 1801; printed; endorsement by TJ.

Bill To provide for the erection and support of a Light-House on Cape Poge, at the north-easterly part of Martha's Vineyard, 21-28 Jan. 1801; printed; endorsement by TJ.

Bill To provide for the more convenient organization of the Courts of the United States, 21 Jan.-7 Feb. 1801; printed; notations, emendations, and endorsement by TJ.

Bill To continue in force the acts laying duties on licences for selling wines and foreign distilled spirits by retail, and so much of the act laying certain duties on snuff and refined sugar, as respects a duty on refined sugar; on property sold at auction, and on carriages for the conveyance of persons, 21 Jan.-23 Feb. 1801; printed; endorsement by TJ.

Motion on votes [on Convention of 1800], 23 Jan. 1801; entirely in TJ's hand; notations by TJ. Variant text printed in JEP, 1:372-3.

Motion to amend Journal of the 23d. of January, 26-27 Jan. 1801; notations and endorsement by TJ.

Motion relative to question on Ratification of a Treaty with modifications, 26 Jan.-3 Feb. 1801; notation and endorsement by TJ. Printed in JEP, 1:374.

Motion for a new Rule relative to questions decided &c., 27 Jan.-3 Feb. 1801; notation and endorsement by TJ. Printed in JEP, 1:374.

Bill Regulating the grants of land appropriated for the refugees from the British provinces of Canada and Nova Scotia, 29 Jan.-12 Feb. 1801; printed; endorsement by TJ.

Bill, To discharge Samuel Lewis, senior, from his imprisonment, 29 Jan.-19 Feb. 1801; printed; endorsement by TJ.

Bill To allow the transportation of goods, wares and merchandize to and from Philadelphia and Baltimore, by the way of Appoquinimink and Sassafras, 29 Jan.-26 Feb. 1801; printed; endorsement by TJ.

Committee Report on amendment to a bill, entitled "An act to erect a mausoleum to George Washington," 30 Jan. 1801; printed; notation by TJ.

Petition of Nath. Waldron and others of State R. Island, 2-5 Feb. 1801; endorsement by TJ.

Minutes on the French Convention, 3 Feb. 1801; notations and emendations by TJ. Variant printed in JEP, 1:376-7.

Bill Making the port of Biddeford and Pepperrelborough, and the port of New-Bedford in Massachusetts, ports of entry for ships or vessels arriving from the cape of Good Hope, and from places beyond the same, 3-12 Feb. 1801; printed; endorsement by TJ.

Bill To incorporate the persons therein named, and their associates, as a Mine and Metal Company, 3-28 Feb. 1801; printed; endorsement by TJ.

Committee report on bill concerning the district of Columbia, 4 Feb. 1801; notation by TJ. Printed copy, [4 Feb. 1801], notations and emendations by TJ.

Mr. Hillhouse's motion to amend the bill, entitled "An act to provide for the more convenient organization of the courts of the United States," 4 Feb. 1801; printed; notation by TJ.

Motion of Mr Hillhouse on judiciary, 5 Feb. 1801; notation by TJ.

Bill Giving a right of pre-emption to certain persons who have contracted with John Cleves Symmes, or his associates, for lands lying between the Miami rivers, in the territory of the United States, north-west of the Ohio, 6-25 Feb. 1801; printed; emendations and endorsement by TJ.

Bill To add to the district of Massac on the Ohio, and to discontinue the districts of Louisville in the state of Kentucky and Palmyra in the state of Tennessee, and therein to amend the act, entitled "An act to regulate the collection of duties on imports and tonnage," 6-27 Feb. 1801; printed; emendations and endorsement by TJ.

Motion of Mr Hillhouse on the Judiciary, 6 Feb. 1801; endorsement by TJ.

Mr Nicholas's motion on Judiciary, 6 Feb. 1801; endorsement by TJ. Printed in JS, 3:121-2.

Amendment to Bill Regulating the grants of land appropriated for the refugees from the British provinces of Canada and Nova Scotia, [7-10 Feb. 1801]; notation by TJ.

Motion by Mr Morris on mode of examining the votes for President and Vice President, 9 Feb. 1801; emendations by TJ.

Motion prescribing to the House of Reps. a mode of procedure on choosing by ballot a President of the U.S., 9 Feb. 1801; notation by TJ.

Resolution, to notify the House of Reps. of the time and place for counting the votes for President of the United States, 9 Feb. 1801; emendations by TJ. Printed in JS, 3:123-4.

Motion for opening Galleries, 10 Feb. 1801; entirely in TJ's hand; notation by TJ. Printed in JS, 3:124.

Bill to establish the district of Bristol, and to annex the towns of Kittery and Berwick to the district of Portsmouth, 16 Feb. 1801; emendation and endorsement by TJ. Printed copy, 16-18 Feb. 1801; emendations and endorsement by TJ.

INDEX

"A.B." (pseudonym): letter from, 506-9; apprehensive of TJ's election, 506-9
Abeille Americaine, 320n
Abert, Geneviève Marie. *See* La Marche, Madame de
abolition: southern states will not dismantle slavery, 155, 295; Africa furnishes little hope to "friends of freedom," 168; in Del., 497n; advocated, 582n
Abraham (ca. 1740-1818, Abram, TJ's slave), 417
Abram (b. 1794, TJ's slave), 164
Abridgment of the Public Permanent Laws of Virginia (Edmund Randolph), 471, 472n
"Account of the Capitol in Virginia" (Thomas Jefferson), 335n
Adair, Douglass, 382n
Adams, Abigail: quoted, 201n; relationship to Cranch, 377
Adams, George: *Micrographia Illustra,* 178

ADAMS, JOHN: letter to, 476

Opinions
thought to be pro-British, anti-French, 196-202; portrays opponents as deluded, 198-9; views of republicanism, 199-200, 202n, 253n; denounces "rage for innovation," 200

Personal Affairs
son-in-law refutes charges, 351-2; relationship to Cranch, 377; relationship to J. Johnson, 477n

Politics
less an aristocrat than TJ, 53; toasted, 60; and C. C. Pinckney candidacy, 91n, 97, 217-18, 229, 263; support for, in New England, 97, 343; 1796 electoral vote, 124, 309n; Paine disdains Adams, 186, 189, 193n; relations with Federalists, 189, 341n, 466; said to misrepresent his opponents, 198-9, 202n; associates republicanism with despotism, 199; weak support for in Del., 217-18; Callender on prospects of, 238; Hamilton's *Letter*, 239, 304n, 422; electoral vote, 263, 271, 300, 306,

307, 309, 322, 324, 347, 357, 358n; Federalists' patronage expectations, 308

President
address to Congress opening session, vii, 248, 250, 601; and proposed military academy, 5n; and recommendations for board of agriculture, 14; replies to addresses on XYZ affair, 34n, 196-202; criticized, 129, 138n, 189, 193n, 196-202, 456, 523n, 574; and establishment of navy, 138n; uses furnishings appropriation to buy horses for President's House stable, 140; late-term appointments, 162n, 296n; receives Ellsworth's resignation, 168n, 323-4n; cabinet politics, 185, 195; and Pickering, 189, 193n, 195, 465-6, 469n, 492; declaration of fast day, 202n; relations with France, 204n, 383n; and prosecution of sedition trials, 210n; and Blount conspiracy, 224; and Ellicott, 224, 321, 548; thought to be avoiding pact with France, 234-5, 244, 248, 252-3; May 1797 address by Senate, 253n; political patronage in Pa., 308, 309n; administration compared to reign of Queen Anne, 315; R. Peale seeks appointment, 316, 317n; submits U.S.-French convention to Senate, 318-19, 323n, 504; appoints chief justice, 324n; makes appointments, 353n, 377n, 443n, 495n, 536, 544n, 563n, 566, 567n, 570n, 577n; and Saint-Domingue, 357n; requests recall of Irujo, 396-7; and fires in government offices, 435-6; relationship with Washington, 436, 439n; low regard for, 436-7; and resolution of electoral tie, 436-7; relationship with Gerry, 465-6, 492; XYZ affair, 465-9, 490-5; Federalists criticize for policy toward France, 490, 492, 494n; mistreated in office, 508; administration marked by bad appointments, 566; and government for D.C., 601; sends correspondence, papers to Congress, 602

[605]

INDEX

ADAMS, JOHN (*cont'd*)

Relations with Jefferson

TJ categorizes Adams's replies to XYZ addresses, 196-202; TJ logs Adams's "Egotisms," 200-1, 202n; statements attributed to TJ, 253n; and appointments, 291-2; TJ hopes to reach an understanding, 323, 436; invites TJ to dinner, 476; TJ reports Adams's views on election, 500

Adams, John Quincy, 296n, 477n

Adams, Louisa Catherine Johnson, 477n

Adams, Samuel: Paine's friendship with, 186; introduces travelers, 244, 250; recommendations for appointments, 349n

Address to the People of the United States (John Beckley), 125n

Ad Lucilium Epistulae Morales (Lucius Annaeus Seneca), 502, 503n

Advice to the People in General, with Regard to Their Health (Samuel Auguste André David Tissot), 178

Advice to Shepherds (Louis Jean Marie Daubenton), 157, 159n

Africa: and linguistic mix on American frontier, 50; Europeans' accounts of, 112, 168; rice of, introduced in U.S., 124, 125n; can give little hope to "friends of freedom," 168; Cape of Good Hope, 603. *See also* Egypt

African Americans: Va. places restrictions on, 482

Age of Reason. Part the Second (Thomas Paine), 190-1, 193n

Aggy. *See* Gillette, Agnes; Hern, Aggy

agriculture: societies for promoting, 8, 10-11n, 125n, 596-7; recommendations for a national board or society, 13-14, 423, 501-3, 560, 596-7; in college curricula, 19n; pests, 21, 43, 185, 206, 297n, 441; toast in praise of, 61n; relationships of land, labor, profit, 85, 121-2, 151-3; crop rotation, 108-10, 164-6; books on, 112, 153, 159n, 178; observations of foreign travelers, 121-2; British improvements to, 149-50; fertilizer, 178, 232n, 407, 441, 545; study of soils, 178; role of, in U.S. economy, 181, 183, 422; cultivation of melons, 206, 306; Mazzei's interest in, 275, 278; threshing machines, 495n; American Board of Agriculture created, 503n

Alabama, 243n, 320n

Albany, N.Y., 58, 198, 411n

Albemarle Co., Va.: postal service, 104, 213; and fire insurance, 104-7; flour mills, 109n, 116; Pen Park estate, 109n; courts, court days, 116, 134, 146, 475, 489; land prices, 116, 144, 242; Birdwood plantation, 117n; land taxes, 128n, 164; parishes of, 128n; potential for sheep raising, 149; and Gabriel's insurrection, 160; clerks, 166n; quality of tobacco from, 209, 301, 546; reputation of lands of, 330; deputy sheriffs, 419n; Tarleton's raid, 452n; surveyors, 592n. *See also* Monroe, James; Monticello

alcoholism, 153, 207

Aldridge, William J.: payments from TJ, 46-7, 472, 473n; letters to, from cited, 47n; supplies groceries, 471, 473n

Alembert, Jean Le Rond d': and *Encyclopédie,* 180

Alexander, Mr., 275, 278

Alexander, Amos: letters to, 15-16, 355-6; letter from, 338; supports TJ, 15-16, 338, 355-6; identified, 16n; letters from cited, 16n, 338n

Alexander, Andrew: letter to, 398-9; letter from, 359-60; trustee of Washington Academy, 359-60, 398-9; identified, 360n

Alexander, Robert, 360n

Alexander the Coppersmith, 308

Alexandria, Bank of, 404n

Alexandria, Egypt, 586

Alexandria, Va.: population of, xxxix; officeholders, 16n; stagecoaches, 16n; churches, 54n; potential home for Du Pont, 65-6, 67, 92, 313, 314; merchants, 140n; schools, 140n; postal service at, 171; and case of *Ranger,* 213n; Darrell and Craven at, 242; newspapers, 330; offers public dinner for TJ, 338, 355-6; hotels, 392n; banks, 404n; poor roads to Washington, 508

Alexandria Mechanical Relief Society, 16n

Algiers: corsairs of, 195; U.S. treaty with, 456

Alien Friends Act (1798): opposition to, 33, 522; and Ky. Resolutions, 381n; and French visitors to U.S., 383n

Allarde, Pierre Gilbert Leroy, baron d', 326, 327, 354

INDEX

Apology for the Bible (Richard Watson, Bishop of Llandaff), 190-1, 193n

"Apotheosis of Washington" (John James Barralet), 420

Appel a l'Impartiale Postérité (Marie Jeanne Phlipon Roland de la Platière), 415

Appendix to the Notes on Virginia Relative to the Murder of Logan's Family: distribution, 8, 11n, 93, 518, 581; published with *Notes,* 219, 334n

Appleton, Thomas, 273, 276-7, 279, 340

Archaeologica Graeca: Or, the Antiquities of Greece (John Potter), 176

Argentina, 218n

Argus (New York), 330n, 376n

"Aristides" (pseudonym), 329, 330n

Aristotle, 479

Arlington, Vt., 197, 198

Armstrong, John (1755-1816): letter from, 245-6; and Kosciuszko's lands, 101, 245-6; identified, 246n

Armstrong, Gen. John: elected to Senate, 315-16; suggested as secretary of war, 566; reports conversation with G. Morris, 590

Arnay, Jean Rodolphe d': *De la Vie privée des Romains,* 177

Arrowsmith, Aaron: maps of North America, 69, 464n; *New and Elegant General Atlas,* 464n

Artemis, temple of, 129, 130n

Arthur, William: letter from, 410-12; asks TJ's religious views, 410-12; identified, 411-12n

artisans: slaves work as, 138n

Asia: languages, 35-7, 134; and origins of American Indians, 134

Asinius Pollio, Gaius, 487, 488n

Ast, William Frederick, 106n

Astronomie (Joseph Jérôme Le Français de Lalande), 180

astronomy: published tables, papers on, 71-2, 89, 147, 157, 255, 346, 479-80; books on, 180, 237, 298-9; data from Ellicott's boundary survey, 224, 336, 479-80; moon, 287, 334, 443; Newtonian theory, 299; meridian at Washington, 321, 346; and common almanacs, 334, 502n; declination of sun, 548, 549n

Astronomy (James Ferguson), 180

Atlas Portatif à l'Usage des Colleges (L'Abbé Grenet and Rigobert Bonne), 180

attorneys: in Ky., 38-9, 41, 561-3, 569-70; in Va., 38-9, 41, 499, 524n; equated with clergy, doctors, 103; in S.C., 208-9n, 348; part of Federalist establishment, 228; in N.H., 348; in Pa., 348, 483; in Del., 370-1; federal district attorneys, 387n; TJ employs, 419n; in Mass., 465; in N.Y., 550-1; read law in Albemarle Co., 561

Augusta Co., Va., 38n, 328n

Aurora (Philadelphia): and rumor of TJ's death, 42n; commentary by, 46n, 435-6n; distribution of, in Va., 104; subscriptions to, 116n; publishes political essays, 135n, 329, 330n, 572n; prints letters, documents, 138n, 202n, 239n, 439n; advertisements, 210n, 212, 213n; Senate prosecution of Duane, 217n; on aspects of presidential election, 221-2, 487; calls Hamilton an intriguer, 304n; reports on Pa. election impasse, 309n, 336n; rumors of Federalist intrigues, 404n. *See also* Duane, William

Austin, William (editor), 201n

Austria: accedes to peace with France, xxxviii, 21-2, 101-2, 186-8, 191n, 192n, 202-3; relations with Louis XVI, 90n; relations with Britain, 187, 191n, 192n; negotiates at Rastatt, 192n; war renewed, ended, 340, 341n, 478, 584; Treaty of Lunéville, 372-3n, 586; releases Lafayette, 427, 430, 431n; and rule of Tuscany, 553, 555; and Naples, 587

Authentic Account of an Embassy from the King of Great Britain to the Emperor of China (George Leonard Staunton), 35, 37n

Aventures de Télémaque (François de Salignac de La Mothe-Fénelon), 502, 503n

Azara, José Nicolás de, 88, 90n

Bache, Catharine Wistar, 17, 39, 69

Bache, William: visits Monticello, 17, 39; knows Niemcewicz, 69; carries correspondence, 104, 202n; hires slaves, 559; TJ reports progress of House balloting to, 579n

bacon, 47, 61, 471

Bacon, Francis: *Historie,* 176; *Essays,* 179

Baer, George, Jr., 46n, 322, 323n, 419n

Bagwell (TJ's slave), 163

138n, 174, 211-12, 233, 235, 236, 238, 240, 250, 254, 255n, 414; jailed at Richmond, 100-1, 129-30, 136-8, 174, 176n, 211-13, 233-4, 235, 236, 254, 399; on U.S. Constitution, 129, 212, 254, 255n; desires press of his own, 130, 137, 233-4; links own future to Republicans', 137, 233; problems with eyesight, uses amanuensis, 137, 138n, 175n, 255n; essay on the navy, 137-8; account of slave conspirators' trials, 174-6; *Political Progress of Britain,* 179; and Madison, 212, 238, 537n; children of, remain in Philadelphia, 213; and *Examiner,* 213n, 233-4, 236, 255n, 399; as "Scots Correspondent," 234n, 255n; seeks, receives financial assistance from TJ, 235, 238, 239-41, 244-5, 254, 450, 470; conflict with Chase, 236; condemned on religious terms, 236-7; "Defence" of TJ, 254-5; and resolution of presidential election, 399; denounced as a supporter of TJ, 519n

Callis, William O., 367n

Calvinism and Universalism (Joseph Young), 237n

Cambacérès, Jean Jacques Régis, 204n

Cambridge, Mass., 200

Camden, N.C., 38n

Camden (Cambden), William: *History of Elizabeth,* 176

"Camillus" (Alexander Hamilton), 426n

Campbell, David, 44, 51n

Campbell, John, 150

Campbell, Samuel, 376

Campbell Co., Va., 104

Campoformio, Treaty of, 373n, 586

Canada: weather observations, 287-8, 443, 448; prospective invasions of, 339, 361n; and alleged British payments to Americans, 352; boundary, 479, 480n, 481n; lands for refugees from, 602, 603

canals: benefits of public investment in, 423; for TJ's mill, 500, 517, 559; Erie, 503n; James River and Kanawha, 503n. *See also* Chesapeake and Delaware Canal Company; James River Company

Canandaigua, N.Y., 7n

Capulets, 370, 371n

Carey, Dr. John, 447

Carey, Mathew: letter to, 447; letter from, 319; prints books, pamphlets, 263n, 345n, 447n, 464n; *School of*

Wisdom, 319, 447; *American Atlas,* 464n; *American Museum,* 571-2

Carlisle, Pa., 201, 348, 434, 483

Carlos (Charles) IV, King of Spain, 51, 52n, 224, 396-7, 480, 548, 549n

Carnot, Lazare Nicolas Marguerite: *Réponse,* 415

Carolina Gazette (Charleston, S.C.), 266n

Carondelet, Francisco Luis Hector, Baron de: governor of Louisiana, 394n

carpenters, 30-1, 57, 64, 70-1

Carr, Mr., 341

Carr, Dabney (TJ's brother-in-law), 99n, 419n

Carr, Hester Smith Stevenson (Hettie, Mrs. Peter Carr), 161, 227

Carr, Jefferson: death of, 116

Carr, Martha Jefferson (Mrs. Dabney Carr, TJ's sister), 98-9

Carr, Mary Jane: not expected to live, 116

Carr, Peter (TJ's nephew): design of residence of, 94; family, 116, 161, 227; joins subscription for Holt, 129n; prospective secretary for TJ, 416-17, 481; letters to, from cited, 417n; TJ reports progress of House balloting to, 579n

Carr, Thomas, Jr., 342

carriage tax, 128n, 602

Carrol, John, 406n

Carroll, Bishop John, 394-5n

Carter, Charles (of Blenheim), 275, 278

Carter, Edward (Ned), 90n

Carter, George (Albemarle Co.), 39

Cartwright, T., xxxix

Cary (b. 1785, TJ's slave), 417

Cary, Sir Henry, Viscount Falkland (attributed author): *History of the Life, Reign, and Death of Edward II,* 176

Castinelli, Giussepi, 554, 555

Cathalan, Stephen, Jr.: consul at Marseilles, 174n

Cathalan, Stephen, Sr., 125n

Cathcart, Mr., 317

Catherine II (the Great), Empress of Russia, 455, 478

Catholic Church: Poor Clares, 392-5; diocese at Baltimore, 394n; Ursuline convent, 394n; seminaries, 395n; allusions to Jesuits, 551-2

Catiline, 441

Catlett, Kemp, 105, 144

cattle, 108, 150, 159n, 164, 166, 452n

Cayenne, French Guiana, 493

INDEX

Holmes (Holms), John: works at Monticello, 31n, 64, 70-1; witnesses indenture, 166; dies from fall, 482, 499

Holstein, 155-6, 159n, 478

Holt, Charles: publishes *Bee,* 7n; subscriptions to pay fine of, 49-50, 117n, 129n, 406n

Holy Roman Empire: titles, 4n, 110, 585n; French wish to reconfigure, 586. *See also* Austria

Homer: never successfully translated, 299

"Homo" (T. Law pseudonym), 270n

Hooke (Hook), Robert, 55n

Hoomes, John: letters to, 504, 540; letters from, 290, 400-1, 515-16; corresponds about politics, 290, 401n, 504, 515-16, 540; identified, 290n; letters from cited, 290n, 401n; sells horse to TJ, 400-1, 489, 504, 515-16, 540; letter to cited, 400-1n; letter from quoted, 515-16n

Hooper, Robert, 601

Hopkins, John, Jr., 374

Hopkins, Samuel (Ky.): and U.S. marshal for Ky., 451-2n; letter from quoted, 451n

Hopkins, Samuel (N.Y.), 591

Horace: *Epistulae,* 167, 168n, 483, 487n; E. Livingston borrows *Odes* of, 550, 551n

Horse-Hoeing Husbandry: or, An Essay on the Principles of Vegetation and Tillage (Jethro Tull), 178

horses: TJ seeks to purchase, 14, 43, 47n, 400-1, 489, 504, 515-16, 540; Fitzpartner, 47n; injuries caused by vehicles and, 70, 505, 568, 573-4; sold by W. Short, 77; military uses of, 102n; in lease agreement, 108, 164, 166; for president's stable, 140; in Ky., 150; good land for, along James R., 152; and hay production, 152; boarding of, in Washington, 260n; arranged for TJ's travel, 263; allusions to, 282, 299, 313-14, 315; Tarquin, 400n, 489; farriers, 406n; equipment for, 465n; for carriage, 489; for riding, 489

horticulture: books on, 112; in educational curricula, 143; collections, 232n

Hottinguer, Jean Conrad: as "X", 466-9

Houston, George Smith: letter from, 134-6; inquires about rumors, 134-6; identified, 135n

Houston, Jane Smith, 135n

Houston, Mary Forman, 135n

Houston, William Churchill, 135-6

Houston, William Churchill (the younger), 135n

Howard, John E., 249n

Hubbard, James (b. 1783, Jame, TJ's slave), 417, 528

Hubbard, Nicholas: and Mazzei's business affairs, 47. *See also* Van Staphorst & Hubbard

Hubbard, Philip (1786-1819, Phill, TJ's slave), 418

Hudson River, 231, 232-3n, 408, 550

Huger, Benjamin, 258n

Hughes, James: certificate of cited, 562n

Hughes, Wormley (1781-1858, TJ's slave): to help clear land, 417; involved in blasting mill canal, 517, 559

Hume, David: *History of England,* 177; *Essays,* 180

Humphreys, Daniel: *Bible Needs No Apology,* 386-7, 446

Humphreys, David: letter from, 162-3; as minister to Portugal, 75-6, 90n; writings, 162; recommends Preble, 162-3; brother, 387; and U.S. relations with Spain, 397n

Hunn, John, 368

Hunter, John, 265

Hurt, John, 17

Husbandry of the Ancients (Adam Dickson), 178

Hutchins, Anthony, 224, 225n

Hutton, Charles: *Mathematical Tables,* 180

Hylton, Daniel L., 70, 175n

Hylton, John, 495

Hylton, Sarah Eppes, 70n

Hylton, William, Sr.: letter from, 495; recommends son for army, 495; visits Monticello, 495n

Impartial History of the late Revolution in France (Jean Paul Rabaut Saint Étienne), 343-5, 415

impeachment, 122, 218n, 381

Independence Day: Republicans honor TJ on, 42-3; Philadelphia Republicans celebrate, 45, 46n; in Raleigh, 60-1; Americans in Spain celebrate, 162n; Federalists scorn TJ on, 442

Independent Chronicle (Boston), 104

India: British-French rivalry in, 192n; economic conditions, 270

Indiana Territory, 563n

INDEX

JEFFERSON, THOMAS (*cont'd*)
most Americans to be Republican,
588-9. *See also* election of 1800

Portraits
bust by Ceracchi, 62n; by R. Peale,
317n; by R. Field, 374n

President
inauguration, xxxv; appointments, 7n,
162n, 296n, 327n, 349n, 435n,
498n, 502n, 592n; and Adams's
appointments, 162n; moves into
President's House, 260n; removes
officers, 328n, 582n; declines to appoint Duncanson, 358n; asks for reversal of Irujo's recall, 397n

President-Elect
music written in his honor, xxxv; receives congratulations, 257, 266,
290, 291, 305, 312-15, 335, 339,
344, 345, 368, 388, 403, 406, 416n,
457, 486, 520, 552, 561, 564, 574,
581; cautioned about entreaties
from S.C., 268, 333, 413; his election presumed, 300, 302-4, 312-15,
354, 361, 396, 422, 435-6n, 448n,
452, 542-4, 583, 584, 587; aspira-
tions for administration, 302-3, 307,
408, 539; begins to assemble cabinet, 302-4, 322, 343, 358, 408-9,
438-9, 537, 566, 596; secrecy of
arrangements, 304, 439, 537; Federalists expect removals from office,
308, 542, 575, 588-9; appointments,
contracts, influence solicited, 313,
314, 316-17, 340, 354, 416-17, 433-
4, 518-19, 533, 534n, 561, 575-7,
582, 587; hopes to reach understanding with Adams, 323, 436; Ky.
marshalship, 327-8, 450-2, 457-8,
460-1, 561-3, 564, 592, 595; needs
to understand Gabriel's insurrection, 330; public celebrations must
be delayed, 338, 355-6; evaluates
potential candidates for office, 347-
9; hopes to continue seeing daughters while he is president, 391-2,
475; recommendations for private
secretary, 416-17, 459-60, 481; and
power to convene Congress, 437;
procedures for interim appointments, 439; urged to claim authority as president, 485-6; importance
of foreign affairs, 489; opponents'
understanding of his positions, ex-

pectations for his presidency, 506-9;
salary payment anticipated, 565;
consequences of delay in Senate approval of appointments, 572, 594;
has support, dedication of all honest
people, 574; policy regarding appointments, 588-9; his election still
in doubt, 590; approached with
deals to settle election, 594

Religion
views on Christianity, xxxvii, 111-12,
167-8, 410-11; accused of atheism,
32, 116, 135n, 229; Va. act for religious freedom, 45, 53-4, 122-3,
124-5n; predicts divine retribution
for slanderers, 98; changes his mind
about clergy holding office, 102-3;
accused of deism, 116, 135n, 230n,
386-7, 446, 506-7; on establishment
of religion, 167; decries "tyranny
over the mind of man," 168; asked
for statement on beliefs, 249,
386-7; and community of scientists,
311; contribution for Georgetown
church, 318n; compiles "Philosophy
of Jesus," 345n; orders pocket
Bible, 376; comments in *Notes on
Virginia*, 386; asked to buy convent
school property, 392-5; his views on
freedom of religion praised, 486;
his views unsettle some people, 507.
See also election of 1800

Scientific Interests
and Count Rumford, 4-5, 311;
R. R. Livingston's system of raising
water, 9, 11n, 120-1; differences
between Europe and America, 18;
must defer, limit his own engagement with scientific topics, 18, 299,
444; prevention of yellow fever,
18-19; comparative studies of languages, 44, 50, 51n, 134, 135n,
243, 449; astronomy, 71-2, 89, 147,
157, 237, 255, 298-9, 334; viewed
Paine's bridge model, 190; collects
information on sewer drains, 230,
232n; successor to Franklin, Rittenhouse as patron of science, 237;
smallpox vaccination, 264-5, 355;
respected as author of *Notes*, 289;
declines, then accepts, continued
presidency of APS, 298, 388,
509-10; all theories are subject
to scrutiny, 299; scientific world
diverse, but "one family," 311;

than Federalists are in New England, 333; oppose wasteful expenditure, 337, 371; all support TJ, 343, 408; TJ's desiderata for changes to federal system, 381-2; happy to have Congress remain inactive, 385; win congressional seats in N.J., 391, 418, 500; could join Federalists to elect Burr, 399; not accustomed to standing firm against threats, 404; absent from Congress, 418, 419n; increasing strength in state governments, 421; in vulnerable, "unjust" situation, excluded from office, 421, 588; in Senate, 422; of Washington, 459; some critical of Gerry, 491, 493; called enemies of religion, 522; growing respect for, 534; compared to Spartans, 571; Dallas a key figure for, 574

Republican Watch-Tower (New York), 376

Revolutions de Portugal (René Aubert de Vertot), 177

Reynolds, James, 577n

Reynolds, Maria Lewis (Mrs. James Reynolds), 577n

Rhea, Jonathan, 367n

Rhine River: left bank ceded to France, 373n

Rhode Island: and election of 1800, vii, 97, 146n, 216, 217n, 234, 236, 250, 263, 322, 324, 332-3, 367n; Republicans in, vii, 229, 343; politics in, 6; addresses on XYZ affair, 199-200; unreliable information from, 250, 342-3; Federalists win, 271; withholds one Pinckney electoral vote, 322, 324; residents petition Senate, 602; and U.S. customs districts, 603

Rhode Island, College of (Brown University), 200

Rhodes. *See* Rodes (Rhodes), Matthew

rice: demand for, in Britain, 30; heavy upland, introduced from Africa to U.S., 124, 125n; and relationship of marshes, pestilence, 124; planters, 208n

Richards, John: handles financial transactions, 64, 114, 139, 302, 312, 405; grocer and John Barnes's agent, 65n; travels between Philadelphia and Washington, 497, 560-1

Richardson, Richard: letter to, 413-14; letters from, 341-2, 597-8; nailery account, 59, 116; witnesses indenture, 166; and Robert Richardson, 255n;

superintends work at Monticello, 341-2, 390-1, 413-14, 471, 488, 597-8; letter from cited, 342n; receives payment, 401, 471, 472; TJ hires slave of, 414, 474n; and Lilly, 417, 598

Richardson, Robert: Callender's amanuensis, 137, 138n, 175n, 255n

Richmond, Va.: artists, xxxvii; TJ's groceries sent by way of, 14, 15, 20, 29, 31, 47, 61, 208, 227, 471-3, 517; commercial, financial relationships with Philadelphia, 17, 30-1, 46-7, 55, 64-5, 71, 127-8, 130, 139, 171, 172, 209, 241, 568; jail, 100-1, 131, 136-8, 145, 212-13, 235-6; newspapers, 125n, 127n, 255, 478; as financial, banking center, 127-8, 130, 241, 251; postal service at, 129, 138, 161, 488; printers, 130, 137, 212, 233, 236, 414; and Gabriel's insurrection, 131, 136-7, 138n, 144-5, 174-6, 212, 295; militia, local guard, 145n, 482n; as market for hay, 152; fires in, 174; XYZ addresses from, 200; price of tobacco at, 209, 235, 240, 245, 251n, 258, 297-8, 301, 546; federal courts in, 212, 213n; as state capital, 220; election results, 244; lacks regular financial connection to Georgetown, 251; presidential electors meet in, 253; lots in, 275, 278; merchants, 374, 473n; tobacco sold at, 402, 450, 546; attorneys, 421n; Rocketts Landing, 471, 472; storage and inspection of tobacco at Shockoe warehouse, 471, 472. *See also* Gibson & Jefferson; Jefferson, George

Ridgely, Nicholas, 371

Rising Sun (sloop), 38

Rittenhouse, David, 237, 363n, 589n

Rittenhouse, Eleanor Coulston, 589n

Rivanna River: boat transport on, 14, 20, 29, 37, 47, 61, 92, 172; and Monticello, Tufton, 108, 110n, 116, 163; mills on, 116, 558; improvement of navigation on, 122, 124n; Shadwell ford, 163

Roanoke River, 90n, 91

Robbins, Jonathan, 33-4

Roberts, Joseph, Jr.: supplies nailrod, 46, 171; letters to cited, 47n, 405n. *See also* Roberts & Jones (Philadelphia)

Roberts & Jones (Philadelphia): supply nailrod, 171-2, 406n; TJ buys stoves from, 172, 405n, 472; letters to, from cited, 172n

Robertson, Dr. William: works of, 176, 177, 178, 231, 233n

INDEX

Saint Hugues, Mother Marie Agnès de. *See* Chevalier, Marie Françoise

St. Julien, Joseph Guyard, Count, 102n, 188

St. Marks, Fla., 51, 52n

Saint Marys River, 548

St. Mary's Seminary (Baltimore), 395n

Saint-Mémin, Charles Balthazar Julien Févret de, xxxvii-xxxviii

St. Petersburg, Russia, 3-4, 40, 222-4, 294

St. Thomas, W.I., 456

Salem, Mass., 141

Sallust: works of, 177

Sally (b. 1792, TJ's slave), 164

Sally (sloop), 115n

salt springs, 150

Sandeman, Robert, 387n

Savannah, Ga., 34n, 232n, 498n

Savery, Thomas, 9, 11n, 121

Sayre, Samuel William, 457, 590, 591n

Sayre, Stephen: letter to, 590-1; letter from, 452-7; recommended for federal office, 433-4; proposes himself as minister for international congress, 452-7, 590-1; acquaintance with TJ, 457n; letter from cited, 457n; TJ's correspondence with, 591n

Scatcherd, James, 376

Schaeffer, Bernard, 577n

School of Wisdom: or, American Monitor (Mathew Carey), 319, 447

Schuylkill River, xxxvii, 206

sciences: in college curricula, 143; government role in collecting, disseminating information, 156, 321; books on, 178, 180; TJ's election a victory for science, 313, 315, 481n; reasoned inquiry under siege by despotism, bigotry, 444, 481n

Scilla. *See* Gillette, Priscilla

Scioto River, 245

Scobell, Henry: *Memorials,* 22, 28n, 283

Scotland: Scots in America, 3n, 232n, 411n; Sinclair in, 13; medical training in, 19n; language, speech, 50; Ariana Randolph in, 64n; Scots as U.S. consuls, 174; histories, 176; universities, 210n, 411n, 510n; strong unity of Caledonians, 333; income tax revenues, 379; Church of, 387n

"Scots Correspondent" (Callender pseudonym), 234n, 255n

Scott, Charles: letter from cited, 452n

Scott, Gustavus, 377

Scott, William, Lord Stowell, 223n

Scourge of Aristocracy, and Repository of Important Political Truths, 262n

Scull, John, 486, 488n

Sedgwick, Theodore, 386n, 419n, 504

Sedition Act (1798): opposition to, 33, 515, 522; prosecutions under, 49-50, 117n, 129n, 210n, 213n, 439n, 442; constrains discussion, 224; bill to continue act in force, 418, 419n, 504, 597n. *See also* Callender, James Thomson

seeds: of muskmelon, xxxvii, 206, 207, 266, 306; from Cummings, 45; of Peruvian winter grass, 49, 128; succory, 49; for wheat, 108, 165-6; sent by post, 128; of varieties of squash, 275, 278; clover, 440-1, 517; cabbage, 471

Selden, Joseph, 131n, 175n

Selection of the Patriotic Addresses, to the President of the United States, 196-202

Seminole Indians, 51-2

Seneca, Lucius Annaeus: *Philosophi opera,* 179; *Ad Lucilium Epistulae Morales,* 502, 503n

"Senex" (Beckley pseudonym), 135n

Seney, Joshua, 365, 366n

serfs, 155-6

Sergeant, Elizabeth Rittenhouse (Mrs. Jonathan Dickinson Sergeant), 589

Sergeant, Jonathan Dickinson, 589n

Serious Considerations on the Election of a President (William Linn), 134-6, 168, 249

Sermons (William Enfield), 179

Sermons of Mr. Yorick (Laurence Sterne), 179

servants, 260, 271

Several Essays in Political Arithmetick (Sir William Petty), 179

Several Methods by Which Meridional Lines May be Found with Ease and Accuracy (Andrew Ellicott), 547-8, 549n, 589

sewers: design of street drains for, 230-1, 232n

Seybert, Adam, 19n

Shadwell (TJ's estate): lease of fields at, 108, 109n, 116, 470n, 473n; mill at, 116; ford at, 163; excavation of mill canal, 500, 517, 559

Shakespeare, William: in M. Carey's reader, 319n; *Romeo and Juliet,* 370, 371n

Sharon, Conn., 58-9, 98

Shawangunk, N.Y., 289, 407, 544

INDEX

livestock, 108; lease of fields at, 108-10, 116, 390-1; adjoins Monticello, 110n; woodlands, 165

Tull, Jethro: *Horse-Hoeing Husbandry,* 178

Tunnicliff, William, 392n

Tunstall, Thomas, 561, 563n

Turgot, Anne Robert Jacques: biography by Condorcet, 180; *Reflexions,* 180

turkeys, 287, 288n, 443-4

turnips, 441

Tuscany, 276, 278, 553-4, 555

Tyler, Anne Contesse, 524n

Tyler, John (1747-1813): letter to, 594-5; letter from, 524-5; introduces nephew, 389, 524-5, 594-5; identified, 524-5n

Tyler, John (1790-1862), 524n

Tyler, John (d. 1773), 524n

Tyler, Mary Marot Armistead, 524n

Tyler, Samuel, 389, 524, 594-5

Uches. *See* Yuchi (Uchee) Indians

UNITED STATES

Army

military academy proposed, 5n; views on standing army, 33, 96, 422; harbor fortifications, 56-7, 66-8, 247; militia preferred over, 60, 173, 339, 422; and executive patronage, 126; armory at New London, Va., 248, 249n; officers of provisional, 309n; War, Navy Departments could be combined, 409; regiments disbanded, 422; fire in War Department office, 435-6; superintendent of military stores, 435n; clerks, functions of War Department, 462-3, 575n; War Department maps, 463; appointments, 495; Armstrong suggested as secretary of war, 566; L. H. Stockton nominated, withdrawn as secretary of war, 566, 567n

Confederation Congress

authorizes monument to Washington, 61-2; admiralty courts, 370, 371n

Congress, Fifth
(4 Mch. 1797-3 Mch. 1799)

and proposed board of agriculture, 14n; Gerry insulted on floor of House, 494, 495n

Congress, Sixth
(4 Mch. 1799-3 Mch. 1801)

opening of 2d session, vii, 115, 116, 216, 243, 248-9, 263; toasted, 61n; elected during XYZ influence on policy, 97; party strengths in, 97, 243; and allowances for consuls, 132-3; act further to suspend commercial intercourse between U.S. and France, 214, 217n; bill for uniform mode of drawing jurors by lot, 214, 217n; and regulation of judges' officeholding, 214, 217n; Ross election bill, 214, 217n, 379n; convenes in new Capitol, 248n; authorization for congressional library, 259; idle, 263, 324, 336, 376, 385; post roads bill, 323, 324n, 336-7; potential bills to direct outcome of presidential election, 358; act to establish uniform system of bankruptcy, 381; and Gérard claim, 384-5; bill for Washington mausoleum, 385, 386n, 601, 602; and budget surplus, 385; possible prolongation of, 404n; bill to continue Sedition Act, 418, 419n, 504, 515, 597n; relief of S. Lewis, 462-4, 574-5, 602; public dissatisfied with, 515; considers continued suspension of trade with France, 540; and western land titles, 603. *See also* District of Columbia; Judiciary Act (1801)

Congress, Seventh
(4 Mch. 1801-3 Mch. 1803)

Republican majorities expected, 6, 95-7, 227, 485; potential role in resolving presidential election, 436-7; dispensation to Dufour for land purchase, 529-33; Senate called for 4 Mch., 572

Continental Congress

Wythe's, P. Randolph's experience in, xxxvi, 21n; members, 415n

Courts

R. R. Livingston laments "arbitrary dogmas" of, 10, 122; Robbins extradition, 33-4; circuit courts, 70n, 213n, 353n; Ware v. Hylton, 70n; suit against E. Randolph, 74-6, 154, 374; importance of trial by jury, 96; impeachment of judges, 122; and indemnification of consuls, 132; chief justiceship, 167, 168n, 322, 323-4n,

UNITED STATES (*cont'd*)
358; marshals, 212, 327-8, 347-8,
349n, 358n, 360n, 450-2, 457-8,
460-1, 561-3, 564, 582, 592; judges'
officeholding, 214, 217n; juries, 214,
217n, 347-8; Pa. Federalists seek judicial appointments, 308; district
court judges, 353n, 525n, 561, 563n;
judicial appointments, 353n, 443n;
chief justice as potential acting president, 358, 375, 385; lasting effects
of judicial appointments, 358, 385;
judges' role in certification of electoral votes, 367n; district attorneys,
387n, 563n, 567n, 570n; judiciary
aligned with executive, 422, 485;
clerks, 561, 563n; Marshall named
chief justice, 570n; Judiciary Act
of 1789, 592; room in Capitol for
Supreme Court, 599, 602. *See also*
common law; Judiciary Act (1801)

Economy
speculation in paper, lands, 7n; use
of hard money, coins, 17, 405; commerce toasted, 61n; agricultural
economics, 85, 121-2, 151-3; values
of securities, currency, 86, 154; role
of commerce, 96; domestic tobacco
markets, 107; transactions in state
currencies, 108, 209, 260n, 400,
402n, 409-10, 413-14, 427, 440,
441ln, 450, 470-2, 473, 499, 534,
535, 558, 573; bank stocks, 158;
Europeans explore commercial
prospects, 161-2n; specie as tender
of contracts, 164; agricultural sup-
plier to industrial, commercial
France and Britain, 181, 183, 325,
326, 438; national currency advocated, 270n; weights and measures,
334, 361-3, 444-5; as market for
British manufactures, 339, 586; relationship of banks' notes in circulation to capital, 350-1; importance of
agriculture, 422, 501; shipping in-
creasingly in foreign hands, 422-3;
potential supply of naval stores to
Britain, 438, 439n; imprisonment
for debt, 462-4, 574-5; trade with
W. Indies, 497n; commercial, banking interests and election intrigue,
500; efforts toward manufacturing
self-sufficiency during American
Revolution, 582n; textile milling,
582n

Executive
likened to a monarchy, 126, 302-3;
fund for furnishings used to purchase horses for president, 140;
social expectations for cabinet, president, 303-4; post roads system
means patronage, favoritism, 337;
use of favors, patronage, 422, 518-19

Foreign Relations
and Spanish authorities in Fla., 51,
52n; boundaries, 55n, 224, 448,
479, 480n, 481n, 548, 549n; avoid-
ance of entangling alliances, 96, 294,
422, 590; consuls as neutrals, 132;
compensation, indemnification of
consuls, 132-4; with Denmark, 156,
293-4; with Spain, 162, 373, 396-7,
424; with Naples and Sicily, 173,
339-40; potential alliance with neutrality league, 186, 189, 195, 204;
with Prussia, 293-4, 296n; with
Russia, 294; aggression against
Britain proposed, 339; diplomatic
relations with Saint-Domingue,
356-7; importance of avoiding war,
372, 422, 438; assuring American
neutrality, 381, 382-4; diplomatic
establishment, 381, 506-7; proposal
to have no resident ministers of
other nations in U.S., 383; no news
from Europe, 385; with Batavian
Republic, 424; dominated by Treasury Department, 424; draw attention, resources from domestic needs,
424; U.S. favors monarchies, not
republics, 424-5; Sayre proposes
multinational agreement, 452-7,
590; with Algiers, 456; nation faces
an agitated international situation,
581. *See also* Convention of 1800;
France: U.S. Relations with; Great
Britain: U.S. Relations with

Government
Digest of the Laws, 364-6; 1792 act
on presidential election, succession,
367, 484-6, 488n; TJ desires council of appointment, 381; need for a
congressional library, 423; German
edition of statutes needed, 424

House of Representatives
petitioned, 132-3, 364-6, 462-4, 529-
33; Republican majority expected,
227; committees, 259n, 364-6, 418,
419n, 436n; party strengths in,

A comprehensive index of Volumes 1-20 of the
First Series has been issued as Volume 21.
Each subsequent volume has its own index,
as does each volume or set of volumes
in the Second Series.

THE PAPERS OF THOMAS JEFFERSON are composed in Monticello, a font based on the "Pica No. 1" created in the early 1800s by Binny & Ronaldson, the first successful typefounding company in America. The face is considered historically appropriate for the Papers of Thomas Jefferson because it was used extensively in American printing during the last quarter-century of Jefferson's life, and because Jefferson himself expressed cordial approval of Binny & Ronaldson types. It was revived and rechristened Monticello in the late 1940s by the Mergenthaler Linotype Company, under the direction of C. H. Griffith and in close consultation with P. J. Conkwright, specifically for the publication of the Jefferson Papers. The font suffered some losses in its first translation to digital format in the 1980s to accommodate computerized typesetting. Matthew Carter's reinterpretation in 2002 restores the spirit and style of Binny & Ronaldson's original design of two centuries earlier.

✧